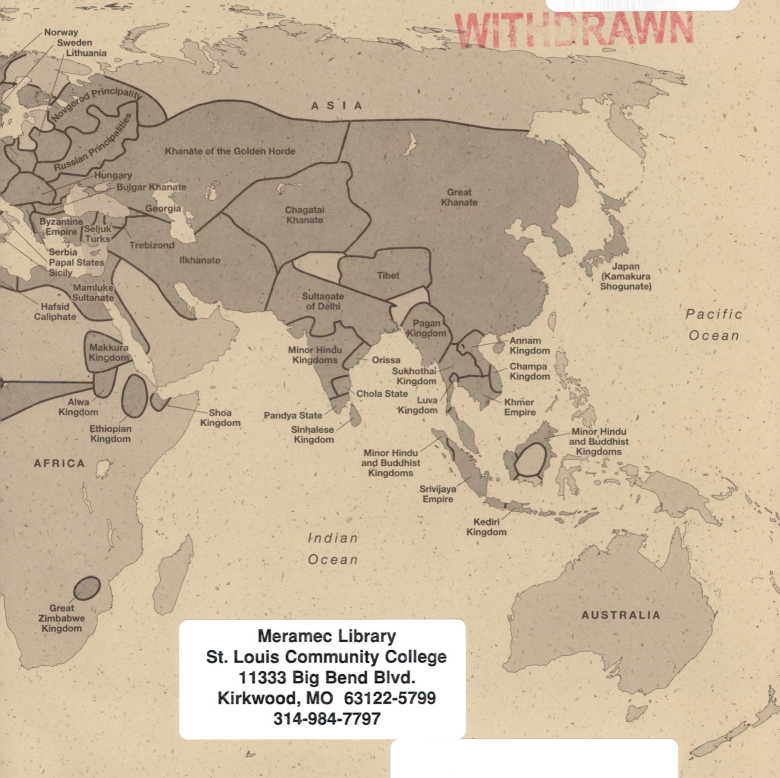

Norway
Sweden
Lithuania

Novgorod Principality

A S I A

Russian Principalities

Khanate of the Golden Horde

Hungary

Bulgar Khanate

Great
Khanate

Georgia

Byzantine
Empire

Seljuk
Turks

Chagatai
Khanate

Trebizond

Serbia
Papal States
Sicily

Ilkhanate

Tibet

Japan
(Kamakura
Shogunate)

Mamluke
Sultanate

Sultanate
of Delhi

Hafsid
Caliphate

Pacific
Ocean

Pagan
Kingdom

Makkura
Kingdom

Minor Hindu
Kingdoms

Annam
Kingdom

Orissa

Champa
Kingdom

Sukhothai
Kingdom

Alwa
Kingdom

Chola State

Luva
Kingdom

Khmer
Empire

Shoa
Kingdom

Pandya State

Ethiopian
Kingdom

Sinhalese
Kingdom

Minor Hindu
and Buddhist
Kingdoms

AFRICA

Minor Hindu
and Buddhist
Kingdoms

Srivijaya
Empire

Indian

Ocean

Kediri
Kingdom

Great
Zimbabwe
Kingdom

AUSTRALIA

ANTARCTICA

WORLD

MONARCHIES

AND DYNASTIES

VOLUME 1

WORLD

MONARCHIES

AND DYNASTIES

VOLUME 1

A–Fo

CONSULTING EDITOR
JOHN MIDDLETON

SHARPE REFERENCE

an imprint of M.E. Sharpe, Inc.

Developed, Designed, and Produced by BOOK BUILDERS LLC

SHARPE REFERENCE

Sharpe Reference is an imprint of M.E. Sharpe, Inc.

M.E. Sharpe, Inc.
80 Business Park Drive
Armonk, NY 10504

Library of Congress Cataloging-in-Publication Data

World monarchies and dynasties / John Middleton, editor.
  p. cm.
Includes bibliographical references and index.
ISBN 0-7656-8050-5 (set : alk. paper)
1. World history. 2. Monarchy—History—Dictionaries. 3. Kings and rulers—History—Dictionaries. I. Middleton, John.

D21 .W929 2004
903—dc22   2003023236

Printed and bound in the United States of America

The paper used in this publication meets the minimum requirements of American National Standard for Information Sciences—Permanence of Paper for Printed Library Materials, ANSI Z 39.48.1984.

BM (c) 10 9 8 7 6 5 4 3 2 1

Endpaper Maps: inside front cover: World Monarchies, 1279 C.E.;
inside back cover: World Monarchies, Present Day
(IMA for BOOK BUILDERS LLC)

CONTENTS

LIST OF FEATURES

Royal Rituals

Maps

PREFACE

Kings and queens have been a staple of historic and sociological writing for centuries, usually in the form of simple biographies. Until recently, "history" was written as a sequence of the often petty doings of kings and queens acting as though they were gods, rulers representing the "spirit" of their peoples.

This simplistic view is outmoded. *World Monarchies and Dynasties* has two aims in bringing royal history up to date. One is to present monarchy as a central political and religious institution, an institution found not only throughout history but throughout the world. The other is to present monarchies, the offices of kings and queens, in all their complexity.

This encyclopedia includes almost 400 accounts of individual monarchs—such as Richard I the Lionheart of England and Emperor Hirohito of Japan—from all continents and periods of history. Although it is, of course, impossible to include accounts of all recorded monarchs, the editors have selected those individuals considered most important, rulers whose reigns or actions significantly impacted history.

World Monarchies and Dynasties also includes more than 450 accounts of royal dynasties—families from the Ming dynasty of China to the rulers of the Roman and Byzantine Empires. Dynasties, the basic units of monarchy, are best understood in terms of their often long histories: a single monarch may have little importance on his or her own but lasting importance as a representative of a dynasty or royal family.

Finally, the central aim of the encyclopedia is to describe and discuss the universal nature of monarchy: the nature of monarchs; beliefs about power and authority; and the divinity or sacredness that defines them as out of the ordinary. These 140 topical articles—such as Tyranny, Regicide, and Divine Right—discuss matters that are often ignored in traditional historical accounts of monarchies and yet are essential if we are to understand kingdoms, the institution of kingship, and the ways in which these institutions define and shape history.

By utilizing the knowledge and expertise of its many contributors and advisers, *World Monarchies and Dynasties* brings together detailed and authoritative discussions about the fascinating and long-lasting phenomenon of monarchy and kingship. In doing so, this encyclopedia will help dispel many of the misperceptions and misunderstandings that still exist about the topic. Moreover, the entries in this encyclopedia provide a wealth of information that is indispensable for anyone interested in one of humankind's longest lasting institutions.

John Middleton

INTRODUCTION

Monarchies are political units ruled by kings or queens, who together may be called monarchs. Monarchies have existed in all periods of history and in virtually all parts of the world. No monarchy is exactly the same as any other, however. Indeed, they display immense variation in size and importance; the nature and history of their dynasties, or ruling families; in the power and authority vested in their monarchs; and in the sacred nature and behavior of their monarchs. These and other features are discussed briefly in this introduction; detailed discussions are found within the entries of the encyclopedia itself.

The Nature of Monarchy

All monarchies, despite their variations, possess certain basic characteristics that are functional, in the sense that most are formed and perpetuated in response to local social, economic, demographic, and political events and circumstances. Other factors prevent the appearance and development of monarchies, while still others—such as conquest, famine, and economic collapse—bring monarchies to a close. Efforts to demonstrate the diffusion of monarchies from a few geographical centers (such as Ancient Egypt or Mesopotamia) have proved to be without foundation, although there are many cases of local diffusion between neighboring areas.

Monarchies are distinct from other forms of political systems, and monarchs are different from other types of individuals or groups who hold political power and authority. It is also essential to distinguish between kingdoms—the domains ruled by monarchs—and kingships—the institutions of monarchy found in particular kingdoms.

In all societies throughout history, members of those societies have exercised political control, either directly or indirectly. Sometimes, this political control has been effective and popular, while other times it has been ineffective and unpopular. Relatively few societies, however, have had kings and queens as rulers.

Because most known societies in history have been without formal kingship, it is important to look carefully at the contexts in which monarchies have appeared. It is especially necessary, and difficult, to see these contexts as they evolve over time—for example, a society may have a monarchy at one period but not at another.

Role of the Encyclopedia

World Monarchies and Dynasties brings together three categories of entries that provide an overview of the various aspects and forms of monarchy. The first category of entries deals with broad conceptual topics—economic, political, sociological, ecological—related to monarchy and kingship, from the Accession and Crowning of Kings to Taxation to Colonialism and Kingship.

The southern Bantu-speaking people of South Africa have a proverb: "the king is a slave." In other words, the monarch is ultimately responsible to the people, and it is the people who decide whether or not a particular monarch or dynasty is to their liking. In this sense, all monarchies are filled with ambiguity, conflict, and contradiction; the conceptual entries in this encyclopedia are concerned with illuminating these issues. In the well-known words of William Shakespeare, "Uneasy lies the head that wears a crown." This is the basic subject matter of this short introduction.

The second category of entries in the encyclopedia is comprised of a long list of several hundred monarchs—individual kings or queens who have ruled over particular realms at various times in history. The editors have made an effort to avoid the old-fashioned "kings and queens" type of history, but, instead, to set the lives and acts of these monarchs in a particular dynastic and sociopolitical context. In doing so, it is hoped that the individual lives of these rulers will take on greater meaning.

The third category of entries in the encyclopedia consists of almost 500 accounts of the royal dynasties to which individual monarchs belong. Because the actions of individual monarchs usually make little sense outside their "family histories," an understanding of dynasties is essential. Monarchs are merely the representatives of royal families that may last for many generations, are engaged in long-lasting conflicts with other monarchies and with many contenders to the throne that often appear, and must deal with the many social factions of any kingdom, from barons and lords jealous of royal authority to the masses who may be oppressed by harsh rule.

The encyclopedia cannot include accounts of all the many thousands of known dynasties and monarchs, although with over 900 articles, it does present a representative selection from all periods of history and from all parts of the world. The selection is based on the comparative interest of the dynasties and monarchs concerned, as well as on the availability of historical and other information about them.

The Two Bodies and "Specialness" of Kings

What is a king or queen? Regnant kings and queens are men and women who act as rulers over kingdoms. They, their children, and their other kin are also royal, but individuals are not regnant until they are made into legitimate rulers by rites of coronation. (Other terms are used in the literature, but "coronation" can cover them all.)

Monarchs are always considered to be essentially different from their subjects and, indeed, from all other people except other monarchs. They are born with the bodies and physical attributes of ordinary human beings; yet neither they themselves nor anyone else considers them to be ordinary people. All human beings are, of course, unique and different from other individuals, but all, except for a few special persons, are essentially similar as ordinary members of their societies.

It is those few special persons that are the concern of this encyclopedia. Mostly, they include kings and queens, various religious leaders and holders of religious authority (such as His Holiness the Pope or the Dalai Lama), and a few people who are often considered to stand outside ordered society altogether (criminals, certain kinds of sick and dying persons, the insane, hermits, and several others).

What all these special categories have in common is that they are made and recognized by members of the society in which they live. A king or queen is made, not born, although there are a few borderline cases. Although monarchs are individuals, they are also persons with specific characteristics that their subjects give to them or recognize in them. This seeming paradox may best be seen in the fact that kings are thought to possess two bodies.

The Kingly Body

Regnant monarchs have both a "body natural" and a "body politic"—they have a normal physical body and, in addition, are ritually given a "body politic" at their coronation. It is important to note that this "body politic" does not belong to monarchs—it is merely bestowed on them and can be taken away should a monarch prove unsatisfactory. All kingdoms have means of removing unworthy monarchs—by deaccession, rebellion, or regicide.

Although this is perhaps a rather simple way of putting it, the owner of the body politic is the state itself. The monarch is made into a sacred person, as distinct from a "natural" individual, by the rituals of election, accession, and coronation. The fact that the transformation from individual to royal person is ritualistic is essential to its efficacy.

The body politic is considered permanent, whereas the body natural exists only as long as the king is alive. This idea is expressed simply in the traditional cry of "The King is dead. Long live the King." This may be understood or translated as "The Kingship endures despite the loss of the temporary holder of the office."

It is a virtually universal notion that the kingdom cannot be without its kingship. For example, when King George VI of England died in 1952, his daughter and successor, Elizabeth II, was in Kenya. Nevertheless, she had to be given the royal oath without delay to signify the continuity of the kingship, even though her actual coronation took place some time later.

The Divinity and Sacredness of Kings

With the doctrine of the king's Two Bodies goes the question of the sacredness and/or divinity of monarchs. The two concepts are frequently confused or conflated, but there are important distinctions between them.

Divinity belongs to God and is only bestowed by God. Sacredness, on the other hand, is given by those ritual personages who have the power to do so because they have been chosen by the people as the representatives of God. The situation appears to be similar throughout the world: monarchs are chosen by the people and then crowned by the chief religious officer recognized by the state.

A clear example of this relationship is that of the Akan kingship in southern Ghana. Among the Akan people, a king is a member of a royal matrilineal clan (he succeeds his mother's brother, not his father). He is chosen by a special committee headed by the queen-mother, who is the senior woman of the royal clan. After being chosen, the king is symbolically put to death, his legal affairs are settled, and his worldly possessions are sequestered. He is then symbolically reborn and carried on a servant's back as though he were a baby. He is given a new name or title, that of one of his ancestors, and is enthroned by the chief ritual figure of the state, whereby he becomes a new and sacred person. If an Akan king breaks any of the rules set for him (most of which involve caring for the welfare of his subjects), he may be dethroned, given a servile wife and a gun, and sent away to live in the forest from which his earliest ancestors are said to have come. It is important that the Akan king comes from the royal clan, the first ancestor of which is said to have come from heaven in a brass pan, thereby showing not his divinity (as God sent him) but his approval by God, which is denied to all other clans.

Monarchs can be thought to have powers that are both given and permitted by God. Although monarchs are not gods themselves, they are sacred—that is "set aside or apart" (in Latin, *sacer*), by the state itself. Some kings—for example, some of those of early Rome—were considered actually to become divine, or they bestowed divinity upon themselves. But such monarchs are rare in history. The phrase "divine right of kings" does not mean that monarchs themselves are gods, but that God is believed to give them certain powers if they are crowned as sacred figures and given authority over their subjects.

Royal Gender and Blood

Kings are male and queens are female. This simple biological statement can be translated into a social one—kings are men and queens are women. It is not quite as simple as either of these statements might imply, however. For example, in the case of regnant queens (not merely nonreigning queens who are the wives of kings), they are widely, though perhaps not always, considered to be men either symbolically or socially. Queen Elizabeth I of England once said that she had "the body of a weak and feeble woman but . . . the heart and stomach of a man." This symbolic ambiguity, the queen as a man, ran throughout Elizabeth's reign. It might be more accurate, however, to say that both regnant kings and queens are neither men nor women but a *tertium quid* (third something). They are set apart from, and thus different from, their subjects.

In perhaps all languages of peoples who have monarchies, there are sayings that regnant kings and queens are also different in their "blood"—not so much physical blood but in the sense of the "blood royal." Blood legitimizes ancestry and descent. Having royal blood does not make the possessor a king or queen—it merely legitimizes them as able to be a ruler if elected and crowned. The ruler's kin (which depends on how a particular society views ancestry, descent, rights of inheritance, and so on) are royal as well because of their royal "blood," and so may be elected and made sacred. Only a few are made sacred, however, and there is always discussion and disagreement as to when royal blood is so diluted that the individual is barely royal at all. The problem of marriage also enters into this discussion. Marriage with nonroyals may dilute the royal blood to a degree that children are barely regarded as royal—hence the efforts of all royal families to marry with other royals or even among themselves. (Marriage of cousins has been a frequent practice among monarchs.)

The Behavior and Adornment of a Monarch

Monarchs are representatives of the people, who make them rulers (and can get rid of them if they have grounds to do so). Monarchs' behaviors show unique position and status. The idioms used here vary immensely from one kingship to another. Most widespread is the idea of being "set apart" from other people: a monarch may wear special and unique clothing, live in a special house or palace, eat special foods, never be seen publicly to eat or drink, never be touched publicly, or never be spoken to directly by ordinary people. A king may be given many wives, concubines, and mistresses to demonstrate his difference from his subjects.

Some rulers walk under umbrellas and wear sandals to show that they may never see the sky or touch the earth, but as sacred individuals are "in-between." Kings are widely held in myth and belief to be associated with the wilderness outside society, the place of divinity, danger, and the asocial. Kings may be allowed to pursue pleasures forbidden to their subjects—for example, their time spent hunting reflects a pursuit of great symbolic importance linking society and wilderness in the royal person.

A monarch who fails to obey such rules may be dethroned and removed, desacralized and made "ordinary" again. A monarch is also widely given mystical or semidivine powers. One such widespread power is the power to cure certain forms of sickness and insanity, such as "the King's Evil" (scrofula).

Throughout much of English history, for example, kings have been thought to have the power to cure by the royal touch.

Kings and queens do not stand alone in isolation. Sacredness is invisible, so their sacredness has to be made visible and physical. This is accomplished by what may be called "adornment"—the ruler is adorned with regalia, clothing, and jewels; with special foods and drink; with courtiers in their royal households and palaces; with powerful and often predatory animals, such as lions and tigers; and with many types of officials, including ambassadors and ministers. Because of such adornments, the actual regnant king or queen may be weak in his or her body natural but powerful in his of her body politic. These sacred qualities stand behind royal authority, which is given to the ruler by the people. History is filled with examples of monarchs who try to keep power to themselves, without its being accepted as legitimate authority by their people. In recent times, much of the ritual and expressions of sacredness of ruling monarchs have come to be thought pointless and even frivolous. Many monarchs have simply been removed by rebellion (the changing of one monarch in favor of another, so that the institution is retained) rather than by revolution (in which the state structure is changed and the monarchy as an institution is abolished).

Yet, many monarchies persist today, despite much popular argument that they are unnecessary or that rulers should become merely ordinary people, like presidents. This argument, however, would seem to misunderstand and misrepresent the real point of monarchy—that it is symbolic of the power of the people themselves, who ultimately control it, yet wish to see in the person of their ruler the power that they, in fact, hold themselves. By keeping the monarchy, people ensure that the state or society itself continues in the form they wish it to be.

The Future of Monarchy

Today, there are fewer monarchies than ever before in history. Monarchies today face two issues: whether they are efficient political institutions, perhaps too expensive or incompetent; and whether kingship as a sacred and ritual institution still makes sense to the members of society. Although many peoples today show little interest in kingship and its sacred nature, and many may consider a secular president all that is needed to serve as a formal figurehead, the many monarchies today continue to have great vitality and popularity, and the monarchs who serve continue to appear as both symbolic and powerful heads of state. Study of this topic yields a vast amount of literature, much of which has been included in *World Monarchies and Dynasties*.

John Middleton

CHRONOLOGY OF DYNASTIES AND KINGDOMS

B.C.E.

3100	Upper and Lower Egypt are united to form earliest known African kingdom; first dynasty of Egypt begins rule
3000s	First ancient Greek kingdom, that of Minoans, established in the eastern Mediterranean region
2334	Founding of kingdom of Akkad, one of world's first monarchies
2000s	Emergence of earliest South Asian kingdoms
1766	The Shang, one of earliest East Asian dynasties, begins rule in China
1750	Death of Hammurabi marks beginning of decline of Babylonian Empire
1680	Beginning of Hittite Empire
1570	End of seventeenth dynasty of ancient Egypt
1400	Emergence of Olmec kingdom in Mexico
1334	Tutankhamun becomes pharaoh of Egypt
1294	Battle of Kadesh between the ancient Hittites and Egyptians
1220	Fall of Hittite Empire
930	Kingdom of Israel split in two, forming kingdom of Israel and kingdom of Judah
767	Beginning of Nubian rule over Egypt
700s	Etruscan kingdoms established in Italy
609	End of Assyrian Empire
550	Start of Persian Empire under Achaemenid dynasty and Cyrus the Great
525	Beginning of first Persian dynasty of ancient Egypt
500s	Establishment of early independent Indian kingdoms
490	Greek victory over the Persians at the battle of Marathon
400s	Major centers of Olmec kingdom of Mexico abandoned
359	Macedonian Empire established by Philip II of Macedon
336	Alexander III, the Great takes the throne of Macedon
330	Conquest of Persian Empire by Alexander the Great
330	Egypt becomes part of Eastern Roman Empire

323	Death of Alexander the Great ends Macedonian Empire
321	Maurya Empire of India founded, ending period of early Indian kingdoms
306	Founding of Ptolemaic dynasty, the first Hellenistic dynasty
300s	Etruscan kingdoms fall to Rome
221	Start of Ch'in dynasty for which China is named
180	End of Maurya Empire in India
100s	Early Southeast Asian kingdoms under Chinese influence
49	Julius Caesar crosses the Rubicon River and launches civil war
37	Establishment of Koguryo kingdom in Korea
30	Death of Cleopatra ends Hellenistic dynasty of Ptolemies
27	Augustus Caesar establishes Roman Empire

C.E.

300s	Beginnings of Hun Empire
300s	Beginnings of Byzantine Empire
300s	Early East Asian kingdoms in Korea struggle for power
313	Edict of Milan issued by Constantine the Great calls for end of persecution of Christians in Roman Empire
320	Gupta Empire of India founded
330	Constantinople founded by Constantine the Great
395	Eastern and Western halves of Roman Empire permanently divided
395	Visigothic kingdom ruled by Alaric I
400s	Leinster kingdom founded in Ireland
400s	Anglo-Saxons establish first English monarchies
410	Alaric, king of Visigoths, conquers city of Rome
450	First of Irish kings of Tara
455	Collapse of Hun empire
476	Fall of western Roman Empire
486	Merovingian-Frankish kingdom established by Clovis I

C.E.

500s	Beginnings of European kingships after fall of Rome
500s	Beginnings of Khmer Empire in Southeast Asia
532	Nika revolt threatens rule of Justinian I in Eastern Roman Empire
552	End of Ostrogothic kingdom in Italy
600s	Beginnings of Turkish Khazar kingdom
632	Death of Prophet Muhammad
632	Beginning of Islamic caliphate under Abu Bakr
667	Collapse of Korea's Koguryo kingdom
710	Beginning of Nara period in Japan
711	Moorish victory ends Visigothic kingdom
714	Carolingian dynasty of France founded by Charles Martel
722	Battle of Covadonga and victory of Asturias kingdom marks beginning of reconquest of Iberian Peninsula from Moors by Christians
732	Earliest evidence of Javan kingdoms
750	Collapse of Umayyad caliphate
751	Carolingian dynasty begins to rule France
751	End of Merovingian-Frankish kingdom and Merovingian dynasty
754	Donation of Pepin marks beginning of papal states
768	Charlemagne begins rule of Frankish kingdom
784	End of Japan's Nara period
794	In Japan, beginning of Heian period, a golden age of culture
800s	Earliest Russian dynasties emerge in Russia
800	Charlemagne crowned emperor of West
802	Angkor kingdom established in Cambodia
814	Death of Charlemagne
862	Rurikid dynasty founded in Russia
870	First ruler of Premysl dynasty, Borijoj I, takes throne of Bohemia
871	Alfred the Great becomes king of Wessex and begins to unite Anglo-Saxon kingdoms of England
900s	Toltec empire established in Mexico
900s	Origins of Habsburg dynasty
960	Sung dynasty founded in China
960	Sung dynasty established in China
962	Establishment of Holy Roman Empire
965	Defeat of Khazar kingdom by Kievan Rus leads to its decline and collapse
969	Fatimid dynasty begins rule in Egypt
987	End of Carolingian dynasty of France
987	Capetian dynasty takes the throne in France marking the beginning of long period of French monarchies
1014	Danish invasion of England by Cnut the Great marks beginnings of greatest period of Viking Empire
1014	Death of Brian Boru, High King who united Ireland
1035	Iberian kingdom of Navarre splits into Navarre, Aragón, and Castile
1044	Pagan kingdom of Burma founded
1057	French Normans first gain control of territory in southern Italy
1066	Norman conquest of England by William I the Conquerer
1072	Norman kingdom of Sicily founded by Roger Guiscard
1085	End of Viking Empire
1087	Death of William I the Conqueror
1131	Angevin dynasty of France rules Crusader kingdom of Jerusalem
1137	Eleanor of Aquitaine inherits the duchy of Aquitaine
1138	Beginning of rule of Holy Roman Empire by Hohenstaufen dynasty
1154	Angevin house of Plantagenet begins rule of England under Henry II
1161	Edward the Confessor of England canonized a saint
1174	Death of last ruler of Toltec empire of Mexico
1179	United kingdom of Portugal emerges
1192	Defeat of Christian crusaders by the Muslim leader Saladin
1194	Rule over the last Norman kingdom in Italy, the kingdom of Naples, goes to Spanish kingdom of Aragón
1200s	Beginnings of Inca Empire
1200s	Formation of Chibcha chiefdoms marks emergence of first South American Monarchies
1206	Mongol Empire founded by Genghis Khan
1215	Magna Carta imposes limits on the English monarchy

C.E.

1224	Death of last powerful Irish king
1238	Founding of Sukhothai kingdom, the first united Thai state
1250	Folkung dynasty rises to power in Sweden
250	Mamluk dynasty begins rule in Egypt
1258	End of Islamic caliphate in the Near East
1269	End of Almohad dynasty of Muslim Spain
1272	Establishment of Bourbon dynasty in France
1273	Beginning of rule of Germany and Austria by Habsburg dynasty
1279	End of Sung dynasty in China
1279	Beginning of Yuan dynasty (Mongol dynasty) in China
1280	Ottoman empire founded by Osman I
1282	English victory marks end of autonomy for Wales
1301	Long-lived Arpad dynasty of Hungary ends
1306	End of Premysl dynasty of Bohemia
1314	Scottish victory over English forces at battle of Bannockburn
1325	Beginning of Aztec Empire in Mexico
1328	Beginning of Valois dynasty rule in France
1336	Founding of Vijayanagar Empire in India
1338	Beginning of Ashikaga shogunate in Japan
1350	Ayutthaya kingdom is founded in Siam
1368	End of Yuan dynasty in China
1368	Ming dynasty founded in China
1370	Central Asian Timurid dynasty founded by Tamerlane
1383	Joao I becomes first ruler of Aviz dynasty of Portugal
1392	Establishment of Choson kingdom in Korea under the Yi dynasty
1397	Kalmar Union unites thrones of Denmark, Norway, and Sweden
1399	Abdication of Richard II; end of rule by the house of Plantagenet in England
1400s	Rise of Medici family in the Italian city-state of Florence
1405	Death of Tamerlane marks beginning of collapse of Mongol Empire
1405	Division of Golden Horde khanate into smaller states
1415	Hohenzollern dynasty begins rule in Germany
1434	Thai capture of Angkor marks beginning of end of Khmer Empire
1435	Treaty of Arras makes duchy of Burgundy independent of France
1453	Conquest of Constantinople by the Ottoman Turks marks end of Byzantine Empire
1455	Beginning of War of Roses in England
1485	Beginning of rule by the House of Tudor in England
1492	Christian conquest of kingdom of Granada, the last Moorish kingdom in Iberia
1502	Safavid dynasty founded in Iran
1509	Henry VIII of Tudor dynasty takes the throne in England
1509	Arrival of Europeans in Southeast Asia begins to influence traditional Southeast Asian Kingdoms
1516	Habsburg dynasty gains throne of Spain under Charles I (Holy Roman Emperor Charles V)
1516	Beginning of united Spanish monarchy under Charles V
1521	End of Aztec Empire in Mexico
1523	End of Kalmar Union in Scandinavia
1526	Conquest of Delhi sultanate by the Mughals
1526	Mughal Empire in India established by Babur
1533	Atahualpa, ruler of Inca Empire, killed by Spanish conquistadors
1534	Henry VIII of England becomes head of English church under the Act of Supremacy
1546	Ivan IV, the Terrible, of Russia becomes first Russian ruler to take the title "tsar"
1547	Death of Henry VIII of England
1556	Akbar the Great begins to rule in Mughal India
1556	Philip II takes the throne of Spain
1558	Elizabeth I of the house of Tudor begins reign in England
1567	James I of England takes the throne, establishing the house of Stuart in England
1572	End of Inca rule in Peru also marks end of indigenous South American monarchies
1588	English defeat of Spanish Armada

C.E.

1598	Death of Philip II of Spain
1603	Death of Elizabeth I marks the end of Tudor dynasty in England
1603	End of Ireland's Leinster kingdom
1605	Death of Akbar the Great of India's Mughal dynasty
1613	Romanov dynasty founded in Russia
1618	Start of Thirty Years' War in Europe
1625	Death of James I of England
1643	Completion of Taj Mahal in India
1643	Louis XIV begins reign in France
1644	End of China's Ming dynasty
1644	Beginning of Ch'ing, or Manchu, dynasty in China
1649	Beheading of Charles I of England ends monarchy and leads to English Civil War
1660	Restoration of monarchy and the Stuart dynasty in England
1670	Rise of Asante kingdom in Africa
1688	"Glorious Revolution" in England removes James II from throne
1700	Bourbon dynasty gains throne of Spain
1701	English Act of Settlement limits monarchical succession to Protestants
1713	Pragmatic Sanction, by which succession in Austrian Habsburg dynasty could pass to a female heir
1714	House of Hanover takes reins of power in England
1715	Death of "Sun King," Louis XIV of France
1724	Hyderabad kingdom founded in India
1737	End of Medici rule in Florence
1740	War of Austrian succession begins
1761	End of Mughal Empire of India
1771	End of Maratha Confederacy in India
1789	Beginning of French Revolution, during which monarchical rule is overthrown in France
1795	Hawaiian kingdom united by Kamehameha the Great
1799	Napoleon I Bonaparte becomes ruler of France
1804	Beginning of Austro-Hungarian Empire under Francis I
1804	Bonapartist Empire established by Emperor Napoleon I
1806	End of Holy Roman Empire
1815	Battle of Watterloo ends the Bonapartist empire of Napoleon Bonaparte

1818	Shaka creates the Zulu kingdom in southern Africa
1821	Death of Napoleon I Bonaparte while in exile on island of St. Helena
1822	Empire of Brazil is founded under the Braganza dynasty
1825	Nicholas I takes the throne of Russia
1837	Queen Victoria, the longest reigning monarch of England, takes the throne
1848	Establishment of a Republic marks end of French monarchies
1855	Death of Nicholas I of Russia
1858	End of India's Mughal Empire
1858	British takeover of India marks end of South Asian kingdoms
1868	In Japan, beginning of Meiji monarchy and Meiji restoration, which restored imperial power after long period of rule by the shoguns
1893	Queen Liliuokalani is deposed, ending independent Hawaiian kingdom
1894	Americans in Hawaii declare a republic, ending Hawaiian monarchy
1901	Death of Queen Victoria ends the house of Hanover in England
1910	End of long-lived Yi dynasty of Korea
1912	Imperial rule ends in China
1917	Russian Revolution ends monarchical rule by Russian dynasties
1917	Beginning of England's house of Windsor
1918	Austro-Hungarian Empire ends as a result of World War I
1918	End of Austro-Hungarian Empire marks end of Habsburg dynasty's rulers in Europe
1918	End of Hohenzollern dynasty in Germany
1921	Beginning of Hashemite dynasty in Jordan
1922	Last Ottoman caliph deposed, marking end of Ottoman Empire
1926	Emperor Hirohito of Japan takes the throne
1936	Edward VIII of England abdicates throne to marry an American divorcee
1945	End of Meiji monarchy in Japan
1949	Last remaining Javan kingdoms absorbed into newly-independent Indonesia

C.E.

1975 Last emperor of Ethiopia deposed, ending more than 700 years of monarchical rule

1989 Death of Emperor Hirohito of Japan

Present Morocco, Lesotho, and Swaziland remain the only African kingdoms

Present Hashemite dynasty continues in Jordan under Abdullah II

Present Bourbon dynasty continues to reign in Spanish monarchy

Present European kingships remain in several European nations

Present English monarchies continue in Great Britain under Windsor dynasty

Present East Asian kingdoms and dynasties continue in Japan under a constitutional monarchy

WORLD MONARCHIES AND DYNASTIES

VOLUME 1

ABBAS THE GREAT (1557–1629 C.E.)

Greatest ruler (r. 1587–1629) of the Persian Safavid dynasty, who drove out the Turks and Uzbeks from traditional Persian territories, established and maintained diplomatic contacts with a number of European nations, and founded the Muslim capital of Isfahan.

The son of Sultan Muhammad (r. 1577–1587), the fourth ruler of the Safavid dynasty, Abbas came to the Safavid throne as shah in 1587 at age thirty. Abbas inherited a Persia that was reeling from foreign attacks launched by indomitable Turks to the north and west, and raiding Uzbeks from the northeast. After making peace with the Turks in 1597, he turned his attention towards his weaker foe, the Uzbeks. After several bitter years of warfare, Abbas successfully overcame the Uzbekis, but his troops and his treasury were exhausted.

Abbas longed to free the northern and western regions of Persia from Turkish control. (The Turks were Sunnis, a different Muslim sect from the Shi'a sect to which Abbas belonged, and the two groups were often at odds). Abbas also wanted to regain the cities of Mosul and Baghdad, but he knew that his sword-bearing Shi'a warriors were no match for the gunpowder of the Turks.

In 1598, two English adventurers, Sir Anthony Sherley and his brother Robert, arrived in Persia and offered Abbas their services. Both men were experienced soldiers and knew the current art of munitions manufacturing. Within a few years, Abbas had thousands of musketmen and 200 pieces of artillery. He was now ready to march.

With this newly armed force, Abbas regained not only the cities of Baghdad and Mosul, but also the northwestern regions of Kurdistan and Azerbaijan. As a result of his victories, the Shi'a faith could now be practiced safely from the Euphrates River to the Indus River. Abbas continued using the talents of Anthony and Robert Shirley as ambassadors to the west, helping Persia establish diplomatic ties to several European nations. Soon Persia had thriving trade routes in silks and spices that went directly to Italy, bypassing the intermediary Turks.

Abbas continued to maintain Persian borders and improve its trade positions, but his primary focus from 1600 until his death was on constructing a remarkable new capital near the ancient city of Isfahan. European travelers in the seventeenth century had found at Isfahan a city "the size of Paris in extent, but only a tenth as populous, for every family had its own house and garden, and there were so many trees that it seemed rather a forest than a city." The city had dozens of colleges, hundreds of public baths, three masonry bridges over the river Zayand, fountains, cascades, and every type of garden. It also had more than a hundred mosques, including the magnificent Masjid-i-Shah, built in 1611–1629, and the equally beautiful, but more delicate, Masjid-I-Sheikh-Lutf-Allah, built by Abbas's father.

Abbas's long forty-two-year reign gave him the opportunity to improve the prosperity of his people. Unfortunately, he became progressively more suspicious and paranoid of his own family in his later years and dealt with them ruthlessly. Upon his death in 1629, he was succeeded by a grandson, Safi I (r. 1629–1642).

See also: SAFAVID DYNASTY.

ABBASID DYNASTY (750–1258 C.E.)

Chief ruling dynasty of the Islamic caliphate, which wrested control from the Umayyad dynasty and provided thirty-seven ruling caliphs between 750 and 1258. The Abbasids claimed legitimacy through descent from al-Abbas, the uncle of the Prophet Muhammad.

The Abbasids launched their bid for power in 718, when they began waging a vigorous propaganda campaign against the ruling Umayyads, particularly among the followers of the Shi'a branch of Islam and the Persians in Khorasan. The Abbasid campaign against the Umayyads culminated in open revolt in

747 under the direction of Abu Muslim, a Persian partisan of the Abbasids.

In 749, the head of the family, Abu al-Abbas (r. 750–754), named himself caliph after observing the gathering support from the Hashimite and Persian factions. Marwan II (r. 744–750), the reigning Umayyad caliph, met this revolt unsuccessfully in a battle near the River Zab. The next year, the Abbasids captured the Umayyad capital of Damascus. Marwan was put to death, and the Abbasids made a rigorous attempt to kill all remaining members of the Umayyad family, thereby justifying the name taken by Abu al-Abbas, al-Saffah (the bloodthirsty).

The Abbasids set about consolidating their power over the Islamic state. Popular leaders who might prove a threat, like Abu Muslim, were put to death. The Abbasids abandoned the old bureaucracy composed of provincial governors and replaced them with administrative civil servants, drawn largely from the Persians, who saw to the day-to-day administrative responsibilities of the Abbasid caliphate. Directing this bureaucracy was an appointed official who held the newly created title of vizier.

Much of the credit for designing this new approach to government must go to al-Saffah's successor, al-Mansur (r. 754–775). During his twenty-two-year reign, this careful ruler established the administrative structure of the new government, reorganized the army, rooted out corrupt officials, and oversaw expenditures so carefully that, upon his death, subsequent Abbasid rulers could afford their reputations for generosity. Al-Mansur also chose the site of the new capital, Baghdad, situated for easy trade along the Tigris and Euphrates rivers. The city prospered in this advantageous location, and subsequent Abbasid caliphs held court there in grand style.

During the reigns of al-Mansur and his successors Harun al-Rashid (r. 786–809) and al-Mamun (r. 813–833), the Islamic caliphate reached its zenith of wealth and power, as these caliphs promoted education, the arts, industry, trade, and commerce.

In time, however, Abbasid power began to decline. One cause of this decline lay in the Abbasid military, which, early in the ninth century, began admitting Turks, Berbers, and Slavs as mercenaries to supplement Arab forces. By the reign of al-Muntasir (r. 861–862), Turkish captains were the main decision makers in the army. These foreign mercenaries had little in common with the people of Baghdad, and they occasionally assassinated caliphs who did not conform to their views.

Meanwhile, territorial disputes rose as the homogeneity of the empire crumbled into squabbling among Arabs, Persians, Berbers, and Jews. When the Abbasid government ceased maintenance of the system of canals that provided irrigation, starvation ensued and taxes to support court luxuries came to be more fiercely resented.

In 945, the Buyids, a family of military adventurers, secured permission from the Abbasid caliph, al-Mustakfi (r. 944–946), to set up a client dynasty to rule in western Iran and Iraq. This policy gave rise over the next hundred years to several other local dynasties, all of which weakened the unity of the caliphate, making it an easier target for the Seljuk Turks in 1055.

In the mid-eleventh century, the Seljuks came to dominate the government at Baghdad. They took the title of sultans and stripped the Abbasids of temporal power, but they left the Abbasids their role as religious leaders and the title of caliph. Members of the Abbasid family held this more limited power as sultans until 1258, when the Mongols seized and sacked Baghdad and overthrew the caliphate. One member of the Abbasid family escaped to Egypt, where members of the dynasty served as puppet caliphs under the Mamluks until the 1500s.

See also: CALIPHATES; HARUN-AL-RASHID; MAMLUK DYNASTY; MAMUN, AL-; MANSUR, AHMAD AL-; SELJUQ DYNASTY; UMAYYAD DYNASTY.

ABD AL-HAMID II (1842–1918 C.E.)

One of the last major sultans of the Ottoman Empire, who was deposed in 1908 by the Young Turk movement. Abd al-Hamid II was born in 1842 and became sultan in 1876. He succeeded his insane brother Murad V (r. 1876), who ruled briefly after their uncle Abd al-Aziz (r. 1861–1876) was deposed by a reformist group of officers intent on leading a constitutional revolution. Abd al-Hamid was initially sympathetic to reforms and agreed to a parliamentary constitution in 1876. However, within a year he suspended the constitution and had the reformist minister Midhat Pasha arrested and killed.

Abd al-Hamid ruled the empire with firm control for the following three decades. As sultan, he pursued a policy of modernization. However, at the same time he rejected the Westernizing impulses of previous rulers, promoting an Islamic ideology based on his religious role as caliph. Abd al-Hamid built railroads and fostered technological and educational advances, but maintained tight political control. He also allied closely with Germany, reorganizing the army in the model of the Prussian military and using German investment to foster development in his indebted empire.

Despite Abd al-Hamid's attempts to strengthen the Ottoman Empire's international position, he was unable to revitalize the regime and effectively oppose Western imperialism. He became known in the West as the Red Sultan after he oversaw the 1894–1896 massacres of Armenians in the empire. Abd al-Hamid's dictatorial rule ended in 1908 with the Young Turk Revolution, which stripped him of much of his power and forced him to submit to the 1876 constitution. He was removed from the throne altogether in 1909 after plotting a counterrevolution, and died in 1918.

See also: OTTOMAN EMPIRE.

ABD AL-RAHMAN (d. 788 C.E.)

First Umayyad emir ("commander") (r. 756–788) of the caliphate of Córdoba, a member of the Umayyad dynasty, who reorganized and consolidated the caliphate and tried to unite the various Moorish groups in Iberia.

Abd al-Rahman belonged to a branch of the Umayyad dynasty that managed to flee Damascus when the Abbasid dynasty overthrew the Umayyad caliphate in 750. The Abbasids had made a concerted effort to kill any living Umayyads, and Abd al-Rahman was lucky to have escaped with his life. He fled across North Africa and eventually found refuge among the occupying Moorish forces on the Iberian Peninsula, where an outpost of the caliphate had been established. He also found an opportunity for political gain there in the rivalry between the two main Moorish factions in Iberia, the Qais and Yaman.

By shifting sides between these two groups, hiring mercenaries, and manipulating the political scene, Rahman built a power base in Iberia. In 756, he defeated the emir of Córdoba, Yusef ben al-Fihri (r. 747–756), taking the city and making it his capi-

tal. In doing so, he established the preeminence of the Umayyad dynasty in Iberia. Although the dynasty would govern Córdoba for 300 years, no ruler would take the title of caliph until the mid-tenth century.

When word spread of Rahman's success, former members of the Umayyad bureaucracy of Damascus flocked to Spain, hoping for employment and opportunities to advance in rank and office. As a result, Rahman's administration soon resembled in structure and capabilities the bureaucracy that the Umayyads formerly maintained in Damascus.

Rahman achieved not only administrative success but military success as well. His armies stopped attempted invasions by the Frankish king Charlemagne (r. 768–814) in 788 and the Abbasid caliph of Damascus. He also made significant strides in consolidating the various Muslim groups in Iberia, although he faced long-standing opposition from the Berbers, Muslim Spaniards, and other Arab factions.

To ratify his power and authority, Rahman embarked on a massive building program, which laid the foundations for the future greatness of the Córdoba caliphate. The most notable building begun during his rule was the Great Mosque of Córdoba ("La Mezquita"), which still stands today. Upon Rahman's death in 788, he was succeeded as emir of Córdoba by his son, Hisham I (r. 788–796).

See also: ABBASID DYNASTY; CALIPHATES; CÓRDOBA, CALIPHATE OF; IBERIAN KINGDOMS; UMAYYAD DYNASTY.

ABDICATION, ROYAL

The renunciation or giving up, formally or in effect, of the rights and duties of the monarch's position. Throughout history, monarchs have abdicated their reigns for various reasons. Abdication of the Crown may be a purely personal decision, or it may be forced on a ruler by external circumstances.

THE ROLE OF RELIGION

In the early Middle Ages, especially in early Anglo-Saxon England, it was not unusual for a king to designate a successor and give up his Crown to pursue a spiritual life. For example, Aethelred I of Mercia (r. 675–704) retired to a monastery in 704. He was succeeded by his nephew Cenred (r. 704–709), who himself abdicated in 709 in order to retire to a religious life in Rome.

Religion often played a role in later abdications as well. Since 1617, Sweden has required its monarchs to belong to the Lutheran Church. However, Queen Christina (r. 1632–1654) of Sweden secretly converted to the Roman Catholic faith. In 1654, she abdicated in favor of her cousin Karl X (r. 1654–1660) and went to live in Rome. Christina chose to abdicate despite the fact that her conversion to Catholicism was not public knowledge and there was no popular pressure for her to give up the throne.

Perhaps the most famous abdication of modern times was due partially to religion as well. Soon after taking the throne of England in 1936, King Edward VIII (1936) announced his intention to marry Wallis Simpson, a twice-divorced American. Many in England felt that because the British monarch was head of the Church of England, he must not marry a divorcee. Although divorce was legal under certain circumstances, it was not considered respectable, and a queen consort who had been twice divorced was deemed unacceptable.

Edward VIII first proposed a morganatic marriage, in which Mrs. Simpson would be his wife but not a queen. Many members of the British government supported this solution, but the prime minister, Stanley Baldwin, opposed Edward marrying Simpson without abdicating. If he had done so, Edward may well have precipitated a constitutional crisis that would have resulted in his being deposed. Forced to choose between Mrs. Simpson and the throne, Edward abdicated on December 11, 1936, in favor of his younger brother, the duke of York, who became George VI (r. 1936–1952).

POLITICAL AND OTHER FACTORS

Kings have also been forced to abdicate as a result of defeat in war or political revolution. In the final few days of World War I, for example, Kaiser Wilhelm II of Germany (r. 1888–1918) fled to Holland, where he abdicated on November 9, 1918, because the Allies, particularly the United States, would not negotiate with a government he headed. After Wilhelm's abdication, Germany never had another monarch.

Tsar Nicholas II of Russia (r. 1894–1917) abdicated his throne in March 1917, submitting to the demands of the Russian Duma, or parliament, and

military generals. These groups hoped that by removing the tsar and his unpopular wife, anarchy could be averted in a nation sinking toward chaos during the beginning stages of the Russian Revolution. Nicholas initially intended to abdicate in favor of his invalid son, the tsarevich Alexei. Instead, he named his brother, Grand Duke Mikhail, as successor, but Mikhail refused the Crown.

Monarchs also abdicate as a form of retirement from the demands of their position. In twelfth-century Japan, where the role of emperor was a highly ritualized one with many restrictions and little real power, emperors frequently resigned the position to the crown prince. They would then assume the position of retired or ex-emperor, a position that sometimes exercised considerable political power.

Retirement from royal duties has also led to a number of modern abdications. In 1980, Queen Juliana of the Netherlands (r. 1948–1980) abdicated in favor of her daughter and heir, Queen Beatrix (1980–), and re-took the title of princess. Juliana's mother, Queen Wilhelmina (1890–1948), had herself abdicated the throne on the fiftieth anniversary of her reign.

Abdications in a modern constitutional monarchy, such as those of Juliana and Edward VIII, take effect through an act of parliament. Legally, this involves what is known as a "demise of the Crown," in which the succession passes to the next in line as though the monarch had died. In a nonconstitutional monarchy, such as that of medieval Japan, there is no parliamentary procedure to follow. Yet, the situation is similar in that the rights and duties of the monarch pass to a successor as though the abdicating ruler had died.

See also: ACCESSION AND CROWNING OF KINGS; BODIES, POLITIC AND NATURAL; INHERITANCE, ROYAL; REIGNS, LENGTH OF; SUCCESSION, ROYAL.

FURTHER READING

Andersson, Ingvar. *A History of Sweden*. Trans. Carolyn Hannay. Westport, CT: Greenwood Press, 1975.

Hall, John Whitney. *Japan from Prehistory to Modern Times*. Ann Arbor: Center for Japanese Studies, University of Michigan, 1991.

Kirby, David. *Northern Europe in the Early Modern Period, 1492–1772*. New York: Longman, 1990.

Spellman, W.M. *Monarchies, 1000–2000*. London: Reaktion Books, 2001.

Stenton, Sir Frank. *Anglo-Saxon England*. 3rd ed. New York: Oxford University Press, 2001.

Taylor, A.J.P. *English History: 1914–1945*. New York: Oxford University Press, 2001.

ABU BAKR (d. 634 C.E.)

Successor of the Prophet Muhammad and the first caliph of the Muslim state (r. 632–634), who helped preserve and strengthen the newly formed Islamic state and set the direction of its future expansion.

Abu Bakr was one of the Arab chieftains who accompanied the Prophet Muhammad to Medina in Arabia in 622. According to tradition, Abu Bakr is said to have been the first male convert to Islam, although that view lacks historical support. Certainly he was a close friend of the Prophet, organizing the pilgrimage to Mecca in 631 and acting as Muhammad's deputy in leading public prayer in Medina prior to Muhammad's death. Abu Bakr was also the father of Muhammad's wife, Aisha, a union that made the ties between the Prophet and Abu Bakr even stronger.

The death of Muhammad in 632 threw the Muslim community into political confusion. Several candidates emerged as potential successors to the Prophet; chief among them were Abu Bakr and Ali, Muhammad's cousin and son-in-law, who was married to Muhammad's daughter Fatima. The majority of Muhammad's followers chose Abu Bakr to be the Prophet's successor.

When Abu Bakr was selected to succeed Muhammad, he took the title *khalifat rasul Allah* ("successor of the Prophet of God"), which was later shortened to *caliph*. This title was clearly distinct from that of Prophet, and those who held it, while leaders of the Muslim community were not regarded as messengers or spokesmen for God. Nonetheless, Abu Bakr and his three immediate successors were regarded as special religious leaders, known collectively as the Rashidun or "Rightly Guided."

Abu Bakr's succession to the leadership of the Muslim state was not universally accepted. Upon Muhammad's death, many of the tribal chieftains reneged on alliances they had formed with the Prophet, unwilling to support either his claims of divine guidance or the political hegemony of Medina. To combat this apostasy, the Muslim community under Abu Bakr's guidance initiated a military action called the *riddah* wars. The success of Abu Bakr's

forces against these factions confirmed the authority of the centralized Muslim rule.

Success in the *riddah* wars encouraged the Muslim military to continue with its policy of conquest, looking outward toward the wealth of Persia, Syria, and Egypt. Thus, although it lasted only two years, Abu Bakr's rule was a critical period in which the direction of Islam's future expansion was firmly established. When Abu Bakr died in 634, he was succeeded by Umar (Omar) (r. 634–644), who had been an adviser to Muhammad.

See also: CALIPHATES.

ACCESSION AND CROWNING OF KINGS

Royal accession is the acquiring of the rank of monarch, the act of reaching the throne and coming into power. Accessions may also mark the start of a new dynasty and its rise to power. Accessions are typically followed, though it can be several months, by coronations, ceremonies celebrating the installation of the new monarch. Accessions in various forms have been around as long as kings and queens; for example, clay tablet records of the accession and coronation of kings dating to 3000 B.C.E. have been found in the ruins of Ur belonging to the ancient Sumerians. The accession of King Solomon has been dated to 970 B.C.E.; he ruled the Hebrews until 930 B.C.E. When a ruling monarch dies or, less commonly, abdicates the throne, a new monarch is selected to the Crown through previously established rules.

In British royalty, the successor to the throne is chosen via rules established at the end of the seventeenth century. The sovereign succeeds to the Crown as soon as the predecessor dies and is immediately proclaimed the (new) monarch at an Accession Council at St. James Palace with the members of the House of Lords, the lord mayor, and leading citizens of London in attendance. The proclamation of the new sovereign is also read in Edinburgh, Windsor, and York. If the new monarch is under eighteen years of age, or if a monarch is ever incapacitated, a regent is appointed to serve until the monarch reaches maturity. For British monarchs, coronations follow the accession after a suitable amount of time has passed, and for the last 900 years have been held at West-

ROYAL RITUALS

ACCESSION OF KING BAUDOUIN

Accession of a new monarch to the throne is most common in the case of the death of the previous monarch, but accession also takes place in the case of the incapacitation or abdication of a monarch. Belgium's King Baudouin (r. 1951–1993) ascended to the throne after the abdication of his father, Leopold III (r. 1934–1951), whose troubled personal life and wartime conduct made him such a controversial and unpopular figure that the future of the monarchy was threatened. Leopold's brother Charles served as prince regent from 1940 until 1950, when the country's voters decided by plebiscite to allow Leopold to resume the throne, which he did, but only briefly. In 1951 he abdicated in favor of his son.

minster Abbey. The current monarch, Queen Elizabeth II, ascended to the throne on February 6, 1952, and was crowned on June 2, 1953.

British accession practices were established long ago with the Bill of Rights in 1689 and in the Act of Settlement in 1701 following the flight of King James II from England in 1688. The Crown was then offered to James's daughter Mary and her husband William of Orange as joint rulers, thereby mandating that Parliament had the power to regulate succession to the throne.

MODERN CHANGES IN ROYAL ACCESSION

Sweden has been a hereditary monarchy since 1523, although the country's current royal family originated in France. When heir to the throne Karl August died in 1810, Danish duke Frederick Christian, a relative of the deceased Karl August, was elected as heir apparent, but pro-French officials resisted his candidacy. The issue was resolved by offering the post to one of Napoleon's marshals, Jean-Baptiste Bernadotte; eventually he was officially recognized by the aging King Karl XIII. Baptiste took the name Karl Johan and was crowned on May 1, 1818.

Not all accession practices are rooted in history. In 1905, when Norway dissolved political ties with Sweden, Norway's citizens passed a national referendum confirming their collective support for the accession of Prince Carl of Denmark and Princess Louise of Sweden and Norway. Norwegians were overwhelmingly in favor of the accession. Prince Karl (r. 1905–1957) agreed and took the name Haakon; he ruled until his death in 1957 and was succeed by Crown Prince Olav (r. 1957–1991), who served as a commander in World War II.

The ruling monarch of Sweden, with only two exceptions—Queen Christina (r. 1632–1654) in the seventeenth century and Queen Ulrika Eleonora (r. 1718–1720) in the eighteenth century—has always been male. Christina became queen at the age of six in 1632, upon the death of her father, the king; she was a brilliant intellectual who in her youth reportedly studied twelve hours per day. As for Ulrika Eleonora, she was born in 1688, ascended the throne after the death of her brother King Karl XII (r. 1682–1718), but soon abdicated in favor of her husband Frederick (r. 1720–1751).

Sweden's Act of Succession went into effect in 1979, amending the constitution to make the first-born the heir to the throne regardless of sex. The Act therefore mandated that the next heir would be Crown Princess Victoria, thus depriving Prince Karl Philip, who was less than a year old at the time, of the Crown.

In dynasties that have ended long ago, as in the case of the Polish royal family, opportunists often try to carve out royal lineage, even though the paths to the defunct thrones are often obfuscated. Pretenders will frequently emerge, trying to prove rights to the lost Crown. In 1832, the Polish constitution establishing a heredity monarchy, written in 1791, was abolished, at which point Poland became part of the Russian Empire. The coronations of the tsar of Russia and the king of Poland were made one and held in Moscow; both were subject to governing by the laws of heredity primogeniture in the male line; if no male heir was left, then the Crown would pass to the female line. After World War I, with the signing of the peace treaty at Versailles, Poland was recognized as an independent republic, and by 1921 the monarchy was no longer mentioned in legal records.

See also: ACCESSION AND CROWNING OF KINGS; BELGIAN KINGDOM; BLOOD, ROYAL; ENGLISH MONARCHIES; PRIMOGENITURE; ELIZABETH II; SWEDISH MONARCHY.

ACHAEANS. *See* MYCENAEAN MONARCHIES

ACHAEMENID DYNASTY

(ca. 550–330 B.C.E.)

Ruling family of the ancient Persian Empire who presided over a period of expansion and great power.

Persia was controlled by the Medes until 550 B.C.E., when Cyrus of Anshan, an Iranian noble, rebelled and took power. Cyrus's victory over the Medes marked the beginnings of the Persian Empire, and his dynasty is known as the Achaemenid after a legendary ancestral king named Achaemenes.

An ambitious conqueror, Cyrus (r. 559–530 B.C.E.) overthrew King Croesus (r. 560–546 B.C.E.) of Lydia (in present-day Turkey) in 546 B.C.E. Then, in 539 B.C.E., he launched a successful attack on the Chaldean Empire of Babylonia. Eventually, Cyrus headed eastward and made inroads into Asia.

Cyrus treated conquered peoples with respect, a policy that became a hallmark of Achaemenid rule. Rather than banish conquered leaders, he allowed them to maintain some autonomy. Nor did he force a new religion or language on conquered people. Such gestures resulted in far less resentment toward Persian rule and a more contented populace, making it much easier to rule the empire. For both his military conquests and for his benevolence, Cyrus is often known as Cyrus the Great.

After Cyrus's death in 530 B.C.E., he was succeeded by his son, Cambyses (r. 529–522 B.C.E.), who continued to expand the Persian Empire. In 525 B.C.E., Cambyses marched into Egypt and conquered it. With this conquest, the Persian Empire became the largest and most powerful in the ancient Near East. Cambyses died in 522 B.C.E. as he was returning from Egypt.

After the death of Cambyses, the throne of Persia was claimed by Darius I (r. 521–486 B.C.E.), who is believed to have been a cousin from another branch of the Achaemenid family. A powerful leader and a strong administrator, Darius brought a level of sophistication to the Persian Empire that had never been seen before. He built roads throughout the empire, created a system of couriers to carry messages, increased trade by digging a channel from the Nile River to the Red Sea, and introduced the use of coins. He also divided the Persian Empire into twenty provinces called satrapies, each with its own ruling governor, or satrap.

Darius I proved to be the last truly great Achaemenid monarch of the Persian Empire. After his death in 486 B.C.E., his successors held onto the empire for another 150 years but faced revolts in Egypt, dissension among the satraps, and attempted encroachments by Greece. In 334 B.C.E., Alexander the Great (r. 336–323 B.C.E.) set out from Greece, conquered Asia Minor, and then marched further eastward into the heart of Persia. Finally, in 330 B.C.E. in a battle with the Achaemenid ruler, Darius III (r. 335–330 B.C.E.), Alexander's much smaller army defeated the previously unrivaled army of the Persian Empire. Darius III fled and was assassinated, bringing the Achaemenid dynasty to an end.

The relative longevity of the Achaemenid dynasty, and the esteem in which it is still held, are due mainly to its two most gifted kings, Cyrus the Great and Darius I. Skilled both militarily and administratively, these two monarchs also brought a tolerant ruling style to bear as their empire expanded. Their strength and farsightedness established the Achaemenid dynasty as a world power. Having provided ancient Persia with a strict set of laws, an established currency and postal service, religious freedom, and a flourishing of the arts and architecture, the Achaemenid dynasty was a high point in the history of the Persian people.

Founded by Darius I around 518 B.C.E., Persepolis was the capital of the Persian Empire during the Achaemenid Dynasty. Built on an immense terrace, which was part natural and part man-made, the capital boasted a magnificent palace complex.

See also: ALEXANDER III, THE GREAT; ARTAXERXES I; ARTAXERXES II; ARTAXERXES III; CAMBYSES II; CROESUS; CYRUS THE GREAT; DARIUS I, THE GREAT; DARIUS II; DARIUS III; LYDIA, KINGDOM OF; MEDES KINGDOM; PERSIAN EMPIRE; XERXES.

FURTHER READING

Asimov, Isaac. *The Near East: 10,000 Years of History*. Boston: Houghton Mifflin, 1968.

Hitti, Philip K. *The Near East in History: A 5000 Year Story*. Princeton, NJ: D. Van Nostrand, 1961.

Perry, Glenn E. *The Middle East: Fourteen Islamic Centuries*. Englewood Cliffs, NJ: Prentice-Hall, 1983.

Sicker, Martin. *The Pre-Islamic Middle East*. Westport, CT: Praeger, 2000.

ACHEH KINGDOM (ca. 1515–1907 C.E.)

Islamic sultanate centered on the Indonesian island of Sumatra that reached its height of power and greatest territorial extent in the early 1600s and developed a reputation as a center of scholarship and trade.

Many historians believe that Acheh was Islam's entry point into the Indonesian archipelago and possibly all of Southeast Asia sometime around the early 1500s. Perlak, the first Islamic kingdom in what is now Acheh, was established in 1504. Much later, in the sixteenth and seventeenth centuries, the port of Acheh became embroiled in European colonial struggles for political and economic dominance.

In the early 1500s, Acheh was a vassal-state of the

pepper-rich port-state of Pidie. Pidie, along with nearby Pasai, came under the influence of the Portuguese and Dutch as a result of the thriving spice trade, which eventually led to the establishment of the Dutch East India Company in 1602.

In reaction to increasing European influence in the region, the sultan of Acheh, Ali Mughayat Shah (r. 1496–1528), declared independence for Acheh around 1515 and issued a call to expel the Europeans. Pidie and Pasai united with Acheh in an attempt to drive out the foreigners.

Acheh reached its pinnacle of power during the reign of Sultan Iskander Muda (r. 1607–1636). At the beginning of Iskander's reign, the sultan launched a naval campaign that gave him control over many of the Indonesian islands. He eventually ruled over all of the major ports on the west coast of Sumatra, most of the east coast of the island, and also the ports of Kedah, Perak, and Pahang on the Malay Peninsula.

After multiple wars with the Portuguese, Acheh finally defeated the Portuguese fleet in 1614 at Bintan on the Malay Peninsula, seriously threatening Portuguese colonial holdings in the Malay region of Malacca. However, an alliance of lesser powers from the Portuguese colonies at Malacca, Johore, and Patani constructed a fleet and devastated the Acheh navy near Malacca in 1629.

Acheh's power was based on trade, and the conflicts with the Portuguese and their colonial allies arose out of Acheh's attempts to gain a monopoly over the highly lucrative pepper trade. Sultan Iskander granted Dutch and British traders a monopoly on the pepper trade, which harmed local traders by banning competing pepper buyers.

Following the loss of Acheh's navy, a number of area chiefs aligned with the Dutch against Acheh. In 1641 the Dutch, with help from these local allies, gained control of Malacca, which eventually led to the loss of Acheh territories on the Malay Peninsula.

During its period of dominance in the early 1600s, Acheh became known as a center for scholarship, and the kingdom attracted well-known Islamic writers. The Acheh system of law administration was also admired by many rulers in the region and provided a model for other Islamic states in Indonesia.

Following Iskandar's death in 1636, Acheh swiftly declined and, combined with increasingly aggressive moves by the Dutch and the lack of another qualified leader, the kingdom soon lost prominence. Despite a

brief alliance in 1641 with the Dutch, the Kingdom continued to decline in influence over the next 200 years.

In 1824, Great Britain and the Netherlands signed an Anglo-Dutch treaty, under which the British ceded Sumatra to the Dutch in exchange for exclusive trading rights on the Malay Peninsula. The treaty guaranteed Acheh's independence, but in 1871, Britain authorized the Dutch to invade Acheh, which they did in 1873, sparking a thirty-year war. Finally, in 1904, the Dutch subdued the rebellious people of Acheh, and in 1907 they forced the last sultan of Acheh into exile, effectively ending the sultanate.

When Indonesia gained independence from the Dutch in 1949, Acheh became an independent province. The following year, however, it was incorporated into the Sumatran province of Utara. The Acheh people continued to press for greater autonomy, waging guerrilla warfare against government forces from time to time. The creation of Acheh as a special district within Indonesia in 1956 did nothing to quell the rebelliousness, which has continued to erupt periodically in violence.

See also: SOUTHEAST ASIAN KINGDOMS.

AETHELRED, THE UNREADY. *See*

ANGLO-SAXON RULERS; EDWARD THE CONFESSOR

AFONSO I (ca. 1109–1185 c.e.)

Also known as Afonso Henriques and Afonso the Conqueror, the first king of Portugal (r. 1139–1185), who campaigned ceaselessly against the Moors and the rulers of the Spanish kingdoms of León and Castile.

A strong military leader, Afonso used his victories over rival states to carve the Portuguese kingdom out of overlapping feudal lands on the Iberian Peninsula. Following his army's victory over the Muslims at Campo de Ourique in southern Portugal in 1139, Afonso declared himself king of Portugal by renouncing fealty to all Spanish kingdoms. His cousin, Alfonso VII of León and Castile (r. 1126–1157), recognized Afonso's rule under the Treaty of Zamora in

1143. However, the papacy did not recognize the sovereignty of an independent Portugal until 1179.

Afonso I was the son of Henry of Burgundy, a French noble who had come to Iberia from France to participate in the reconquista, or reconquest, of Iberia from the Moors. In 1093, Henry was named count of Portugal by Alfonso VI of León (r. 1065–1109) for his support in resisting the Moors. Afonso's mother, the Countess Teresa, was the illegitimate daughter of Alfonso VI of León.

When Henry died in 1112, Teresa became regent for Afonso, who was still only a child. Ambitious in her own right, Teresa ruled the country with her Spanish consort, Fernando Perez de Trava, and refused to acknowledge her son's accession to the throne. In 1128, Afonso, with the support of the Portuguese nobles, challenged his mother and her lover for control of the Crown, defeating them at the battle of Sao Mamede, near Guimares in northwestern Portugal.

Having secured his throne, Afonso began a series of military campaigns to build and secure his kingdom. His victory over the Moors at Campo de Ourique in 1139 secured much of southern Portugal. In March 1147, he captured Santarem (in west-central Portugal) from the Moors, and he took the city of Lisbon in October of that year with help from a mostly English contingent of troops from a passing fleet of 13,000 Crusaders sailing to the Holy Land.

By the time of his death in 1185, Afonso had extended Portuguese territory to the Tagus River, despite recurrent incursions by Moors of the Moroccan Almohad dynasty. To maintain order in his kingdom, Afonso allied with the Knights Templar, the religious military order established during the Crusades to protect pilgrims. He also enlisted monks from the Cistercian order to develop agriculture in sparsely populated areas of his kingdom.

In 1169, Afonso broke his leg during an unsuccessful attack against the Moors at Badajoz in southwestern Spain. Captured by his Castilian son-in-law, King Fernando II (r. 1157–1188 of León), who aided the Muslims, Afonso was ransomed only after renouncing claims to the province of Galicia in the northwestern corner of the Iberian Peninsula, which lies directly north of Portugal.

In 1170, Afonso I knighted his son Sancho, and the two ruled Portugal in tandem until Afonso's death in 1185. Sancho then took the throne as Sancho I (r.

1185–1211). Over the next 200 years, the descendants and successors of Afonso I built up and strengthened the kingdom of Portugal, making it a powerful maritime nation and a leader in exploration.

See also: CASTILE, KINGDOM OF; IBERIAN KINGDOMS; LEÓN, KINGDOM OF; SPANISH MONARCHIES.

AFONSO I, NZINGA MBEMBA

(ca. 1460–1543 C.E.)

Christian ruler (*manikongo*) of the kingdom of Kongo in central Africa from 1506 until his death in 1543.

Afonso I was born Nzinga Mbemba, a son in the royal house of the kingdom of Kongo. The exact date of his birth is uncertain; estimates range from the mid-1450s to the mid-1460s. His father was Nzingu Kuwu, the first Kongo king to make contact with Christian missionaries who arrived in the territory from Portugal. As did many other members of his household, Nzingu Kuwu converted to the newly imported religion, taking the baptismal name of João I. Among the converts was his son, Nzinga Mbemba, who took the Christian name of Afonso in 1491.

Eventually, King João I became disillusioned by the Portuguese, whom he found to be corrupt, and he expelled them from the kingdom soon after his conversion to Christianity. But Afonso, who was then a provincial governor of a province in his father's kingdom, gave the exiled Westerners a safe haven. Afonso maintained close ties with the Portuguese, who came first to trade for ivory and other local goods but stayed to participate in the increasingly lucrative slave trade. When King João died in 1506, Afonso inherited the Kongo throne, and the Portuguese returned to royal favor.

Afonso I used his ties to the Portuguese and his control over the supply of slaves and trade goods to enrich his kingdom and consolidate his power, successfully expanding his realm throughout the region. He manipulated Christian doctrine to strengthen his claim to power, adapting the rituals of the church to further this end. He even invoked divine intervention to explain his victory over his rivals to the throne, using the claim of God's favor to justify the establishment of the dynasty he founded.

Contacts with Westerners and with Christianity had a powerful influence on Afonso I. During his reign, he established schools modeled after those of Portugal and ordered the construction of churches throughout his kingdom. He ordered that the young men of his lineage be educated in Lisbon in Portugal, and one son, Henrique, returned to the Kongo as a Catholic bishop. However, relations with Portugal eventually soured dramatically over disputes regarding the slave trade, so much so that, in 1540, his erstwhile Portuguese allies attempted to have him assassinated. Unlike his father, however, Afonso remained faithful to the Catholic Church until his death in 1543.

See also: KONGO KINGDOM.

AFRICAN KINGDOMS

Diverse kingdoms and tribal societies that have existed in Africa over the course of the last 5,000 years.

The earliest known kingdom in Africa arose along the banks of the Nile River between 3200 and 3000 B.C.E., when a man named Menes founded the first Egyptian dynasty of rulers that became known as pharoahs. If earlier kingdoms existed elsewhere in Africa, there is no direct evidence of them. However, the founder of the first Egyptian dynasty clearly had some concept of a state-like social organization, since it was through his efforts that independent settlements were unified into a larger political unit.

Whether Menes came up with the idea independently or was inspired by knowledge of similar political forms that already existed is a matter of scholarly speculation. Some experts argue that Egypt invented the form, whereas others suggest that the idea of kingship originated in the African interior and was adopted by the pharaohs.

FEATURES OF AFRICAN KINGSHIP

The continent of Africa is immense, and its peoples and resources are highly variable from one region to another. It is therefore no surprise that Africa's human communities would occur in a wide variety of forms. Nonetheless, across the range of Africa's kingdoms—indeed, across the range of kingdoms the world over—there are a number of features shared in common. First is the fact of hierarchical organization, with a single authority—be it a king, queen, or pharaoh—at the top. Second, there is generally an appeal to some extraworldly sanction that legitimizes the authority of the ruler. This is frequently expressed in religious terms: the ruler (and his or her

ROYAL RITUALS

POLYGYNOUS MONARCHS

One way in which African kings have played a symbolic role as a unifying force in society has been through marriage. In many of Africa's monarchical societies, the king has been expected to take many wives, a practice known as polygyny. (Polygamy simply means the taking of multiple spouses, male or female, while polygyny refers specifically to multiple wives; polyandry means the taking of multiple husbands.)

By selecting wives from a wide range of clans within the society, the king forms marital alliances across the diverse regions, clans, and ethnic groups within his kingdom. These alliances serve both as a symbol of the kingdom's unity, and as a form of insurance for the king himself, for through such marriages he makes potential rivals or dissidents into kin, reducing the likelihood that they will become disloyal. This practice was commonly employed in the east African Kingdom of Buganda, whose king used marital alliances with the important families of his border territories to reduce the possibility of revolt among these far-flung, and thus difficult to control, regions of his kingdom.

AFRICAN KINGDOMS AND STATES, 1500–1800

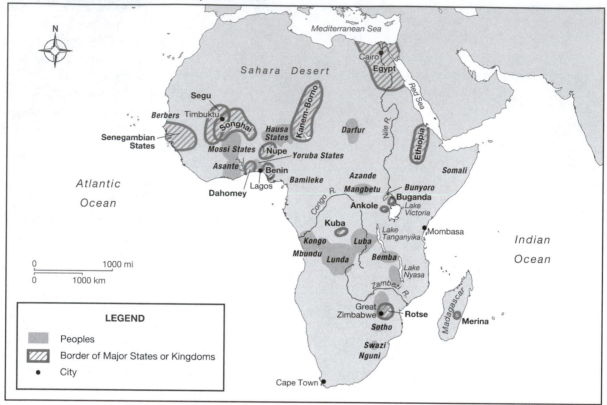

immediate line of descent) is believed to be related to a deity. Alternatively, the ruler's legitimacy may be based on a claim of kinship to an important, perhaps founding, ancestor of the community.

Whatever the basis for a monarch's claim to legitimacy, ritual and other public display represent important aspects of kingship. The ruler is not only an administrator of a state, but also a symbolic figure in whose person the identity of an entire people is made manifest. This is why, even today, when nearly all of Africa's traditional kingdoms have lost their political power, members of royal lineages have nonetheless retained great symbolic importance in terms of ethnic pride and identity.

CONDITIONS FOR THE RISE OF AFRICAN KINGDOMS

Large-scale political units such as kingdoms, which in Africa have encompassed populations as great as a million people, could not arise in a vacuum. Certain preconditions needed to be met before human populations began to organize themselves into communities that extended beyond small, kinship-based settlements. The most important of these preconditions, clearly exemplified by the rise of the kingdom

of Egypt, is the presence of enough resources—especially a stable and abundant food supply—to support a large number of people. The pre-kingdom communities that united to form pharaonic Egypt achieved this precondition in two ways: their early economy was based largely on fishing, thanks to the abundance provided by the Nile, and on the use of domesticated plants and animals, which came early to the region, probably introduced from the Near East.

The importance of surplus resources for the formation of kingdoms in Africa—or anywhere else in the world—should not be underestimated. Without an abundant, reliable supply of the necessities of life, communities cannot grow very large, and everyone in the community must spend most, if not all, of their time securing the livelihood of their households. This in turn means that each member—or at least each adult member—of the group is of equal importance to the survival of the whole. The best provider, or the strongest or cleverest individual, might enjoy a status within the group as "first among equals." Thus, that person's opinions might be given greatest consideration when the group is making decisions as to where to settle, what game to hunt, and so forth. As long as the group is relatively small, however, there is little need for that privileged position to extend to a broader administrative role. That function can, and usually does, remain within the purview of the heads of individual households.

When communities grow larger, and when settlements grow more dense, an authority that extends beyond individual households becomes necessary. This does not necessarily give rise to the need for a ruler of the order of a king. A particularly strong or respected individual could easily fulfill such an administrative need, as could someone with the reputation for wisdom or spirituality. As long as the problems to be resolved are largely or exclusively internal to the group, the need for a unifying concept beyond shared kinship and community life remains small. But when a community grows large enough that it interferes with the territorial claims of other groups—as occurred in the Nile Valley around 3200 B.C.E.—it becomes more important to forge a group identity distinct from that of rival neighbors.

This need for an identity, however, need not be initiated by intergroup competition or rivalry. It can just as easily arise from concerns that are not in dispute. For example, the pre-kingdom settlements of West Africa that participated in the trans-Saharan trade came to recognize that they could better exploit their advantages by organizing into a state. Such organization improved their ability to deal with traders and enabled them to support a military that could ensure their acquisition of trade goods from their neighbors. Such unity called for a strong leader whose authority extended beyond the internal conduct of the community to the control of that community's neighbors. This is one theory for the rise of the kingdom of Mali in the 1200s C.E. (founded by Sundjata Keita) and for the kingdoms of Takrur (in

As early as the first century C.E., Europeans had limited knowledge about the kingdoms and states of North and West Africa. This map, published in Strasbourg in 1522, is based on the second-century account of geographer Ptolemy of Alexandria.

Senegal) and Kanem (on the shores of Lake Chad), both of which arose in the late 600s C.E.

Finally, in addition to the indigenous monarchies of Africa, some kingdoms were formed through the intervention of outsiders. In other words, some African kingdoms were "made" rather than "born," and among the earliest of these were the kingdoms that arose in North Africa. One example is the kingdom of Numidia (in present-day Algeria), created by Rome in the second century B.C.E. Its ruler, Masinissa, was just one of many local chiefs, each of whom led a largely nomadic community that earned its livelihood through raiding the trans-Saharan trade caravans and sedentary communities along the North African coast. When Rome extended its empire to North Africa and sought to secure its newly acquired territory, it made a deal with Masinissa to pacify the region. In return for his loyalty to Rome, he was given the title of king and granted authority over a much greater territory than he could have secured for himself (with Roman troops to enforce his claims).

THE POWER AND SYMBOLISM OF KINGS

The role of a king in Africa involved more than the execution of administrative and leadership skills. Kings—and in rare cases, queens—served as the incarnations of their people's histories; as mediators between their communities and the gods, ancestors, and/or forces of nature; as defenders of the principles and values that their citizens held dear; and as an emblem of their community's continuity over time. But no one individual, with his or her personal loyalties and concerns, could fulfill all these functions. To act as such a potent symbol for all the populace, the ruler must at least appear to stand apart from normal preferences and prejudices. He or she must appear to represent all the various interests of the people. Therefore, African monarchs have employed a variety of rituals and symbolic items intended to lift them from the average citizenry and create a privileged office that transcends intragroup rivalries and competing interests.

Kingly regalia, for instance, can serve this function. Among the Asante of West Africa, one well-known ritual possession of the kingdom is the Golden Stool, a sacred object on which no one may sit. Among many peoples, the king's clothing and personal accessories, such as ornate headdresses, fly whisks, or special robes, spears, crowns, or necklaces, serve a similar function. Among many African kingdoms, certain locations are dedicated to the office of the king, commemorating the reigns of the current ruler's ancestors. Among the many peoples whose ancestral kings are honored by such shrines are the Lozi of Zambia.

Ritual occasions are another way that the African monarch is marked as different from the average citizen. Among many African peoples, the king is expected to make a regular circuit of his territory, stopping at villages and towns and ancestral shrines along the way to hold court and hear from the people, or to hold ceremonies of a religious nature. Allowing himself (or herself) to be seen by the people reinforces the immediacy of the king's authority. A monarch's role may also include direct intercession with gods, ancestors, or natural forces on behalf of the people. The queens of the Lovedu, for example, have traditionally been associated with the rain and are believed to embody—and ensure—the fertility of the people and of their land.

ROYAL ADVISERS AND SUCCESSION TO THE THRONE

To fulfill the duties of a monarch, the occupant of the throne must rely on the assistance of others, such as court officials, military advisers, and generals. It would seem logical that such assistants would best be drawn from the ranks of the royal family. However, this is also the group from which a monarch's successor must be chosen. Upon the death of a ruler, succession is generally restricted to descendants of that king, or at least to members of the royal lineage—a brother, an uncle, or (more rarely) a sister, wife, or mother. The close proximity of these relatives to the throne results in a conflict of interest: a ruler's relatives might be valuable allies and agents of the monarch, if their loyalty is certain, but they may also be dangerous rivals if they seek the power of the throne prematurely.

In order to reduce the potential for intrigue and treachery among courtiers and advisers who might covet the throne, a variety of strategies have been developed. For instance, among the Ganda of the Buganda kingdom—who honor patrilineal descent (descent through father)—the danger of relying on the support and advice of a rival claimant to the throne is mitigated by the practice of employing only maternal relatives (who are by definition ineligible to rule). This arrangement serves the interests of both ruler and advisers, for royal advisers can lay claim to their privileged position of courtiers only so long as the king remains upon the throne. An alternative approach, employed by the Bagirmi of Chad, among others, is to appoint nonrelatives—often slaves who may not even be of the same ethnic group as the monarch and his people—as military and political officials. These individuals, who have no prospect whatsoever of ascending to the throne in the normal order of things, are therefore trusted to advise and to act solely in accordance with the interests of the king.

Strategies for choosing a successor to the throne upon the death of a monarch are also somewhat variable across the range of African kingdoms. In some cases, as among the pharaohs of Egypt, succession is dictated by birth order and parentage: the firstborn son of the "first" or "true" wife (always a sister or half-sister of the pharaoh) was the presumptive heir to the throne. Among other peoples, however, no such formal mechanism of inheritance existed. A king might designate a favorite as the heir to the throne, or no heir might be named. The virtue of the former strategy is to provide a clearly understood order of succession: the monarch's chosen successor is known well before he or she ever takes office. However, such designation in advance of the death or retirement of the monarch has its drawbacks. Others who believe they also have a claim to the throne may protest the choice, possibly through violence against the king or his designee. On the other hand, supporters of the designated successor may decide not to wait for the reigning monarch to die or retire and may hasten matters by assassinating the ruler in order to clear the way for the heir.

To avoid such difficulties, some rulers have simply not designated any heir, leaving the people or, more likely, the elders and other leaders, to select a new ruler on their own. Such a situation can also arise if the current ruler dies unexpectedly, or if he or she leaves no traditionally appropriate heir. When there is no designated or traditional heir to the throne, the result is often a violent period during which various claimants attempt to take the throne by force. When one claimant succeeds in securing the throne, it is not uncommon for that monarch to eliminate potential rivals by killing those who might challenge his or her right to rule.

MODERN AFRICAN KINGDOMS

Today only three nations in Africa still retain a monarchical form of government: Morocco in North Africa and Lesotho and Swaziland, both in southern Africa. The Alawi dynasty has reigned in Morocco since the seventeenth century C.E. The kingdom of Lesotho differs from traditional African monarchies in that its king serves a largely symbolic role, while actual governance falls to constitutionally elected officials: a prime minister and parliament.

Swaziland, on the other hand, is the last nation in Africa to be ruled by an absolute monarch. The current hereditary king, Mswati III (r. 1986–), came to the throne in 1986. His mother served as regent between 1982, when the previous king died, and 1986, when Mswati came of age. Unlike the king of Lesotho, Mswati has direct control over Swaziland's government, and in large part he personally appoints the officials who serve in the nation's parliament. Although there is political pressure within Swaziland to do away with the absolute power of the king and move to a more democratic form of government, such efforts have so far met with no real success.

Kingships below the national level still exist within many of Africa's nation-states. For example, among the Zulu of southern Africa and the Yoruba and Asante of western Africa, the traditional office of kings is still recognized. However, these localized kingdoms have no true political power at the national level. Instead, they serve as local, ethnically specific symbols of unity and identity.

See also: ASANTE KINGDOM; BAMBARA KINGDOM; BENIN KINGDOM; ITSEKERI KINGDOM; KANEMBU-KANURI KINGDOM; KONGO KINGDOM; LOVEDU KINGDOM; LOZI (OR ROTSE) KINGDOM; LUBA KINGDOM; LUNDA KINGDOM; MALI, ANCIENT KINGDOM OF; MANGBETU KINGDOM; MBUNDU KINGDOMS; MERINA KINGDOM; MOSSI KINGDOMS; NUPE KINGDOM; NYORO KINGDOM; SHILLUK KINGDOM; SONGHAI KINGDOM; SOTHO (SUTO) KINGDOM; ZANZIBAR SULTANATE; ZULU KINGDOM.

AHAB (d. 853 B.C.E.)

King of Israel (r. ca. 874–853 B.C.E.), a contemporary of the prophet Elijah, who allowed the worship of the god Baal alongside the traditional Jewish worship of Yahweh.

Ahab was the seventh king of the kingdom of Israel. (At this time, the land of the Hebrews was divided into two kingdoms, Israel in the north and Judah in the south.) Ahab's father, king Omri (r. 885–874 B.C.E.), secured a marriage for his son to Jezebel, the daughter of the king of Sidon (in Phoenicia), thus reaffirming a political connection with Phoenicia that had been missing since the days of King Solomon (r. 970–931 B.C.E.). This alliance, along with tributary relationships established between the Gilead, Bashan, and Moab tribes of Israel, established the potential for a peaceful rule.

Despite the possibility of peace at home, Ahab fought continuing wars and skirmishes with the encroaching Syrians throughout his life. The aggressive Assyrians remained a constant threat as well. In 855 B.C.E., Ahab combined forces with the Syrians and defeated the encroaching Assyrian ruler, Shalmaneser III (r. 858–824 B.C.E.), at Karkar on the Orontes River, demonstrating to the Assyrians that Israel would not be easily overrun. Aside from these persistent problems with the Syrians and Assyrians, however, Ahab's reign was generally quite peaceful. His alliance with King Jehoshaphat (r. ca. 873–849 B.C.E.) of Judah helped maintain friendly relations with that less-powerful kingdom to the south.

Ahab's wife, Queen Jezebel, aroused strong opposition in Israel, especially from the prophet Elijah, because of her worship of the Canaanite god Baal. According to the Hebrew historian Josephus (first century B.C.E.), Ahab allowed Jezebel to participate in and promote the worship of Baal in Israel. Ahab himself participated in these ceremonies, specifically using the brazen serpent (made by Moses and kept in the Temple of Solomon) in the worship rituals. Critics also accused Ahab of excessive luxury— he built a room made entirely of ivory for his "painted queen," who may have used Egyptian styles of facial makeup, which were seen as decadent by many Hebrews.

The prophet Elijah made much of Ahab's un-Jewish ways, and Jezebel more than returned the prophet's antipathy. After Ahab confiscated the vineyard of a friend of Elijah's, the prophet cursed the king and his wife. Shortly thereafter, Ahab was slain in battle with the Syrians. He was succeeded by his son, Ahaziah (r. 853–852 B.C.E.).

See also: ISRAEL, KINGDOMS OF; JUDAH, KINGDOM OF.

AHMADNAGAR KINGDOM
(1494–1636 C.E.)

One of five Muslim states located on the Deccan, a plateau in south-central India, that was almost continuously at war with other states.

Around 1500, as the Bahmani sultanate began to decline, the Deccan broke up into five Muslim states. A Bahmani noble, Malik Ahmad Nizam Shahi (r. 1494–1509), took control of territory on the Sini River, centered at the site of the ancient town of Bhingar. Malik named the territory Ahmadnagar (or Ahmednagar) and founded the Nizam Shah dynasty. Malik built a great fort at Ahmadnagar (which the British used in the 1940s to jail Indian nationalist leader, Jawaharlal Nehru).

Throughout the reign of the Nizam Shahi dynasty, the Ahmadnagar kingdom was constantly at war. Ahmad's son, Burhan Nizam Shah (r. 1509–1553) aligned himself with the Hindu Vijayanagar Empire against other Deccan states. He was succeeded by Hussain Shah (r. 1553–1565), who reversed that policy, signing a treaty with the other Muslim states of the Deccan in an effort to keep any one state from dominating the area and for their mutual survival. In 1565, the Deccan states of Bijapur and Golconda acted with Ahmadnagar to destroy the city of Vijayanagar and its forces at the battle of Talikota.

Between 1500 and 1600, Chand Bibi, the queen dowager of Bijapur, gallantly resisted attacks by the Mughal dynasty from the north. When the state of Berar ceded to the Mughals in 1596, Mughal emperor Akbar the Great (r. 1556–1605) was able to annex the greater part of the Deccan. Ahmadnagar fell to the Mughals after the queen's death, but the Shahi dynasty and a part of the state of Ahmadnagar remained until the fall of Deccan city of Daulatabad in 1633 and the coming of the Mughal emperor Shah Jahan (r. 1628–1658) to the region in 1636.

During the Mughal decline in the eighteenth century, the states of the Deccan experienced numerous rivalries and conflicts over succession. In 1759, the Peshwas of the Maratha Confederacy gained control of Ahmadnagar, which was ceded to the Maratha chief Daulat Rao Sindhia (d. 1827) in 1797.

When the Peshwas signed the Treaty of Bassein with Great Britain in 1893, agreeing to British protection and the presence of British soldiers in Peshwa lands, Sindhia objected. In response, the British captured Ahmadnagar in 1803 and returned it to the Peshwas. Ahmadnagar remained neutral during the third Maratha war (1817–1818) when the British crushed the Peshwas and all other opposing forces in southwestern India. Ahmadnagar became part of the nation of India when it gained its independence from Great Britain in 1947.

See also: AKBAR THE GREAT; BAHMANI DYNASTY; GOLCONDA KINGDOM; INDIAN KINGDOMS; JAHAN, SHAH; MUGHAL EMPIRE; VIJAYANAGAR EMPIRE.

AHMOSE I (ca. 1560–1546 B.C.E.)

Pharaoh of Egypt (r. ca. 1570–1546 B.C.E.) and founder of the Eighteenth dynasty, the greatest achievement of which was driving the Hyksos out of Egypt.

When Ahmose was ten years old, he inherited the contested throne of Egypt from his brother, Kamose (r. ca. 1576–1570 B.C.E.). Kamose, like his father Seqenenre Tao II (r. ca. 1591–1576 B.C.E.) before him, had died while fighting to drive out the Hyksos, a nomadic people of Semitic origin from western Asia who had ruled Egypt since the beginning of the Fifteenth dynasty (ca. 1668–1560 B.C.E.).

Ten years after assuming the throne, Ahmose massed his troops and captured Memphis, Egypt's traditional capital. The Hyksos, however, were based in Avaris. Ahmose I left his mother, Queen Ashotep, to oversee the government from Thebes and proceeded to lay siege to the city of Avaris.

The siege of Avaris was interrupted by a rebellion in Upper (southern) Egypt, which Ahmose was forced to quell before he could proceed with his plans. Having successfully stopped the rebellion, he returned to capture Avaris. The surviving Hyksos fled to Palestine, where Ahmose later pursued them.

First, however, Ahmose chose to lead his troops south into the land of the Nubians, who had been allies of the Hyksos. Ahmose conquered Nubia as far south as the Second Cataract of the Nile near the fortress of Buhen, and he appointed a governor to administer the region and secure the riches of the Nubian gold mines for Egypt. While Ahmose was in Nubia, Egypt was once more threatened by insurrection, which was put down by Queen Ashotep.

Once Ahmose had finished strengthening his borders, he turned to domestic matters. Ancient records show that Ahmose granted lands to veterans of his campaigns as well as to various members of his family. Several inscriptions from the period refer to cedar found in Syria, suggesting that Ahmose resumed trade with that country. Inscriptions also reveal that he restored temples and erected new ones.

Ahmose I, like many of the Egyptian pharaohs, married his sister to keep his supposedly divine bloodlines pure. His sister-wife, Ahmose-Nefertiri, became the first "God's Wife of Amun," an important religious and political role that continued until the Twenty-Sixth dynasty (ca. 664–525 B.C.E.). Together, Ahmose and Nefertiri had numerous children, many of whom died young. His third son, Amenhotep I (r. 1551–1524 B.C.E.) inherited the newly reunited Egypt upon Ahmose's death in 1546 B.C.E.

See also: DIVINITY OF KINGS; EGYPTIAN DYNASTIES, ANCIENT (EIGHTEENTH TO TWENTY-SIXTH); HYKSOS DYNASTY; NUBIAN KINGDOMS.

AKAN KINGDOMS (1700s–1900s C.E.)

Group of independent kingdoms that arose in western Africa in response to the growth of the trans-Saharan and, later, Atlantic trade.

Until about the seventeenth century, the sub-Sahelian region bounded on the west by the Bandama River (in present-day Ivory Coast) and the Volta River (in present-day Ghana) and extending southward to the Atlantic coast was populated by small, clan-based communities of people known as Akan. Beginning in the 1400s, however, several factors conspired to encourage the transformation of these independent communities into larger political units, eventually giving rise to the formation of what are now known collectively as the Akan kingdoms, Of these, the two most powerful were the Fante and Asante kingdoms.

The Akan peoples shared several characteristics that facilitated the rise of states. Among them were matrilineal descent, shared religious beliefs, and a common linguistic tradition. In addition, all these communities gained their livelihood by forest cultivation. Perhaps most important to the eventual rise of states in the region, however, was gold, which was present in rich deposits throughout their territory. It was this highly prized commodity that attracted the trans-Saharan traders to extend their routes southward into Akan territory.

IMPACT OF TRADE

By the middle of the 1400s, the arrival of trading specialists eager to exploit the availability of gold had led to the founding of a series of important trade centers within Akan territory. Here the precious mineral was exchanged for fabrics, leather goods, brassware, and other items, brought from as far away as Turkey. To better control access to the increased wealth available through trade, and to defend the gold-producing lands from takeover by rival peoples in the region, many of the previously independent Akan communities began to coalesce into larger political units. This was especially true along the northern border, where forest and savannah (grasslands) meet. This coalescing of communities gave rise to the earliest Akan states. First among those formed was the Bono state, which was centered upon the wealthy trading town of Begho.

Later in the fourteenth century, additional impetus toward state formation was provided when a new group of outsiders arrived in Akan territory from the south. These were the Portuguese, who landed on Akan shores in 1471 and drew the region into the Atlantic trade with Europe. The Portuguese were followed in short order by traders from France, England, and the Netherlands, among others.

These new commercial interests were principally drawn by the region's gold, and, in return, they introduced new crops such as maize, manioc, and groundnuts, brought from their possessions in the new world. The new crops greatly transformed local agriculture, permitting a rapid population expansion that further encouraged the development of more sophisticated political organization in the region.

RISE OF STRONG LEADERS

With the introduction of firearms by European traders, the means of conquest and consolidation were vastly enhanced as well, and strong leaders arose who were eager to gain greater control over the now highly lucrative gold trade. Among these militaristic leaders was Awurade Basa, who in the 1500s waged a series of wars of conquests against his neighbors in what is now southern Ghana. His efforts sparked a great population movement, as refugees fled the area of conflict.

These refugees settled in communities to the south and east and founded small states of their own. By the mid-1600s, there were dozens of such small states scattered throughout the southern portion of Akan territory. Among these, the Denkyira, who arose in the center of the region, was perhaps the most powerful, but in the east another kingdom, called Akwamu, was dominant during roughly the same period.

Over the next 100 years, the gold trade continued to enrich the various states of the Akan region and was largely controlled by the Denkyira and Akwamu rulers. These kings only increased their wealth and power as a new commodity, slaves, grew in importance to their European trade partners. However, within Denkyira, many communities were beginning to revolt, and by the start of the 1700s a confederation had been formed among the more powerful local chiefdoms.

This confederation, called Asante, was led by Osei Tutu (r. ca. 1701–1717). Osei Tutu succeeded in overthrowing the Denkyira king in 1701 and became Asantehene, or king of Asante. The capital of this new state was created at Kumasi. A similar revolt occurred in Akwamu, which was overthrown around 1730 by a confederacy led by the Akyem. The Asante state achieved supremacy throughout most of Akan territory, demanding and receiving tribute from the less powerful kingdoms of the region until they were dissolved by the British in 1900–1901.

See also: ASANTE KINGDOM; OSEI TUTU.

FURTHER READING
McCaskie, T.C. *State and Society in Pre-Colonial Asante.* New York: Cambridge University Press, 1995.

Shillington, Kevin. *History of Africa.* New York: St. Martin's Press, 1989.

AKBAR THE GREAT (1542–1605 C.E.)

Third emperor of the Mughal dynasty of India, who is remembered as an enlightened ruler who preached tolerance for his non-Muslim subjects and established a highly efficient system of government.

The grandson of Babur (r. 1526–1530), the founder of the Mughal dynasty, Akbar became ruler of India in 1556 upon the accidental death of his father, Humayun (r. 1530–1540; 1555–1556). Only thirteen years old at the time, Akbar did not take full charge of the empire. Instead, a "protector" or regent, Bairam Khan, controlled the government. By the time Akbar turned eighteen, he was impatient to assume greater control over his realm. He dismissed

ROYAL RITUALS

THE JIZYA TAX

During the expansion of Islam into non-Islamic lands, the *jizya* tax caused a great deal of resentment among non-Muslims. This special tax, levied on unbelievers (infidels), was a form of protection money, the payment of which earned non-Muslim subjects the right to security and freedom from molestation within a Muslim realm. Although the levy was generally small, it was graduated to accommodate different economic levels, and it exempted the unemployed and impoverished. Nonetheless, many non-Muslims perceived the tax to be a form of humiliation. This is why Akbar's revocation of the *jizya* was such a profoundly popular act: by eliminating the tax, Akbar was signifying the equality of his Muslim and non-Muslim subjects.

Bairam Khan in 1560 and sent him on a pilgrimage to Mecca; the regent was killed by an Afgani assassin along the route.

Bairam's dismissal and death did not lead to greater autonomy for Akbar, however, because one of his father's wives, Maham Anaga, and her son, Adam Khan, assumed power. Akbar chafed under these circumstances, finally deciding to take charge by force. He had Adam Khan killed in 1562, and Maham Anaga died soon afterward, leaving the twenty-year-old Akbar in full control of his empire.

Even before Akbar gained full autonomy, his rule had been marked by military success. In the year following his father's death, factions in the city of Delhi rebelled, and Akbar took decisive action to foil this challenge. In the second battle of Panipat in 1556, Akbar faced a challenger named Hemi, whom he successfully vanquished. With this victory, the Mughal dynasty was firmly established in power on the Indian continent.

The Mughal Empire expanded further during the rule by Akbar's regents. But it was only after 1564, when Akbar ruled in his own right, that the empire achieved truly impressive territorial gains. By 1601, Akbar had managed to expand the imperial borders in all directions, conquering Kashmir in the north, Orissa and Bengal in the east, Sindh in the west, and Kandesh and Varhad in the south. Despite these impressive gains, Akbar never succeeded in bringing the southernmost part of the Indian subcontinent into the empire.

To control his empire, Akbar instituted a system of government that relied on a division of the territory into provinces, each of which was ruled by an appointed governor. He won over the Rajput states in northwestern India by applying a policy of rewards and punishments. To create ties of loyalty, he took wives from among the noble classes of his subject states. According to some reports, these political marriages numbered more than five thousand.

Akbar's biggest problem was winning the acceptance of his Hindu subjects, something that his father and grandfather had never achieved. To accomplish this, Akbar made many political marriages to Hindu women, and he earned much goodwill by not requiring these wives to convert to Islam. Akbar also abolished the special tax levied upon non-Muslims (a significant break with normal Muslim practice), and he exempted the empire's Hindu territories from Muslim Shari'a law, permitting them to administer justice through their own Hindu court systems.

Akbar's grandfather Babur was considered a great scholar, but Akbar was an unlettered man. Nonetheless, during his reign he developed a great interest in the various cultures and religions represented within his empire. From the first, he proved to be more tolerant of the religious practices of his non-Muslim subjects, as evidenced by his abolition of the tax normally imposed on unbelievers. Over time, Akbar also became interested in discovering the common threads among the different religions of his subjects. He even went so far as to sponsor theological debates

One of India's preeminent rulers, Akbar the Great expanded the Mughal Empire to unprecedented size. This scene from an illustrated manuscript, circa 1630, shows Akbar symbolically passing the crown from his son, Jahangir, to his grandson, Shah Jahan.

within the palace, inviting Hindus, Jains, Buddhists, and others, including Jesuit priests from the Portuguese colony of Goa.

Such theological explorations ultimately led Akbar to create a personal religion, called *Din-i Ilahi* ("religion of God"), over which he presided as prophet. He required his courtiers and ministers to practice this new religion, which caused outrage among the orthodox Islamic clergy. These new beliefs bordered on apostasy, and one of his own sons became so infuriated by Akbar's apparent rejection of Islam that he attempted an insurrection. The rebellion failed, but Akbar realized that a return to accepted Islamic belief and behavior was necessary if he wished to retain his rule. He thus returned to more conventional religious practice.

During his reign, Akbar managed to hold together a coalition of widely disparate states, but he could not ensure that his religious and political tolerance would survive him. When Akbar died in 1605, his son Salim, who assumed the royal name Jahangir (r. 1605–1627), reversed most of his father's policies, reinstituting the non-Muslim tax and imposing Shari'a law throughout the realm. Jahangir's successor, his son Shah Jahan I (r. 1628–1658), continued the Islamicization of the imperial territory.

See also: BABUR; JAHAN, SHAH; JAHANGIR; MONGOL EMPIRE; POLYGAMY, ROYAL.

AKHENATEN (ca. 1350–1334 B.C.E.)

King of ancient Egypt (r. ca. 1350–1334 B.C.E.), a member of the Eighteenth dynasty, known for his attempt at religious reform.

Akhenaten, known originally as Amenhotep IV, changed his pharaonic name to honor the sun-god, Aten. He inherited the throne after serving as co-regent with his father, Amenhotep III (r. 1385–1349 B.C.E.). Akhenaten's wife, Nefertiti, who may have served with him as his co-regent (r. 1379–1358 B.C.E.), gave him six daughters. Among his other wives was Kiya, by whom he probably fathered Tutankhamen (r. 1334–1325 B.C.E.).

Akhenaten is important for his religious revolution. When he took the throne, Amun-Re was the chief divinity of ancient Egypt and had been for generations. Foreign gods, such as the Canaanite goddess Astarte, had also gained acceptance in Egypt, while the influx of foreigners into the empire made others argue for a more universal god. The concept of the sun's rays, giving life to the empire, had also begun to take root.

Akhenaten embraced this idea of one universal god. He thus abolished ancient Egypt's polytheism and established the sun-god, Aten, as the only god. He also established a new capital for his empire at Armana, where he founded an artistic school emphasizing the sun. Akhenaten also maintained that idols could not properly convey the majesty of Aten.

Akhenaten imposed his regime through terror. Around the eighth year of his rule, he began a persecution of the powerful priesthood of the ancient god Amun. He ordered that altars and religious objects everywhere be defaced and that the god Amun's name be erased. He apparently imposed his order with force, for surviving personal icons also show defacing. As a result of these policies, Akhenaten's regime became increasingly unpopular. Moreover, he showed little interest in statecraft or diplomacy, and his focus on religion cost Egypt its empire, as some of its provinces broke away.

Akhenaten died of uncertain causes in his seventeenth year as pharaoh and was succeeded briefly by his son Semenkhkare (r. 1336–1334 B.C.E.). Some think he had Marfan's disease, a genetic condition that causes unusually long limbs and congenital heart disease. Others think he was killed. After his death, his name was erased from Egypt's monuments and statues by his son and successor, Tutankhamen, who restored the old gods, partly because a famine made people believe that they were offended. Surviving references call Akhenaten "that heretic" or "the rebel."

Early Egyptologists viewed Akhenaten as a prophetic figure who, like the biblical prophets, was rejected by religious and political authorities of his time. More recent scholars, however, consider him politically calculating. By Akhenaten's time, the priesthood of Amun had become very powerful, and the pharoahs were unsure of their loyalty. By moving the capital to Armana and rejecting the old gods, Akhenaten sought to weaken the priests and concentrate power in his own hands. His new name implies this idea. *Amenophis* means "The god Amun is content"; *Akenaten* means "He who is effective on Aten's behalf." With Akhenaten as Aten's son, no priests were needed because the people worshiped Aten through worshiping Akhenaten.

See also: EGYPTIAN DYNASTIES, ANCIENT (EIGHTEENTH TO TWENTY-SIXTH); TUTANKHAMEN.

AKKAD, KINGDOM OF

(ca. 2334–2154 B.C.E.)

One of the oldest civilizations in the world and the founding kingdom of a vast Mesopotamian Empire.

In the fourth millennium B.C.E., a number of agricultural states began to form in the river valleys of Mesopotamia ("land between rivers") in what is now present-day Iraq. One of these early sedentary cultures was Akkad, located where the Tigris and the Euphrates rivers came the closest to one another.

Akkad was named after its capital city, Agade, built around 2335 B.C.E. by Akkad's first king, Sargon of Akkad (r. ca. 2334–2279 B.C.E.). Sargon rose from humble beginnings to create the first empire in history, uniting Akkad with Sumer, another culture that shared the Tigris and Euphrates River Valley. Sargon called his empire "the land of Sumer and Akkad."

An ancient artifact, the Sumerian king list, shows that the first five rulers of Akkad—Sargon, Rimush (r. ca. 2278–2270 B.C.E.), Manishtusu (r. ca. 2269–2255 B.C.E.), Naram-Sin (r. ca. 2254–2218 B.C.E.), and Shar-kali-sharri (r. ca. 2217–2193 B.C.E.)—ruled for a total of 142 years, although Sargon alone held the throne for fifty-six years. During this time, Akkad was the commercial and cultural center of the Middle East. The empire was connected by a system of roads, and a regular postal service was in operation.

Until Sargon, records from Akkad had been written in Sumerian. During his reign, however, the cuneiform writing of the Sumerians was adapted to fit the Akkadian language, and the resulting records have revealed Akkadian as the oldest known Semitic language. Cuneiform spread with the empire and was adopted in other states, including the kingdom of Elam, located to the west of Akkad. Akkadian artwork also came into its own during this period, and the surviving examples of the ancient cylindrical seals and stone reliefs are exquisite examples of their type.

The position of women in Akkadian society is difficult to determine. It seems that some Akkadian temples had priestesses rather than priests, and some of these priestesses were literate. Many historians consider the priestess Enheduanna, the daughter of Sargon, to be the first named author, because she has been identified as the writer of two long hymns. There is evidence indicating that Akkadian women also held jobs as midwives, nurses, singers, dancers, and musicians. Other records indicate that some women managed family lands and engaged in commerce.

After the death of the fifth king of Akkad, Shar-kali-sharri, in a palace coup, the Akkadian Empire lasted only about forty more years. Records from the period are sparse, and the exact chronology of the kindgom's decline is unclear. Surviving inscriptions suggest that internal strife over the succession may have played a role in weakening Akkad. But it is clear that the final blows came as a result of an external attack from the nomadic Amorites from the northwest and the Gutians, a mountain people from the East. Less than two centuries after Akkad had forged the world's first empire, Mesopotamia reverted to a series of independent city-states, not to be united again until the third dynasty of Ur was established around 2112 B.C.E.

See also: NARAM-SIN; SARGON OF AKKAD.

AKSUM KINGDOM

(ca. 6 B.C.E.–1150 C.E.)

The first of the Ethiopian kingdoms, originating as a result of the migration of Arab traders who sought new sources of ivory and slaves along the coast of northeastern Africa in around the sixth century B.C.E.

When Arab traders arrived in northeast Africa in the first millennium B.C.E., some settled in the territory of indigenous Tigre and Amhara peoples, intermarrying with the locals. Among the most important of the coastal settlements they founded was Adulis, through which most of the region's wealth passed on the way to markets in Persia and India. As the settlements grew in wealth and size, however, greater political organization was needed, and in the first century C.E. a true kingdom was founded, with its capital at the inland city of Aksum.

RISE OF THE KINGDOM

The rise of a kingdom from a handful of small trading towns was due, in part, to a growing population, which required the creation of greater central authority, as did the management of the profits of the ivory and slave trade. Equally important was the fact that these settlements had set themselves the goal of breaking the existing trade monopoly in the region. This had long been under the control of the kingdom of Meroe, located to the northeast, lying just south of the fifth cataract of the Nile.

An old and powerful kingdom, Meroe had dominated Ethiopia and other parts of northeastern Africa for centuries. By around 200, however, it had begun to decline. The young kingdom of Aksum, advantageously located and with its great trading port of Adulis, was able to take advantage of Meroe's waning power in the region, extending its own raids for ivory and slaves into territory that once was exclusively the preserve of the Meroitic kings.

Thus, Aksum's advance in power and stature was closely linked to its success in controlling trade with the Arabian Peninsula and points east, and by the fortuitous timing of Meroe's decline, to which its own economic competition contributed. By 300, Aksum was the preeminent power in the region and had become a center for art and learning. Attracting missionaries from the Alexandrian (Coptic) Church, King Ezana of Aksum (r. 320–350) greatly desired to forge strong trading ties with the Greeks, which then was the greatest power in the region. This may have been his reason for adopting Christianity in the name of his people. He also enjoyed great military success, using his powerful army to expand his kingdom westward and northward, and ultimately conquering Meroe itself.

PROSPERITY AND DECLINE

Aksumite kings ruled their central territories directly but merely extracted tribute from their outlying provinces. This light-handed rule did not ensure tranquility throughout the kingdom, as remote districts frequently rebelled. Nonetheless, the taxes collected on all trade goods passing through the port cities, over which the kings held tight control, were enough to provide enormous wealth to the rulers.

By the sixth century, Aksum had extended its power across the Red Sea to include present-day Yemen. The kings used missionaries and the church to forge a national unity, but this soon came into conflict with a new, rival religion in the region with the birth of Islam and its rapid spread throughout Arabia. By 800, the kingdom had lost much of its power, and its monopoly over regional trade was broken.

Aksum continued to prosper for several more centuries, although less grandly than in the past. Around 1150, the Aksumite kings were overthrown by a rival clan, who installed a new ruling family for the kingdom. This was the Zagwe dynasty, which held the reins of power until 1270. The Zagwe were then overthrown by Amharic rebels and replaced by a new ruling lineage, the Solomonids. This dynasty claimed ancestral ties to the old Aksumite kings as well as to King Solomon and the Queen of Sheba, and it used the Christian Bible as justification for rule.

See also: AMHARA KINGDOM; NUBIAN KINGDOMS.

FURTHER READING
Munro-Hay, Stuart C. *Aksum: An African Civilisation of Late Antiquity.* Edinburgh: Edinburgh University Press, 1991.

ALARIC I (370–410 C.E.)

King of the Germanic Visigoths (r. 395–410), whose conquest of the city of Rome in 410 signaled the end of the Western Roman Empire.

When Alaric was born in 370 on an island in the Danube River, his parents foresaw their son's greatness, naming him from the Gothic word *Ala-Reiks*, or "Master of All." Alaric went on to rule the Germanic kingdom of the Visigoths on the Danube River, and later in the Roman province of Illyria along the coast of the Adriatic Sea.

Alaric was born into a particularly troubled time. Under attack from the east by the invading Huns, the Visigoths moved into Roman territory in 376 with the permission of the Eastern Roman emperor Valens (r. 364–378). In return for the privilege of living in the new territory, the Visigoths agreed to serve in the Roman army against the invading Huns.

In 394, Alaric took command of the Visigothic troops serving under Emperor Theodosius I (r. 379–395). The following year, after Theodosius died, and after the Visigoths had suffered a decade of neglect and near starvation, Alaric broke his allegiance with the Romans and turned west. His troops revolted against the Romans, and Alaric claimed the title of king of the Visigoths.

Led by Alaric, the Visigoths hounded western Roman forces throughout Southern Europe and into the Italian Peninsula over the next decade. During an invasion of Italy in 408, Alaric laid siege to the city of Rome, but the siege was raised after he reached an agreement with the Roman Senate. In 410, the Visigoths invaded Italy again, this time successfully sacking Rome, the first time the western imperial capital had been captured since 390 B.C.E., when it had been sacked by the Celtic Gauls.

Alaric died while planning further incursions into Roman territory in Sicily and North Africa. After his death, the Visigoths reached an agreement with the western emperor, Honorius (r. 395–423), which allowed them to settle in southern Gaul (present-day France). From there, the Visigoths moved into the Iberian Peninsula and established a Christian kingdom in Spain.

See also: ROMAN EMPIRE; THEODOSIUS I, THE GREAT; VISIGOTH KINGDOM.

FURTHER READING

Brion, Marcel. *Alaric The Goth*. Trans. Frederick H. Martens. New York: R. M. McBride, 1930.

ALAUNGPAYA DYNASTY

(1752–1885 C.E.)

Burmese dynasty (also known as the Kongbaung dynasty) that led Myanmar (Burma) in an era of expansionism that lasted from the mid-1700s to the 1880s. The collapse of the dynasty as a result of increasing British military dominance of the region signaled the end of Myanmar's independence for more than sixty years.

The Alaungpaya dynasty was founded by a Burmese leader named Alaungpaya (r. 1752–1760), son of a village headman, who gained control of upper Myanmar and the Shan states of central Myanmar in 1752 and assumed the title of king, establishing a capital at Rangoon. By 1759, Alaungpaya had conquered the Indian state of Manipur, which bordered Myanmar in the northwest, as well as the Mon people of the delta region of the Irrawaddy River. He also conquered and destroyed Pegu, the Mon capital.

Also in 1759, Alaungpaya responded to Siamese attempts to incite rebellion in Myanmar with an invasion of their territory. He captured the ports of Moulmein, Tavoy, and Tenasserim and surrounded Ayutthaya, the capital of Siam, the following year. During the siege of Ayutthaya, Alaungpaya was mortally wounded and died while his army retreated. He was succeeded by his son Naungdawgyi (r. 1760–1763), who ruled for only about three years.

In 1767, Alaungpaya's second son, Hsinbyushin (r. 1763–1776), mounted a successful invasion of Siam and succeeded where his father had failed. After mounting a fourteen-month siege against Ayutthaya, the capital city fell and the Myanmar armies sacked the city entirely.

Hsinbyushin's armies occupied much of the Shan and Lao states as well as the Manipur kingdom in India. During the period between 1766 and 1769, China, fearing the growing power of Myanmar, invaded the county four times but was held off by Hsinbyushin.

Bodawpaya (r. 1782–1819), another son of Alaungpaya and sixth king of the dynasty, launched frequent but unsuccessful campaigns to recapture

Ayutthaya, which the Siamese had reoccupied after its initial defeat. His grandson and successor, Bagyidaw (r. 1819–1837), was defeated by the British in the First Anglo-Burmese War (1824–1826). In the resulting Treaty of Yandabo (1826), he was forced to cede several coastal regions to British India.

Myanmar continued to lose territory and authority to the British, and in 1852, King Pagan (r. 1846–1853), the ninth ruler of the Alaungpaya dynasty, was defeated by the British in the Second Anglo-Burmese War (1852), leading to the loss of southern Myanmar.

By 1878, the struggle between Myanmar and the British was at a peak. Britain, fearing the rising power of the French in Southeast Asia, launched a Third Anglo-Burmese War (1885) to gain full control of the region. The victorious British annexed all of Burma and deposed the current king, Thibaw (r. 1778–1885), ending the rule of the Alaungpaya dynasty.

See also: AYUTTHAYA KINGDOM; BURMESE KINGDOMS; MANIPUR KINGDOM; PEGU KINGDOMS; SIAM, KINGDOMS OF; THIBAW.

ALBERT I (1250–1308 C.E.)

King of Germany (r. 1298–1308) and duke of Austria and Styria (r. 1282–1298), a member of the powerful Habsburg dynasty, who was a capable military leader and competent administrator.

Albert I was the son of King of Germany Rudolph I (r. 1273–1291), the founder of the Habsburg dynasty and king of the Germans. Toward the end of Rudolph's reign, the German princes, or electors, became afraid of the growing power and independence of the Habsburgs. Thus, after Rudolph's death in 1291, the electors, led by Archbishop Gerhard Mainz, acted to prevent the Crown from becoming hereditary.

Instead of choosing Albert to succeed his father, the German princes elected the duke of Luxemburg, Adolph of Nassau (r. 1292–1298), as King of Germany. Adolph took the throne in 1292. Before long, however, Pope Boniface VIII became dissatisfied with Adolph, who had allied with Edward I of England (r. 1272–1307) against Philip IV of France (r. 1285–1314).

In 1298, with the support of the pope and most of the princes, Albert deposed Adolph. Adolph's forces met those of Albert at the battle of Gollsheim, where Adolph was defeated and killed. With Adolph's death, the princes elected Albert as king. Meanwhile, Albert's son, Rudolph III (r. 1298–1307), took over the duchy of Austria.

It was politically important for Albert's authority to be recognized by Pope Boniface VIII, who had helped Albert get elected. But after the removal of Adolph, Boniface became concerned about the relaxation of tensions between France and Germany, and he wanted Albert to renounce all imperial rights to northern Italy. Albert refused, and Boniface refused to recognize Albert's Crown.

Boniface started to organize what was left of Adolph's supporters against Albert. This greatly annoyed Albert, who then arranged a marriage between his son and the daughter of King Phillip IV of France. Albert also supported the towns along the Rhine River in a toll struggle against the German imperial electors, who were backed by the pope. The electors revolted, but Albert suppressed the uprising.

In 1303, the pope needed Albert's support in the papal struggle against France, and an agreement was negotiated between Albert and the papacy. In return for recognition by the pope, Albert would acknowledge that only the pope had the right to bestow the imperial Crown of the Holy Roman Empire. Albert promised that none of his sons would be elected German king and emperor without papal consent.

Free from his disagreement with the pope, Albert turned his attention to his empire. In 1301, King Wenceslaus II of Bohemia (r. 1278–1305) and Poland (r. 1300–1305) claimed the Hungarian succession for his son, Wenceslaus III (r. 1301–1305). Fearful of a possible alliance between Bohemia and France, Albert marched into Hungary in 1304. The situation changed, however, when Wenceslaus II died in 1305. His son, Wenceslaus III, the last ruler of the Premysl dynasty, withdrew to his kingdom of Bohemia. When Wenceslaus III was murdered in 1306, Albert claimed both Bohemia and Moravia for his son, Rudolph (r. 1306–1307).

In 1307, Albert attempted to claim the region of Thuringia, but his forces were defeated at the battle of Lucka. Meanwhile, Albert's son Rudolph died the same year, leaving Bohemia to Henry of Carinthia (r. 1307–1310). Revolts in Swabia, the Swiss cantons, and the Rhineland later in the year forced Albert to turn his attention to the west. In 1308, a group of conspirators, including a nephew, Duke John of Swabia, assassinated Albert I. His successor on the throne, elected by the German princes, was Henry of Luxembourg, who ruled as Henry VII (r. 1308–1313).

See also: HABSBURG DYNASTY; HOLY ROMAN EMPIRE; PHILIP IV, THE FAIR; RUDOLF I.

FURTHER READING

Heer, Friedrich. *The Holy Roman Empire.* London: Weidenfeld & Nicolson, 1968.

ALEXANDER I (1888–1934 C.E.)

King of Yugoslavia from 1921 to 1934, who was a key figure in the Balkan Wars and World War I.

Born in the Balkan state of Montenegro on December 16, 1888, Alexander was the second son of King Peter I (r. 1903–1921), ruler of the kingdom of the Serbs, Croats, and Slovenes. Educated largely in Russia, Alexander became crown prince of Serbia in 1909 after his older brother, George, renounced his succession to the throne. In 1904, Alexander joined the imperial forces of Russia, and he later gained distinction as a leader of Serbian forces fighting against the Ottoman Turks during the Balkan Wars of 1912–1913.

Some historians speculate that Alexander may have been linked to the Serbian Black Hand society, the organization credited with masterminding the assassination of Archduke Franz Ferdinand of Austro-Hungary on June 28, 1914, an event that led to the start of World War I. This is unproven, however. During the war, Alexander led Serbian forces and petitioned Allied governments to combine forces and form a "greater Serbia" comprised of the kingdoms of the Serbs, Croats, and Slovenes. This unification ultimately occurred on December 1, 1918, with Alexander acting as regent of the kingdom for his father, who was in exile in Geneva, Switzerland.

Alexander took the throne upon the death of his father in 1921, and on August 3, 1929, he renamed the kingdom Yugoslavia. The change led to some problems, however. Croat nationalism caused great ethnic and religious turmoil within the country. In an effort to overcome dissent, Alexander abolished parliament and declared a dictatorship on January 6, 1929.

In 1931, Alexander declared an end to the dictatorship and proclaimed a new constitution, keeping the majority of the power to himself, however. He improved diplomatic relations with other Balkan states, but his authoritarian control and centralized authority led to increased dissent and tensions within Yugoslavia as separatist factions of Croats and Macedonians fought for a return to democracy.

While on a diplomatic visit to France in 1934, Alexander was assassinated by a member of a Croatian terrorist organization. He was succeeded on the throne by his son, Peter II (r. 1934–1945).

See also: CROATIAN KINGDOM; MONTENEGRO KINGDOM; SERBIAN KINGDOM.

ALEXANDER I, TSAR (1777–1825 C.E.)

Russian emperor who ruled from 1801 to 1825 and who expelled Napoleon from Russia in 1812.

Alexander Pavlovich was the grandson of Catherine II (r. 1762–1796) and the oldest son of Paul Petrovich and Maria Fedorovna. As empress, Catherine had isolated Alexander from his parents because she wanted him to succeed her rather than her own son Paul, whom she disliked. To prepare Alexander for the throne, she hired the Swiss republican Jean Francoise de La Harpe to instruct him in European politics, history, and philosophy. Under La Harpe's tutelage, Alexander embraced the need for a Russian constitution and renounced governmental corruption and serfdom.

Despite Catherine's plans, her son Paul seized the throne when she died in 1796. Unlike Catherine's Westernized, opulent court, the court of Paul I (r. 1796–1801) was despotic, militant, and crude. He imprisoned anyone suspected of disloyalty and initiated unprovoked wars with England and France. Consequently, in 1801, conspirators led by Count Petr von Pahlen plotted his overthrow. Assured that his father would not be harmed, Alexander assented. When the conspirators brutally murdered Paul, Alexander was distraught and initially refused to reign. However, Pahlen convinced him that Russia would collapse without a recognizable leader, and Alexander reluctantly became emperor.

As tsar, Alexander I initially demonstrated an increased liberalism. He released his father's prisoners, reestablished personal rights for the nobility, dis-

Tsar Alexander I of Russia secured a powerful position in European affairs—and his place in history—through his role in the defeat of Napoleon. After Alexander's reported death in 1825, rumors persisted that he was living as a hermit in Siberia. In 1926, the Soviet government opened his tomb in St. Petersburg and found it empty.

Paul's murder may have disillusioned Alexander. His early plans clearly appeased Pahlen and the other conspirators. But when Alexander eventually felt secure enough, he dismissed Pahlen from his government and halted most reforms. In addition, Alexander inherited Catherine's paternalistic attitude toward the Russian subjects and believed that only he could implement reform.

Despite his domestic failures, Alexander achieved tremendous foreign success. He recognized that Napoleon posed a powerful threat and actively tried to prevent French expansion across Europe. At first Alexander failed. Napoleon crushed the Russian forces, led by Alexander himself, first at Austerlitz in 1805, then at Friedland in 1807. After these disasters, Alexander negotiated a treaty with France.

The treaty forced Russia to accept Napoleon's Continental System. This arrangement blocked all European trade with England, thereby crippling Napoleon's greatest enemy. But the system also decimated Russia's economy because England was the largest importer of Russian iron and timber. Still, Alexander honored the agreement because it gave him time to rebuild and strengthen his army.

In 1812, Alexander denounced the treaty with France. When Napoleon invaded, the Russian army surprisingly retreated and burned all the villages and cropland in its path, eliminating potential supplies for the French. Although Napoleon ransacked Moscow, the oncoming winter threatened his forces. While Napoleon retreated, the Russian army relentlessly attacked, finally trapping and defeating the French at the Berezina River in 1812. Ignoring his advisers, Alexander pursued Napoleon to France and triumphantly entered Paris along with the English and Austrian armies in 1814.

Alexander then formed a Holy Alliance among all European kingdoms except England and the Vatican. The alliance emphasized the precepts of "Justice, Christian Charity, and Peace." Alexander believed that Russia's collective suffering during France's dominance and its subsequent victory were divine experiences. Yet most European rulers ignored the treaty because they rejected Alexander's perceived mysticism.

Violent rebellions in Spain and Italy subsequently undermined Alexander's own belief in the alliance and also solidified his resistance to a Russian constitution. Dismayed, Alexander allowed his chief of staff, Aleksei Arakcheev, to control government pol-

mantled the Secret Chancellery, and significantly increased educational funding. He also commissioned his close adviser, Michael Speransky, to draft a "Charter for the Russian People" which was intended initially to increase the Senate's power to levy taxes and write laws. Eventually, Speransky proposed the creation of an elected parliament that would be empowered to introduce legislation and veto the tsar's laws. Furthermore, Alexander accepted an early plan to abolish serfdom.

The emancipation plan largely failed because landowners refused to voluntarily free their serfs and provide them with land. This failure presaged a lack of fulfillment in Alexander's other designs. He ultimately forbade a constitution and dismissed Speransky. Alexander did restructure individual ministries, but he limited the powers of their administrators. In total, Alexander abandoned his earlier liberalism.

icy. Although Arakcheev reduced governmental corruption, he sadistically refused to alleviate harsh conditions among both the serfs and the military.

In 1824, an underground group, the Decembrists, planned Alexander's overthrow. However, Alexander died before they could act. The new tsar, Nicholas I (r. 1825–1855), crushed the infant rebellion in 1825, but the possibility of a successful revolution had arisen.

Alexander transformed the Russian army into an imposing force. But he neither abolished serfdom nor implemented a constitution, and his passion as a ruler dissipated as his reign continued. Consequently, Alexander squandered the chance to reform Russian society and quell the rebellious fervor that swept across Russia for the next century.

See also: CATHERINE II, THE GREAT; NICHOLAS I; ROMANOV DYNASTY.

FURTHER READING

Hartley, Janet M. *Alexander I.* New York: Longman, 1994.

McConnell, Allen. *Tsar Alexander I: Paternalist Reformer.* New York: Thomas Y. Crowell, 1970.

ALEXANDER II (1818–1881 C.E.)

Russian emperor (r. 1855–1881) who emancipated the serfs in 1861.

Alexander Nikolaevich was the oldest son of Tsar Nicholas I (r. 1825–1855) and Aleksandra Feodorovna. Nicholas, distressed by his own poor education, scrupulously prepared Alexander to become tsar. He assigned two distinguished tutors, General Merder and the poet Vasily Zhukovsky, to instruct his son. In 1837 and 1838, Alexander made extensive tours through Russia and Western Europe. After returning, he served as a diplomat and headed State Council meetings when Nicholas was absent.

Consequently, when Nicholas died in 1855, Alexander had already acquired substantial political experience. Upon assuming the throne, he immediately halted the Crimean War (1853–1856), which had crippled the Russian military and economy. In 1856, Alexander signed the Treaty of Paris, which eliminated Russia's coveted military positions in the Black Sea and restricted Russia's European influence.

Russia subsequently used its alliance with Prussia to maintain strength in Europe.

Domestic troubles were far more pressing for Alexander. Serfdom had finally crippled the Russian economy. Russia badly needed factories to modernize its economy, but no independent labor existed because the serfs were legally bound to Russia's vast rural estates. At the same time, landowners were unable to introduce modern agricultural equipment and techniques because of the serfs' lack of education. Farming had become unproductive and unprofitable, and landowners were finally willing to entertain plans to eliminate serfdom.

In 1861, Alexander signed an act to free the serfs. The act established local committees to determine how much land each family of serfs would be allocated. The government compensated individual landowners for their lost land and the value of their serfs and issued forty-nine-year mortgages to the serfs to repay the expenditure. Peasant communes were used to collect the taxes and arbitrate any disputes. Because the serfs were not given the amount of land they had formerly farmed, many believed the landowners were disobeying the actual law.

The emancipation necessitated other essential social reforms. In 1864, Alexander approved the formation of *zemstvos,* locally elected bodies charged with maintaining the infrastructure and administering schools, hospitals, and other public institutions. That same year, Alexander also reformed the judicial system. To recognize the newly freed serfs, laws were rewritten to provide equality for all individuals, jury trials, due process, and an independent judiciary. The military was also thoroughly reformed. In 1874, conscription was expanded to include all men over the age of twenty. The term of service was also reduced from fifteen years to six to attract the liberated serfs into the military.

As a part of his reforms, Alexander also increased public freedoms. He eliminated the Third Section, the oppressive secret police force his father had developed. In 1865, he passed a new censorship law that greatly decreased government control of publications. Also, under Alexander, the Russian government promoted the building of railroads, factories, and other modern facilities.

Because of these reforms, many members of the Russian upper class expected Alexander to radically alter the government, replacing the monarchy with an elected, representative body. However, Alexander shared the autocratic views of his ancestors. Although he recognized the need to abolish serfdom and modernize the economy, Alexander never intended to relinquish the tsar's undisputed power.

In response, members of the educated elite formed a group called Land and Liberty which, during the 1870s, adopted a populist policy designed to instigate a lower class revolution. Although the peasant class was generally dissatisfied with its social condition, they remained loyal to Alexander because he had freed them from serfdom. In 1879, exacerbated by their failure to start a peasant revolt, members of Land and Liberty formed the People's Will Party. Their goal was to terrorize the government and assassinate Alexander.

The People's Will Party narrowly missed assassinating Alexander on two occasions. In 1880, group members planted a bomb in the dining room of the Winter Palace before a state dinner for the prince of Bulgaria. The bomb prematurely detonated before Alexander arrived, but dozens were killed in the blast. Alarmed, Alexander repealed many of the freedoms he had granted in the preceding decades. But he also accepted a plan to allow elected representatives to serve on the State Council.

In March 1881, a bomb blast overturned Alexander's carriage as he traveled to the Winter Palace. As he emerged from the wreckage, a second blast fatally wounded him. He was taken to the palace where he soon died. Although Alexander had introduced greater reforms than any previous monarch, his attempts to preserve Russia's autocratic government led to his assassination.

See also: NICHOLAS I; ROMANOV DYNASTY.

FURTHER READING

Christian, David. *Imperial and Soviet Russia.* New York: St. Martin's Press, 1997.

Lincoln, W. Bruce. *The Great Reforms.* DeKalb: Northern Illinois University Press, 1990.

Smith, David. *Russia of the Tsars.* London: Ernest Benn, 1971.

Wieczynski, Joseph L., ed. *The Modern Encyclopedia of Russian and Soviet History.* Vol 1. Gulf Breeze, FL: Academic International Press, 1976.

ALEXANDER III. *See* ROMANOV DYNASTY

ALEXANDER III, THE GREAT

(356–323 B.C.E.)

Ruler of ancient Macedon (r. 336–323 B.C.E.) whose military genius and towering ambition enabled him to spread his empire throughout southern Asia and the Middle East in a little over a decade.

Alexander the Great is one of the most famous and culturally significant figures of the ancient world, yet many of the facts of his life are colored by legend and rumor. References, stories, and myths about Alexander appear in numerous cultures, and his life became the subject of frequent romantic poetry and prose in Africa, Asia, and Europe. Over the course of subsequent history, Alexander's reign became a sort of morality tale, a story of one man's desire to conquer the world and how this hubris led to his downfall.

While there is little historical evidence to show whether or not Alexander sought world domination, this view of him is the one most commonly held, even today. That he was a man of remarkable energy and drive, and that he stands among the greatest military leaders in history, are perceptions beyond dispute. It is also generally agreed that Alexander was the person most responsible for the spread of Hellenistic culture and ideals throughout much of the ancient world.

EARLY LIFE AND RISE TO POWER

Alexander's ambitions and political skills were honed from a young age. Born in 356 B.C.E., he was the son of King Philip II of Macedon (r. 359–336 B.C.E.), who was himself a great military tactician. During Philip's reign, Macedon emerged as the most prominent of the Greek city-states, and Philip's successful wars against the other principalities allowed him to effectively unify Greece.

Alexander's mother was Olympias, the daughter of a local chieftain from Epirus in northwestern Greece. Alexander was reportedly much closer to his mother than his father, who had scorned Olympias for one of his other wives. Alexander's later cultural sophistication is said to have been attributable to his mother's influence. The education of the young prince was given much priority, and the great philosopher Aristotle was installed as his tutor.

Alexander's career began unexpectedly early. Philip was assassinated, probably by rivals, in 336

ROYAL RELATIVES

OLYMPIAS

The wife of King Philip II of Macedonia and mother of Alexander the Great, Olympias was the daughter of Neoptolemus, the head of the small kingdom of Epirus. Olympias married Philip in 359 B.C.E. and gave birth to Alexander in 356 B.C.E.. Her marriage to Philip was by all accounts cold, and it dissolved to the point of Philip claiming a new wife in 337 B.C.E., at which point Olympias took Alexander and moved to Epirus.

Philip's assassination in 336 B.C.E. has been blamed on Olympias, but there is very little evidence to prove this accusation. Her son's accession to the throne was a source of great pride for her, for she and Alexander were quite close. Consequently, Alexander's decision to make his general, Antipater, ruler of Macedon while he was in Asia did not please Olympias, and the queen made several attempts to take control of the kingdom herself. Upon Alexander's death in 323 B.C.E., Olympias was left with few protectors in Macedon, so she fled to Epirus.

The civil wars that engulfed the Macedonian Empire after Alexander's death gave Olympias an opportunity to return to the throne. The queen rallied a large army and ordered the execution of many of her rivals, including some close relatives. She battled fiercely with Antipater's son Cassander, the leader of the major opposition, but ultimately was forced to surrender in 316 B.C.E. Shortly thereafter, Olympias was executed on Cassander's orders.

B.C.E., bringing his son to the throne at the age of twenty. The young Alexander was greatly respected, and the military quickly signaled their support for him.

In 335 B.C.E., Alexander led his army on a march into Thebes when that city revolted against Macedonian rule. The astonishing speed and utter ferocity with which Alexander's forces quelled the Thebans ensured that rebellion would not spread to the rest of Greece.

Alexander's father had long contemplated an attack on the Persian Empire to the east, and the young king set about putting this plan in motion almost immediately after putting down the uprising in Thebes. In 334 B.C.E., Alexander set sail with his troops for the Hellespont, one of the straits separating Greece from Anatolia (present-day Turkey), thus beginning his march through Asia.

CONQUEST BEGINS

The Persians under King Darius III (r. 335–330 B.C.E.) seriously underestimated the strength of Alexander's forces, and the Macedonian king was able to take much of the peripheral territory of the Persian Empire with minimal effort. The Macedonians then turned southward toward Syria, where they hoped to secure the Mediterranean coastline. There, Alexander and his troops met direct opposition from Darius's forces for the first time but quickly sent the Persians fleeing. The Persians offered a portion of their empire to Alexander if he would lay down his arms, but he refused and made it known that his intention was to take the whole of the Persian Empire. His next step was to march toward Egypt.

Initial Successes

Persian forces in Gaza and Tyre along the eastern Mediterranean coast held out much longer against the Macedonians than previous forces had. As punishment, Alexander had their people sold into slavery after his eventual victory in 332 B.C.E. Alexander then took Egypt without spilling a drop of blood, for the Egyptians saw the Macedonians as their liberators from Persian oppression.

The military genius Alexander III of Macedonia, known as Alexander the Great, built an empire that stretched from the Adriatic Sea to India. This mosaic, found in the ruins of Pompeii, Italy, depicts Alexander in 333 B.C.E. at the Battle of Issus, where he defeated the Persian ruler Darius III.

It was in Egypt that the idea began to circulate that Alexander was a god-like figure, adding to the legends rapidly multiplying around him. The Egyptian occupation also witnessed the founding of the city of Alexandria, which would become one of the major commercial centers of the Mediterranean region. With the Mediterranean finally under his control, Alexander turned eastward and began his march across Persia.

In 331 B.C.E., Alexander met Darius's troops again, this time outside the city of Nineveh near the village of Guagamela in upper Mesopotamia. Darius had brought together an enormous army to face Alexander, but the Macedonians were again victorious. The Greeks then marched south to Babylon and the royal city of Persepolis. Having escaped death, Darius led Alexander on a rapid chase toward the

Caspian Sea, only to be murdered by his own men in 330 B.C.E.

Alexander continued eastward to the region of Bactria in central Asia, but his own men began to chafe at their leader's despotic generalship, and some started to plot against him. Alexander responded to this insurgency with great severity, a decision that helped quiet his men for the short term but added to a growing list of complaints against him.

Developing Unrest

Alexander intended not merely to rout the Persian Empire but to make the world Greek. As a result, he established local governments and educational institutions throughout his growing empire. While these served the purpose of spreading Hellenistic culture around the Mediterranean, they were frequently run by lackluster officials, leading to general dissatisfaction. Alexander also pushed for the cultural integration of Greeks and former Persians, which was met with skepticism and resistance on both sides. As impressive as his empire was in scope, it was becoming increasingly fragile at its core.

THE HEIGHT OF EMPIRE

Alexander's growing awareness of his empire's internal discord did little to stop his march, which turned eastward in pursuit of Bessus, the Persian satrap, or governor, of Bactria, who was finally caught in the spring of 328 B.C.E. Alexander then continued toward India, routing clan after clan and spreading Greek ideals, as well as his own legendary status, across southwest Asia.

The Macedonians fought what many historians consider their greatest battle in 326 B.C.E., when Alexander brilliantly subdued the army of Porus, one of the most powerful Indian rulers. The Macedonian victory was so impressive that Porus became an ally of Alexander, and he was installed as a local governor upon the departure of the Macedonians.

Alexander continued eastward, hoping to take all of India. His men, however, refused to continue their endless march, and a standoff of several days between Alexander and his troops convinced the king that he should begin the march homeward. After exploring portions of India's Punjab region, the Macedonians tried to follow the Indian Ocean on their return trip west. Finding this route impassable, they were forced inland to the Gedrosian Desert, where starvation and dehydration killed many of the troops.

The Macedonians finally arrived at the Iranian city of Susa in the spring of 324 B.C.E.

REBELLION, DEATH, AND COLLAPSE

In Susa, Alexander enacted a series of administrative reforms to strengthen his delicate empire, though he would not live long enough to see them put in place. He again courted the displeasure of his troops by forcing some of them to marry Persian women and by removing several popular military leaders from his ranks. This led to a brief mutiny near the town of Opis, which Alexander put down quickly and relatively peacefully. The death of Alexander's lifelong friend Hephaistion in the autumn of 324 B.C.E. sent the king into a period of intense mourning and psychological distress. The end of that year saw him move his men southward to Babylon.

By this point, Alexander had assumed god-like status in the eyes of many, including, to some extent, his own people. Many inhabitants of the empire, however, began to grow weary of Alexander's overzealous personal ambitions, and as the reforms he promised were slow in coming, general discontentment continued to rise.

Alexander, however, was more concerned with further exploration than in internal reforms and set about planning an ocean voyage around the Arabian Peninsula to Egypt to take place in the summer of 323 B.C.E. Before he could embark, however, Alexander caught a terrible fever. As he lay on his deathbed, he ordered each member of the Macedonian army to pay a final visit to him.

Alexander died in June 323 B.C.E. at the age of thirty-three. The Macedonian Empire collapsed into civil war almost immediately after his death. However, the educational, cultural, and commercial links that Alexander had forged between the Mediterranean, the Middle East, and southern Asia formed the backbone of the later Roman Empire.

See also: DIVINITY OF KINGS; EGYPTIAN DYNASTIES, PERSIAN, HELLENISTIC, AND ROMAN; GREEK KINGDOMS, ANCIENT; HELLENISTIC DYNASTIES; MACEDONIAN EMPIRE; MILITARY ROLES, ROYAL; PERSIAN EMPIRE; PHILIP II OF MACEDON.

FURTHER READING

Lane Fox, Robin. *Alexander the Great.* New York: Penguin, 1994.

ALEXANDRA (1872–1918 C.E.)

Last tsarina of Russia, wife of Tsar Nicholas II (r. 1894–1917). Alexandra was born Alix Victoria Louise Beatrice, princess of Hesse-Darmstadt, a grand duchy of the German Empire, in 1872. Her mother Alice was a daughter of Queen Victoria of Great Britain. When Alexandra visited Russia in 1889, the heir to the Russian throne, the Tsarevich Nicholas, fell in love with her. Nicholas and Alexandra Feodorovna, as she became known in Russia, were married shortly after the death of Nicholas's father, Tsar Alexander III (r. 1881–1894) in 1894. The couple eventually had five children—Olga, Tatiana, Maria, Anastasia, and Tsaravich Alexei, who had hemophilia.

Alexandra's anxiety over Alexei's illness led the tsarina to depend for guidance and support on a self-declared holy man and faith healer named Rasputin. Rasputin's excessive influence at court was only one of many problems in imperial Russia at that time, which included growing movements for social change ranging from the moderate to the extreme. Tsar Nicholas often relied on Alexandra for advice, but during World War I suspicions that the German-born tsarina was pro-German undermined the tsar's authority. When Nicholas went to the battlefront to take command of the army in 1915, Alexandra assumed control of the government in St. Petersburg. However, because of Rasputin's influence over the tsarina, the monk was the primary decision-maker until his assassination in 1916. By 1917, Russia was in a state of chaos; Nicholas abdicated in March, but this did not resolve the situation. The Bolsheviks emerged as the victors in the Russian Revolution of November 1917. The imperial family was arrested, imprisoned, and executed in July 1918.

See also: NICHOLAS II; ROMANOV DYNASTY; RUSSIAN DYNASTIES; VICTORIA.

ALFONSO V, THE MAGNANIMOUS (1396–1458 C.E.)

King of Aragón and Sicily (r. 1416–1458) and of Naples (as Alfonso I, r. 1442–1458), who played an important part in Italian politics and became a great patron of the arts and literature.

Alfonso's father, King Ferdinand I of Aragón (r. 1412–1416), was also the ruler of Catalonia, Valencia, and Sicily. Educated at the Castilian court, Alfonso followed his father to Aragón when Ferdinand became king in 1412. Alfonso married his cousin, Maria of Castile, in 1415, but they had no children.

Alfonso succeeded to the thrones of Aragón and Sicily upon his father's death in 1416. He gained the name "Magnanimous" (or "noble of mind") when he destroyed a list of nobles who had opposed him. Alfonso was known for his generosity and charm, as well as his shrewd mind, political ability, and love of learning.

In 1420 Alfonso, eager to follow Aragón's tradition of Mediterranean expansion, set out to win the island of Corsica. The childless Joanna II (r. 1414–1435), queen of Naples, asked Alfonso to become her adopted heir in return for his assistance against Louis III of Anjou (1417–1434). To those who opposed this risky venture, Alfonso replied, "No one has ever yet won glory without danger and difficulty."

In 1423, however, Joanna transferred her favor from Alfonso to Louis. On her death in 1435, Alfonso claimed the kingdom of Naples, but Duke René of Anjou (1434–1480), Louis's successor, opposed Alfonso, aided by the pope and Dule Filippo Maria Visconti of Milan. In 1435, Genoese troops captured Alfonso and turned him over to Visconti, but he charmed his captor and they formed an alliance.

In 1442, Alfonso defeated René, made a triumphal entry into Naples, and established his royal court there. He never again returned to Aragón, delegating his brother Juan to rule there as regent. Alfonso also had his wife Maria rule as regent in Catalonia. While in Italy, Alfonso had an illegitimate son, Ferdinand, with his mistress, Lucrezia de Alagno. He legitimized Ferdinand and made him his rightful heir to Naples.

Alfonso's court in Naples was known as a center of Renaissance learning and culture. He gave new vigor to the administration, which had become inefficient under previous weak rulers. His neglect of problems in Aragón, however, led to social and economic unrest there, which his successors later had to face and resolve. Upon his death in 1458, Alfonso V was succeeded as king of Naples by his son, Ferdinand I (r. 1458–1494), and as king of Aragón by his brother, Juan (John) II (r. 1458–1479).

See also: ARAGÓN, KINGDOM OF; NAPLES, KINGDOM OF; SICILY, KINGDOM OF.

ALFONSO X, THE WISE

(1221–1284 C.E.)

Medieval king of Castile and León (r. 1252–1284), noted for his patronage of the arts and scholarship, who also continued with the Christian reconquest of Iberia from the Moors.

Alfonso was the son of King Ferdinand III (r. 1217–1252) of Castile and León, and Beatriz, daughter of German king Philip of Swabia (r. 1198–1208), through whom Alfonso had a claim to the throne of the Holy Roman Empire.

When Ferdinand died in 1252, Alfonso succeeded to the throne and continued Ferdinand's campaign to drive the Moors from Iberia. In 1262, Alfonso conquered the southern Iberian city of Cádiz from the Moors, but two years later his Moorish subjects there revolted. Alfonso's insistence on royal authority also led to a rebellion among the nobles of Castile and Leon.

Despite attempts to reclaim Moorish territories and anti-Semitic legislation, Alfonso welcomed both Islamic and Jewish scholars to his court. Under his patronage, fifty astronomers gathered at the city of Toledo in 1252 and created the Alfonsine tables, an improvement on the study of planetary movement made by the ancient Greek astronomer Ptolemy. Alfonso also continued legal reforms begun by his father. The *Siete Partidas*, compiled by a group of jurists between 1251 and 1265, streamlined existing Castilian law and has been described as "the most important law code of the Middle Ages."

A patron of schools and universities, Alfonso supported schools in a number of cities, including Seville and Salamanca, whose university became one of the greatest in Iberia. Alfonso also focused his attention on literature, music, and games, including chess. Under his influence, the Castilian dialect spoken in his kingdom became paramount as the language of Spanish literature.

Despite his accomplishments as a patron and reformer, Alfonso was criticized for lavish spending and was accused of weakness because of his interest in the arts and science. He was also involved in political intrigue. Through his mother, Beatriz, he hoped to claim the title of King of Germany. Although supported by one faction of German princes, Alfonso faced opposition from the pope and Spanish antagonism toward his ideas, and he renounced the claim to the German crown in 1275.

That same year, Alfonso's eldest son Ferdinand died while fighting the Moors. Subsequently, civil war erupted between supporters of Ferdinand's heirs and allies of his brother Sancho. In 1282, Sancho's supporters at the Cortes (the Spanish parliament), declared Alfonso deposed. The dispute over the succession, unsettled at Alfonso's death in 1284, ended with Sancho's accession to the throne later that same year as Sancho IV (r. 1284–1295).

See also: CASTILE, KINGDOM OF.

ALFRED THE GREAT (849–899 C.E.)

King of Wessex (r. 871–899) who is credited with unifying the different kingdoms of Anglo-Saxon England and with being the first real king of all England. During his reign, Alfred proved to be an excellent warrior, an able negotiator, and an admirable administrator, strengthening the security of the state, building roads and towns, implementing a uniform law code, and establishing schools.

When Alfred ascended the throne in 871, he took over a country already at war with Danish invaders. His initial attempts at routing them were so unsuccessful that, only a month after becoming king, a defeat at Wilton forced him to pay tribute to save his throne.

Years of conflict against the Danes followed, finally culminating in a decisive victory against Danish forces at Edington in 878. Alfred was able to dictate terms in the subsequent Peace of Wedmore, limiting the Danes to an area that came to be called the Danelaw, which comprised East Anglia and East Mercia. Alfred ruled over the remaining territory, making himself king not only of Wessex, but of East Anglia and the western part of Mercia as well.

Having established the boundaries of his kingdom through war, Alfred set about maintaining them by negotiating cordial relations with the Welsh, building new forts and reinforcing old ones, reorganizing his army, and building a navy, complete with ships of his own design. Far-sighted in his approach to social issues, he devised laws to ensure legal protections for the poor while setting aside an eighth of the state revenues for education and an eighth for charitable relief.

Concerned that the Danish incursions were a judgment from God on the English for letting the cause of education fail, Alfred provided a personal example of scholarship to inspire his subjects. With only a limited knowledge of Latin, Alfred arranged in 887 to study under a scholarly Welsh priest named Asser. Alfred then laboriously translated Pope Gregory's *Pastoral Care* into English and saw to its distribution among the bishops of his country, many of whom had little Latin. Translations of other works, including Bede's *Ecclesiastical History of England*, and Boethius's *Consolation of Philosophy*, are also attributed, in part or in whole, to the king. These personal efforts, and the many other works translated into English under his patronage, put Alfred well ahead of his fellow European monarchs in recognizing the importance of the vernacular languages in making learning more accessible.

It was not only Alfred's accomplishments, but also his temperament that set him apart from other monarchs. He combined personal modesty with effective leadership, even-handed administration, and concern for the welfare of his people. It is perhaps as much for his noble character as for his unification of warring states that he is frequently referred to as the first king of England.

See also: ANGLO-SAXON RULERS; DANISH KINGDOM; EDUCATION OF KINGS; KENT, KINGDOM OF; LITERATURE AND KINGSHIP; NAVAL ROLES; NORTHUMBRIA, KINGDOM OF; SUSSEX, KINGDOM OF; WESSEX, KINGDOM OF.

ALMOHAD DYNASTY (1130–1269 C.E.)

Islamic family that ruled much of North Africa and Spain in the 1100s and 1200s.

What later became known as the Almohad dynasty was actually begun as an Islamic religious movement in the 1100s. During the time of Almoravid rule in North Africa, Muhammad ibn Tumart (r. 1121–1130), a messianic leader in southern Morocco, became dismayed by what he saw as the people's lost connection to their Islamic faith. Tumart began preaching in Morocco about moral reform and oneness with God. His movement was called Almohad (in Arabic, *al-Muwahhidun*, which means monotheists). By the 1120s, his movement had attracted many Arab and Berber followers in the nearby mountains.

The Almohad religious message was soon broadened into a political movement, with the removal of the Almoravid dynasty as its central goal. In 1133, Tumart was succeeded by Abd al-Mu'min (r. 1133–1163), a Berber disciple of Tumart's, as leader of the Almohads. Al-Mu'min took the title of caliph and thus founded the Almohad dynasty.

An ambitious leader, al-Mu'min conquered Morocco in the 1140s and took over rule of Islamic Spain in the 1150s. With these conquests, he reigned over all the former territory of the Almoravid dynasty. Al-Mu'min also added territory in eastern Algeria and in Tunisia to the Almohad kingdom.

Al-Mu'min and the first caliphs who succeeded him were strong administrators who ran their kingdom in an organized and efficient manner. Although they maintained control, they did allow tribal representatives some participation in government. The Almohads also are known for their cultural contributions, particularly in the field of architecture. Caliph Yakub al-Mansur (r. 1184–1198), in particular, built the Hassan Tower in Rabat, Morocco, and the Giralda Tower in Seville, Spain.

Although the Almohads managed to maintain a united Islamic kingdom for more than two centuries, internal struggles between members with different tribal affiliations, as well as uprisings of Christians in Spain, brought about tensions and disorder. The decisive battle of Las Navas de Tolosa in southern Spain in 1212, in which Christian Spanish kings defeated the Almohads, marked the beginning of the end of Almohad power in Spain. By 1232, the Almohads had completely ceded their control in Spain.

Some years earlier, Caliph Muhammad an-Nasir (r. 1199–1213) had divided the Almohad kingdom in Africa into two administrative districts, roughly divided by tribe. The western half was comprised mostly of Morocco and Algeria, while the eastern half was comprised mostly of Tunisia. The leader of the Hafsid dynasty was placed in charge of the eastern area. The Hafsids used this position of power to gain independence from the Almohads, and by 1230 they had formed a separate kingdom and monarchy. In the west, the Marinids and Ziyanids, local tribes in Morocco and Algeria, gradually gained control over

their regions and formed separate, independent kingdoms. By 1269, the Almohad dynasty had come to an end.

See also: ALMORAVID DYNASTY; HAFSID DYNASTY; IBERIAN KINGDOMS.

ALMORAVID DYNASTY

(ca. 1042–1172 C.E.)

Ethnic Berber dynasty that united Muslim lands in Spain and Northwest Africa in the Middle Ages.

Emerging from the torrid borderlands of the Sahara Desert region of Morocco, the Almoravids drew on their fierce Berber fighting spirit to establish a short-lived, religiously inspired Islamic dynasty. At their peak, the Almoravids ruled a vast swath of territory that stretched from the trading towns of sub-Saharan West Africa to the borders of Catalonia in northern Spain, laying the groundwork for the even larger Berber Empire of their successors, the Almohads.

When Islam first came to Morocco in the eighth century, the native Berber tribesmen of the region had been subject to foreign overlords for many centuries—Carthaginians, Romans, Visigoths, and Byzantine Greeks. But they were never tempted to modify their tribal perspective until their new Arab overlords introduced them to Islam. Once the original Arab empires in the region disintegrated, leaving a power vacuum, the Berbers used Islam to fashion an ideology of conquest and rule.

In the 800s and 900s, the nomadic tribes of the Berber Sanhaja clan parlayed their position at the northern end of the trans-Sahara trade route to build a powerful trading confederation. They profited by exchanging salt and manufactures for gold and slaves from the kingdom of Ghana. One of the Sanhaja chiefs, Yahya ibn Ibrahim, made a pilgrimage to Mecca in 1035, influenced by a wave of revivalism led by the Sunni branch of Islam that was sweeping the Muslim world. Yahya returned to North Africa accompanied by a Moroccan teacher, 'Abd Allah ibn Yasin, who was determined to purify what he perceived to be the lax, uninformed Islam of the region. Those who joined them in their *ribat* (fortress) retreat became known as *al-murabitun*, "the people of the retreat" (in the Latin transliteration, the name became Almoravids).

Yahya proclaimed a *jihad,* or holy war, in 1042. By his death in 1159, the Almoravids had conquered all of southern Morocco. His successors, abu Bakr ibn 'Umar (r. 1056–1061) and Yusuf ibn Tashufin (r. 1061–1106), conquered all of North Africa as far east as Algiers, ruling from the newly founded capital of Marrakesh. They also launched a *jihad* against pagan Ghana in 1076, putting an end to that 500-year-old trading state. Yusuf ibn Tashufin adopted the title Commander of the Faithful, and managed to get official recognition for the Amoravid regime from the caliphate in Baghdad.

The backbone of the new Almoravid state was a Berber army with as many as 100,000 troops. A system of salaried judges, schooled in the new Muslim legal trends, helped govern the country effectively. One of the most popular reforms of the new order was to abolish all taxes on Muslims, except for those explicitly mentioned in the Koran. Unfortunately, there were few Christians in Morocco to pay the non-Muslim head tax. Consequently, the government was under constant pressure to find new territories to conquer, since 20 percent of the spoils of war went to the treasury.

Almoravid military success attracted the attention of the beleaguered Muslim Taifa states of Andalusia in southern Spain. These local kingdoms had emerged following the collapse of the Ummayad caliphate. The Taifa states were under growing military pressure from the Christian rulers to their north, who exacted large annual tribute payments. In 1085, King Alfonso VI of Castile (r. 1065–1109) conquered the Moorish city of Toledo, the first major Muslim loss in Spain in more than three hundred years. In a panic, the Muslim rulers of Seville, Granada, and Badajoz traveled to Africa to enlist Yusuf's support.

In four separate expeditions starting in 1086, Yusuf turned back the Christian tide and united most of Muslim Spain under Almoravid rule. Valencia was taken after the death of the Christian hero El Cid in 1102, and the last Christian holdout, Saragossa, fell to the Almoravids in 1110. The Balearic Islands in the western Mediterranean were seized as well; they were to remain the last Iberian stronghold of the Almoravids.

Yusuf's son, Ali ibn Yusuf (r. 1106–1142), ruled the entire Almoravid kingdom from Marrakesh; his brother Tamim governed Andalusia in his name from Granada, the regional capital. The Almoravid dynasty's initial popularity soon waned, however. The top ruling class was drawn entirely from the Sanhaja tribe, who stood out in the streets of Muslim Spain because of their unusual clothing—males wore a face veil that concealed all but their eyes.

When military expansion ceased after 1018, the Almoravids were forced to introduce new taxes. Moreover, the religious tolerance that characterized earlier Muslim eras in Andalusia began to dissipate. Few Jews were able to enter government service, many Arabic-speaking Christians were forcibly removed to Morocco, and church properties were seized.

In the 1130s, a rival group, the Almohads, began to amass support in the Atlas Mountains of Morocco. More puritanical than the Almoravids, but just as willing to use the promise of tax reform to undermine the current rulers, the Almohads conquered all their predecessors' African realms by 1145. By 1160, they had pushed their control of North Africa as far east as Libya.

Most of Andalusia fell to Almohad rule after 1148. Saragossa, the last Almoravid stronghold on the Spanish mainland, fell in 1172, although a line of Almoravid princes continued to rule on the island of Majorca in the Balearic Islands until the late twelfth century.

See also: ALMOHAD DYNASTY; CALIPHATES; GHANA KINGDOM, ANCIENT; TAIFA RULERS.

AMBASSADORS

The highest ranking diplomatic officials, who usually reside in the foreign country to which they are sent. The word "ambassador" comes from the Latin *ambaxator* (from *ambactiare*, "to go on a mission") and was first used in thirteenth-century Italy. The practice of rulers sending representatives to other states is a very old one, however.

In past centuries, when travel and communications were difficult, personal meetings and negotiations between monarchs were not always possible, and were often considered inadvisable. Such meetings were difficult to arrange—the rulers had to meet on neutral ground (perhaps a bridge or stream between their territories); immense retinues had to accompany the rulers as a sign of their rank; and during times of war, there was always the fear that one ruler might harm or abduct the other.

Not all societies have had the same concept of an ambassador. In some cultures, the ambassador was not considered equal in dignity to the sovereign he was addressing. But in Western Europe ambassadors sent by monarchs represented the person of their sovereign and were supposed to be treated with the same dignity due the ruler.

The embassies of ancient Greek city-states often consisted of a large delegation, which did not always represent the state as such. Often, each envoy would represent a different opinion or faction within the state and would argue its case. In republican Rome, the Senate reserved for itself the right to choose and send diplomatic delegations, and continued to do so during the period of the Roman Empire, although the emperor often received ambassadors personally. In the Byzantine Empire, the emperor made himself appear as exalted as possible before ambassadors as a means of intimidation; they had to bow before him as his throne rose up to a great height before them by means of a mechanical device.

In medieval Western Europe, the idea of an ambassador as the representative of the sovereign developed gradually. The earliest type of envoy, a *nuntius* (messenger), did not have any power to act on his own; this power was allowed to the *procurator*, who could actually conduct negotiations. A *procurator* could also represent the sovereign ceremonially, as ambassadors later did. Kings in the Middle Ages became increasingly conscious of their rank and dignity and might send a *procurator* to kneel and perform the humiliating act of feudal homage to an overlord for a territory, as Richard II (r. 1377–1399) of England did for the region of Guienne in France. Medieval canon lawyers argued that ambassadors could not be harmed because this would be considered *lesa majestatis*, or harm to the person of a sovereign.

The custom of resident ambassadors began in Renaissance Italy. Also called *ordinary ambassadors*, they were expected not so much to represent a monarch as to gather political information about their host country. Sometimes, however, *extraordinary ambassadors* were sent to negotiate with a monarch on particular occasions, which were treated with greater ceremony on both sides.

Originally, it was not only European sovereign states or monarchs that had ambassadors; cities could send them to the Holy Roman emperor. In the sixteenth century, however, Emperor Charles V (r. 1519–1558) insisted that only the diplomats sent by crowned heads of state and the Republic of Venice should be called ambassadors.

Because he represented a monarch, an ambassador was usually a person of high status. In medieval Europe, ecclesiastics were sometimes chosen to serve as ambassadors. In seventeenth-century France, it was generally thought that an ambassador should be a noble, though there were many exceptions.

As diplomacy began to be considered a profession, many of these ideas were codified. In 1716, François de Callieres, a French diplomat, wrote a treatise called *De la maniere de négoicier avec les Souverains* (On Negotiating with Sovereigns). In this document, he stipulated that ambassadors did not have to uncover their heads in front of the sovereign because they represented another sovereign, whereas lower-ranking diplomats, such as envoys and resident ministers, were required to bare their heads. It was because of this association of ambassadors with royalty that the United States did not appoint diplomats of ambassadorial rank until 1893.

Modern developments in diplomacy, including instantaneous communication by phone and teleconferencing, the ease of international flight, the growth of roundtable conference diplomacy, and the founding of the United Nations, have made personal negotiation among world leaders easier and reduced the mystique of an ambassador as representing the person of a sovereign. Yet, ambassadors continue to perform their other functions, including social and cultural exchange and representing their country's interests and its citizens abroad.

See also: Courts and Court Officials, Royal; Diplomacy, Royal; Oaths and Oath-taking; Regalia and Insignia, Royal.

FURTHER READING
Hamilton, Keith A., and Richard Langhorne. *The Practice of Diplomacy: Its Evolution, Theory, and Administration.* New York: Routledge, 1995.

AMENHOTEP IV. *See* AKHENATEN

AMERICAN KINGDOMS, CENTRAL AND NORTH

Kingdoms that developed in Central and North America since approximately the twelfth and fourteenth centuries, respectively. The native American kingdoms of Central and North America shared three main qualities: a centralized political organization, control over several tribes, and relatively vast territories. In Central America, the political entities that exhibited these qualities were those of the Aztecs or Mexicas, and the Purépechas or Tarascos. In North America, the Iroquois League of Nations, and the Huron, Powhatan, and Creek Confederacies developed a kingdom-like political organization. The autonomous evolution of these kingdoms was interrupted by the gradual arrival of Europeans beginning in the early sixteenth century.

CENTRAL AMERICA

By the time the Spaniards arrived in Mexico in 1519, the different native groups of Mexico shared at least three characteristics. First, they relied on military expansion both to impose tribute over the peoples they subjected and to obtain sacrificial victims. The significance of war was indicated by the role assigned to war deities, as well as by the defensive location and architecture of many settlements. Second, the practice of long-distance trade provided native groups with access to diverse food staples and luxury goods. This was evidenced by the high status of merchants and the existence of settlements that specialized in commerce. Finally, the Mexican civilizations shared common iconographic symbols and artistic techniques. These included the use of light-blue lines and stepped architectural borders, and depictions of local fauna and flora.

The Aztecs

Between the twelfth and sixteenth centuries, two powerful states developed in the territory of Mexico. The first one was the Aztec Empire, which controlled the central and southern area of Mexico, with its capital city of Tenochtitlan. The other state was the Purépecha Empire, which controlled the east-central area of Mexico, with its capital city of Tzintzuntzan.

Studies indicate that the Aztecs originated in the north Mexican plateau. The Aztec origin myth claimed that they came from the island of Aztlan, north of the Valley of Mexico. In 1168, Huizilopochtli, their sun and war god, led them out of Aztlan toward the south. They arrived in the Valley of Mexico in 1248. Once there, they became vassals of the chiefdom of Culhuacán. Human sacrifices were an important aspect of Aztec religion, and as part of one of these rituals, they killed the daughter of the chief of Culhuacán. As a result, the Aztecs were forced to take refuge at an island on Lake Texcoco, where they founded the city of Tenochtitlan around 1325.

After settling at Tenochtitlan, the Aztecs became vassals of the Tepanecs, whose capital city was Atzcapotzalco. Around 1400, the Aztecs joined forces with the city of Texcoco, and successfully rebelled against the Tepanecs. In 1428, Tenochtitlan, Texcoco, and Tlacopan formed the "Triple Alliance." Under the rule of Moctezuma I (r. 1440–1468), the Aztecs and their allies began a rapid territorial expansion. By the mid-fifteenth century, the Triple Alliance had taken over the city of Azcapotzalco. It then proceeded to conquer Tlaxcala and Huejotzingo, located east of the Valley of Mexico. Gradually, the Aztecs became the main power within the Triple Alliance. According to some scholars, by the early sixteenth century Tenochtitlan reached a peak of 200,000 inhabitants. The Aztecs not only exacted tribute from the peoples that they conquered, but also demanded a number of sacrificial victims.

The Tarascos or Purépechas

The other large state that the Spaniards encountered when they arrived in Mexico was the Tarasco or Purépecha Empire. According to some scholars, this group had similar origins to the Aztecs. Their origin myth claimed that they came from northern Mexico and that they arrived at the Lake Pátzcuaro basin around the thirteenth century. Their leader was called Ire-Ticátame, and their main deity was Curicaueri, who represented fire.

Until the fifteenth century, the Purépechas were divided into various hereditary chiefdoms. The most important cities were Pátzcuaro, Cuyuacán or Ihuatzio, and Tzinzunzan. The first king who succeeded in unifying the Purépechas was Tariácuri, who ruled from 1300 to 1350 approximately. When he died, the kingdom was divided among his son, Hiquingaje, and his nephews, Hirepan and Tangáxuan, who took control of Pátzcuaro, Cuyuacán, and Tzintzunzan, respectively.

In the second half of the fifteenth century, Tangaxuan was able to unify the kingdom again. One of his successors, King Tzitzipandácuri (r. ca. 1454–1479), increased the territory of the Purépecha Empire. The Purépechas achieved a great mastery of pottery and metallurgy. In alliance with the Matlatzincas, the Purépechas were able to resist the Aztecs and remain independent, while other peoples fell under the control of the Aztecs.

Spanish Conquest

In 1519, Spanish conqueror Hernán Cortés disembarked on the eastern coast of Mexico. After establishing alliances with Cempoaltecas and Tlaxcaltecas, two native groups that were enemies of the Aztecs, he arrived at Tenochtitlan. Emperor Moctezuma II (r. 1502–1520) welcomed Cortés, believing he was an envoy of the Aztec deities. The Spaniards took advantage of the situation and captured Moctezuma. A group of Aztec nobles rebelled against the Europeans, killed Moctezuma, and appointed a new emperor, Cuauhtémoc. In 1521, the Spaniards defeated the rebels, captured Cuauhtémoc, and consolidated their control over the Valley of Mexico. Meanwhile, the last Purépecha emperor, Tangoxoan II (r. ?–1525), surrendered peacefully to Cristóbal de Olid, one of Cortés's lieutenants.

NORTH AMERICA

The European settlers who established themselves in eastern North America in the seventeenth century had contact with four major indigenous groups: the Iroquois League of Nations, and the Huron, Powhatan, and Creek Confederacies. All of these native groups had sedentary settlements and were located in river valleys. Their main agricultural products were corn, beans, and squash, a combination of crops that originated in Mesoamerica and that allowed them to make a broader use of their environment.

Iroquois peoples were one of the largest native linguistic groups in the Eastern Woodlands. They were divided into the Iroquois League of Nations and the Huron Confederacy. The Iroquois League occupied the territory of modern upstate New York. Between the fourteenth and fifteenth centuries, various Iroquois villages began to ally with neighboring towns in an attempt to solve conflicts and ease trade among each other. This led to the gradual formation of the Iroquois league, which was already established by the early sixteenth century. According to the Iroquois tradition, the founder of the league was chief Deganawidah. The Iroquois league was comprised of the Mohawk, Oneida, Onondaga, Cayuga, and Seneca nations.

The Huron Confederacy occupied the modern territory of Ontario (Canada) and was formed around 1420 by the Attignounstan and Attingneenognahac nations. The purpose of the confederacy was to avoid violent conflicts and allow peaceful commercial relations between the groups. Two other nations, the Arendahronon and the Tohonaenrats, joined the Huron Confederacy during the second half of the sixteenth century. Each nation was governed by its own council, and each sent representatives to a confederacy council.

In 1609, French explorers and colonists established Quebec on the St. Lawrence River. Some years later, in 1624, the Dutch established Fort Orange, at the location of present-day Albany, New York. Both the Huron and Iroquois established commercial relations with the European settlers, mainly trading animal furs. By the late seventeenth century, however, the Iroquois had exhausted most of their animal stock. Seeking more resources, they began the "Beaver Wars" against the tribes of the Ohio River Valley region to the west. The power of the Iroquois declined afterward, owing to war, epidemics, and outmigration.

The Powhatan Confederacy occupied the territory of present-day southeastern Virginia. It comprised about thirty-two tribes, including the Pamunkey, Mattapony, and Chickahominy, all of which belonged to the Algonquin linguistic group. When the British established the settlement of Jamestown in 1607, the chief of the confederacy was Wahunsonacock, or "Powhatan." By this time, there were around two hundred Powhatan palisaded settlements. Initial relations between the natives and the British were peaceful, but they changed when the Europeans began to take land away from the Powhatan. The natives attacked the British in 1608, 1622, and 1644, but they were defeated.

The Creek Confederacy occupied the southeastern part of the present-day United States. It comprised around fifty-two tribes, including the Muskogee, Yuchi, and Hitchitee. All of these tribes belonged to the Muskogean linguistic group. These different tribes formed the confederacy primarily to resist attacks from northern natives, as well as to face the threat posed by the Europeans after they arrived.

The first explorer who had contact with the Creek was the Spanish explorer Hernando de Soto, around 1540. The Spanish established some religious missions among the Creek, but they never managed to establish completely peaceful relations with the tribes. From the 1670s onward, the British succeeded in establishing trading links with the Creek, driving the Spanish missions out of their territory.

See also: AZTEC EMPIRE.

FURTHER READING

Fenton, William N. *The Great Law and the Longhouse: A Political History of the Iroquois Confederacy.* Norman: University of Oklahoma Press, 1998.

Pollard, Helen Perlstein. *Tariácuri's Legacy: The Prehispanic Tarascan State.* Norman: University of Oklahoma Press, 1993.

Roundtree, Helen C., and E. Randolph Turner III. *Before and After Jamestown: Virginia's Powhatans and Their Predecessors.* Gainesville: University of Florida Press, 2002.

Smith, Michael Ernest. *The Aztecs.* 2nd ed. Malden, MA: Blackwell, 2003.

AMHARA KINGDOM

(ca. 1270–1936 C.E.)

Former kingdom of east Africa that became a province of Ethiopia in 1936, named for the Amhara people who lived there. The Amhara people have been the dominant group through much of Ethiopia's history. Rulers of the Amhara kingdom are known as the Solomonids because they claimed direct descent from Solomon's son Menelik I, first emperor of Ethiopia. From 1270 until the fall of Haile Selassie I in 1974, Ethiopian rulers were descendants of the Amhara dynasty.

The Amhara kingdom arose in the same region as the once great kingdom of Aksum, which declined sometime around 900. Amhara rulers share their descent from Solomon and the queen of Sheba with the Aksumite kings. From the tenth to the thirteenth centuries, the Zagwe dynasty ruled in Ethiopia. The Zagwe kings were considered usurpers by those in the Solomonic line. In 1270, Emperor Yekuno Amiak (r. 1270–1285) conquered the Amhara region and proclaimed the reestablishment of the ancient Solomonic dynasty.

In order to ensure that later kings would be of the Solomonic dynasty, Yekuno's male children were placed in a secure mountain location and guarded by several hundred warriors. There they studied in isolation, in anticipation of their selection as heirs to the kingdom. Yekuno's grandson, Amda Seyon (r. 1314–1344) was successful in gaining control over all the Christian districts of Ethiopia that had been fragmented during the Zagwe period.

The Solomonic rulers had a negative impact on the development of urban centers throughout Ethiopia, preferring to move with their courts from district to district. The tent cities they erected had an advantage in that they could easily be dismantled when it became necessary to move on; however, such a policy did not encourage art and architecture. An additional advantage of a peripatetic royal court was that it enabled the king to maintain a close relationship with his subjects, who were welcome to approach his court whenever it was in their vicinity.

The Muslim population throughout the region continued to grow and challenged the Christian leadership of Ethiopia. The first serious defeat of the Amhara was during Emperor Ba'eda-Maryan's reign (r. 1468–1478), but the Ethiopians were able to regroup and maintain their kingdom. Later, Lebna Dengel (r. 1508–1540) forestalled conquest by Somali Muslims led by Ahmed Gran in the early 1530s by allying himself with Portugal. After these attacks, Lebna sought to centralize his power and established a capital at Gondar. After Lebna's death, however, his sons weakened Amhara by internal strife over the succession. The Amhara were able to withstand the attacks of the Muslim Turks and defeat them in 1543, but Ethiopia became an isolated Coptic Christian nation.

During the reign of Tewodros II (r. 1855–1868), Ethiopia clashed with Europeans, notably the British and Germans, who were intent upon colonizing the nation. Tewedros managed to retain at least nominal independence, but Ethiopia was now seen as strategically important, particularly because of its proximity to the Suez Canal, which was under construction in the 1860s.

In the late nineteenth century, Menelik II (r.

1889–1911) was able to reassert Amhara rule over much of the former empire and set boundaries that remain generally intact in modern Ethiopia.

See also: AKSUM KINGDOM; HAILE SELASSIE I; MENELIK II.

FURTHER READING

Levine, Donald N. *Greater Ethiopia: The Evolution of a Multiethnic Society.* Chicago: University of Chicago Press, 2000.

Pankhurst, Richard. *The Ethiopians: A History.* New York: Blackwell Publishers, 2001.

ANDHRA KINGDOM

(ca. 235 B.C.E.–175 C.E.)

Ancient kingdom in India whose rulers modeled themselves and their government on the great Maurya Empire.

The Andhra kingdom was the domain of the Satavahana dynasty. Around 271 B.C.E., a leader named Simuka (r. ca. 235–212. B.C.E.) became the first Satavahana monarch when he overthrew the Kanvas dynasty and gained control of the Upper Deccan region. Simuka established a capital at Pratisthana and consolidated his control over the area. Initially, the Andhra kingdom encompassed only the land between Godavari River and the Krishna River.

EARLY RULERS

Simuka and his two successors, Krishna (r. ca. 212–195 B.C.E.) and Satakarni I (r. ca. 195–193 B.C.E.), used the powerful Maurya Empire as a model for their government. Like the Mauryas, Simuka adopted the Hindu doctrine of *dharma,* which outlined the religious and moral rights and responsibilities of individuals and guided the way to social order and virtue. According to *dharma,* every monarch was required to be pious and just and was responsible for such diverse areas as agriculture, forestry, defense, and industry.

To help him fulfill his duties, Simuka appointed a council of ministers to oversee the government's various departments. A department was created for each activity in the kingdom, such as salt mining, weaving, and pasturage. Among the ministers, the treasury minister and tax revenue minister were the most powerful. With such careful delegation of

power, Simuka and his successors tightly controlled the kingdom during its first century of existence.

After the death of Sakatarni I around 193 B.C.E., the Andhra kingdom entered a long and perilous period during which invasions by nomadic peoples from Central Asia weakened the kingdom and reduced its size. Eventually, in the second century C.E., an Indo-Greek dynasty known as the Western Satraps established a satrapy, or colony, near Maharashtra to the west of the Andhra kingdom. The Satavahana monarchs retained power only by pledging allegiance to the invaders.

THE KINGDOM'S GREATEST RULER

In the mid-first century, the Satavahana monarch, Gautamiputra Satakarni (r. ca. 70–95), rallied the Andhran citizenry and regained control of the entire kingdom. Gautamiputra Satakarni is recognized as the most influential Satavahana monarch. During his reign, he reunited the various states of the Upper Deccan. He also conquered significant portions of western and central India. Under his leadership, the Andhra kingdom came to encompass all the land from the Krishna River in the south to the kingdom of Malwa in the north, and from the province of Berar in the east to the Konkan coast in the west.

Freed from the threat of invasion, the Andhran economy expanded dramatically. Gautamiputra Satakarni closely regulated all aspects of the kingdom's economy. He established farming villages, called *grihas,* which contained between 30 and 1,000 families. Farmland surrounded the communities, and each family was responsible for farming a portion of the land. Open pastures lay beyond the farmland, and again, each family was responsible for supervising the cattle upon their section. Each village was assigned a carpenter, blacksmith, potter, barber, horseman, and excavator. A superintendent, accountant, police captain, and doctor formed the village council and oversaw daily affairs.

Gautamiputra Satakarni also encouraged the expansion of the artisan class in the Andhra kingdom. Woodworkers, leatherworkers, stonemasons, painters, confectioners, weavers, and jewelers all proliferated during his reign. Often, members of a profession would inhabit the same area of a city, and their shops would be grouped together.

Mining became the Andhra kingdom's most valuable industry. The monarchy controlled all mines and profited greatly from the extraction of gold, silver, copper, lead, tin, iron, diamonds, and other precious stones. Under Gautamiputra, the monarchy monopolized the salt industry; constructed its own cotton, oil, and sugar factories; and strictly regulated alcohol production.

The Satavhana monarchy also controlled all trading in the kingdom. Goods could not be sold in the same community where they were manufactured; instead, the government erected public markets where the goods were sold and traded. All sellers were required to have a license issued by the government, and the government set the quantity and prices of the goods that could be sold. Merchants attempting to skirt the regulations were heavily punished.

The Andhran economy became very prosperous largely because of Gautamiputra's expert control and management. He combined this skill with military prowess to completely dominate the kingdom. However, his successors struggled to maintain this dominance. Their inability and ineffectiveness, combined with the reemerging threat of invasion, gradually weakened the kingdom during the second century.

DECLINE AND FALL

The Satavahanas briefly regained the power lost by Gautamiputra's successors during the reign of Yajna Sri Satakarni (r. ca. 128–157). Yajna returned Satavahana authority across the Andhra kingdom and restored the monarchy to its former position, but he died without leaving a direct heir. After his death, the kingdom was divided into several principalities ruled by different members of the royal family. Predictably, these principalities easily succumbed to invasion by other states, most notably Maharashtra, and the Andhra kingdom steadily dissolved. By the fourth century, only fragments of the once vast kingdom remained.

See also: INDIAN KINGDOMS; MAURYA EMPIRE; SATAVAHANA DYNASTY; SCYTHIAN EMPIRE.

FURTHER READING

Auboyer, Jeannine. *Daily Life in Ancient India.* London: Phoenix, 2002.

Shastri, Ajay Mitra. *The Age of the Satavahanas.* New Delhi: Aryan Books International, 1999.

ANGEVIN DYNASTIES (909–1491 C.E.)

Two dynasties of a French noble house that played an important role in England, France, Italy, Jerusalem, and Hungary during the Middle Ages. From the eleventh to the fifteenth centuries, the influence of the Angevin dynasties extended to a great part of Europe.

FIRST DYNASTY

The Angevin dynasty—which included the House of Plantagenet in England—began with the counts of Anjou in France, from which the term *Angevin* derives. In the mid- to late 900s, Geoffrey Greymantle (r. 960–987) of Anjou acquired territory in the French regions of Maine and Touraine. This policy of expansion was also pursued by Geoffrey's son, Fulk Nerra (r. 987–1040), who gained the title count of Anjou in the late 900s. Both Fulk Nerra and his son and successor, Geoffrey Martel (r. 1040–1060), had to defend their realm against the powerful duchy of Normandy.

Count Fulk V (r. 1109–1129) of Anjou, the great-grandson of Fulk Nerra, married the daughter of Baldwin II (r. 1118–1131), ruler of the Latin kingdom of Jerusalem, which had been captured by the Crusaders in 1099. Fulk succeeded Baldwin as king of Jerusalem in 1131, bringing the Angevins to power in this Crusader kingdom. The title king of Jerusalem remained in the Angevin family until 1186, when Baldwin the V died without an heir.

The Angevin line came to the throne of England through the marriage of Matilda, the daughter of Henry I of England (r. 1100–1135), to Geoffrey Plantagenet, the son of Count Fulk V of Anjou. When Henry I died in 1135, Matilda claimed the throne of England but lost it to her cousin, Stephen of Blois (r. 1135–1154), who seized control after Henry I's death. However, on Stephen's death in 1154, Geoffrey's and Matilda's son became Henry II (r. 1154–1189), the founder of the Angevin Plantagenet dynasty in England.

In 1152, Henry II married Eleanor of Aquitaine, gaining that region of southwestern France. Along with Normandy, the English Angevins now claimed a good part of France. After the death of Henry II in 1189, he was succeeded by his son Richard I, the Lionheart (r. 1189–1199). By 1204, Richard's successor, his brother John (r. 1199–1216), had lost the county of Anjou as well as almost all his other French lands to King Philip II, Augustus of France (r. 1180–1223), and the region of Anjou came under the control of the French Crown. The Angevin line continued in England until Richard II (r. 1377–1399) was deposed by Henry IV (r. 1399–1413), of the House of Lancaster, in 1399.

SECOND DYNASTY

The second Angevin dynasty began as a branch of the Capetian dynasty of France. In 1246, the Capetian monarch Louis IX (r. 1226–1270) invested his youngest brother Charles with the counties of Maine and Anjou as his *apanage* (lands allotted to the younger brothers of a king as their inheritance). Charles also acquired the important territory of Provence through his marriage to Beatrice, daughter of Count Raymond Berenger V of Provence (r. 1209–1245).

A man of vast ambition, Charles received his chance for empire-building in 1266, when Pope Urban IV asked him to lead a campaign against King Manfred of Sicily (r. 1258–1266), who was an enemy of the papacy. Charles defeated Manfred in battle and gained the Crown of Sicily as Charles I (r. 1266–1285) in 1266, bringing the Angevin line to that kingdom. Charles paid little attention to Sicily, however, leaving it to the care of French nobles. The Sicilian people revolted against French rule in 1282, and the kingdom was claimed by Pedro III of Aragón (r. 1276–1285), who had backed the revolt. However, the Angevin dynasty continued to rule the kingdom of Naples in southern Italy until 1435, when the kingdom of Aragón seized control after the death of Joanna II (r. 1414–1435), the last Angevin ruler of Naples.

A Hungarian branch of the Angevin dynasty had its roots in the marriage of Charles II of Anjou (r. 1285–1290) to Mary, the daughter of King Stephen V of Hungary (r. 1270–1272). When the last ruler of the Arpad dynasty, Andrew III of Hungary (r. 1290–1301), died in 1301, Charles II's grandson, Charles Robert, pressed his claim to the throne. He eventually became King Charles I of Hungary (r. 1307–1342). In addition, Charles married Elizabeth, the daughter of King Ladislaus I of Poland (r. 1305–1333). Their son, Louis I (r. 1342–1382), succeeded his father as king of Hungary, becoming one of the greatest medieval rulers of Central Europe. In 1370, Louis also became king of Poland after the

death of his uncle, Casimir III (r. 1333–1370), who had named Louis his heir.

Louis had no male heirs. His daughter Mary succeeded to the throne of Hungary as Mary I (r. 1382–1395). After her death, she was succeeded by her husband Sigismund (r. 1387–1437), whose succession marked the end of Angevin rule in Hungary. Louis's other daughter became Queen Jadwiga of Poland (r. 1383–1399). The succession of her husband Ladislas II (r. 1386–1434) as sole ruler after her death in 1399 marked the end of Angevin rule in Poland. Ladislas was the founder of the Jagiello dynasty in Poland.

Meanwhile, the Angevin dynasty was drawing to a close in France as well. In 1360, Anjou became a duchy under Duke Louis I (r. 1360–1384) of the House of Valois, the son of King John II of France (r. 1350–1364), thus ending Angevin rule of Anjou. In 1491, with the death of Duke Charles I of Maine, a descendant of Charles II of Naples, the Angevin line in France died out, and Anjou, Maine, and Provence became permanent domains of the French crown.

See also: ANJOU KINGDOM; AQUITAINE DUCHY; ARPAD DYNASTY; CRUSADER KINGDOMS; FRENCH MONARCHIES; HENRY II; JAGIELLO DYNASTY; LOUIS I, THE GREAT; NAPLES, KINGDOM OF; PLANTAGENET, HOUSE OF; SICILY, KINGDOM OF; VALOIS DYNASTY.

FURTHER READING

Bachrach, Bernard S. *State-Building in Medieval France: Studies in Early Angevin History.* Aldershot, Hampshire, Great Britain/Brookfield, VT: Variorum, 1995.

Dubabin, Jean. *Charles I of Anjou: Power, Kingship and Statemaking in Thirteenth-Century Europe.* New York: Longmans, 1998.

Gillingham, John. *The Angevin Empire.* 2nd ed. London: Arnold; New York: Oxford University Press, 2001.

ANGKOR KINGDOM (802–1431 C.E.)

A Khmer state, located in northwestern Cambodia, that thrived culturally and politically for more than six hundred years as the heart of the Khmer Empire and is regarded as the peak of Cambodian civilization.

The Angkor kingdom was established in 802 when the Khmer leader Jayavarman II (r. 802–850) declared himself a king with divine powers. His successors also enjoyed the status of absolute monarch, which may have contributed to the stability of the civilization. The first capital of the kingdom, established by Yasovarman I (r. 889–900), was centered around the temple of Phnom Bak Kheng.

Suryavarman II (r. 1113–1150) is considered one of the greatest Khmer rulers. He conquered several states of the Champa kingdom in neighboring Vietnam, as well as parts of central Thailand. He also waged war against the Vietnamese state of Nam Viet. In addition to expanding his kingdom's territory, Suryavarman II is also credited with building what is considered the greatest architectural achievement in Southeast Asia, the temple complex of Angkor Wat ("Angkor temple"), located southeast of the capital at Phnom Bok Kheng. Dedicated to the Hindu god Vishnu, the imposing Angkor Wat remains standing today and is the largest religious structure in the world.

Following the reign of Suryavarman II, the Angkor kingdom went through a period of wars with the Champa kingdom. The Chams were finally sacked under the reign of Jayavarman VII (r. 1181–1220), considered the last great ruler of the Angkor kingdom. Unlike his Hindu predecessors in Angkor, Jayavarman VII was a devout Mayana Buddhist.

During his reign, Jayavarman VII built several temples, including the new Khmer capital at Angkor Thom ("great Angkor"), as well as more than 100 hospitals and a network of roads to improve the infrastructure of the Angkor kingdom.

By the beginning of the thirteenth century, the Angkor kingdom had fallen into decline. The spread of Theravada Buddhism into Southeast Asia challenged Angkor's kingship system by discounting the legitimacy of divine rule. Eventually, around 1431, a Thai army captured Angkor Thom, sacked the city, and enslaved much of its population and relocated them to the Thai kingdom of Ayutthaya. After this defeat, the Thais came to dominate the region.

See also: AYUTTHAYA KINGDOM; CAMBODIAN KINGDOMS; CHENLA EMPIRE; KHMER EMPIRE; VIETNAMESE KINGDOMS.

ANGLO-SAXON RULERS

(400s–1066 C.E.)

Leaders of Germanic tribes who ruled small kingdoms in England from the fifth century until 1066.

In the middle of the fifth century, hordes of pagan invaders descended upon southern England from Germany. According to the *Anglo-Saxon Chronicle* (probably written in the late 800s), the first Saxon invaders were the warlords Horsa and Hengist (r. 455–488), who established the kingdom of Kent around 450. As they invaded, the Anglo-Saxons drove the Celtic Britons into Wales and Cornwall and established small Anglo-Saxon kingdoms that eventually covered most of the area that is modern-day England.

The invaders were members of three Germanic tribes: the Angles, the Saxons, and the Jutes, and they spoke a Germanic language that we now call Anglo-Saxon or Old English. Originally, they worshiped the Norse gods, such as Thor and Odin, but in the seventh century they were converted to Christianity after the Kentish king Ethelbert I (r. 560–616) married the Christian princess Bertha, daughter of the Frankish king in France.

Anglo-Saxon rule was less centralized than most early medieval monarchies. Early Anglo-Saxon social structure consisted of a warlord, called an ealdorman or eorl (alderman or earl), surrounded by his followers, called thegns (thanes), who were like knights. Anglo-Saxon society was somewhat democratic—the Anglo-Saxons did not follow strict rules of dynastic succession, and power was sometimes shared among several family members—but they did practice slavery. Anglo-Saxon government also developed the institution of the *witan* or *witenagemot*, a council of noblemen who advised the king. The *witan* bore some resemblance to the modern-day House of Lords.

At its height, Anglo-Saxon England was divided into seven separate kingdoms: Wessex, Essex, Sussex, Mercia, Northumbria, East Anglia, and Kent. These kingdoms often battled over territory and often temporarily conquered each other. All England was permanently united when the kings of Wessex obtained dominance over the other Anglo-Saxon kingdoms in the ninth century under Alfred the Great.

Alfred the Great of Wessex (r. 871–899) was perhaps the most famous Anglo-Saxon ruler, earning his title defending his kingdom against Viking invaders and encouraging learning. During his reign, he became overlord of the other Anglo-Saxon kingdoms. One of the more infamous Anglo-Saxon kings was Ethelred II "The Unready" (r. 979–1013, 1014–1016), whose poor judgment and lack of military skill placed England in the hands of invading Danes led by Sven Forkbeard for a brief time between 1013 and 1014.

Wessex faced another crisis some fifty years later. When Edward the Confessor (r. 1042–1066) died in 1066, there was some dispute over who should be his successor. Harold Godwinson, earl of Wessex, became the next king of England as Harold II (r. 1066). However, many believed the title rightfully belonged to William, duke of Normandy (who may have been promised by his cousin, Edward the Confessor, that he would inherit the English throne).

William decided to act, and he invaded England with an army of 7,000 followers. He defeated Harold and his Anglo-Saxon forces at the battle of Hastings on October 14, 1066 and was crowned King William I (r. 1066–1087) on December 25, 1066. The Norman conquest ended the Anglo-Saxon period of English history and inaugurated the Norman era.

The Normans brought to England a new hierarchical social structure, new codes of chivalry, and a new language, Norman French. Modern-day English is a synthesis of the Anglo-Saxon and the Norman French languages, just as English culture is an amalgamation of Anglo-Saxon and Norman traditions.

See also: ALFRED THE GREAT; EDWARD THE CONFESSOR; KENT, KINGDOM OF; MERCIA, KINGDOM OF; NORMAN KINGDOMS; NORTHUMBRIA, KINGDOM OF; WESSEX, KINGDOM OF; WILLIAM I, THE CONQUEROR.

FURTHER READING

Black, Jeremy. *A New History of England.* Reading: Sutton, 2000.

Yorke, Barbara. *Kings and Kingdoms of Early Anglo-Saxon England.* London: Seaby, 1990.

ANJOU, HOUSE OF. *See* ANGEVIN

DYNASTIES

ANJOU KINGDOM (ca. 1060–1500 C.E.)

Kingdom in southern Italy ruled by a branch of the French Angevin family during the Middle Ages.

The French first gained a presence in southern Italy when the Norman nobleman, Robert Guiscard, and his brother, Roger d'Hauteville, gained control of territory there in 1057 after expelling the Byzantines from the area. Hoping to extend their holdings, the Normans turned to the island of Sicily, which was then under Arab Muslim rule.

Invasions of northern Sicily by Robert and the Normans began in 1060, but it was 1090 before the last Muslim stronghold fell and the island came completely under Norman French control. The two brothers, Robert and Roger, then divided their holdings on the mainland and in Sicily between themselves, with Roger becoming Count Roger I of Sicily (r. 1072–1101).

Roger's older son, Simon (r. 1101–1105), inherited the title upon the death of his father. But Simon died before reaching adulthood, leaving the throne to his younger brother, Roger II (r. 1105–1154). When Roger I reached maturity, he united Sicily with his uncle's territory on the mainland, forming what became known as the kingdom of Two Sicilies. Roger II was crowned king of this united realm in 1130. When Roger II died in 1154, he was succeeded first by his son, William I (r. 1154–1166), and then by his grandson, William II (r. 1166–1189).

William II had no male heirs, and when he died in 1189, a struggle for succession arose. Holy Roman Emperor Henry VI (r. 1191–1197), a member of the German Hohenstaufen dynasty, claimed the throne in the name of his wife Constance, who was the daughter of Count Roger I. Henry took the throne of the Two Sicilies in 1194, thereby bringing the kingdom into the Holy Roman Empire. When Henry died in 1197, his son Frederick II (r. 1194–1250) inherited his father's titles as emperor and king of Sicily.

In 1266, Pope Clement IV reclaimed sovereignty over Italy and deposed the Hohenstaufens in favor of Charles of Anjou, the youngest brother of King Louis IX of France (r. 1226–1270). Charles invaded Italy and defeated Manfred (r. 1258–1266), the current ruler of the kingdom at the battle of Benevento. Mandred died in the battle, and Charles of Anjou took the throne as Charles I (r. 1266–1285).

A member of the Angevin dynasty, Charles ruled as king of both Naples and Sicily. But he was a cruel and unpopular ruler. In 1272, in an event called the Sicilian Vespers, the Sicilians revolted against Angevin rule and accepted Manfred's son-in-law, King Peter III of Aragón (r. 1226–1285), as their sovereign. This revolt separated Sicily from the mainland, and for the next several generations, Sicily was ruled by Aragón, while Naples remained under the rule of the French Angevin descendants of Charles I.

In 1443, King Alfonso V of Aragón (r. 1416–1458) reunited the kingdom of Two Sicilies (Sicily and Naples) under his rule. When he died in 1458, he left his Sicilian title to his son Ferdinand I (r. 1458–1494). Under the Treaty of Blois, signed in 1505 by Louis XII of France (r. 1498–1515) and Ferdinand II of Aragón (r. 1479–1516), the kingdom of Sicily and Naples was granted to Spain, which exploited the region and allowed it to become one of the poorest in Europe.

See also: ALFONSO V, THE MAGNANIMOUS; ANGEVIN DYNASTIES; ARAGÓN, KINGDOM OF; FERDINAND II AND ISABELLA I; FREDERICK II; FRENCH MONARCHIES; HOHENSTAUFEN DYNASTY; NAPLES, KINGDOM OF; NORMAN KINGDOMS; SICILY, KINGDOM OF.

ANKOLE KINGDOM

(ca. 1450 C.E.–Present)

One of several kingdoms to arise during the fifteenth and sixteenth centuries in what is now the nation of Uganda.

The kingdom of Ankole is one of the best known of the states to arise in present-day Uganda, along with the Nyoro and Toro kingdoms. The founders of Ankole were Hima cattle pastoralists, who traditionally lived in separate, lineage-based societies. Individual settlements were governed by clan chiefs, but around the middle of the 1400s, one of these, Ruhinda, rose to dominance and established himself as *mugabe*, or paramount ruler over all the Ankole clans.

The coalescence of the Ankole clans into a single political unit was largely motivated by the defensive needs of the people. State formation had been ongoing in the region during the previous century, and this presented a problem for the independent pastoralist settlements, none of which could withstand an attack on its own. By banding together under a single leader, to whom each constituent clan settlement was obligated to provide troops when the need arose, all of the clans enjoyed greater security. As paramount ruler, Ruhinda did not project his authority into day-to-day administration of individual Ankole settlements; this responsibility remained in the hands of the clan chiefs.

Succession to the Ankole throne was hereditary, and for more than five hundred years there appears to have been an orderly transition of power from father to son, except for a few occasions when, due to the untimely death of a reigning *mugabe*, power passed to a sibling. This occurred, for example, during the reign of Kitera (r. ca. 1650–1674), who died without having sired a son, leaving the throne to his brother Rumongye. Subsequent kings followed the father-to-son pattern of inheritance.

Ankole kings managed to maintain the independence of their people until 1901, when Great Britain claimed the region as a colonial possession and the kingdom came under British control. To facilitate administration throughout the region, the British broke traditional lines of succession, selecting individuals from within the royal lineages that they felt they could best control. Thus, Kahaya II (r. 1901–1944) was installed as king of the Ankole in 1901, although he was a nephew of the previous *mugabe*, not a son.

Under British rule, the authority of both kings and clan chiefs was subordinated to colonial administrative policies, and the *mugabe* became primarily a ritual office. Nonetheless, the institution of kingship was permitted to carry on throughout the years of colonization, and it survived into the post-independence period. In 1967, however, Uganda's prime minister, Dr. A. Milton Obote, abolished all the traditional kingdoms of the nation. In 1993, then-President Yoweri Museveni restored the traditional kingships, and John Patrick Barigye (r. 1993–present), twenty-seventh in the line of Ankole kings, was restored to the throne.

See also: NYORO KINGDOM; TORO KINGDOM.

ANNAM, KINGDOM OF. *See*

VIETNAMESE KINGDOMS

ANNE (1665–1714 C.E.)

Final monarch of the embattled House of Stuart, who reigned as queen of England and the newly formed United Kingdom of Great Britain from 1702 until her death in 1714. Historically perceived as feeble and somewhat irrelevant to the political developments of her time, Anne has risen to a place of prominence in British history thanks to recent historical scholarship, which has recast her as a strong and intelligent ruler.

The second daughter of James II (r. 1685–1688) and Anne Hyde, the first of James's two wives, Anne came of age during a time of great religious controversy in England, which came to a head with the so-called Glorious Revolution of 1688. James, a Catholic, was deposed and driven from England in 1688 by his son-in-law, William of Orange (later William III, r. 1689–1702), and his daughter, Mary (Mary II, r. 1689–1694), both Protestants. Anne, who was also a Protestant, supported her sister and brother-in-law in their bid for the throne, and she became queen upon William's death in 1702. The year before Anne became queen, Parliament had passed the Act of Settlement, which ensured that the Crown would remain in Protestant hands, even if it had to leave the House of Stuart.

Among the most notable events of Anne's reign was the War of the Spanish Succession (1701–1713), and its counterpart in North America known as Queen Anne's War (1702–1713). The Mediterranean-based War of the Spanish Succession ended well for the British, who were able to prevent France from extending its reach throughout Southern Europe. Queen Anne's War, which was part of an ongoing struggle between the British and the French in North America, had a much more mixed outcome, as the Canadian settlements of Port Royal and Acadia fell into British hands, but the major city of Quebec remained firmly in French control.

Anne also oversaw the 1707 Act of Union, which was part of the attempt by the Protestant-controlled Parliament to keep a Catholic from ascending to the throne. The Act united the kingdoms of England and Scotland as the United Kingdom of Great Britain, thus circumventing any attempt by the Scots to support Anne's exiled Catholic half-brother, James the Old Pretender, in a bid for the Crown.

Although Anne endured nearly twenty pregnancies during her lifetime, she left no descendants upon her death in 1714. In accordance with the Act of Settlement, the Crown went to her nearest Protestant relative—George I (r. 1714–1727), elector of the House of Hanover, and great-grandson of James I.

See also: ENGLISH MONARCHIES; GEORGE I; HANOVER, HOUSE OF; JAMES I OF ENGLAND (JAMES VI OF SCOTLAND); JAMES II; QUEENS AND QUEEN MOTHERS; STUART DYNASTY; WILLIAM AND MARY.

ANTIGONID DYNASTY. *See*

HELLENISTIC DYNASTIES

ANTIOCHUS III, THE GREAT (241–187 B.C.E.)

The sixth ruler of the Seleucid dynasty of the Hellenistic Middle East, who helped to restore the Seleucid Empire to a semblance of glory after a period of decline.

The son of Seleucis II (r. 246–226 B.C.E.), Antiochus III succeeded his brother, Seleucus III (r. 226–223 B.C.E.), in 223 B.C.E. Most of his energies as ruler went into a series of wars, beginning with an unsuccessful conflict with the old rivals of the Seleucids, the Ptolemies of Egypt. The Ptolemies defeated Antiochus at the battle of Raphia in 217 B.C.E.

Antiochus's most successful military endeavor, and the one that made his reputation, was a series of campaigns from 212 to 205 B.C.E. to reassert Seleucid power in Persia and Central Asia. During those campaigns, Antiochus won the submission of the kings of Armenia, Parthia, and Bactria, and led his armies to the border of India.

The death of Ptolemy IV of Egypt (r. 222–204 B.C.E.) in 204 B.C.E., and the accession of the infant Ptolemy V (r. 204–180 B.C.E.), opened up opportunities in Palestine and Phoenicia, which Antiochus exploited in an alliance with the king of Macedon, Philip V (r. 221–179 B.C.E.). Antiochus's victory in 200 B.C.E. at the battle of the Panium permanently ended Ptolemaic rule in Syria and Palestine. He next invaded Asia Minor, where he captured Ptolemaic possessions. Antiochus's continued expansion eventually brought him into conflict with the rising power of the Mediterranean, the Roman Republic, particularly after he crossed into Europe from Asia Minor in 196 B.C.E. In 195 B.C.E., Antiochus welcomed as an adviser the Carthaginian general Hannibal, the enemy of the Romans.

Antiochus and the Romans clashed in Greece, which Antiochus invaded in 192 B.C.E. as an ally of the Aetolian League, a group of Greek city-states. Defeated by the Romans at Thermopylae in 191 B.C.E., he retreated to Asia Minor, where he was defeated again at the battle of Magnesia in 190 B.C.E. by a Roman force under the command of Lucius Cornelius Scipio. This was the last great battle between a Hellenistic empire and Rome. The peace treaty of Apamea between Rome and Antiochus in 188 B.C.E. forced him to withdraw from western Asia Minor and disband his navy and elephant force. The treaty also required Antiochus to give hostages to the Romans, including his son, the future Antiochus IV (r. 175–164 B.C.E.). He also had to expel Hannibal from his kingdom and pay a large indemnity. Antiochus was murdered at Susa in 187 B.C.E. while on another expedition to the East. He was succeeded by his brother, Seleucis IV (r. 187–175 B.C.E.).

See also: HELLENISTIC DYNASTIES; PTOLEMAIC DYNASTY; SELEUCID DYNASTY.

AQUITAINE DUCHY (670–1453 C.E.)

Medieval duchy in southwestern France that became one of the richest French regions and a center of medieval art, courtly literature, and chivalry.

The region of Aquitania was originally a part of the ancient land called Gaul by the Romans. Julius Caesar (r. 49–44 B.C.E.) conquered the people of the region, known as the Aquitani, in 56 B.C.E. Subsequent conquerors of the region were the Visigoths, who invaded in the fifth century C.E., and the Franks under Clovis I (r. 481–511), who conquered the region in 507.

For a century and a half after the Frankish conquest, Aquitaine more or less managed its own affairs while Frankish overlords dealt with problems of succession. From 670 the dukes of Aquitaine ruled with little outside interference, but in 718, Duke Eudes of Aquitaine (r. 688–725) sought assistance from Charles Martel (r. 714–741), king of the Franks, to quell a Moorish invasion.

By 781, the Frankish ruler Charlemagne (r. 768–814) had eliminated opposition from the nobles of the Aquitaine duchy and transformed the area into a kingdom for his son, Louis, who ruled as Louis I (r. 781–840). For the next two centuries, control of Aquitaine shifted back and forth between Aquitainian dukes and the kings of the Carolingian dynasty. The situation was complicated by successive invasions by Normans and Muslims, which weakened Carolingian control over the duchy.

By the early tenth century, Carolingian control over Aquitaine had all but vanished, and the counts of Poitiers, Auvergne, and Toulouse all claimed the title duke of Aquitaine. Count William I of Poitiers finally secured the title, becoming William III of Aquitaine (r. 935–963) in 935. His descendants ruled the area into the eleventh century, during which time Aquitaine expanded its borders and became one of the leading powers in Western Europe.

When the last duke of Aquitaine, William X (r. 1127–1137), died in 1137, the kingdom passed to his daughter, Eleanor of Aquitaine. Through her marriage to the French king, Louis VII (r. 1137–1180), Aquitaine became part of France. Following their divorce, however, Eleanor married Henry Plantagenet, count of Anjou, who became King Henry II of England (r. 1154–1189).

Subsequently, a lengthy struggle evolved between England and France for control of the duchy. For a number of years, England held the duchy as vassals of the French Crown, but France eventually gained supremacy during the Hundred Years' War (1337–1453) and took control of Aquitaine. At that point, the duchy was renamed Guyenne, and it was absorbed into the regions of Gascony and Guyenne as a province of France.

At the height of its power, the Aquitaine duchy was one of the wealthiest regions in Western Europe. Its great wealth made it a cultural center for art, architecture, and literature, and traveling poets called troubadours composed courtly poetry for the court of the Aquitaine dukes. The Aquitaine court also became associated with the chivalric traditions of the time.

See also: ELEANOR OF AQUITAINE; HENRY II.

FURTHER READING

Sauvigny, G. de Bertier de, and David H. Pinkney. *History of France.* Arlington Heights, IL: Forum Press, 1983.

Koenigsberger, H.G. *Medieval Europe, 400–1500.* Burnt Mill, England: Longman Group UK Limited, 1987.

Tierney, Brian, and Sidney Painter. *Western Europe in the Middle Ages, 300–1475.* 6th ed. New York: McGraw-Hill, 1999.

ARABIA, KINGDOMS OF

(ca. 1000 B.C.E.–600 C.E.)

Small kingdoms established in the coastal regions of the Arabian Peninsula that flourished between about 1000 B.C.E. and 600 C.E.

In ancient times, the inhabitants of the Arabian Peninsula were mostly nomadic peoples who formed tribes for protection and for survival. By about 1000 B.C.E., however, a number of small, cohesive Arabian kingdoms had been organized in the region. Although information about these kingdoms is limited, it is believed that they prospered as a result of trade in spices and the skills of their innovative merchants.

The best-known of the Arabian kingdoms was Saba (Sheba), in the southwestern part of the Arabian Peninsula, with its capital at Ma'rib. The kingdom of Saba existed from about the tenth to the second century B.C.E. The Sabaeans were well-known traders, responsible for introducing Indian spices to the ancient Romans. They also traded locally grown frankincense and myrrh via regional caravan routes using domesticated camels. Sabaean traders traveled as far north as present-day Syria and beyond the Persian Gulf. To help feed the population of the kingdom, the Sabaeans built elaborate dams to irrigate crops. The legendary queen of Sheba mentioned in the Bible is said to be from Saba.

Around the second century B.C.E., the Himyarite kingdom apparently succeeded Saba as the predominant economic force in the southern Arabian Peninsula. The Ethiopians tried unsuccessfully to invade Himyarite territory in the fourth century C.E., and in the sixth century, they succeeded in conquering the kingdom.

In the northern part of the Arabian Peninsula, in southern Transjordan (present-day Jordan), the Nabataean kingdom arose sometime before the third century B.C.E. Its capital of Petra was a wealthy and highly civilized city. The Nabataean kingdom included present-day Jordan as well as much of present-day Syria, including the important city of Damascus. Also traders, the Nabataeans carried on an extensive trade that reached as far as the Mediterranean Sea. The kingdom eventually became a vassal state of Rome, and in the second century C.E., it was reduced to the status of province of the Roman Empire.

See also: HADRAMAWT KINGDOMS; SABAEAN KINGDOM; SHEBA, QUEEN OF.

ARACHOSIA KINGDOM

(520–155 B.C.E.)

Ancient kingdom in Afghanistan, located near the current Afghan city of Kandahar, that was originally established as part of the Persian Empire.

During the sixth century B.C.E., the ruler of the Persian Empire, Darius I (r. 521–486 B.C.E.), divided the eastern portion of his empire into four territories and installed loyal satraps, or governors, to govern each one. The southernmost of these four territories was Arachosia.

Arachosia remained under Persian control until 331 B.C.E. when Alexander the Great (r. 336–323 B.C.E.) confronted Darius III or Persia (r. 335–330 B.C.E.) at the battle of Gaugamela. Arachosian cavalry, led by their satrap Barsaentes, comprised a significant portion of the Persian army. But the invading Greeks defeated the Persians, forcing Darius to flee the advancing Greeks.

Initially, Alexander pursued the defeated Darius. But three of the Persian satraps, including Barsaentes, betrayed Darius and assassinated him. They then defied Alexander and declared autonomy for their regions. Thus, Alexander was forced to individually defeat each of the satraps. In 329 B.C.E., he finally entered Arachosia, executed Barsaentes, and founded the city of Alexander-in-Arachosia.

After Alexander's death, his empire was divided among his most prominent generals. Seleucus, a general in charge of Babylon, gained control of the eastern region, which included Arachosia. Seleucus I (r. 312–281 B.C.E.) struggled to suppress repeated rebellions in the region. These efforts weakened his forces, and in 305 B.C.E. he was unable to stop invading forces from the Mauryan Empire of India. A subsequent treaty divided Arachosia between the two empires, although the Greeks retained control of the city of Alexander-in-Arachosia.

Rebellions and invasion had left the forces of Seleucus irreparably weakened, and the Mauryan emperors continued to expand their control of the region. By 250 B.C.E., the Greeks had been expelled from Arachosia, and Mauryan dominance over the kingdom lasted until 232 B.C.E. Seleucus's successors, most notably Antiochus III (r. 223–187 B.C.E.) and Demetrius I (r. 162–150 B.C.E.), briefly regained control of Arachosia between 209 and 155 B.C.E. They also crossed the Indus River and decimated the remnants of the Mauryan Empire.

The final Seleucid ruler, Menander (r. 114–90 B.C.E.), who ruled the Indo-Greek kingdom of Bactria, reunited all of Afghanistan. But Menander faced a growing threat in the west from the Parthian kingdom. The Parthians marched eastward and, like Alexander the Great, conquered any forces they encountered. After the Parthian victory over the Indo-Greeks, the Afghan territories lost their individual identities and ceased to exist.

See also: ALEXANDER III, THE GREAT; DARIUS I, THE GREAT; INDO-GREEK KINGDOMS; MAURYA EMPIRE; MENANDER; SELEUCID DYNASTY.

ARAGÓN, HOUSE OF

(ca. 1050–1504 C.E.)

Medieval dynasty that ruled the kingdom of Aragón on the Iberian Peninsula (in what is present-day Spain), as well as the county of Catalonia and the kingdoms of Naples, Sicily, and Sardinia.

The House of Aragón was established by Ramiro I (r. 1035–1063), an illegitimate son of Sancho III of Navarre (r. 1004–1035), whose kingdom was partitioned following his death in 1035. For nearly sixty years, the kingdom of Aragón was united with the kingdom of Navarre under the rule of Ramiro's successors: Sancho I (r. 1076–1094), Peter I (r. 1094–1104), and Alfonso I (r. 1104–1134).

Navarre and Aragón separated again in 1134 with the accession of Ramiro II "the Monk," (r. 1134–1137), the brother of Alfonso I. Three years later, the house of Aragón was united with Catalonia as a result of the marriage of Ramiro's daughter Petronilla to Raymond Bergengar IV (r. 1134–1162), count of Barcelona.

As a result of this union, Aragón acquired various holdings in southern France, most notably Montepellier, Provence, and Roussillon. But the House of Barcelona, as the dynasty now styled itself, lost these French holdings during the reign of Pedro II (r. 1196–1213), who was defeated in 1213 during the papal struggle against heresy known as the Albigensian Crusade. However, Aragón and Catalonia remained united under his descendants.

Under James I (r. 1213–1276), Aragón and Catalonia conquered the Balearic Islands and Valencia from the Moors. James's son, Pedro III (r. 1276–1285), expanded the family's holdings in 1282, becoming King Peter I of Sicily as a result of his marriage to Constance, the heir of king Manfred of Sicily (r. 1258–1266). This territorial acquisition, along with control of the Balaeric Islands, provided the House of Aragón with considerable influence in the western Mediterranean.

Peter's grandfather, Pedro II of Aragón (r. 1196–1213), had pledged himself a papal vassal, but Peter refused to give homage to the pope, who excommunicated him and organized a crusade against Aragón. This troublesome situation alienated members of the Aragónese nobility, who forced Peter to grant them a "general privilege" that defined the rights and duties of the aristocracy and allowed annual meetings of the cortes, or representative assembly. Under Pedro IV (r. 1336–1387), the Aragónese monarch once again restricted the power of the nobility.

The far-flung holdings of the House of Aragón were seldom united under one ruler. Various branches of the dynasty ruled different territories, often warring with their relatives for supremacy. For example, in 1276 the Balearic island of Majorca became a separate kingdom under James I (r. 1276–1311), the son of James I of Aragón (r. 1213–1276). It remained separate until 1343, when Pedro IV conquered the island and restored it to the kingdom of Aragón. Sicily was separate from Aragón from 1296 to 1409, until it was reunited with the Aragónese monarchy by King Martin (r. 1395–1410) of Aragón.

The house of Aragón ended with King Martin of Aragón, who died without a male heir in 1410. After a two-year interregnum, during which Aragón was without a monarch, Aragónese nobles chose Martin's nephew, Prince Ferdinand of Castile, to be their king.

The reign of Ferdinand I (r. 1412–1416) marks

the beginning of the reign of the House of Trastamara in Aragón. Ferdinand's son and successor, Alfonso V (r. 1416–1458), conquered Naples and united various Aragónese holdings. More interested in the culture of the Italian Renaissance than in Aragón, Alfonso shifted the center of Aragónese power to the kingdom of Naples. His son, Ferdinand II (r. 1479–1516) married Isabella of Castile (r. 1474–1504), uniting Aragón and Castile into one kingdom.

See also: ALFONSO V, THE MAGNANIMOUS; ARAGÓN, KINGDOM OF; FERDINAND II AND ISABELLA I; JAMES II OF ARAGÓN; SICILY, KINGDOM OF; TRASTAMARA, HOUSE OF.

ARAGÓN, KINGDOM OF

Christian kingdom in the northeastern part of the Iberian Peninsula (in present-day Spain) that emerged in the eleventh century and played an important part in the reconquest of Iberia from the Moors, who had conquered most of the peninsula beginning in the 700s.

Conquered by the Visigoths in the late fifth century, the region of Aragón came under Moorish control in the early eighth century. Around 850, the Carolingian rulers of France expelled the Moors from the area, and Aragon came under the rule of the kingdom of Navarre. Upon the death of the Navarrese king, Sancho III (r. 1000–1035), in 1035, Navarre was divided into three separate kingdoms: Navarre, Aragón, and Castile.

AN INDEPENDENT KINGDOM

The first ruler of an independent kingdom of Navarre was Ramiro I (r. 1035–1069), the illegitimate son of Sancho III of Navarre. During his reign, Ramiro fought unsuccessfully against the Moors at Saragossa, and he died fighting the rival Castilians. Ramiro's son, Sancho I (r. 1069–1094) continued the campaign against the Moors. While visiting Rome on a pilgrimage in 1068, he also agreed to hold Aragón as a vassal of the papacy.

Crusading activities against Muslims were very important to the medieval Aragónese monarchy. Like other medieval Iberian rulers, the Aragónese kings supported the Crusades in the Middle East, but the primary military efforts were aimed at fighting the Moors in Iberia. Alfonso I (r. 1104–1134), known as

Alfonso the Battler, actively recruited knights from other parts of Europe to fight the Moors, rewarding the survivors with fiefs in the conquered territories. Under Alfonso, Aragón extended its territory southward, capturing Saragossa from the Moors in 1118. His raids into the Moorish province of Andalucia, the southernmost region of Iberia, helped boost the morale of Christians as they struggled with the reconquest.

Alfonso had no direct heir, and his will stipulated that the kingdom of Aragón would be left to the knightly orders of Crusaders, the Knights Templar and Knights Hospitalers. This idea never came close to being carried out, however. Instead, Alfonso's brother Ramiro, a monk, was recalled from his monastery by Aragónese nobles upon the death of his father in 1134. Crowned as Ramiro II (r. 1134–1137), he married, fathered a daughter, Petronilla, and then abdicated and returned to his monastery in 1137.

A TURNING POINT

Petronilla's marriage, arranged shortly after her birth, was a turning point for the Aragónese monarchy. Her husband was Raymond Berenguer IV (r. 1131–1162), the count of Barcelona, whose domains included all the regions of Catalonia. Raymond and Petronilla ruled the merged kingdom jointly until Raymond's death in 1162; Petronilla then reigned alone until 1164, when she abdicated in favor of her son, Alfonso II (r. 1164–1196).

The union between Aragón and Catalonia, along with the territory of Valencia, which had been conquered from the Moors, was referred to as the "Crown of Aragón." In 1319, King James II (r. 1291–1327) of Aragón declared this union indissoluble, but the regions maintained their separate institutions, laws, languages, and customs. Each continued to develop along separate paths, which sometimes caused friction between them. Catalonia, different from Aragón culturally and much more economically dynamic, brought the Aragónese monarchs into a closer relationship with France, with which Catalonia had had close ties for centuries.

The "Crown of Aragón" continued to expand after its union with Catalonia. In 1229, James I, the Conqueror (r. 1213–1276) captured the island of Majorca from the Moors, and the kingdom of Majorca, which included the other Balearic islands, was united with Aragón. Sometimes Majorca was ruled directly by Aragón, while other times it was in the hands of a cadet branch of the Aragónese ruling house.

Sicily had a similar fate. In 1282, Pedro III of Aragón (r. 1276–1285) became king of Sicily based on a claim through his mother Constance, the daughter of King Manfred of Sicily (r. 1258–1266). Sicily subsequently passed in and out of the hands of the main line of Aragónese monarchs and was finally permanently united with the Crown of Aragón in 1409. Aragónese power even briefly extended to Greece, where Catalan adventurers established small feudal lordships and acknowledged the Aragónese ruler as their overlord.

NATURE OF ARAGÓNESE RULE

Aragón did not have an absolute monarchy—in contrast to its neighbor, the kingdom of Castile. Aragónese royal authority was limited by the need of the king to obtain the consent of the three *cortes*, or parliaments, of Aragón, Catalonia, and Valencia. As in medieval England, the combination of the king's need for money for wars, and the nobility's control over the purse strings, increased the power of these assemblies. In 1287, Aragónese nobles, in the *Privileges of the Union*, required the king to consult them before choosing royal councilors. The document also limited the right of the king to proceed judicially against a noble without the consent of an official, the *justicia*, who was chosen from the nobility and dedicated to their interests rather than the interests of the king. The famous "Oath of the Aragónese," which allegedly set conditions of the king's tenure on the throne based on his respect for the rights of the nobles, is a sixteenth-century myth. But it reflects Aragónese political traditions.

MERGING KINGDOMS

The direct line of Aragónese–Catalan monarchs ended in 1410, with the death of Martin I (r. 1396–1410). Electors chosen by the *cortes* offered the throne to Ferdinand of Antequera, a member of the Trastamara dynasty of Castile. Ferdinand was connected to the Catalan dynasty of Aragón through his mother Eleanor, the daughter of Peter IV of Aragón (r. 1336–1387). Ferdinand assumed the throne in 1412 as Ferdinand I (r. 1412–1416). His son, Alfonso V, the Magnanimous (r. 1416–1458), added Naples to the Aragónese possessions, although

he later left it to his illegitimate son, Ferrante, rather than to his heir and successor, his brother John II (r. 1458–1479) of Aragón.

Ultimately, Aragón and Castile were brought even closer together in 1469 through the marriage of Isabella I of Castile (r. 1474–1504) and Ferdinand II of Aragón (r. 1479–1516), the son and heir of John II. Ferdinand and Isabella ruled their kingdoms jointly, although the union of crowns was a personal one, not a formal, political union. The union of the two kingdoms was not finalized until 1516, with the accession of Charles I (r. 1516–1556), the grandson of Ferdinand and Isabella (and who was perhaps better known as Emperor Charles V of the Holy Roman Empire). The merger of Aragón and Castile under Charles marks the beginning of a process that resulted in a unified kingdom of Spain. Despite Castilian dominance, Aragón retained its separate institutions and identity until 1716, when King Philip V (r. 1700–1746) of Spain abolished all remaining special privileges enjoyed by the Aragónese.

See also: ALFONSO V, THE MAGNANIMOUS; ARAGÓN, HOUSE OF; CASTILE, KINGDOM OF; CATALONIA, COUNTY OF; CHARLES V; FERDINAND II AND ISABELLA I; JAMES I OF ARAGÓN; JAMES II OF ARAGÓN; NAPLES, KINGDOM OF; SICILY, KINGDOM OF; SPANISH MONARCHIES; TRASTAMARA, HOUSE OF.

FURTHER READING

Cawsey, Suzasnne F. *Kingship and Propaganda: Royal Eloquence and the Crown of Aragon, c. 1200–1450.* Oxford: Clarendon Press, 2002.

ARAMEAN KINGDOMS

(1100–732 B.C.E.)

Mesopotamian states founded by the Arameans, a Semitic tribespeople who abandoned their desert existence sometime in the second millennium B.C.E. and adopted a settled existence in the ancient Near East. The most important of the Aramean kingdoms was Aram-Damascus, which controlled much of present-day Syria as well as parts of Iraq and southeastern Turkey. The kingdom faded from history after 732 B.C.E., when Assyria conquered the Aramaic capital of Damascus. The Aramaic language, a Semitic language, flourished for additional centuries as a lingua franca of administration and trade.

Around the twelfth century B.C.E., large numbers of Aramean nomads began migrating westward into Mesopotamia and Babylonia. Tiglath-Pileser I of Assyria (r. ca. 1116–1076 B.C.E.) claimed to have fought twenty-eight battles against the Aramean newcomers. Evidently, the Arameans withstood his attacks and strengthened their connections with another Semitic tribe, the Hebrews. According to biblical tradition, Isaac and Jacob took Aramean wives from the kingdom of Padan Aram.

Toward the north of the region, Padan Aram and other Aramean kingdoms took shape slowly, through peaceful settlement as well as conquest. By about 1000 B.C.E., the Neo-Hittite state of Til Barsip had been transformed into the Aramean kingdom of Bit Adini. Other Aramean states that took shape in the years that followed were Ya'diya, Bit Agusi, Bit-Bahiani, Bit-Adini, Hamath-Lu'ash, Bit-Gabbari, and Geshur. By the early ninth century B.C.E., these moderate-sized kingdoms contained fortified royal cities. There were also a number of smaller Aramean kingdoms, including Bit Zamani, Bit-Asalli, and Bit-Halupe.

Further south, Arameans established themselves in Damascus and Zobah, areas that had escaped Egyptian rule late in the reign of Pharaoh Rameses III (r. ca. 1198–1166 B.C.E.). Zobah and Damascus fell to the Israelites around 1000 to 965 B.C.E., when the army of King David (r. 1010–970 B.C.E.) defeated King Hadadezer of Zobah and his allies. During the reign of David's son, King Solomon (r. 970–931 B.C.E.), however, a servant of Hadadezer's named Rezon retook Damascus and declared himself ruler of the kingdom of Aram-Damascus.

The kingdom of Aram-Damascus prospered. King Ben Hadad I (r. ca. 880–842 B.C.E.) annexed land from Israel in 878 B.C.E. and may even have made Israel a tribute-paying vassal state. In 853 B.C.E., he joined with King Ahab of Israel (r. 874–853 B.C.E.) and King Ikhuleni of Hamath to defeat Shalmeneser III of Assyria (r. 858–824 B.C.E.) at the battle of Qarqar (853 B.C.E.). Although Damascus fell to the Assyrians in 842 B.C.E. and Ben Hadad was assassinated, his successor, a commoner named Hazael (r. 842–806 B.C.E.), managed to restore Damascus's dominance by conquering most of the land of Philistia and all of Israel. Not until the reign of Hazael's son, Ben Hadad II (r. 806–750 B.C.E.), did the balance of power swing back in favor of Israel.

The Aramean kingdoms lying to the north of Damascus, closer to Assyria, did not fare as well. Assyria had absorbed a number of lesser Aramean states. In the 850s B.C.E., Shalmeneser III defeated King Khayan of Ya'diya and King Akhuni of Bit Adini, and the powerful Bit Adini became an Assyrian province. Other kingdoms eventually suffered the same fate. Geshur fell to Tiglath-Pileser III, and the Assyrians in 734 B.C.E. Bit Agusi succumbed to the Assyrians around 740 B.C.E..

Fearing for his kingdom, King Rezin of Aram-Damascus set aside traditional quarrels with the Israelites and joined them in a coalition against Assyria, but the Assyrians had become too powerful. In 732 B.C.E., Tiglath-Pileser III sacked the city of Damascus, killed Rezin, and deported the surviving residents. Soon after, the Aramean kingdoms all became Assyrian provinces under the collective name Aram Naharain.

Although the Arameans had lost their political power, their language survived. Assyrian rulers employed Arameans as scribes, and Aramaic-speaking merchants carried the language along trade routes throughout the Near East. Aramaic became the common trade language of the Fertile Crescent, and Darius I the Great of Persia (r. 521–485 B.C.E.) declared it the official language of his empire. In widespread use as a vernacular language in the time of Jesus, Aramaic was still spoken in remote villages in Syria thousands of years later. Beginning in 280 B.C.E., the Arameans became known as the Syrians, when a popular translation of the Bible, the Septuagint, used the term *Syria* in place of *Aram*.

See also: ASSYRIAN EMPIRE; BIBLICAL KINGS; DARIUS I, THE GREAT; DAVID; SYRIAN KINGDOMS; TIGLATH-PILESER III.

ARENAS, ROYAL

An area for public contests or exertions in which royal or imperial personages can display symbols of their wealth and power and interact more directly with their population. Arenas have been used throughout the ages as venues for public display of royal events.

In Ancient Rome, the emperors regularly frequented two large arenas—the Colosseum and the Circus Maximus. The emperors sometimes used the events held in these great arenas to distribute a share of grain to the citizens of Rome, a tradition that helped keep the people of Rome content. Emperor Commodus (r. 180–192) even appeared as a gladiator in the Colosseum and fought with wooden weapons. He awarded himself a fee of one million sestertii (Roman coins worth approximately 2 million dollars today) for his appearance.

Citizens sometimes used gatherings at arenas as a means of expressing their dissatisfaction to the emperor. During Commodus's reign, frustration over a grain shortage led to a riot at the Circus Maximus in 190. The people believed that an imperial adviser, Cleander, was hoarding grain in order to increase his own wealth. The riot spilled out of the Circus, and the people converged on a villa where the emperor was staying. Commodus accepted their demands that Cleander be killed and his body turned over to the mob.

In the Americas, arenas that hosted the Mesoamerican ball games were often owned and visited by Mayan kings. The rulers themselves sometimes played ball at these ball courts, taking on the persona of a god. At the Mayan city of Chichen-Itza in the Yucatán region, thirteen ball courts still remain, one of which, the Great Ball Court, appears to have been owned by the king. A variety of ceremonies may have been held at this arena, including inauguration ceremonies for new kings and possibly human sacrifices.

In Southeast Asia, the Tiger's Arena (or Ho Quyen) was built in 1830 for the emperor of Vietnam. It included a staircase and an imperial box where the emperor and his family could watch fights between tigers and elephants. The fights were partially symbolic in nature—the elephants represented the might of the emperor and the tigers that of his adversaries. Such fights were carried out until 1904.

In England, horse races have been held on royal land since 1711. That year, Queen Anne, a dedicated racing enthusiast, founded the Royal Ascot racecourse. The racecourse included a royal stand, which by 1845 included a two-story structure, private lawn, and an area for celebrations. The racecourse at Ascot is still used today.

See also: AMERICAN KINGDOMS, CENTRAL AND NORTH; CAESARS; HUNTING AND KINGSHIP; MAYA EMPIRE.

ARLES KINGDOM (933–1380 C.E.)

Medieval kingdom in France, under the nominal control of the Holy Roman Empire, which became part of France in the late fourteenth century.

The kingdom of Arles was established in 933, when Rudolf II (r. 912–937), king of Transjurane Burgundy (in what are now Switzerland, Savoy, and Franche-Comté), gained control of Provence and established his capital at the Provençal city of Arles. This kingdom, called Arles or Arelate, was also known as the second kingdom of Burgundy, to distinguish it from the powerful kingdom of Burgundy, which had existed in the previous century.

Rudolph III of Arles (r. 993–1032), the grandson of the kingdom's founder, had no heirs and decided to leave the kingdom to his nephew, German king and Holy Roman emperor, Henry II (r. 1002–1024). However, Henry died nearly a decade before Rudolf, who named no other heir.

On Rudolph's death, Holy Roman Emperor Conrad II (r. 1024–1039), though only distantly related to Rudolf by blood, claimed Arles for the German Crown and marched his troops into the kingdom and occupied it in 1033. The Burgundian nobles preferred the rule of this distant emperor to the intrusive authority of Odo II of Champagne, the nephew of Rudolf III, who had a much stronger claim to the throne. The nobles thus elected Conrad as king of Arles, and he was crowned in Geneva in 1034.

Conrad's crowning marked the beginning of the rule of the Holy Roman emperors over the so-called three kingdoms of Germany, Italy, and Burgundy. Arles was important to the emperors because it contained vital routes connecting the territories they ruled. However, because of the vastness of their lands, and because the Burgundian nobility continued to resist imperial rule, the emperors were often able to exert only nominal control over Arles.

Conrad II appointed his son, Henry III (r. 1039–1056), as king of Arles, but most often the emperors ruled through imperial vicars. Occasionally, they even went outside their own realms in search of a subordinate king. In 1193, for example, Holy Roman Emperor Henry VI (r. 1190–1197), seeing that Philip II Augustus of France (r. 1180–1223) threatened control of some Burgundian provinces, appointed Richard I of England (r. 1189–1199) king of Arles, but Richard died before he could be crowned.

In 1378, the Holy Roman emperor, Charles IV (r. 1355–1378), made the dauphin Charles, heir to the French throne, the imperial vicar for the kingdom of Arles. When the dauphin later became King Charles VI of France (r. 1380–1422), sovereignty over Arles passed to the French Crown. With this transfer of power, Arles effectively ceased to exist as a separate, independent kingdom.

See also: BURGUNDY KINGDOM; CONRAD II; CONRAD III; HOLY ROMAN EMPIRE; PHILIP II, AUGUSTUS; RICHARD I, LIONHEART.

ARMENIAN KINGDOMS

(ca. 500s B.C.E.–1375 C.E.)

Series of kingdoms in Armenia, a region between the Black and Caspian seas, which had a unique culture that blended Iranian social and political structures with Hellenistic and Christian literary traditions.

The history of the Armenian kingdoms features a long legacy of invasions, conquests, and struggles for power in an area that often served as a bridge between different cultures and civilizations. Despite numerous invasions and conquests, the kingdoms of Armenia managed not only to survive but also to develop a unique culture, with distinct art and architectural styles and a national alphabet.

In the late third century C.E., during the reign of Tiridates III (r. 287–298), the Armenians were also among the first people to adopt Christianity as a state religion. In 653, they were introduced to Islam when the region was conquered by Arab forces. During the thirteenth and fourteenth centuries, Mongols invaded Armenia twice and established Islamic dynasties as well. The region came under Turkish rule in 1375, and in the fifteenth century, most of what is now present-day Armenia became a part of the Ottoman Empire. When not controlled by outside conquerors, independent Armenian dynasties ruled.

The Armenian people first came into Asia Minor in the 700s B.C.E. and invaded the ancient state of Urartu, which had flourished in the region since the thirteenth century B.C.E. The Armenians began to intermarry with the native peoples, and by the 500s B.C.E., they had formed their own nation.

In 330 B.C.E. Armenia was conquered by Alexander the Great (r. 336–323 B.C.E.). After his death in 323 B.C.E., Armenia became a part of the Syrian

kingdom of the Seleucid dynasty, which was founded by Seleucus Nicator, one of Alexander's generals. Armenia remained part of the Syrian kingdom until it declared independence in 189 B.C.E. under the native Artaxiad dynasty, founded by Artaxias I (r. ca. 200–159 B.C.E.).

The greatest king of the Artaxiad dynasty was Tigran II, also known as Tigranes, or Tigran the Great (r. 95–56 B.C.E.). Under the rule of Tigranes and his successors, the Armenian kingdom reached its greatest size and influence, stretching from the Mediterranean Sea northeast to the Mtkvari River in present-day Georgia. Tigranes and his son, Artavazd II (r. 56–33 B.C.E.), made Armenia a center of Hellenistic culture, and during their reigns Armenian culture, art, and architecture also flourished. Tigranes's ambitions, however, ultimately led to conflict with the Roman Empire, which conquered the region in 69 B.C.E. and made Armenia a Roman province. Armenian kings continued to rule but only as vassals to Rome.

In 63 C.E., a Parthian prince named Tiridates (r. 63–98) became king of Armenia, founding a new ruling dynasty, the Arsacids. Tiridates defeated the Roman forces in Armenia and was recognized as king by the Emperor Nero (r. 54–68). In the centuries that followed, Armenia maintained some measure of independence, despite the fact that it was sought after by the Byzantines, Persians, Mongols, and Turks.

Armenia adopted Christianity in the late 200s, when Saint Gregory the Illuminator, the son of a Parthian nobleman, performed a series of miracles that convinced the pagan ruler of Armenia, Tiridates III, to convert to the religion. His conversion predates the acceptance of Christianity by Emperor Constantine the Great (r. 307–337) in 312, thus making Armenia the first established Christian kingdom in the East.

In the fourth century, the Persians overran Armenia and began a period of Christian persecution that fueled a nationalistic spirit among the people. Fostered by numerous martyrs to the Christian faith, Armenians made several attempts to gain independence. Each period of independence was short-lived, however.

Early in the fifth century, Saint Mesrop, also known as Mashtots, created an Armenian alphabet that eventually became the basis for a national literature. At the same time, religious and historical works began to be written as part of an effort to consolidate the influence of Christianity.

From the fifth to seventh century, Armenia experienced a golden age in which political unrest coincided with the development of a national literary tradition and a strong religious life. Part of the Byzantine Empire during this period, Armenia remained an imperial province until the mid-seventh century. Finally, in 653 the Byzantines, finding the region increasingly difficult to govern, ceded Armenia to the Arabs, who introduced Islam to the region.

In 806, the Bagratid dynasty was established in Armenia, first as governors and ultimately as kings of a semiautonomous state. During the rule of the Bagratid kings, from 886 to 1045, Armenia experienced the longest period of independence in its history. During that time, the development of Armenian art and culture continued to develop and flourish.

Reconquered by the Byzantines in 1046, Armenia was then overrun by the Seljuk Turks following their defeat of the Byzantines at the battle of Manzikert in 1071. The conquest by the Muslim Seljuks started a mass exodus of Armenians from their native lands. In 1080, these exiles established a new kingdom in Cilicia, a region bordering the Mediterranean Sea in Asia Minor (present-day Turkey).

This new Armenian kingdom, sometimes known as Little Armenia, frequently allied itself with Christian powers of the West, particularly during the period of the Crusades. However, the kingdom finally fell to the Mamluk Turks in 1375, bringing an end to Armenian independence. Shortly afterward, the Mongols, under the great conqueror Tamerlane (r. ca. 1370–1405), seized the original region of Armenia from the Seljuks and massacred much of the population.

See also: BYZANTINE EMPIRE; ROMAN EMPIRE; SELEUCID DYNASTY; SELJUQ DYNASTY.

ARPAD DYNASTY (ca. 889–1301 C.E.)

Dynasty that ruled Hungary and an expanded Hungarian empire for nearly five hundred years during the Middle Ages.

The Arpad dynasty is virtually synonymous with the early history of the Magyar people (as Hungarians call themselves). Arpad rulers led the Magyars from their initial incursion into Central Europe in the late 800s until 1301, by which time Hungary had become a powerful and important European state.

The Magyars were originally a seminomadic tribal confederation speaking a language related to Finnish. Before about 895, they lived in the lands north of the Black Sea, an area that had long been a staging ground for peoples invading Europe and the Middle East. At that time, under pressure from enemy tribes, the Magyars began moving westward over the Carpathian Mountains. Some sixty thousand strong, they were led by a chieftain named Arpad (d. 907), who became the founder of the Arpad dynasty.

Arpad, the semilegendary subject of many Hungarian poems and romances, had been chosen by his fellow chieftains as a temporary leader to head the campaign of conquest. By wile and brute force, he and his immediate descendants managed to establish the principle of hereditary rule.

Decades of turmoil followed the Magyar's march westward, during which their raids reached as far as Spain. But the bulk of the population put down permanent roots in the Pannonian Plain (central Hungary), where the Arpad family consolidated its hold as princes or dukes.

A decisive defeat at the hands of German king Otto I (r. 936–973) in 955 near Augsburg, Germany, convinced the Arpads to abandon foreign adventures. Under the dukes Taksony (r. 955–972) and his son Geza (r. 972–997), the Arpads centralized administration, settled towns, encouraged trade, and persisted in efforts to weaken the separate tribal identities that existed among the Magyars. Geza strengthened the Arpad's pro-Western and anti-Byzantine orientation by inviting Otto I (r. 962–973), now Holy Roman emperor, to send Christian missionary bishops to his dominions.

All these policies bore fruit during the reign of Geza's son, Stephen I (r. 997–1038), who was recognized as the first king of Hungary by Pope Sylvester II (r. 999–1003) and crowned in the year 1001. The long, peaceful reign of Stephen I was marked by vigorous policies of administrative reorganization and Christianization. He was canonized as Saint Stephen by the Roman Church in 1083 and is still considered the patron saint of Hungary as well as the greatest ruler of the Arpad dynasty.

Stephen's successors built on the firm foundation that he and his forebears had established. Laszlo (r.

1077–1095) and Kalman (r. 1095–1116) expanded the kingdom into the Balkan region of Croatia, while Bela III (r. 1173–1196) controlled Serbia farther south, as well as the Galician region to the northeast of Hungary. The thirteenth century was less generous to the Arpad kings, however, and great nobles gained power at their expense. Bela IV (r. 1235–1270) rallied Hungary after the devastating Mongol invasion of 1241–1242, but the great defensive castles built by the nobles at his request were eventually used to defy royal power. The dynasty ended in 1301, when Andrew III (r. 1290–1301) died without an heir.

See also: OTTO I, THE GREAT; STEPHEN I (SAINT STEPHEN).

ART OF KINGS

Works of art depicting or owned or commissioned by monarchs all over the world from ancient to modern times.

ROLE OF ROYAL ART

The arts have always been a way to exalt royal qualities. In all ages and civilizations, imperial images have tended to represent particular themes, such as the sovereign himself and members of his court, life in the palace, or the ruler's war exploits. Surviving Egyptian art works, for instance, are mainly architectural accomplishments, frescoes on tombs, and objects and sculptures made by artists and artisans who served the pharaohs and other royalty. Most of them are sculpted or painted depictions of the pursuits of monarchs, such as the ceremonial and leisure activities of the court; funerary rites; the diligent work of peasants and farmers, which represented the affluence of the kingdom; and military conquests of the kings. Similarly, steles and sculptures in carefully carved bas-relief decorating the palaces of ancient Mesopotamian realms like Assyria and Babylonia celebrated imperial glory by illustrating war and hunting scenes. In Rome, royal art used the same tradition, exhibiting portraits of the emperors and images of their exploits to display the power of the empire to the Italic, Latin, and barbarian peoples it ruled.

In Africa as well, art has been used to represent aspects of a monarchy's history and to expand and perpetuate royal power. But rather than portray war or court scenes, most works of African royal art focus on the monarch himself. Many illustrate the intrinsic contradiction between individual rulers and the concept of kingship; that is, the ruler is a human being who will therefore eventually die, whereas a kingdom is a lasting political structure. Thus, many royal portraits of African kings in Dahomey (current Benin), Kuba (current Congo), and Benin (current Nigeria) depict the kings as the embodiment of beauty and perfection, of ideal age and body size, in perfect health, and of calm demeanor. Some large African kingdoms such as Benin, Dahomey, Ashanti, and Kuba had court artisans—sculptors, smiths, founders, embroiderers, weavers, sculptors, jewelers—who dedicated their work to the royalty. They belonged to guilds that were protected by the king, and their art became distinct from the more popular arts.

PORTRAITS

In Egypt, portraits—sculpted, on frescoes, or in bas-relief—were intended to preserve the image of the pharaoh and his court. They were usually full-length, and the figures looked at ease. Exact resemblance was not a goal. Rather, portraits gave an impression of a vigorous and passionate, yet wise, pharaoh. The Romans, on the other hand, strove for identical resemblances in their portraits, which celebrated the greatness of the emperor and were placed in public places. The head was the main part of the Roman royal portrait.

Later, portraits came to be fashionable in Europe in the form of paintings. In England, in the 1600s, most painted pictures were, in fact, portraits. Under Henry VIII, a typically English style of portraiture started to emerge following the development of this art form in other European countries. Henry VIII's royal art collection included many portraits, but at the time they were seen more as royal advertisements than as valuable works of art. They were even used to negotiate marriages. Henry VIII possessed a number of royal portraits, such as of Henry V, Henry VI, Edward IV, and Richard III. The subjects of the Tudor portraits can be identified by coats of arms, inscriptions, and badges. Jewelry, costume, and insignia indicated rank and affluence. Most of the portraits were head-to-shoulder rather than full-length. Royal portraits often hung in the king's dwellings and in those of loyal subjects. Henry VIII was the first king to have an art collection as we know it, although his intent—like that of other rulers throughout the centuries—was to magnify his own glory.

See also: BENIN KINGDOM; HENRY VIII; KUBA KINGDOM; TUDOR, HOUSE OF.

ARTAXERXES I (464–424 B.C.E.)

A king from the Achaemenid dynasty who ruled the Persian Empire during its later, decadent era.

Artaxerxes I (r. 486–464 B.C.E.) took the throne of the Persian Empire after the assassination of his father, Xerxes I (r. 485–465 B.C.E.), by killing off his two brothers. Throughout his reign, Artaxerxes I was forced to devote much of his efforts to fighting rebellions and navigating palace intrigues, but he managed to maintain Persian predominance. Faced with a major rebellion in the Persian province of Egypt in 459 B.C.E., Artaxerxes I suppressed it, but only after five years of intense effort.

Around 448 B.C.E., the Greeks of the city-state of Athens sent a fleet to aid a rebellion against Persian rule in Cyprus. The Greek fleet won a great victory, but at the Treaty of Callias that ended the war, Artaxerxes negotiated favorable terms—Athenian recognition of Persian power in Asia Minor (persent-day Turkey). When Athens broke the treaty in 439 B.C.E., Persia won a series of battles that further strengthened its position in the West.

Despite the intermittent warfare with Greece, important cultural exchanges occurred between the two countries during the reign of Artaxerxes I. The king also played an important role in supporting the revival of Judaism in Jerusalem

By the time of Artaxerxes I, the Persian imperial court had grown dramatically in size and opulence. Most of the Achaemenid kings sired scores of illegitimate sons, and they and their descendants—at least those who escaped bloody succession struggles—taxed the resources of the state. After Artaxerxes I's death in 424 B.C.E., three of his sons claimed the throne. Darius II (r. 423–404 B.C.E.) eventually triumphed over his brothers, Xerxes II (r. 424 B.C.E.) and Sogdianus (r. 424 B.C.E.), following the murder of these other two claimants to the throne.

See also: ACHAEMENID DYNASTY; ARTAXERXES II; ARTAXERXES III; PERSIAN EMPIRE.

ARTAXERXES II (436–359 B.C.E.)

King of Persia (r. 404–359 B.C.E.) whose long reign was punctuated by repeated military challenges. Although Artaxerxes II emerged successful from most of these challenges, his loss of Egypt in 404 B.C.E. marked the beginning of the end for the Persian Empire.

Artaxerxes II was the son and successor of Darius II (r. 423–405 B.C.E.). Troubles at the very start of his reign were a portent of things to come. During his coronation, Cyrus the Younger, one of the king's many Achaemenid relatives, tried to assassinate him and seize the throne. Forgiven and sent to a provincial post in Asia Minor, Cyrus nonetheless continued to plot against the king. In 401 B.C.E., Cyrus marched eastward with 10,000 Greek mercenaries

During the rule of Artaxerxes II, of the Achaemenid Dynasty, Persian power was on the decline. Upon his death in 359 B.C.E., Artaxerxes was placed in this rock tomb at the royal capital of Persepolis.

in hopes of seizing the empire, only to be defeated and killed at the battle of Cunaxa.

Artaxerxes II also faced a rebellion in Egypt that broke out during his succession struggle and resulted in the loss of that land soon after he took the throne. Artaxerxes II spent much of his reign preparing to reconquer the province, but the Egyptians repelled a major invasion by his Greek mercenaries in 374 B.C.E. News of the defeat encouraged an uprising by several provincial satraps, or governors. Although the satraps were defeated, Artaxerxes II allowed them to remain in their posts; this leniency may have further weakened royal authority. After Artaxerxes died in 359 B.C.E., he was succeeded by his son, Artaxerxes III Ochus (r. 359–338 B.C.E.).

See also: ACHAEMENID DYNASTY; ARTAXERXES I; ARTAXERXES III; PERSIAN EMPIRE.

ARTAXERXES III (d. 338 B.C.E.)

Persian ruler (r. 359–338 B.C.E.) who centralized and strengthened his empire through harsh and bloody means.

The son of Artaxexes II (r. 404–359 B.C.E.), Artaxerxes III came to the throne as a result of tawdry and violent intrigues. To win and secure power, he murdered many of his relatives, including some eighty brothers who were killed in one day. Artaxerxes III continued a policy of terror throughout his reign. As an indication of the political climate at the highest Persian ranks, Artaxerxes took the family of his new commander-in-chief as hostages in order to ensure the commander's loyalty.

In 351–350 B.C.E., Artaxerxes III tried unsuccessfully to retake Egypt, which had been lost during the reign of his father. Emboldened by Persian defeat, the cities of Phoenicia and Palestine rose up in rebellion but were brutally suppressed. Artaxerxes III led a final, more successful invasion of Egypt in 343 B.C.E. Persian rule was restored there, but this lasted only until the end of Artaxerxes's reign five years later.

In 338 B.C.E., King Philip II of Macedon (r. 359–336 B.C.E.) pushed aside Persian troops in Thrace and proceeded to subdue all of Greece. That same year, the powerful court eunuch Bagoas, Artaxerxes's military commander, had Artaxerxes III poisoned, and he then placed the king's son Arses (r.

337–336 B.C.E.) on the throne. In killing Artaxerxes, Bagoas spared the king from living to see the collapse of the empire following the massive invasion by Alexander the Great (r. 336–323 B.C.E.) in 331 B.C.E.

See also: ACHAEMENID DYNASTY; ALEXANDER III, THE GREAT; ARTAXERXES II; DARIUS III; PERSIAN EMPIRE; PHILIP II OF MACEDON.

ARTHUR, KING

Legendary king of Britain and founder of the Round Table, celebrated in medieval legend, who is said to have initiated the search for the Holy Grail.

The bold figures of Arthur, Queen Guinevere, Merlin, Lancelot du Lac, and the knights of the Round Table are best known as heroes of Arthurian romance and literature. However, historical sources support the existence of one or more early British leaders who may have served as the model for this celebrated monarch.

THE LEGENDARY ARTHUR

There are three major sources for the Arthur of legend: the twelfth-century *History of the Kings of Britain* by Geoffrey of Monmouth; a cycle of Arthurian romances by the medieval French poet Chretien de Troyes; and *Le Morte d'Arthur* by the fifteenth-century English author Sir Thomas Malory.

Writing only seventy years after the Norman conquest in 1066, English chronicler Geoffrey of Monmouth catered to the values and desires of his audience, the Anglo-French ruling class, in his account of the legendary Arthur. From Geoffrey, we learn that Arthur and his Britons defeated not only the Saxons, but eventually Rome itself. It is also in Geoffrey that we first find a number of other characters and places in the Arthurian legend—Uther, Ygraine, the castle Tintagel, Avalon, and, most importantly, the wizard Merlin. Merlin's exploits include moving "the Giant's Dance" to its current location at Stonehenge.

In the medieval French *jongleur* tradition of wandering minstrels, Chretien de Troyes never pretended to write history. Instead, he wove together Celtic myths and borrowed heavily from *Layamon*, a version of Arthurian stories by the twelfth-century Norman-French poet, Wace. In his medieval ro-

The legendary King Arthur and his Knights of the Round Table, models of chivalry in the Middle Ages, have appeared in countless depictions over the centuries. This is from an illustrated manuscript published by Antoine Verard in Paris around 1490.

mances, Chretien presented Lancelot, Camelot, and the Holy Grail as parts of the Arthurian legend for the first time.

It was, however, a lonely, imprisoned English knight, Sir Thomas Malory, who used Chretien de Troyes, Geoffrey of Monmouth, and other sources to create the most widely known version of the Arthurian legend, *Le Morte d'Arthur*, which was published in 1485, after the author's death.

In Malory, King Arthur is the son of Uther Pendragon. According to legend, Uther disguises himself as Gorlois, duke of Cornwall, and fathers Arthur with Gorlois's wife, Ygraine. As Gorlois is conveniently killed in battle that same evening, Uther takes Gorlois's kingdom and wife for his own. When Ygraine has a son, Arthur, the wizard Merlin collects the baby as repayment for having magically transformed Uther into Gorlois on the night of the child's conception, and he takes Arthur away to be fostered in secret by the rural knight, Sir Ector. Approximately twenty years later, the young Arthur pulls the mystical sword Excalibur from a stone and is proclaimed the rightful king of Britain.

Arthur later marries Guinevere, the daughter of King Leodegrance, and is given an enormous Round Table as a wedding gift. He decides to take advantage of the table's egalitarian shape (which allows no one to sit "higher" or "lower" than anyone else) and founds the chivalric order known as the Knights of the Round Table. This order, dedicated to defending virtue and the helpless, becomes the key feature of Arthur's court at Camelot.

But Arthur's reign is undermined by two forces. First, the greatest knight of the group—Sir Lancelot du Lac, a Frenchman from the castle Joyeuse Garde in France—falls in love with Guinevere, who returns his affection. At the same time, Arthur and the Knights share a vision of the Holy Grail—the cup from which Jesus Christ drank at the Last Supper. The knights of the Round Table are urged to give up all other pursuits to search for the Grail. Many Knights die or are captured during their quests, weakening the kingdom just as Arthur's illegitimate son, Modred (fathered with Arthur's half-sister, Morgause), brings Lancelot's and Guinevere's affair to Arthur's public attention.

As Lancelot and Guinevere escape to France and Joyeuse Garde, Modred organizes armies to attack the dispirited Arthur, hoping to take the throne. However, Lancelot returns at the last moment and helps Arthur defeat Modred. Mortally wounded in this last battle, Arthur does not die on the battlefield but is borne off by the mystical Lady of the Lake to Avalon, an enchanted island in the west.

Such is the Arthur of legend.

THE HISTORICAL ARTHUR

In the latter half of the twentieth century, considerable investigations were made into the possibility of an historical King Arthur. Evidence was unearthed that several real figures might have served as inspiration for the renowned fictional ruler.

When the Roman legions left Britain in the early sixth century, the wealthy and civilized southern part of Britain soon felt pressure from raiding Teutonic tribes. These invasions increased in frequency and magnitude for the next two centuries. It is Gildas, a contemporary sixth-century British monk, who first names an Arthur-like figure, Ambrosius Aurelianus, as the *Dux Bellorum*, or warlord, who rallied the Britons against the invading Saxons. Among the cited victories of Amabrosius is the battle of Mons Badonicus.

Another Arthur (or perhaps the same figure) is mentioned in the *Historia Brittonum*, a chronicle from the early ninth century. Nennius, the compiler of this work, is thought to be reliable; however, he unfortunately insists that Arthur (not Aurelianus) single-handedly slew 960 men at the battle of Mons Badonicus.

An entirely different—and more magical—Arthur appears in Welsh traditions as early as the eighth century in the *Annales Cambriae*, as well as in the more popularly known *Mabinogion*, a fourteenth-century collection of Welsh tales that probably date from as much as a thousand years earlier. The Arthur in these works is a magical Celtic king who is assisted by Merlin and other supernaturally endowed denizens in fighting enemies far stranger than the Saxons.

Who then is King Arthur—a mythical Celtic hero, a Roman general, or the first king-of-all-Britain? Original documentary sources and archaeological evidence are sketchy and remain in dispute. Nonetheless, in literature and the popular imagination, Arthur will continue as the enduring symbol of the noble and doomed monarch.

See also: MYTH AND FOLKLORE.

FURTHER READING

Alcock, Leslie. *Arthur's Britain.* London: Penguin, 1971.

Malory, Sir Thomas. *Le Morte d'Arthur.* New York: Macmillan, 1970.

White, T.H. *The Once and Future King.* New York: Penguin, 1987.

ASANTE KINGDOM (1670–1901 C.E.)

Kingdom in West Africa that, at the peak of its power, controlled a wide swath of territory that included much of southern Ghana and extended into the present-day states of Togo and Ivory Coast.

The Asante kingdom arose around 1670, when a powerful leader named Osei Tutu began to gather a strong enough following among local Akan chiefdoms to overthrow the then dominant Denkyira people and assume control over the local trade. Osei accomplished the overthrow of the Denkyira in a war that lasted from 1699 to 1701. With his ultimate victory over the Denkyira, Osei Tutu (r. 1685–1717), who succeeded his uncle as ruler of the Ku-

masi state in 1685, consolidated power and established a new seat of government at Kumasi.

To legitimate his claim to rulership, Osei relied not only on the might of his military, but also on the development of rituals and institutions that brought his people together. First among these was the Golden Stool, a ritual object used in the installation of a ruler (*asantehene*). The concept of the ritual stool, shared by many of the Akan peoples within the Asante kingdom, symbolized the broader authority of the Asante king over local leaders. Osei also introduced other important rituals designed to unite the disparate peoples under Asante rule, giving everyone a common set of cultural elements to define their shared membership in the state.

At the time the Asante kingdom was created, Europeans were avidly seeking to trade with the local populations for gold and slaves. Whoever could control the trade goods sought by Europeans stood to gain a great advantage over their neighbors, for they would receive modern weaponry in return. Osei Tutu and his successors understood this relationship very well. The slave trade, in particular, provided the Asante with the wherewithal to create the strongest military force in the region.

The Asante's military strength enabled them to be the most efficient in raiding for slaves to sell to European and to subdue and incorporate their neighbors into their state. By 1750, the Asante kingdom reached its maximum extent, and the work of consolidation began in earnest. Over the next fifty years, the kingdom became highly centralized. In 1807, however, the Asante kingdom faced crises on several fronts. The most notable of these crises was the British abolition of the slave trade and increasing unrest among groups along the borders of the kingdom, which ushered in a new round of regional warfare.

By the 1820s, war with its neighbors was causing a severe drain on the resources of the Asante kingdom. Adding to the pressure were ever-increasing incursions of British colonialists into Asante territory. Despite several armed clashes with the British, the Asante managed to reach an agreement with them, but this was violently breached when the Asante attempted, in 1863, to retake territory the British had claimed. Although the Asante enjoyed initial success in the clashes that followed, the British eventually won, and, in 1901, Britain annexed the kingdom as part of its Gold Coast Colony. Although the Asante state retained its own institutions and structure, it became subordinate to the larger British colonial administration. The Asante never again achieved the status of an independent state.

See also: AFRICAN KINGDOMS; OSEI TUTU.

FURTHER READING

McLeod, Malcolm D. *The Asante*. London: Oxford University Press, 1981.

ASHIKAGA SHOGUNATE

(1338–1573 C.E.)

The 250-year span in Japan following the Kamakura period (1185–1333), which was marked by growing decentralization, splintered administrative control, and constant civil war. The Ashikaga shogunate includes the Dual Monarchies period, during which two emperors ruled Japan between 1336 and 1392.

Ashikaga Takauji (r. 1305–1358) established the Ashikaga shogunate in 1338 and became its first shogun. Initially, Takauji sided with Emperor Go-Daigo (r. 1318–1339) in a campaign to reestablish direct imperial power after the domination of the Kamakura shoguns. The alliance between Takauji and Go-Daigo was instrumental in bringing down the Kamakura shogunate, and the emperor was temporarily successful in the Kemmu Restoration of 1333.

Three years later, however, unhappy with Go-Daigo's growing independence and the emperor's failure to name him shogun, Takauji switched his allegiance to a rival emperor. Faced with these shifting alliances, Emperor Go-Daigo moved his imperial court south to the Yoshino Mountains near the old imperial city of Nara. The ensuing civil disorder led to the sixty-year period of Dual Monarchies (1336–1392), with a Northern Court in Kyoto and a Southern Court in Yoshino. Allied with Kyoto, Takauji had the northern emperor name him shogun in 1338, the post that Go-Daigo had denied to him in 1335.

THE MUROMACHI PERIOD

By 1378, the Ashikaga shogunate had set up headquarters in the Muromachi section of Kyoto, and the period that followed was thus known as the Muromachi period. This 250-year span, which ended in

Ashikaga Shogunate	
TAKAUJI	1338–1358
YOSHIAKIRA	1359–1367
YOSHIMITSU	1369–1394
YOSHIMOCHI	1395–1423
YOSHIKAZU	1423–1425
YOSHINORI	1429–1441
YOSHIKATSU	1442–1443
YOSHIMASA	1449–1474
YOSHIHISA	1474–1489
YOSHITANE	1490–1493
YOSHIZUMI	1495–1508
YOSHITANE (RESTORED)	1508–1522
YOSHIHARU	1522–1547
YOSHITERU	1547–1565
YOSHIHIDE	1568
YOSHIAKI	1568–1573

1573, was a period of violent conflict among Japan's many warring clans.

Although the shogunate had successfully curtailed imperial power, Takauji's successors were poor leaders, and the shogun was never able to wield tight central control. The *daimyo*, or large feudal owners, followed their own course, either in league with or against the powerful local *shugo* families, the bureaucratic constable class that had built up power under the preceding Kamakura shogunate. In some cases, the daimyo themselves became the most powerful shugo families in their areas. By the late twelfth century C.E., a single shugo might exercise control over as many as ten or eleven of the 66 provinces in Japan.

By the outbreak of the Onin War (1467–1477), a struggle between two powerful warlords who sought control of Japan, there were nearly 260 independent daimyo armies vying to exploit the explosive political situation. Order degenerated even further following the war, and the next hundred years became known as the *sengoku jidai*, or Warring States era, during which the provincial warlords marched endlessly to and fro in support of ever-changing loyalties.

Takauji Rulers

Takauji's grandson, Ashikaga Yoshimitsu (r. 1369–1395), is considered one of the most capable of the lackluster Ashikaga rulers. In 1392, he reunited the dual imperial courts by reneging on his promise to alternate succession between Northern and Southern claimants to the throne. To curb the power of the shugo, Yoshimitsu forced them to reside in Kyoto under his watchful eye. He built the famous Kinkakuji, or Golden Pavilion palace, there, reopened trade with China, and encouraged Chinese cultural influences.

Muromachi Cultural Legacy

Despite the civil disorder of the period, the Ashikaga shoguns lived in splendor during much of the Muromachi era. In particular, the shoguns Yoshimitsu and Yoshimasa (r. 1445–1490) were renowned for their love of art and dedicated patrons of the arts.

The cultural legacy of the Ashikaga warrior society included the pervasive influence of Zen Buddhism. In contrast to the disorder that characterized society, the Zen ideals of simplicity, restraint, discipline, and meditation inspired a lively culture that came close to, if it did not match, the refined achievements of the Heian period (794–1185).

The Muromachi artistic ideals still permeate modern Japanese culture. The elegant and restrained arts of the tea ceremony (*chanoyu*) and flower arranging (*ikebana*) came into their own during the Muromachi period. Painting, poetry, and landscape gardening flourished, and the classical Noh dance-drama was born. The Noh plays of Japan, with their masks and stylized speech and gestures, were often about the tragedies of military life and the rewards to be found in the afterlife.

WINDS OF CHANGE

Despite the volatile political situation, trade and crafts manufacturing grew during the Muromachi period and helped enrich the coffers of provincial leaders. By the early fourteenth century, money rather than rice had become the main currency of exchange; the trend increased as trade with China expanded.

During the Ashikaga period, Japanese sailors carried on extensive maritime commerce (and piracy)

along the Chinese and Korean coastline as well as with the lands of Southeast Asia. Among the many port towns that developed to accommodate coastal trade was the free city of Sakai (modern Osaka), which was governed by local merchants.

The ravages of the Onin War left both the Ashikaga shogunate and the imperial court in Kyoto impoverished. By the mid-sixteenth century, change was in the air. Nothing gave events a larger push than the arrival in 1542 or 1543 of an off-course Chinese junk on a small island off Kyushu. The passengers included three Portuguese traders, who brought with them Christianity and, of greater historical import, sophisticated muskets, or guns. Japanese artisans were quick to replicate these weapons, which played a significant role in the successful consolidation of power in 1578 by the warlord Oda Nobunaga (r. 1568–1582), whose dictatorship ended the Warring States period and marked the end of the Ashikaga shogunate.

See also: Minamoto Rulers; Kamakura Shogunate; Oda Nobunaga; Yamato Dynasty; Yoritomo.

ASHURBANIPAL (d. 627 B.C.E.)

Last great Assyrian monarch (r. ca. 668–627 B.C.E.), who was a patron of the arts as well as a military leader.

Ashurbanipal was one of the younger sons of King Esarhaddon of Assyria (r. 680–669 B.C.E.). In 672 B.C.E., Esarhaddon named Ashurbanipal crown prince, hoping to avoid conflicts over succession to the throne. Taking his duties seriously, Ash-urbanipal assumed an active role in the royal administration. Sometime later, however, perhaps pressured by another of his wives, Esarhaddon appointed an older son, Shamash-shum-ukin, as his successor in Babylon, which was controlled by Assyria. This decision by Esarhaddon was later to prove a source of conflict.

When Esarhaddon died in 669 B.C.E., Ashurbanipal had little difficulty in succeeding to the throne with his mother's backing. Even though his brother received a lesser kingdom, Ashurbanipal had little doubt of his brother's loyalty. Ashurbanipal was far more concerned with internal strife elsewhere in the empire.

Within the first few years of his reign, Ashurbanipal responded successfully to an Egyptian rebellion, and he laid siege to the Phoenician city of Tyre, winning with it control of Cilicia and Syria. Threatened by advances of the people known as the Cimmerians along the northern borders of his empire, Ashurbanipal allied with the Scythian ruler Madyes (r. mid-600s B.C.E.) and turned back the Cimmerians.

In 652 B.C.E., the Assyrians killed an usurper in the neighboring state of Elam, and Ashurbanipal backed the succession of the Elamite princes Humbanigash and Tammaritu to the throne of that kingdom. Ashurbanipal's brother, Shamash-shum-ukin, perhaps seeing his brother's failure to impose direct Assyrian rule on Elamas a sign of weakness, decided to move against him.

Shamash-shum-ukin set up a plot with leaders in Phoenicia, Lydia, Egypt, Elam, and the Arab and Chaldaean tribes, all of whom agreed to rebel at the same time. Had this plan succeeded, it would likely have brought down the Assyrian Empire. When Ashurbanipal discovered the plan, he was forced to act against his brother in Babylon, although he did his best to avoid putting Shamash-shum-ukin in direct danger. This was all in vain: when Ashurbanipal took the city in 648 B.C.E., his brother committed suicide.

Disturbed by the destruction of Babylon resulting from his siege, Ashurbanipal had the city restored under his personal direction, and appointed a local Chaldaean noble as governor. Ashurbanipal was not yet through dealing with the repercussions of his brother's treachery, however; it would take another nine years before he finally subdued the Arab tribes and Elam.

Ashurbanipal was not only a soldier, but also a great supporter of the arts. He built palaces filled with sculptures depicting his historical and ceremonial activities. He collected two glorious libraries in the Assyrian capital of Nineveh, with volumes that numbered in the tens of thousands and topics that ranged from religion to natural science, history, and fable.

The remains of Ashurbanipal's great libraries have revealed much of what is known of ancient Akkadian, Sumerian, and Assyrian literature, including the great epics of the legendary hero Gilgamesh and the Mesopotamian creation story. In the end, Ashurbanipal's libraries were his most lasting legacy; his empire, so carefully protected and so thoughtfully organized, crumbled completely within eighteen years of his death in 627 B.C.E.

See also: AKKAD, KINGDOM OF; ASSYRIAN EMPIRE; ESARHADDON; PHOENICIAN EMPIRE; SYRIAN KINGDOMS.

ASIAN DYNASTIES, CENTRAL

(ca. 500s B.C.E.–1600 C.E.)

Kingdoms and empires covering the present-day countries of Afghanistan, Kazakhstan, Kyrgyzstan, eastern Russia, Tajikistan, Turkmenistan, and Uzbekistan, as well as portions of Pakistan, Kashmir, China (Xinjiang province), Mongolia, Iran, and Iraq.

Central Asia is largely comprised of a series of steppes and deserts, stretched like horizontal belts across the continent of Asia. Great temperate forests lie to the north of this region, while a number of mighty mountain ranges, including the Altai, Tianshan, Pamir, Kunlun, Karakoram, and Himalayas, lay generally to the south. The area also contains several major rivers, lakes, and seas.

EARLY EMPIRE FORMATION

By the fifth century B.C.E., various small states and city-states in Central Asia began to be conquered by great empires from the west and east of the Central Asian steppes. This included acquisitions by the Persian Empire of the Achaemenids (545–330 B.C.E.), the Macedonain Empire of Alexander the Great (336–323 B.C.E.), the Seleucid Empire (ca. 305–238 B.C.E.), the Greco-Bactrian kingdom (ca. 246–130 B.C.E.), and the Parthian Empire (247 B.C.E.–224 C.E.).

In the Persian and Macedonian empires, local rulers paid taxes and tribute to the central government in exchange for maintaining their status and authority. Buddhism came to Central Asia in the third century B.C.E. During the same period, the Han Chinese extended their control from the east over thirty-six city-states in the Xinjiang region.

During this period of annexation and conquest, empires allowed the development of ever-longer trade routes. Over time, the longest trade route connecting China to Europe became known as the "Silk Road," because of the exquisite Chinese silks, as well as other valuables, that moved over it. The wealth of the Silk Road funded the rise of native, Central Asian monarchies beginning in the early centuries C.E. In 53 B.C.E., the Parthians defeated the Romans and gained control of the Silk Road.

By the first century C.E., Central Asia had both settled cities and a variety of nomadic tribes that raided or conquered settled populations. Among these nomadic tribes were the Sarmatians, Hephthalites, Chionites, Huns, and Turkish tribes of the steppes. New empires began to arise in Central Asia at this time, including the Kushan Empire (ca. 78/142–280), the Sasanian Empire (ca. 226–651), the Chorasmian and Sogdian kingdoms (200s–700s), the Hephthalite kingdoms (ca. 450–565), the Hunnic Empire (300s–400s), and the Juan-Juan Empire (ca. 400–552).

MUSLIM RULE

In 651, the city of Merv (in present-day Turkmenistan) became the first Islamic conquest in Central Asia when it fell to invading Arabs. An ever-expanding Islamic empire in Central Asia was controlled first by the Umayyads (661–750), followed by the Abbasids (750–819), the Tahirids (820–869), and the Saffarids (869–900). In Tajikistan/Afghanistan, the area was divided between the Muslim Samanids (ca. 900–1000) and the Ghaznavids (977–1186). The Sogdian and Chorasmian kingdoms controlled Turkmenistan and Uzbekistan until the eighth century. In Kyrgyzstan and Kazakhstan, a Turkish khanate replaced the Juan-Juan Empire in 552 and ruled until 744 or 745. That khanate later fell under the power of the Uighur kingdom (744–840 and ca. 850–1218).

As the Chinese Tang Empire fractured in the tenth century, regional kingdoms such as the Uighurs and Xixia (1032–1227) came into power. Other regional rulers included the Ghurid dynasty (1000s–1215), the Khwarazm-Shah dynasty (1157–1231), the Qarakhanid dynasty (ca. 1000–1140), and the Qarakhitai dynasty (1124–1211). The Mongols conquered all these Central Asian kingdoms in the thirteenth century, ruling from 1215 to 1227.

The Chaghatay khanate (ca. 1227–1363) and the Timurid dynasty (ca 1370–1507) were both Mongolian dynasties. In 1370, Timur Leng—also known as Tamerlane (r. 1370–1405)—the first ruler of the Timurid dynasty, conquered most of western Asia, southern Russia, and India during a thirty-five-year reign.

After 1500, the Mongolian dynasties came into increasing conflict with the Shaibanids, an Uzbek dynasty that had seized control of the central part of Asia and Khwarazm from the Timurids. In the east, Mongol clans were continuously at war for control. In 1507, Khorasan, the capital of the Timurids, fell to the Shaibanids. Babur (r. 1526–1530), the last surviving member of the Timurids, fled to India, where he founded the Mughal Empire. Shaibanid power declined after 1598, as the khans of Khiva and Bukhara took over their lands.

See also: ABBASID DYNASTY; ACHAEMENID DYNASTY; GHAZNAVID DYNASTY; GHUR DYNASTY; HUN EMPIRE; KHWARAZM-SHAH DYNASTY; MONGOL EMPIRE; MUGHAL EMPIRE; SAFFARID DYNASTY; SAMANID DYNASTY; SASANID DYNASTY; SELEUCID DYNASTY; UIGHUR EMPIRE; UMAYYAD DYNASTY.

FURTHER READING

Soucek, Svatopluk. *A Short History of Inner Asia*. New York: Cambridge University Press, 2000.

Tapsell, R.F. *Monarchs, Rulers, Dynasties and Kingdoms of the World*. New York: Facts on File Publishing, 1983.

ASOKA (c. 299–232 B.C.E.)

Third ruler (r. 268–232 B.C.E.) of the Maurya dynasty (321–180 B.C.E.) of India, who is credited with elevating the then local religious movement of Buddhism to a truly world religion and with unifying nearly all of the Indian subcontinent under one rule for the first time in history.

The son of Emperor Bindusara (r. 297–272 B.C.E.), Asoka was born in approximately 299 B.C.E. in a region then known as Magadha (present-day Bihar). Asoka's grandfather, Chandragupta Maurya (r. 321–297 B.C.E.), founded the Maurya dynasty and had controlled a territory that stretched north and east from the Ganges River Valley. During his own rule, Bindusara extended that territory southward into the Indian subcontinent. Chandragupta, and his son after him, were relentless in their pursuit of empire, waging wars of conquest against their neighbors and steadily expanding the territory they controlled.

When Bindusara died around 272 B.C.E., Asoka's accession was by no means certain; he faced a number of rival claimants to the throne. His solution was simple but brutal: he had all his rivals killed, includ-

Indian Emperor Asoka of the Maurya Dynasty united most of the subcontinent under one rule for the first time. His support of Buddhism significantly spread that religion. To help educate his people about Buddhist principles, Asoka had stone pillars erected and inscribed with edicts. This pillar dates from the third century B.C.E.

ing at least one of his brothers. Asoka's singleminded use of violence on this occasion appalled the public, however, and it took several years—until 268 B.C.E.—before he was formally permitted to take the throne. At that time he took the royal name Devanampiya Piyadasi, which means "beloved of the gods."

The beginning of Asoka's reign seemed to foretell a continuation of the expansion-by-conquest policies of his predecessors. Like them, he led his armies into battle, and it seemed that there was no one who could withstand his military might. Between about 261 and 260 B.C.E., however, he underwent a great conversion, one that led him to abandon the battlefield and turn to more peaceful policies.

Asoka's was a religious conversion. The faith he followed in his early years is uncertain, although it is known that his grandfather, Chandragupta, was a Zoroastrian who later converted to Jainism. Sometime around 263 B.C.E., Asoka became interested in Buddhism, which was then a localized religious sect. His Buddhist studies did not at first dissuade him from waging wars, but after a particularly bloody battle for the conquest of Kalinga (now Orissa), Asoka appears suddenly to have revolted against the

destruction and loss of life. From that time forward he rejected violence as a means of expanding his empire.

Asoka's commitment to nonviolence (*ahimsa*) and other aspects of Buddhist teachings seems undeniably sincere, for throughout the remainder of his reign he sent out missionaries to spread the word of this religion, including (according to some sources) his own son and daughter. To further educate the populace in Buddhist principles, Asoka ordered the construction of great stones and pillars throughout his realm, on which were inscribed what have come to be known as "Asoka's Edicts"—pronouncements on particular aspects of Buddhist teachings.

Freed of the need to wage constant war, Asoka committed himself to improving the lot of his subjects, establishing schools, roads, and medical centers throughout his empire. During his rule, India prospered economically as well, and the arts flourished. By virtue of his enlightened rule, and through the efforts of his missionaries, he managed to achieve greater success in expanding his empire than either his father or grandfather, ultimately incorporating the whole of the Indian subcontinent and Ceylon (now Sri Lanka) into his empire without further wars.

Although personally committed to Buddhism, Asoka preached tolerance for other religions. Unfortunately, his tolerance did not earn him support from the Brahmins (the Hindu priestly class), because their ritual sacrifice of animals was something that Buddhist principles did not allow. This conflict was never successfully resolved during Asoka's reign, and friction between Buddhists and Hindus ultimately led to the downfall of the Maurya dynasty in 180 B.C.E. For his part, Asoka spent the final years of his reign outside the public sphere, immersing himself more and more in his religious studies.

As long as Asoka lived, he was able to maintain stability in his empire, despite ongoing religious rivalries, through the force of his character and through the judicious use of his army and elaborate political bureaucracy. His successors were less successful, however. Asoka died in 232 B.C.E., and he was succeeded by his grandson, Dasaratha (r. 232–224 B.C.E.). The Maurya dynasty survived only another forty-seven years after Asoka's death. In 185 B.C.E. it was overthrown by Pusyamitra Shunga, an upstart rebel leader from a rival family who had the aid of the Hindu Brahmins and other dissatisfied groups within the populace. With the accession of Pusyamitra (r. 185–151 B.C.E.), the Maurya dynasty came to an end and the Shunga dynasty assumed control of India.

See also: AURANGZEB; CHANDRAGUPTA MAURYA; INDIAN KINGDOMS; MAURYA EMPIRE.

ASSYRIAN EMPIRE (ca. 1269–609 B.C.E.)

An empire established by warrior-kings that dominated the ancient Near East around the beginning of the first millennium B.C.E.

Throughout nearly the entire history of the Assyrian Empire, its power came from the strength and ferocity of its army, both in conquering new lands and maintaining control over conquered people. The Assyrian king, as commander-in-chief of the army, spent a great deal of effort and attention on his army and, except in rare cases, not as much on the organization and administration of his empire. Revolts among the Assyrian rulers' inner circle were not uncommon, causing disorder that weakened the empire, sometimes crucially. Consequently, though incredibly powerful for much of its existence, the Assyrian Empire also experienced periods of weakness during which its territory was diminished.

ORIGINS AND RISE TO POWER

In 1365 B.C.E., the city-state of Ashur in upper Mesopotamia gained independence from the powerful kingdom of Mitanni. The warrior who accomplished this was Ashuruballit (r. ca. 1363–1328 B.C.E.), who took the title Great King and claimed equal status with the rulers of Babylon, Egypt, and other Near Eastern states.

Ashuruballit's kingdom became known as Assyria, which means "land of Ashur." It was not until about ninety years later, however, during the reign of Ashuruballit's grandson, Shalmaneser I (r. ca. 1273–1244 B.C.E.), that Assyria became a great power and the Assyrian Empire is said to have begun. Shalmaneser extended Assyrian territory west to the borders of Asia Minor, while his successor, Tukulti-Ninurta I (r. ca. 1243–1207 B.C.E.), made gains east, north, and south until Assyria dominated all of Mesopotamia.

The rule of Tiglath-pileser I (r. ca. 1114–1076 B.C.E.) marks the origin of the Assyrian monarchy's reputation for ferocity and cruelty in battle. His legendary methods of fighting became the hallmark of all succeeding Assyrian kings. Although Tiglath-pileser I gained prominence for Assyria through his military dominance, after his death, those whom he had brutally controlled rose up in revolt. Subsequently, Assyria went into a 150-year period of decline under a series of weak and undistinguished kings, until it occupied merely a strip of land along the Tigris River.

CHANGING FORTUNES

The Assyrian decline ended in the ninth century B.C.E. with a succession of stronger monarchs who recaptured lands for the empire. They also rebuilt the army, which would be used by Ashurnasirpal II (r. 883–859 B.C.E.) to the detriment of all those in his path. Ashurnasirpal refined the skill of human cruelty, and his brutality surpassed that of Tiglath-pileser I. He used the spoils of his conquests to establish a new capital at Calah. Ashurnasirpal also created a highly centralized state by reorganizing provinces and appointing provincial governors loyal to the monarchy.

After the death of Ashurnasirpal and his son and successor, Shalmaneser III (r. 858–824 B.C.E.), Assyria entered a period of turmoil, stagnation, and decline as weak rulers once again allowed the state to sink into near obscurity. This period of decline ended in 745 B.C.E. with a monarch from a new royal family under whom Assyria experienced a remarkable rebirth. This ruler took the name Tiglath-pileser III (r. 744–727 B.C.E.), possibly to indicate continuity with earlier centuries.

A brilliant military planner, Tiglath-pileser III also had a talent for organization. After spending some time reorganizing the empire and training a professional army, he focused on returning Assyria to the formidable stature it had held earlier. He defeated the kingdom of Urartu, conquered the kingdom in Syria and the Phoenician city-states, and even took the mighty kingdom of Babylon and placed it under his control. Under Tiglath-pileser III, the Assyrian Empire grew to be the most powerful in the ancient world.

The rule of the new royal family was brief, however, lasting only twenty-three years until it was overthrown by a new king from a new dynasty, Sargon II (r. 722–705 B.C.E.). During his reign, Sargon put down several rebellions and conquered new territory for Assyria. His son and successor, Sennacherib (r. 705–681 B.C.E.), continued the policies. He also chose the ancient city of Nineveh to be a new capital.

PEAK OF POWER AND FINAL DECLINE

The Assyrian Empire reached its peak under the rule of Sennacherib's son Esarhaddon (r. 680–669 B.C.E.). In 671 B.C.E., Esarhaddon made a bold offensive against Egypt and conquered the Nile Delta and Memphis, one of Egypt's most ancient and important cities. At its peak, the empire that Esarhaddon ruled stretched for more than one thousand miles, from Egypt to Iran.

This period of greatness was short-lived, however. After the death of Esarhaddon's son and successor, Ashurbanibal (r. 668–627 B.C.E.), the Assyrian Empire began declining once again because it lacked strong leadership. Civil war weakened the empire, and enemies who had long bristled under brutal Assyrian control and despised the Assyrians eagerly turned on the weakened state and gained their independence.

Around 612 B.C.E., the Medes people of Iran joined forces with the Chaldeans of Babylonia and captured and completely destroyed the Assyrian capital of Nineveh. Three years later, in 609 B.C.E., the Medes and Babylonians crushed Assyrian troops under the last Assyrian ruler, Ashuruballit II (r. 611–609 B.C.E.), bringing the Assyrian Empire to a final end.

See also: ASHURBANIPAL; ESARHADDON; MEDES KINGDOM; MITANNI KIMGDOM; SARGON II; SENNACHERIB; SHALMANESER II; SHALMANESER V; TIGLATH-PILESER III.

ASTURIAS KINGDOM

(ca. 718–910 C.E.)

Medieval kingdom along the northwestern coast of the Iberian Peninsula, near the Bay of Biscay, that provided the initial impetus for the *reconquista*, or reconquest, of Iberia from the Moors.

Located in a ruggedly mountainous and well-forested region of the Iberian Peninsula, the kingdom of Asturias resisted invasion and conquest throughout most of its history. The kingdom had its origin in the early 700s, when Muslim invaders (known as the Moors) swept through the Iberian Peninusla, sending Christians fleeing before them. Many of the refugees found safety in the rugged Cantabrian Mountains of Asturias.

Sometime between 718 and 722, the Asturians, under the leadership of the Visigothic leader, Pelayo (r. ca. 718–737), defeated the Moors at the battle of Covadonga. Pelayo established the kingdom of Asturias and became its first monarch. Covadonga, the first great victory of Christians over Moors, became a legendary rallying point in the Christian reconquest of the Iberian Peninsula.

Asturian kings continued to lead the battle against Moorish domination of Spain, expanding their territory as they did so. Around 725, Pelayo's son-in-law Alfonso conquered the province of Galicia to the west and recaptured the province of León from the Moors. In 739, he became King Alfonso I of Asturias (r. 739–757). Further conquests by his successors extended Asturian territory to include sections of Navarre and Vizcaya. In the tenth century, the capital city of Asturias moved from Oviedo to León. Subsequently, the kingdom was referred to as León, with Asturias taking a secondary role as a province in the Leonese kingdom.

Alfonso III, the Great, of León (r. 866–910) expanded Asturian territory to include parts of Castile and Portugal. During his reign, one of the most celebrated events in Spanish cultural and religious history occurred. According to legend, a star guided a shepherd to a marble coffin in the mountains. Inside were the remains of a body believed to be Saint James, one of the twelve Apostles of Jesus. The site became the location of a chapel dedicated to Santiago de Compostela ("St. James of the Field of the Star"), who became the patron saint of Spain. A cathedral eventually replaced the chapel, and Santiago de Compostela became an important destination for Christian pilgrims throughout the Middle Ages and afterward.

In the thirteenth century, the kingdom of Asturias and León was joined to the much larger kingdom of Castile under King Ferdinand III (r. 1217–1252). In 1388, King John I of León and Castile (r. 1379–1390) made Asturias a principality under his son, the future Henry III (r. 1379–1406). Subsequent heirs to the throne were given the title prince of Asturias, and this is the title of current heirs to the Spanish throne.

See also: CASTILE, KINGDOM OF; IBERIAN KINGDOMS; LEÓN, KINGDOM OF; SPANISH MONARCHIES.

FURTHER READING

Tierney, Brian, and Sidney Painter. *Western Europe in the Middle Ages, 300–1475.* 6th ed. New York: McGraw-Hill, 1999.

ATAHUALPA (ca. 1500–1533 C.E.)

Last free ruler (r. 1532) of the Inca Empire, who was killed by Spanish conquistadors during the conquest of Peru.

In the final years of the fifteenth century, Huayna Capac (r. 1493–1524), known as the Great Inca, conquered the kingdom of Quito. To better ensure peace with this new addition to the Incan Empire, he took one of the daughters of the Quito ruler as a concubine, and with her he fathered a son named Atahualpa. Although by all accounts the favorite child of the Great Inca, Atahualpa was legally ineligible to inherit the empire, for only a son of pure Incan blood could take the imperial throne.

The imperial heir, Atahualpa's half-brother Huascar, was of proper birth: both his father and mother were directly descended from the founding Great Inca, Manco Capac (r. ca. 1200). Nonetheless, Huayna Capac saw to it that Atahualpa received a proper royal education in religion, culture, and science, along with training in the art of war. At about age thirteen, Atahualpa became his father's constant companion as the Great Inca toured his empire, fought in battles, and held court.

In 1524 Huayna Capac lay dying. Unable to place the empire into the hands of Atahualpa, his favorite son, he showed his favor by designating Atahualpa king of Quito, the homeland of Atahualpa's mother. Atahualpa thus had royal status, although he was subordinate to the new Great Inca, his half-brother Huascar (r. 1524–1532).

For a few years, there was peace between Atahualpa and Huascar, but soon Atahualpa began nursing greater ambitions. In the first years of the 1530s, he began amassing an army with which to challenge Huascar's rule. In 1532, Atahualpa's forces succeeded in capturing and imprisoning Huascar, and Atahualpa proclaimed himself Great Inca.

Atahualpa retired to the healing waters of a spa near the village of Cajamarca to recover from wounds received in battle. There he learned that a small army of strangers had entered Inca territory. These were Spanish conquistadors, led by Francisco Pizarro, who came to conquer the region and convert the inhabitants to Christianity. With only a handful of soldiers and a few priests, Pizarro needed to employ trickery to achieve his goals.

Upon arriving at Cajamarca, Pizarro hid his army in ambush and sent a messenger to request an audience with the Great Inca. When Atahualpa arrived he found only a Dominican friar, who demanded that the emperor convert to Christianity. Atahualpa refused, providing Pizarro with an excuse to attack. The terrifying devastation caused by cannonballs, musketry, and armed cavalry—none of which had ever before been seen in the region—threw Atahualpa's troops into a panic, and in less than two hours the battlefield was littered with the bodies of thousands of Incan soldiers. Atahualpa was taken to Cuzco, the Incan capital, and thrown into prison by the Spaniards.

Aware that he could not hold his newly conquered territory with only a few soldiers, Pizarro decided to install a puppet ruler from among the indigenous people. The logical choice was between Atahualpa and Huascar. Atahualpa knew that his life depended upon being chosen, so he offered to ransom his life with a room filled with gold and silver.

Having already experienced Spanish treachery once, however, Atahualpa decided to ensure his survival by eliminating his rival, Huascar. From his prison cell he ordered the execution of his half-brother. This decision backfired, however, for Pizarro used the assassination as the pretext to charge Atahualpa with fratricide, along with other offenses such as polygamy (a common practice among the Inca nobility) and idolatry (because Atahualpa had refused to convert to Christianity).

Put on trial, Atahualpa was quickly found guilty and condemned to death by burning at the stake. In an attempt to avoid death by fire, the Incan ruler agreed to be baptized into the Catholic Church. This earned him leniency: Instead of dying by fire, he was instead strangled on July 26, 1533. Others of his line ruled for brief periods, always under the control of the Spanish, but with the death of Atahualpa, the Inca Empire effectively ended.

See also: HUAYNA CAPAC; INCA EMPIRE; SOUTH AMERICAN MONARCHIES; VIRACHOCHA.

ATHALIAH (842–836 B.C.E.)

First and only queen of Judah in ancient Palestine, who was killed by Yahwists (followers of the Hebrew Bible) in a revolt led by priests against her rule and her support of the worship of Baal.

Descended from the line of King Omri of Israel (r. 885–874 B.C.E.), Athaliah was the daughter of King Ahab (r. 874–853 B.C.E.) of Israel and his wife Jezebel, a Phoenician princess and worshiper of Baal. Ahab arranged a marriage between his daughter Athaliah and Jehoram (r. 847–841 B.C.E.), son of the king of Judah, in order to cement good relations between that country and Israel. But this goal was lost in the series of bloody political massacres described in the Hebrew Bible.

Athaliah's mother Jezebel (Jez-Baal), whose name later came to mean "wicked woman," established the worship of Baal in Israel. This move was unpopular with the Yahwist populace. In addition, Jezebel acquired a great vineyard for her husband by plotting the murder of its owner. In 841 B.C.E., Elisha, a disciple of the prophet Elijah, incited a revolt against Jezebel and her followers, choosing Jehu (r. 841–814 B.C.E.), who later became king of Israel, as their leader. The followers of Baal were tricked into meeting at their temple and were massacred. The Yahwists then converted the temple of Baal into a latrine.

Athaliah's family, the royal family of Israel, was also murdered during the revolt. Athaliah's mother, Jezebel, was thrown out a window by her own attendants and was trampled to death by the rebels' horses. Athaliah's son, King Ahaziah of Judah (r. 841 B.C.E.), had chosen this inconvenient time to visit his Israelite relatives, and was killed in the revolt as well.

The Bible describes Athaliah's response to this bloodbath and, in particular, to the death of her son. She ordered all the available men of the royal line to be slaughtered, thereby decimating, as she thought, the royal line of Judah. Her grandson Jehoash, however, was saved by his aunt Jehosheba and hidden away for six years, during which period Athaliah ruled over Judah.

Little is known about Athaliah's actual reign. The Bible, the main historical source for the period, describes only the beginning and end of her reign. It is clear, however, that Athaliah introduced the religion of her mother into Judah. Once more, this was an unpopular move with the local priests, and after six years of rule by a Baalist monarch, the priests of Yahweh and the Judaean army, commanded by the priest Jehoiada, plotted a revolt. Surrounded by guards and priests, Athaliah's grandson, Jehoash (r. 813–797 B.C.E.), was brought in secret to the temple of Jerusalem where he was crowned king of Judah.

The Bible asserts that Athaliah first learned of the rebellion when she heard the applause of the masses immediately after her grandson's crowning, at which point, according to the Bible, "Athaliah rent her clothes, and cried, 'Treason, treason,'" and went into the temple. Loath to have the queen killed in a temple, Jehoiada had Athaliah taken out of the palace area through the stable door and slain with a sword. Seven-year-old Jehoash now began his reign as king of Judah.

See also: BIBLICAL KINGS; ISRAEL, KINGDOMS OF; JUDAH, KINGDOM OF; JUDAISM AND KINGSHIP.

ATHENS, KINGDOM OF

(ca. 900–404 B.C.E.)

Ancient Greek kingdom based in the city-state of Athens that later became the birthplace of democracy.

Between about 1400 and 1200 B.C.E., early Greek kings in the Mycenaean monarchies served as priests, judges, and military leaders. Although they were powerful, independent rulers, they also sought the counsel of aristocrats in society on important matters. In the city-state of Athens, kings were held accountable to the *Areopagus,* a council of nobles named for the hill on which they met.

GOVERNMENT BY THE RICH

By the eighth century B.C.E., the power of kingship in Athens had passed over to the *Areopagus,* and the city-state became an oligarchy, a government ruled by a small group of individuals. Government by the nobles of the *Areopagus* resulted in the rich of Athens getting richer, while the poor were sometimes sold into slavery. Justice was harsh, and only members of the Areopagus knew the laws. The country became unstable and prone to revolution.

Around 621 B.C.E., a member of the *Areopagus* named Draco (r. ca. 620–594 B.C.E.) was elected to curb abuses of power by reviewing and writing down the laws. The code of laws Draco established were very harsh; death was the penalty for many crimes, including the theft of vegetables. Despite Draco's codification of the laws, Athens remained unstable.

THE REFORMS OF SOLON

In 594 B.C.E., the *Areopagus* and the people of Athens handed over all political power to a statesman named Solon (r. 594–559 B.C.E.). They gave him a mandate to be a peacemaker and to prevent any future economic disparity in Athens. Solon's attempt to do this resulted in a limited form of democracy.

Solon lightened the penalties for offenses, retaining the death penalty only for homicide. He redeemed all forfeited land and freed all citizens who had been enslaved because of their indebtedness. Solon divided Athenian society into four classes based on wealth. The two wealthiest classes were allowed to serve on the *Areopagus*. The third class was allowed to elect a council of 400 individuals to balance or check the power of the *Areopagus*. The fourth class, the poor, were allowed to participate in an assembly that voted on affairs brought to it by the council and to elect local magistrates. They also were permitted to participate in a new judicial court that heard civil and military cases.

Athenians praised Solon for his reforms, although his economic policies took decades to implement. However, the slow pace of reform led to anger and disenchantment among the nobles and many other Athenians, and within a few years, Athens began to collapse into anarchy.

PEISISTRATUS, ATHENS' FIRST TYRANT

Taking advantage of the unstable situation, the statesman Peisistratus attempted to restore order around 560 B.C.E. A brilliant military leader and clever politician with a powerful mercenary army, Peisistratus staged a coup d'état, took control of the *Areopagus* and declared himself *Tyrannos* ("tyrant"), which meant "chief" or "master" in the Anatolian languages of western Asia Minor (present-day Turkey). In ancient Greece, the tyrant was not a violent despot but a leader who considered himself an absolute ruler and did not need the advice of the aristocracy.

As Tyrant, Peisistratus (r. ca. 560–527 B.C.E.) increased the power of the assembly and used all his own power to make sure that the model of government established by Solon worked smoothly. He built public buildings in and around Athens and sought to reform Athenian religious practices. He settled people on tracts of farmland, providing them with seed to grow food, and he rewarded the industrious with tax-free status. Peisistratus also devoted his government to cultural reform, encouraging poets and artists to make Athens a sophisticated and dynamic society.

FALL TO SPARTA

Upon the death of Peisistratus in 527 B.C.E., the tyranny went to his son, Hippias (r. 527–510 B.C.E.). But a wealthy family named Alcmaeonid, which had been exiled by Peisistratus, plotted against Hippias and asked the city-state of Sparta for assistance. Sparta's king, Cleomenes I (r. 520–489 B.C.E.) attacked and captured Athens in 510 B.C.E., forcing Hippias to flee to exile in Persia.

The Spartans installed a leader named Isagoras as archon, or chief civil official in 508 B.C.E., but the Athenian people wanted the statesman Cleisthenes to serve instead. Isagoras was swept from power in a popular uprising, and Cleisthenes (r. 508–502 B.C.E.) was installed as ruler of Athens.

GOVERNMENT BY THE PEOPLE

As archon, Cleisthenes began a series of major reforms that produced the first true Athenian democracy. Based on the principle of *Isonomia* (equality of rights for all), Cleisthenes enfranchised all free men living in Athens and Attica (the area surrounding Athens) as citizens and established a council with executive and administrative powers that would be the chief arm of government. Every citizen over the age of thirty was eligible to sit on this council, whose members would be chosen by lot. An Assembly, which included all male citizens, was allowed to veto any of the council's proposals and was the only branch of government with power to declare war.

Ostracism was another element of Athenian democracy introduced by Cleisthenes. Once per year the Assembly could vote to ostracize, or expel, citizens from the state for a period of ten years. Ostracism helped guarantee that any individuals who contemplated seizing power would be removed from the country before they could precipitate a civil war. In 487 B.C.E., Hipparchus, son of Charmus of Collytus, became the first Athenian citizen to be ostracized.

THE DELIAN LEAGUE

In 478 B.C.E. Athens created a confederation of states called the Delian League, formed to protect members from the Persian Empire. The league consisted of most of the Greek city-states, most of the Aegean Islands, many cities in Chalcidice (a peninsula in eastern Macedonia), the shores of the Hellespont and Bosporus, some of Aeolia (northwestern Asia Minor), most of Ionia (the western coast of Asia Minor), and other Greek and non-Greek cities in southwestern Asia Minor.

The fifth century B.C.E. was Athens' golden age of architecture, literature, and philosophy. While the statesman Pericles (ca. 495–429 B.C.E.) was building the Parthenon and long walls to the seaport of Pireaus, the Greek dramatists Aeschylus, Sophocles, and Euripides were writing plays and the philosophers Socrates and Plato were teaching.

The Delian League's early naval successes and imperialistic expansion frightened the city-state of Sparta, the main rival of Athens, and led to the Peloponnesian War (431–404 B.C.E.). In 404 B.C.E. Sparta, with the help of Persia, defeated Athens and disbanded the Delian League. Athens, exhausted from the struggle, went into a demographic and financial decline from which it would never really recover.

END OF THE KINGDOM OF ATHENS

In the early second century B.C.E., Sparta imposed the reign of the Thirty Tyrants on Athens. But poor management led to a revival of Athenian influence and a new naval league, which grew to include fifty states by the time the Spartans were defeated by the Boeotians in 371 B.C.E. The victory of Philip II of Macedon at the battle of Chaeronea in 338 B.C.E. ended any thoughts of reviving the empire. Athens continued as a center of culture and philosophy for many years but would never again be a separate kingdom.

See also: GREEK MONARCHY; MINOAN KINGDOMS; SPARTA, KINGDOM OF; TYRANNY, ROYAL.

FURTHER READING

Van der Kiste, John. *Kings of the Hellenes: The Greek Kings 1863–1974.* Dover, NH: Sutton, 1999.

ATTALID DYNASTY. *See* HELLENISTIC

DYNASTIES

ATTILA (ca. 406–453 C.E.)

Leader of the Huns (r. ca. 434–453), who was called the "Scourge of God" because of his army's fierce horse-mounted archers and his tactics of wholesale slaughter.

Attila ruled the Huns for nearly twenty years, during which time he terrorized all of Europe and much of Asia. When Attila was born, around 406, the people known as the Huns were already a power to be reckoned with in their territory between the Volga and Don rivers (in present-day Russia). Nomads and horse breeders, the Huns developed into a formidable fighting force because of their great skill as mounted archers.

Earlier kings of the Huns had established the group as the dominant people of the steppes. During Attila's childhood and youth, then-king Roas (also called Rugilas) successfully demanded that the Eastern Roman Empire, ruled then by Theodosius I (r. 379–395), pay tribute to avoid attack. Although not politically or economically sophisticated, the Huns were well organized and highly sought after as mercenaries. This, together with the tribute they collected, permitted them to amass great wealth.

RISE TO POWER

As a young man of the steppes, Attila was trained as a warrior, but he was destined to something much grander than a simple warrior's fate. As one of Roas's nephews, Attila was in line to inherit the throne, as was his elder brother, Breda. These two young men therefore were groomed for leadership. In 433 or 434, Roas died and leadership of the Huns fell to Attila and Breda jointly. At the age of twenty-seven, Attila was more than up to the challenge of rule.

The Huns did not devote much energy to creating permanent settlements or political institutions; they attacked their neighbors, extracted tribute, and then moved on. Attila's predecessors had made occasional forays outside the Hun homeland, but Attila had grander ambitions. He intended to conquer the world. Some scholars claim that Attila's first efforts were directed to the East, toward China but that he was repulsed at the borders. Whether or not this is true, it is undisputed that in 441–442, Attila secured all the territory between his homeland and the Danube River. By 447, he had marched his armies through Illyria (on the Balkan Peninsula) and had

The Hun ruler Attila was known as just to his own people but savage in the treatment of his enemies. The Romans, whom he attacked repeatedly in the mid-fifth century C.E., referred to him as the "Scourge of God."

moved on toward Constantinople, the capital of the Eastern Roman Empire. Sometime prior to this, Attila had assumed sole leadership of the Huns, having murdered his brother to eliminate any interference to his rule.

Attila's seemingly unstoppable march on the Eastern Roman Empire was not complete, however. Although he laid siege to Constantinople, he never managed to capture the city. Still, he succeeded in forcing Theodosius II (r. 408–450) to beg for mercy. Attila was finally persuaded, in 447, to call off his troops in return for the payment of huge amounts of tribute. Three years later, however, Theodosius II died and was succeeded by Marcian (r. 450–457), who refused to be intimidated by Attila's threats.

LOOKING TO THE WEST

Rather than mount a new campaign against Constantinople, Attila turned his attention to the West. According to legend, this move came about because of discord between the Western Roman emperor, Valentinian III (r. 425–455), and the emperor's sister, Honoria. Honoria was supposedly caught in a compromising situation with a servant. The emperor

ordered the servant be summarily killed, and Honoria was placed in confinement. Knowing of his great reputation as a warrior, Honoria is said to have surreptitiously sent a message to Attila, begging him to come to her aid. Attila, misreading this message as a proposal of marriage, demanded that Valentinian grant him half of the territories comprising the Western Empire, calling it his marriage dowry. When Valentinian failed to meet this demand, Attila is said to have invaded solely to claim his rightful property.

For this invasion, Attila augmented his fighting forces with warriors recruited from the peoples he conquered along the way: Ostrogoths, Burgundians, and Alans (all Germanic peoples). By the time he reached the heart of Gaul, Attila's army was said to have numbered between 300,000 and 700,000 men, although this may well be exaggerated. His forces included infantry and the famous mounted archers of the Huns. The army sacked and torched every major settlement they encountered on their westward march, and they appeared to be unstoppable. However, in 451, at the battle of Chalons (in the western part of present-day France), Attila met his match in the Roman general, Aetius.

Aetius had prepared for the coming of the Huns by recruiting allies from the Visigoths, who lived in the Chalons region. In 451 he and his army faced Attila on the battlefield near the town of Troyes. Aetius forced Attila back eastward, all the way across the Rhine. This setback seems to have been enough to change Attila's plans, for he gave up his westward assault and turned his attention to Italy and the western imperial capital of Ravenna.

In 452 Attila began his Italian campaign, again leaving devastation in his wake. He failed in his ultimate objective of conquering Ravenna, however, although the reasons for this failure are unclear. Some sources say that Attila was turned back because epidemics were raging in Italy at the time. Others say that Pope Leo I (r. 440–461) saved the day, claiming that the fearsome Hun was himself terrified by the power of the Church, as represented by its pontiff. For whatever reason, Attila did not follow through on his invasion plans for Italy.

Rather than marching straight back to his home territory, however, Attila took time out to acquire a new wife, named Ildico. This was in 453, and the now forty-seven-year-old bridegroom celebrated his marriage night with a huge, raucous feast, during which he became exceedingly drunk. What happened next is another matter of conjecture. Some say that Attila died of a stroke in his wedding bed. Others claim that, passed out in a drunken stupor, he failed to awaken when he developed a nosebleed and drowned in his own blood. With his passing, so also passed his empire.

See also: HUN EMPIRE; OSTROGOTH KINGDOM; ROMAN EMPIRE; VISIGOTH KINGDOM.

AUGUSTUS (63 B.C.E.–14 C.E.)

First emperor of Rome (r. 27 B.C.E.–14 C.E.) who established a system of government known as the Principate and laid the foundation for a great empire.

Born Gais Octavias (also called Octavian) in 63 B.C.E., the future Augustus was the grandnephew and adopted son of Julius Caesar (r. 49–44 B.C.E.), as well as his heir. After Caesar's assassination in 44 B.C.E., Octavian, the soldier and politician Mark Antony, and a general named Lepidus shared power, forming a government known as the Second Triumvirate. Each man controlled part of the army.

GAINING CONTROL

The elderly Lepidus soon retired, leaving Antony and Octavian to fight a civil war (ca. 37–31 B.C.E.) for control of Roman territory. Antony went to Egypt, where he allied with Queen Cleopatra (r. 51–30 B.C.E.), who had allied years earlier with Julius Caesar. Octavian rallied support in Rome and won a great victory over the forces of Antony and Cleopatra at the naval battle at Actium in Greece in 31 B.C.E. Antony and Cleopatra fled back to Egypt, where they committed suicide the following year.

Octavian spent the next few years consolidating power, becoming the wealthiest and most powerful citizen of the Roman Republic. Although the ideal of republican rule still existed, not to be officially cast off for several centuries, the Roman Republic had fallen and was replaced by a de facto monarchy. In 27 B.C.E., the Senate proclaimed Ocatavian *Imperator* and *Augustus*, a title he adopted as ruler of the empire.

POLICIES

Augustus left much of the republican government in place, ruling through personal influence and coercion. Since Augustus took the title *princeps* ("first cit-

Augustus, the first Roman emperor, set his people on a course of expansion and imperial greatness. This statue, known as the Augustus of Prima Porta, depicts him as a victorious general. Discovered in the ruins of a villa that belonged to Augustus's second wife, Livia, the statue is believed to have been commissioned by his adopted son, Tiberius, around 15 C.E.

izen"), this period in Roman history is known as the Principate.

The Roman Republic had never instituted a system of checks and balances between its civilian government and the military, relying instead on the loyalty and honor of individual soldiers and their leaders. The successes of Augustus as a military leader during the civil war, combined with his vast wealth, allowed him to control the army and the Roman treasury.

Augustus instituted a number of reforms and public works, financed with his own money, to maintain public support. These included establishing the first firefighting force in Rome, increased military benefits, and construction of the Forum of Augustus (a huge complex of buildings centered on a temple to the Roman god of war, Mars). As the Roman historian Tacitus said of Augustus, he "won over the soldiers with gifts, the populace with cheap corn, and all men with the sweets of repose."

Augustus maintained and perpetuated his power by appealing to traditional Roman values. He did not, for example, claim absolute authority. To do so would have violated basic political values deeply embedded in the Roman Republic. Instead, he ruled through the respect traditionally due a man of wealth and accomplishment in Roman society. Augustus's attempts at social reform reflected this traditionalism. He believed that one of Rome's faults was its moral decay. To combat this, he outlawed adultery. The law remained controversial, as Augustus regularly slept with the wives of his political rivals. His own daughter Julia was exiled from Rome after being caught in another man's bed.

LEGACY

An important part of Augustus's legacy was the *Pax Romana*, a time of peace and great prosperity that Rome experienced in first century C.E. This peace lasted, despite the rule of a series of inept and insane emperors, such as the infamous Caligula (r. 37–41) and Nero (r. 54–68), the last of Augustus's direct line.

Those who followed in Augustus's footsteps illustrated the fundamental weakness of the governmental system that Augustus had established. In forming a monarchy, Augustus created the need for effective leadership for the system to work. Without it, Rome fell into decadence and decay. Other capable rulers would eventually follow, but too few to ensure continued peace and stability for the empire.

See also: CAESARS; CALIGULA; CLEOPATRA VII; EMPERORS AND EMPRESSES; JULIO-CLAUDIANS; NERO; ROMAN EMPIRE.

FURTHER READING

Tacitus. *The Annals of Tacitus*. Trans. Alfred John Church and William Jackson Brodribb. Franklin Center, PA: The Franklin Library, 1982.

AURANGZEB (1618–1707 C.E.)

The last great ruler (r. 1658–1707) of the Mughal Empire in India, whose military and economic policies both expanded and weakened the empire.

Aurangzeb was the third son of the Mughal emperor, Shah Jahan I (r. 1628–1658). When his father became very ill in 1658, Aurangzeb and his three brothers began battling for succession to the throne. All four of the young men had impressive governing experience as well as military forces.

Shah Jahan had designated his oldest son, Dara Shikoh, as his successor. But Aurangzeb, with his great military and administrative capabilities, as well as his desire for power, fought hard for the throne and won. His ruthless tactics involved the deaths of his brothers and the imprisonment of his father until Shah Jahan died in 1666.

During his long forty-nine-year reign, Aurangzeb—whose kingly name was Alamgir ("world conqueror")—expanded the Mughal Empire to its greatest extent by means of war and clever politics. He borrowed a method used by his great-grandfather Akbar (r. 1556–1605) of reconciling with his enemies and then putting them into his service. His main military thrust was leading Mughal forces to conquer areas of the Deccan region of India. After gaining control of the Golconda and Bijapur kingdoms, he assaulted the Maratha chieftains, whose territories he annexed without ultimately conquering the Marathas. However, these military campaigns were a steady financial drain that affected the overall administration of the empire.

Aurangzeb was a zealous Muslim as well as an aggressive warrior, and he was extremely intolerant of other religions. That fanaticism led to tensions and dissatisfaction that were factors in the collapse of the Mughal Empire. Aurangzeb forced Islam on his people, prohibiting any drinking or gambling, and imposing the *Shari'a* (Islamic religious law, based on the Qu'ran) as the basis of law throughout the empire.

This emphasis on Islamic law did not endear the emperor to the Hindus in his realm, who had their own religious law. Aurangzeb also revoked all taxes that Islamic law or custom did not designate, thereby depriving the empire of a necessary revenue source. Aurangzeb responded to the financial shortfall by reestablishing the *jizya*, a tax on nonbelievers that was traditional in other Muslim states. Since most of the Mughal people were Hindu, the imposition of this tax provoked rebellions throughout the empire.

As the empire grew larger, it became more unmanageable, and Aurangzeb had few dependable leaders who could handle the more remote areas of the realm. This lack of effective leadership in the periphery of the empire also contributed to a weakening of Mughal rule.

Soon after Aurangzeb died in 1707, the problems of the Mughal Empire began to compromise its power and influence in India. The inability of Aurangzeb's successors to handle these problems led to the eventual collapse of Mughal rule.

See also: ASOKA; GOLCONDA KINGDOM; JAHAN, SHAH; MUGHAL EMPIRE.

AUSTRO-HUNGARIAN EMPIRE

(1804–1918 C.E.)

Name given to the territories and peoples under the control of the Austrian monarchy in the nineteenth and early twentieth centuries. The Austrian monarchy struggled to maintain the empire against both internal conflicts and foreign challenges for the entirety of its existence. This combination of domestic and international opposition eventually led to the collapse of Austria-Hungary in World War I.

ORIGINS

Although the Austro-Hungarian monarchy did not legally come into existence until 1867, the empire, in effect, began in 1804 when Francis II of the Holy Roman Empire declared himself Francis I (r. 1804–1835), emperor of Austria. Before this time, Austria was an archduchy, albeit a powerful one inasmuch as its location in Central Europe made it a continual route of passage. The powerful Habsburg dynasty had ruled Austria from the Hofburg Imperial Palace in Vienna for centuries, and the archduchy was thus in control of hereditary territories scattered throughout Europe. Because of these possessions, the notion of an Austrian Empire was in existence long before Francis's accession as emperor.

WAR WITH FRANCE

In the wake of the French Revolution in 1789, many of the monarchical powers surrounding France feared that the antiroyalist rebellion would spread to their own kingdoms and duchies. These nations indicated that they would go to war with Revolutionary France to protect themselves and, if possible, restore the French royal family to the throne. France, eager to spread its revolutionary ideals and outraged at being threatened, declared war on its neighbors, with Austria the first to come under attack. This series of conflicts, known as the French Revolutionary Wars, lasted for the next decade and resulted in the weakening of Austria and the collapse of the Holy Roman Empire in 1806.

The ruler of Austria at this time, Francis II (r.

ROYAL RELATIVES

FRANZ FERDINAND (1863–1914)

Although the tensions and conflicts that exploded into World War I were forged decades earlier, it is the assassination of Franz Ferdinand that is most frequently cited as the precipitating cause of the war. After the mysterious death of Franz Joseph's only son in 1889, Franz Ferdinand became the heir to the Austro-Hungarian throne. Seeing the nationalist tensions he was going to inherit, Franz Ferdinand made it his life's work to try to create a third section of the monarchy, one that gave voice to the Slavs. These actions made him immensely unpopular among both the Austro-Hungarians and the Serbians, who were agitating for an independent and unified Slavic nation. Disdain for Franz Ferdinand's cause led Gavrilo Princip, a member of a Serbian nationalist group, to assassinate the Austrian heir and his wife while they were in a motorcade in Sarajevo. Austria-Hungary used this act as justification for declaring war on Serbia, eventually drawing Germany and the rest of Europe into the fray.

On June 28, 1914, shortly after leaving the city hall in Sarajevo, Yugoslavia, Archduke Franz Ferdinand, heir to the throne of the Austro-Hungarian Empire, and his wife were shot and killed. The assassin was a Serbian nationalist named Gavrilo Princip.

1792–1835), was the head of the Habsburg dynasty. Faced with losing his own empire and fearful of seeing the Habsburgs driven out of Austria forever and replaced by the French, Francis declared himself emperor of Austria. This did little to change his situation, since Emperor Napoleon I (r. 1804–1815) of France defeated the Austrians several times over the next few years. Only with the allied defeats of Napoleon in 1814 and 1815 by Britain, Prussia, Russia, and Sweden was order restored to Austria.

OPPRESSION AND CONSEQUENCES

An authoritarian ruler, Francis quashed reform movements with an oppressive administration. Making himself prime minister, he oversaw all aspects of his administration from the Imperial Palace in Vienna, constantly stifling dissent. Francis was aided by his foreign minister, Prince Clemens Metternich, who handled Austria's international dealings. Metternich, though a brilliant statesman and diplomat, had a zeal for repression in domestic matters, and he helped Francis centralize the government, much to the frustration of his ethnically diverse subjects.

After Francis died in 1835, many of his oppressive policies were continued by his eldest son, Ferdinand (r. 1835–1848), who succeeded to the throne upon his father's death. An epileptic who was also plagued by attacks of insanity, Ferdinand wielded little actual power. Instead, his reign was dominated politically by Prince Metternich and a regent council known as the Staatsconferenz. In the late 1840s, an antiroyal, pro-nationalist fever swept across Europe. This revolutionary fervor severely affected Austria, owing to the tight control that Francis and Metternich had exercised over the people. In 1848, the Austrian capital of Vienna was on the verge of revolt. Ferdinand was persuaded to abdicate the throne in order that a stronger leader might put down the growing insurgency. Ferdinand fled the city, leaving behind his nephew, Franz Josef, to take the throne.

THE REIGN OF FRANZ JOSEF

With the close support of the Roman Catholic Church, Franz Josef (r. 1848–1916) solidified the tenuous Austrian monarchy almost immediately, enabling him to set his sights on foreign affairs. As the new emperor, Franz Josef achieved several quick successes. In 1849, he stopped a rebellion in Hungary and beat back Victor Emmanuel II (r. 1849–1861), the king of Sardinia, who was leading a movement against Austrian rule for an independent and unified Italy. Soon after, however, events took a turn for the worse when the German state of Prussia, in a move aimed at accelerating German unification, went to war with Austria over a jointly administered territory in the summer of 1866. Prussia smashed the Austrians in just seven weeks, thus marking Germany's supremacy over Austria in European affairs. The Prussians took no territory from Austria, however, and in doing so put themselves in a position to secure Franz Josef as a future ally.

Domestic troubles became more of a concern for Franz Josef than his foreign problems, however, as the Hungarians under Austrian control pushed for independence. The emperor, unwilling to fight a civil war, agreed to a compromise in 1867 that created a dual monarchy known as Austria-Hungary. Thus, Franz Josef also became the king of Hungary, which had its own internal administration outside the control of Austria. Both parts of the kingdom followed Franz Josef's lead as head of state, and the Austrian government dictated foreign affairs for the entire empire.

The dual monarchy of Austria-Hungary was beset by serious problems. Widespread ethnic discrimination on the part of German and Hungarians, aimed at a variety of Slavic groups that lived in the empire, led to pockets of nationalist unrest throughout Austria-Hungary. Franz Josef was especially eager to contain such unrest because his brother, Emperor Maximilian of Mexico, had been killed in a Mexican nationalist uprising in 1867. Russian support for the agitating elements in Austria-Hungary led Franz Josef to join an alliance with Germany and Italy in 1879. This alliance was opposed by a coalition of Britain, France, and Russia, creating deep lines of tension that pushed Europe toward world war.

DECLINE AND FALL

In 1908, Austria-Hungary annexed the regions of Bosnia and Herzegovina from Serbia. This action generated a great deal of resentment among the Serbs and almost led to war. Although fighting was at first avoided, it seemed inevitable. When a Serbian nationalist assassinated Franz Josef's nephew and heir, Franz Ferdinand, on June 28, 1914, war erupted soon afterward. World War I pitted Austria-Hungary and its allies, Germany and the Ottoman Empire, against Great Britain, France, Belgium, Russia, and, eventually, the United States.

Emperor Franz Josef did not live to see the end of World War I, passing the Crown to his grandnephew Charles (r. 1916–1918) in 1916. Charles's main role as wartime emperor was to try to negotiate a peace settlement with the Allies. By the autumn of 1918, with Austria-Hungary on the verge of collapse, Hungary seceded from the empire, leaving Charles in control of only Austria, which he quickly surrendered. As part of the surrender, Charles abdicated the throne and fled Austria, thereby marking the end of the Austro-Hungarian Empire.

See also: DUAL MONARCHIES; FRANZ JOSEPH; HABSBURG DYNASTY; NATIONALISM; POWER, FORMS OF ROYAL.

FURTHER READING

Macartney, C. A. *The Habsburg Empire, 1790–1918.* New York: Macmillan, 1969.

Mason, John. *The Dissolution of the Austro-Hungarian Empire, 1867–1918.* New York: Longman, 1997.

AVADH KINGDOM. *See* OUDH KINGDOM

AVANTI KINGDOM

(flourished ca. 500s–300s B.C.E.)

Ancient kingdom of northern India, located in the area of the present-day Madhya Pradesh state, which was one of the main kingdoms in northern India during the time of Gautama Siddhartha, the Buddha.

The capital of the Avanti kingdom, Mahismati (probably what is now Godapura), was founded around 600 B.C.E. Before long, however, the capital shifted to Ujjayini (in the vicinity of modern-day Ujjain). The Avanti kingdom was conveniently located on the trade routes between northern and southern India and the port of Bharukaccha (now Bharuch) on the Arabian Sea.

Avanti became one of northern India's four greatest powers by the time of Buddha in the sixth to fifth centuries B.C.E. It was then ruled by King Pradyota the Fierce (r. ca. 400s B.C.E.), who was powerful enough to be a threat to the Magadha kingdom.

In the fourth century B.C.E., Chandragupta Maurya (r. 321–297 B.C.E.), the founder of the Mauryan Empire, conquered Avanti and annexed it to his realm, which stretched from Afghanistan and the Himalayas in the north to the southern edge of Central Asia. The Avanti capital, Ujjayini, became one of the Hindus' seven holy cities. Famous for its physical beauty and prosperity, it also became a gathering place for early Buddhism and Jainism (an ancient branch of Hinduism that rejects the notion of a supreme being and advocates a deep respect for all living things).

After 50 B.C.E., as the Magadha Empire weakened, the Sungas, Andhrabhrtyas, and Sakas vied for control of the Avanti kingdom. Ujjayini became the affluent capital of the western Saka state in the second century C.E. under Rudradaman I (r. ca. 100s C.E.).

Around 390 C.E., the Sakas were overthrown by Chandragupta II (r. 376–415 C.E.) (also known as Vikramaditya) of the Gupta dynasty, who established his royal court at Ujjayini. At an unknown date, the Malava tribe moved to Avanti, and eventually its name supplanted that of the Avantis to designate that land.

See also: CHANDRAGUPTA MAURYA; GUPTA EMPIRE; INDIAN KINGDOMS; MAGADHA KINGDOM; SUNGA DYNASTY.

AVIZ DYNASTY (1385–1580 C.E.)

Portuguese kings descended from João I (1385–1433), who established autonomy from Spain at the battle of Aljubarrota in August 1385. The Aviz family was extraordinarily interrelated because kings so often married nieces and first cousins, including their royal Spanish relations.

The Aviz dynasty had its roots in the early 1200s, when King Afonso II (r. 1211–1223) of Portugal granted the district of Aviz in central Portugal to a branch of knights as reward for driving the Moors from Portugal. In 1383, one of the knights of the Order of Aviz, as they became known, led a revolution to prevent the Spanish princess, Beatriz of Castile, from gaining the throne. This knight, John,

established himself as King João I, becoming the first ruler of the Aviz dynasty.

The direct descendants of João I ruled Portugal until the death of his great-grandson, João II (r. 1481–1495) in 1495. Thereafter, the Aviz ruled through the heirs of João's cousin, Manuel I (r. 1495–1521). In 1580, upon the death of the last Avis ruler, Henry the Cardinal (r. 1478–1580), Philip II (r. 1556–1598) of Spain—the nephew and one-time son-in-law of João III (r. 1521–1557)—became Philip I of Portugal after Spain took control of the country. Portugal remained under Spanish rule until the Bragança dynasty reestablished the monarchy sixty years later.

The Aviz dynasty launched the Age of Discovery, as Portuguese navigators began searching for new routes sailing to the east. The golden age of Portugal reached its apex under the Aviz ruler, Manuel I (r. 1495–1521), an especially impressive feat considering that only about 1.5 million of an estimated 10.35 million Iberians were Portuguese in the 1500s.

Following the lead of Henry the Navigator, the son of João I, Portuguese trader adventurers like Bartholomew Dias and Vasco da Gama set sail in their fast caravel ships. In 1494, under the Treaty of Tordesillas, Spain recognized Portuguese claims to all landfalls east of a longitude 370 leagues west of the Cape Verde Islands in the Atlantic Ocean.

By 1515, the Portuguese had established colonies or trading posts in the Azores, Madeira, Brazil, and Goa on the coast of India. They also had established trading centers in Sierra Leone, Ghana, the Congo, Malaysia, and Indonesia, and were trading with the Ethiopians and the Chinese. Sugar, spice, African gold, and other imports enriched Lisbon.

During the reign of João II, the monarchy brought to heel the increasingly wealthy nobles of Portugal. Among these were the Braganças—an illegitimate line of the Aviz dynasty descended from João I and a daughter of Nuno Alvares Pereira. The Braganças gained popular support by expanding the system of the king's magistrates. João I was succeeded by Manuel I.

Manuel I successively married two daughters of Ferdinand II and Isabella I, the rulers of Spain. In return, he adopted the Spanish policy of expelling Jews and Muslims from Portugal, although he hedged this policy by giving two decades of grace to "new Christian converts," during which their conversions were not to be questioned. Manuel courted aristocratic loyalty with overgenerous stipends to nobles.

After the late 1550s, the economy of Portugal suffered from the burden of royal grants, the cost of overseas administration, falling world prices for goods, heavy loan payments, the loss of trading monopolies to other Europeans, and the effects of the Inquisition. When Manuel's grandson Sebastian I (r. 1557–1578) died while invading Morocco in 1578, his celibate great-uncle, Cardinal Henry, took the throne and ruled for two years. Henry was the last of the Aviz line of Portuguese monarchs.

See also: BRAGANÇA DYNASTY; IBERIAN KINGDOMS; PHILIP II; SPANISH MONARCHIES,

AVONGARA. *See* AZANDE KINGDOMS

AWAN DYNASTY (ca. 2350–2150 B.C.E.)

An early dynasty of ancient Elam in Mesopotamia, around the time of the Akkadian Empire in the third millennium B.C.E., which was an important center of power. Although scholars are not certain exactly where the Awan dynasty was based, it was most likely near the city of Susa in present-day southern Iran.

Not much is known about the Awan dynasty, since little has been discovered of the Elamite civilization. According to some ancient sources, the Awan dynasty consisted of twelve kings who ruled during a period of approximately two hundred years. Luhhishan, the eighth king, was forced to submit to King Sargon of Akkad (r. ca. 2334–2279 B.C.E.) around 2300 B.C.E. Although the Awan kings revolted regularly against Akkad, they remained under Akkadian control for decades. We know that Naram-Sin of Akkad (r. 2254–2218 B.C.E.), made a treaty with King Khita of Awan around 2220 B.C.E.

The last king of the Awan dynasty, Puzur-Inshushinak, successfully revolted against the Akkadians and created an independent empire for the Elamites around 2200 B.C.E. However, shortly after Elam gained independence, the Awan dynasty came to an end. It is not known for certain, but some scholars believe that, after their revolt against the Akkadians, the Elamites were overrun by the Gutians, a nomadic people who invaded Mesopotamia from the Zagros Mountains to the east and caused the collapse of the Akkadian Empire.

See also: AKKAD, KINGDOM OF; NARAM-SIN; SARGON OF AKKAD.

FURTHER READING
Sasson, Jack M., Editor in Chief. *Civilizations of the Ancient Near East.* Peabody, MA: Hendrickson, 2000.

AYMARA KINGDOMS

(ca. 1200–1500 C.E.)

South American polities that developed in the Altiplano plateau region surrounding Lake Titicaca in Peru and Bolivia. These kingdoms, founded by the Aymara peoples, emerged after the collapse of the Tiwanaku Empire in the thirteenth century. In the late fifteenth century, the kingdoms were conquered by the Inca, who turned the Aymara region into the "Collasuyu," one of the four administrative units that composed the Incan state.

After the demise of the Tiwanaku Empire (ca. 500–1200), a number of Aymara polities appeared in the Altiplano, the high plateau region in the central Andes Mountains. According to available historical evidence, by the early sixteenth century there were at least twelve Aymara kingdoms: Canchi, Cana, Colla, Lupaca, Collagua, Ubina, Pacasa, Caranga, Charca, Quillaca, Omasuyu, and Collahuaya. Internal and external conflicts occurred frequently among the kingdoms, and Aymara rulers built a number of fortified hilltop sites, or *pukaras*, to help defend their realms. The majority of the population of the Aymara kingdoms lived in villages that surrounded these stone fortifications.

Each Aymara kingdom and village was divided into two moities, or *parcialidades*, each of which had its own chief, or *kuraka*. One of the *kurakas* was considered to have more power than the other, but they exercised authority in a complementary manner. At the local level, the *kurakas* performed religious and military duties, and were also responsible for apportioning the available land among the members of the community.

The Aymara kingdoms practiced an extensive agriculture, complemented by pastoralism that involved the tending of herds of alpaca, vicuna, and other Andean hooved animals. According to some scholars, the Aymara also practiced an "archipelago system," in which dependent colonies were established in different ecological areas of the kingdoms. In this way, the Aymara had access to goods from different natural environments, helping to sustain their populations. The Aymara economies also included the production of pottery, stone tools, and textiles made from the wool of their herd animals.

The most powerful Aymara states were Colla and Lupaca, the capitals of which were Hatuncolla and Chucuito, respectively. When the Inca began their expansion toward the Altiplano in the early fifteenth century, the chief of the Colla was Zapana, and the chief of the Lupaca was Cari. Cari allied himself with the Inca and killed Zapana. The Inca consolidated their rule over the Aymara kingdoms in the late fifteenth century, and, in 1538, the Aymara people were conquered by the Spanish conquistadors, Hernando and Gonzalo Pizarro.

See also: INCA EMPIRE; SOUTH AMERICAN MONARCHIES; TIWANAKU KINGDOM.

AYUTTHAYA KINGDOM

(1350–1767 C.E.)

Kingdom of Siam, whose capital was the town of Ayutthaya, located in present-day central Thailand, approximately fifty-five miles north of Bangkok.

Founded by Ramathibodi I (r. 1350–1369) around 1350, Ayutthaya was a small city-state at the northwest border of the powerful Khmer Empire. Ramathibodi and his successors expanded Ayutthaya's power so much that it became one of the strongest states in Southeast Asia, spreading across all of modern Thailand except in the far east and far north, and along the mountain ranges in the southeast of modern Myanmar (formerly Burma).

The rise of Ayutthaya was largely due to the breakdown of Khmer and Mon control, the destruction of the Pagan kingdom in Burma, and the failure of the Vietnamese to move quickly southward along the east coast of Indochina to face the fierce resistance of the Cham peoples.

The kingdom of Ayutthaya was successful in a number of wars with nearby domains. In 1431, it drove back the Khmer and captured their capital of Angkor. Several years later, in 1438, it conquered the weakened Sukhotai kingdom and made it a province of Ayutthaya. The town of Ayutthaya, sometimes called Krung Kao ("ancient capital"), continued to thrive for more than four hundred years, and at its peak of power and prosperity in the mid-1400s to mid-1500s, it probably had hundreds of thousands of inhabitants.

Ayutthaya became one of the most prosperous and sophisticated cities of its era. Even though it was located inland, it was convenient to reach for ocean-bound ships sailing up the Chao Phraya River. It thus became a flourishing international marketplace visited by many European and Asian traders in the sixteenth and seventeenth centuries.

Ayutthaya's power was threatened by Burmese troops beginning in 1569, when they overpowered and sacked large parts of the kingdom. King Naresuan (r. 1590–1605) managed to win back the kingdom's independence, but wars with the Burmese continued. In 1767, Burmese troops invaded again, and Ayutthaya was unable to recover. The king, royal family, and many captives were taken to Myanmar, and all Ayutthayan records and works of art were destroyed.

See also: ANGKOR KINGDOM; BURMESE KINGDOMS; CHAMPA KINGDOM; KHMER EMPIRE; SOUTHEAST ASIAN KINGDOMS; SUKHOTHAI KINGDOM.

AYYUBID DYNASTY (ca. 1171–1250 C.E.)

A family of sultans and princes of Kurdish origin who governed much of the Muslim heartland for eighty years from power bases in Egypt and Syria, and succeeded in leaving a lasting imprint on the Middle East.

The Ayyubid military, political, economic, and cultural achievements helped restore and defend Muslim civilization in its orthodox Sunni form against strong challenges from European Christians and Shiite Muslim sects. Under their patronage, Egypt became the dominant cultural center of the Arab world.

ORIGINS OF THE DYNASTY

The Ayyubids came to power at a time of Muslim weakness and disunity in the face of the Christian

Crusader challenge. Local governors in Syria and northern Iraq were able to organize holding actions, but in the 1160s, Egypt itself was in danger of falling to the Western European Christian armies. In desperation, the sultan in Cairo, a member of the ruling Fatimid dynasty, sent a plea for help to the emir of Damascus, Nur al-Din. Nur dispatched his best general along with the general's young nephew, Salah al-Din (or Saladin, as he came to be known in Europe).

A brilliant warrior, Saladin (r. 1175–1193) followed up victories against the Crusaders in Egypt by overthrowing the Fatimids in 1171, and then taking over Syria and northern Iraq as well after the death of Nur al-din in 1174. He soon added Yemen, western Arabia, and most of Palestine to his dominions, installing relatives to govern as princes in his behalf. The dynasty Saladin established was called the Ayyubid dynasty, named after his father, Ayyub (Job).

One of Saladin's first acts as sultan was to restore Egypt to the dominant Sunni religious tradition (the Fatimids had been fervent Shiites). He declared loyalty to the caliph in Baghdad and launched what became the characteristic Ayyubid program of religious building projects. Eventually, some sixty-three *madrasa*s (religious colleges) were built in Damascus alone under Ayyubid patronage, and similar institutions were established throughout Syria and northern Iraq. In Cairo, the Ayyubids endowed major schools of Islamic law, and erected Sufi learning centers (*khanaqa*s) and tombs to honor Muslim saints. They brought to Egypt Sunni teachers and judges, who composed pious tracts lauding Saladin and his successors. This literature helped mobilize popular religious fervor behind the anti-Crusader *jihad*.

Saladin's dramatic victories over the Crusaders, culminating in the recapture of Jerusalem in 1187, were not consistently duplicated by his successors. On the contrary, Ayyubid sultans and princes developed a policy of accommodation with the remaining Crusader states. Jerusalem itself, where Ayyubid rulers had subsidized extensive public works, was abandoned in 1219; Sultan al-Kamil Muhammad II (r. 1218–1238) even ceded a demilitarized Jerusalem to Holy Roman Emperor Frederick II (r. 1212–1250) in 1229. The Ayyubids feared that a decisive victory would only invite further European military intervention. They also discovered that trade with Italian merchant colonies on the Levantine coast and with Europe itself could be a lucrative source of revenue.

ACHIEVEMENTS

The political stability created by the Ayyubids in Syria and their administrative reforms in Egypt fostered prosperity and economic growth. In Egypt, the Ayyubids won popular support by abolishing all taxes not specifically authorized in the Koran (Muslim scriptures). They also installed the *iqsa* system there, in which agricultural areas were granted for life to military supporters in exchange for tax revenues. Under the Ayyubids, the Red Sea became the chief spice route linking the Far East, the Muslim world, and Europe.

Cairo flourished under the Ayyubids, defended by a new Citadel (1187) and expanded walls. By opening the old Fatimid royal city to general development, Saladin is said to have created the Cairo of today. The Citadel of Aleppo, built in the early twelfth century, also survives as a testament to Ayyubid monumental architecture.

The Ayyubid era is also known for fine ceramics and inlaid metalwork, often produced in Mosul in northern Iraq. Impressive examples of Ayyubid enameled glass and elaborate woodcarving are featured in museums to this day.

DECLINE AND FALL

Despite the best efforts of sultans such as al-Adil Abu Bakr I (r. 1199–1218), al-Kamil Muhammad II, and al-Salih Ayyub (r. 1240–1249), infighting in Syria gradually undermined Ayyubid power. Slave soldiers, known as mamluks, purchased from lands north of the Black Sea, increasingly supplemented the Ayyubid armies of free Turks and Kurds, Bedouin mercenaries, and jihad volunteers.

Under Sultan al-Salih, the dependence on Mamluk forces proved fatal. When Al-Salih died in 1249 during a Crusader advance under King Louis IX of France (r. 1226–1270), his remarkable Turkish slave wife, Shajar al-Durr ("tree of pearls"), led the defense of Egypt until his son, Turan Shah, could return from a military campaign in Iraq and repel the invaders.

Mamluk conspirators soon killed Turan Shah and proclaimed Shajar the new sultan (r. 1250). As such, Shajar issued coins with her image and inserted her name into the weekly prayers. But both the Syrian Ayyub princes and the caliph in Baghdad deemed the idea of a female ruler unacceptable, and Shajar was forced to marry the Mamluk general Aybak. She remained the effective ruler, however, until her murder in 1259. By 1260, the remaining Ayub princes in Syria were finally defeated and deposed by the new

Mamluk sultan Baybars, bringing an end to the Ayyubid dynasty.

See also: CRUSADER KINGDOMS; FATIMID DYNASTY; MAMLUK DYNASTY; SALADIN.

FURTHER READING
Hillenbrand, Carole. *The Crusades: Islamic Perspectives.* New York: Routledge, 2000.
Hourani, Albert H. *A History of the Arab Peoples.* Cambridge, MA: Belknap Press of Harvard University Press, 1991.
Lapidus, Ira M. *A History of Islamic Societies.* New York: Cambridge University Press, 1988.

AZANDE KINGDOMS

(1500s–1800s C.E.)

Kingdoms formed by African groups that settled in southern Sudan in the 1500s. The Azande people, who still exist today, are basically an ethnic mixture originating from the Ambomu people, a group that lived on the Mbomu River (which marks the current boundary between northern Zaire and southern Central African Republic).

The rulers of the Ambomu, the Avongara clan, defeated several other peoples, probably in the first half of the 1700s, and assimilated them culturally and politically into their realm. At first, the Ambomu occupied all the lower official positions in the kingdoms, but gradually foreigners joined them and peoples from different ethnicities and cultures became part of a group of kingdoms that shared the same language, institutions, and lifestyle.

During the conquests by the Avongara clan in the eighteenth century, members carved out their own kingdoms, and wars between the various kingdoms were not uncommon. The political structure of the Azande kingdoms was very hierarchical. Zandeland, for instance, was split into several self-ruling chiefdoms. Each had a pyramidal structure of authority, with chiefs at the top, then subchiefs, deputies, and lastly heads of homesteads. The homestead was the primary political, economic, and social unit in the Azande kingdoms. The aristocratic Avongara clan had absolute authority, and the highest positions that common people could attain were as deputies or homestead heads.

Class distinctions were characteristic of Azande society. The Avongara clan discriminated strictly between chiefs and commoners, and most of the Azande groups made further distinctions between conquerers, the conquered, and slaves. Political, social, and economic standing was based solely on birth; but the politically high-ranking Avongara kept that distinction by well-thought-out political and military means. For instance, the ruler's court in each kingdom was centrally located, with roads leading from it to the courts of lower-level chiefdoms and homesteads.

The Azande settled in family groups in scattered homesteads with areas of cultivated land or forest between them. Several homesteads comprised a village, and groups of villages formed communities. The Azande economy was based mainly on farming, and the people were very knowledgeable about growing food plants, including vegetables, maize, and fruits.

The Azande also were known for their skill as artists and craftsmen. They were especially famous for their knives, spears, and shields, which helped them prevail over their neighbors and broaden the reach of their culture. Other Azande crafts included metalworking, pottery, basketry, net-weaving, smelting, and ivory- and wood-carving.

Of particular interest is the speculation that the Azande practiced cannibalism. There is evidence that some of them did, but also that the original Azande—the Ambomu and the ruling Avongara clan—did not.

See also: AFRICAN KINGDOMS.

AZTEC EMPIRE (1300s–1521 C.E.)

The last of the major indigenous empires to dominate the Mesoamerican region before the arrival of the Spanish conquistadors.

For centuries, the Valley of Mexico in south-central Mexico had been home to a succession of powerful states that flourished for a time and then collapsed. The last of these states to arise in the region was that of the Aztec, who dominated the area from the fourteenth to the sixteenth centuries, achieving the peak of their development during the last hundred years of their rule.

EARLY DEVELOPMENT OF AZTEC STATE
The Aztec first entered the Valley of Mexico during the latter half of the eleventh century. According to

ROYAL RITUALS

AZTEC SACRIFICE

The religion of the Aztec called for blood sacrifice, a practice shared by other peoples of the region but which the Aztec carried out on an unprecedented scale. Although simple blood-letting (which did not result in death) was common, the most important sacrifice, which provided the most nourishment for the gods, required the offering of a still-beating heart. The preferred victim was a war captive who had distinguished himself by great bravery on the battlefield. He was held down on a ceremonial altar, his heart was cut out and presented to the gods, and his body thrown down the steps. The bodies of particularly esteemed victims would be carried down the steps rather than thrown.

their own written records, the Aztec supposedly originated somewhere in the north, on an island called Aztlan, and traveled south at the command of one of their gods, Huitzilopochtli. At the time of their arrival in the Valley of Mexico, the region was controlled by the Toltecs, who had long dominated the area but whose power was on the decline due to frequent uprisings among their subject peoples. In 1171, the Toltec were overthrown by one such uprising, in which the Aztec participated.

For a time after the fall of the Toltec, the great ceremonial centers that they had built were abandoned, and small independent states sprang up throughout the Valley of Mexico. None of these states grew large enough to dominate the entire region, but many were able to assert control over their neighbors. The Aztec settled near one of these small states, which was centered around the town of Culhuacan. The people of Culhuacan found some of the Aztec practices offensive, particularly the Aztec fondness for human sacrifice, and attacked them. As a result, the Aztec became subjects of the Culhuacan, but some escaped this fate and fled to establish a new settlement, called Tenochtitlan, on an island in Lake Texcoco.

The bulk of the Aztec population remained as tribute-paying subjects of the Culhuacan for many decades, until they committed the unpardonable offense of sacrificing a member of the ruling family. For this offense they, too, were driven from the region and joined their fellows at Tenochtitlan. Among this group was a powerful and influential leader named Tenoch (r. 1325–1375), who is considered to be the first Aztec emperor. Under his leadership, the settlement at

Tenochtitlan became a great city. Tenoch also formed a large army, which he hired out to neighboring peoples as mercenaries. By the end of Tenoch's rule, the city of Tenochtitlan, with its ceremonial centers, ball courts, and markets, was complete.

Rise and Fall of the Empire

The kingdom ruled by Tenoch remained limited in scope. It was his successor, Acamapichtli (r. 1372–1391), who earned the distinction of converting the kingdom into an empire, for he was the first to begin a successful campaign of conquest against neighboring states, settlements, and tribes. By the time of the fourth Aztec king, Itzcoatl (r. 1427–1440), the Aztec controlled the whole Valley of Mexico. Itzcoatl also expanded the city of Tenochtitlan and built roads and a great causeway that ran from the island to the mainland.

Moctezuma (Montezuma) I (r. 1440–1468) succeeded Itzcoatl in 1440 and ruled for the next twenty-eight years. His reign was marked by a series of successful conquests, adding substantially to the territory under Aztec control. By the end of his reign, he had pushed the imperial borders well past the Valley of Mexico and extended Aztec control to include parts of the present-day Mexican states of Veracruz, Guerrero, and Puebla.

Through the reigns of the next three Aztec emperors, the stability of the region was maintained, but the days of further imperial conquest were nearly over. The Aztec rulers concentrated instead on collecting tribute from their subjects. As high priests in the Aztec religion, they also officiated over rituals, in-

THE AZTEC AND MAYA EMPIRES

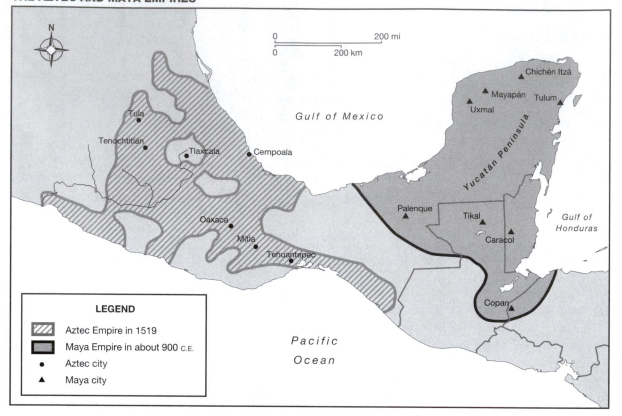

cluding human sacrifice practiced on an astonishing scale. The Aztec made such sacrifices to appease the gods, and they believed that without human sacrifice the "animating spirit" of all life would cease. With the accession of Moctezuma II (r. 1502–1520) around 1502, however, this stability was shaken as the conquered peoples upon whom the Aztec depended for tribute and slaves began to revolt.

This revolt is not surprising because by this time the Aztec sacrificial ceremonies demanded large numbers of sacrifices. In fact, Moctezuma II's predecessor, Ahuitzotl (r. 1486–1502), is said to have officiated at the sacrifice of 20,000 victims in a single ceremony, celebrating the successful conclusion of a major battle. Although the most valuable sacrifices were war captives, subject states and settlements also were required to supply a share of sacrificial victims. This caused deep resentment that led, ultimately, to rebellion.

Moctezuma II could perhaps have restored order to the empire given enough time and a sufficiently powerful army. However, a final disaster struck during his reign: the arrival of the Spanish conquistador, Hernando Cortés, in 1519. Some Aztec thought that

Cortes was a legendary god who had promised to return one day, and this made them reluctant to oppose him. Ultimately, however, it was the inherent weakness of the Aztec state—caused by the hostility of the subordinate peoples and the fact that Aztec military success was based on numbers, not strategy—that rendered the Aztec incapable of withstanding the Spanish, who brought firearms, cannon, and cavalry, none of which had ever been seen before. Within a year of the arrival of the Spanish, Moctezuma II had been deposed and killed. He was succeeded by his brother, Cuitlahuac (r. 1520), who ruled for less than a year. Cuitlahuac was followed on the throne by Cuauhtemoc (r. 1520–1521), who witnessed the destruction of Tenochtitlan by the Spanish in 1521. With the destruction of its great capital city, the Aztec Empire was no more.

Life in the Empire

At its peak, prior to the reign of Moctezuma II, the Aztec Empire extended over much of Mexico. Its heart and essence, however, was the lake city of Tenochtitlan. During the empire's heyday, the city was home to between 100,000 and 300,000 inhabi-

Aztec Empire

TENOCH	1325–1372
ACAMAPICHTLI	1372–1391
HUITZILIHUITL	1391–1416
CHIMALPOPOCA	1416–1427
ITZACOATL	1427–1440
MOCTEZUMA I	1440–1468
AXAYACATL	1468–1481
TIZOC	1481–1486
AHUITZOTL	1486–1502
MOCTEZUMA II*	1502–1520
CUITALAHUAC	1520
CUAUHTEMOC	1520–1521

*Indicates a separate alphabetical entry.

This Aztec calendar, known as the Sun Stone, is one of Mexico's most famous symbols. Carved in 1479 during the reign of the sixth Aztec ruler, the massive stone slab, measures about 12 feet in diameter and weighs nearly 25 tons. It was dedicated to the sun, the principal Aztec deity.

tants. The population required huge amounts of maize and other provisions, which necessitated the development of an extremely efficient form of agriculture, called *chinampa*. In *chinampa*, reeds were spread over the waters of the lake, and soil was then spread on top of them. The result was a system of floating gardens, and fully half of the city's population was employed in farming these man-made plots.

The remainder of the city's population was divided into *calpulli*—trade and craft specialists whose occupation was defined by the family to which they belonged. These economic divisions, similar in form and function to castes, were rigidly defined, unlike the social classes, of which there were two: *macehualles* (commoners) and *pilli* (nobles). These social divisions were not defined by kinship; an individual could become *pilli* through merit, usually through valor in war, or through marriage.

At the very top of the social, political, and religious hierarchy was the king, called *tlacatecuhtli* (which means "chief of men"). Beneath the king were members of the nobility and priestly classes, after which came the commoners. This hierarchy was specific to the city, however. Subject peoples did not participate except to send goods, including maize, slaves, crafts, and, of course, sacrificial victims. Order within the city of Tenochtitlan was maintained by a straightforward system of punishments. Nearly all crimes were capital offenses, and for the few that did not incur the penalty of death, punishment was nonetheless severe: extreme beatings and mutilation were common.

A Modern Legacy

The fall of the Aztec Empire marked the end of the great indigenous Mesoamerican civilizations. The memory of the great power of the Aztec, however, remains strong throughout Mexico. The idea of the original Aztec homeland, Aztlan, has become a potent symbol of ethnic pride, both within Mexico and in Mexican-American communities in the United States.

See also: MAYA EMPIRE; OLMEC KINGDOM; TOLTEC EMPIRE.

FURTHER READING

Coe, Michael. *The Aztecs*. Norman: University of Oklahoma Press, 1973.

Davies, Nigel. *The Ancient Kingdoms of Mexico*. New York: Penguin. 1982.

BABAR. *See* BABUR

BABENBERG DYNASTY (976–1246 C.E.)

Rulers of the Mark and Duchy of Austria, first appointed in 976 by Holy Roman Emperor Otto II (r. 973–983), probably as repayment for support against an uprising in the duchy of Bavaria.

The original title given to Leopold I (r. 976–994), the founder of the Babenberg dynasty, was margrave of Austria (the "eastern mark"). The family origins were rooted in the waning institutions of the Frankish Carolingian empire of the ninth century: "margraves" presided over "marks," or frontier areas, which they were charged with defending, alongside but below in rank to hereditary dukes or counts. Success for Babenbergs was closely connected to the success of the Holy Roman emperors in their efforts either to best the pope in controlling the Roman Catholic Church or subdue contending noble families.

Margrave Leopold I was succeeded by his son, Henry I (r. 994–1018); his brother, Adalbert (r. 1018–1055); and his nephew, Ernst (r. 1055–1075). Unlike his predecessors, Margrave Leopold II (r. 1075–1095) quarreled with the Holy Roman emperor, Henry III (r. 1039–1056), but despite setbacks, passed on his domain to his son Leopold III, "the Saint" (r. 1095–1136).

Leopold III benefited from his astute positioning during the investiture controversy, in which the emperors disputed with the popes over the right to make church appointments. Leopold sided with Emperor Henry IV (r. 1056–1105) and married Henry's widowed daughter Agnes, thus enhancing his stature with ties to the imperial family. Nevertheless, Leopold declined the imperial crown in 1125. Canonized in 1485, he is the patron saint of Austria.

Through marriage ties, Leopold IV (r. 1136–1141) added the duchy of Bavaria to the Babenberg realm. But his brother and successor, Henry II (r. 1141–1172), gave the duchy back to Bavaria in 1156 in return for promotion to duke of Austria by Emperor Frederick I Barbarossa (r. 1152–1190). This exchange helped to diffuse conflict between the imperial Hohenstaufen dynasty and their rivals, the Welfs. Leopold IV extracted several favors from the emperor, including the right to female succession (or, if no heir, to name a candidate for successor) and the right to approve the exercise of other jurisdictions (including ecclesiastical) within Babenberg domains.

Duke Leopold V (r. 1177–1194) went on Crusade in 1181 and 1190, quarreled with and then captured Richard I of England (r. 1189–1199) as Richard returned in disguise from the Holy Land, and subsequently exacted a handsome tribute from English nobles for Richard's release.

In 1192, the Babenbergs inherited the duchy of Styria in southeastern Austria. Duke Leopold VI "the Glorious" (r. 1198–1230) who succeeded his brother Frederick I (1194–1198) on the throne, presided over a time of great prosperity in the duchy of Austria. However, his son and successor, Frederick II "the Warlike" (r. 1230–1246), was very unpopular because of his harsh policies. Frederick II had no male heir, and his death in battle in 1246 marked the end of the Babenberg line.

See also: HOHENSTAUFEN DYNASTY; HOLY ROMAN EMPIRE.

BABUR (1483–1530 C.E.)

Founder and first ruler (r. 1526–1530) of the dynasty of Mongol warriors known as the Mughals. The Mughal dynasty was the greatest Muslim dynasty in Indian history, and the empire Babur established was the foundation of the golden age of Islam in India.

Born Zahir ad-Din Muhammad and known as "The Tiger," Babur was descended on his mother's side from the great Mongol conqueror Genghis Khan (r. 1206–1227). On his father's side, he was descended from Tamerlane (r. 1370–1405), the great warrior who captured and ruled an enormous empire that included present-day Pakistan, Central Asia, and Iran.

Founder of the Mughal Dynasty in 1526, Babur laid the foundation of a golden age of Islam in India. His memoirs, known as the *Baburnama,* constituted the first true autobiography in Islamic literature. This illustration is from a version of the *Baburnama* published in 1589–1590.

Like his ancestors, Babur came from relatively humble origins but became one of the most outstanding conquerors of his era. Starting out as ruler of the minor kingdom of Fergana in Turkestan around 1495, Babur first extended his realm by attacking Afghanistan and taking over Kabul in 1504. He then began to create the Mughal Empire by conquering Ibrahim II Lodi (r. 1517–1526), the sultan of Delhi, at the battle of Panipat in 1526. Although Babur's army was smaller than Ibrahim's, it consisted of excellent horsemen who were able to defeat the sultan's more numerous troops in just half a day.

Babur expanded Mughal rule with a victory over the powerful Rajputs of India under Rana Sanga of Mewar (r. 1509–1527) at the battle of Kanwar in 1527. The Mewar dynasty had continued to exist despite hundreds of years of Muslim attacks and rule, and Sanga was highly respected as a battle-proven leader of Hindu India's resistance to Mughal dominance.

At the battle of Kanwar, Sanga surrounded Babur's forces with his much larger army, but Babur boosted the morale of his struggling troops by smashing his golden wine goblets and giving away the pieces to the poor. He then ordered all his wine to be poured into the ground, and he swore never to drink the forbidden liquor again. Meanwhile, Rana Sanga made the mistake of waiting too long before attacking, losing some of his allies before the major battle ensued. As a result, Babur won the battle, and Sanga was fatally wounded and forced to flee.

Babur crushed an attempt to bring down the Mughal dynasty in 1529, when he defeated the Afghans of eastern Uttar Pradesh and Bihar. After that victory, Babur ruled all of northern India. He made Agra the capital of his Mughal Empire, which stretched from Kabul and Kandahar in the west to Bihar in the east, and from the Himalayas in the north to Gwalior in the south. Besides owing success to military prowess and skilled soldiers, Babur's victories also were due to technological advantages, such as the earliest use of muskets and artillery among the Muslim conquerors. These weapons were not highly developed, but they were far superior to those of the Hindustan armies.

Babur's reign ended after only four years, when he died in 1530 and was succeeded by his son Humayun (r. 1530–1540), a much less successful ruler. But Babur left behind an interesting memoir, the *Baburnama,* which tells about his ideas, beliefs, and the exploits of nearly forty years. This handwritten document may be the most comprehensive description of life in Central Asia at that time.

See also: GENGHIS KHAN; LODI KINGDOM; MUGHAL EMPIRE; RAJASTHAN KINGDOM; TAMERLANE (TIMUR LENG).

FURTHER READING

Keay, John. *Into India.* Ann Arbor: University of Michigan Press, 1999.
Wolpert, Stanley. *A New History of India.* 7th ed. New York: Oxford University Press, 2003.

BACTRIAN KINGDOM. *See* INDO-GREEK KINGDOMS

BAGIRMI KINGDOM

(ca. 1500 C.E.–Present)

Kingdom founded in the early 1500s in the Lake Chad region, situated between the rival kingdoms of Borno and Wadai.

Spoken tradition holds that the Bagirmi kingdom was founded by Dala Birni, who led his Barma people to the lands between Borno and Wadai in the early sixteenth century and created a settlement called Massenya. Dala Birni became the first Bagirmi king. The newcomers quickly made a name for themselves locally as capable warriors, in particular because of their use of cavalry.

The local peoples of the region, living as they did between two powerful states, turned to the newly arrived Barma warriors for protection. Soon, however, the protected communities became subordinate to, and then subsumed into, the growing Bagirmi state, particularly as the military mounted raids in search of captives for use as slaves.

The Barma ruler, called the *Mbang*, quickly amassed a territory that included not only Barma but also Arab and Fulani peoples, and its original settlement of Massenya became the capital of a full-fledged kingdom. In the final years of the 1500s, successors to *Mbang* Dala Birni converted to Islam and insisted that their subjects do the same. Nonetheless, the origins of the kingdom were pre-Islamic. The ruler was believed to descend from two supernatural sources, *mao* and *karkata*, and elements of Barma pre-Islamic ritual and beliefs remained prominent on such occasions as the king's installation and funerals.

In the 1600s, the Bagirmi kings adopted a policy of direct conquest of neighboring peoples, and over the next two centuries they extended their rule well into the north and west. Inevitably, this came to the attention of the rulers of the powerful Wadai state, who feared that the Bagirmi would soon begin encroaching on their territory. Wadai's response was predictable, and in 1806, the Bagirmi ruler, Guadang, was defeated by the forces sent from Wadai, abruptly curtailing any Bagirmi advances in that direction.

Any hope of further territorial expansion by the Bagirmi meant that they had to confront their neighbors in Wadai and Borno. Throughout the 1800s the Bagirmi kings sent numerous armies out to war, struggling to assert their kingdom's supremacy in the region. Soon, however, they were faced with a new obstacle in their path toward regional dominance.

In the late 1800s, France, hoping to establish a stable colonial presence in the Lake Chad region, sent soldiers and administrators to pacify the kingdoms there. At first, the Bagirmi king tried to play a diplomatic game, playing the French and rival regional powers against one another in hopes of maintaining autonomy and perhaps even expanding its influence. But this policy was unsuccessful, and in 1912 the kingdom was absorbed into the French colonial empire.

With the imposition of direct rule by France, the Bagirmi *Mbang* and his officials were reduced to little more than figureheads and cultural curiosities. In 1960, the newly independent nation of Chad abolished all kingdoms within its territory, including Bagirmi, but the kingdom was restored in 1970 and has been ruled since then by Yusuf Muhammad (r. 1970–present), the twenty-sixth *Mbang*.

See also: AFRICAN KINGDOMS; KANEMBU-KANURI KINGDOM.

FURTHER READING

Reyna, S.P. *Wars Without End*. Hanover, NH: University Press of New England, 1990.

BAHMANI DYNASTY (1347–1518 C.E.)

Muslim dynasty that ruled the Deccan plateau in central India for nearly two hundred years.

The Bahmani dynasty was established in the 1340s when a group of nobles rebelled against the Delhi sultanate and gained control of Daultabad in central India, the stronghold of Delhi's ruling Tughlug dynasty. The nobles were led by Hasan Zafar Khan, a former officer of the Delhi sultan, who assumed the royal name Alauddin Bahman Shah (r. 1347–1359), and founded the Bahmani kingdom.

Hasan expanded the new Bahmani kingdom through war and conquest. During his twelve-year reign, he gained control over the Deccan plateau, which stretched across central India. Hasan established a new capital at Gulbarga and divided the kingdom into four territories, each possessing its own governor, army, and civil administration.

When Hasan died in 1359, his son, Muhammad I (r. 1359–1375), succeeded him as Bahmani sultan.

Muhammad pursued his father's aggressive policies and launched repeated campaigns against the kingdom of Vijayanagar, Bahmani's southern neighbor. Muhammad's motives for war were both religious and strategic. Vijayanagar was a Hindu kingdom, not Muslim like Bahmani, and it occupied two key forts at the Bahmani border. Although Muhammad and his immediate successors secured numerous concessions from Vijayanagar, the steady warfare gradually weakened their dynasty.

Consequently, in 1422, Vijayanagar finally defeated Bahmani and regained its lost lands. Embarrassed by this defeat, the Bahmani ruler, Firuz (r. 1397–1422), abdicated the throne in favor of his brother, Ahmad I (r. 1422–1436). In 1425, Ahmad orchestrated a decisive victory over Vijayanagar, recaptured the forfeited Bahmani lands, and extracted a massive tribute. To strengthen Bahmani, Ahmad encouraged Turks, Persians, and Arabs to emigrate to his kingdom. These newcomers steadily advanced in the government and military, ultimately causing unrest among the native nobility.

This animosity exploded during the reign of Muhammad III (r. 1463–1482). Muhammad was an extremely weak ruler who relied upon his minister, Mahmud Gawan, to run the government. Gawan was loyal and highly effective, but he was a foreigner who had immigrated to the kingdom. Jealous of Gawan's power, the Indian nobles forged letters showing a secret alliance between the minister and Vijayanagar. Muhammad foolishly believed these letters, and, in 1481, he ordered Gawan to be executed.

When Muhammad died in 1482, his young son, Mahmud (r. 1482–1518), was unprepared to rule. Open violence soon erupted between the Deccans and foreign immigrants. Because Mahmud was a weak ruler, the governors of the various Bahmani territories each proclaimed their independence. Although the monarchy retained control of a small area around the capital city of Bidar until 1538, the dynasty effectively crumbled after Mahmud's death in 1518.

See also: INDIAN KINGDOMS; TUGHLUQ DYNASTY; VIJAYANAGAR EMPIRE.

BALDWIN I (1058–1118 C.E.)

Also known as Baldwin of Boulogne, member of the First Crusade and first king of the Frankish kingdom of Jerusalem (r. 1100–1118). Under Baldwin, the Franks secured control of Palestine that lasted 200 years.

Baldwin was the son of Eustace II, count of Boulogne. His older brother, Godfrey (usually known as Godfrey of Bouillon), was widely regarded as the greatest European knight of the First Crusade. Because he was instrumental in taking Jerusalem from the Muslims, both his fellow knights and the representatives of the Church selected Godfrey as the first Defender of the Holy Sepulchre, a title that he preferred to that of king of Jerusalem, the newly created crusader state in Palestine.

In 1098, while Geoffrey was fighting for Jerusalem, Baldwin had gone to the assistance of Toros, the Christian prince of Edessa in Macedonia. Instead of helping Toros, Baldwin duped the ruler and then coerced him into abdicating in Baldwin's favor.

Upon Godfrey's death in 1100, Baldwin began a campaign for the Crown of Jerusalem. Godfrey, allying with the Church, had kept a close watch on villainous and unruly behavior in Jerusalem, and many of the Frankish knights were unhappy with these restrictions. Baldwin promised them a freer hand. He was successful in winning favor and was chosen as the second Defender of the Holy Sepulchre in 1100. Shortly thereafter, he was crowned the first king of Jerusalem. His election to the throne marked a shift in power among the Christian crusaders, a shift toward secular goals and military means instead of religious ones.

Baldwin continued the struggle against the Muslims, and by 1112, he had succeeded in taking all the major coastal cities of Palestine and Syria except for Ascalon and Tyre. In 1115, he built the formidable castle Krak de Montrèal (in present-day Jordan) to guard the southern reaches of his realm. After defeating the Muslim rulers of Palestine, Baldwin created an able administration that helped maintain Frankish control of Palestine and Syria until the end of the Third Crusade in 1192.

See also: CASTE SYSTEMS; CHRISTIANITY AND KINGSHIP; CRUSADER KINGDOMS; FRANKISH KINGDOM.

BAMBARA KINGDOM

(1660–1893 C.E.)

Successor to the Songhai Empire as western Africa's dominant political power; also called the Segu state, after the name of its capital.

Until the end of the sixteenth century, the Bambara were one of many subject peoples paying tribute to the great Songhai Empire. Then Moroccan invaders conquered Songhai and broke the empire up into smaller units. The Bambara comprised one of these units, which were governed by political appointees of the Moroccan sultan. The sultan, however, found it difficult to retain control over his possessions in West Africa because they were so far from the center of his power on the North African coast. From amid the chaos, a new state emerged in 1660, centered on the city of Segu on the banks of the Niger River.

The Bambara were the largest ethnic group in this region, a people who had retained its traditional animist religions even while its rulers (the Songhai *askiyas* and Moroccan governors) promoted Islam. Oral tradition holds that a Bambara leader named Mamari Kulubali developed a following among the young men with whom he had undergone his rites of initiation into manhood. He and his followers left their home village and established a community of their own. From this base they began raiding their neighbors, gaining local fame as fierce warriors. Young men from other peoples in the area came to join Mamari's band, but the newcomers were considered subordinate to the original Bambara group. As Mamari's following grew ever larger, he took for himself the title of *faama*, which translates as "ruler" or "king."

The kingdom established by Mamari was distinctive in that it was almost entirely militarized. Recruitment of new members was achieved primarily through capture during raids, and these same raids were the principal source of the state's revenues. In effect, the business of this kingdom was war, and war alone. With the wealth gained through their military raids, the Bambara employed the neighboring Somono to provide fish and river transport, the Fulani to provide cattle, and other local groups to work their farms. They also traded their surpluses for horses and weapons. By the end of Mamari's rule, the Bambara had become the most powerful military force in the region.

The cohesion of the Bambara kingdom, however, was due largely to the charisma of its leader. When Mamari died (in 1754 or 1755) the kingdom entered a decade of great upheaval, as competing factions sought to claim the throne. In 1765, a new king finally emerged to lead the Bambara. This was Ngolo Jara (r. 1765–1790), who ruled for the next twenty-five years. His reign was a continuation of Mamari's militarist policies. When Ngolo Jara died in 1790, there was again no clear successor to the throne. His three sons each claimed the title, and the Bambara kingdom was plunged once more into a long, bloody civil war.

Around 1795, Monzon Jara (r. ca. 1795–1808) was finally recognized as the legitimate king of the Bambara. Unlike his predecessors, Monzon Jara did not rely on the military as his sole means of ensuring order in the kingdom. Instead, he attempted to create a more centralized authority, with the administrative seat in the capital at Segu. The military was put to work reclaiming territories that had been lost during the confusion of the civil war. He also made a point of clearly designating his son, Da Monzon, as his successor. As a result, his approximately thirteen-year reign was a time of relative stability and prosperity.

Da Monzon (r. 1808–1827) took the throne in 1808. He continued his father's successful policies of centralization and was strong enough to maintain control over the kingdom throughout his reign. He was the last to succeed in doing so, however. After his death in 1827, a series of weaker rulers gradually lost control of their subject territories, and by 1860 the kingdom was in a greatly weakened condition.

In 1860, a devout Muslim named 'Umar Ibn Sa'id Tal, known as "Al Hajj," was becoming a powerful force in the region. Al Hajj had dedicated himself to spreading Islam and eradicating paganism wherever he found it. He attacked and conquered the Bambara kingdom in 1862. He died two years later, however, and his successors were unable to maintain order in the kingdom. The traditional Bambara ruling clan sought to regain the throne by forming an alliance with the French, who were looking to establish a colony in the region. In 1890, the French siezed the territory, reinstated the Bambara kingship, and appointed Mari Jara (one of Da Monzon's sons) (r. 1890) as the new ruler, expecting him to be compliant to French rule. Within the year, however, Mari Jara was executed by French colonial authorities for fomenting rebellion, and he was replaced by a member of a rival clan. This new appointed king, Bojan (r. 1890–1893), never gained the support of the people, and in 1893 the French simply replaced the kingship with direct colonial rule.

See also: GHANA KINGDOM, ANCIENT; MALI, ANCIENT KINGDOM OF; SONGHAI KINGDOM.

FURTHER READING

Roberts, Richard. *Warriors, Merchants, and Slaves: The State and the Economy in the Middle Niger Valley, 1700–1914.* Stanford, CA: Stanford University Press, 1987.

BAMILEKE KINGDOMS

(1500 C.E.–Present)

Approximately one hundred small kingdoms (more properly, chiefdoms) collectively called Bamileke, located in the grasslands region of what is now the Western District of Cameroon in west-central Africa.

The name "Bamileke" is the result of misunderstanding and mispronunciation. When German explorers in Cameroon came across the first of these polities in the 1800s, they asked their guide and interpreter what these people might be called. The interpreter, who came from an ethnic group that lived to the west, responded with a phrase from his own language: *mba lekeo*, which roughly translates as "the people who live over there." The name, mispronounced and miswritten, came into use, and today the Bamileke continue using the term to refer to themselves (at least when speaking to outsiders). The single name, however, is misleading, for it implies a unity among the many independent Bamileke kingdoms that has no basis in fact.

FORMATION OF THE KINGDOMS

The people who became the Bamileke originated somewhere to the north of the lands they now occupy and moved southward under pressure from the rise of the Tikar kingdom in northern Cameroon. In the early 1500s, other pressures arose, as Fulani people (from present-day Nigeria) began pressing southward into the central grasslands where the Bamileke peoples had settled. The formation of centralized states probably originated at this time, when individual Bemileke settlements discovered they could better resist Fulani conquest by organizing into more unified states.

These states proliferated throughout the region, each independent of the others, over the next 300 years. By the late 1880s, when German colonists arrived to claim the whole of Bamileke territory, the borders of the individual kingdoms had long been set and included Bafang, Bafoussam, Bangwa, Nsaw, and Wum, among many others. Although all the kingdoms speak dialects of a parent Bantu language, the relationship is not very close, and many of the dialects spoken are mutually unintelligible.

BAMILEKE SOCIETY

Bamileke chiefdoms continue today, although the rule of the kings is subordinate to the national government of Cameroon. The kingdoms share a number of physical and cultural features. Each is divided into a number of small administrative units containing a handful of individual villages. At the heart of each kingdom is the royal compound, with the royal palace, the houses of the king's wives, and meeting houses for use by the king and his court.

The king and the queen mother are the pinnacle of Bamileke society. Below them are nobles, royal servants, and commoners, in that order of social rank and importance. A fourth category of subjects, slaves, was once important, but slaves are no longer permitted by law. At the service of the king were secret societies—male-only groups whose members underwent special initiation rites that set them apart from the rest of society and who were charged with seeing that the king's will was carried out.

The king is viewed as a divine figure, responsible for protecting the health and prosperity of the people. His divinity, however, comes from his office. That is, he gains his divinity only through the rituals that lead up to his coronation. These rituals are intended to transform him from man to god, beginning with a mock "capture" after which he is imprisoned for nine weeks in a special ritual building. His emergence from this hut symbolizes his rebirth as a divine being. Even so, he is truly recognized as king only after he has sired one child of each gender.

The jurisdiction of Bamileke kings today is limited by the rule of the Cameroon state, which assumes all authority over criminal matters. However, subjects still consult their Bamileke kings for help in local civil matters.

See also: AFRICAN KINGDOMS; TIKAR KINGDOM.

FURTHER READING

Fowler, Ian, and David Zeitlyn, eds. *African Crossroads: Intersections Between History and Anthropology in Cameroon.* Providence, RI: Berghahn Books, 1996.

BAMUM KINGDOM. *See* TIKAR KINGDOM

BANGKOK KINGDOM

(1700s C.E.–Present)

Kingdom located in present-day capital of Bangkok in central Thailand, ruled by the Rama dynasty, which was transformed from an absolute monarchy to a constitutional monarchy in 1932.

The establishment of the Thai, or Rama, dynasty at Bangkok took place in the midst of chaos two decades after the fall of the Thai kingdom of Ayutthaya to the Burmese in 1767. The new dynasty began with P'ya Taksin (r. 1767–1782), a half-Chinese general who fought his way out of the Burmese siege of Ayudhya in 1767 with 500 followers.

The disappearance of the Ayutthaya royal family after the Burmese siege left a power vacuum that Taksin took up as he struggled to drive out the Burmese and reunify Siam. By 1776, Taksin had succeeded in reuniting Siam, but his reign was marked by a long series of brutal and exhausting campaigns against the Burmese and others. The stress of endless battles eventually led to Taksin's insanity.

In the early 1780s, a series of rebellions broke out in Ayutthaya with the intention of dethroning the insane king, and rebel leaders placed General Chakri, a well-liked figure, on the throne. In 1782, Chakri rushed back to Ayutthaya from a campaign in Cambodia and acted to put down the rebellions that still plagued the kingdom. Upon his return, he was welcomed and hailed as the new ruler by the people.

Taking the title Rama T'ibodi (Rama I) (r. 1782–1809), Chakri became the founder of the Rama dynasty of Bangkok, which continues to rule Thailand to the present day. Chakri moved the capital of the Thai kingdom to modern Bangkok, away from the old capital of Thon Buri in the Menam basin. By the time Rama I died in 1809, Thailand had completely recovered from the devastation caused by the constant wars with Burma and had become more powerful than before.

The Bangkok kingdom became known for its strong and adaptable monarchy. Bangkok kings, such as Mongkut (Rama IV) (r. 1851–1868) and his son, Chulalongkorn (Rama V) (r. 1868–1910), carried out modernizing projects, such as building efficient communication and transportation infrastructures, which enabled Thailand to retain its sovereignty during a time when other Southeast Asian countries were becoming European colonies. Thailand became the only nation in Southeast Asia to retain its royal monarchy despite the incursion of Western colonial powers and the Japanese Occupation following the outbreak of World War II.

The current Bangkok ruler is Rama IX (Bhumibol Adulyadej) (r. 1946–). Like his predecessors, he continues to be an important symbol of national identity in the modern state of Thailand.

See also: AYUTTHAYA KINGDOM; CHULALONGKORN; MONGKUT (RAMA IV); SOUTHEAST ASIAN KINGDOMS.

BANU KHURASAN

(500s B.C.E.–Present)

Large area in southern Asia, mainly in northeastern Iran, that contains a number of different ethnic groups resulting from centuries of successive invasions. The historical area of Banu Khurasan extended from the Oxus River in the north to the Caspian Sea in the west, and from the central Iranian deserts in the south to the mountains of central Afghanistan, and possibly the Indian border, in the east.

In the sixth and fifth centuries B.C.E., Banu Khurasan was first part of the Persian Achaemenid Empire. It then became part of the Parthian Empire in the first century B.C.E. Its name, bestowed by the Persian Sassanid dynasty early in the third century B.C.E., means "Land of the Sun." The Arabs conquered Banu Khurasan around 650 C.E. and settled there in large numbers, producing a mixture of Islamic and eastern Iranian cultures. Between 821 and 999, the region regained its independence under the Tahirid, Saffarid, and Samanid dynasties. It then became part of the Ghaznavid, Seljuq, and Khwarezm-Shah kingdoms but was taken over by the Mongol ruler Genghis Khan in 1220 and then by the Turkic conqueror Tamerlane around 1383.

The Iranian Safavid kings, who ruled from 1502

to 1722, defended Banu Khurasan from attacks by the Uzbeks, and the Afghans occupied the region from 1722 to 1730. Persian king Nadir Shah (r. 1736–1747), who was born in Khurasan, overthrew Afghan domination, and the city of Meshed became the capital of his Iranian empire. Meshed remains the capital and major city of modern-day Khurasan.

See also: ACHAEMENID DYNASTY; GHAZNAVID DYNASTY; KHWARAZM-SHAH DYNASTY; NADIR SHAH; PARTHIAN KINGDOM; SAFAVID DYNASTY; SAFFARID DYNASTY; SAMANID DYNASTY; SASANID DYNASTY.

BARCELONA, COUNTY OF. *See*

CATALONIA, COUNTY OF

BARGHASH IBN SA'ID EL-BUSAIDI (ca. 1833–1888 C.E.)

Member of the Busaid dynasty of Oman, who ruled as sultan of Zanzibar from 1870 to 1888.

One of three sons of Sultan Seyyid Sa'id (r. 1804–1856), Barghash ibn Sa'id was born in Zanzibar around 1833. His father, who inherited the Busaid sultanate of Oman in 1804, moved his capital to Zanzibar in 1832. There he created a thriving commercial empire, the economy of which depended largely on the spice trade and trade in ivory, but soon came to include slaves. Seyyid's rule ultimately extended well into the east African mainland, and his subjects included coastal Bantus as well as Omani, Persian, and Indian immigrants who settled the region in pursuit of trade.

When Seyyid died in 1856, his middle son, Majid, was designated heir to the throne. But both the elder son, Thuwaini, and younger son, Barghash, bitterly contested their brother's succession. The three vied for power for the next fourteen years, with first one, then another, briefly gaining ascendancy. Barghash ultimately took over the rule of Zanzibar in 1870, at a time when the government was saddled with a highly corrupt ministerial class that fought hard to protect its own interests. Barghash also faced increasing pressure from the European colonial powers, for both Britain and Germany coveted Zanzibar for its wealth and its strategic location on the eastern coast of the African continent.

In addition to these political pressures, Barghash faced an even greater challenge when, early in his reign, a hurricane struck the island of Zanzibar and, in a single stroke, devastated the spice economy upon which much of the country's wealth was based. He succeeded in restoring prosperity, largely through the great slave markets of Zanzibar. But in 1873 the British forced him to outlaw slave trading, which dealt a second devastating economic blow to his nation's wealth and power.

Barghash sought to establish Zanzibar as a truly autonomous state, not merely a commercial center. The times were against him, however. Germany laid claim to the parts of Zanzibari territory that lay on the African mainland, and Barghash was unable to reassert control over those lands. As a result, Barghash found his sultanate reduced in territory to just its offshore islands, leaving Zanzibar vulnerable to further imperialistic claims by European powers. By the time of Bargash's death in 1888, the power, wealth, and prestige of the independent sultanate of Zanzibar was a thing of the past. In 1890, the sultanate became a British protectorate.

See also: ZANZIBAR SULTANATE.

BARODA KINGDOM (1721–1948 C.E.)

A kingdom in west-central India, part of the Maratha Confederacy, which was ruled by the Gaekwar dynasty from 1721 until the kingdom was absorbed into the Republic of India in 1948.

Located in the Gujarat state of west-central India, the kingdom of Baroda was established in the early eighteenth century by the Maratha military commander Pilaji Rao Gaekwar (r. 1721–1732) and his son, Damaji Rao I (r. 1732–1768). In 1721, Pilaji defeated Mughal armies in the area and took over large sections of Gujarat. Pilaji and his son were supposed to consolidate power and collect taxes for the peshwa, the administrator of the Maratha Confederacy. Instead, they took advantage of conflicts between Maratha nobles, in particular between the Dabhude family and the peshwa, to declare independence.

In the 1750s, the Maratha peshwa recognized the right of the Gaekwar family to control large parts of Gujarat. Damaji Rao I set up a capital at Baroda and became one the most powerful rulers in the region.

Although Baroda had gained independence, it was still necessary for the peshwa to step in and stop a succession dispute after Damaji died in 1768.

After several years of conflict, the peshwa appointed Fateh Singh (r. 1771–1789) to rule Baroda as regent, but Fateh soon turned to the British East India Company for help in maintaining order in the kingdom. British soldiers moved in and Fateh Singh signed a treaty giving the British government control of all external matters, while Baroda kept control of internal affairs except for succession disputes.

In 1873, the British released Malhar Rao Gaekwar (r. 1873–1875), who had been thrown into prison by his late ruling brother, Khande Rao (r. 1856–1870), and allowed him to rule Baroda. Within a year, however, the British accused Malhar of trying to poison their viceroy, Lord Northbrook. Nothing could be proved at the trial, but Northbrook deposed Malhar Rao on the grounds of gross misrule and tyranny and exiled him to Madras in 1875. His predecessor's widow was then permitted to adopt an heir from among the family descendants. She chose the son of a farmer, twelve-year-old Shrimant Gopalrao Gaekwar, who ruled as Sayaji Rao III (r. 1875–1939).

Under British tutelage, Sayaji Rao III, the last Gaekwar ruler of Baroda, became a model prince, and he was a frequent visitor to London. Much decorated by England, he died in 1939. Less than a decade after his death, in 1948, Baroda, which had been a British garrison town since the beginning of the nineteenth century, formally became part of independent India.

See also: MARATHA CONFEDERACY.

BASIL I (ca. 813–886 C.E.)

Byzantine emperor, known also as Basil the Macedonian, who ruled (r. 867–886) during the medieval period.

Basil I was descended from Armenians and Slavs who settled in Macedonia centuries earlier. In 856, he became the favorite of Byzantine emperor Michael III (r. 842–867), who helped him in 866 to assassinate Bardas, Michael's uncle and chief minister. Michael then declared Basil co-emperor.

Within a short time, however, Basil began to lose Michael's favor. Basil thus had the emperor mur-

dered in 867 and proclaimed himself the sole Byzantine ruler. Basil's accession to the throne marked the beginning of the Macedonian dynasty of Byzantium, which lasted until 1056.

A capable ruler, Basil I reformed the finances of the empire and introduced a new law code, the Basilica, which modernized the Byzantine legal code established centuries earlier by the emperor Justinian I, the Great (r. 527–565). An advocate for the poorer classes, Basil I also restored the prestige of the Byzantine military. Byzantine art and architecture flourished during Basil's reign, but so did dissension between the Roman and the Eastern Christian churches, fueled in part by continuing differences over iconclasm, the religious use of images. Upon his death in 886, Basil I was succeeded by his son and co-regent since 870, Leo VI (r. 886–912).

See also: BYZANTINE EMPIRE; JUSTINIAN I.

BASIL II (ca. 958–1025 C.E.)

Byzantine emperor (r. 976–1025) who ruled during the medieval period, at a time when the schism, or split, between the Roman and Eastern Christian churches widened dramatically.

Known as Bulgar Slayer because of his military exploits against the Bulgarians, Basil II and his brother, Constantine VIII (r. 1025–1028), were the sons of Byzantine emperor Romanus II (r. 969–963). From 960 and 972, respectively, the brothers served as co-regents with their father. They jointly succeeded to the throne in 976, after a thirteen-year period in which the empire was ruled by two generals who had usurped power. When they took the throne, Constantine served as emperor in name only, while Basil actually ruled.

Basil II was primarily a soldier. Between 976 and 989, he successfully suppressed a series of revolts by Byzantine landowners. In the process, he revived and strengthened the laws directed against landowners that had been established decades earlier by Emperor Romanus I (r. 920–944).

In 1018, Basil II annexed Bulgaria, and he later extended the eastern frontier of the Byzantine Empire through conquest and diplomacy. His military powers and diplomatic skills gained him great political and territorial strides. During his reign, however, the division between the Roman and the Eastern churches, which had already led to serious friction between religious factions, widened, creating a significant rift within the Christian faith.

Basil II died in 1025 and was succeeded by his brother, Constantine VIII, who ruled as sole emperor from 1025 to 1028.

See also: BYZANTINE EMPIRE.

BASQUE KINGDOM (834–1515 C.E.)

Early kingdom established in the ninth century in present-day northern Spain and southwestern France, whose struggle against the Muslims marked the beginnings of the *reconquista*, the reconquest of Iberia from the Moors.

In 297, the area that became the Basque kingdom gained its first taste of independence when the Romans granted the Basques some degree of autonomy. The region later became the duchy of Gascony in 602. The Basque state of Gascony remained united until 717, when it lost two of its provinces to the Franks. The Basques later became vassals of the Franks during the reign of the Frankish king, Charlemagne (r. 768–814).

The rise of a Muslim state in Iberia, which began in 711, weakened the Franks enough that the Basques were able to defeat Charlemagne's armies in 778 at Roncesvalles in the Pyrenees Mountains. This success eventually led to an independent and reunited Basque kingdom, which emerged in 824 with the formation of the Basque kingdom of Navarre under Iñigo Arista (r. 824–851).

After the kingdom of Navarre was formed, it had to fight to maintain its independence. When the Muslims of Córdoba, led by Abd al-Rahman II (r. 822–852), defeated the Basques and the Muslim Visigoth ruler Banu Qasi in 842, the sovereignty of Arista's fledgling kingdom was in jeopardy. The danger forced the young Basque kingdom to try to maintain its independence by resisting the Cordobans and allying with Muslim opponents of Córdoba.

The Basque kingdom's fight for survival lasted throughout the tenth century and was intensified by the continuous need to keep at bay other invaders from the north, the Vikings. By the beginning of the eleventh century, the Basque kingdom of Navarre was united with its neighbor, the kingdom of Aragón, through marriage. A further alliance with the county of Castile in 1002 helped the Basques defeat the Muslim Cordobans, who had destroyed the city of Pamplona three years earlier in 999.

The victory over the Cordobans in 1002 heralded a period of expansion and solidification of the Basque kingdom under Sancho III, the Great (r. 1004–1035). Sancho III gained a claim to the county of Castile through his wife, Munia, who inherited that land after her brother, Garcia II (r. 1017–1029), was murdered. Eventually, Sancho's son, Ferdinand (r. 1029–1065), joined Castile and León through his marriage to Sancha, the daughter of King Alfonso V of León (r. 990–1028). Sancho was also an ally of the county of Barcelona, and Navarre and Barcelona created a united front across the Spanish border with France.

Upon Sancho's death in 1035, his kingdom was divided among his sons. Garcia III (r. 1035–1054) received Navarre, Ferdinand received Castile and later León, and Ramiro I (r. 1035–1069) inherited Aragón. This division of Sancho's acquisitions initiated a drive by Ferdinand for control of Navarre. This resulted in Garcia's death in 1054, at which point Navarre fell under Castile's control.

A little over a decade later, in 1067, Navarre received help from Aragón in repelling Castile. But Castile re-invaded Navarre in 1076 after the Navarrese king, Sancho IV (r. 1054–1076), the son of Garcia III, was murdered. Despite efforts by Castile to gain control, the king of Aragón, Sancho Ramirez (r. 1069–1094), was chosen to be king of Navarre, and Navarre became a protectorate of Aragón.

Navarre and Aragón expanded throughout the twelfth century. From this region, expansion into the eastern Iberian Peninsula was accomplished at the expense of the Muslim Almoravid and Almohad dynasties. However, the united expansion of Navarre and Aragón did not continue past the death of Alfonso I (r. 1104–1134) in 1134, at which point the kingdom was split back into its original two parts.

In 1200, the king of the Basque kingdom of Navarre, Sancho VII (r. 1194–1234), had his title usurped by an invasion by Castile. This led to the division of Navarre and its subjugation to the kingdom of Castile. This conquest, however, did not prevent Navarre from allying itself willingly with Castile to ward off Muslim attacks a decade later, in 1211.

Navarre, now much reduced in size, allied itself with England in 1137, after Eleanor of Aquitaine married King Henry II of England (r. 1154–1189). This marriage brought Gascony, the Basque duchy that had remained separate from Navarre and was a part of Aquitaine, out of French control and into English control.

In 1159, Henry II relinquished Aquitaine to the French. By late in the thirteenth century, the Basque kingdom had been transferred through marriage to the control of the French king, Philip IV (r. 1285–1314), and France retained the territory until 1328.

For Navarre, much of the fourteenth century was spent being used as a tool in political maneuvering between rival states and leaders in England, France, Aragón, and Castile. During this time, the northern Basque region of Gascony experienced a nearly twenty-year period of civil war, between 1343 and 1360. In 1379, Navarre's political position stabilized again with the forced political union of the kingdoms of Castile and Navarre.

The death of Navarre's king in 1441 led to a civil war in which the Basque nobility split their support between rival claimants to the throne. The civil war lasted until Castile invaded in 1512. Castile, with assistance from Aragón, took control of much of the country and resisted a French attempt to liberate Navarre. In 1515, Castile ended Navarrese autonomy by annexing the kingdom and creating the kingdom of Spain. The new Spanish rulers later solidified this arrangement by putting down an uprising in 1531 that was supported by the French.

The northern Basque provinces of Gascony remained independent throughout this period, even though Gascony was located within the borders of France. In the Treaty of the Pyrenees in 1659, the French relinquished all their claims to Navarre, leaving the former Basque kingdom officially divided between France and Spain. Since then, the Basque provinces of Spain have struggled to maintain some degree of autonomy within the Spanish nation.

See also: ARAGÓN, KINGDOM OF; CASTILE, KINGDOM OF; CÓRDOBA, CALIPHATE OF; IBERIAN KINGDOMS; NAVARRE, KINGDOM OF; SANCHO III, THE GREAT; SPANISH MONARCHIES.

FURTHER READING

Mayo, Patricia Elton. *The Roots of Identity: Three National Movements in Contemporary European Politics.* London: Allen Lane, 1974.

BATHS, ROYAL

Luxurious and opulent places for royalty to relax, bathe, and sometimes be entertained. Throughout the world, and as early as the ninth century B.C.E. when the Celtic prince Bladud established the town of Bath in England at the site of natural hot springs, monarchs and other royalty have indulged themselves in restorative and opulent baths.

The Romans developed baths with hot and cold water systems, built on natural mineral springs, to ease the battle wounds of soldiers. The baths began to foster a communal spirit complete with vendors and entertainment, and the citizens of Rome began to enjoy the baths as well. Emperors and members of the upper class not only had their own private baths, but they also enjoyed the public bathhouses. Emperor Caracalla (r. 211–217) had a bath constructed that covered almost 28 acres and had more than 1,600 marble seats. The great baths of the emperor Diocletian (r. 284–305) had room for three thousand.

On the whole, Roman royalty accorded greater ceremony with respect to bathing and baths than did the Greeks. Some emperors opted to exercise before a bath, but for the most part, bathing was a luxurious experience. Slaves were available to slather an oil mixture on the royal's body, next the oil was rubbed in to release dirt, and then the oil and dirt were scraped off with a metal instrument called a strigel.

In South America, both the Incan and the Aztec dynasties conceived of baths as royal luxuries. For the Incan royalty, baths were located within the palace confines and were very grand in scale. They were made with large, carved, well-fitting stones that the newly arrived Spanish thought were constructed without mortar. Hundreds of Incan women adorned in ornamental finery would be found in the baths. When a young girl entered puberty, she would undertake a period of retreat, abstaining from certain foods and making use of the purifying baths.

The Aztec royals used the *ternascal* ("sweatbaths") as a source of hygiene for women to relieve labor pains and to purge illness. In the Aztec palaces, the *ternascal* was located in a separate room, detached from the palace; some were adorned with the figurines of the fertility goddess Xochitquetzal, sug-

Built by the Emperor Caracalla around 212–216 C.E., the extensive Baths of Caracalla in Rome were staggering in complexity and opulence. The central building measured 750 feet by 400 feet, and the facility could accommodate up to 1,600 bathers, as well as sporting events and theatrical entertainment. Today, opera performances are staged at the site.

gesting an additional use for the baths. The royals believed that the baths were intended to be enjoyed by men and women together; in a 1564 court case, royals defended their practice of mixed bathing much to the shock of the recent Spanish arrivals living in the community.

The town of Aachen, well known in the Middle Ages for its healing, natural-sourced hot water and steam (located in present-day Germany), was taken over by the Frankish king Charlemagne (r. 742–814) in 768. According to legend, Charlemagne's horse had injured its hoof and was healed when the hoof was placed in a hot spring. Charlemagne then decided to set up his residence in Aachen, building a spacious facility on the site of old Roman baths. It is believed that he visited the baths daily, often with family members and court officials. Charlemagne buoyed the popularity of the baths, which dissipated after his death in 814.

BATU KHAN (d. 1255 C.E.)

Grandson of the Mongolian leader Genghis Khan (r. 1206–1227) and founder of the Golden Horde, whose campaigns as Mongol military leader threatened all of Europe in the thirteenth century.

Batu was the son of Juchi, who was a son of the great Genghis Khan (r. 1206–1227). When Juchi predeceased his father in 1227, his military endowment passed to Batu. In 1235, Batu was elected commander of the western Mongol armies and led campaigns to invade and conquer Europe. He first sent the bulk of his armies to Russia, bringing all of Russia under Mongol control by 1240. During this campaign, the Mongols thoroughly razed Kiev, the cultural capital of the principality known as the Kievan Rus.

After subjugating Russia, Batu turned his attention to Central Europe. Splitting his forces, he sent one army to Poland under the leadership of his chief general, Subutai, and he led another army himself toward Hungary. Both armies were victorious, and by 1242, Batu added Hungary, Poland, and the Danube River Valley to the areas under his control.

Batu next prepared to invade Western Europe—an invasion that most scholars believe would have ravaged much of the continent. However, in 1242, he received word of the death of Ögödei, the Mongol khan (lord), and was recalled to Karakorum in central Asia to participate in the choice of a successor. Batu thus withdrew his armies from Europe.

After participating in the election of the new khan, Batu returned to Russia and established the Kipchac khanate, which came to be known as the Golden Horde. He chose an area on a lower stretch of the Volga River to found his capital city of Sarai Batu. Batu died in 1255, while preparing for further military conquests.

See also: Genghis Khan; Mongol Empire; Yuan Dynasty.

Baudouin (1930–1993 C.E.)

King of Belgium (r. 1951–1993), who helped rebuild his nation after World War II and worked hard to alleviate poverty in Belgium and around the world.

Baudouin Charles Leopold Axel Marie Gustave was born in 1930, the eldest son of King Leopold III of Belgium (r. 1934–1951), and Astrid, a Swedish princess. Befitting a member of a modern royal family, Baudouin received an excellent education and was regarded as an eager student and quick learner by his teachers.

In May 1940, when Germany invaded Belgium after the start of World War II, Baudouin's father, King Leopold III, recognized the futility of trying to resist the Nazis and surrendered. Leopold and his family were held under house arrest for most of the war. After the war ended in 1945, the place of Belgium's royal family in their postwar nation was uncertain. Leopold and his family, including Baudouin, went into voluntary exile in Switzerland until 1950, when Leopold III returned as king.

Because of questions about his conduct during the war, Leopold III faced strikes and violent protests when he returned to Belgium. In order to avoid further disruption in his country and to save the monar-

chy, Leopold abdicated in 1951, and his son Baudouin ascended the throne. In 1960 Baudouin wed Doña Fabiola Mora y Aragón, a Spanish noblewoman. They had no children.

During Baudouin's reign, the Belgian Congo, Belgium's principal colony in Africa, was granted independence. In 1976, Baudouin began the King Baudouin Foundation, the aim of which is to study and alleviate poverty around the world. This foundation remains active today, issuing publications and funding antipoverty projects as well as artistic endeavors. Baudouin also promoted the cause of the North Atlantic Treaty Organization (NATO) and served at the forefront of efforts to develop greater integration of Europe economically, politically, and socially.

A very religious man, King Baudouin was adamantly opposed to abortion. In 1990, when the Belgian parliament passed a law to liberalize abortion, Baudouin refused to sign the legislation, which was necessary for the bill to become law. To enable passage of the bill, the parliament had to declare the king unable to rule on April 4, 1990, while it signed the bill into law. The next day, they rescinded their ruling on the king, declaring him capable of reigning, and he resumed his place on the throne.

Baudouin died of a heart attack in the south of Spain in 1993, after reigning in Belgium for forty-two years. He was succeeded by his brother, Albert II (r. 1993–).

See also: Belgian Kingdom.

Behavior, Conventions of Royal

Behaviors expected and exhibited by monarchs as a result of their position and role as rulers of their society or symbolic head of their nation.

The behavior expected and exhibited by monarchs has varied greatly among different monarchical cultures. One important difference is that between monarchs who are expected to maintain their distance from their subjects and cultivate their own exalted status, and monarchs who are expected to be on an equal footing with their subjects.

At one extreme are the contemporary monarchs of Scandinavia and the Netherlands, often referred to as "bicycling monarchs" for their lack of pomp or elaborate entourage. These monarchs cultivate an image of equality with the average person in their countries and demonstrate a detachment from politics to maintain royal status in a generally egalitarian political context. At the other extreme are rulers who are almost completely separated from society outside a small circle of family and courtiers and who cultivate an image of detachment. The imperial house of Japan has maintained such a role of separateness for much of its history.

Periods of transition from a more egalitarian to a more remote monarchy can be fraught with peril. The pretensions to divinity of Alexander the Great (r. 336–323 B.C.E.) and his adoption of Persian court etiquette generated much resentment among Macedonians and Greeks, who remembered the more informal monarchy of his father, Philip II of Macedon (r. 359–336 B.C.E.). The Emperor Augustus (r. 27 B.C.E.–14 C.E.), in managing Rome's transition from a republic to a monarchy, was careful not to behave too much like a king for fear of antagonizing Romans. For example, as emperor he continued to dress in homespun cloth rather than adopting an elaborate costume with regal insignia.

Another difference exists between warrior societies, such as those of the Romans, Mongols, and Assyrians that prize physical vigor in a ruler, and societies that accept and even encourage physical passivity in a ruler. The Chinese imperial office, for example, was often torn between a Confucian Chinese model of a physically passive ruler and a Central Asian model of a vigorous monarch. This was particularly true during the rule of dynasties with a Central Asian origin, such as the Mongol Yuan dynasty and the Manchu Ch'ing (Qing) dynasty.

Religion also affects standards of monarchical behavior. Generally, monarchs are expected to publicly conform to the duties of their faith, and they scrupulously attend or even preside over religious rituals. However, excessively religious behavior can be perceived as incompatible with other royal responsibilities. Devout early medieval rulers, such as the Carolingian ruler Louis the Pious (r. 814–840) or Edward the Confessor of England (r. 1042–1066) were often perceived as weak or insufficiently ruthless to be successful rulers, more suited to be monks than kings. Other medieval kings, notably Louis IX of France (r. 1226–1270), combined strict and sincere religious observance with highly successful domestic and foreign policies.

Accession to the throne is often expected to lead to a change in behavior, in favor of greater remoteness and self-discipline. Kings who continue to indulge in youthful frivolities at the expense of their royal duties, whatever those duties happen to be, receive virtually universal condemnation. A famous literary example is found in the history plays of William Shakespeare, where the irresponsible youth Prince Hal (in *Henry IV*) is transformed into the noble yet bloodthirsty King Henry in *Henry V*. In West Africa, the Yoruba people require each new ruler to go through a series of ceremonies in which he bids farewell to his mother, family, friends, and members of his peer group before assuming rulership—a ritual that signifies his new status as a person apart from society.

See also: EDUCATION OF KINGS; ETIQUETTE, ROYAL; KINGLY BODY; MILITARY ROLES, ROYAL; RELIGIOUS DUTIES AND POWER; SECLUSION OF MONARCH.

FURTHER READING

Bertelli, Sergio. *The King's Body: Sacred Rituals of Power in Medieval and Early Modern Europe.* Trans. R. Burr Litchfield. New rev. ed. University Park: Pennsylvania State University Press, 2001.

Pemberton, John, and Funso S. Afolayan. *Yoruba Sacred Kingship: A Power Like That of the Gods.* Washington, DC: Smithsonian Institution Press, 1996.

BELGIAN KINGDOM

(1831 C.E.–Present)

Ruling monarchy that came to power after the Belgian people won their independence from the Netherlands in 1831, following a violent uprising. A constitutional monarchy, the Belgian kingdom is one of the few European monarchies still in existence.

ORIGINS

The formation of modern Belgium has its roots in the Napoleonic Wars of the early 1800s, when the region was occupied by France. As the defeat of Napoleon Bonaparte became imminent, the major European powers convened to decide how best to split up and control the areas under French influence. This meeting, known as the Congress of Vienna (1814–1815), made the territory of Belgium part of

King Albert II, reigning monarch of Belgium, took the throne in 1993 upon the death of his older brother, King Baudouin. King Albert and his Italian-born wife, Queen Paola, have three children. The eldest, Prince Philippe, is heir to the throne.

the kingdom of the Netherlands, under King William I (r. 1815–1840).

Tensions arose immediately because the Belgians viewed William I and the Dutch as occupiers. Although Belgium's population was significantly larger than that of the Netherlands, Belgium had very little say in governmental matters. The situation worsened when William and the Dutch-dominated government tried to enforce legislation that was openly hostile to the Belgians and favorable to Holland, such as establishing Dutch as the national language. The situation came to a head in 1830 on the anniversary of William's accession, when mob fighting broke out in the Belgian city of Brussels. The revolt spread rapidly

and was handled so poorly by the Dutch that the Belgians won their independence in less than six months.

After creating a constitution with a parliamentary government and limited royal power, Belgian officials voted to name Leopold of the House of Saxe-Coburg-Gotha as the new king of an independent Belgium. Leopold, who was chosen both for his personal character and the fact that his accession created a neutral state in Western Europe, took the throne as Leopold I (r. 1831–1865) in 1831.

STABILITY AND EXPANSION

Leopold had much popular support and was widely respected both in Belgium and throughout Europe.

Very well educated, he not only helped preserve the fragile kingdom but also set Belgium on a course of industrial, cultural, and economic development that benefited the fledgling nation far into the future. Leopold's death in 1865 was an occasion of great mourning throughout Belgium. Upon his death, the Crown passed to his son, Leopold II (r. 1865–1909). Unlike his venerated father, Leopold II was held in an ambiguous light by his people. On one hand, during his reign, Belgium became ever wealthier as a result of its industrial successes. However, Leopold kept much of this wealth for himself and tarnished the Belgian Crown with his passion for financial gain at any moral cost. In this vein, Leopold II is best known for his personal role in beginning Belgian colonial expansion into the African Congo, from which he extracted wealth at the great expense of its African inhabitants.

Leopold II had no immediate heirs, and upon his death in 1909, he was succeeded by his nephew, Albert I (r. 1909–1934). Shortly after Albert came to the throne, the tensions that had threatened peace across Europe for decades exploded into World War I. Almost immediately after the declarations of war in 1914, Germany invaded neutral Belgium, an act that further galvanized support for Germany's Allied opponents. Albert personally led the Belgian army, and the fierce and heroic resistance of the Belgian people greatly helped the Allied cause. Away from the battlefield, Albert was a well-liked and respected ruler who worked to liberalize Belgian social institutions and improve conditions in both Belgium and its African colony.

Upon Albert's early death in a mountaineering accident in 1934, the throne passed to his son, Leopold III (r. 1934–1951). The reign of Leopold III was resolutely unpopular, in marked contrast to that of his father. When Belgium was faced with another German invasion, this time in 1940 at the start of World War II, Leopold III refused to defend his country and surrendered to Germany. Many Belgians saw Leopold's decision to surrender as an act of collusion with the Nazis, and his return to power at the end of the war was greeted with such popular disdain that he was forced to abdicate to his son, Baudouin (r. 1951–1993), in 1951.

King Baudouin was as respected as his father had been disparaged. Best known for his efforts to repair social inequalities, Baudouin oversaw the dismantling of Belgium's colonial empire as the Congo in Africa gained its independence in 1960. Baudouin died suddenly in 1993, and the Crown passed to his brother, King Albert II (r. 1993–). Albert has maintained Baudouin's role as an emissary of social justice and equality.

See also: COLONIALISM AND KINGSHIP; NATIONAL IDENTITY; NETHERLANDS KINGDOM; POSTCOLONIAL STATES; SAXE-COBURG-GOTHA DYNASTY; WILLIAM I.

FURTHER READING

Kossmann, E.H. *The Low Countries, 1780–1940.* New York: Oxford University Press, 1978.

BEMBA KINGDOM (1800s C.E.)

One of many states that arose in east-central Africa during the nineteenth century in response to the development of trade on the Swahili coast of East Africa.

In the nineteenth century, the success of the Swahili trading empire along the east coast of Africa gave rise to a great deal of wealth, not only for the Swahili but also for those peoples who traded with them. As new trade routes pushed further and further into the African interior, many of the communities the traders encountered coalesced and developed centralized governments to take better advantage of the new economic opportunities that became available. Some of these new states were motivated by the desire to improve their control over locally produced trade goods, and others by the need to gain greater control over access routes to trading centers. The Bemba, who lived in the forests of what is today northern Zambia, took a much more direct approach.

The Bemba lived in stockaded villages headed by chieftains. Since their arrival in the region in the seventeenth century, they had earned a reputation for fierceness because they were prone to staging raids on the lands and livestock of their neighbors. As the Swahili cities on the coast attracted increasing numbers of trade caravans with goods from the interior, it was only natural that these, too, would become targets of Bemba warriors.

With the wealth gained from raids on trade caravans, the Bemba were able to become traders themselves, buying European weapons and thus vastly increasing their military might. In the early 1800s, the stockaded villages of the Bemba were consolidated into a unitary state, under the leadership of the first Bemba king, Chilufya Mulenga (r. ?–1820). It is believed that Chilufya came from Luba territory and that he was one of the many members of that kingdom's ruling dynasty who were scattered when the Luba state split apart in the early years of the nineteenth century.

Under Chilufya Mulenga, the Bemba became an important power in the region, but the militaristic focus of the kingdom made it inherently unstable. Wars of succession were common, and the reigns of individual kings were generally short. The kingdom faced constant challenges from its neighbors, particularly from the Ngoni kingdom, which was attempting to expand its holdings into Bemba territory.

Although the Bemba were never conquered, by the late 1800s they were eclipsed by the Ngoni, whose superior military force enabled them to achieve regional dominance. The Ngoni did not have long to savor their newly ascendant position in the region, however. By 1900, the British South Africa Company, under Cecil Rhodes (British colonialist and entrepreneur, and founder of the colony of Rhodesia), had taken control over the entire territory. The colonial administration considered traditional kingdoms to be a liability, and Bemba rulers were stripped of their political and military powers by the start of the twentieth century.

See also: AFRICAN KINGDOMS; LUBA KINGDOM; LUNDA KINGDOM; NGONDE KINGDOM.

FURTHER READING

Roberts, Andrew D. *A History of the Bemba.* Madison: University of Wisconsin Press, 1973.

BENIN KINGDOM

(1000s–1897 C.E.)

Powerful kingdom located in the forest and coastal region of present-day Nigeria, which is known today largely for its magnificent metal artworks.

Prior to the eleventh century, the region east of the modern Nigerian city of Lagos was home to Edo-speaking peoples who lived in communities that were headed by local chiefs. However, political and economic factors combined to inspire many of these communities to draw together into a more centralized, unified state that soon became one of the most powerful forces in the region.

This bronze plaque, dating from sometime in the mid-sixteenth to mid-seventeenth century, depicts a court servant of the Benin Kingdom. The Benin people of West Africa were renowned for their metal artwork, which they often used for trade.

ORIGINS OF THE KINGDOMS

Some scholars argue that the rise of the kingdom of Benin was influenced by state formation that was occurring elsewhere in the region in the early years of the eleventh century. For one thing, the rise of Benin occurred at about the same time that the Yoruba kingdom at Ife was coming to power to the west. In addition, aspects of Benin kingship reflect practices found among the Yoruba. The Benin king bore the title *oba* (the Ife rulers were called *alefins*) but claimed to trace his descent from Oduduwa, the culture hero said to have founded the Yoruba people.

Whatever the kingdom's origins, Benin did not begin a policy of expansion until some four centuries after its founding. In the middle of the fifteenth century, Oba Ewuare (r. ca. 1440–1473) created a powerful military force with which to conquer neighboring lands and ultimately gained control over the whole of the Niger Delta and westward to Lagos. To ensure that his subject territories remained loyal to the Benin throne, he appointed governors to administer the newly conquered lands and maintain order among the peoples, supplanting the traditional local chiefs.

There is little information regarding the degree of stability enjoyed by the rulers of Benin before the reign of Ewuare. But it may be that wars of succession occurred with some frequency, for Ewuare began a practice of designating his successor while he still held the throne himself. This policy served to eliminate the disorder and confusion that often follows the death of kings, as various rival claimants fight among themselves to claim the right to rule.

EXPANSION AND WEALTH

The period of Benin expansion, which continued throughout the second half of the fifteenth century, coincided with the arrival of the Portuguese at Lagos, bringing Benin into contact with a much expanded trading network. The Portuguese, who were already trading with Akan kingdoms further up the coast, sought goods that would bring them much Akan gold. Benin was oversupplied with war captives, thanks to its campaigns of conquest, and was more than willing to trade them to the Portuguese as slaves. This slave trade continued until Benin had reached the limits of its expansion and thus no longer had a surfeit of captives for trade. Nonetheless, the kingdom remained a trading partner with the Portuguese, offering items such as ivory and pepper.

The Benin king used the wealth acquired through trade not only to support his army, but also to underwrite artistic expression. He commissioned works of brass and copper that celebrated the reigning *oba*. Artworks in these metals, as well as works in ivory, were also created for trade. The king tightly controlled the secrets of brassworking and other artistic methods, ensuring that Benin kept a monopoly on the production of these trade goods.

PERIOD OF DECLINE

The kingdom of Benin remained relatively stable until the eighteenth century. At that time, the administration of the now far-flung empire broke down, and the kingdom was wracked with civil wars.

With the restart of war in Benin territory, the rulers again began taking captives, which were once again offered for sale into the Atlantic slave trade. Decades of civil unrest followed. The disruption was further aggravated as more and more people discovered the profits to be made in the slave trade, a discovery that led many to turn from their normal pursuits to become raiders in search of captives.

By the late 1800s, Benin was significantly weakened, and it was thus easily annexed by Great Britain, which made it part of its colony of Nigeria. In 1897, after looting the capital city (also named Benin), the British brought the power of the *obas* to an end.

See also: AFRICAN KINGDOMS; YORUBA KINGDOMS.

FURTHER READING

Ryder, Alan: "Benin State and History." In *Encyclopedia of Africa South of the Sahara*, John Middleton, ed. New York: Charles Scribner's Sons, 1997.

BERAR KINGDOM (1490–1574 C.E.)

Kingdom in central India that began as a province of the Muslim Bahmani kingdom but that eventually gained a short period of autonomy in the late fifteenth and early sixteenth centuries.

Berar originated in the mid-fourteenth century as a province in the Bahmani kingdom. To manage their large kingdom, the Bahmani monarchs had divided it into four provinces; Berar occupied the northeast region of the kingdom. Initially, the Berar province contained two territories: Gawil in the north and Mahur in the south. Each of these territories had a major fortress, and the two combined to protect Bahmani's northern frontier.

GAINING INDEPENDENCE

During the late fifteenth century, the Bahmani kingdom slowly crumbled as a result of internal unrest, and the provincial governors increasingly rejected Bahmani control. In 1490, during the reign of the last major Bahmani monarch, Mahmud Shah (r. 1482–1518), Berar became the first province to declare its independence. The provincial governor, Fathullah, adopted the royal appellation Imad-ul Mulk (r. 1490–1504) and became the first monarch of the Berar kingdom.

Berar did not sever all ties with Bahmani, however. In deference to the Bahmani sultan, Imad-ul Mulk and the other governors refused to adopt any divine appellations or to declare themselves as heavenly chosen rulers. They also maintained close economic ties with Bahmani and used Bahmani currency instead of issuing their own. Furthermore, the former provinces united their forces to battle their common enemies, the Vijayanagar Empire and the kingdom of Orissa.

DEALING WITH OTHER STATES

When the last Bahmani sultan died in 1538, the relationship among the former provinces became increasingly fractious because each sought to dominate the Deccan region. Although Berar possessed the imposing fortresses at Gawil and Mahur, their overall military strength was weak. The three other former Bahmani provinces—Ahmadnagar, Bijapur, and Golconda—had much larger armies and threatened repeatedly to invade Berar in order to gain a larger presence in the region.

Because of their military weakness, the Berar monarchs relied upon diplomacy to prevent any encroachments upon their territory. During the late 1400s and early 1500s, Imad-ul Mulk and his successors negotiated highly fluid alliances with Ahmadnagar, Bijapur, and Golconda, pledging fealty to whichever state currently appeared to gain control over the region. Berar loaned whatever limited military forces it had to attacks against Vijayanagar and Orissa, and the kingdom also maintained its traditional role in defending the Deccan's northern frontier.

The Berar monarchs also offered substantial tributes to their neighbors to curb the possibility of invasion. Portions of Berar were agriculturally rich, and the kingdom used its crop surpluses to appease the surrounding kingdoms. Berar also operated some highly productive mines, which yielded both gold and silver. The Berar rulers often utilized these precious metals to preserve the kingdom's freedom.

Because of its central location, Berar was a key trading center. Goods from other Indian states and China arrived in Berar, and traders from as far away as Portugal and Italy frequented the kingdom's markets. Great amounts of ivory, spices, cotton, silk, and jewelry passed through the cities and trading centers of the kingdom. The Berar government heavily taxed the trading industry and used the income to pay tribute to its potential enemies.

FALL OF THE KINGDOM

Despite its prosperity and attempts to maintain autonomy, the Berar kingdom ultimately failed to keep its independence. The kingdom's military weakness and crucial geographic location made it too inviting a target. In 1574, forces from the Ahmadnagar kingdom invaded Berar and quickly subdued it.

With this defeat, Berar lost its brief autonomy and was incorporated into the Ahmadnagar kingdom. But its status as a province of Ahmadnagar was also fleeting. In 1596, in an effort to appease the rulers of the encroaching Mughal Empire, the Ahmadnagar ruler ceded Berar to the Mughal sultan, Akbar I, the Great (r. 1556–1605). Berar thus became part of the rapidly expanding Mughal Empire and fully lost its identity as an independent state.

See also: AHMADNAGAR KINGDOM; BAHMANI DYNASTY; GOLCONDA KINGDOM; INDIAN KINGDOMS; MUGHAL EMPIRE; VIJAYANAGAR EMPIRE.

BERENGAR, RAYMOND. *See*

CATALONIA, COUNTY OF

BETSIMISARAKA KINGDOM

(ca. 1751 C.E.–Present)

Kingdom along the eastern coast of the island of Madagascar, established in the eighteenth century, which was one of three great states formed after the early 1700s.

The island of Madagascar has been home to a great many ethnic groups, drawn not only from the African mainland but also from various Arab states, Malaysia, and Oceania. The first arrivals may have come to the island as much as fifteen hundred years ago, and there is archaeological evidence that attests to an Arab presence as early as 900. The result of all this immigration was a highly diverse population that gave rise to a great many individual kingdoms.

Three of these kingdoms rose to particular prominence. Of these, the Merina kingdom of the highland region and the Menabe kingdom on the western coast became powerful in the early nineteenth century. The Betsimisaraka, who lived along the eastern coast of Madagascar, founded their kingdom somewhat earlier, in the mid-1700s. Betsimisaraka lands stretched for approximately four hundred miles along the coast, in a narrow band from the Bemarivo River in the north to the Mananjary River in the south.

According to oral tradition, the Betsimisaraka territory was settled by the early immigrants from the Middle East, who came to the island sometime before 1000. These immigrants intermarried with Africans who had come to Madagascar from the African mainland. Until the last half of the seventeenth century, these people occupied several distinct settlements, each with its own political center and ruling elite. The economy of these early states was based on trade.

Sometime toward the end of the seventeenth century, the northernmost of the Betsimisaraka states received a visitor—a British-born sea captain named Thomas Tew who, by all accounts, was a pirate. Tew is said to have been received with such great favor by the local ruler, a woman named Antanavaratra Rahena, that he fathered a son with her. Tew returned to the sea, but his son, Ratsimilaho, remained behind to be raised in the ruling household.

Antanavaratra Rahena died sometime around 1710, and her son succeeded her as ruler of the northern Betsimisaraka. Although the new king was still only in his mid- to late teens, he proved both politically and militarily able. He quickly succeeded in drawing the two other Betsimisaraka groups into a confederation, and it is this larger political organization that has come to be known as the Betsimisaraka kingdom. The kingdom grew in power and wealth, largely because of its control over the busy port city of Toamasina and the access this provided to the flow of gold and ivory from the Swahili trade centers on the East African coast.

The reign of King Ratsimilaho (r. ca. 1710–1756) was a time of great prosperity, but his successors proved less capable. After his death in 1756, the power and wealth of Betsimisaraka waned steadily. By the early 1800s, the Merina kingdom of the highlands had extended its control over most of the island, and Betsimisaraka was but one of many lesser kingdoms that submitted to Merina dominance.

See also: AFRICAN KINGDOMS; MADAGASCAR KINGDOMS; MERINA KINGDOM.

FURTHER READING

Kottack, Conrad Phillip, Jean-Aime Rokotoarisoa, Aidan Southall, and Pierre Verin, eds. *Madagascar: Society and History*. Durham, NC: Carolina Academic Press, 1986.

BEYEZID II (1447–1512 C.E.)

Ottoman sultan (r. 1481–1512) best known for his consolidation of Ottoman sovereignty in Eastern Europe and for his benevolence towards the Jews. Beyezid II was born in 1447 in the Greek region of Thrace, the heartland of Ottoman-ruled territory in Europe. The son of Mehmed II (r. 1451–1481), Beyezid was a child five years of age when his father defeated the last Byzantine stronghold and made Constantinople the new Ottoman capital. When Mehmet II died in 1481, Beyezid was appointed his successor, triumphing over a challenge by his brother Cem, who also sought the throne.

During Beyezid II's reign, the Ottoman Empire established or tightened its control over such areas as Herzegovina, the Crimea, and Greece. He helped make the empire a major sea power, building a navy capable of competing with that of the Republic of Venice, a constant rival and occasional enemy. Called "the Sufi" (a term referring to members of Islamic mystical religious orders) because of his strong religious devotion, Beyezid strengthened Islamic institutions by financing the construction of public works and mosques. In 1492, when Ferdinand and Isabella of Spain expelled the Jews from Iberia, Beyezid welcomed the skilled, educated, and prosperous community of exiled Jews into his empire, where they flourished and contributed to Ottoman wealth and power. Beyezid's later reign was marred by a power struggle between his two sons and potential heirs, Selim and Murad. In 1512, Beyezid abdicated in favor of Selim (r. 1512–1520) and died a month later.

See also: MEHMED II, THE CONQUEROR; OTTOMAN EMPIRE; SELIM I, THE GRIM.

BHAGNAGAR KINGDOM. See

HYDERABAD KINGDOM

BHARATPUR KINGDOM

(1722–1947 C.E.)

Former Hindu state in India, located south of the city of Delhi and bordering on the Mathura and Agra districts, which was known for its strong army.

The rulers of Bharatpur traced their history back to the eleventh century to the Tomara clan of Delhi and the Jadon clan of Bayana, princely landowning families (Rajputs). Toward the end of the reign of Emperor Aurangzeb (r. 1658–1707) of the Mughal Empire, these families were plundering the countryside and consolidating their power. In 1722, the Mughals recognized Bharatpur as a self-governing kingdom.

Bharatpur rose to importance under Suraj Mal Jat (r. 1751–1764) who plundered Delhi in 1753. In 1756, Suraj Mal received the title of Raja ("Prince") and subsequently joined the great army of the Maratha Confederacy, contributing about 30,000 troops. By 1763, Suraj Mal had taken the city of Agra, and it was estimated that he had a formidable military force of 60,000 to 70,000 men.

In 1803, Ranjit Singh Bahadur Farzand Jung (r. 1778–1825) of Bharatpur broke the Treaty of Bassein (1802) by siding with the Maratha Confederacy against the British. In response, the British under Lord Lake made four unsuccessful attempts to storm the fort of Bharatpur, in 1804 and 1805, before withdrawing. A new treaty guaranteed Ranjit Singh his land and protection in return for a large sum of money paid to the British East India Company.

In 1825, a dispute over the right of succession led Raja Durjan Sal (r. 1825–1826) to seize the fort at Bharatpur. A British force of 20,000 men under Lord Combermere took the fort a year later, demolished it, and placed Balwant Singh Bahadur Jung (r. 1826–1853), the son of the former Raja, on the Bharatpur throne.

Over the next fifty years, the British tightened their hold on the administration of Bharatpur. This was made even easier when, in 1853, a three-year-old boy, Jaswant Singh Bahadur Jung (r. 1853–1893), inherited the Crown. He ruled under a council of regency until he received full powers in 1872.

In 1895, the British deposed Maharaja Ram Singh (r. 1893–1900) because he had arranged the murder of one of his personal attendants. He was succeeded by his infant son, Brijendra Sawai Kishen Singh (r. 1900–1929), who reigned under the regency of his mother, Maharani Sri Maji Sahiba Bibiji Girraj Kaur, until he reached the age to rule alone in 1918. Bharatpur became part of the new nation of India when it gained its independence from Great Britain in 1947.

See also: INDIAN KINGDOMS; RAJASTHAN KINGDOM; SOUTH ASIAN KINGDOMS.

BHUTAN KINGDOM

(747 C.E.–Present)

Small landlocked kingdom of south-central Asia, located on the eastern rim of the Himalayas between India in the south and Tibet in the north, which for centuries was jointly controlled by both a Buddhist spiritual leader and a temporal leader.

EARLY PERIOD

The earliest documented history of the Bhutan kingdom concerns Guru Padsambhava, also called Guru Rinpoche, a Buddhist master who is said to have traveled over the mountains from Tibet to Bhutan flying on the back of a tigress. According to tradition, Guru Rinpoche founded the Nyingmapa religious school and was even thought to be the second Buddha.

Over the following centuries, many great Buddhist masters preached in Bhutan, so the religion had become very widespread there by the eighth century. Although Bhutan was originally a sectarian state, the lama (teacher) and administrator Shabdrung Ngawang Namgyal unified it in the seventeenth century under the Drupka Kagyupa sect of Mahayana Buddhism.

The mountainous country of Bhutan existed as an isolated kingdom as late as the first half of the twentieth century. Its rough mountains and thick forests made access from the outside world nearly impossible, and Bhutan's rulers fostered its isolation by forbidding foreigners to enter the country.

In 1907, Bhutan's first king, Sir Ugyen Wangchuck (r. 1907–1926), was elected, beginning the country's system of democratic monarchy. In the decades that followed, nearby nations whose trade could benefit from access to Bhutan succeeded in penetrating the country, and the new outside contacts led to modernization of the economy and social system.

CHINESE AND BRITISH DOMINANCE

Even though it was isolated for centuries, Bhutan was invaded a number of times. In 1720, a Chinese imperial army attacked Tibet and made both Tibet and Bhutan vassal states. In 1864–1865, the British defeated the Bhutanese, who signed a treaty giving Great Britain control of Bhutan's southern border passes. The treaty also consented to British guidance in external (but not internal) affairs in exchange for receiving an annual subsidy.

In 1949, Bhutan signed a treaty with recently in-

For centuries, the tiny Asian kingdom of Bhutan had a feudal-like society and was isolated from the rest of the world. King Jigme Singye Wangchuk, who took the throne in 1972, continued the policy of modernization begun by his father, King Dorji Wangchuk.

dependent India, which allowed that country to assume Britain's role in regard to Bhutan. In addition to receiving an annual subsidy from India, Bhutan was given a piece of land in Assam called the Dewangiri.

When the People's Republic of China occupied Tibet in 1950, Bhutan strengthened its relationship with India, hoping to forestall China's attempts to occupy Bhutan as well. When China threatened to gain sovereignty over some Bhutanese territory, India fortified its defensive troops along Bhutan's border with Tibet in the north. Construction began on a road network within Bhutan going toward India, and the first cars to use these roads marked the end of Bhutan's traditional isolation.

MODERN TIMES

Starting in the early 1960s, King Jigme Dorji Wangchuk (r. 1952–1972) launched a program to build up Bhutan's primitive economy and modernize its feudal-like social system. He constructed new roads and hospitals, and he set up secular schools as an option for education other than Buddhist monasteries. He also updated Bhutan's governmental structure, which eventually became a constitutional monarchy.

When Jigme Dorji Wangchuk died in 1972, his son Jigme Singye Wangchuk (r. 1972–present) became king at the early age of seventeen. Still ruler of the country, he is considered a competent and active ruler who has continued his father's efforts to modernize and to develop Bhutan without losing its strong cultural traditions or natural environment.

See also: BUDDHISM AND KINGSHIP.

FURTHER READING

Cooper, Robert. *Bhutan: Cultures of the World.* New York: Benchmark Books, 2001.

BIBLICAL KINGS (1010–586 B.C.E.)

Rulers of the ancient kingdoms of Israel and Judah, whose deeds are featured in the Bible.

To be a leader in war was the first requirement of a biblical king. Israel instituted a monarchy when the Philistine army threatened the Hebrew tribes in the early eleventh century B.C.E. Prior to 1020 B.C.E., leadership had come from charismatic tribal or clan chiefs, sometimes called judges, who could rally their people to conduct warfare against small bands of unorganized enemies. However, faced with the powerful army of the Philistines and realizing that the only thing they had in common was their religious belief in God, the people of Israel sought a strong military leader to protect and guide them.

THE FIRST BIBLICAL KINGS

Most Israelite leaders, such as the judge Gideon, refused to take the powers of kingship, agreeing with religious leaders that God alone was king. As tension mounted, however, a charismatic warrior named Saul accepted the title as the Hebrews' first king (r. ca. 1020–1010 B.C.E.).

Israel's greatest king was Saul's successor, King David (r. ca. 1010–970 B.C.E.), who was known for his brilliant military exploits. All other biblical kings stood in the military shadow of Saul and David.

In the early days of the Israelite monarchy, the royal household differed little from the other chief houses of the nation. King Saul continued to live in his ancestral estate and stopped working his fields and came forward only when required to do so. During David's forty-year reign, however, the Hebrews established an empire, with its capital at Jerusalem. Jerusalem began to resemble the capitals of other ancient Near Eastern kingdoms, with a royal court and a government bureaucracy. Moreover, the Hebrew people started to support the monarchy and such grandeur through taxes and forced labor.

COMMERCE

In times of relative peace, the biblical kings turned their energies toward the economy of Israel. King David, for example, expanded his territory to include major trade routes in Egypt, while his son and successor, King Solomon (r. 970–931 B.C.E.), after consolidating his political power in 965 B.C.E., developed commerce and shipping. As the kingdom's wealth and splendor increased, so did taxation, corruption, and unrest among the people. After the death of Solomon around 931 B.C.E., the ten northern tribes revolted and set up their own kingdom of Israel in the north. The Kingdom of Judah was in the south.

SUCCESSION

Traditionally, the Hebrews hand over power from father to son. When Gideon died, for example, his son Abimelech succeeded him as judge. But this did not happen in the case of Saul, who was invited by the people to be king. Saul thought that his son Jonathan should replace him as king, but the people chose David instead while Saul was still on the throne. David did not pass the power to his son Adonijah but gave the Crown to his younger son, Solomon. In later years, the succession in the kingdom of Judah remained in the house of David, and the northern kingdom of Israel followed the same pattern, except for those frequent occasions when violence and revolution destroyed the royal house and brought a new ruler to the throne.

HIGH PRIESTS AND JUDGES

The Hebrew people expected the biblical kings to be their high priests and supreme judges in all matters. This was based on a nomadic tradition, in which the head of the family was expected to be the oracle of God who would judge all matters. Moses took this role during the formation of the twelve tribes, and he passed it down to the clan or tribal chiefs when they settled in the land of Canaan in Palestine.

Saul had held the trust of the people until David took it from him. King Solomon built the temple in Jerusalem, which was the center and rallying point of the Hebrew religion. But he lost the people's respect for him as a judge because of his oppression of the poor, injustice in the law courts of Jerusalem, and the introduction of pagan practices into religion.

ROYAL CORRUPTION

Solomon's legacy of royal corruption continued with his successors. Some were adventurous murderers, such as the military officer, King Zimri (r. 885 B.C.E.), who killed his predecessor and ruled as king of Israel for only seven days. Others were treacherous and worshiped other gods. Athaliah (r. 841–836 B.C.E.), the only reigning biblical queen, worshiped Baal and seized power after her son died by massacring all but one of the heirs to the throne, whom a priest had hidden in the temple. At times, such acts of despotic violence went by unchallenged. However, after a few years of Athaliah's rule, a temple guard dragged the queen from the temple and killed her. Then Joash (r. 836–796 B.C.E.), the missing heir, was crowned king at the age of seven.

On other occasions, ancient Hebrew law and customs exercised considerable restraint on the biblical kings. When Naboth refused to sell his vineyard to King Ahab (r. 874–853 B.C.E.), the king was unable to force him to sell. However, Ahab was able to condemn Naboth before a military tribunal and then took the land.

Some kings were able to rise above the corruption. King Jehohshaphat (r. 867–846 B.C.E.) set up a complete legal system, with judges in all the larger cities and courts of appeal in Jerusalem. Other rulers attempted religious reform, and King Omri (r. 885–874 B.C.E.), though spiritually deficient, brought peace and prosperity to the land.

END OF THE KINGDOMS

The kingdoms of Israel and Judah were located between the larger and more powerful kingdoms of Mesopotamia, to the northeast, and Egypt, to the southwest. In 722 B.C.E. the Assyrians conquered Israel and dispersed the ten tribes of Israelites throughout the Middle East. The kingdom of Judah continued for more than a century, caught up in a power struggle between the Assyrians, the Egyptians, and the Babylonians. In 597 B.C.E., the Babylonian king of Mesopotamia, Nebuchadrezzar II (r. 604–562 B.C.E.), captured Jerusalem and deported 10,000 of its inhabitants to Babylon.

King Zedekiah (r. 596–586 B.C.E.) was left in Judah to serve Babylon, but he and the people of Judah rebelled. Nebuchadrezzar attacked Judah again in 588–587 B.C.E. Zedekiah was forced to watch the murder of his sons, and then he was blinded and taken to Babylon. Nebuchadrezzar then destroyed Jerusalem in 586 B.C.E., bringing the kingdom of Judah to an end.

See also: ASSYRIAN EMPIRE; COMMERCE AND KINGSHIP; DAVID; ISRAEL, KINGDOMS OF; JUDAH, KINGDOM OF; SOLOMON.

FURTHER READING

Galil, G. *The Chronology of the Kings of Israel and Judah.* Leiden: Brill Academic Publishers, 1996.

Grottanelli, C. *Kings and Prophets: Monarchic Power, Inspired Leadership, & Sacred Text in Biblical Narrative.* New York: Oxford University Press, 1999.

BIDAR KINGDOM (1518–1619 C.E.)

An independent kingdom that emerged in central India after the dissolution of the Bahmani dynasty in the early sixteenth century.

In 1518, upon the death of Mahmud (r. 1482–1518), the last powerful Bahmani monarch, four major Bahmani territories—Ahmadnagar, Golconda, Berar, and Bijapur—declared their independence. Only the land around the Bahmani capital of Bidar remained under the control of Mahmud's weakened descendants in the Bahmani dynasty.

A government official named Kasim Barid assumed control of Bidar and installed one of Mahmud's children as a puppet monarch. Consequently, Kasim and his son, Amir, preserved the illusion of Bahmani control until the last Bahmani descendant died in 1527. With the Bahmani line ended, Amir appointed himself ruler of Bidar, as Amir Barid Shah I (r. 1527–1542) and started his own dynasty, the Baridshahi.

The Baridshahi dynasty never attained lasting stability, however, because fierce rivalries soon arose among the kingdoms of Bidar, Bijapur, Ahmadnagar, and Golconda. Because Bidar was the smallest kingdom, it faced repeated threats from its more powerful neighbors. In 1531, Bijapur invaded Bidar and claimed the majority of its land. In response, Bidar allied with Ahmadnagar to resist the Bijapur forces. After Bijapur defeated the allies, however, Bidar readily changed sides and agreed to support Bijapur in an approaching conflict with Golconda.

In 1542, Bidar again seized a dubious opportunity. Convinced that Bijapur had been weakened by incessant warfare, the new Bidar monarch, Ali Barid Shah I (r. 1543–1579), forged an alliance with Ahmadnagar and again invaded Bijapur. The plan had disastrous consequences for Bidar. Ahmadnagar betrayed the hapless Ali Barid, seized control of Bidar, and divided the small kingdom with Bijapur. When the alliance between Ahmadnagar and Bijapur deteriorated, the Golconda ruler, Jamshid Qutb Shah (r. 1543–1550), intervened. In 1548, he negotiated the return of Ali Barid to the Bidar throne and positioned Bidar as a buffer state between Ahmadnagar and Bijapur.

A common threat eventually allayed the hostilities among the various kingdoms. The kingdom of Vijayanagar, the bitter adversary of the former Bahmani state, sought to capitalize on the widespread dissension among the former Bahmani territories and crush them. In 1565, Bidar, Ahmadnagar, Golconda, and Bijapur formed a confederacy to counter the kingdom of Vijayanagar. Their combined forces defeated the invaders in a massive battle at Talikota in January 1565.

Under the auspices of the confederacy, however, Bidar gradually lost its autonomy. Instead of using military action against Bidar, the much larger Bijapur used its size to gradually absorb the smaller kingdom. In 1619, Bidar officially lost its independence and became part of Bijapur.

See also: AHMADNAGAR KINGDOM; BAHMANI DYNASTY; GOLCONDA KINGDOM; INDIAN KINGDOMS; VIJAYANAGAR EMPIRE.

FURTHER READING

Majumdar, R.C., ed. *The Mughal Empire.* Bombay: Bharatiya Vidya Bhavan, 1974. Vol. 7 of *The History and Culture of the Indian People.*

Srivastava, Ashirbadilal. *The History of India: 1000 A.D.– 1707 A.D.* Jaipur: Shiva Lal Agarwala, 1964.

BIMBISARA. *See* MAGADHA KINGDOM

BINDUSARA. *See* ASOKA

BLOIS-CHAMPAGNE DYNASTY

(928–1391 C.E.)

Two powerful, related noble families of medieval France, who played a leading role in French history. Among the descendants of the counts of Blois was a king of England, Stephen (r. 1135–1154). The counts of Champagne, descended from the younger sons of the counts of Blois, were poets, Crusaders, and patrons of the arts. Both lines were ancestors of kings of France.

THE FAMILIES OF BLOIS AND CHAMPAGNE

The counts of Blois and Champagne both established themselves on lands near the royal domains of France in the tenth century. The two families were first joined by the marriage of Liegard, daughter of Count Herbert II of Champagne (d. 943), and Thibault I of Blois (d. 975).

In the eleventh century, the lands of the two families were united under Thibault III of Blois, who also ruled Champagne as Thibault I (r. 1066–1089). But the Blois-Champagne domains were divided again in 1093, when Thibault's son and successor, Hugues (r. 1093–1125), became count of Troyes, and Hugues's brother Etienne-Henri (r. 1089–1102) became count of Blois-Chartres-Meaux. Hugues was the first in his family to officially take the title count of Champagne.

In 1083, Etienne-Henri had married Adele, the daughter of William I, the Conqueror (r. 1066–1087) of England. Their son, Stephen of Blois, later became king of England. Meanwhile, since Hugues had declared his own son illegitimate, Etienne-Henri's son Thibault II (r. 1125–1152) became heir of both Champagne and Blois.

CHAMPAGNE AS A CULTURAL AND LITERARY CENTER

Thibault II issued special protections for merchants from Italy and other parts of Europe who came to trade in Champagne, and he instituted a regular yearly cycle of market fairs for the county. This was the origin of the great medieval fairs of Champagne, where staple goods and luxury items were traded by merchants from all over Europe.

Thibault's son, Count Henry I (r. 1152–1181), endeared himself to King Louis VII of France (r. 1137–1180), when he served with the king on the Second Crusade. Henry married Marie de France, the daughter of Louis by his first wife, Eleanor of Aquitaine. Henry, who became known as "The Liberal" because of his generosity to the clergy, was the first count of Champagne to be well-educated and to speak Latin. Marie was well-read in vernacular literature.

At their court in Champagne, Henry and Marie became well known for their patronage of writers, including the great medieval poet Chrétien de Troyes, who is known for creating the first literary version of the Arthurian legend about King Arthur and the Knights of the Round Table. Marie held "courts" in which she and her ladies debated questions of love and knightly chivalry.

In addition to patronizing art and literature, Henry followed his father's support of yearly trade fairs. He also increased the wealth of Champagne by encouraging many large merchant families of Italy and Northern Europe to establish branch houses in the county.

LATER DESCENDANTS

Henry's brother Thibault, count of Blois, married Alice, the second daughter of Louis VII of France and Eleanor of Aquitaine. With this marriage, Blois and Champagne split permanently. Thibault's descendants became counts of Chatillon as well as of Blois. After Louis VII divorced Eleanor in 1152, the French king married Adele, the sister of Henry and Thibault, and she thus became an ancestor of the future kings of France.

After the death of Henry I in 1181, Marie of Champagne served as regent for her sons. The older son, Henri II (r. 1181–1197), distinguished himself on Crusade. He married Isabella I, the queen of Jerusalem, and died in Jaffa in 1197. His younger brother, Thibault III (r. 1197–1201), inherited the county and helped organize the Fourth Crusade before his early death in 1201. Thibault's wife, Blanche of Navarre, became regent for their baby son, Thibault IV (r. 1201–1253). Blanche was an energetic and efficient administrator who strengthened the power of the counts against the vassal barons.

Thibault IV was known as *le Chansonnier* ("The Singer") because of his skill at poetry. In 1234, he inherited the Crown of the kingdom of Navarre (r. 1234–1253) on the death of his mother Blanche. His son Thibault V (r. 1253–1270) (also Thibault II of Navarre) became very close to King Louis IX of France (r. 1226–1270) and married the king's daughter, Isabel. The pious couple accompanied Louis on Crusade in 1270 and died with him there. Thibault was succeeded by his brother Henry III (r. 1270–1274). When Henry's only son predeceased his father, Henry's daughter Jeanne inherited the county and then ruled it (r. 1274–1305) after her father's death.

UNION WITH FRANCE

In 1285, Jeanne married the future king Philip IV (r. 1285–1314) of France; but Champagne remained separate and independent. However, in 1314, Champagne became part of the royal domain of France when Jeanne's and Philip's son became King Louis X (r. 1314–1316). Blois was purchased by Louis I, duke of Orleans, in 1391. More than 100 years later, in 1498, Louis's grandson, Duke Louis IV of Orleans, became King Louis XII of France (r. 1498–1515), and Blois was united with the French Crown.

See also: FRENCH MONARCHIES; LOUIS VII; LOUIS IX (ST. LOUIS); NAVARRE, KINGDOM OF; STEPHEN; WILLIAM I, THE CONQUEROR.

BLOOD, ROYAL

Term used in many societies to describe physical descent from royalty, a quality that is usually considered necessary for succession to the throne. As a source of life and power, blood often has a ritual connotation, and this is especially true for royal blood. In the Akuapem kingdom in Ghana, for instance, the king's throne, or Black Stool, derives its power from the blood of a member of his lineage poured onto it.

The qualities considered necessary for kingship are thought to pass through the blood to one's descendants. For example, the early Germanic tribes in Europe chose as king the man they thought could best represent their descent groups before the gods.

(The English word "king" originally came from *cyn* or *kin*.) The man they chose was thought to possess *Heil*, good fortune or charisma. In time, this quality came to be considered hereditary in the blood, and kings were selected from descendants of a king. In many societies where the original kings were considered gods, royal blood is divine blood that is passed to the first king's descendants.

Many rulers have sought to connect a new dynasty to an old one by blood lineage. For example, at the death of the last Carolingian king, Louis V (r. 986–987) in 987, Hugh Capet (r. 987–996) was chosen king in preference to the late king's brother, even though he was not in the direct blood line. However, Capet's successors in the Capetian dynasty found it advantageous to marry into the Carolingian line in order to legitimize their rule through a blood lineage.

Royal blood extends to the whole family, not just to those considered eligible for the throne. Beginning in the fourteenth century in France, the Capetian kings, in order to strengthen the legitimacy of their dynasty, began to call the sons, brothers, and uncles of the sovereign "princes of the blood" or "of the blood royal"; the daughters, sisters, and aunts were called "princesses of the blood."

To be of royal blood, one must be a descendant of a royal lineage, but not all blood descendants of a monarch are legally entitled to inherit the kingship. Kingship most often descends through the male line, in many cases through primogeniture, or inheritance by the first-born son.

Kings often marry women of royal blood to preserve that blood in the children. For this reason, in some societies, marriages take place not only within royalty, but within the same family or kin group (a practice called endogamy). Some of the pharaohs of ancient Egypt practiced brother-sister marriages. In the Eighteenth dynasty (ca.1570–1293 B.C.E.), a pharaoh might marry his half-sister, as was the case with Tutankhamen (r. ca. 1332–1322 B.C.E.) and his wife Ankhesenamun.

Marriage between full brother and sister was practiced only in the Ptolemaic dynasty (323–30 B.C.E.).

Brother-sister marriage in ancient Egypt preserved a concentrated bloodline and imitated the marriage of the brother and sister deities, Isis and Osiris. Marriage to a sister could also prevent her from becoming a political rival or allow her to keep her assets from a previous marriage within the family.

During the fourteenth and fifteenth centuries C.E. among the Incas of Peru, the emperors also married their sisters in order to preserve the royal blood, apparently in imitation of their ancestor, Manco Capac (ca. 1200), the mythical first Inca emperor, who married one of his sisters.

Succession to the kingship is often forbidden if the bloodline is considered diluted. In European monarchies, according to a custom of Germanic origin, children born of a morganatic marriage (a marriage between a man of royal blood and a woman of lower rank) are disqualified from ruling.

Many people try to prove that their bloodline is royal in order to claim that they are descended from royalty. The publication of royal pedigrees and peerage books in England and elsewhere indicates the fascination that royal blood still holds.

See also: ACCESSION AND CROWNING OF KINGS; INCEST, ROYAL; INHERITANCE, ROYAL; MARRIAGE OF KINGS; PRIMOGENITURE.

FURTHER READING

Hallam, Elizabeth M., and Judith Everard. *Capetian France, 987–1328*. 2d ed. New York: Longman, 2001.

Hindley, Geoffrey. *The Royal Families of Europe*. New York: Carroll & Graf, 2000.

Shaw, Ian, ed. *The Oxford History of Ancient Egypt*. New York: Oxford University Press, 2002

BODIES, POLITIC AND NATURAL

In *The King's Two Bodies: A Study in Mediaeval Political Theology*, Ernst H. Kantorowicz places the concept of the king's two bodies "in its proper setting of medieval thought and political theory." He begins his analysis with reference to Edmund Plowden, a sixteenth-century lawyer whose *Reports* (1571) has been described as "the chief Elizabethan source for the metaphor of the king's two bodies." Plowden writes:

> For the King has in him two Bodies, *viz.*, a Body natural, and a Body politic. His Body natural (if it be considered in itself) is a Body mortal, subject to all Infirmities that come by Nature or Accident, to the Imbecility of Infancy or old Age, and to the like Defects that happen to the natural Bodies of other People. But his Body politic is a Body that cannot be seen or handled, consisting of Policy and Government, and constituted for the Direction of the People, and the Management of the public weal, and this Body is utterly void of Infancy, and old Age, [. . .] So that [the King] has a Body natural, adorned and invested with the Estate and Dignity royal; and he has not a Body natural distinct and divided by itself from the Office and Dignity royal, but a Body natural and a Body politic together indivisible.

Plowden's *Reports* was written as part of a legal controversy regarding a monarch's right to own land. Queen Elizabeth had asked for clarification regarding her right to lease the duchy of Lancaster a piece of land owned by the Lancastrian kings as private property and not as property of the Crown. According to Plowden and his fellow lawyers, a king (the monarch was always referred to as a king in these documents, even though she was a queen) did not share a subject's freedom to own or dispose of property by giving it to his children in his will: the monarch could not own land in his body natural because his body natural was indivisible from his body politic, and the body politic never died. At the "demise" of a king's body natural, the body politic migrated to the body natural of the succeeding king. Lawyers used the metaphor of the king's two bodies in order to deal with the paradox that individual monarchs died, but the Crown survived. The lawyers were formulating an idea of the state as a perpetual corporation, and when they spoke of the body politic, they referred to a specific quality: the essence of corporate perpetuity.

In referring to both this metaphysical concept of the king's two bodies and to the older collective metaphor of the realm as a political body with the king as its head, Plowden and his fellow lawyers combined two distinct but related medieval theories of monarchy, and thereby facilitated a distinction between the king who was the realm and so above the law and the king who was a subject under the law. Both of these concepts of the body politic were current in the early seventeenth century. While succession anxieties brought on by Elizabeth's advancing age led to an emphasis on the state as a perpetual corporation, the ambitions of James I to unify England and Scotland brought numerous allusions to Britain as a single body with James as its head.

The idea of the two bodies of rulers can be traced, in some ways, to ancient Roman belief about the Caesars. On the day of a triumphal parade, the victorious general or ruler would ride a glorious chariot and be dressed like the Roman god, Jupiter. When the general or ruler arrived at the Capitol, the slave riding with him would hold a crown over his head and whisper, "*Memento quod es homo* (Remember that you are a man)." On the other hand, it was clear that the Caesars were considered divine in their own right. As early as 7 B.C.E., Roman altars were dedicated to the *genius* (talent) of Augustus. Caligula had temples and priests that sacrificed to his *numen* (divine will). In the Caesars' capacity as *Pontifex Maximus* (greatest priest), the ruler offered sacrifices and received them as well.

Around 1100 C.E., a theological and political treatise was written by an unknown cleric from Normandy. This monk, commonly referred to as the "Norman Anonymous," emphasized another dual nature of kingship. In this text, the king is not like other men in his natural body. He is a "super-man" with special qualities not given to ordinary people. The king is also a "shadow" or imitator of Christ, based on Christian doctrine. In this way, the king is seen as divine and becomes a god-like being through his coronation, when he receives his ability to rule from heaven. The ideal of the king having a human nature and being made divine by grace served as the foundation for the later doctrine of the "king's two bodies."

The king also was considered a religious figure in the Middle Ages, since he ruled with the grace of heaven. He was a mediator between his people and heaven, as well as a sacred representative. Many kings wore clerical symbols, such as a sacred ring, to signify their religious aspects. The crossover between the church and the state led to ongoing challenges of authority between popes and kings during the medieval period. While the Church was Christ's mystical body, the kingdoms were considered "holy empires" inasmuch as kings under divine grace ruled them. Kingly power should maintain Christian rule by punishing evil-doers, issuing laws, summoning men for military service, and creating order in society.

In nearly every culture where there are both kings and gods, people have considered how these powers relate. Rulers connect themselves to gods to show they are more than just regular human beings. Many kings gain the right and authority to rule from one or more divine powers. Christianity believes that a divine power, or god, is an all-powerful, eternal being without faults. The problem with making kings into gods in Christian belief is the obvious fact that kings, as human beings, get sick, old, and eventually die just like everyone else.

In other belief systems, divine powers are born, have lives, change, are vulnerable, and can die. So kings can have both divine power and the qualities of their gods without any of the difficulties presented by Christian beliefs. For example, in Fiji, rulers were made from "different clay" than their subjects, so the king could be considered to be divine without people wondering what made him so different. Hawaiian kings were believed to have spiritual power, or *mana*, within their bodies that would harm commoners if they got too close. This *mana* was believed to come from the supernatural lineage of the chiefs. In Japan, imperial persons were considered to be sacred. In these societies, authority to rule comes from supernatural forces within rulers.

In general, cultures believed their kings were related to the divine powers in three ways. First, the ruler could claim to be a direct descendant of a god or become a god upon death. Egyptian pharaohs are an example. Second, the ruler could be described as having divine attributes or possessing sacred symbols, without actually being considered a god. For example, those who held the royal drum ruled the Ankole kingdom of East Africa. In early China, rulership belonged to those who had the *ting* tripods. Finally, a ruler might achieve divinity only on occasion by summoning god-like forces to himself, as needed to do battle, for example.

In many cultures, kings provide the central communication channel between gods, humans, and, in many cases, royal ancestors. The ruler determined how people should approach the god or gods. He also interpreted the divine will of the supernatural forces. The Mayan kings were examples of this type of rulership. In the eighth-century Byzantine Empire, emperors attempted to use the title "priest-king" but the pope forbade them from using the title.

In some cultures, the ruler's life cycle and mortality may become symbolic attributes of higher, more cosmic cycles and patterns. The birth, life, marriage, and death of the ruler become symbols for the life cycle of the universe, such as the sacred kings of Egypt and Persia. In this process, the king's mortality and human weaknesses are diminished, and his natural body, like his political body, becomes eternal.

See also: ACCESSION AND CROWNING OF KINGS; AUGUSTUS; CALIGULA; DIVINITY OF KINGS; EGYPTIAN DYNASTIES, ANCIENT (EIGHTEENTH TO TWENTY-SIXTH); ELIZABETH I; GENDER AND KINGSHIP; KINGLY BODY; SACRED KINGSHIPS.

FURTHER READING

Kantorowicz, Ernst H. *The King's Two Bodies: A Study in Mediaeval Political Theology.* Princeton, NJ: Princeton University Press, 1957.

BONAPARTIST EMPIRE

(1804–1815 C.E.)

Territories and peoples under French control during the reign of Emperor Napoleon I (who ruled as emperor 1804–1815). In a little less than two decades in the late 1700s and early 1800s, Napoleon was able to dominate most of Western Europe, and in doing so, he forever altered the course of European history.

ORIGINS AND EARLY SUCCESS

Napoleon's conquest of Europe actually began before he became emperor with his victories in the French Revolutionary Wars (1792–1802). Anxious to make sure that the antiroyal rebellion of the French Revolution did not spread throughout Europe, several major European powers in the 1790s indicated that they would go to war with revolutionary France to protect surrounding territories. France, in turn, declared war on these nations, unleashing a decade of warfare that dominated European affairs.

As general of the French army in Italy in 1796, Napoleon drove back the occupying Austrians in a quick-moving campaign that stunned the European military establishment. Acting independently, without sanction of the French government, Napoleon concluded a peace treaty with the Austrians that included the cession of Belgian territories to France. These would remain in French control for the entire life of the Bonapartist Empire.

As Napoleon swept through the Austrian lands in 1796–1797, his popularity soared both in France and abroad. The Italian people viewed him as a liberator and defender of freedom, while the French saw him as extending the ideals of the Revolution. The financial gains and imperial glory France reaped from these campaigns also were a factor in Napoleon's popularity with the French government, a popularity that would prove invaluable in the coming years.

With the continent under his control, Napoleon turned to Great Britain, which remained the only European nation that could effectively challenge French power. While attacking British trade routes in Egypt in 1798–1799, Napoleon saw an opportunity for a power grab unfolding in France. The government, known as the Directory, was blamed for the defeats of the French army on the continent, where many of the territories gained by Napoleon had been regained by other European powers. The French people also were growing disgusted with the Directory because of its increasingly repressive actions against internal opposition. Napoleon returned to France from Egypt and, along with two high-ranking officials, staged a coup in autumn 1799, thereby taking control of the government as first consul.

As first consul, Napoleon consolidated his power, shutting out any opposition that was likely to arise from within France. Externally, he again went to war with the Austrians, reclaiming territories for France and reasserting French dominance on the continent. Once Germany and Switzerland were under his control, and the Italian lands were back in his grasp, Napoleon faced no real challenge from any European nation except Great Britain. Meanwhile, in France, the wildly popular leader was seen as restoring the glory to a nation torn by revolt. With overwhelming support, Napoleon was elected life consul in 1802, essentially solidifying his dictatorship.

THE EMPIRE EXPANDS

France and Britain were evenly matched militarily, with the French army dominant on land and the British navy superior on the sea. As a result, war between the two nations drew to an uneasy stalemate between 1803 and 1805. With the situation in Europe fairly stable, Napoleon was overwhelmingly elected emperor in 1804, thus marking the official beginning of the Bonapartist Empire. Conflict resumed the next year, however, as Napoleon's continued expansion in Italy brought new hostilities with a coalition of Austria, Britain, Prussia, and Russia.

MARIE LOUISE (1791–1847)

Not nearly as well known as Napoleon's first wife Josephine, Marie Louise was the daughter of Austrian emperor Francis I. Her marriage to Napoleon in 1810 was essentially an insurance clause enacted between Napoleon and her father, who felt that linking his family with that of the French emperor's was the best way to maintain his own empire. Marie Louise showed very little interest in Napoleon after the birth of their child, Napoleon II. In fact, she did not return to France from her family home in Austria when Napoleon mounted his unsuccessful bid to reestablish the empire in 1815. Awarded the Duchy of Parma at the Congress of Vienna, Marie Louise was unable to secure any real inheritance for her son, whom she left alone in Vienna. She was a moderate ruler of no real distinction, and her small territories were eventually absorbed into the kingdom of Italy.

Although the British continued to dominate the French at sea, Napoleon's forces seemed unstoppable on land, quickly moving against Austria and Russia in the winter of 1805. By the summer of 1807, Napoleon forced Alexander I of Russia (r. 1801–1825) and Frederick William III of Prussia (r. 1797–1840) into a treaty that gave him their support as well as much of their territory. A renewed offensive by the Austrians was handily defeated in 1809, thus solidifying French power on the continent.

IMPERIAL ADMINISTRATION

With the empire secure, Napoleon began filling the leadership posts of the kingdoms under his control with people he thought would remain loyal to him and willing to accept French domination. In the end, however, few of these people stood by Napoleon in times of crisis, including Jean-Baptiste Bernadotte, for whom Napoleon secured the throne of Sweden in 1810 only to have him side with Napoleon's enemies soon after. Napoleon's brother Louis was made king of Holland in 1806 but was later driven out by Napoleon himself, since Louis would not cooperate with French plans to enforce a trade blockade against Britain. Another of the emperor's brothers, Jérôme, was given the Crown of Westphalia, a German kingdom, in 1807, but quickly drove his small province so deep into debt that Napoleon was forced to recall him. Most disastrously, Napoleon's brother Joseph

was put in charge of the Naples kingdom in 1806, where he accomplished few of his ambitious projects, and then the Spanish Crown in 1808, which he lost through an unwinnable guerrilla war in Spain and in a military debacle with Britain. Napoleon's sisters worked out somewhat better, however; Elisa of Tuscany and Caroline of Naples were both effective rulers.

Despite mishandling by Napoleon's chosen administrators, the Bonapartist Empire reached its peak by 1810. At that point, France controlled most of Spain and Portugal, all of Italy save for Sicily, Poland, Switzerland, all of the Low Countries north of France, and the western German kingdoms. The royal line of succession was also secure, since Napoleon had divorced his first wife, Josephine, and married a second, Marie Louise (the daughter of emperor Francis I of Austria), who bore him a son, styled Napoleon II, in 1811.

One of the most noticeable features of the Bonapartist Empire was its use of the Code Napoléon, an organized legal system set up under Napoleon's reign. The Code laid out different areas of legal jurisdiction over individuals and was applied uniformly across the empire. Despite this ostensibly egalitarian legal system, the Bonapartist Empire was anything but, as Napoleon consolidated power in France and forced local administrators to follow French dictates. Citizens were allowed almost no participation

THE BONAPARTIST EMPIRE, 1812

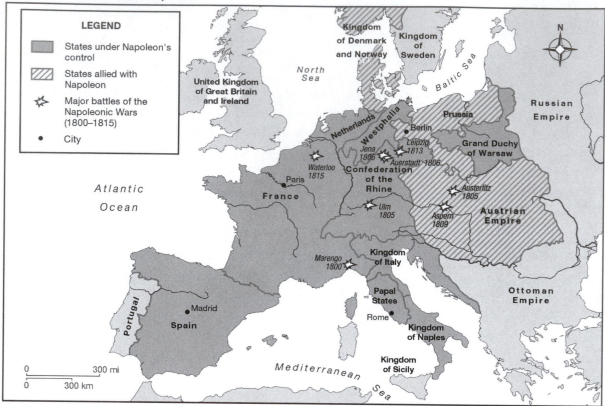

in the governmental process, and virtually every institution—from churches to schools to museums—was ultimately under the authoritarian control of Napoleon and his administrators. This tightly controlled empire, however, was on the verge of collapse from external pressures just as it was at its most extensive.

THE EMPIRE COLLAPSES

Napoleon, furious at Alexander I of Russia for refusing to follow his plan for a trade blockade of Britain, launched an attack on Russia in the summer of 1812. Despite having a huge army at his command, Napoleon was unable to defeat the Russians and was forced to retreat by the end of the year, having lost half a million soldiers. With the French military weakened, the states controlled by the empire began to revolt, forming a coalition, along with Austria, Britain, and Russia, to beat back the French. Napoleon, facing enemies on all sides, refused to surrender and finally abdicated in the spring of 1814 as the allied forces marched into Paris. The empire was finished, and Napoleon was forced into exile on the island of Elba.

Although Napoleon staged a counterattack a year later and thus reestablished the empire for 100 days, he was quickly and decisively beaten in the battle of Waterloo in June 1815. The defeated ruler was once again placed in exile, this time on the island prison of St. Helena, located in the south Atlantic off western Africa. The allied forces, meeting at the Congress of Vienna, drew up plans for a newly divided Europe. These plans, which were based on the idea that a balance of power was the best way to ensure peace, marked a decisive moment in European diplomacy and cooperative political action, and set the stage for the nationalist movements that came to dominate Europe during the rest of the century.

See also: AUSTRO-HUNGARIAN EMPIRE; CONQUEST AND KINGSHIPS; EMPIRE; MILITARY ROLES, ROYAL; NAPOLEON I (BONAPARTE); NATIONALISM.

FURTHER READING

Asprey, Robert. *The Reign of Napoleon Bonaparte.* New York: Basic Books, 2001.

BORNU EMPIRE. *See* KANEMBU-KANURI KINGDOM

BORU, BRIAN (ca. 940–1014 C.E.)

Ard Ri (high king) of Ireland (r. 1002–1014), who is credited with driving off the Vikings that had invaded Ireland in the century prior to his rule.

A younger son of Cennedig (Cenn-tig), chief of the Dal Cais tribe in the area of Munster, Brian Boru was born around 940. In the century before Brian's birth, Ireland had been invaded by Norse marauders, who eventually established a number of Viking settlements—including Dublin and Waterford—along the Irish coast. When Brian was just a child, he witnessed first-hand the violence of the Vikings, for his home village was raided and most of its inhabitants, including Brian's own mother, were killed.

Many Irish chieftains sought to avoid attacks by the Vikings by entering into treaties with these interlopers. This was the tactic adopted by Brian's brother, Mahon, when he inherited the chieftainship of the Dal Cais upon the death of their father, Cennedig. Brian, however, could not accept such a truce, so he gathered to himself several brave men and abandoned his brother's chiefdom, preferring to fight the Vikings wherever he found them.

Brian's reputation grew to legendary status as he and his followers harried the Vikings throughout southern Ireland. In time, others who chafed under the heavy-handed rule of the Vikings sought him out and joined his cause. Ultimately, even Mahon renounced his treaties with the Vikings and lent support to his brother. With so great a force at his command, Brian was able to drive most of the Vikings from southern Ireland, pushing them back to a handful of coastal settlements in the north.

Unfortunately, the Viking leader Ivar (sometimes called Imar) did not accept defeat, and sometime between 976 and 978 he returned to the attack, capturing and killing Mahon. The death of the Dal Cais chief elevated Brian to the head of the clan, and he was no more willing to tolerate a Viking presence in Ireland now than he had been previously. He called upon all the other chiefs of southern Ireland to rally to his flag, and they again expelled the Vikings. In the meantime, Brian also set about rebuilding the churches and libraries that the Vikings had destroyed.

Soon Brian had succeeded in unifying all the southern Irish clans under his rule. In the north, another strong ruler, Malachy, had done the same, but Malachy did not have the great popular support that Brian enjoyed, and in the late 900s (possibly 998), Malachy ceded his territory to Brian's rule. Thus did Brian Boru become the first Ard Ri, or high king, to unify all of Ireland.

The death of Brian Boru is attributed to one of his wives, Maelmora, who is recorded in legend as being both the most beautiful woman in all of Ireland and the most evil. Brian married her sometime after the turn of the eleventh century, but he left her a few years later. Enraged by his abandonment, she is said to have called upon the Vikings, offering to help them retake Ireland if they would kill Brian in return. Whatever their actual reasons, the Vikings did indeed return to Ireland in 1014.

Brian Boru's final battle took place on April 23, 1014, on the fields of Clontarf near Dublin The battle was fierce, and when it was over there were 4,000 Irishmen lying dead on the field. Despite the devastating Irish losses, the Vikings fared even worse. It is said that not more than twenty Vikings remained alive after this battle. During the battle, while the now aging Brian was praying in his tent, a Viking leader named Brodar came looking for him. Again, history and legend may be intertwined, but legend holds that even after Brodar struck Brian a mortal blow, the great Irish king swung his own blade and sliced the Viking's head from his shoulders. Brian Boru is celebrated today as one of Ireland's greatest heroes and as the only ruler to truly unify the entire island.

See also: IRISH KINGS; MEATH KINGDOM; MUNSTER KINGDOM.

BOUDICCA (BOADICEA) (d. 61 C.E.)

Warrior queen of the Iceni, a British tribe in Roman Britain, who led a ferocious and brutal, but ultimately unsuccessful, rebellion against the Romans.

By the reign of the Roman emperor Claudius (r. 41–54), many of the Celtic natives of Britain had accepted Roman rule and appreciated the advantages that accompanied Roman occupation, including good roads, efficient law courts, improved sanitation and water supplies, and burgeoning trade. However, the weight of Roman rule varied depending upon local enforcement and the directives of the current colonial governor.

Prasutagus, the chief (or king) of the Sussex-based tribe, the Iceni, was a reasonable and peace-loving ruler. He paid his taxes and tributes to Rome without complaint and counseled his people to work with the Romans in Britain. Unfortunately, the military governor of Britain, Caius Suetonius Paulinus, saw the colony of Britain as merely an opportunity for increasing his own wealth and prestige through ruinous taxation and continued military conquests.

Upon Prasutagus's untimely death in the year 60, his wife, Queen Boudicca, objected when Paulinus levied heavy taxes. The queen was publicly beaten and scourged for her protest. As Boudicca was recovering from her humiliation, she learned that her two daughters had been raped by the Roman officials who had ordered her punishment.

Boudicca, a red-haired woman of imposing size and demeanor, swore revenge and pledged to drive the Romans from her homeland. She bided her time and, though she traveled extensively over the next two years giving fiery speeches to many tribes, she was careful never to speak in front of Romans or their servants. She counseled all Britons to remain subservient until the time was ripe, then to rise up as one to overthrow their Roman overlords.

Boudicca's chance came in 61, when Paulinus decided to mount a large-scale attack against the island of Mona (now Anglesey in northwestern Wales), the sacred island and stronghold of the Druids. While the Roman legions were engaged at Mona, Boudicca organized a huge army of Britons, perhaps numbering one hundred thousand or more, and led it against the single legion of Roman troops that remained garrisoned at Camulodunum (Colchester) in the south of Britain.

Boudicca and her forces easily defeated the Roman garrison and mercilessly slew as many of the Romans—men, women, and children—as she could find in the Roman towns of Camulodumum, Verulamium (St. Albans), and Londinium. Estimates of the Roman dead run as high as seventy thousand.

In the midst of these massacres, Paulinus returned from a successful campaign on Mona. He carefully organized his men and waited for Boudicca's army to come to him (near modern-day Fenny Stratford). Though greatly outnumbered, the Romans, with their better discipline, tactics, and training, won the day. As many as eighty thousand Britons were left dead in the bloodiest battle yet to take place on British soil. Defeated, but not conquered, Queen

Boudicca took poison while standing in her war chariot next to her two daughters.

See also: CLAUDIUS; GENDER AND KINGSHIP; QUEENS AND QUEEN MOTHERS; ROMAN EMPIRE.

BOURBON DYNASTY

(1272 C.E.–Present)

Royal family, established in France, that has played an important role in a number of European monarchies, including those of Spain, Sicily, and the duchy of Parma in northern Italy. The Bourbon dynasty was originally a branch of the Capetian dynasty, the royal house of France that ruled continuously from 987 to 1328. Today, the Bourbon family continues to sit on the throne in Spain.

BEGINNINGS OF THE DYNASTY IN FRANCE

The Bourbon line was established in 1272 when Robert of Clermont, a son of king Louis IX of France

King Henry IV of France was the first king of the Bourbon Dynasty, a noble house founded over three hundred years earlier. A Huguenot, or French Protestant, Henry IV gave up his faith to reduce Catholic-Protestant conflict in his kingdom.

ROYAL PLACES

VERSAILLES

Louis XIV, the Sun-King, oversaw the construction of the magnificent palace of Versailles. Versailles began as a hunting lodge, built by Louis's father, Louis XIII, in 1624. Expansion of this retreat, which began in 1669, would occupy the Sun-King for the remainder of his life. The construction of the palace was an extravagance that consumed as much as 5 percent of the royal budget each year. When it was finished, Versailles contained the finest paintings, sculptures, and furnishings available, and the palace grounds included large terraces and magnificent gardens. Versailles became the official residence of the French king in 1682. Following the French Revolution, Louis Philippe turned the palace into a museum. The palace contains more than 700 rooms and 67 staircases and is set on more than 1,800 acres of parkland.

(r. 1226–1270), married Beatrice, the heiress of Bourbon. Bourbon was the seat of the Bourbonnais, a region in central France whose rulers were descended from Adhemar, a Frankish noble of the ninth century. In 1327, Robert of Clermont's son Louis became the first duke of Bourbon (r. 1327–1342), a hereditary title that passed from father to eldest son. The title died out in 1527 with the death of Duke Charles III (r. 1505–1527) of Bourbon, who had no male heirs.

A cadet branch of the dynasty, the Bourbon-Vendôme line, was established in 1548 with the marriage of Antoine de Bourbon, son of Duke Charles of Vendôme, to Jeanne d'Albret, the daughter of King Henry II of Navarre (r. 1517–1555). As a result of this marriage, the Bourbon family inherited considerable territory in southern France, and, in 1555, Jeanne became queen of Navarre (r. 1555–1572), with Antoine as her consort.

The son of Antoine and Jeanne, Henry of Navarre, became the first Bourbon king of France as Henry IV (r. 1589–1610), following the death in 1589 of French king Henry III (r. 1574–1589), who had no male heirs and was the last ruler of the House of Valois. All subsequent kings of France traced their lineage back to Henry of Navarre and the Bourbon line.

FRENCH BOURBONS

Henry IV of France was a prominent Huguenot Protestant leader prior to his marriage in 1572 to Margaret of Valois, the sister of Charles IX of France (r. 1560–1574). However, following the St. Batholomew's Day massacre of Protestants in 1572, Henry gave up his faith in order to save his life during a period of intense Catholic-Protestant conflict in France.

Although Henry subsequently returned to Protestantism, he renounced it again in 1593 in order to secure greater support for his reign. Nevertheless, in 1598, Henry established some religious freedom for Protestants with the Edict of Nantes. A religious fanatic assassinated Henry in 1610.

After Henry's death, his wife, Marie de'Medici, served as regent for their son, Louis XIII (r. 1610–1643). Louis was overshadowed by his mother, and later by the powerful Cardinal Richelieu and Richelieu's successor, Cardinal Mazarin. Richelieu's policies greatly increased royal authority and the centralization of the French government.

King Louis XIV (r. 1643–1715), the son and successor of Louis XIII, ruled France as an absolute monarch, undermining the power of the French nobles and further centralizing the government. Louis XIV emphasized grandeur, building a magnificent palace at Versailles, and he became known as the "Sun-King" because of the extravagance of his court.

Following the death of Louis XIV in 1715, the Crown went to his great-grandson, Louis XV (r. 1715–1774), whose principal adviser, André Hercule de Fleury, restored order to the national finances, reversing many of the economic problems

Bourbon Kings of France

HENRY IV*	1589–1610
LOUIS XIII	1610–1643
LOUIS XIV*	1643–1715
LOUIS XV*	1715–1774
LOUIS XVI*	1774–1793
LOUIS XVII	1793–1795
LOUIS XVIII	1814–1824
CHARLES X	1824–1830

Bourbon Kings of Spain

PHILIP V	1700–1746
LOUIS I	1724
FERDINAND VI	1746–1759
CHARLES II	1759–1788
CHARLES IV	1788–1808
FERDINAND VII	1814–1833
ISABELLA II	1833–1868

ALFONSO XII	1874–1885
ALFONSO XIII	1886–1931
JUAN CARLOS*	1975–PRESENT

Bourbon Kings of the Two Sicilies

FERDINAND I	1816–1825
FRANCIS I	1825–1830
FERDINAND II	1830–1859
FRANCIS II	1859–1860

Bourbon Dukes of Parma

PHILIP	1748–1765
FERDINAND	1765–1802
CHARLES II	1847–1849
CHARLES II	1849–1854
ROBERTO	1854–1859

*Indicates a separate alphabetical entry.

---

remaining from the reign of Louis XIV. Upon Fleury's death in 1743, Louis XV chose not to replace him, relying instead on the advice of court favorites, most notably his mistresses, Madame de Pompadour and the Comtesse Du Barry. Louis's weakness as a king resulted in growing influence for the aristocracy and increasingly serious fiscal problems for the government.

The extravagance and short-sightedness of the Bourbon kings of France were compounded by the indecisiveness of Louis XVI (r. 1774–1792) and led directly to the French Revolution. Although Louis made some effort to accept the new political order, the intrigues of the royal court and his queen, Marie Antoinette, undermined his attempts. In 1792, Louis XVI and his family were imprisoned by revolutionaries, and on January 21, 1793, the king was guillotined. Louis's heir, his eight-year-old son Louis

Charles, was given the title Louis XVII (r. 1793–1795), but the young boy died in prison two years later, in 1795, without ever actually taking the throne.

The Bourbon monarchy in France was later restored when, in 1814, a brother of Louis XVI, the comte de Provence, assumed the title of Louis XVIII (r. 1814–1824) after the rule of Napoleon Bonaparte. Initially, Louis XVIII seemed interested in reform, granting a constitutional charter, and appointing moderate ministers. However, ultraroyalist factions gained control, and when his nephew, the duc de Berry, was assassinated by them in 1820, Louis allowed reactionary factions to take control of the government. The result was a deterioration of civil liberties and increased abuses of power by the wealthy classes.

Following the death of Louis XVIII in 1824, his

brother Charles took the throne as Charles X (r. 1824–1830). An extreme reactionary, Charles attempted to restore the *ancien regime* (the old order) of royal authority that had been established in the Middle Ages, but he failed dismally. Following the July Revolution of 1830, Charles X abdicated, ending the rule of the Bourbon kings of France.

SPANISH BOURBONS

The Bourbon dynasty came to power in Spain in 1700. Before his death that year, the childless Charles II (r. 1665–1700), the last Habsburg ruler of Spain, designated Philip of Anjou, the grandson of Louis XIV of France, as his heir. However, Philip's claim to the throne was contested by other Habsburg claimants, resulting in the War of the Spanish Succession (1701–1714), in which France and Spain were allied against England, the Netherlands, and the Holy Roman Empire. Although Spain ultimately lost much of its power as a result of the war, Philip became the first Bourbon ruler of Spain as King Philip V (r. 1700–1746).

The Bourbons remained the royal family of Spain for the next three centuries. Throughout their rule, Spain experienced a number of violent upheavals. In the mid-1800s, struggles over succession led to the Carlist Wars (1833–1840; 1873–1876). The greatest upheaval was the Spanish Civil War (1936–1939), which led to the establishment of a military dictatorship under Generalissimo Francisco Franco.

In 1931, King Alfonso XIII (r. 1886–1931) of Spain was deposed, and a republic was established. Alfonso had designated his son, Don Juan, as successor, but Juan was unable to take the throne while Spain was under Franco's military dictatorship. However, he succeeded in placing his son, Juan Carlos, under the supervision of General Franco, who groomed the Bourbon heir as his own successor. In 1975, after the death of Franco, Juan Carlos was restored to the Spanish throne as a constitutional monarch, reinstating the Bourbon line in Spain.

BOURBONS IN NAPLES AND SICILY

The Bourbon line was established in Naples and Sicily in 1759 when Ferdinand (r. 1769–1825), the son of Charles III of Spain (r. 1759–1788), succeeded to the throne of the two kingdoms after his father became king of Spain. Ferdinand then revived the kingdom of Two Sicilies (Sicily and Naples), which had been united under one rule for nearly 200 years be-

ginning in 1519. However, the two kingdoms were not officially merged until 1816.

Objections to Ferdinand's policies led to a popular uprising in 1820, after which Ferdinand was forced to grant the kingdom a constitution. In 1821, however, with help from Austria, Ferdinand restored absolute monarchy in the kingdom and this continued under his Bourbon successors, Francis I (r. 1825–1830), Ferdinand II (r. 1830–1859), and Francis II (r. 1859–1860). In 1860, Sicily was captured by the republican forces of the Italian patriot leader Giuseppi Garibaldi. Francis II was deposed in 1860, ending a little more than 100 years of Bourbon rule. The following year, the kingdom of Two Sicilies was merged with the kingdom of Italy.

BOURBONS IN PARMA

The duchy of Parma and Piacenza in northern Italy was created in 1545 by Pope Paul III (r. 1534–1549), who bequeathed it to his son, Pier Luigi Farnese. The Farnese family ruled Parma and Piacenza until 1731, when the duchy passed through the female line to the Bourbons of Spain. When Duke Antonio of Parma (r. 1727–1731) died that year, Charles I (r. 1731–1736) assumed the throne. Charles was the son of Antonio's niece, Elizabeth Farnese, and King Philip V of Spain (r. 1700–1746).

In 1736, Charles I was forced to give up Parma to Austria, which kept control of the duchy until 1748. Under the Treaty of Aix-la-Chapelle (1748), which ended the war of the Austrian Succession (1740–1748), the duchy was restored and Charles's younger brother, Philip, became duke, reestablishing the house of Bourbon-Parma. Parma remained under Bourbon control until 1802, when Napoleon annexed the duchy as part of France. It was restored to the Bourbons in 1847 under Duke Charles II (r. 1847–1849), but when Robert of Parma (r. 1854–1859) was deposed in 1859, Bourbon rule ended. The following year, the duchy was united with the kingdom of Italy.

See also: FRENCH MONARCHIES; NAPLES, KINGDOM OF; SICILY, KINGDOM OF; SPANISH MONARCHIES.

FURTHER READING

Carr, Raymond. *Spain 1808–1975*. Oxford: Clarendon Press, 1982.

Seward, Desmond. *The Bourbon Kings of France*. New York: Barnes and Noble, 1976.

BRAGANÇA DYNASTY

(1640–1910 C.E., Portugal; 1822–1889 C.E., Brazil)

Descendants of an illegitimate son of João I (r. 1385–1433) and the ruling family of Portugal and its colonies for nearly three hundred years.

The Portuguese Braganças were a wealthy and powerful dynasty. As nearly absolute rulers, they helped Portugal regain its independence from Spain, stabilized Portugal's overseas empire, and carried out numerous public works projects. Although their power diminished greatly after the Napoleonic Wars (1803–1815), they maintained their hold on the Portuguese throne, despite internal political upheavals, for nearly a century more. Although Portugal and Brazil are now republics, the Braganças continue to assert their claims to the thrones of both countries.

THE THRONE OF PORTUGAL

In 1640, Philip IV of Spain (r. 1621–1665), who ruled Portugal as King Philip III (r. 1621–1640), was facing a revolt in Catalonia and demanded soldiers and money from his Portuguese subjects. A number of noble landowners objected to these demands and persuaded the eighth duke of Bragança to replace Philip on the Portuguese throne. Ruling as João IV (r. 1640–1656), this first Bragança king spent much of his reign raising money to resist the Spanish armies at home and Dutch encroachments on Portuguese colonies abroad. He also reduced the power of the Portuguese Inquisition.

João IV died in 1656 and was succeeded by his son, Afonso VI (r. 1656–1667), who was partially paralyzed and may have been mentally impaired. The key event of Afonso's reign was the marriage of his sister Catarina to Charles II of England (r. 1660–1685). In return for a sizable dowry, colonies, and trade concessions, Portugal received military aid from England. Still, Spain did not recognize Portugal's independence until February 1668.

Under Afonso's brother, Pedro II (r. 1683–1706), Portugal increased religious toleration in its colonies. Trade with India revived somewhat, and small shipments of settlers to Mozambique helped strengthen Portugal's presence in southeast Africa, which would continue into the mid-twentieth century. In 1697, prospectors struck gold in Brazil. This find, and the discovery of diamonds in 1728 under João V (r. 1706–1750), contributed to the perception that Portugal's ruling family was the richest in the world. It was also powerful, ruling without a Cortes, or parliament, from 1689 to 1822.

During the eighteenth century, Bragança rulers and their ministers abolished slavery within Portugal (it remained legal in the colonies until 1869); introduced reforms in law, education, and commerce; encouraged intellectual endeavors; and helped Lisbon recover from the terrible earthquake of 1755. The century ended with João VI (r. 1816–1826) becoming regent in 1799 for his mother María I (r. 1777–1816), who had sunk into deep depression and mental illness.

EXILE AND DECLINING FORTUNES

In 1807, Napoleon invaded Portugal. João VI fled to Brazil with his mother Queen María, his wife, and their children. Thus began a steep decline in the power of Portuguese rulers. The king returned to Lisbon in 1821 to find his power circumscribed by a constitution. The following year, his son Pedro declared Brazil's independence from Portugal and ruled Brazil as Pedro I (r. 1822–1831). João's death in 1826 ushered in a succession crisis that pitted Pedro's young daughter, the future María II (r. 1834–1853), against her uncle Miguel. The succession struggle lasted for years and further reduced the prestige and power of the Bragança dynasty.

The Bragança dynasty ruled Brazil until 1889, when Pedro II (r. 1831–1889) was deposed and the country became a republic. Meanwhile, despite their diminished importance in Portugal, the Braganças in that country weathered a succession of parliamentary governments, as well as several popular revolts and economic crises. Agitation for a republic, however, grew loud. In 1908, King Carlos I (r. 1889–1908) and his eldest son were assassinated. Two years later, a group of army officers instigated an uprising, and Manuel I (r. 1908–1910) was forced to abdicate, ending the monarchy in Portugal.

See also: HABSBURG DYNASTY; IBERIAN KINGDOMS; JOÃO (JOHN) VI; PEDRO I; PEDRO II.

BRAHMARSI-DESA KINGDOM

(ca. 1500–1000 B.C.E.)

Kingdom in northern India that was founded by Indo-Aryan migrants from central Asia in the second millennium B.C.E.

Around 2000 B.C.E., nomadic invaders from Central Asia forced groups of Indo-Aryan peoples from their original homeland between the Caspian Sea and the Black Sea. As the tribes scattered across Asia, the Aryans pushed the farthest east. After crossing the rugged Hindu Kush Mountains (in present-day Kashmir and Afghanistan), the migrants settled in the Brahmavarta and Kurukshetra regions of northern India and established the Brahmarsi-Desa kingdom.

The name Brahmarsi-Desa means "the land of divine sages," and although many details about the kingdom remain unknown, it retains an exalted position in Indian history. According to tradition, Kurukshetra was the site of the legendary holy war between the Kauravas and the Pandavas, two groups whose struggle for power forms the main theme of the great Hindu epic, the *Mahabharata*. The region of Brahmavarta was the Holy Land of seven great rivers, including the Indus and the sacred Ganges River.

Of perhaps even greater importance, however, was the role of the Aryan priests of the Brahmarsi-Desa kingdom, who crafted the works known as the Vedas ("Books of Knowledge"), which preserved Aryan history, religious rites, songs, poems, and social customs. The Vedas were passed down orally through successive generations until they were first transcribed around 600 B.C.E. They eventually became the most revered works in Indian Hindu culture.

The Vedas describe how the Aryans arrived in India and battled the native population for supremacy. They describe the bamboo homes of the Aryans, reveal that the Aryans formed villages with surrounding farmland, and used chariots and bronze weapons in battle. The Vedas also describe how the Aryans introduced the Sanskrit language to India.

Most importantly, the Vedas describe the four social castes that became the basis of Indian society. Priests and the most learned members of Aryan society occupied the highest caste, known as the Brahman. Members of the military and the ruling family belonged to the Kshatriya caste. The Vasiya caste consisted of artisans and farmers, while peasants and servants constituted the lowest caste, the Sudra. These caste distinctions have lasted thousands of years and into the modern era.

The Aryans of the Brahmarsi-Desa kingdom gradually assimilated with the indigenous population of northern India. Native Indians adopted the caste system and many of the beliefs contained in the Vedas, while the Aryans converted to Hinduism and adopted many Indian social customs. By about the tenth century B.C.E., the Aryans no longer lived in homogenous communities, and the Brahmarsi-Desa kingdom dissolved into the various states that existed before the rise of the Maurya Empire, India's first great empire, in the fourth century B.C.E. Although the Brahmarsi-Desa kingdom disappeared, its Aryan founders had introduced social philosophies and ideas that had a permanent impact on the subsequent civilizations of India.

See also: INDIAN KINGDOMS; MAURYA EMPIRE; SOUTH ASIAN KINGDOMS.

BRAZIL, PORTUGUESE MONARCHY OF (1822–1889 C.E.)

Kingdom in Brazil formed as a result of the invasion of Portugal by the armies of Napoleon Bonaparte, which served as a monarchy in exile for Portuguese rulers.

Brazil had been a colony of Portugal since 1494, when Pope Alexander VI interceded between Spain and Portugal to settle their competing claims to territory in the Americas with the Treaty of Tordesillas. The colony of Brazil came to represent an enormous source of wealth for the Portuguese throne, and over the centuries a great many Portuguese nationals settled there. Thus, in 1807, when the prince regent of Portugal, João VI (r. 1799–1816 as regent), found himself facing the armies of Napoleon as they marched on Lisbon, Brazil seemed a logical destination to which to flee.

João's regency had been dictated by the infirmity of his wife, Maria I (r. 1777–1816), who was the acknowledged Portuguese sovereign but was deemed unfit to rule because she suffered from dementia. Maria died nine years after the royal family's flight to Brazil, and João became full sovereign. He established Rio de Janiero as the new seat of the exiled Portuguese government and raised the status of the colony to that of kingdom. These measures were intended to be temporary, until the military situation with Napoleon could be resolved. But even after Napoleon was expelled from Portugal, João remained in Brazil, returning home only in 1821 at the command of the Cortes (Portuguese parliament).

In 1824, Emperor Pedro I of Brazil declared independence from Portugal and issued the kingdom's first constitution. Two years later, upon the death of his father, King João VI of Portugal, Pedro renounced the Portuguese throne in favor of his daughter, Maria II. He later abdicated the Brazilian throne, passing it to his son, Pedro II.

When João returned to Portugal, he left the administration of Brazil in the hands of his son, Pedro I (r. 1822–1831).

Pedro was not content to let Brazil remain subordinate to Portugal, regardless of centuries of history. Within a year of taking the throne, he declared Brazil to be fully independent from Portugal, and in 1824, he promulgated the kingdom's first constitution. When his father João died in 1826, the Cortes demanded that Pedro return to Lisbon to assume the throne there. Forced to choose, Pedro abdicated his Portuguese throne to his daughter, Maria, who later became Maria II (r. 1834–1853).

Pedro's decision did not secure his rule in Brazil, however, for he had lost the support of the people with a disastrous war against Argentina in 1828, during the course of which he lost a large tract of territory (now the country of Uruguay). In 1831, Pedro was forced to abdicate the Brazilian throne to his son, Pedro II (r. 1831–1889), who was then only five years old.

During the early years of Pedro II's rule, Brazil was governed by a regency, but he was allowed to assume full sovereignty at age thirteen. Pedro II was a popular ruler throughout much of his reign, but Great Britain's abolition of the lucrative Atlantic slave trade in 1807 had undermined the foundation of the Brazilian economy. The later years of his reign saw a rising popular demand for establishing a republic in place of the monarchy. In 1889, a revolutionary movement led by Brazilian military leader Manuel Deodoro de Fonseca succeeded in overthrowing the monarchy, ending nearly four hundred years of Portuguese rule.

See also: João (John) VI; Pedro I; Pedro II; South American Monarchies.

FURTHER READING

de Costa, E.V. *The Brazilian Empire: Myths and Histories.* Chicago: University of Chicago Press, 1985.

BRETAGNE DUCHY (936–1532 C.E.)

Duchy in northwest France (Brittany) that was ruled by a succession of dukes with varying degrees of independence from France.

After the Romans departed Gaul (France) in the fifth century, the region of Bretagne, or Brittany, was settled by Celtic peoples from Britain and Ireland. Since then, the region has remained quite independent from the rest of France in terms of its language and culture. Although Bretagne became a province of France in 1532, the desire for political independence continued to surface within the region.

The people of Bretagne first tasted independence from all foreign powers in 846, when a Breton warrior named Nomenoë led them in a revolt against the Carolingian ruler Charles the Bald (r. 843–877), the king of the West Franks. This independence was short-lived, however. In 921, the Vikings conquered the region of Bretagne, and then, in 933, the area was conquered by the Normans.

During this period of conquest by foreigners, many Bretons fled to England. One of them, Alan Barbetorte, a descendant of ancient Breton royalty, returned to Brittany in 936 and led a successful campaign to oust the Normans. Barbetorte then established a government in the captured town of Nantes and ruled Bretagne as Duke Alan I (r. 937–952).

When Alan I died in 952, there was no clear

choice of a successor since his only legitimate son died shortly thereafter. This led to a succession rivalry that continued until 1066, when Hoël, the count of Nantes and Cornouaille, reunited much of Bretagne through inheritance and marriage.

Although some internal discord remained in the duchy, a prosperous period began that lasted until another disputed succession in the early 1300s resulted in civil war. Duke Jean III (r. 1312–1341) of Bretagne had no legitimate children, and upon his death in 1341, succession passed to his niece Jean de Penthievre and her husband, Charles de Blois. Jean's uncle, Jean de Montfort, the son of Duke Arthur II of Bretagne (r. 1305–1312), was her rival for the throne. Charles de Blois ruled from 1341 to 1364, but throughout his reign control of the duchy was contested in the War of the Bretagne Succession.

In 1369, during a war between France and England, Jean de Montfort openly declared his support for England and sought refuge there. Charles de Blois allowed French troops to occupy Bretagne, but the independent-spirited Bretons welcomed Montfort back to rid them of the French, which he did with English assistance. Finally, in the second Treaty of Guerande (1381), France recognized Montfort as duke of Bretagne.

Peace with France ushered in a period of prosperity and peace for the duchy, which was marked by opulence and heraldry. This culminated in the marriage of the duchess of Bretagne to the king of France. Anne (r. 1488–1514), the daughter of Francis II of Bretagne (r. 1458–1488), became duchess upon her father's death in 1488, and she was the last ruler of an independent Bretagne. In 1491, Anne married King Charles VIII of France (1483–1498), but the duchy of Bretagne remained her personal property. After Charles died in 1498, Anne married King Louis XII of France (r. 1498–1515).

When Anne died in 1514, her daughter Claude inherited the title duchess of Bretagne. Claude, the wife of King Francis I (r. 1515–1547) of France, transferred Bretagne to her husband at the time of their marriage, on the condition that their son Francois be made duke. After her death, France continued to rule Bretagne until 1532, when it was formally incorporated into France as a French province, marking the end of the independent Bretagne Duchy.

See also: CAROLINGIAN DYNASTY; FRANCIS I; NORMAN KINGDOMS.

BRITTANY. *See* BRETAGNE DUCHY

BROOKE, SIR JAMES (RAJAH)

(1803–1868 C.E.)

Rajah of Sarawak (r. 1841–1868), a kingdom that occupied the northeast portion of the island of Borneo, who played an important role in gaining the country's independence.

James Brooke, the first rajah of Sarawak, was the son of an officer in the British East India Company. Born in Benares, India, on April 29, 1803, Brooke spent the first part of his life there. When he was twelve years old, his parents sent him home to England for schooling, while they remained on duty in India. School did not agree with the young James, however, and he ran away after attending for only two years. As soon as he was old enough, Brooke applied for and received a commission in the British army. He was sixteen years old at the time.

Brooke found the military more to his liking, and he received regular promotions. When war broke out against British colonial rule in Burma in 1824, he put together a volunteer force ready to fight, but he was shipped home less than a year later after being wounded in battle. After spending a few years in England, he began traveling, visiting China and other places in Asia and Southeast Asia.

In 1839, Brooke offered his military skills to the sultan of Brunei, who was having trouble with rebellious factions in Sarawak, which was then under the sultan's rule. It took nearly three years, but Brooke succeeded in pacifying the rebel forces. The sultan rewarded him in 1842 by giving him the title "White Rajah" of Sarawak.

Sir James's rule as rajah of Sarawak lasted twenty-six years, during which time he dealt with numerous rebellions and embarked on a campaign of territorial expansion. Desirous of autonomy, he sought to break ties with Brunei, and he achieved some measure of success in 1850, when the United States recognized Sarawak's independence. It would be another fourteen years, however, before Britain did the same. By then Sir James was seriously ill.

Some years earlier, Sir James had received a visit from one of his nephews, Charles Anthony Johnson. After schooling and a stint in the Royal Navy, Charles had joined his uncle in Sarawak in 1852 and offered his services. When Sir James suffered his first stroke a few years later, he relied heavily on his nephew. When continued ill health forced Sir James to return to England, he named Charles his successor. At this point, Charles abandoned the surname of his birth and took the name Brooke instead.

Sir James returned to Sarawak in May 1868 but was never truly able to return to rule. He suffered a final stroke in June of that year, and Charles succeeded him as rajah. Sir Charles (r. 1868–1917) ruled Sarawak for the next forty-nine years, during which time his country became a British protectorate in 1888. The last independent rajah of Sarawak was Charles Vyner Brooke (r. 1917–1946), the son of Charles Anthony Johnson Brooke, who ceded the country to Great Britain as a colony in 1946.

See also: SOUTHEAST ASIAN KINGDOMS.

BUDDHISM AND KINGSHIP

Impact of Buddhist belief on the concept and practice of kingship on monarchies in Asia. The Buddhist idea of kingship, based on the extensive body of Buddhist literature, focused on the moral and political authority and legitimacy of the Buddhist king.

Buddhism first developed as a philosophy that challenged the limitations of the early Hindu beliefs in providing a means of salvation for peoples belonging to the lower castes of society. Because knowledge was an essential aspect of Hinduism, only the upper class of Brahmans possessed the means of salvation, for they were the only ones in Hindu society who knew the rituals of the sacrificial ceremonies.

The doctrines developed by Gautama Siddhartha, a prince of the Sakya people who became known as the Buddha upon his attainment of enlightenment, allowed the common people a chance to attain enlightenment regardless of their station in life. His teachings spread far and wide throughout South Asia, Southeast Asia, Central Asia, and East Asia after his death in around 486 B.C.E. Although little was known for certain about the Buddha's life, later Buddhist writings by his followers contained colorful and vivid descriptions of his life. These included a collection of the Buddha's sermons in the *Sutta Pitaka* (a Pali Buddhist text containing 10,000 discourses given by the Buddha) and literary works such as Asvaghosa's *Buddhacarita* (written around the fifth century C.E.).

BUDDHIST COUNCILS AND SPREAD OF BUDDHISM

The Buddha's teachings did not appear to contain any explicit instructions on the concept of kingship; this concept would only be described in later Buddhist scriptures commissioned by kings and written under the auspices of the Buddhist councils and monastic orders.

According to tradition, the first general council on Buddhist teachings was held soon after the Buddha's death, at which the Buddha's disciples, Upali and Ananda, recited the Buddha's sermons on matters of doctrines and ethics. A century later, a second council was held at which a schism, or split, occurred forming the two main branches of the Buddhist order, the Sthaviravadins or Theravadi ("Lesser Vehicle") and Mahayana ("Greater Vehicle").

By the time of the third council, held under the patronage of King Asoka (r. 268–232 B.C.E) of the Indian Maurya Empire in third century B.C.E., many Buddhist works of later composition were already added into the Buddhist religious traditions. Ac-

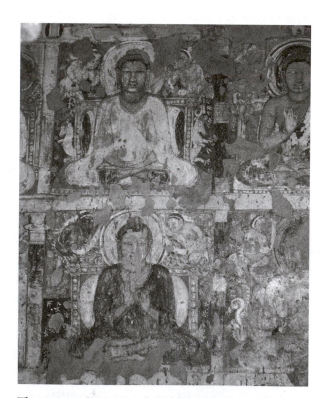

This image of two seated Buddhas, from the interior of the Ajanta caves in India's Maharashtra state, was painted in the fifth century during the Gupta Dynasty. By the sixth century, Buddhism had begun to wane in India. This was followed by a resurgence of Hinduism and then Islam.

cording to ancient Ceylonese and Burmese chronicles, it was at the third religious council that Mogaliputta Tissa, one of the Buddhist Council leaders, sent missionaries to spread the Buddhist faith to various regions from Southeast Asia to Central Asia and China.

ELEMENTS OF BUDDHIST KINGSHIP

Several themes comprise the key elements of Buddhist kingship: *chakravartin* (universal monarch), *dharmaraja* (defender and protector of Buddhism), and *devaraja* (divine kingship). According to Buddhist literature, the essential relationship between the king and his dominions is one based essentially on a social contract between the king and his people. The king's authority is thus limited not only by sacred law but also by his moral obligations to the people. A Buddhist king gains legitimacy because he is both a protector of the people and the defender of the Buddhist faith.

Buddhist rulers in Ceylon (Sri Lanka), India, and kingdoms in Southeast Asia exercised the idea of the universal monarch, or *chakravartin* ("turner of the wheel of sovereignty"), to justify their conquests of regions beyond the boundaries of their domains. One of the key roles of the king was to spread Buddhism throughout his empire and to regions that were not already Buddhist.

The motif of Buddhist king as a conqueror was probably derived from the story of Asoka, a great conqueror of the Mauryan Empire (268–232 B.C.E.), which stretched from the borders of Persia to Central Asia in the northeast. According to tradition, Asoka converted to Buddhism after his bloody campaign at the battle of Kalinga in 257 B.C.E. He then became the ideal model of Buddhist kingship because of his role as conqueror and supporter of the Buddhist faith. Ashoka was known for his extensive development of structures to facilitate the spread of Buddhism, such as the building of shelters and expansion of transportation and communications networks. Another example of the appropriation of the idea of *chakravartin* to justify territorial conquests is represented in the sixteenth-century invasion of the northern Thai kingdom of Ayudhya (in present-day Thailand) by King Bayinnaung (r. 1551–1581) of the Toungoo kingdom in Burma.

Another important element of Buddhist kingship is the king's role as the *dharmaraja*——the defender and protector of Buddhism. According to Buddhist ideals, the king should not only fulfill his duty as defender and protector of the Buddhist religion, but he must also act as the upholder of moral and political hierarchy and order of his kingdom. As the *dharmaraja*, the king must adhere to ten kingly virtues, five common precepts (or rules), and eight precepts on holy days.

The king's duty as a *dharmaraja* includes the patronage of monastic orders and the convening of general Buddhist councils to ensure that rules of monastic discipline have been followed. Asoka held the third general council in the third century B.C.E., and King Kaniska I (r. 78–102 C.E.) of the Kushan dynasty of northern India and Afghanistan held a fourth council during the first or second century C.E.

The third universal feature of Buddhist kingship is the idea of the king as a divinity, or *devaraja*. The idea of *devaraja* is probably best exemplified in the importance of the king's role as a *bodhisattva*—a being who has chosen to delay his attainment of enlightenment in order to help his people in their pursuit of salvation. This concept of kingship is present in both the Theravada and Mahayana branches of Buddhism. In the T'ang dynasty (618–907) of China, the popularity of the Goddess of Mercy, or Guanyin, a representation of the Buddhist deity Avalokitesvara, attests to the importance of not only the *bodhisattva* but also personalities associated with the deity. The T'ang ruler, Empress Wu Tse T'ien (r. 684–705), claimed her status as the *bodhisattva* who would bring salvation to her people. The faces on the Bayon, a temple complex in Cambodia dating from the twelfth to thirteenth century, was thought to represent the then king of Angkor, Jayavarman VII (r. ca. 1181–1219) as a *bodhisattva*.

In the mainland Southeast Asian region there is an additional element of Buddhist kingship that refers to the king as a *kammaraja* (possessor of good merit). Burmese religious texts, such as the *Sasanavamsa* ("History of the Buddhist Religion"), suggest that the Burmese kings justified their legitimacy to rule by their possession of good *kamma*, or merit (also known as *karma*). Burmese chronicles, such as the eighteenth-century *Glass Palace Chronicle*, describe how some characters, such as a cucumber farmer named Kunhsaw, were able to usurp the throne by killing the Burmese king because of their good karma. Karma is not constant, however; it has to be earned. Kunhsaw was eventually killed when a fallen pillar hit him because he ran out of good merit.

EXTENT OF THE BUDDHIST RELIGION

Buddhism spread over an extensive area of Asia, especially in the first millennium. However, the faith would wane in India by the fifth or sixth century paving the way for a resurgence of Hinduism and then Islam, which was brought to the Indian subcontinent by the Mughals. Theravada Buddhism, however, prevails in Sri Lanka and the mainland Southeast Asian countries of Burma, Thailand, and Cambodia, whereas Mahayana Buddhism retains its prominence in parts of China, Japan, and Korea. A third branch of Buddhism, the Vajrayana School, predominates in Tibet. These regions still share the Buddhist conception of kingship.

See also: CASTE SYSTEMS; DIVINITY OF KINGS; HINDUISM AND KINGSHIP; ISLAM AND KINGSHIP; LEGITIMACY; RELIGIOUS DUTIES AND POWER; SACRED KINGSHIPS.

BUGANDA KINGDOM. *See* GANDA KINGDOM

BULGARIAN MONARCHY

(681–1014, 1186–1396, 1878–1944 C.E.)

Kingdom that ruled over part of the Balkan region and the eastern Mediterranean sporadically over a period of thirteen centuries. The long history of Bulgaria can be divided into five distinct periods: First Bulgarian Empire (681–1014), Byzantine occupation (1014–1186), Second Bulgarian Empire (1186–1396), Ottoman occupation (1396–1878), and Third Bulgarian State (1878–present).

THE BEGINNINGS OF A KINGDOM

The first Bulgarian kingdom began with the migration of Slavic peoples into the Balkan Peninsula in the 500s and 600s. Among these people were the Bulgars, a Turkish group who came from north of the Black Sea, conquered the Slavic tribes of the region, and founded the first Bulgarian kingdom in 681.

The Bulgars intermarried with the Slavs and became absorbed into the Slavic culture. In the 800s, during the reign of Prince Boris I Michael (r. 852–889), the Bulgars adopted Christianity, creating a common tradition among the people that encouraged greater organization as well as growth and development. Boris's son, Simeon (r. 893–927), continued to advance Bulgaria geographically, culturally, and intellectually. He doubled the size of the kingdom, expanded educational opportunities, supported the arts of painting and music, and funded massive building projects.

Simeon's successors, however, did not prove to be strong leaders, and Bulgaria began to lose territory to encroaching invaders. In 1014, the Byzantine emperor Basil II (r. 976–1025), after winning a battle over the Bulgarian army, ordered 14,000 prisoners to be blinded. This earned him the title of "Bulgar slayer" and led to a period of Byzantine occupation that lasted until 1185.

RETURN AND FALL OF THE KINGDOM

In 1185, two brothers, Ivan and Peter Asen, led a revolt against Byzantine rule. Their victory marked the start of the second Bulgarian kingdom. During the reign of Ivan Asen II (r. 1218–1241), Bulgaria once again rose to power, dominating much of the Balkan region. At the end of the century, however, a series of peasant revolts weakened the kingdom and permitted easy invasions by Serbs, Mongols, and, ultimately, a successful attack and subsequent occupation by the Ottoman Turks in 1396.

Although the Ottomans occupied Bulgaria for the next five centuries, the country's history and customs were preserved in its monasteries. In the 1700s, a monk named Paissy used ancient texts to write a history of the Bulgarian people. He used this history to encourage Bulgarians to remember their rich history, thus beginning a national revival. Paissy also urged the expansion of education as primary in importance.

The independent Bulgarian Orthodox Exarchate was formed in 1870, and the April Uprising, launched by revolutionaries in 1867, ultimately led to the start of the Russo-Turkish War. This conflict, which lasted from 1877 to 1878, ended with the signing of the Treaty of San Stefano, in which Bulgaria was made an autonomous principality and greatly enlarged, marking the rise of the third Bulgarian kingdom.

THIRD BULGARIAN KINGDOM

The history of the third Bulgarian kingdom is characterized, in part, by its conflicts. In 1885, during the reign of Prince Alexander (r. 1879–1886), the

Bulgarians formed a union with the north Balkan regions, which led to an attack by Serbia. Bulgarian forces were victorious over the Serbs, but Alexander abdicated the throne in 1886 because he had lost the favor of Russia, one of his previous supporters.

In 1887, Ferdinand I (r. 1887–1918) of the House of Saxe-Coburg-Gotha succeeded to the throne of Bulgaria, taking the title of tsar in 1908. By that time, much of the land gained by the San Stefano Treaty had been lost, and Ferdinand made it the focus of his reign to regain the lost territories. To this end, he formed an alliance with Serbia, Montenegro, and Greece in 1910.

This allegiance forced Turkey, during the First Balkan War in 1912, to relinquish its Balkan territories. However, the alliance fell victim to infighting, which led to Bulgaria's defeat in the Second Balkan War of 1913. Bulgaria again lost land during World War I, giving up territory to Serbia and Greece. There was much domestic opposition to the war, and when Bulgaria's military position crumbled, Ferdinand abdicated and fled to Germany. His son, Boris III (r. 1918–1943), became king.

During World War II, Boris III of Bulgaria allied with Germany, though reluctantly. In spite of this allegiance, Bulgaria did not send forces into combat during the war, nor would it agree to send its Jewish population to the death camps in Poland. Boris died in 1943, leaving the throne to his six-year-old son, Simeon II (r. 1943–1946).

MODERN BULGARIA

In September 1944, the Soviet Union invaded and rapidly occupied Bulgaria, abolishing the monarchy and forcing the boy king, Simeon II, into exile to Spain. A communist group, led by Georgi Dimitrov and known as the Fatherland Front, seized power in 1946.

After World War II, Bulgaria became a satellite state of the Soviet Union, and it adopted a Soviet communist-style government. Communist rule lasted until November 10, 1989, when Prime Minister Todor Zhivkov was removed from office by democratic reformers, leading to the formation of a parliamentary democracy.

Simeon II returned to Bulgaria in 2001, founding a political party that won half the parliamentary seats in the election that year. As Bulgaria's democratically elected premier, he instituted economic reforms and worked to secure Bulgaria's admission into the North Atlantic Treaty Organization and the European Union.

See also: BYZANTINE EMPIRE; OTTOMAN EMPIRE.

FURTHER READING

Genov, Nikolai, and Anna Krasteva. *Recent Social Trends in Bulgaria, 1960–1995.* Montreal: McGill-Queen's University Press, 2001.
Tsvetkov, Plamen S. *A History of the Balkans: A Regional Overview from a Bulgarian Perspective.* San Francisco: EM Text, 1993.

BUNDI KINGDOM

(ca. 1300s–1948 C.E.)

Kingdom in northwest India, in the region known as Rajastan, which was home to one of the many Rajput clans of northern and central India.

The former princely state of Bundi, known historically as Haraoti, was established in the fourteenth century by the Hara branch of the Chauhan dynasty, one of the various Rajput clans that claimed connection with ancient Hindu epics. The kingdom took the name of its principal town, Bundi, which had been named after Bunda, a thirteenth-century chieftain.

The state of Bundi was founded around 1342 by Rao Dewa, a Hara chief who captured the town from a group called the Minas. The state remained relatively unimportant, however, until the time of Rao Surjan (r. ca. 1554–1583), who succeeded to the chieftainship in 1554. In return for his cooperation and allegiance, the Mughal emperors of Delhi gave Rao Surjan the title "Raja," or prince. This princely title would pass to successive rulers of Bundi.

The Mughals also gave Bundi a considerable amount of territory, part of which came to be known as the kingdom of Kota. (Modern Kota is a walled city in northwestern India, just east of the Chambal River.) At first, Kota was granted to the eldest son of the Bundi ruler. In 1624, however, the Mughal ruler, Jahangir (r. 1605–1627), partitioned Bundi and made Kota an independent state. As a result, the territory of the Bundi kingdom was greatly reduced in size. In 1625, Rao Madho Singh (r. 1625–1656), the son of the ruler of Bundi, took the throne of Kota.

Despite its reduced size, Bundi continued to play an important role in Indian history. In the early 1700s, the Bundi ruler, Budh Singh (r. 1706–1729), was awarded imperial recognition for helping Bahadur Shah I (r. 1707–1712) gain the Mughal throne in the succession struggle that erupted after the death of Bahadur's father, Aurangzeb (r. 1658–1707).

In 1804, Raja Bishan Singh of Bundi (r. 1770–1821) gave valuable assistance to the British in their disastrous retreat before the armies of the Maratha Confederacy. In revenge, the Marathas continually ravaged Bundi until 1818, when the kingdom was placed under British protection.

In 1821, Bishan Singh was succeeded by his son, Ram Singh (r. 1821–1889). Ram Singh exemplified the Rajput gentleman. A disciple of Balak Singh, the founder of the Sikh movement for independence (known as the Namdhari movement), he instilled a sense of self-worth and dignity in his followers. He continued to enjoy the favor of the British government during the Sepoy Mutiny (1857–1858) and was much honored for his support of the British during that uprising against British colonial rule. A year after India gained its independence from Great Britain in 1947, Bundi became part of the Indian state of Rajasthan.

See also: AURANGZEB; INDIAN KINGDOMS; JAHANGIR; KOTA KINGDOM; MUGHAL EMPIRE; RAJASTHAN KINGDOM.

BUNYORO KINGDOM. *See* NYORO KINGDOM

BUREAUCRACY, ROYAL

A system of specialized officials who execute the monarch's will and the administrative functions of the royal government. Derived from the French word for "desk" or "office" (*bureau*), royal bureaucrats were divided into an organizational hierarchy with a centralized chain of command. In Europe, bureaucracies were organized by function into groups or departments, such as finance, commerce, security, and justice. Bureaucracies also included royal experts in all areas, from medicine to manufacturing, who advised the monarch on all sorts of issues. Bureaucracies were intended to regularize government and apply the dictates of royal law uniformly to all the ruler's subjects. They also were used to increase and consolidate the ruler's political and financial power.

ORIGINS OF BUREAUCRACIES

Most of the world's monarchies throughout history have had some form of bureaucracy. Indeed, the earliest governments of ancient Mesopotamia had officials who developed writing to help the king collect taxes and administer his government. Generally, as both populations and territories grew, so too did royal bureaucracies. Rulers usually expanded bureaucracies to consolidate political power and to increase their ability to collect taxes. They usually consolidated their power by undercutting the power of the landed nobility, while increases in revenue were usually used to fund military activities.

ROYAL REVENUE

Bureaucracies were often expanded to meet the need for more royal revenue. For example, when the European monarchs in the seventeenth century needed money for their numerous wars, many expanded their bureaucracies to centralize power and increase royal revenues. Not only had there been more warfare in the wake of the religious changes in the sixteenth century, but new military technology demanded larger armies and equipment. Monarchs needed much more revenue to fund these armies and a larger bureaucracy to collect the money. This process was self-perpetuating, however. The buildup in bureaucracy and royal revenue also fueled warfare and the military aggrandizement of the state, as in the case of the territorial wars between Louis XIV of France (r. 1643–1715)) and the Habsburg Empire.

SURVEILLANCE AND CENSORSHIP

The desire to apply royal law in a uniform manner and to regularize government meant that royal bureaucrats needed to collect information on their subjects. During the Ch'ing dynasty (1644–1912) in China, the government used surveys and audits to gauge the effectiveness of the royal administration.

Most rulers also used the bureaucracy to ensure that all subjects followed a uniform ideology, whether it be an "official" religion, philosophical school, or view of history. Censorship or ideological repression was a common function of royal bureaucracies.

BUREAUCRATS

Rulers frequently employed bureaucrats from outside the traditional elite classes to consolidate power in new territories or to increase power in an existing kingdom. Louis XIV of France, for example, hoped to centralize his power by replacing many of his noble officers with educated non-nobles in the seventeenth century. These bureaucrats answered directly to a few central officials appointed by the king. Not born to privilege, all owed their position to the king and were quite loyal to him. It was also hoped that non-noble officials would apply royal law fairly to all subjects, not just to the privileged few.

Not all bureaucracies were formed with educated commoners, however. In the nineteenth century, the rulers of the African kingdom of Merina used talented individuals from their traditional aristocracy to staff their bureaucracy. Regardless of origins, royal bureaucrats were expected to bring the expertise of a university education (usually) and real-world experience to the royal government and to give the ruler advice. The French had a Council of Commerce in the eighteenth century made up of top merchants and businessmen to give the Crown advice on commerce and manufacturing matters. Most rulers had several royal physicians who provided not only personal medical care but also recommendations on public sanitation and hygiene law.

Most of the world's royal bureaucracies shared some common characteristics: centralization of power and administration, use of select talented officials, common ideology, militarism, and a desire to impose a uniform application of the laws on all subjects. The early Ch'in dynasty (221–207 B.C.E.) of China typified this sort of administration. Shi Huang Ti (Shihuangdi) (r. 221–210 B.C.E.), the first emperor, developed a centralized bureaucracy of talented officials, established an administrative system of prefectures, expanded his army and territories, suppressed rival thought systems, built roads, and established a uniform writing system. He laid the foundation for future Chinese rulers by using the bureaucracy to consolidate power and increase revenue.

See also: COUNCILS AND COUNSELORS, ROYAL; COURTS AND COURT OFFICIALS, ROYAL.

BURGUNDY KINGDOM

(300s–534; 800s–1030 C.E.)

A medieval kingdom and duchy of northern France, Belgium, and the Netherlands, first established in the fourth century and later reincorporated in the seventh century as the kingdom of Jurane-Burgundy.

ORIGINS

The kingdom of Burgundy originated among the Germanic Burgundians, one of many Germanic peoples who moved into the northern Roman Empire in the early centuries C.E. Like the Franks, another Germanic people, the Burgundians were *foederati*, or confederated allies of Rome, not its enemies.

During the fifth century, the Burgundians enjoyed relative independence from Rome under their king, Gundobad (r. ca. 473–516), often serving in the armies of the Western Roman Empire and influencing imperial succession until the disintegration of the empire in 476. By the middle of the sixth century, however, Burgundy had fallen under the control of the Merovongian Franks. The next 300 years were characterized by warfare among the several Frankish kingdoms.

Philip the Good, duke of Burgundy from 1419 to 1467, allied his duchy with England against King Charles VII of France, a traditional rival. During wars between the two nations, Philip's forces captured the French heroine Joan of Arc and handed her over to English authorities for trial.

JURANE-BURGUNDY

After the fall of the Carolingian Frankish Empire in the ninth century, most of Burgundy once again became an independent state, the kingdom of Jurane-Burgundy. But the intervening centuries had erased a coherent sense of identity, and the kingdom failed to prosper.

The last king of an autonomous Burgundy, Rudolph III (r. ca. 993–1032), died in 1032 without an heir. Upon his death, Burgundy was divided, with most of the region becoming part of the Holy Roman Empire and a smaller part being absorbed by France. This division continued into the late Middle Ages, with the territories and titles of Burgundy being hotly contested between France and Germany.

DUCHY OF BURGUNDY

The French portion of Burgundy became the semi-autonomous duchy of Burgundy in 1032, when a grandson of the French Capetian ruler, Hugh Capet (r. 987–996), was given the duchy after Rudolph III's death. The Capetians ruled for the next 300 years, a period that was the most stable and prosperous in Burgundian history.

The duchy's stability changed after 1361, when the last Capetian duke of Burgundy, Philip de Rouvres (r. 1347–1361), died without an heir. The title went to King John II of France (r. 1350–1364), member of the Valois dynasty, who gave the duchy to his son, Philip the Bold (r. 1363–1404).

Philip the Bold added to Burgundian territory through an advantageous marriage in 1369 to Margaret of Flanders, who brought significant areas of northern France (Franche-Comte, Flanders, and Artois) into the ducal domain. Philip's son and successor, John the Fearless (r. 1404–1419), used the increased power of Burgundy earned by his father to vie unsuccessfully for the throne of France.

The unrest caused by John's efforts to gain the throne of France weakened that country as well as Burgundy. John was assassinated in 1419 and succeeded by his son, Philip the Good (r. 1419–1467), who allied himself with the English against the French king, Charles VII (r. 1422–1461). It was Philip the Good who turned Joan of Arc over to English authorities.

Burgundy and France eventually made peace following the Treaty of Arras in 1435, which made Burgundy a powerful and virtually autonomous realm within France. Philip also acquired Namur, Luxembourg, and Holland, which, together with Flanders and Artois, formed what was known as the Burgundian Netherlands.

The last duke of Burgundy of the Valois line, Charles the Bold (r. 1467–1477), followed in his father's footsteps by waging war to expand Burgundian territory. Like his father, Charles dreamed of a truly independent Burgundian kingdom. He succeeded in uniting parts of the Low Countries and Switzerland with Burgundy before being killed in battle in 1477.

Charles the Bold left no male heir, and his daughter Mary (r. 1477–1482) inherited his titles. However, under Burgundy's law of primogeniture (inheritance by the oldest son), a woman could not rule alone. As a result, Mary was married to the future Holy Roman emperor Maximillian I (r. 1493–1519), and the Burgundian Netherlands thus passed into the hands of the Austrian Habsburg dynasty.

The duchy of Burgundy itself never fell under Habsburg imperial control, however, because the French king, Louis XI (r. 1461–1483), successfully claimed it for France. As a result, duke of Burgundy became a Habsburg title, but the duchy of Burgundy was absorbed into the kingdom of France.

See also: CAROLINGIAN DYNASTY; FLANDERS, COUNTY OF; FRANKISH KINGDOM; FRENCH MONARCHIES; HABSBURG DYNASTY; HOLY ROMAN EMPIRE; MEROVINGIAN DYNASTY.

BURMESE KINGDOMS

(ca. 1 B.C.E.–1886 C.E.)

Kingdoms and dynasties that ruled Burma (now Myanmar) that shared borders and cultural influences with India and China. Burma's early history is the story of conflict between the various ethnic groups that migrated down the Irrawaddy River from the north, including the Mon and the Pyu peoples, the Shan (T'ai), and the Burmese.

ORIGINS

Beginning in the first century B.C.E. and continuing until the ninth century C.E., people known as the Pyu, devout Buddhists who also worshiped the Hindu god Vishnu, established city-kingdoms in the region that later became Burma. These city-kingdoms prospered because of their location along trade routes between China and India.

Various Pyu dynasties ruled the city-kingdoms in Burma during this period. The Vikrama dynasty (673–718) ruled from old Prome, or Sri Ksetra, which was situated at the fertile mouth of the Irrawaddy River. The Vikrama dynasty enjoyed a powerful rule in the Irrawaddy Valley until the T'ai people invaded from Nanchao, near Yunnan, China, between 760 and 832. After the T'ai invasion, the Pyu moved northward and eventually disappeared from historical records.

People known as the Mon, originally from western China, also migrated into the region and established states there. They, in turn, were defeated by southward-migrating people who formed the kingdom of Pagan.

THE PAGAN KINGDOM

In 1044, King Anawrahta (r. 1044–1077), a Burman military leader who used elephants on a large scale in warfare, founded the great Pagan (Bagan) kingdom and empire (1044–1287). Anawrahta was the first ruler to unify most of Burma. He exerted his influence throughout the central Irrawaddy River Valley and to the south, where he captured the Mon kingdom of Thaton in 1057 and deported its entire population to Pagan. The capture of Thaton brought the Pagans into direct contact with the Mon's rich Indian cultural heritage and opened a window to Buddist centers overseas.

Kyanzittha (r. 1084–1112), Pagan's third king, enjoyed a peaceful reign and heightened the prestige of the city of Pagan by building the famous Ananda Pagoda and restoring the most sacred place in the Buddist world, the Mahabodhi Temple at Bodhgaya. He made increasing contacts with the outside world, especially with China. In 1287, the Pagan kingdom, under Narathiahapate (r. 1254–1287), fell to the Mongols led by Kublai Khan (r. 1260–1294), who ruled as emperor of China.

SHAN DOMINATION

From the fourteenth to mid-sixteenth centuries, the kingdoms of the Shan (1364–1555) and the Mon (1353–1539) competed for dominance in Burma. Thadominbya (r. 1364–1368) was the first king of the Shan kingdom. The Shan kingdom was fraught with conflict until reunification with Burma in 1555. The Mon kingdom at Pegu, founded by Wareru (r. 1287–1296), was relatively peaceful. Its greatest ruler, Dammazedi (r. 1472–1492), was honored as a saint at his death.

TOUNGOO AND KONBAUNG DYNASTIES

Established by a Burman leader named Minkyinyo (r. 1486–1531), the Toungoo dynasty flourished from 1486 to 1752. Minkyinyo's son and successor, Tabinshwehti (r. 1531–1550), unified Upper and Lower Burma in 1539 when he conquered the Mon people and made the port city of Pegu his capital. Tabinshwehti failed, however, in his attempt to capture Siam, and the kingdom began to fall apart after his death in 1550.

Tabinshwehti's brother-in-law, Bayinnaung (r. 1550–1581), conquered Ayuthia, the Siam capital, and other Shan states, including the ancient capital of Ava, between 1554 and 1568. Bayinnaung restored Pegu as a great commercial center and, in 1555, he reunited much of Upper and Lower Burma. However, with the accession of Bayinnaung's son, Nandabayin (r. 1581–1599), Siam reasserted its independence and the Toungoo dynasty began to decline.

By the 1600s, many Westerners were living and trading in Burma's seaports. In 1613, a Portuguese mercenary named Philip de Brito y Nicote, who served as governor of the province of Syriam, became ruler of Lower Burma. De Brito held control until his defeat by Bayinnaung's grandson, Anaukpetlun (r. 1605–1648) in 1613.

Anaukpetlun's successor, King Thalun (r. 1629–1648), moved the capital of Upper Burma from Pegu to the more isolated Ava in 1635, while Lower Burma had greater contact with European traders. Thalun's reign was peaceful, and he improved the kingdom's revenues. But his dynasty grew weak when Manchu forces chased Yung-Li (Yong-Li), the Ming claimant to the imperial throne of China, to Burma and battled on its soil. The Mons took this opportunity to rebel. They established their dynasty at Pegu and captured Ava in 1752, ending the Toungoo dynasty.

The last Burmese dynasty, the Konbaung dynasty, was founded by Alaungpaya (r. 1753–1760) in 1752 and continued until 1886. Alaungpaya ("embryo Buddha"), a great warrior, recaptured Ava from the Mons only a year after its fall, and he soon reunited Upper and Lower Burma. In 1755, Alaungpaya occupied Dagon, the site of the revered Shwedagon Pagoda, and established Yangon (Rangoon) there, the capital of modern Burma. During his reign, Alaungpaya conquered the Manipur kingdom in northeastern India and, in Burma, the Shan kingdom of Mai, and the states of Syriam and Pegu.

CONFLICTS WITH THE BRITISH

King Bodawpaya (r. 1782–1819), a younger son of Alaungpaya, seized the Burmese throne in 1782 from his nephew, Maung Maung (r. 1782). Bodawpaya assassinated all possible rivals, moved his capital to Amarapura in northern Burma, and conquered and annexed Arakan, a province bordering Bengal in India. The Arakanese, however, revolted against Burmese rule. They fled into territory held by the British East India Company and attempted to reconquer Arakan from there, succeeding in 1811.

In 1821 King Bagyidaw (r. 1819–1853), Bodawpaya's grandson and successor, attacked Manipur and Assam, worsening relations with the British through a succession of border incidents. Britain sent forces from India and claimed victory over the Burmese king during the First Anglo-Burmese War (1824–1826), forcing Bagyidaw to relinquish rights to Manipur and other states between Burma and British India.

Burma's dynastic legacy ended with Thibaw Min (1878–1885), who took the throne in 1878 as an inexperienced nineteen-year-old ruler. The British deposed Thibaw in 1885, annexed his kingdom, and forced him into exile in India. Soon after, in January 1886, all of Burma became a province of British India.

See also: ALAUNGPAYA DYNASTY; MANIPUR KINGDOM; MON KINGDOM; PAGAN KINGDOM; PEGU KINGDOM; SHAN KINGDOMS; THIBAW; TOUNGOO DYNASTY.

BUSAID DYNASTY. *See* BARGHASH IBN

SA'ID EL-BUSAIDI

BUYID (BUWAYHID) DYNASTY
(945–1060 C.E.)

An Islamic dynasty that ruled western Iran and parts of present-day Iraq during the tenth and eleventh centuries. The dynasty took its name from a Muslim leader named Buyeh, whose three sons—Ali (r. 932–949), Hasan (r. 947–977), and Ahmad (r. 936–967)—founded the ruling line by their military takeover of several Persian provinces and then Baghdad itself.

Buyid rulers took a variety of titles and honorifics, but none took the title of caliph, which was reserved for members of the ruling Abbasid dynasty for nearly three hundred years. The Buyid rise to power, however, did alter the character of the Abbasid caliphate, as Abbasid power became decentralized, residing more in vassal dynasties supported by local military. How much obeisance these individual rulers felt they owed the caliph varied from ruler to ruler, depending on the military strength of the respective parties.

After the death of Buyeh's sons, rule continued to be split among family members and provinces until 977, when it was consolidated briefly under Adud ad-Dawlah (r. 949–983). The Buyid dynasty reached its zenith during that time, as Adud ad-Dawlah increased the holdings of the domains, established diplomatic relations with the Samanids, Hamdanids, Byzantines, and Fatimids, and had a dam built across the Kur River near Shiraz. The arts also flourished during this period of Buyid rule, with exquisite pottery, metalwork, and patterned silks.

Growing discord among later Buyid leaders contributed to the eventual decline of the dynasty, especially after the death of Abud ad-Dawlah in 983. After his death, instability in the economy, military ranks, and political leadership increased dramatically. The dynasty ended in 1055, when Tughril Beg (r. 1038–1063), the founder of the Seljuk dynasty, removed the final Buyid ruler, Abu Nasr al-Malik ar Rahim (r. 1048–1055),

See also: ABBASID DYNASTY; FATIMID DYNASTY; SAMANID DYNASTY; SELJUQ DYNASTY.

BYZANTINE EMPIRE (330–1453 C.E.)

Eastern successor to the Roman Empire, also called the Eastern Roman Empire or Later Roman Empire, which outlived its predecessor by a thousand years. At the height of the Byzantine Empire, it ruled the Balkan Peninsula, Greece, the Greek islands of the Aegean and Mediterranean, and Asia Minor (present-day Turkey).

ORIGINS OF THE EMPIRE

It is easy enough to say when the Byzantine Empire came to an end—on May 29, 1453, when, after a two-month siege, the outnumbered defenders of the Byzantine capital of Contantinople succumbed to an overpowering assault by the Ottoman Turks. This was only the second time that the massive, thousand-year-old walls of the ancient city had been breached by force. The previous occasion was in 1204, when the Christian forces of the Fourth Crusade, diverted from their destination to the Holy Land because of their desire for riches, sacked and plundered the city and established the short-lived Latin Empire (1204–1261).

While its end is clear, it is more difficult to establish the beginning of the Byzantine Empire. One could date its founding to 330, when Emperor Constantine I, the Great (r. 307–337), refounded and rebuilt the ancient Greek city of Byzantium on the Bosporus Strait, renaming it Constantinople.

One could also set the date of the empire's founding at 395, when the eastern and western halves of the Roman Empire were permanently divided, never again to be reunited. Or one might mark the start of the Byzantine Empire with Emperor Justinian I (r. 527–565), whose reign saw the last attempt, undone at his death, to reconquer the western portion of the old Roman Empire.

Finally, the date of the empire's beginning could be placed in the early seventh century, when Greek replaced Latin as the language of government and administration in the Eastern Empire, and the imperial title was changed from the Latin imperator, Caesar, and Augustus to the Greek basileus (king).

In any event, the long-lived and resilient Byzantine Empire preserved the memory of Ancient Rome throughout its existence. Surviving innumerable assaults and a multitude of foes, it helped preserve and spread Roman political traditions, Hellenic (Greek) culture, and Christian beliefs. Thanks to the Byzantines, Christianity spread to the Balkans and to Russia. The empire fulfilled its cultural mission even at the end, when, on the eve of the Ottoman conquest, an exodus of Byzantine scholars to Italy infused the budding Renaissance with more ancient Greek learning and ideas than the West had ever known before.

Between the late fourth century and mid-sixth century, the Western Roman Empire was subject to invasions by a number of groups, including the Visigoths under Alaric (r. 395–410), the Huns led by Attila (r. 445–453), and the Slavs, Bulgars, and Persians. Meanwhile, the Eastern Roman Empire

THE BYZANTINE EMPIRE, ca. 565 C.E.

Byzantine Empire (ca. 330–1453 C.E.)

Dynasty of Theodosius

ARCADIUS	395–408
THEODOSIUS II	408–450
MARCIAN	450–457

Dynasty of Leo

LEO I	457–474
LEO II	474
ZENO THE ISAURIAN	474–475
BASILISCUS	475–476
ZENO (RESTORED)	476–491
ANASTASIUS I	491–518

Dynasty of Justin

JUSTIN I	518–527
JUSTINIAN I, THE GREAT*	527–565
JUSTIN II	565–578
TIBERIUS II CONSTANTINE	578–582
MAURICIUS	582–602
PHOCAS	602–610

Dynasty of Heraclius

HERACLIUS	610–641
CONSTANTINE III	641
HERACLONAS	641
CONSTANS II	641–668
CONSTANTINE IV	668–685
JUSTINIAN II	685–695
LEONTIUS	695–698
TIBERIUS III	698–705
JUSTINIAN II (RESTORED)	705–711
PHILIPPICUS	711–713

ANASTASIUS II	713–715
THEODOSIUS III	715–717

Syrian Dynasty

LEO III, THE SYRIAN	717–741
CONSTANTINE V	741
ARTAVASDUS	741–743
CONSTANTINE V (RESTORED)	743–775
LEO IV	775–780
CONSTANTINE VI	780–797
IRENE*	797–802
NICEPHORUS I	802–811
STAURACIUS	811
MICHAEL I	811–813
LEO V, THE ARMENIAN	813–820

Amorian Dynasty

MICHAEL II, THE AMORIAN	820–829
THEOPHILUS	829–842
MICHAEL III	842–867

Macedonian Dynasty

BASIL I, THE MACEDONIAN	867–886
LEO VI	886–912
ALEXANDER	912–913
CONSTANTINE VII	913–959
ROMANUS I	920–944
CHRISTOPHER	921–931
ROMANUS II	959–963
NICEPHORUS II PHOCAS	963–969
JOHN I TZIMISCES	969–976
BASIL II*	976–1025
CONSTANTINE VIII	1025–1028
ROMANUS III	1028–1034

Macedonian Dynasty (continued)

MICHAEL IV, THE PAPHLAGONIAN	1034–1041
MICHAEL V	1041–1042
ZOE AND THEODORA (JOINTLY)	1042
CONSTANTINE IX	1042–1055
THEODORA (AGAIN)	1055–1056
MICHAEL VI	1056–1057
ISAAC I COMNENUS	1057–1059

Ducas Dynasty

CONSTANTINE X DUCAS	1059–1067
EUDOCIA	1067–1068
ROMANUS IV	1068–1071
EUDOCIA (AGAIN)	1071
MICHAEL VII	1071–1078
NICEPHORUS III	1078–1081

Comnenian Dynasty

ALEXIUS I COMNENUS	1081–1118
JOHN II	1118–1143
MANUEL I	1143–1180
ALEXIUS II	1180–1183
ANDRONICUS I	1183–1185

Angelus Dynasty

ISAAC II ANGELUS	1185–1195
ALEXIUS III	1195–1203
ISAAC II (RESTORED)	1203–1204
ALEXIUS IV	1203–1204
ALEXIUS V DUCAS	1204

Lascarid Dynasty

THEODORE I LASCARIS	1204–1222
JOHN III	1222–1254
THEODORE II	1254–1258
JOHN IV	1258–1261

Palaeologan Dynasty

MICHAEL VIII PALAEOLOGUS	1261–1282
ANDRONICUS II	1282–1328
MICHAEL IX	1295–1320
ANDRONICUS III	1328–1341
JOHN V	1341–1376
JOHN VI CANTACUZENUS	1347–1354
MATTHEW CANTACUZENUS	1353–1357
ANDRONICUS IV	1376–1379
JOHN V (RESTORED)	1379–1391
JOHN VII	1390
MANUEL II	1391–1425
JOHN VIII	1425–1448
CONSTANTINE XI	1448–1453

Rulers of the Latin Empire

BALDWIN I	1204–1205
HENRY	1205–1216
PETER OF COURTENAY	1217
YOLANDA	1217–1219
ROBERT OF COURTENAY	1221–1228
BALDWIN II	1240–1261

*Indicates a separate alphabetical entry.

began to develop a distinct culture and society of its own that combined Roman political tradition with Hellenistic culture and Christian beliefs. Violent religious controversy became chronic, and political divisions marked much of Byzantine history as well.

Byzantine power grew significantly under Justinian I and his wife, Empress Theodora. During their reign, Byzantine armies checked the Persian threat from the east and recovered parts of Italy and Africa. Justinian's greatest accomplishment, however, was his codification of Roman law into the Justinian Code.

Much of the gains made by Justinian were lost under his successors. Italy was lost to the Lombards in the late sixth century, while Muslim conquests in the mid-600s and early 700s took Syria, Palestine, Egypt, and Africa from the empire. The seventh century, meanwhile, was marked by the increasing Hellenization of the empire, as Greek culture and traditions supplanted the traditions of Rome.

In 800, the crowning of Charlemagne (r. 768–814), king of the Franks, as emperor of the West, ended once and for all the primacy of Byzantium over Europe.

Along with the political division of east and west came a religious division between the Roman and Eastern Orthodox churches. This culminated with the complete break between the two branches of the Christian faith in 1054, when the Roman pope, Leo IX, excommunicated Michael Cerularius, the patriarch (or bishop) of the Eastern Orthodox Church in Constantinople. Although Constantinople remained a center of both Roman and Greek civilization, Byzantium lost all claim to religious or political universality and became essentially a Greek monarchy.

Between 867 and 1025, the Byzantine Empire entered a new period of power and splendor. Its emperors regained control of the Balkans and pushed the eastern borders of the empire as far as the Euphrates River in present-day Iraq. During this period, Russia also became an outpost of Byzantine culture, having adopted Eastern Orthodox Christianity from the Byzantines.

A period of anarchy and decline began in the mid-eleventh century. The Seljuk Turks increased their attacks against the empire at this time, and with the Turkish victory at the battle of Manzikert in 1071, the Byzantines lost most of Asia Minor permanently. The powerful Republic of Venice began challenging Byzantine commercial dominance in the eastern Mediterranean during this period, and the Bulgars and Serbians gained their independence.

The rulers of the Comnenian dynasty (1081–1185) oversaw further disintegration of the Byzantine Empire. Then, in 1204, the Byzantines suffered the devastating attack on Constantinople by the forces of the Fourth Crusade. Having captured the Byzantine capital, the crusaders established the Latin Empire, which included Thrace, Macedonia, and Greece. The remainder of the empire also split up in a series of independent states, among the most notable of which were Nicaea, Trebizond, and Epirus.

In 1261, Emperor Michael VIII Palaeologus (r. 1261–1282) conquered most of the Latin Empire and founded the Palaeologan dynasty. However, the empire was soon attacked again from all fronts, including the Italian city-state of Venice, the kingdom of Naples, the kingdoms of Serbia and Bulgaria, and the empire of the Ottoman Turks. At the same time, the Byzantine Empire began to disintegrate from within, as ambitious nobles sought land and privileges, religious orders fought each other, and the Church and state vied for power.

By 1453, the Ottoman Turks had completely encircled the dramatically weakened Byzantine Empire, which consisted only of Constantinople and some surrounding territory. The Ottoman sultan, Mehmet II the Conqueror (1451–1481), surrounded the Byzantine capital with his troops in the spring of 1453, and after a fifty-day siege, the city fell to the Turks. The fall of Constantinople marked the end of the Byzantine Empire and the last remaining vestige of the ancient Roman Empire.

BYZANTINE INSTITUTIONS

Among Byzantine institutions, three stand out as being especially important: the army, the Church, and the imperial Crown. Each played a vital role in the history, organization, and administration of the empire.

The Military

From the seventh century, the very organization of the empire was military in scope. At that time, military districts, termed *themes* and commanded by a *strategus* (general), replaced the existing provinces that had been established centuries earlier under Rome.

The best soldiers in the empire came from the Balkan region and Asia Minor (or Anatolia). When Asia Minor was overrun by the Seljuk Turks in the eleventh and twelfth centuries, Byzantium lost its best source of troops, and the empire was fatally crippled as a result.

The Byzantine Empire frequently resorted to the employment of mercenaries, most notably Varangian warriors from Scandinavia and Russia, who formed the palace guard in the capital city. For a time, the Norwegian chieftain Harald Hardraada (who, as king of Norway, died while attempting to conquer England in 1066), served as a high-ranking Varangian officer at Constantinople.

When the Ottomans attacked Constantinople in 1453, Genoese and other European volunteers did their best to stem the Turkish tide. By then, in fact, they outnumbered the native Greek contingent in the military. The Byzantine navy, on a par with the army at its best, was famously equipped with Greek Fire, an inflammable, napalm-like substance squirted out of tubes at hostile warships.

The Church

The Eastern Orthodox Church, formally severed from allegiance to Rome in 1054, had been going its separate way for centuries before then. By the ninth century, the eastern and western (Roman) churches had already established different cultures, each with separate doctrines, forms of worship, and rites.

With its leadership in Constantinople under imperial oversight, the Eastern Orthodox Church was far more dependent on the emperor than the Roman papacy was on the kings and princes of Western Europe. The term *caesaropapism* has been coined to denote the strength of imperial control over the Eastern Church.

Another feature differentiating Eastern Christianity from that of the West was the divisive squabble over the nature of Christ, with some groups, particularly the Arian Christians, stressing His human nature, while others, the Monophysites, stressed His divine nature. A series of church councils grappled with this divisive issue, but the uncompromising positions of the contending groups persisted. The prevalence of Monophysitism in the eastern provinces of the Byzantine Empire facilitated their conquest by the Arabs in the seventh century because it fostered antagonism toward the central government.

Even more hard-fought was the bitter and long-lived iconoclastic controversy, which pitted supporters of icons (religious pictures and images) against those who (in Muslim and Jewish fashion) deemed icons to be blasphemous. The controversy was most acute during the eighth and ninth centuries, when icon-supporting monks rioted with their opponents in Constantinople. Even the imperial family was divided by the controversy; Constantine V (r. 741–775) persecuted icon-supporting monks relentlessly, while his daughter-in-law, later the Empress Irene (r. 797–802), supported them with equal fervor.

Imperial Power

The power of the Byzantine emperor was theoretically absolute. However, the history of the Byzantine throne is marked by a long procession of usurpations, depositions, civil war, and murders, and emperors had to be sensitive to the demands and needs of many diverse groups.

The position of emperor in the Byzantine Empire was open to talented individuals. Hereditary rule was often buttressed by the appointment of an heir as co-regent, or junior emperor. But an unworthy occupant of the imperial throne could be swiftly set aside.

Byzantine monarchs sometimes arose from the lowest classes of society, gaining their position through talent and skill. For example, Emperor Justin I (r. 518–527), the uncle of Justinian I, was an illiterate Balkan peasant, perhaps a swineherd. Emperor Leo III, the Syrian (r. 717–741), was of humble origin, as was Michael II (r. 820–829), the founder of the Amorian dynasty. Emperor Basil I, the Macedonian (r. 867–886), founder of the long-lived Macedonian dynasty, was a peasant's son raised in poverty.

Imperial power did not protect the emperor from threats against his life. The emperor's palace in Constantinople was filled with court intrigue and was the scene of a number of spectacular and grisly murders, most notably those of emperors Leo V (r. 813–820), Michael III (r. 842–867), Nicephorus II (r. 963–969), and Andronicus I (r. 1183–1185).

Sometimes, mutilation occurred instead of death, with emperors losing their noses. But when the amputated nose of Justinian II (r. 685–695) proved to be no barrier to his reaccession to the throne (705–711), blinding became the fate of former monarchs who were not killed upon their deposition.

At times, two political factions known as the Blues and Greens (who took their names from the colors worn by circus charioteers) were instrumental in determining the succession to the throne; they would riot and then proclaim an emperor of their choosing. In 532, for example, the Blues and Greens started a riot, burned public buildings, and proclaimed a new emperor. But the forces of the current ruler, Justinian I, attacked the rebels and killed thousands of them, keeping Justinian on the throne.

The rapid turnovers on the imperial throne contributed to instability, but also, paradoxically, to the renewal and reinvigoration of imperial power, as talented or skilled new rulers took power and strove to gain popular support. Unlike many other monarchies around the world, no families of shoguns (as in Japan) or mayors of the palace (as in the Frankish kingdom in Western Europe) ever eclipsed the Byzantine emperor.

Another notable feature of Byzantine imperial power was the emergence of women as sovereigns in their own right, which was unheard of in Ancient Rome. The first female Byzantine ruler was Irene (r. 797–802), the ambitious widow of Emperor Leo IV (r. 775–780), who seized the throne after blinding her own son, Constantine VI (r. 780–797) when he was deposed. Viewed in the West as a monstrous usurpation of power, Irene's action facilitated the claims of Charlemagne to the title of emperor, and he was crowned emperor of the West three years later in Rome.

The power of the Byzantine throne reached its zenith under Emperor Basil II, the Bulgar-slayer (r. 976–1025), whose conquest of Bulgaria was followed by the blinding of thousands of Bulgarian captives. The strangest Byzantine regime occurred in 1042, when Basil's two nieces, Zoe (r. 1042) and Theodora (r. 1042, 1055–1056), briefly reigned together. Theodora retired when Zoe took a third husband, Constantine IX (r. 1042–1055), but she resumed the throne on Constantine's death and reigned for a year on her own.

The longest-lived Byzantine dynasty was that of the Palaeologi (1261–1453), which ended with the death of Constantine XI (r. 1448–1453) during the final Ottoman siege of Constantinople. As the Byzantine Empire neared its end, the later Palaeologan emperors journeyed to the West to plead for European aid, having been reduced to pitiable suppliants. In the end, the dynasty survived the empire itself—from 1305 to 1533, the northern Italian state of Montferrat was ruled by a cadet branch of the Palaeologi, offspring of a western princess and a Byzantine emperor.

RELATIONSHIP WITH THE WEST AND LEGACY

Some degree of hostility had long marred the relationship between Europe and the East. The Byzantines, termed "Romans" by themselves but "Greeks" by Western Europeans, saw the West as virile but uncouth. Western Europeans, termed "Latins" by themselves but "Franks" by the Byzantines, viewed the East as cultured but effete.

The Eastern Empire could not forget the horrors of 1204, when European crusaders sacked and plundered Constantinople. Nor could the West ignore the allure of Byzantine wealth. In fact, a major factor in the economic strength of the Byzantine Empire was the remarkable gold solidus, or nomisma. This coin, first issued by Constantine I in the fourth century, maintained its value with only small fluctuations until the eleventh century. Its existence spurred the revival of gold coinage in the West, including the florin in Florence and the ducat in Venice.

Like China, the Byzantine Empire was a radiating culture, influencing its neighbors even when they sought to eclipse its power. Bulgaria, Serbia, and Russia all derived their Christianity from Byzantium. They adopted a modified Greek alphabet, the Cyrillic, to translate the Bible into the Slavic tongues. The title "tsar," used in all three states, was the Slavonic form for the Greek term *basileus,* or ruler.

Any weakening in Byzantine power brought fierce competition over the Byzantine legacy. For example, during the Latin Empire in the thirteenth century, when legitimate rule was transferred from Constantinople to Nicaea in Asia Minor, rival successor-states sprang up at Trebizond on the Black Sea (1204–1461) and, briefly, at Thessalonica (1224–1246). These states were ruled by members of Byzantine imperial families, with rulers called *basileus* modeled after the rulers of Byzantium. After the fall of Constantinople in 1453, Moscow viewed itself as the Third Rome, heir of Old Rome on the Tiber River in Italy and of New Rome (Constantinople) on the Bosporus Strait.

Toward the end of the eighteenth century, English historian Edward Gibbon wrote of Byzantine culture as one long night of debasement and decline: "In the revolution of ten centuries, not a single discovery was made to exalt the dignity or promote the happiness of mankind." Today, however, Byzantine culture is fervently admired and avidly studied, and its legacy is clearly evident.

In art, the Byzantine legacy can be seen in the magnificent mosaics of Ravenna, Italy, and the Holy Wisdom church in Istanbul (formerly Constantinople). Although not as well known, Byzantium's literary legacy includes two outstanding works: the *Chronographia* of Michael Psellus, an account of court life during the eleventh century, and the *Alexiad* of Anna Comnena, which relates the story of her father, Emperor Alexius I (r. 1081–1118).

Complementing these latter works is the report of Liudprand, tenth-century bishop of Cremona, of his diplomatic mission to the Byzantine court. Liudprand describes the imperial throne, set about with chirping mechanical birds and roaring mechanical lions, which rose into the air while the startled envoy paid homage to the emperor. Echoes of such Byzantine splendor can be found as far afield as the poems of Irish poet William Butler Yeats and the plays of American playwright Tennessee Williams, for Byzantium, like all great cultures, has its place in myth as well as in history.

John Morby

See also: BASIL I; BASIL II; COMNENIAN DYNASTY; CONSTANTINE I, THE GREAT; EMPERORS AND EMPRESSES; EMPIRE; IMPERIAL RULE; IRENE; JUSTINIAN I; MEHMED II, THE CONQUEROR; OTTOMAN EMPIRE; PALAEOLOGAN DYNASTY; THEODORA.

FURTHER READING

Comnena, Anna, et al. *The Alexiad of Anna Comnena.* Trans. E.R. Sewter. New York: Penguin, 1979.

Kazhdan, Alexander, ed. *The Oxford Dictionary of Byzantium.* 3 vol. New York: Oxford University Press, 1991.

Psellus, Michael. *Fourteen Byzantine Rulers: The Chronographia of Michael Psellus.* Trans. E.R. Sewter. London: Penguin Books, 1966.

CAESARS

The family name and title of Roman emperors of the Julian *gens* (clan), which later became one of the titles of all Roman emperors. Caesar was originally the family name of Gaius Julius Caesar (c. 100–44 B.C.E) and was first used as an imperial title by the Emperor Augustus (r. 27 B.C.E.–14 C.E.).

The development of the Roman imperial succession represented something of a paradox. While the Romans stressed family, tradition, and ancestors, they also admired leadership based on merit. Moreover, they had detested the idea of a hereditary monarchy since the establishment of the Roman Republic around 500 B.C.E. Adopting the name of the revered leader Julius Caesar helped the first emperors legitimize their rule and also resolved the paradox in true Roman fashion. The Caesars became a new *gens*, or clan, that emperors entered upon taking the throne, even when they gained their rule not by inheritance but through appointment by a predecessor or acclamation by the army. Later, "Caesar" became a title for an emperor's designated heir or for a subordinate emperor.

THE JULIO-CLAUDIAN DYNASTY

The title "Caesar" derives from Gaius Julius Caesar, the renowned military leader and dictator of Rome. Shortly before his assassination in 44 B.C.E., Caesar adopted his young great-nephew, Gaius Octavius,

The title "Caesar" came from the family name of Gaius Julius Caesar, portrayed by this marble bust. Though not an emperor, Julius Caesar laid the groundwork for imperial rule by consolidating power during his brief tenure as consul and dictator of Rome.

who, according to Roman custom, then assumed the name Gaius Julius Caesar Octavianus. When Octavian became Rome's first emperor, Caesar Augustus, in 31 B.C.E., the aura surrounding the name of the deified Julius Caesar aided his claim to power. His rival Mark Antony claimed that Augustus owed all of his success to the name Caesar. Augustus and his successors are known as the Julio-Claudian dynasty.

Augustus, who had no male children, formally adopted his stepson Tiberius Claudius Nero, who became known as Tiberius Claudius Caesar (r. 14–37 C.E.). Tiberius was succeeded in the same fashion by Caligula (r. 37–41), Claudius (r. 41–54), and Nero (r. 54–68). Claudius was the first Caesar not to be formally adopted by his predecessor.

THE FLAVIAN AND ANTONINE DYNASTIES

Titus Flavius Vespasianus, or Vespasian (r. 69–79), a renowned general who was acclaimed emperor by the army in 69, founded the Flavian dynasty, but not without difficulty, for some senators objected to passing the imperial title through a family of lesser rank. Nevertheless, according to the *Lives of the Twelve Caesars* by the ancient Roman historian Suetonius, Vespasian insisted that "his sons would succeed him or he would have no successor." He appointed his son Titus (r. 79–81) as Caesar and emperor designate. Beginning with the Emperor Trajan (r. 98–117), the standard formula for an emperor's titles became *Imperator Caesar (name and other titles) Augustus*.

During much of the second century, childless emperors selected and trained talented men from outside their family as Caesars. By adopting Antoninus Pius in 138, Hadrian (r. 117–138) began the line of Antonine emperors: Antoninus Pius (r. 138–161), Marcus Aurelius (r. 161–180), and Commodus (r. 180–192). From Trajan in 98, no emperor had a son of his own blood inherit his title until Commodus succeeded Marcus Aurelius in 180.

CAESARS AS SUBORDINATE RULERS

"Caesar" became the title for a subordinate acting emperor in 293, when Diocletian (r. 284–305) and Maximian (r. 206–305) established a tetrarchy (system of four rulers). Such a system was necessary to govern the now enormous Roman Empire. Both Diocletian and Maximian ruled as Augustus, and each chose a Caesar as his assistant: Maximian selected Constantius I (r. 305–306), and Diocletian selected Galerius (r. 305–311). Each Caesar and each Augustus was assigned his own capital city and the administration of a portion of the empire.

This system did not last long, however. Maximian's choice of Constantius as Caesar had angered Maximian's own son, Maxentius (r. 306–312), who declared himself emperor in 306. Galerius's new Caesar, Maximinus Daia (r. 310–313), declared himself Augustus in 310. The resultant warfare ended only when Constantius's son, Constantine I (r. 323–337), became sole emperor in 323. Constantine in turn gave the title "Caesar" to his three sons and two nephews, only to have their reigns end in fratricidal warfare after his death in 337.

The use of the title "Caesar" continued after the division of the Roman Empire into eastern and western halves, each with a separate emperor, in 364. By this time, however, the meaning of "Caesar" as a designation for the imperial heir had diminished, since emperors often elevated their sons to the rank of Augustus when they were mere children. Long after the fall of Rome in 476, the imperial significance of the title "Caesar" survived in two forms that derived from it, the German title "Kaiser" and the Russian "Tsar."

See also: AUGUSTUS; DIOCLETIAN; JULIUS CAESAR; JULIO-CLAUDIANS; TSARS AND TSARINAS.

FURTHER READING

Grant, Michael. *The Roman Emperors: A Biographical Guide to the Rulers of Imperial Rome, 31 B.C.–A.D. 476.* New York: Barnes and Noble, 1997.

Scarre, Christopher. *Chronicle of the Roman Emperors: The Reign-by-Reign Record of the Rulers of Imperial Rome.* New York: Thames and Hudson, 1995.

CALIGULA (12–41 C.E.)

Roman emperor (r. 37–41) known primarily for his financial and sexual excesses and his cruel and ruthless reign. Caligula's brief rule ended when he was murdered by one of his own guards.

Born Gaius Caesar Germanicus, Caligula was the son of the Roman general Germanicus, who was the nephew of the emperor Tiberius (r. 14–37), the brother of future emperor Claudius (r. 41–54), and the grandson of Livia, the widow of Emperor Augustus (r. 27 B.C.E.–14 C.E.). His mother was Agrippina, the granddaughter of the emperor Augustus. Born while his father was away fighting in northern campaigns, the precocious young Gaius became a favorite of his father's legionaries, who gave him the affectionate nickname Caligula, meaning "little boot."

A few years before his death, the emperor Tiberius named Caligula as his heir. In 37, Tiberius fell ill and was presumed dead; the Senate quickly declared Caligula to be emperor. Tiberius began to recover, however, so Caligula employed one of the imperial guards to smother the emperor. Despite this bloodthirsty start, Caligula began his reign auspiciously. He lowered taxes, provided games and spectacles for the Roman populace, and recalled many of those exiled by Tiberius.

Whether Caligula's pleasant beginning was sincere or calculating, it was short-lived. The remainder of Caligula's rule was a bizarre mixture of self-indulgence, foolishness, and violent excesses. As his reign progressed, his actions became increasingly unpredictable and extreme. Caligula's devotion to racing led him to appoint his favorite horse, Incitatus, a senator. He conducted a military campaign against Neptune, the god of the sea, and declared victory to the Roman Senate when he revealed casks of seashells supposedly taken as tribute from his hapless opponent.

Such antics were matched by Caligula's sexual escapades. One of the emperor's favorite activities was to declare a divorce for a woman of his choosing and then force his attentions upon her for a brief time. His sexual interests ranged beyond married women to handsome young men, and perhaps even to his own sisters.

Caligula's passion for his siblings fit with his view of himself as a god. He greatly admired the ancient Pharoanic system of Egypt, in which kingship and godhead were equal. Caligula set up his own religion, complete with priests, in the ancient temple of Castor and Pollux, where he could often be found reprimanding Jupiter or in the embrace of an invisible moon goddess.

Over and above these eccentricities, Caligula's financial extravagances quickly bankrupted the state treasuries carefully built up by his predecessors, Tiberius and Augustus. To increase his revenues, Caligula regularly condemned wealthy senators and nobles for wholly fabricated treasons and confiscated their estates.

Within four years of Caligula's ascendancy, Rome was in its worst state—both financially and psychologically—since the civil wars of the previous century. Through his ruthlessness and cruelty, he managed to maintain control over the people and the Roman Senate. However, the emperor made a fatal error in underestimating the pride of his force of bodyguards, the Praetorians. Each night, Caligula gave a new password to the officer of his personal guard. The emperor enjoyed the petty humiliation of forcing this man to repeat lewd phrases as the passwords to his fellows. On one night in 41, this insult proved too much for the Praetorian tribune, Cassius Chaerea, who stabbed and killed the emperor in a dark passage.

Caligula had no named heirs, but the Praetorians quickly found a replacement to ensure their continued employment. They proclaimed as emperor Caligula's uncle Claudius, who had had little political involvement up to this time and did not want to assume leadership. The assassination of Caligula and the proclamation of Claudius as emperor by the Praetorians marked the beginning of a new era of Roman politics; the Senate's power was long dead, and now the Roman military began its ascendancy.

See also: AUGUSTUS; BEHAVIOR, CONVENTIONS OF ROYAL; CAESARS; CLAUDIUS; DIVINE RIGHT; DIVINITY OF KINGS; INCEST, ROYAL; JULIO-CLAUDIANS; REGICIDE; ROMAN EMPIRE; TIBERIUS.

CALIPHATES

Religious and political organization of the Muslim world under one leader, known as the caliph, which began in southwest Asia in the seventh century.

The caliph is considered the rightful successor to the prophet Muhammad, the founder of Islam, even though Muhammad's directions for the future leadership of Islam have been subject to wide debate since the time of his death in 632. While various Muslim political and religious leaders have styled themselves as caliphs into the twentieth century, the caliphate itself ceased to be a significant political organization in the thirteenth century.

ORIGINS AND EARLY YEARS

The death of the prophet Muhammad in 632 precipitated an early crisis for the young Islamic world, as

Caliphates

ORTHODOX CALIPHATE

ABU BAKR*	632–634
UMAR	634–644
UTHMAN	644–656
ALI	656–661

Umayyad Dynasty

MU'AWIYA I	661–680
YAZID I	680–683
MU'AWIYA II	683–684
MARWAN I	684–685
ABD AL-MALIK	685–705
AL-WALID I	705–715
SULAYMAN	715–717
UMAR II	717–720
YAZID II	720–724
HISHAM	724–743
AL-WALID II	743–744
YAZID III	744
IBRAHIM	744
MARWAN II	744–750

Abbasid Dynasty

ABU AL-ABBAS AL-SAFFAH	750–754
AL-MANSUR	754–775
AL-MAHDI	775–785
AL-HADI	785–786
HARUN AL-RASHID*	786–809
AL-AMIN	809–813
AL-MA'MUN	813–833

AL-MU'TASIM	833–842
AL-WATHIQ	842–847
AL-MUTAWAKKIL	847–861
AL-MUNTASIR	861–862
AL-MUSTA'IN	862–866
AL-MU'TAZZ	866–869
AL-MUHTADI	869–870
AL-MU'TAMID	870–892
AL-MU'TADID	892–902
AL-MUKTAFI	902–908
AL-MUQTADIR	908–932
AL-QAHIR	932–934
AL-RADI	934–940
AL-MUTTAQI	940–944
AL-MUSTAKFI	944–946
AL-MUTI	946–974
AL-TA'I	974–991
AL-QADIR	991–1031
AL-QA'IM	1031–1075
AL-MUQTADI	1075–1094
AL-MUSTAZHIR	1094–1118
AL-MUSTARSHID	1118–1135
AL-RASHID	1135–1136
AL-MUQTAFI	1136–1160
AL-MUSTANJID	1160–1170
AL-MUSTADI	1170–1180
AL-NASIR	1180–1225
AL-ZAHIR	1225–1226
AL-MUSTANSIR	1226–1242
AL-MUSTA'SIM	1242–1258

*Indicates a separate alphabetical entry.

his direction for how believers were to proceed politically after his death were ambiguous, and his only direct descendants had died in infancy. The two major branches of Islam, Sunni and Shii, arose from the controversy over Muhammad's successor.

Shiite Muslims believe that the only rightful successor to Muhammad was Ali (r. 656–661), the prophet's nephew and son-in-law, who became the fourth caliph in 656. Since Ali's descendants were killed, Shiites question the legitimacy of any caliphs who followed him. The Sunni branch of Islam, which became the politically more dominant of the two, holds that Muhammad's proper successor was Abu Bakr (r. 632–634), the prophet's father-in-law. Upon Muhammad's death, Abu Bakr was elected as the first caliph by a group of Muslim elders. Since the majority of early Muslims believed in the legitimacy of Abu Bakr, his succession in 632 is considered to be the effective beginning of the caliphate.

Abu Bakr served as caliph for only two years, but his reign was crucial because it saw the further unification of Muslims on the Arabian Peninsula and the beginning of the expansionist policies that allowed Islamic rule to eventually spread throughout the Middle East, North Africa, and even into Europe.

Abu Bakr was succeeded by Umar (r. 634–644), who is often credited with creating the Islamic state through his shrewd administrative reforms and impressive military conquests. Umar was assassinated by a Christian slave in 644, leading to the election of Uthman (r. 644–656) as his successor. Uthman's reign as third caliph saw the caliphate extend throughout North Africa and into southeastern Europe. Uthman's military successes, however, were complicated by his policy of distributing the monetary and political spoils of war to his family and close friends, which alienated many Muslims. In the summer of 656, he was captured and assassinated in his home in Medina by a group of disaffected Muslims, thus bringing the prophet's son-in-law Ali to the caliphate, as the fourth caliph.

Ali's five-year rule as caliph is known largely for the internal opposition he faced. Aishah, a wife of Muhammad and daughter of Abu Bakr, challenged Ali's right to succeed to the caliphate and staged an unsuccessful revolt in 656. Five years later, Ali was assassinated by the Khawarijis, a group of dissatisfied ex-supporters. His death led to the caliphate of his main rival, Muawiyah I (r. 661–680), who founded the Umayyad dynasty.

Muawiyah had pressured Ali's son Hasan, who had been proclaimed caliph, to abdicate the title in order to avoid a costly war. Hasan's death in 669 was considered a murder by Shiites, and they believe that Muawiyah was responsible. Hasan's brother, Husayn, challenged Yazid I (r. 680–683), Muawiyah's son and successor, for the caliphate in 680, but was badly defeated and killed by the Umayyads at Karbala that same year. His death marks a great holy day for Shiites and the source of much internal controversy among Muslims.

GROWTH AND DECLINE

The Umayyad dynasty continued the spread of the Islamic caliphate throughout Asia, North Africa, and Southern Europe, but it began to face internal opposition from tribal leaders. The Umayyads were challenged and defeated by the Abbasid family, which took the caliphate in 749 and began its own dynasty under as-Saffah (r. 750–754). Under the Abbasids, the caliphate reached its greatest extent, expanding across Asia and vastly increasing its wealth and power. The Abbasid caliphs Harun al-Rashid (r. 786–809) and al-Mamun (r. 813–833) are credited with encouraging the impressive scientific and cultural advances that mark the early Abbasid period.

Abbasid ascendancy did not last long, however, as internal rivalries began to weaken the Islamic Empire. From the ninth century onward, a variety of local dynasties appeared, especially in Persia (modern-day Iran). These groups were ostensibly under the oversight of the Abbasids, but actually chafed under Abbasid rule, and pushed to establish more local authority. Among these local kingdoms established were those of the Buyids, Fatimids, Saffarids, Samanids, Seljuqs, and Ayyubids.

Although some of these kingdoms professed loyalty to the Abbasid rulers, in reality, the caliphate was in serious decline. The end of the Abbasid caliphate came in 1258, when the Mongols under Hulagu Khan attacked the Abbasids at their capital of Baghdad, killing the current caliph, al-Mustasim (r. 1242–1258).

Although a variety of local leaders, including the head of the Ottoman Turks, assumed the title of caliph in the years that followed, no caliph was ever recognized outside of his home dominion, thus making the caliphate merely a title with little political significance. The defeat of the Ottoman Empire in World War I, and the deposition of the last Ottoman caliph, Abdul-Majid II (r. 1922–1924), in 1924 signaled the official end of the title of caliph and of the caliphate.

See also: ABBASID DYNASTY; ABU BAKR; BUYID (BUWAYHID) DYNASTY; FATIMID DYNASTY; HARUN-AL-RASHID; ISLAM AND KINGSHIP; MAMUN, AL-; OTTOMAN EMPIRE; SAFFARID DYNASTY; SAMANID DYNASTY; SELJUQ DYNASTY; SULTANATES; UMAYYAD DYNASTY.

CALUKYA (CHALUKYA) DYNASTY (ca. 543–1070 C.E.)

Actually two Indian dynasties—the Western Calukyas, who were emperors in the Deccan region from 543 to 757 and then again from around 975 to 1189; and the Eastern Calukyas, who reigned in Vengi (in eastern Andra Pradesh) from around 624 to 1070.

The Western Calukya dynasty was established in 543 by Pulakesin I (r. 543–566), known as the Great Lion. Pulakesin founded the city of Vatapi (present-day Badami) and made it his capital. His sons and successors, Kirtivarman I (r. 566–597) and Mangalesa (r. 597–609), expanded the kingdom after military victories against various neighbors.

The greatest Calukya ruler was Kirtivarman's son, Pulakesin II (r. 609–642). During his more than thirty-year reign, he strengthened Badami's control of Maharashtra and took over extensive sections of the Deccan region. Around 624, Pulakesin II conquered the kingdom of Vengi and presented it to his brother, Kubja Vishnuvardhana (r. 624–641), who was the first ruler of the Eastern Calukyas. The Eastern Calukyas continued to rule Vengi for more than four centuries, from around 624 to 1073.

King Narasimhavarman I (r. ca. 630–668) of the Hindu Pallava dynasty in southeastern India overpowered and killed Pulakesin II in 642, destroying Vatapi in the process. The next Calukya ruler, Pulakesin's son Vikramaditya I (r. 655–680), took up the battle against enemies in the south and largely restored the dynasty's previous glory. His great grandson, Vikramaditya II (r. 733–746), was another successful warrior; but he and his son were defeated around 753 by the Hindu Rastrakuta dynasty.

When the Rastrakuta dynasty collapsed around 975, the powerful Calukya leader, Tailapa (r. ca. 975–997), established the second Western Calukya dynasty, with its capital at Kalyana. Tailapa's principal accomplishment was restraining the Paramara dynasty, which ruled over the kingdom of Malwa from the ninth to thirteenth centuries.

Between 993 and 1021, the Calukyas suffered many attacks by the Cola dynasty of southern India, and eventually, around 1156, the Calukya dynasty was replaced by the Kalacuri family, which originally came from central and western India. The Calukya dynasty was restored again briefly by Somesvara IV (r. 1184–1200), but he was defeated by the Hindu Yadavas of central India, the Hoysala dynasty from the southern Deccan, and the Kakatiyas of Warangal, around 1200, bringing the Calukya dynasty to an end.

See also: COLA KINGDOM; INDIAN KINGDOMS; KALACURI DYNASTIES; PARAMARA DYNASTY; RASTRAKUTA DYNASTY.

CAMBODIAN KINGDOMS

(ca. First Century–1800s C.E.)

Kingdoms that occupied the area that is present-day Cambodia from the first to the nineteenth century. The early Cambodian kingdoms thrived culturally and economically, reaching their peak of power and greatness with the Angkor kingdom during the tenth and eleventh centuries. This golden era of Cambodian history was followed by several centuries of decline, ending in a period of Vietnamese and Thai domination that lasted until 1863, when the French established Cambodia as one of its Southeast Asian protectorates.

EARLIEST KINGDOMS

The earliest of the Cambodian kingdoms, the kingdoms of Funan and Chenla, were strongly influenced by frequent contact with Chinese and Indian sea merchants. Both kingdoms flourished culturally and politically as a result of this contact.

The Funan kingdom was established in the first century. In the third century, under Fan Shih-man (r. 205–225), Funan conquered many of its neighbors and extended its rule to the lower reaches of the Mekong River. In the sixth century, Funan was conquered by its rival and neighbor, the Chenla kingdom

Angkor Wat, an elaborate temple complex in the capital of the Khmer Empire (now Cambodia), was completed about 1150 C.E. Dedicated by King Suryavarman II to the Hindu god Vishnu, the temple contains some of the most beautiful bas-relief carvings in Southeast Asia.

of the Khmer people. The Chenla state later grew into one of the greatest early kingdoms of Cambodia, the Angkor kingdom.

THE ANGKOR KINGDOM

The Angkor kingdom rose out of the Chenla kingdom when King Jayavarman II (r. ca. 802–850), a descendant of a Chenla king, ascended to the throne in 802 and declared himself ruler of a new empire, which became known as Angkor.

The Angkor Empire thrived for the next 300 years. Its rulers undertook vast public works projects, building numerous religious temples. Under the reign of King Jayavarman VII (r. ca. 1181–1219), the Angkor Empire conquered the neighboring Champa kingdom (which occupied the region of present-day central Vietnam). Jayavarman VII is known for rebuilding the city of Angkor, called Angkor Thom, and turning it into a crowded and wealthy metropolis.

The Angkor Empire also saw several centuries in which Hindus and Buddhists coexisted in peace. Although the Mahayana Buddhist kings of Angkor ruled the empire with what they claimed were divine powers, they also tolerated the nation's large Hindu population, which had occupied the region since the first century when the Funan kingdom came into contact with Indian sea traders who practiced Hinduism.

The Angkor kings capitalized on their divine powers and mobilized the population to work for the kingdom. Eventually, however, the Angkor kingdom fell into decline when missionary monks from Burma began spreading a new branch of Buddhism. This new Buddhist sect, Theravada Buddhism, caught on quickly, and by the end of the 1200s the majority of the population had converted. Unlike Mahayana Buddhism, Theravada Buddhism did not recognize the divine right of the Angkor kings, leaving the rulers with less control over the people.

FOREIGN DOMINATION

By the fourteenth and fifteenth centuries, the Angkor Empire was replaced by a smaller Khmer kingdom, which was centered further south with its capital at present-day Phnom Penh. Little is known of this period in Cambodian history, except that the Siamese captured the city of Angkor in 1431.

From the fifteenth century until 1863, when the French established a protectorate over the region, Cambodia was dominated by the more powerful states in Vietnam and Siam (Thailand). In the early 1620s, the ruling Nguyen family of Southern Vietnam cut off Cambodian access to foreign trade, and in the following century, Thai overlords ruled the country.

The Cambodian monarchy was relatively weak during the seventeenth century, enduring a series of attempted coups and countercoups by rivals within the ruling family over who controlled Phnom Penh. The monarchy often had to rely on Vietnam or Siam for support against their internal enemies.

After two centuries of dependence on its more powerful neighbors, Cambodia accepted a French protectorate in 1863 under King Norodom (r. 1860–1904), though it remained a kingdom with a ruling monarch. French control lasted for nearly a hundred years. In 1953, under the rule of Norodom Sihanouk (r. 1941–1955; 1991–2004), Cambodia gained its political independence from France.

See also: ANGKOR KINGDOM; CHENLA EMPIRE; FAN SHIH-MAN; FUNAN KINGDOM; NGUYEN (HUE) DYNASTY; VIETNAMESE KINGDOMS.

FURTHER READING

Chandler, David. *A History of Cambodia.* 3rd ed. Boulder, CO: Westview Press, 2000.

CAMBYSES II (d. 522 B.C.E.)

One of the lesser of the Achaemenid rulers of ancient Persia (r. 529–522 B.C.E.), who added Egypt to the realm.

The founder of the Achaemenid dynasty of ancient Persia was a legendary figure named Achaemenes. The first historical ruler of the dynasty, Cyrus I (r. 640–600 B.C.E.), was king of Anshan, a city in the Fars region of Iran. His son, Cambyses I (r. 600–559 B.C.E.), came to dominate all the Persian tribes, and Cambyses's son and successor, Cyrus the Great (r. 559–530 B.C.E.), assumed the title of king of all the Persians.

In 530 B.C.E., Cyrus the Great's son, Cambyses II, succeeded to a throne that was vastly more powerful and glorious than that of his grandfather and namesake. Thanks to the achievements of his father and other forebears, Cambyses II was now king of a vast empire that extended from Afghanistan to the borders of Greece and Egypt.

Cambyses had served an apprenticeship in 538 B.C.E. as nominal king of Babylon, where he presided over ancient religious rites that played a central role in the civilization of Mesopotamia. Designated co-monarch just before his father's death in 530 B.C.E., Cambyses was determined to continue the family tradition of expansion.

In 525 B.C.E., Cambyses crossed the Sinai Peninsula into Egypt at the head of a large imperial army that included contingents from across the empire. He quickly defeated Pharaoh Psammetichus III (r. 526–525 B.C.E.), bringing an end to Egypt's Twenty-Sixth Dynasty and, symbolically, to three thousand years of Egyptian cultural and political independence.

Cambyses remained in Egypt for three years, extending his control past the borders of Nubia to the south and as far as the Greek colonies in Cyrene to the west. He would have attacked the city-state of Carthage as well, but his Phoenician vassals, whose ships would have been essential to the venture, refused to cooperate in an attack on a city that had been founded by the Phoenicians.

Cambyses declared himself pharaoh of Upper and Lower Egypt, and set about reorganizing Egyptian religious life. He drastically reduced the revenues of some of the ancient temple complexes, earning him the enmity of their priests.

Learning of a rebellion back home in Persia, Cambyses left Egypt in 522 B.C.E. However, he died before he reached home, possibly of an infected wound, or possibly, as some ancient accounts have it, by suicide.

Cambyses II's historical reputation suffered at the hands of the ancient Greek historian Herodotus, who wrote of the king's supposed madness and his insensitivity to the religious traditions of Babylon and Egypt. The Greek philosopher Plato portrayed him as the spoiled product of a soft court upbringing. One Iranian tradition even has Cambyses murdering his brother Bardiya, a possible rival to the throne. Nevertheless, during his relatively brief reign Cambyses II managed to expand and consolidate the new Persian Empire.

See also: ACHAEMENID DYNASTY; CYRUS THE GREAT; DARIUS I, THE GREAT; EGYPTIAN DYNASTIES, ANCIENT (EIGHTEENTH TO TWENTY-SIXTH); EGYPTIAN DYNASTIES, PERSIAN, HELLENISTIC, AND ROMAN.

CANUTE I, THE GREAT. *See* CNUT I, THE GREAT

CAPET, HUGH (ca. 938–996 C.E.)

King of France from 987 to 996 and founder of the Capetian dynasty. Capet was elected king, but with the support of the Church he was able to ensure that the position became hereditary. The name Capet came from a distinctive cape or cap that he wore, though the sobriquet, or nickname, is not contemporary.

Hugh Capet was the son of Hugh the Great, the count of Paris and duke of the Franks. When Hugh Capet was elected to succeed his father in 956, during the reign of the Carolingian king Lothair (r. 954–986), he began to create alliances with the Holy Roman emperors Otto II (r. 973–983) and Otto III (r. 983–1002) and with the archbishop of Reims. When Lothair's heir, Louis V (r. 986–987), died in 987 (the last ruler of the Carolingian dynasty), Hugh had sufficient support and power to claim the French throne by election. There was a rival Carolingian claimant, Charles of Lorraine, but Hugh became king with support from the Norman dukes.

Much of the reign of Hugh Capet was devoted to attempting to increase and consolidate the power of France, as well as his own position as king. This struggle precipitated a number of rebellions, including that of Eudes I, count of Blois, which Capet was able to put down successfully.

In 969, Hugh Capet had married Adelaide of Poitou, an action that was at least partly political, helping to improve relations with the powerful duchy of Aquitaine in southwestern France. He ensured the succession within his own family line by crowning his son Robert II (r. 996–1031) co-regent in 987.

Hugh Capet died of what was likely smallpox at about age fifty-eight, but the dynasty he founded ruled France through his direct descendants until 1328. The Capetian dynasty then continued to rule through its Valois and Bourbon branches until the French Revolution, and then again until 1848. The Capetian line, through its related branches, also continued in the kings of Spain (after 1700), the kings of Naples (from 1734 to 1860), and in other royal European houses.

See also: BOURBON DYNASTY; CAPETIAN DYNASTY; FRANKISH KINGDOM; FRENCH MONARCHIES; VALOIS DYNASTY.

CAPETIAN DYNASTY (987–1328 C.E.)

French royal house named for Hugh Capet, a descendant of Robert the Strong, the marquis of Neustria and count of Anjou and Blois. Capetian rule was marked by a great expansion of royal authority and the beginnings of modern France.

In 888, Eudes (r. 888–898), the son of Robert the Strong, was elected to replace the deposed Carolingian king Charles II (r. 885–888). Over the ensuing years, power shifted between the Robertians and the Carolingians. Eudes's brother, Robert I (r. 922–923), was elected king in 922. When Robert died the next year, his son Hugh the Great refused the Crown, which then passed to Robert's son-in-law, Rudolf (r. 923–936). After Rudolf's death in 936, the throne returned to the Carolingians, who ruled for the next fifty-one years.

In 987, Hugh Capet (r. 987–996), the son of Hugh the Great, was elected king by the nobles and clergy and was crowned on July 5 of that year. His election as king marks the beginning of the Capetian dynasty as the royal house of France.

Hugh's election to the kingship reflected the conditions of the era, when the king was usually considered first among equals by other princes. Although French princes might swear fealty to the king, the balance of power was in constant flux as rival princes struggled to increase their holdings and influence. Because hereditary succession was not assured at this time, kings from Hugh Capet to Louis VII (r. 1137–1180) made their eldest sons joint kings and had them rule alongside them. Except for Louis VI (r. 1108–1137), Capetian kings-in-waiting down to 1179 were crowned while their fathers were still alive.

Insistence on primogeniture (inheritance by the eldest son) helped secure Capetian power. Diplomacy, war, and marriage also extended their territory. When Hugh Capet was elected, his kingdom was mostly confined to the Île-de-France, a relatively small area around Paris. By 1328, the kingdom covered much of modern France. The Capetians also laid the organizational foundation for the *parlement* of Paris, which served as the supreme court of France until the late eighteenth century.

Although often reviled by historians for his gluttony, sensuality, and greed, King Philip I (r. 1060–1108) had a significant impact on the success of the Capetian dynasty, largely because of his efforts to subordinate unruly rival princes. Philip was particularly successful in manipulating rivalries within the Norman family of William the Conqueror, enabling him to minimize their power in Normandy and other French territory.

Philip's great-grandson, Philip II Augustus (r. 1180–1223), continued the policy, winning back French territory held by the English kings Richard I Lionheart (r. 1189–1199) and his brother John (r. 1199–1216). Considered by many as the greatest Capetian ruler, Philip II became king at age fourteen and ruled for forty-six years. A brave war leader and skilled diplomat, he used feudal law to great advantage to increase his power and that of his successors.

Another notable Capetian monarch was Louis IX (r. 1226–1270) who led the Seventh Crusade in 1248. Captured by the Muslims in Egypt, he eventually returned to France, where he was noted for his piety and his encouragement of the arts and education. Louis IX died on crusade in 1270 and was canonized as Saint Louis in 1297.

Louis IX's mother, Blanche of Castille (ca. 1188–1252), played a significant role in the Capetian dynasty. She served as regent from 1226 to 1234, during her son's minority, and again from 1248 to 1252 while Louis IX was away on crusade. Blanche's most serious challenge as regent came from powerful barons who revolted in 1226. Through diplomatic skill and personal acumen, she quashed the rebellion. For the remainder of her life, Blanche was actively involved in the government of her son's kingdom.

King Philip IV, the Fair (r. 1285–1314), was handsome and well educated, and under his leadership the Capetians reached the pinnacle of their power. Philip was especially skilled in delegating tasks to his advisers, a practice that has led some historians to claim he was manipulated by his subordinates. Though religious, Philip taxed the Church heavily to finance his ventures. During his reign, Pope Clement V moved the papacy to Avignon, beginning the so-called Babylonian captivity of the papacy.

The direct line of Capetian kings ended with the death of Charles IV (r. 1322–1328) in 1328. However, the succeeding Valois and Bourbon dynasties, from which French kings were drawn until 1848, descended from Capetians.

See also: BOURBON DYNASTY; CAPET, HUGH; CAROLINGIAN DYNASTY; FRENCH MONARCHIES; VALOIS DYNASTY.

FURTHER READING

Fawtier, Robert. *The Capetian Kings of France: Monarch and Nation, 967–1328.* New York: St. Martin's, 1969.

Hallam, Elizabeth M., and Judith Everard. *Capetian France, 987–1328.* 2d ed. New York: Longman, 2001.

CARACALLA. *See* ROMAN EMPIRE

CAROLINGIAN DYNASTY

(714–987 C.E.)

Frankish dynasty that succeeded the Merovingian dynasty, eventually ruling all of present-day France, the Low Countries, most of Germany, and parts of northern Spain and northern Italy.

The Carolingian dynasty was named for Charles Martel (r. 714–741), one of the "mayors of the palace" under the Merovingian kings. In the later years of the Merovingian dynasty, kings of the Frankish kingdom exercised little real power. Instead, the mayors of the palace (*major domo*), who had started out as highly placed officials, ruled the kingdom.

GAINING LEGITIMACY

By the time of the last Merovingian king, Childeric III (r. 743–751), the Carolingians were sufficiently powerful to legitimize their authority. In 751, Charles Martel's son, Pepin III, also known as Pepin the Short (r. 751–768), wrote to Pope Zacharias and stated a case for why he should be ruler of the Frankish kingdom.

Since the Carolingians had supported the papacy against its enemies, Zacharias gave Pepin the support he desired. In 751, Pepin assembled nobles and powerful clergy at the city of Soissons and was declared king of the Franks. His predecessor, Childeric II, was thus deposed and sent to a monastery. Three years later, the new pope, Pope Stephen III, traveled to France and personally anointed Pepin as king.

MAINTAINING STABILITY

The Frankish kingdom reached its peak of power and greatest extent under the Carolingian dynasty, particularly under Charlemagne (r. 768–814), one of the greatest rulers of the Middle Ages. A crucial component of Carolingian success was the close relationship with the Roman Church and the papacy. This relationship went back to the time of Pepin II (r. 680–714), a powerful "mayor of the palace" and the father of Charles Martel. Pepin II helped the papacy acquire its first territory, which became known as the Donation of Pepin and laid the foundation for the beginnings of the Papal States.

Good luck also helped the Carolingians. When Pepin III died in 768, he followed Frankish tradition and divided his kingdom between his two sons, Carolman and Charles (Charlemagne). But Carolman

THE CAROLINGIAN EMPIRE

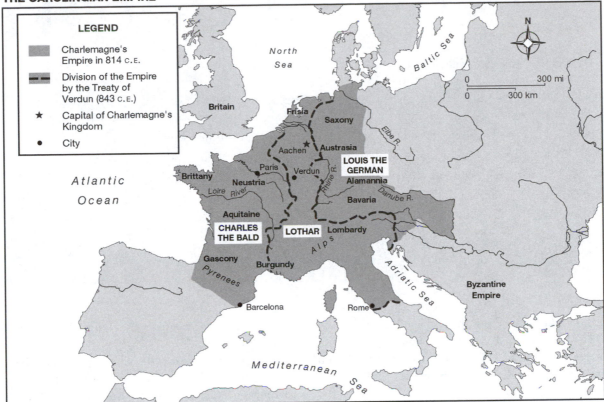

died in 771, and the entire kingdom went to Charles, removing the possibility of the type of dynastic wars that had plagued the Merovingians in the preceding centuries. In addition, Charlemagne lived to age seventy-two. This longevity provided the kingdom with consistency and relative stability, also ensuring Charlemagne's prominent place in history. King of all Franks from 768, he was crowned emperor of the West in 800.

AFTER CHARLEMAGNE

On Charlemagne's death, Charlemagne's sole surviving son Louis inherited the throne, once again keeping the empire intact. Louis I (r. 814–840), known as Louis the Pious, maintained the close relationship between the Carolingians and the Church, although this caused contention among the nobles. In an effort to avert factionalism among his descendants, Louis made his eldest son Lothair associate emperor in 817. He also attempted to balance Frankish tradition with dynastic needs. Although he ordered the kingdom split among his three sons, Lothair, Pepin, and Louis the German, he made it clear that Louis and Pepin would be subordinate to Lothair.

This precarious situation was complicated by the existence of a fourth heir, Charles the Bald, the product of Louis's second marriage. Charles's mother, Judith of Bavaria, urged Louis to give her son territory equal to that of his half-brothers. When Louis attempted to create a kingdom for Charles, Louis the German and Pepin revolted. Conflict between father and sons continued from 822 to 833. Louis was deposed in favor of Lothair twice, but each time he was restored to the throne.

A KINGDOM DIVIDED

Louis died in 840. Three years later, in 843, his three surviving heirs (Pepin had died in 838) split the Carolingian kingdom into three parts under the terms of the Treaty of Verdun (843). Charles the Bald received the western portion, which included much of present-day France; Lothair's kingdom was a narrow strip stretching from Frisia in the north to Burgundy in the south; and the remainder of the kingdom, the easternmost portion, went to Louis the German.

Louis the German and his successors ruled much of what is present-day Germany until the Carolingian line there died out in 911. The aristocracy of the

ROYAL PLACES

CAROLINGIAN ARCHITECTURE

On a visit to Ravenna in early 801, Charlemagne was impressed by buildings constructed under the Byzantine emperors. Determined to imitate the splendor of Ravenna's Church of San Vitale, he returned home to his own palace at Aachen (Aix-la-Chapelle) and ordered the erection of a chapel. Charlemagne's chapel arose as one of the finest examples of Carolingian architecture. Like San Vitale, it was surmounted by an ocatgonal dome. Inside was a circular, two-storied colonnade, decorated with gold and silver, as well as bronze railings and doors. The chapel was dedicated by Pope Leo III in 805. Destroyed by Viking raiders, the Palace Chapel was rebuilt in the tenth century.

east Frankish kingdom then elected Conrad I (r. 911–918), duke of Franconia, as king. Conrad's successor, Henry I (r. 919–936), established the Saxon dynasty, which ruled Germany and the Holy Roman Empire until 1024.

On Lothair's death in 855, his kingdom was further divided among his heirs. Charles the Bald was able to reunite much of the territory with his own and ruled as Charles II (r. 843–877). He was also crowned emperor of the West in 875. But Charles and his descendants were ineffectual rulers. Like the Merovingians, they were at the mercy of the land-holding nobles who held much of the real power within the kingdom.

CAROLINGIANS IN THE WEST

Under Charles II, the Carolingians in France had to deal with a growing threat—the Vikings. Viking raids had begun near the end of Charlemagne's reign and continued throughout the tenth century. Charles first paid tribute to Norse invaders and then turned to military solutions. In 862 he built a fortified bridge near Pîtres in an effort to protect Paris from Viking invaders. He also entrusted the Bretons with the defense of what is now northern France.

The Viking invasion proved unstoppable, however, although the Norsemen (Vikings) did make some concessions. In 911, under the Treaty of St. Clair-sur-Epte, Rollo, the leader of the Viking invaders, agreed to convert to Christianity in exchange for land in what is now Normandy. He

also agreed to recognize the king of France as sovereign.

The campaign against the Vikings proved a mixed blessing for the Carolingians. Robert the Strong, the marquess of Neustria, who led the defense of French territory for Charles II, was so popular and amassed so much power that his family rivaled that of the king. In 888, Robert's son Eudes (Odo) (r. 888–893), the count of Paris, who had defended Paris from the Norse raiders three years earlier, was elected king by the nobles. The Carolingian ruler, Charles III (r. 893–923), regained the throne in 893, but the brother-in-law of Eudes, Raoul (r. 923–936), gained the throne of France in 923.

Charles's branch of the Carolingian dynasty was restored in 936 under Louis IV (r. 936–954). But the power behind the throne was Hugh the Great, a nephew of Eudes. Hugh's son, Hugh Capet (r. 987–996), succeeded to the throne after the death of the childless Louis V (r. 986–987), the last ruler of the Carolingian dynasty. Hugh Capet established the Capetian dynasty of France.

See also: CAPET, HUGH; CHARLEMAGNE; FRANKISH KINGDOM; LOTHAIR I; LOUIS I, THE PIOUS; MARTEL, CHARLES; MEROVINGIAN DYNASTY; PEPIN THE SHORT (PEPIN III); SAXON DYNASTY.

FURTHER READING
Fichtenau, H. *The Carolingian Empire*. New York: Harper and Row, 1964.

Ganshof, F.L. *The Carolingians and the Frankish Monarchy*. Ithaca, NY: Cornell University Press, 1971.

CARTHAGE, KINGDOM OF

(flourished 800–146 B.C.E.)

Kingdom in North Africa (near modern Tunis) founded by the Phoenicians in the ninth century B.C.E., and renowned for its naval control of the western Mediterranean and wars with the early Roman Republic.

FOUNDING OF CARTHAGE

Sometime in the eighth or ninth century B.C.E., Phoenician sailors from the city-states of Phoenicia along the coast of Palestine discovered vast mineral wealth on the Iberian Peninsula. These Semitic adventurers—close cousins of the ancient Jews in language and culture—constituted the most powerful naval force on the Mediterranean of that time.

Iberia was a long way from Tyre, however, and intermediate posts were required for provisioning, repairing, and ultimately for trading. The ports established on the North African coast included Utica (present-day Utique), Leptis Magna (now Lebda), and Hippo Diarrhytus (now Bizerte). Phoenicia's most famous colony, Carthage, was founded for this purpose ten miles from modern Tunis on an ideally situated promontory that enjoyed an almost perfect, sheltered, shallow bay and, behind it, the fish-filled Lake of Tunis. Although this account of the founding of the city-state does not coincide with the Roman legend of Queen Dido of Carthage escaping the clutches of her would-be suitor, King Pygmalion of Tyre, our only source for that romantic legend is the *Aeneid* by the Roman poet, Virgil.

CARTHAGINIAN CULTURE

Although Carthage was respected and feared throughout the Mediterranean world for its robust trade and powerful navy, its culture was not admired. For example, even in ancient times the Carthaginians were reviled for their practice of human sacrifice. Worship of the god Baal Haaman (similar to the Phoenician god Baal) and the goddess Tanit (probably a native Libyan fertility goddess) required regular sacrifice of children, whose bones have been found under thousands of sacred columns throughout Carthage and her colonies.

Politically, Carthage began with supreme power residing in its kings, but the power of these rulers became diluted during the fifth century C.E. From that time on, political decisions were made by *shufets*, or judges, and by a ruling council. Although these positions were elected, eligible candidates came from only the richest families of Carthage.

RELATIONSHIP WITH ROME

The Carthaginians sailed throughout the western Mediterranean. They mined ores in Iberia (present-day Spain), traded with the Greeks in Massilia (Marseilles) and Magna Graecia (southern Italy), subjugated the islands of Corsica and Sardinia, exchanged goods with the Etruscans in Italy, and even ventured as far as the tin mines of Cornwall in southwestern England. It was probably through their contact with the Etruscans that the Carthaginians become known to the Romans.

In the third century B.C.E., Rome consolidated its power and control over the central Italian Peninsula. During the same time, Carthage became wealthier and more powerful from its Iberian and Sardinian mines, as well as from trade with the Greeks and the East. However, Roman and Carthaginian spheres of influence overlapped very little until both countries decided to expand into Sicily.

Sicily was the logical geographical point of contention for the two young empires. The highly fertile island sits in the middle of the strait that extends from the toe of Italy across to the Carthaginian Peninsula jutting out from North Africa. When Hiero, the tyrant of Syracuse, assaulted the mercenaries of Campania, the Mamertines, in their recently taken stronghold of Messana on Sicily, they appealed to both Carthage and Rome for assistance. The Carthaginians were first to respond, but they disappointed the Mamertines by forming an alliance with Hiero. The Romans soon appeared and took the side of the Mamertines. The First Punic War between Rome and Carthage had thus begun (264 B.C.E.). (The term *Punic* comes from the Latin word for Phoenicia.)

The war moved across Sicily into North Africa and then into Italy. It was the first time the Romans had fought at sea. Their success was limited until they devised a method to use their legionnaires as marines and, through imaginative boarding techniques, turned sea battles into land battles at sea. After several reverses of fortune for both sides, the Carthaginians lost the battle of the Aegadian Islands and sued for peace in 241 B.C.E. The Romans accepted the peace offer, and the Carthaginians were forced to leave Sicily, paying a large war indemnity as well.

Carthage chafed under the heavy fines imposed at the end of its first war with Rome. Carthage's best general, Hamilcar Barca, repaired to Iberia, to gather funds and train troops for an eventual counterstrike. In 218 B.C.E., Hamilcar's son Hannibal initiated a campaign that became the sixteen-year Second Punic War.

One of history's greatest military geniuses, Hannibal defeated the Romans again and again for the first fourteen years of the war. His crossing of the Alps with elephants is legendary, although ultimately it proved of little military significance. His masterful victory at the battle of Cannae in 216 B.C.E. was the worst defeat the Romans had ever suffered. However, Hannibal never felt his position was strong enough to attack and hold the city of Rome, and the lack of support he received from Carthage required him to return to North Africa in 203 B.C.E.

Not long thereafter, the Roman commander Scipio met Hannibal on the plain of Zama, where Hannibal suffered his first but also final defeat. With this defeat, the war and the competition between the two empires were over. Rome took all of Carthage's warships and elephants, as well as demanding (and receiving) 10,000 gold talents per year for the next fifty years. Carthage's commercial and military viability had been destroyed.

The Romans had not forgotten the humiliations they had suffered under Hannibal, and in 149 B.C.E., the Roman senator Marcus Cato (the Elder) whipped the Roman Senate into a xenophobic frenzy and launched the Third Punic War. The only action in this "war" was a three-year siege of the city of Carthage, which adamantly refused to surrender. In 149 B.C.E., the Romans broke through the city's walls, sold all living survivors into slavery, and "left not one stone on top of another." The kingdom of Carthage had come to an unusually final end, as Cato told the Senate, "Cartago delenda est"—"Carthage is no more."

See also: PHOENICIAN EMPIRE; ROMAN EMPIRE.

CASIMIR III (1310–1370 C.E.)

King of Poland (r. 1333–1370), known as Casimir the Great, who played an important role in shaping the kingdom of Poland and strengthening royal power. Casimir brought stability to his kingdom through a temporary peace he negotiated with the German Teutonic Knights, a religious-military order, in the Treaty of Kalisz (1343).

The last ruler of the Piast dynasty, Casimir was the son of the king Wladislaus Lokietek (r. 1320–1333) of Poland, and Jadwiza, princess of Kalisch, a protectorate in central Poland. In 1335, at the Congress of Visegrad, Casimir agreed to let John of Luxembourg rule the Polish region of Silesia as a semiautonomous state on the condition that John renounce all claims to the throne of Poland. Casimir officially recognized John's power in 1339, at the same time consolidating his rule over Poland.

Casimir pursued policies of domestic reform that angered the Polish nobility while alleviating the condition of the poor, causing him to be known as "king of the peasants." During his reign, he brought much of the Polish nobility under his control with severe laws against tyranny and oppression. He codified Polish law, giving peasants and Jews increased rights, and, in 1364, he founded the University of Krakow.

Casimir's treaty with the Teutonic Knights in 1343 allowed him to consolidate his own territories, and he later expanded his realm by acquiring, through diplomacy, much of the duchy of Galich-Vladmir in present-day Russia. Casimir died without an heir in 1370 and was succeeded by his nephew, King Louis I of Hungary (r. 1370–1382).

See also: LOUIS I, THE GREAT; PIAST DYNASTY.

CASIMIR IV (1427–1492 C.E.)

King of the united kingdoms of Lithuania and Poland, who reigned from 1440 to 1492.

A member of the Jagiello dynasty, Casimir IV became ruler of Lithuania in 1440 upon the death of his cousin, Sigismund (r. 1432–1440). A few years later, he inherited the throne of Poland when his brother, King Ladislaus III (r. 1434–1444), died without heir. As a result, the kingdoms of Poland and Lithuania were united. He united them even more closely by placing them on an equal footing, enacting similar laws and policies for each.

Like his predecessor and namesake Casimir III (r. 1333–1370), Casimir IV forged a peace with the Teutonic Knights. With the Treaty of Torun (1466),

Poland gained territory from the knights, who also officially recognized Polish sovereignty. In 1467, Casimir IV created the first Polish legislative assembly, and taking a different approach than Casimir III, he consolidated power by increasing aristocratic rights and privileges.

In 1454, Casimir IV married Elizabeth of Austria, a member of the Austrian Habsburg line, bringing Poland into the complicated picture of European monarchical succession. The marriage also made his family of six sons and seven daughters eligible for Habsburg titles. Casimir's son, Ladislaus I, became king of Bohemia in 1471 and king of Hungary in 1490, ruling both until his death in 1516. Three of Casimir's other sons followed him to the throne of Poland: John I (r. 1492–1501), Alexander I (r. 1501–1506), and Sigismund I (r. 1506–1548).

See also: CASIMIR III; HABSBURG DYNASTY; JAGIELLO DYNASTY; LITHUANIAN, GRAND DUCHY OF.

CASTE SYSTEMS

A complex social hierarchy, sometimes quite rigid in its organization, that ranks the status of individuals within their own society or cultural network.

In societies where the caste system exists, such as in India, an individual's caste is determined at birth, and he or she remains in that particular group until death. People sharing the same caste also share the same levels of wealth and status, and they participate in the same occupations and have the same cultural mores, religious rituals, and social customs. Caste also determines details of daily living, such as diet. Although those within a caste live a homogenized lifestyle and upward mobility is nearly impossible, the specific duties and nuances of castes have varied over time and place.

Karma and reincarnation are important components of the caste system in India. Karma suggests that one's status in the current life depends upon the quality of deeds performed in previous lives, and so those born in higher castes believe that their royal status is due them. Those in lower castes accept their condition as necessary repayment for past ethical misdeeds, and they faithfully adhere to the rules of their castes in hopes of achieving a better status in the next lifetime.

The caste system has existed for thousands of years, but no record exists of its origins. Some scholars believe that the caste system began in the hunter/gatherer period of history, as a survival mechanism. For example, stronger members of the tribe would become hunters, while others, less physically able, would care for the young or prepare food. As time passed, the categories of work in early societies became more distinct and the caste system began to evolve.

Although caste systems have existed in many cultures and eras, castes are an important element of Hinduism, and the most well-known caste system began to form in India over three thousand years ago. Around 1500 B.C.E., Aryan religious leaders first formulated the specific duties and rules governing caste in a work called the *Code of Manu*. This code differentiated among four broad categories of individuals and assigned each a color (varna).

The top class, the Brahmins, was assigned the color white. Brahmins served as the priestly and/or scholarly class of individuals. The next class, the Kshatryas, was given red, and it consisted of rulers, nobles, and warriors. Yellow was assigned to the Vaishyas, and these individuals served as the merchant class. Black was reserved for the Shudras, the working and laboring class of society. Below these castes were the untouchables, who performed the lowest of job duties and were considered impure. The untouchables entered homes by separate entrances and drank water from separate wells.

The term *caste* itself first came into use in the sixteenth century, when Portuguese merchants and travelers visited India. The Portuguese word *casta* means "race" or "lineage." Many Indians, however, still use the term *jati* to indicate the caste system. In the late seventeenth century, Guru Gobind Singh, a leader of the Sikhs, attempted to weaken the caste system in India. At that time, Indian surnames indicated caste. By giving all women the last name *Kaur* and all men the last name *Singh*, Guru Singh hoped to eliminate class distinctions. In the twentieth century, the Indian political and spiritual leader, Mahatma Gandhi, attempted similar reform. He renamed the untouchables *Harijans*, which means "Children of God." Gandhi would eat with and associate with the Harijans, in a symbolic attempt to raise their status within India.

Caste systems similar to India's operate in other Hindu countries such as Sri Lanka (Ceylon) and Nepal. Feudal Japanese society also was based on castes. The Japanese emperor and other nobility were *shoguns*, with the warrior (*samurai*) class and laborers ranked below them in the social hierarchy. The class of outcasts in Japan was called *burakumin*. Ancient China also had a highly developed caste system based on occupations, though the classes were somewhat less rigid than those of India or Japan. The Chinese ruling class, or Mandarins, was made up of the most highly educated in society, who sometimes were able to rise from lower classes by devoting themselves to learning.

In medieval Europe, feudalism served a function similar to that of the caste system. Kings were at the top of the social pyramid, with lesser nobles beneath them. The system depended on a large base of commoners who were under the control of those in the upper classes. Individuals had limited social mobility in feudal Europe, and the Church supported the system.

With a caste structure operating to support the hierarchy and to limit change, it can be a potent tool for those in power. In modern times, the government of India has attempted to abolish the caste system, but it has not been entirely successful. India's constitution, written in 1950, officially bans the caste of untouchables, but untouchables continue to live and face discrimination in that nation.

See also: CLASS SYSTEMS AND ROYALTY; FEUDALISM AND KINGSHIP; HINDUISM AND KINGSHIP; RIGHTS, CIVIL.

CASTILE, KINGDOM OF

(ca. 880–1506 C.E.)

Medieval and Renaissance period kingdom on the Iberian Peninsula that eventually became the foundation of the kingdom of Spain.

Covering most of the central Spanish plateau, the meseta, Castile can trace its beginnings to the settlement of the city of Burgos in 880. From 712 to 755, the territory had been under the Moorish caliphate, and it was then ruled by the caliphate of Córdoba until around 800. The region of Cantabria and the Basque provinces of Alava and Vizcaya were part of Castile, which was named for the many castles that protected the territory from Moorish incursions.

AUTONOMY AND MERGERS

Castile was a county of the kingdom of León from 910 to 1029, but it enjoyed considerable local autonomy from 930 onward. Among the notable rulers of the county of Castile at that time were Fernan Gonzalez (r. 930–970), Garcia of the White Hands (r. 970–995), Sancho I of the Good Laws (r. 995–1017), and Garcia II Sanchez (r. 1017–1029).

In 1029, Castile was joined to the kingdom of Navarre, whose king, Sancho III (r. 1000–1035), later separated it and willed it to his son, Ferdinand I the Great (r. 1035–1065), as an independent kingdom. Two years after Ferdinand I became king of Castile in 1035, he seized control of León and became its king.

The unification of the kingdoms of Castile and León lasted until 1230, and the territory it covered during this period is now referred to as Old Castile. The territory called New Castile incorporated lands reclaimed by successive Castilian kings during the *reconquista*, the period during which Iberian Christians reclaimed the peninsula from Moorish rule.

In 1065, Sancho II the Strong (r. 1065–1072) drove his younger brother Garcia out of Galicia, the territory in the northwest corner of the Iberian Peninsula, which he had inherited from his father, Fernando I. Galicia was then incorporated into the kingdom of Castile.

CASTILE AND LEÓN

King Ferdinand III (r. 1215–1252) permanently unified the kingdoms of Castile and León in 1230 and campaigned actively for the *reconquista*. He reconquered Córdoba from the Moors in 1236, Jaén in 1246, and Seville in 1248. With the occupation of Murcia by Ferdinand in 1243, all of Moorish Spain except the kingdom of Granada in the south had been reclaimed by Christian forces.

In 1252, Ferdinand III was succeeded as king of Castile and León by his son, Alfonso X (r. 1252–1284). Meanwhile, in 1254, Ferdinand's daughter Eleanor married King Edward I of England (r. 1272–1307), bringing as her dowry the French territories of Ponthieu and Montreuil as well as a claim to Gascony.

Enhancing Castile's prominence was the declining influence of the Iberian kingdoms of Catalonia—Aragón and Valencia. Also indicative of the growing power of the Castilian kings was the election, in 1257, of Alfonso X of Castile (r. 1252–1284) as Holy Roman emperor by a faction of German princes who opposed another contender, Richard, earl of Cornwall. Pope Alexander IV and Spaniards opposed his election, however, so Alfonso X never traveled to Germany to claim the imperial throne and he renounced all claim to it in 1275.

CASTILE AND ARAGÓN

During the reign of King Sancho I of Navarre (r. 925–970), the county of Aragón was attached to the kingdom of Navarre. But Aragón became a separate kingdom on the death of Sancho III (r. 1004–1035) in 1035. During the thirteenth century, the kingdoms of Castile and Aragón were the two most powerful kingdoms on the Iberian Peninsula; by the fifteenth century, the rulers of Castile had gained supremacy.

In 1474, Isabella I, the Catholic (r. 1474–1504), inherited the kingdom of Castile. The kingdom had initially passed to her half-brother, Henry IV (r. 1454–1474), upon the death of their father, John II (r. 1405–1454) in 1454. But when Henry died, civil war erupted between supporters of his daughter, Juana la Beltraneja, and the supporters of Isabella. Isabella's side won the succession struggle, helped by supporters of her husband, Ferdinand II of Aragón (r. 1479–1516), whom she had married in 1469.

With the accession of Isabella and Ferdinand to the thrones of Castile and Aragon, the two most powerful kingdoms in Spain were united. In 1492, Ferdinand and Isabella conquered Granada and drove the last remaining Moors from the Iberian Peninsula. The succession of their grandson as Charles I, king of Spain (r. 1516–1556), and later as Holy Roman Emperor Charles V (r. 1519–1558), confirmed the merger of the two kingdoms, along with Navarre, which had been annexed by Aragón in 1515. The merger of the two kingdoms, together with the rule of Charles I, is usually considered the beginning of the kingdom of Spain.

See also: ARAGÓN, KINGDOM OF; CATALONIA, COUNTY OF; FERDINAND II; IBERIAN KINGDOMS; NAVARRE, KINGDOM OF; SPANISH MONARCHIES.

CATALONIA, COUNTY OF

(801–1479 C.E.)

County in northeastern Iberia that eventually merged with the kingdom of Aragón in the late twelfth century.

The history of the county of Catalonia begins in the ninth century, when the area became part of the Spanish March of Charlemagne (r. 768–814), a frontier border region of his Frankish Empire. Ruled by French counts, Catalonia was ostensibly subservient to the Frankish Empire. But the counts of Catalonia generally ruled independently of the Franks, and in 991, under Count Borrell II (r. 947–993), they completely rejected Frankish supremacy.

From 1131 to 1162, Catalonia was ruled by Raymond Berengar, the count of Barcelona. Through his marriage to Petronilla, the daughter of Ramiro II of Aragón (r. 1134–1137), Raymond also ruled the kingdom of Aragón. Catalonia and Aragón remained under the control of Raymond's descendants until 1410, when the last count of Barcelona died.

By this time, Catalonia was the dominant partner in its union with Aragón. Much of Catalonia's power stemmed from its economy, especially its active maritime trade. Since Greek and Roman times, the area had been an important trading center on the western Mediterranean; by the late Middle Ages, it was nearly as prominent as Genoa and Venice. Trade helped expand the interest of Catalonia's rulers, as well as foster the growth of cities and the development of a prosperous and powerful merchant class.

In 1410, Martin I (r. 1356–1410), the last count of the Barcelona dynasty, died. Under the Compromise of Caspe, the House of Trastámara assumed power, with Ferdinand I (r. 1412–1416) as king. Because Trastámara interests were more closely linked to those of Aragón, Catalonia's influence in the union began to wane. This began to cause feelings of resentment and dissatisfaction among many in Catalonia.

Dissatisfaction reached the point of rebellion in 1462, four years after John II (r. 1458–1479) assumed the throne of Aragón. In 1472, John finally put down the rebellion and a peasants revolt in Catalonia. With the marriage of John's son, Ferdinand II (r. 1479–1516), to Isabella I of Castile (r. 1474–1504), the new kingdom of Castile-Aragón further eclipsed Catalan sovereignty. In addition to the shift in political power, changes in trade routes, frequent pirate attacks on the coast of Catalonia, plagues, and famine undermined the region's economy.

During the 1500s, Catalonia was eclipsed by Castile. Although Catalonia kept its autonomy and its Generalitat, or legislative assembly, diverging interests reinforced a separatist movement that lasted from the seventeenth century onward. Resentment simmered for years, reaching a boiling point as a result of the Thirty Years' War (1618–1648). Outraged by atrocities committed by Castilian troops in their territory during that war, Catalonian peasants revolted in 1640, attacking royalist troops in Barcelona. Catalonians later sought and received the protection of King Louis XIII of France (r. 1610–1643), but the revolt was put down by King Philip IV of Spain (r. 1621–1665) in 1650.

Catalonia's opposition to the interests of the Spanish monarchy again became apparent during the War of Spanish Succession (1701–1714). Catalonia supported Archduke Charles of Austria rather than Philip of Anjou, both of whom were vying for the Spanish throne. In 1713, Philip laid siege to Barcelona, finally defeating the city's forces after eighteen months in September 1714. In retaliation for the resistance, Philip, who became Philip V of Spain (r. 1724–1746), ended Catalonian autonomy, disbanded the Generalitat, and abolished the official use of the Catalan language. In 1768, under King Charles III of Spain (1759–1788), the teaching of the Catalan language also was forbidden.

The forces of French emperor Napoleon Bonaparte (r. 1804–1815), occupied Catalonia between 1808 and 1813. During his invasion of Spain, Napoleon offered Catalonia a degree of independence and official status for the Catalan language in exchange for support. But the Catalonians refused, and the region remained a mere province of the Spanish kingdom. It has remained a part of Spain ever since. In December 1979, Catalonia achieved a measure of independence within the modern Spanish republic when the Spanish government established the region as an autonomous community.

See also: ARAGÓN, KINGDOM OF; CASTILE, KINGDOM OF; IBERIAN KINGDOMS; SPANISH MONARCHIES.

FURTHER READING

Koenigsberger, H.G. *Medieval Europe, 400–1500.* New York: Longman, 1987.

Tierney, Brian, and Sidney Painter. *Western Europe in the Middle Ages, 300–1475.* 6th ed. Boston: McGraw-Hill College, 1999.

CATHERINE II, THE GREAT

(1729–1796 C.E.)

German princess, wife of Russian tsar Peter III (1762), who deposed him and ruled from 1762 to 1796, during which time she opened Russia to the cultural influences of Europe. Catherine's greatest legacy was in continuing the efforts of Peter I, the Great (r. 1682–1725) to end Russia's isolation from Europe.

EARLY LIFE

Tsarina Catherine II, known as Catherine the Great, was born Sophie Frederika Augusta in 1729, the daughter of German prince Christian August von Anhalt-Zerbst. In 1742, Christian succeeded his cousin as Prince of Anhalt-Zerbst, a small principality in Germany.

In 1741, Elizabeth (r. 1741–1762), daughter of Tsar Peter the Great, became tsarina by overthrowing the infant tsar Ivan VI (r. 1740–1741), who was the nephew of her cousin, the Tsarina Anna (r. 1730–1740). Elizabeth then designated her own nephew Peter as her successor, and, in 1744, she chose German princess Sophie to be Peter's bride on the recommendation of King Frederick II of Prussia (r. 1740–1786).

In order to marry Peter, Sophie converted from the Lutheran religion to the Russian Orthodox faith, taking the Russian name of Ekaterina Alexievna. Ekaterina, or Catherine, threw herself wholeheartedly into becoming Russian, studying the language and culture. In 1745, she and Peter were married, but their relationship became the subject of much speculation when she failed to produce an heir. After two miscarriages, Catherine finally had a son, the future tsar Paul I (r. 1796–1801), but it was rumored that the father was actually her lover, Sergei Saltykov.

Catherine became fervently Russian, while her husband Peter held unpopular pro-German attitudes and openly admired everything Prussian. The two became utterly estranged, and Catherine continued to make alliances within the court, forming her own power base in opposition to Peter's. She also had a series of lovers, often men who were of some political use to her.

When Tsarina Elizabeth died in 1762, Peter took the throne as Peter III (r. 1762). Almost immediately, he antagonized the court and the nation by ending Russia's involvement in the Seven Years' War against Prussia and entering into friendly relations with that country. Catherine, along with her lover Grigori Orlov and his brothers, seized power with the backing of the army later that year. The senate, the army, and the synod (the body that headed the church) offered her their allegiance. Forced to abdi-

Russia was transformed under the rule of Catherine the Great, who continued the program of Westernization begun by Peter the Great and expanded the Russian Empire by approximately 200,000 square miles. Catherine's reign, from 1762 to 1796, was one of the most prosperous periods in Russian history.

cate, Peter was imprisoned and murdered soon thereafter.

CATHERINE AS MONARCH

As tsarina, Catherine increased the power of the nobility but never lost control over them, continuing to manipulate factions at court. A keen student and a patron of the arts, she increased the influence of European learning and culture on that of Russia.

Catherine prided herself on being a ruler influenced by the principles of the Enlightenment. She began a commission to reform Russian law and government, but it came to nothing and her policies instead strengthened autocratic rule. In 1762, she confiscated the lands of the Russian church, using the revenue to enhance the state treasury. To strengthen her support among the aristocracy, Catherine confirmed their privileges by a charter in 1789.

The institution of serfdom reached its most se-

vere form during Catherine's rule; in addition to its expansion among Russian peasants, it was also imposed on previously free peasants in newly acquired regions, such as the Ukraine. Serfs could be punished by their masters, sent to Siberia, and even sold. Such policies led, in the 1770s, to several unsuccessful peasants' revolts. The largest rebellion, in 1773 and 1774, was led by the army officer Yemelyan Pugachov, who declared serfdom abolished and claimed to be Tsar Peter III. Pugachov was captured and executed in 1775.

Between 1768 and 1774, Russia was at war with the Ottoman Turks and, in the negotiated peace that followed, it gained important ports on the Black Sea. War with the Ottoman Empire made Russia the dominant power in the Middle East, but Catherine's efforts to break up the Ottoman realm had only limited success, such as the annexation of the Crimea in 1783.

Under Catherine, Russia also invaded Poland at the invitation of a conservative faction of the Polish nobility following the 1791 Polish civil war and constitutional crisis. In 1795, after a period of division, uprising, and conflict, Poland was divided between Russia, Prussia, and Austria. Russia also gained control of Lithuania and the Ukraine.

Catherine had a number of favorites after her lover, Grigori Orlov. The most influential of her lovers was Grigori Potemkin, who remained her close associate and adviser, helping choose her future lovers after their own romantic affair ended. She took little interest in her son Paul, whom she disliked intensely. Instead, she gave her grandson Alexander the attention and education due an heir. It was rumored that Catherine meant to designate Alexander her successor, but she died of a stroke in 1796 without doing so. Paul succeeded his mother and changed the laws of inheritance to prevent women from ever ruling Russia again.

See also: ALEXANDER I; PETER I, THE GREAT; QUEENS AND QUEEN MOTHERS; ROMANOV DYNASTY; RUSSIAN DYNASTIES.

FURTHER READING

Alexander, John T. *Catherine the Great: Life and Legend.* New York: Oxford University Press, 1989.

Erickson, Carolly. *Great Catherine.* New York: Crown, 1994.

Freeze, Gregory L., ed. *Russia: A History.* New York: Oxford University Press, 1997.

CERA (CHERA) DYNASTY

(ca. 20 B.C.E.–1000 C.E.)

Also known as the Kulasekhara, a dynasty that ruled the ancient Kerala kingdom on the southwestern, or Malabar, coast of India, an area noted for its spices and religious tolerance.

In ancient times, the Cera (Chera) dynasty reigned over a small section of the southwestern coast of India known as the kingdom of Kerala, one of the three Tamil states. Kerala means "home of the Ceras." The two other Tamil states in this southern part of India were the Chola kingdom and Pandya kingdom.

The first inhabitants of Kerala were probably animists, who believed in the existence of spirits and demons and maintained that all natural phenomena have souls. As Indo-Aryans moved into India from the north, they drove Dravidian peoples east and then into southern India. This movement of peoples caused regular warfare among local chieftains in the Kerla region, which led to the establishment of a community of warriors, called Nairs, some of whom were trained as suicide squads. The preoccupation of men with warfare led to the development of a complex social pattern in Kerala called *marumakkathayam*, which allowed women to inherit family property. This practice continued in southwestern India until modern times.

Proximity to the Arabian Sea made Kerala an important international trading center. Roman gold, Italian wine, and other products found in the region testify to the extensive foreign trade that took place there. The Ancient Romans traded generously for Indian spices, especially pepper. Later, the Arabs took Indian spices in return for Arabian horses. Jews and early Christians established colonies in Kerala, and some believe that Thomas, the apostle of Jesus, visited there in the first century of the Common Era.

By about 200 C.E., the northern Aryan sage, Agastya, had established himself as a cultural hero in Kerala. Agastya was revered as the Brahman (priestly) incarnation of a god who brought Sanskrit civilization to South India. The Cera princes of Kerala were very powerful in the fourth and fifth centuries, but their aggressive impulses were held in check by the neighboring Cholas.

From the mid-sixth century to the ninth century, the Chalukya, Pallava, and Pandya dynasties fought a long series of wars in southwestern India. Nonetheless, the period was marked in Kerala by a revival of Hinduism and the advance of the fine arts. The great Hindu philosopher and religious reformer, Shankara (Shankaracharya), was born in Kerala around 790. He simplified Brahmanic Hinduism and reestablished the values of the old Hindu religion.

From about 850, the southern area of Kerala was taken from the Ceras, first by the Cholas and later by the Chalukyas of the Deccan region. By about 1000, the Cera dynasty was present only in the form of local chieftains.

See also: CALUKYA (CHALUKYA) DYNASTY; COLA KINGDOM; INDIAN KINGDOMS; PANDYA DYNASTY.

CETSHWAYO (1832–1884 C.E.)

Zulu king from 1872 to 1879 and from 1883 to 1884, who struggled to resist European advances on his kingdom.

Cetshwayo kaMpande was born in 1832. His father, Mpande, was the brother of King Dingane (r. 1828–1840), who succeeded Shaka Zulu to the throne; his mother was Ngqumbazi. Like Shaka before him, Dingana had no offspring, and upon his death, rule of Zululand passed to Cetshwayo's father.

Succession to the Zulu throne normally went to the first-born son of the king's "great wife." The great wife was appointed by the king, which meant that the current ruler had nominal control over the disposition of the kingship upon his death. When Mpande took the throne, he initially favored Cetshwayo as his successor, but at some point he changed his mind and selected another son, Mbuyazi, as heir. Cetshwayo, however, challenged his brother's right to rule and killed Mbuyazi in battle in 1856, long before Mpande's own death.

King Mpande could not ignore Cetshwayo's obvious ambition to rise to the throne. To secure his own continued survival, the king offered Cetshwayo effective rule over the Zulu nation but retained the title of king. Upon Mpande's death in 1872, Cetshwayo was well-placed to claim the throne. He rose to power during a dangerous time, however. Both the British in Natal and the Afrikaners of the Transvaal wanted to annex Zulu territory.

Cetshwayo sought to protect Zululand's autonomy by allying himself with the interests of the British, but this strategy backfired when, in 1877, the British annexed the Transvaal and began looking to Zululand as its next colonial objective. Cetshwayo's resistance to colonization led to the outbreak of the Anglo-Zulu War in 1879, which ultimately resulted in victory for the British that same year.

To preclude the possibility of rebellion, the British exiled Cetshwayo to Cape Town, South Africa. The deposed king did not accept his exile meekly, however. Instead, he traveled to Britain to argue for his reinstatement to the Zulu throne. Although Cetshwayo faced strong opposition from colonial officials, who attempted to paint him as a vicious dictator, he succeeded in reclaiming his throne in 1883.

Cetshwayo could not hold power for long, however, for members of the British colonial office were vindictive and had long memories. At their urging, Cetshwayo's political rivals were encouraged to rebel, and the result was civil war among the Zulu. Forced to flee to a part of Zululand controlled by Natal, Cetshwaya died there in exile in 1884.

See also: SHAKA ZULU; ZULU KINGDOM.

CHAHAMANAS DYNASTY. *See*

CHAUHAN DYNASTY

CHALDEAN EMPIRE. *See*

NEBUCHADREZZAR II

CHAKRI DYNASTY (1782–Present)

The current ruling dynasty of Thailand (formerly Siam), which has been in power since the eighteenth century.

The Chakri (Chakkri) dynasty was established in 1782 by General Chaophraya Chakri, who proclaimed himself king of Siam after the death of King Taksin. P'ya Chakri ruled the country as King Buddhayodfa (Rama I) (r. 1782–1809). Soon after taking the throne, Rama I moved the capital city from Thonburu to Bangkok, where he built the Temple of the Emerald Buddha, or Wat Phra Kaew. During his reign, Siam repelled several attacks by neighboring Burmese forces.

Following the reign of Rama I, Siam underwent a process of social and economic modernization. Throughout much of the eighteenth century, Siam had followed an isolationist policy toward the West. However, under the rule of Rama II (r. 1809–1824), the country began to establish relations with Europe.

In 1826, under Rama III (r. 1824–1851), the third ruler of the Chakri dynasty, Siam signed the Burney Treaty, which allowed British merchants modest trading rights in the kingdom. The country signed a similar agreement with the United States in 1833.

King Mongkut, also known as Rama IV (r. 1851–1868), led Siam through a period of increased contact with the West, signing treaties with European powers that made Siam the only county in Southeast Asia to avoid European colonization. Under the leadership of King Prajadhipok (Rama VII) (r. 1925–1935), the country was transfomred from an absolute monarchy to a constitutional monarchy. In 1939, during the reign of King Ananda Mahidol (Rama VIII) (r. 1935–1946), the country changed its name from Siam to Thailand, meaning "land of the free." The current Chakri monarch, King Bhumibol Adulyadej (Rama IX) has ruled Thailand since 1946.

See also: SIAM, KINGDOMS OF.

CHAMPA KINGDOM

(Second–Seventeenth Centuries C.E.)

Ancient Indochinese kingdom (known as *Lin-yi* in Chinese) on the east coast of present-day Vietnam. It lasted longer than almost any other kingdom in history.

The Champa kingdom was founded by the Cham when the Chinese Han dynasty broke up in 192. The Cham were a Malay people whose culture was very Indianized.

The kingdom stretched about three hundred miles, from beyond Hue in the north to Camranh Bay in the south. It originally consisted of four small states named after areas of India: Amaravati (Quang Nam), Vijaya (Binh Dinh), Kauthara (Nha Trang), and Panduranga (Phan Rang). They all struggled to get hold of land that the Chinese occupied in Vietnam. At its peak, the population of Champa reached about two and a half million people, divided into two clans: Narikel Vamsa (Coconut Clan), which mainly ruled the northern part of the kingdom, and Kramuk Vamsa (Betelnut Clan), which was mostly in the south.

Champa was unified by its first major king, Bhadravarman, around 400 C.E. During his rule, My Son, one of the most famous Cham monuments in Vietnam, developed into a religious center—which it remained until the thirteenth century. Nearly all of the temples at My Son were devoted to Cham kings associated with Hindu gods, particularly Shiva, who was considered the creator and guardian of Champa's dynasties. Many of the towers at My Son were destroyed during the Vietnam War in the 1960s.

In retaliation for the many Cham raids on Chinese territories, the Chinese attacked Champa in 446 and took control of the region. In the sixth century, Champa was able to regain dominance and flourish economically and artistically for many years despite attacks by the Chinese, Javanese, and Khmer. Notably, under Indravarman II, founder of the Indrapura (sixth) Champa dynasty in 875, complex temples and palaces were built. In the tenth century, the Vietnamese started fighting with Champa, and they took over the Cham capital, Amaravati, in 1000. Harivarman IV, who established the ninth Cham dynasty in 1074, withstood additional assaults by the Vietnamese and Cambodians. In 1145, the Khmers raided and took control of Champa. In 1147, the Cham king Jaya Harivarman I successfully fought off the Khmer domination, and in 1177 the Chams sacked Angkor, the Khmer capital in Cambodia. They fell under Cambodian rule again between 1190 and 1220, and were invaded by the Vietnamese Tran kings and the Mongols in the thirteenth century. In 1312, Champa became Vietnam's vassal state for a short time. King Che Bong Nga (r. 1360–1390) won back Champa's independence by pillaging Hanoi in 1371, but the kingdom weakened after his death. By the end of the fifteenth century, it was virtually devastated by the continuing battles. Its capital, Vijaya, was captured by the Vietnamese emperor Le Thanh Tong in 1471, and the Vietnamese annexed and absorbed all of Champa by the seventeenth century.

See also: HAN DYNASTY; VIETNAMESE KINGDOMS.

CHAMPASSAK KINGDOM

(1500s–1900s C.E.)

Buddhist kingdom located in central Laos which became a part of French Indochina in the late nineteenth century.

The earliest known kingdom bearing the name Champassak dates back to the sixteenth century. Early accounts of the kingdom and its kings are sparse, however. Documentary evidence records the reign of a king named Khajanam in 1550. Khajanam might have been the founder of the Champassak dynasty, but little else is known about him or his successors.

The modern Champassak kingdom rose to prominence in the eighteenth century with the reigns of King Soysisamout (r. 1713–1737) and his son King Sayakoummane (r. 1738–1791). King Soysisamout built his new capital on the island of Khong, which controlled the water route of the Mekong River. This was an important move because it not only guaranteed Champassak's control of the Mekong, an important source of commerce, but it also ensured that the kingdom enjoyed the natural defenses provided by the river. King Soysisamout also introduced new ideas of government to his growing kingdom, as more vassals pledged allegiance to the king. By the time of his death in 1738, he had left a strong state to his son, King Sayakoummane.

It was Sayakoummane who created the sovereign nation of Champassak by unifying the diverse parts of his kingdom. His reign became the longest in Champassak history. The king was a devoted Buddhist, and his practice of nonviolence made him successful in his unifying campaigns. At the same time, his staunch Buddhist attitude also led to the outbreak of many rebellions against his rule.

The greatest danger, however, came from Sayakoummane's brother. In 1758, a disagreement between the king and his eldest brother led the latter to raise an army and attack the Champassak capital. The king fled the city and lived in exile for two years before he was reinstated through the assistance of the Queen Mother. Sayakoummane's problems were assuaged temporarily in 1768 with the death of his brother, but other problems emerged.

In the 1770s, King P'ya Taksin of Thailand (r. 1767–1782) embarked on a campaign to unite all

Thai territory. He sent an army against Champassak in 1777 on the pretext that Sayakoummane had failed to aid Taksin's ally, Phra Vorarat, a former minister of Vientiane. Rather than fight the Thai forces, Sayakoummane fled the kingdom. Captured by the Thais in 1778, he was taken to Bangkok as a prisoner. Two years passed before Sayakoummane was returned to Champassak to rule as a vassal of Thailand.

By 1780 Champassak had completely lost its independence to Thailand. In the latter part of Sayakoummane's reign, the kingdom was divided among competing factions. The king died from a stroke in 1791. The Thai king, Rama I (r. 1782–1809), wanting to maintain Thai control over Champassak, placed Sayakoummane's son, Fay Na (r. 1791–1811), on the throne as a figurehead. Two other relatives of King Sayakoummane were made senior ministers to retain the loyalty of the people.

Although appointed by Rama I as a figurehead, Fay Na refused to be a mere puppet subjected to the manipulation of the Thais. He tried to re-create the once glorious kingdom of Champassak by establishing a new capital and building monuments, including a *vihara*, or Buddhist hall, to house the image of the Crystal Buddha, an important symbol of Buddhist kingship. Fay Na's death in 1811 signaled the last attempt made by a Champassak king to assert independence from the Thais. Champassak had also lost the Crystal Buddha to the Bangkok monarchy.

Fay Na was followed by a string of weak kings who had troubled reigns marked by revolts and increasingly limited powers. After 1829, Bangkok was able to exert tighter rein over Champassak by placing Thai commissioners in the kingdom to oversee its government. Even before this, however, the latter Champassak kings had relinquished their autonomy to rule, subjecting themselves to the authority of the Thai monarchs.

Champassak remained a dependency of Thailand until 1893, after which it was governed by the colonial French administration. Ceded to the French in the Franco-Siamese Treaty of 1893, Champassak became a protectorate of French Indochina. The French continued to endorse the puppet government of the Champassak kings until 1934, when they abolished the monarchy and gave the current Champassak ruler, Chao Ratsadanay (r. 1900–1934), the title of the governor of Champassak.

See also: BANGKOK KINGDOM; BUDDHISM AND KINGSHIP; SIAM, KINGDOMS OF; SOUTHEAST ASIAN KINGDOMS.

FURTHER READING

Manich Jumsai, M.L. *History of Laos, Including the History of Lannathai, Cheingmai.* New York: Paragon Book Gallery, 1967.

Simms, Peter, and Sanda Simms. *The Kingdom of Laos: Six Hundred Years of History.* Surrey: Curzon Press, 1999.

Stuart-Fox, Martin. *A History of Laos.* New York: Cambridge University Press, 1997.

———. *The Laos Kingdom of Lan Xang: Rise and Decline.* Bangkok: White Lotus Press, 1998

CHANDELLA DYNASTY

(ca. 850–1202 C.E.)

The last Hindu rulers of Bundelkhand, a kingdom in the central Ganges Valley area of northern India, known especially for its architecture.

The first known ruler of the Chandella dynasty was Nannuka (r. ca. 831), whose ancestors were probably humble vassals of the once powerful Pratihara Empire. The Pratiharas, in turn, were descendants of Huna invaders, who controlled much of northern India by the sixth century.

Scholars believe that the Chandellas were originally members of the Gond and Bhar families who, once they had come to power as royalty, claimed to be descendants from Chandra, the moon god. The Chandella claimed that Chandra had taken human form and fathered the first of their line by a Brahman girl. As such, the Chandella claimed Kshatriya, or warrior, caste status.

The Chandellas came into prominence while the Pratihara leaders, faced with a steady decline in their power and authority, were attempting to defend all of India from Muslim incursions from Afghanistan. The province that the Chandellas ruled, Bundelkhand, was then known by its ancient name, Jejakabhukti, which was the nickname of Jayaskati (r. ca. 850–?), the grandson of Nannuka. Jejakabhukti extended from the Jumna River in the north to the Vindhya Mountains in the south, an area that is now part of the present-day Indian state of Vindhya Pradesh.

The most important ruler of the Chandella dynasty was its seventh king, Yasovarman (r. ca. 925–954). As the Pratihara Empire continued to decline, Yasovarman, also known as Lakshavarman, captured the famous hill fort of Kalanjar, which became the stronghold of his growing kingdom. Yasovarman won victories over scattered remnants of the Pratihara Empire, including some lands held by the Pala dynasty of Bengal and the Paramara dynasty of Malawa. He made Mohaba his capital and built a magnificent temple there dedicated to the god Vishnu.

The Chandella dynasty reached its peak during the reign of Yasovarman's son and successor, Dhanga (r. ca. 954–1003), who consolidated the kingdom's power. A poet and a great patron of the arts and architecture, Dhanga supported the construction of many temples during his reign. Also a capable statesman, in the late tenth century he joined with a federation of Hindu princes under Jaipal (r. ca. 965–1002), the king of the Punjab, to resist the Muslim advances of Mahmud Ghaznavi (r. 998–1030) in the northern Punjab. Mahmud defeated the federation's forces around 990, and Dhanga's army withdrew to reconsolidate in Jejakabhukti.

During the short, relatively peaceful reign of Dhanga's son and successor, Ganda (r. 1003–1018), more temples were built, adding to the architectural legacy of the Chandella dynasty. However, by 1018, Muslim military forces had reached Jejakabhukti, and Ganda's son and successor, Vidyahara (r. 1018–1022), had to face invasions by Mahmud Gaznavi. Nevertheless, Vidyahara continued his dynasty's patronage, building the famous Kandariya Mahadeva Temple of Khajuraho for the god Siva.

After the reign of Vidyahara, Chandella power began to fade. In the north, the Kalacuri dynasty came to power and established the kingdom of Chedi (1158–1181), taking away Chandella territory between the Narmada and Godavari rivers. Moreoever, Muslim attacks continued to threaten Chandella stability. A succession of Chandella rulers—including Vijayapala (r. ca. 1022–1051), Devavarman (r. ca. 1051), and Kirttivarman (r. 1070–1098)—focused their attention on maintaining the strategic forts of Mohaba, Ajayagerah, and Kalanjar. Experiencing a brief resurgence of power, Kirttivarman defeated Karna (r. 1063–1093), chief of the Chedi kingdom, and joined with other Hindu dynasties to fight against the Muslims under Mahmud of Ghazni.

The last ruler of the Chandella dynasty was Paramardideva (r. ca. 1166–1202), who lost the Kalanjar fort and many other parts of the Chandella kingdom to the Rajput leader, Prithviraja Chauhan (r. ca. 1150–1192). In 1202, Paramardideva handed over power to the Muslim leader, Shah Abuddin Ghuri (r. 1163–1203), marking the end of the Chandella dynasty.

See also: INDIAN KINGDOMS; MAHMUD OF GHAZNA; PALA DYNASTY.

FURTHER READING

Mahajan, Vidya. *Ancient India.* New Delhi: S. Chand, 1976.
Prakash, Vidya. *Khajuraho: A Study in the Cultural Conditions of Chandella Society.* New York: Apt Books, 1982.

CHANDRAGUPTA MAURYA

(d. 297 B.C.E.)

Founder of the imperial Maurya dynasty and first emperor (r. 321–297 B.C.E.) to centralize most of India under one ruler. Chandragupta established the groundwork for the great Maurya Empire, which was larger and more powerful than any previous Indian kingdom and which lasted nearly 150 years.

Chandragupta was born to a poor family in northern India. As a youth, he was sold as a slave to a shrewd Brahman official named Canakya, an expert in Indian statecraft who instructed Chandragupta in military strategy. With Canakya's guidance, Chandragupta gathered enough soldiers to defeat the Nanda dynasty of Magadha and assume control of that kingdom around 325 B.C.E. After the agents of Alexander the Great (r. 336–323 B.C.E..) withdrew from the Punjab region, Chandragupta also took over that area around 322 B.C.E. The following year he unified the areas under his control politically, forming the Mauryan Empire.

Between 305 and 304 B.C.E., Chandragupta resisted a series of attacks by Seleucus I Nicator (r. 312–281 B.C.E.), the Macedonian ruler, and founder of the Seleucid dynasty, who controlled territories in northwestern India conquered by Alexander the Great. Chandragupta managed to push the border of Macedonian-controlled territory farther west.

Afraid that he would lose his whole realm, Seleucus apparently made an offer of peace in exchange for his daughter's marriage to Chandragupta. Seleucus also relinquished control of Afghanistan, Beluchistan, and areas east of the Sindhu River. With those territories under his control, Chandragupta is said to have then conquered almost all of India with a force of 600,000 soldiers. His empire eventually stretched from Afghanistan and the Himalayas in the north to the southern edge of Central Asia.

The Maurya Empire founded by Chandragupta was the first successfully united Indian state. It was run effectively, with limited dictatorship at the top and democratic principles in the cities and villages. Maurya rule was a peaceful time, with thriving trade and general affluence based on bountiful agriculture, plentiful water, and mineral riches.

Guarded by Chandragupta's strong military, Indian merchants were able to transport goods by land throughout India and as far away as Burma, China, Greece, and Rome. The Mauryans thus started the trade routes that subsequently made Indian jewels, spices, and fabrics well known throughout the ancient world. Cities prospered from trade, and a rich class of Indian merchants emerged. The capital of the Maurya Empire, Pataliputra, became famous for its wealth and splendid imperial palace, buildings, and parks. The government also standardized weights and measures, established the first use of money in northern India, and took over matters of taxation, sanitation, and famine relief.

Chandragupta's final years were a less happy time, however. A harsh famine overwhelmed India. Despairing over the hunger that ravaged his people and empire, Chandragupta fasted and starved himself to death around 297 B.C.E. Upon his death, he was succeeded by his son, Bindusara (r. 297–272 B.C.E.), who further expanded the Mauryan Empire and took control of southern India as far as the city and province of Mysore.

See also: INDIAN KINGDOMS; MAURYA EMPIRE; SELEUCID DYNASTY.

CHAO DYNASTIES

(453–228 B.C.E., 304–329? C.E., 319–352 C.E.)

Three dynasties that emerged during turbulent times to rule a small area in northeast China.

The first Chao state came to power during the Warring States period (ca. 403–221 B.C.E.) of the Later Chou dynasty (771–221 B.C.E.). During this violent and turbulent time, feudal states battled for supremacy within the decentralized Chou state. At the beginning of the Later Chou period, in the eighth century B.C.E., some 200 states vied for control of China. Over time, a handful of these states managed to absorb or conquer the rest.

By the 200s B.C.E., several powerful states had emerged in China. Among these states were the Ch'in in the west, the Jin in the north, the Ch'i in the east, the Chu in the south, and the Yan in the northeast. In 453 B.C.E., the Jin state broke up into the Chao, Wei, and Han states. In 228 B.C.E., the powerful Ch'in state, led by Shih Huang Ti (Shi Huangdi), China's first emperor (r. 221–210 B.C.E.), conquered the Zhao. By 221 B.C.E., the Ch'in had succeeded in defeating all rival states to unite China under the Ch'in dynasty.

Two more Chao dynasties emerged during the chaotic Sixteen Kingdoms period (301–439 C.E.), when north China was ruled by a series of short-lived kingdoms founded by non-Chinese invaders from the northern steppes. The first of these brief Chao dynasties, founded by Xiongnu peoples, was known initially as the Han state (304–329?). The nomadic Jie founded an overlapping dynasty, the Posterior or Later Chao (319–352). The Posterior Chao practiced Buddhism and helped spread their religion among the tribes of northeast China. The earliest known Chinese Buddhist image dates from the Posterior Chao dynasty.

See also: CH'IN (QIN) DYNASTY; CHOU (ZHOU) DYNASTY; WEI DYNASTIES.

CHARLEMAGNE (ca. 748–814 C.E.)

Greatest of the Frankish rulers, who ruled as both king of the Franks (r. 768–814) and emperor of the West (r. 800–814). One of the most famous and most powerful of medieval rulers, Charlemagne ruled over a domain that included present-day France, the Low Countries, and parts of Germany, Italy, and Spain. The Frankish Empire he established became the basis for the Holy Roman Empire, and it played an important role in spreading Christianity across Central Europe.

EARLY LIFE AND RULE

Charlemagne was the son of Pepin the Short (r. 751–768), the founder of the Carolingian dynasty, and the grandson of Charles Martel, a "mayor of the palace" for the kings of the Merovingian dynasty. When Pepin the Short died in 768, his kingdom was divided between his sons, Carolman and Charles.

The Frankish tradition of dividing kingdoms among sons had created tremendous problems for rulers in the past. But the death of Carloman in 771 eliminated divisiveness within the kingdom because Charles became king of all the Franks. During a rule that lasted more than forty years, Charles extended Frankish power, became emperor of the West, served as precursor of the Holy Roman emperor, and laid the foundations for modern France. Following his death in 814, he became known as Charles the Great, or Charlemagne.

Tall, strong, and fair, Charlemagne brimmed with vitality. He loved to hunt and swim, and he located the capital of his kingdom at Aachen so he could bathe in the natural hot mineral waters there. During his lifetime, Charlemagne had four wives and five mistresses, and fathered eighteen children.

To consolidate his kingdom, Charlemagne engaged in frequent military activities. His conquest of the Lombard kingdom of the Italian Peninsula in 774 allowed him to expand his own holdings while assisting the papacy by providing it with military protection against the Lombards. During seven campaigns in Spain beginning in 778, Charlemagne expanded Frankish rule and, in 795, created the Spanish March, a frontier province with Barcelona as its capital. Charlemagne also subdued all the remaining Germanic tribes of Germany.

In 778, while returning from the first expedition to the Spanish March, a Frankish rearguard under the command of Charlemagne's nephew, Roland, was ambushed by Basque mountaineers in the Pyrenees Mountain pass of Roncevalles and annihilated. *The Song of Roland*, which commemorated the event, became the first epic poem of the Middle Ages.

COMMANDING AN EMPIRE

By 800, Charlemagne's military campaigns had extended his Frankish kingdom to include most of the European territory formerly held by the ancient Roman Empire. The papacy at this time was increasingly worried about domination by the Byzantine Empire, which was hostile to the Roman Christian Church. With a woman, the Empress Irene (r. 797–802), on the Byzantine throne at Constantinople, the time seemed ripe for a radical move.

In December 800, Charlemagne was in Rome. He had traveled to Italy to support Pope Leo III against challenges to papal authority by various nobles, including relatives of Leo's predecessor, Pope Adrian I. On Christmas night, while Charlemagne was praying in the Basilica of St. Peter, Leo produced a gold crown and placed it on the Frankish ruler's head. Charlemagne was hailed by the crowd as "Charles the Augustus, crowned by God the great and peace-bringing Emperor of the Romans."

The new emperor of the Romans may have had some mixed feelings about this honor, since he did not use the title for several years. In the meantime,

ROYAL RITUALS

JURY SYSTEM

The jury system so familiar to the Western world today has its roots in the Frankish empire of Charlemagne. When Charlemagne's representatives traveled through the kingdom to ensure that his laws were being enforced or to mete out justice, they sometimes summoned prominent citizens to give their opinions of the matter. These collective decisions on crimes or land ownership were called *jurata*. Adopted and altered by the Normans and later the English, the *jurata* developed into the verdicts of modern juries.

Charlemagne, a member of the Frankish Pepin Dynasty, came to rule over most of Europe and was crowned Roman emperor in 800 C.E. Among the treasures of Aachen Cathedral, the emperor's palace church and site of his tomb, is this jeweled reliquary bust, dating to 1350.

however, Charlemagne persuaded the Byzantine ruler to recognize his new position as ruler of the West. Acceptance of Charlemagne as emperor of the Romans shifted the locus of power from the Byzantium Empire to Northern Europe. But Leo's action would also have repercussions for successive emperors, setting a precedent that enshrined in the papacy the right to bestow the title of emperor.

ACCOMPLISHMENTS

Because of his long rule, Charlemagne was able to consolidate and maintain power. Although he was more than competent in military matters, it was his administrative ability and support of learning that helped his empire survive.

Compared to previous Frankish monarchs, Charlemagne had a good education. He read and spoke Latin fluently, understood some Greek, and

had an appreciation of mathematics and astronomy. Moreover, he constantly strove to improve his knowledge, and during his meals he had someone read scriptures or historical texts aloud.

Charlemagne understood the value of education for his people as well. With the assistance of Alcuin, a Saxon monk sent to Charlemagne by King Offa of Mercia (r. 757–796), he established many schools connected to monasteries and cathedrals. The model school attached to the imperial palace at Aachen was open both to the children of nobles and to children of more humble station; Charlemagne and members of his family also attended. Charlemagne's appreciation of learning also extended to the preservation of ancient texts, many of which were copied by monks under his patronage.

Charlemagne was actively involved in the government of his far-flung empire. Once each year, he summoned nobles and bishops to discuss the business of his empire. His decisions were promulgated as ordinances called *capitularies*, with counts and bishops in various territories assigned to carry out his instructions. As a safeguard, Charlemagne also sent out *missi dominici* ("emissaries of the master"). The task of these two-man teams, one a layman, the other a bishop, was to ensure that the *capitularies* were being carried out.

When Charlemagne died on January 28, 814, he left a strong and united Frankish Empire, but this unified realm did not last long. Charlemagne was succeeded on the throne by his son, Louis the Pious (r. 814–840), whom he had designated co-emperor in 813. Upon Louis's death, the empire that Charlemagne built was once again partitioned among Louis's sons.

See also: CAROLINGIAN DYNASTY; FRANKISH KINGDOM; LOUIS I, THE PIOUS; MARTEL, CHARLES; MEROVINGIAN DYNASTY; PEPIN DYNASTY; PEPIN THE SHORT (PEPIN III).

FURTHER READING

Boussard, J. *The Civilization of Charlemagne*. Trans. Frances Partridge. New York: McGraw Hill, 1968.

Collins, Roger. *Charlemagne*. Toronto: University of Toronto Press, 1998.

Koenigsberger, H.G. *Medieval Europe 400–1500* Burnt Mill, England: Longman Group UK Limited, 1987.

Sauvigny, G. de Bertier de, and David H. Pinkney. *History of France.* Trans. James Friguglietti. Arlington Heights, IL: Forum, 1983.

CHARLES I (1600–1649 C.E.)

British monarch (r. 1625–1649) of the Stuart dynasty whose conflicts with Parliament led to the English Civil War.

Charles I was the second son of King James VI (r. 1567–1625) of Scotland and Anne of Denmark. In 1603, his father inherited the English Crown as James I (r. 1603–1625), and the family moved to London. Charles thus spent his early years in the English court, indulging in pleasures such as hunting and the arts.

When James I died in 1625, Charles was crowned king, his older brother Henry having died several years earlier. Soon after his coronation, Charles married Princess Henrietta Maria, a sister of the French king Louis XIII (r. 1610–1643). Charles inherited his father's belief in the divine right of kings, as well as James's conflicts with Parliament and with the Puritans.

Almost immediately upon his taking the throne, Charles became involved in struggles with Parliament over his foreign and financial policies. These conflicts continued and intensified, leading Charles to dissolve Parliament in 1626. The next year, he resummoned Parliament in an attempt to resolve the conflicts, but he was unable to force the body to bend to his will and thus adjourned Parliament again in 1629, an adjournment that lasted eleven years.

One of the major sources of conflict between Charles and Parliament was money. Charles inherited his father's love of extravagant spending, which Parliament did not want to finance. Religion was also a source of disagreement: the Stuarts' brand of Anglicanism was too close to Catholicism for the many Puritans in Parliament. Ultimately, Charles's conflicts with Parliament were a power struggle: Charles wanted to rule the country single-handedly, while Parliament believed that England was ruled jointly by both a monarch and a legislative body.

Another source of trouble for Charles came from his dealings with Scotland, his native land. In 1637, he attempted to impose an Anglican prayer book on largely Presbyterian Scotland. The Scots responded by creating a National Covenant to protect their

The second ruler of England's Stuart Dynasty and a believer in the divine right of kings, Charles I struggled fiercely with Parliament, a conflict that eventually led to the outbreak of civil war. Shown in this portrait by Sir Anthony van Dyck, Charles I was found guilty of treason and executed at Whitehall Palace in 1649.

faith, which led to war between Charles and the Scots in 1639. In April 1640, Charles finally summoned Parliament again, to ask for aid in financing his war with Scotland. When this so-called Short Parliament refused, Charles dismissed it again the next month. The next Parliament, called by Charles in November 1640, became known as the Long Parliament because it served through the long period of the English civil war.

Charles needed Parliament to approve the funding for his war, but the resentment that the members of Parliament felt against the king for his lack of respect for their authority came to a head, and England erupted into civil war in 1642. For the next four years, Charles led his Royalist armies against the Parliamentarians from his royal court, which was now centered at Oxford. In 1646, he was captured by the Scottish army and handed over to Parliament.

Charles escaped the following year, however, and fled to the Isle of Wight, where he made an alliance with the Scots. This led to a second civil war, in which Charles's royalist forces were again defeated. Taken prisoner again, Charles was tried and found guilty of high treason. He was executed by beheading on January 30, 1649.

After Charles's death, England was led by Oliver Cromwell, one of the Puritan leaders of the Parliamentary army, who ruled as Lord Protector of England until his death in 1658. Cromwell's son Richard then took over as Lord Protector of England. Richard was an ineffective leader, however, so in 1660 the English invited Charles's son, Charles II (r. 1660–1685), to return from exile on the European continent and take the throne.

See also: CHARLES II; JAMES I OF ENGLAND (JAMES VI OF SCOTLAND); JAMES II; STUART DYNASTY.

CHARLES II (1630–1685 C.E.)

British monarch (r. 1660–1685) of the Stuart dynasty, whose return to the throne after the English Civil War ushered in the period known as the Restoration.

Born in London in 1630, Charles II was the eldest son of King Charles I (r. 1625–1649) and Henrietta Maria. His royal childhood was disrupted by his father's troubles with Parliament; by the time Charles was twelve years old, his father was fighting a civil war against his own Parliament in a struggle for control of the nation.

As soon as Charles was old enough, in 1645, he went to the aid of his father in battle. After his father's execution in 1649, the Scots proclaimed him Charles II, but the English Parliamentarians did not. After a brief, failed attempt to lead the Scots against the armies of the Parliamentary general, Oliver Cromwell, Charles fled to France in 1651. For the next decade, Cromwell ruled England in a period known as the Interregnum ("between monarchs"). A strict Puritan, Cromwell condemned such frivolities as the theater and dancing and forbade them in his realm.

When Cromwell died in 1658, power passed to his son Richard, who became Lord Protector of England. Richard Cromwell, however, lacked the energy or experience to rule effectively, and his Protectorate collapsed in the spring of 1659. Hoping to restore order and stability, the English people invited Charles back as their king. In 1660, Charles II returned from the Continent for his coronation.

The period that began when Charles II took the throne in 1660 is known as the Restoration because the Stuart dynasty was restored to power. The Restoration was an era of scientific discovery, theatrical brilliance, and moral laxity. In contrast to the oppressive policies of Oliver Cromwell, Charles reopened the theaters, encouraged the arts, and ushered in more tolerant policies, such as allowing women to perform on the stage. Charles also supported greater religious toleration.

In his personal life, Charles II was a notorious womanizer and libertine, leaving at least fourteen illegitimate children but not a single legitimate heir.

In foreign affairs, Charles endorsed the Navigation Acts, which regulated trade with England's colonies. These acts contributed to the outbreak of a series of wars with the Dutch and strained relations with the American colonies.

One of the more remarkable incidents of Charles's reign was an anti-Catholic affair known as the Popish Plot (1678). Titus Oates, a former Protestant clergyman, claimed that the Catholics intended to murder Charles, allowing his Catholic brother James to become king. News of the supposed plot set off a wave of anti-Catholic paranoia in England and led to a movement to exclude James from the line of succession. This movement failed: when Charles died in 1685, the Crown passed to his brother James II (r. 1685–1688), the last of the Stuart kings of England.

See also: CHARLES I; JAMES I OF ENGLAND (JAMES VI OF SCOTLAND); JAMES II; STUART DYNASTY.

CHARLES III (1716–1788 C.E.)

Monarch of the independent kingdoms of Naples and Sicily, and king of Spain; known for the prosperity enjoyed by the Spanish under his rule. Described by historians as an "enlightened despot," Charles III was able to push through a series of administrative reforms and physical improvements in his kingdoms— including a network of roads and canals—that enabled Spanish trade to expand and flourish.

A member of the royal family of Bourbon, Charles was born in 1716 to King Philip V of Spain (r. 1700–1746) and his wife, Elizabeth Farnese of Parma. Elizabeth was a powerful woman whose influence over her husband was so great that many described her as the real ruler of Spain, rather than Philip V. After being named duke of Parma by his mother, Charles obtained the kingdoms of Naples and Sicily (later known as the Two Sicilies) by virtue of the Spanish victory in the War of the Polish Succession (1733–1735). He was crowned king in 1734.

Charles's rule in Naples and Sicily was effective, but the relative smallness of the two kingdoms prevented his enthusiasm for reform from having much impact. With the 1759 death of Ferdinand VI (r. 1746–1759), Charles's half brother and reigning monarch of Spain, Charles passed on the kingdoms of Naples and Sicily to his son Ferdinand (later Ferdinand I of the Two Sicilies, r. 1816–1825) and took the throne as the new king of Spain.

Among Charles's many internal reforms as king of Spain were the limits he placed on the legal powers of the Catholic Church. By removing many privileged and powerful Jesuits from Spain, Charles was able to slow the progress of the Spanish Inquisition, though it would not be stopped until well into the next century. These actions, coupled with his economic and administrative improvements, earned Charles respect at home and abroad.

Charles's foreign policy decisions were less successful, however, especially his support of a virtually defeated France in the waning days of the Seven Years' War (1756–1763), a choice that cost Spain a great deal of its North American territory, which it lost to Great Britain. Charles was able to redeem himself later by supporting the American colonies against Britain in the American Revolutionary War (1776–1783), and thereby regaining some of Spain's former lands.

Charles III outlived his wife, Maria Amelia of Saxony, by more than twenty years. At his death in 1788, the Spanish throne passed not to his oldest son, who was mentally retarded, but to his second son, who became Charles IV (r. 1788–1808).

See also: BOURBON DYNASTY; FERDINAND I; NAPLES, KINGDOM OF; SICILY, KINGDOM OF; SPANISH MONARCHIES.

CHARLES IV (1316–1378 C.E.)

Much loved and respected king of Bohemia (r. 1346–1378), as well as monarch of the Holy Roman Empire (r. 1346–1378). Charles is best known for his efforts to modernize Central Europe, which led to the rise of Prague as a vitally important city, and for eas-

ing the political tensions that plagued the relationship between the papacy and the Holy Roman Empire.

Charles IV was the son of John of Luxemburg, the king of Bohemia (r. 1310–1346), and princess Elizabeth of Bohemia. John, who became king of Bohemia in 1310, rarely spent any time there, as he was closely allied with France in the Hundred Years' War (1337–1453). John's death in battle in 1346 brought Charles to the Bohemian throne.

Although Charles was elected to the imperial throne in 1346 (but not crowned Holy Roman emperor by the pope until 1355), most of his energy was spent on strengthening Bohemia, which had been rocked by internal disputes during his father's reign. In an attempt to boost both economic and cultural growth, Charles founded the University of Prague (also known as Charles University) in 1348. He also greatly extended the size of Prague by annexing and developing nearby land; much of modern Prague is actually part of this extension. Not all of Charles's reforms were successful, however. The influential upper classes of Bohemia stopped Charles's plan to codify and organize the Bohemian legal system. Despite such setbacks, Charles was able to ensure that Bohemia remained stable and prosperous throughout his reign.

In an attempt to prevent future disputes over royal succession—and thus protect the legacy of his own family—Charles issued the Golden Bull of 1356. This law removed the influence of the Catholic Church over the electoral process of the Holy Roman Empire and placed the power to name a sovereign in the hands of seven princes. While this document established the framework of a constitution for the Holy Roman Empire, its rejection of centralized forms of government promoted the regional autonomy that kept Germany in a state of disunity for the next 500 years.

Charles's death in 1378 was a blow to Central Europe, and the ensuing reign of his son and successor Wenceslas (r. 1378–1419), who ruled as both king of Bohemia and Holy Roman emperor, was beset by both internal and external disputes.

See also: ELECTION, ROYAL; HOLY ROMAN EMPIRE; WENCESLAS IV.

CHARLES V (1500–1558 C.E.)

Holy Roman emperor (r. 1519–1558) and (as Charles I) king of Spain (r. 1516–1556), a member of the powerful Habsburg dynasty, who inherited one of the largest and most powerful realms in the history of Europe

Charles V was the son of Philip I of Castile (r. 1504–1506) and grandson of Emperor Maximilian I (r. 1493–1519) on his father's side. His grandparents were Ferdinand II of Aragón (r. 1479–1516) and Isabella I of Castile (r. 1474–1504). Elected Holy Roman emperor in 1519, Charles became the only Habsburg ruler to inherit all of his illustrious family's various titles. The territories under his direct control included Austria, several German states, the Low Countries, and Spain, including all of the latter's possessions in Italy and the New World.

From early in his reign, Charles faced numerous challenges from both inside and outside his empire. In the face of the united power Charles represented, all of Europe banded together in rival alliances. Most notably, France and the Ottoman Empire forged an opposing alliance, the first between a Catholic and a Muslim country.

Confrontation with this alliance remained an expensive stalemate throughout Charles's reign. Charles himself formed an alliance with Great Britain in 1520 when he signed the Treaty of Gravelines with King Henry VIII of England (r. 1509–1547). In 1521 he invaded northern Italy, which was then controlled by France. Charles extracted the major cost of this venture from the kingdom of Spain, and the resentment there grew until the Spanish revolted in 1521. The rebels began to fight among themselves, however, and their cause was lost in a bitter class struggle that was put down by Charles's forces.

Inside his domains, Charles also faced the problem of religious division brought on by the Protestant Reformation. In 1521, at age twenty-one, Charles heard Martin Luther's profession of faith at Worms in 1521. It did not take long for disgruntled German princes to use the establishment of Protestantism as a battle cry against Catholic Habsburg rule. From 1525 on, Charles waged unsuccessful war against German Protestant princes determined to rule their own lands. This resulted in the Peace of Augsburg in 1555, which allowed each prince to determine the religion of his land.

Faced with mounting financial problems and continuing political conflict, the devoutly Catholic Charles resigned all his titles between 1556 and 1558 and withdrew to a monastic-style retreat. His realms were divided between his son Philip II (r. 1556–1598), who became king of Spain, and his brother Ferdinand I (r. 1558–1564), who became Holy Roman emperor and ruler of the Austrian Habsburg domains. Charles died quietly in 1558.

See also: FERDINAND II AND ISABELLA I; HABSBURG DYNASTY; MAXIMILIAN I; PHILIP II; SPANISH MONARCHIES.

CHARLES VI (1685–1740 C.E.)

Holy Roman emperor (r. 1711–1740) whose rule was overshadowed by international conflict, which prevented his empire from achieving lasting stability. Born into the influential Habsburg dynasty, Charles was the son of Holy Roman Emperor Leopold I (r. 1658–1705), whose reign had been similarly war-torn, and Eleanora, a Palatine princess. Like his brother, Emperor Joseph I (r. 1705–1711), Charles was raised with an appreciation of the arts, a lifelong passion that fostered a great deal of cultural achievement during his reign.

Even before he came to the throne, Charles's life was surrounded by violence, a result of his father placing him at the center of what came to be known as the War of the Spanish Succession (1701–1714). When Spanish king Charles II (r. 1665–1700) failed to produce an heir to the throne, Leopold I claimed that monarchy for his son Charles on the basis of a marriage that connected the two royal families. However, on his deathbed in 1700, Charles II named a French prince, Philip V (r. 1700–1746), as the new Spanish king, thus provoking war. Charles went so far as to lead an army into Spain in 1704 to take the throne by force, but he was unsuccessful.

Meanwhile, the sudden death of his brother Joseph I from smallpox in 1711 placed Charles on his father's throne. After being crowned sovereign of the Holy Roman Empire, as well as king of Hungary and Bohemia, Charles continued to war against France and Spain, capturing several Spanish territories, including Sicily.

As Holy Roman emperor, Charles was concerned with instituting educational reforms as well as encouraging support for the arts. Much of the royal treasury, however, went toward military expenses, to finance a series of wars over a span of twenty years with the Ottoman Empire in defense of Charles's eastern lands. These wars were costly, and Charles was never able to maintain a firm grip on his outlying territories.

Charles's death in 1740 brought only more violence to the empire and to Europe. Charles had no male heirs, and in a decree known as the "pragmatic sanction" made shortly before his death, he named his daughter Maria Theresa as his successor. The choice of Maria Theresa was fiercely challenged by France, Spain, and Prussia, leading to the War of the Austrian Succession (1740–1748). Although the war left Maria Theresa firmly in control of her hereditary lands, she lost large amounts of territory.

See also: AUSTRO-HUNGARIAN EMPIRE; HABSBURG DYNASTY; HOLY ROMAN EMPIRE; LEOPOLD I; MARIA THERESA; SUCCESSION, ROYAL.

CHARLES VII (1403–1461 C.E.)

King of France (r. 1422–1461) from the House of Valois who expelled the English from France and ended the Hundred Years' War (1337–1453).

One of the most influential monarchs in French history, Charles VII created France's first permanent standing army, established the right of the Crown to levy taxes, and broke the power of feudal lords. He did not attack the feudal lords directly, but weakened their power by using prosperity, forgiveness, and his own popularity to strengthen the monarchy and the sense of French nationalism. Charles also established the liberty of the French Catholic Church with the Pragmatic Sanction of Bourges (1438), which sharply limited papal authority over the church in France. Known as "The Victorious" because of his military victories over the English, Charles was also called the "Well-Served" for the able ministers who oversaw the rebuilding of France after the end of the Hundred Years' War.

Charles VII was the son of King Charles VI (r. 1380–1422) of France and Isabella of Bavaria. His father, who suffered recurrent bouts of insanity after 1392, played little role in government from that time on. This created a power vacuum, which resulted in the division of the government between rival factions led by the king's two brothers, the dukes of Burgundy and Orleans. The Burgundian faction took control of the capital of Paris in 1418, and Charles fled to Bourges in southern France. In 1420,

Philip the Good, the duke of Burgundy, signed the Treaty of Troyes with his English allies. This treaty named King Henry V of England (r. 1413–1422) as heir to the French throne.

When Charles VI died in 1422, Charles VII claimed the throne, despite the terms of the Treaty of Troyes. His claim was recognized by southern France, which he ruled from his capital at Bourges. The English, however, from their base of power in northern France, laid siege to Orleans, a key city of Charles's realm. A peasant girl, Joan of Arc, claimed that she had been ordered by God to rid France of the English. This both inspired the soldiers in Charles's army and galvanized Charles VI into action against the English.

Under the leadership of Joan of Arc, Charles's troops freed Orleans from the English, and Charles, now recognized as heir and successor, was crowned king at the city of Reims in 1429. Charles ended the Burgundian-English alliance by signing the Treaty of Arras with Philip of Burgundy in 1435. By 1453, he had reclaimed all the English-held territories in France except Calais. With the French victory at the battle of Castillon in 1453, the Hundred Years' War came to an end.

Charles's willingness to pardon English sympathizers helped reunite his kingdom. France's standing army, established to fight the English and financed by taxation, became useful in peacetime to assert the king's sovereignty and end the power of the feudal lords. With Charles controlling the strongest army, he did not have to fear rivals or make concessions to them.

During his reign, Charles surrounded himself with able advisers, including his wife, Yolanda, and his mistress, Agnes Sorel. Although heir to a weakened kingdom, Charles left a much strengthened kingdom to his son, Louis XI (r. 1461–1483), who succeeded to the throne upon Charles's death in 1461.

See also: BURGUNDY KINGDOM; FRENCH MONARCHIES; LOUIS XI; VALOIS DYNASTY.

CHAUHAN (CHAHAMANAS) DYNASTY (ca. 600s–1192 C.E.)

Rajput dynasty of central and northern India that fought the most decisive battle in Indian history.

The Chauhan dynasty was one of the four great

Rajput dynasties, located in the desert region of the east-central Rajasthan state, west of the city of Jaipur. The Rajputs (meaning "son of a king") were landowners from a wide variety of families in central and northern India. In the seventh century, Raja Ajay Pal Chauhan (r. 600s), ruler of one of the eight Chauhan families, established the city of Ajmer as the Chauhan capital.

In the twelfth century, the Chauhan ruler Vigraha (r. ca. 1150–1165) conquered the whole of northern India up to the Himalayas, including the city of Delhi and the eastern part of a region in northwestern India known as the Punjab. The greatest ruler of the Chauhan dynasty, however, was Prithviraj III (r. 1177–1192).

A devout Hindu, Prithviraj III came to the throne as a youth and is best known for his conflict with the Muslim invader, Muhammad of Ghuri (r. 1173–1206). In 1186, Muhammad captured Fort Lahore in the Punjab, and for the next five years the armies of Muhammad and Prithviraj stood face to face along a line that is near the present-day India-Pakistan border. Prithviraj moved against the Muslims in 1191 but was intercepted by Muhammad's main army at Tarain, about 150 miles north of Delhi.

In the battle, one of Prithviraj's vassals, Govinda-raja of Delhi (r. 1100s), fought with Muhammad. Govinda managed to pierce Muhammad's arm with his spear. A young officer leapt into Muhammad's saddle, and they rode off the battlefield. The Muslim troops, fearing that their leader was dead, broke off the fight. It could have been a rout, but Prithviraj let them go and went on to recapture Lahore.

Muhammad regrouped and gathered more soldiers. By the middle of 1192, he confronted Prithviraj, again on the field of Tarain, with 120,000 horsemen. Backed by the largest Rajput army ever assembled, 300,000 Rajasthan horsemen, Prithviraja announced to the Muslims that he would consider a truce.

Muhammad agreed to the truce, and Prithviraj's forces rejoiced at their easy victory, celebrating long into the night. At dawn the next day, however, Muhammad's archers entered the Hindu camp to kill the sleeping soldiers. The Hindu forces rallied, fought off the archers and pursued the Muslims on elephants. Wave after wave of Muslim archers attacked the advancing column.

Many Hindu soldiers died during this attack, but their forces rallied and killed a few archers as they retreated. By sunset, Prithviraj and his tired army were certain of victory. It was then that 12,000 of the best Muslim horsemen, led by Muhammad, ploughed through the Hindu ranks. In the disorder and panic that followed, Prithviraj, Govinda, and 100,000 Rajasthan soldiers were killed. The heart of India was now open to the Muslim invaders.

A branch of the Chauhan dynasty established the state of Bundi in the state of Rajasthan in the fourteenth century. In 1625, the state of Kotah broke away from Bundi under a separate branch of the dynasty. Both Bundi and Kota were absorbed into the Republic of India after India gained its independence from Great Britain in 1947.

See also: BUNDI KINGDOM; INDIAN KINGDOMS; KOTA KINGDOM; RAJASTHAN KINGDOM.

CHAVIN EMPIRE (fl. 900–200 B.C.E.)

First unified state in north-central Peru, known primarily for its distinctive artistic style.

The Chavin Empire derives its name from the elaborate temple site of Chavin de Huantar, a religious and economic center in the highlands of northern Peru. Chavin de Huantar is the largest example of the culture's nonresidential temple sites. What the inhabitants of the empire might have named themselves has been lost, for only archaeological remains have survived to tell their story.

Archaeological evidence suggests that sometime before 900 B.C.E., northern and central Peru were populated by small agricultural communities in the early stages of developing the technologies of pottery, lithics (stonework), and weaving. By the ninth century B.C.E., however, the Chavin style, remarkable for its unique combinations of human, feline, serpentine, crocodilian, and avian characteristics, had become the standard throughout the region. Examples of Chavin artwork have survived primarily in stone sculpture, although there are also a few surviving ceramics, textiles, and goldwork.

The Chavin religion seems to have centered around the chief Chavin deity, the so-called smiling god, a medusa-like human figure with the vicious fangs of a jaguar. Temples to this god and others were constructed primarily of adobe and stone, and there is evidence that human sacrifice played a part in some of the rituals. Convincing people of the power of authority and ritual seems to have been a significant priestly task.

The influence of the Chavin culture gradually spread from Cajamarca in the north to Ayacucho in the south. Over time, however, other cultures arose in the Andean region that began to challenge Chavin society and influence its customs and traditions. By around the second century B.C.E., the influence of the Chavin Empire had declined dramatically, as typified by the artistic replacement of Chavin styles with those of the Nazca culture.

See also: CHIMU EMPIRE; HUARI (WARI) EMPIRE; INCA EMPIRE; MOCHE KINGDOM; NAZCA KINGDOM.

CHENLA EMPIRE (500s–800s C.E.)

Khmer state, a predecessor of the Angkor kingdom of Cambodia, which flourished from the sixth to early ninth centuries and covered the area of present-day western Cambodia, southern Thailand, southern Vietnam, and southern Laos. According to ancient Chinese historical records, the Chenla Empire first emerged as a vassal state of the Funan kingdom, one of the earliest kingdoms in Southeast Asia. But Chenla overran the Funan state in the early to mid-500s and gained its independence.

Like the Funan kingdom, the Chenla civilization was strongly influenced by Indian and Chinese sea merchants, who frequently brought foreign goods and ideas to the region. The Chenla people relied on coastal trading to support their economy, and they subsisted primarily on rice farming.

Sculptures and architectural remains show the influence of Indian artistic and political thought on the Chenla Empire, although some art with uniquely Khmer qualities was also beginning to appear. This style would later evolve into the elaborate Khmer art celebrating Hindu gods that was characteristic of the period of the Angkor kingdom. Archeological ruins from the time also suggest that Hinduism was becoming more popular than Buddhism during the Chenla period. Decorative sculptures and religious shrines are inscribed with Sanskrit and early Khmer writing.

Jayavarman I (r. ca. 657–681) is considered one of the most prominent rulers of the Chenla Empire. Historians credit him with conquering territory stretching over central and upper Laos and with consolidating power over the lower Mekong River Delta

region and the area surrounding the great Tonle Sap Lake in central Cambodia. Jayavarman I died without an heir, which brought about a period of instability that may have led to the division of the Chenla Empire into two separate and independent provinces—an inland region and a coastal region.

These two states were named Land Chenla (or Upper Chenla) and Water Chenla (or Lower Chenla). Chinese historical annals indicate that "Land Chenla" thrived as a powerful military and economic force that occasionally sent envoys to the Chinese T'ang dynasty. "Water Chenla," on the other hand, suffered periods of instability and became a vassal of the kingdom of Java. Sanskrit and Khmer writings from the time indicate that Upper and Lower Chenla were later broken up into a number of smaller provinces.

During the eighth century, the navy of the powerful Java Empire conquered the Chenla states. But Prince Jayavarman II (r. 802–850) fought successfully against the Javanese, establishing the Angkor kingdom and declaring himself a king with divine powers. The formation of the Angkor kingdom and the rise of the Khmer Empire marked the end of the Chenla Empire.

See also: ANGKOR KINGDOM; CAMBODIAN KINGDOMS; FUNAN KINGDOM; SOUTHEAST ASIAN KINGDOMS; VIETNAMESE KINGDOMS.

CHERA DYNASTY. *See* MYSORE KINGDOM

CHIANGMAI (1200s–1500s C.E.)

Buddhist kingdom located in northern Thailand founded in the late thirteenth century, the control over which was long disputed between Burma and the kingdom of Ayudhya (Ayuthia), the predecessor of the modern state of Thailand.

The city of Chiangmai in northern Thailand was founded in 1296 by Mangrai (Meng Rai) (r. 1296–1318), a sworn ally of King Rama Kamhaeng of Sukhothai (r. 1275–1317) and Ngam Muang of Phu Kam Yao (r. 1258–1298), after they defeated the Mons of Haripunjaya, another kingdom in northern Thailand. The site for the city had apparently been chosen four years earlier by Mangrai and his allies, but the actual founding of Chiangmai was not carried out until the Mons had been completely subjugated.

Mangrai ordered the construction of Wat Chiang Man, which marked the site of the new city. Chiangmai became not only an important political center but also a cultural center in the decades to follow. According to ancient records, Mangrai went to Pegu, the capital of the Mon kingdom of Burma, where he married a Mon princess. On his return to Chiangmai, he brought with him artisans from Burma. Mangrai's death in 1315 set off a series of succession disputes among his three sons.

In the late fourteenth century, the kingdom of Ayudhya began extending its power northward, bringing it into direct conflict with Chiangmai. Ayudhya made two attempts, in the 1410s and 1442, to bring Chiangmai under its control, capitalizing on the chaos caused by succession disputes in Chiangmai. Both attempts were unsuccessful, as the Chiangmai army inflicted severe defeat on the Ayudhya Siamese.

When Prince Ramesuan of Ayudhya, also known as Boroma Trailokanat (r. 1444–1488), came to power in 1444, it marked the beginning of a long series of incessant wars between Ayudhya and Chiangmai. Trailok tried all means to weaken Chiangmai, including attempts in 1467 and 1468 in which he sent a Burmese monk and Brahmin priest to sow dissension in the Chiangmai court. Wars between Ayudhya and Chiangmai escalated and became more complicated in the fifteenth and sixteenth centuries, as the Laotian kingdom of Luang Prabang and the Burmese kingdom also became involved in the struggle.

The Burmese, under the leadership of King Bayinnaung (r. 1551–1581) of the Toungoo dynasty, fought a long series of wars with the Thais that culminated in the successful defeat of not only Luang Prabang and Chiangmai but also Ayudhya in the 1560s. Chiangmai fell to the Burmese, and its king was captured and taken back to Pegu in 1565. The Burmese appointed a regent to administer Chiangmai and left a Burmese garrison to oversee control of the kingdom. Chiangmai remained a vassal of Burma until the rise of the Bangkok kingdom in the eighteenth century.

See also: AYUTTHAYA KINGDOM; BANGKOK KINGDOM; BURMESE KINGDOMS; LUANG PRABANG KINGDOM; SOUTHEAST ASIAN KINGDOMS; TOUNGOO DYNASTY.

FURTHER READING

Coedes, George. *The Indianized States of Southeast Asia.* Honolulu: University of Hawaii Press, 1970.

Hall, D.G.E. *A History of South-East Asia.* New York: St. Martin's Press, 1981.

Wyatt, David. *Thailand: A Short History.* New Haven, CT: Yale University Press, 1984.

CH'IEN LUNG (QIANLONG)

(1711–1799 C.E.)

Chinese Ch'ing emperor (r. 1736–1796) who doubled the size of the Chinese Empire during the longest reign in Chinese history. Ch'ien Lung (Qianlong) was the son of Xiao Sheng, a Manchu noblewoman, and Emperor Yongzheng (r. 1723–1735). Named Hongli at birth, he was a favorite of his grandfather, the great Ch'ing emperor Kangxi (r. 1661–1722), who took him hunting and had him tutored by an eminent Chinese scholar. Yongzheng wanted Hongli to succeed him, and he groomed his fourth son for the role of emperor. To ensure that no one else claimed the throne upon his death, Yongzheng wrote down his wish in a document kept locked in a box in the palace. At his father's death in 1736, the twenty-five-year-old Hongli became the fourth Ch'ing emperor, assuming the title Ch'ien Lung and beginning a sixty-year reign. By his two wives, Xiao Xian and Xiao Yi, Ch'ien Lung would have seventeen sons and ten daughters.

CHINESE TRADITION MEETS MANCHU STRENGTH

Like the Ch'ing rulers before him, Ch'ien Lung was not ethnic Chinese. He was descended from the tribesmen of Manchuria, a region to the northeast of China. The fierce Manchu warriors had seized power from the Ming dynasty in 1644. To win Chinese acceptance of foreign Manchu rule, the Ch'ing deliberately maintained many of China's traditions and institutions. Ch'ien Lung continued this strategy, taking pains to uphold both Manchu and Chinese customs. In keeping with China's Confucian tradition of filial piety, Ch'ien Lung staged elaborate public displays of devotion to his mother. He sponsored the *Four Treasuries,* a massive collection of classical Chinese philosophy, history, and literature that totaled 36,000 volumes.

Ch'ien Lung also upheld many Manchu traditions, including the male Manchu hairstyle of shaving the front of the head and growing a long braid, or queue. A strong man, he preserved Manchu military traditions with annual hunting expeditions to Inner Mongolia.

CONQUEST AND PROSPERITY

Ch'ien Lung presided over the Ch'ing dynasty at the height of its power. A conscientious ruler, he rose early each morning to attend to state business. His greatest achievement was the conquest of vast territories to the west—now Xinjiang province—that doubled the size of the Chinese Empire. In 1751 he brought Tibet under Ch'ing control. Ch'ien Lung's empire dominated neighboring nations, forcing them to participate in a tributary system. This Chinese custom required emissaries from foreign states to *kowtow* (touch their foreheads to the ground) before the emperor, thereby recognizing China's superiority. Under Ch'ien Lung's reign, the growing European appetite for Chinese tea, silks, and porcelain brought vast amounts of silver into China through trade. Improvements in agriculture led to a population explosion.

Ch'ien Lung nursed a genuine passion for Chinese art and literature, and the emperor devoted his afternoons to reading, writing, and painting. During his reign he published more than 42,000 poems. He also collected great works of Chinese painting and calligraphy and commissioned new work from the finest artists and architects of his day. He was also a fan of Western art and had the Italian Jesuit painter Giuseppe Castiglione design him a magnificent European-style summer palace.

CORRUPTION AND DECAY

Despite outward appearances of greatness, the latter years of Ch'ien Lung's reign were marked by crisis. Ch'ien Lung left many important decisions to his councillors. Widespread government corruption, failed military campaigns, and land shortages caused by population growth led to internal unrest and a series of domestic uprisings.

Pressure from the West increased at this time. Ch'ien Lung espoused the ancient Chinese view that China resided at the center of the world and that all other nations were inferior. (The Chinese word for China, *Zhongguo,* literally means "middle kingdom.") Foreign traders therefore met with constant restrictions when trading with China. Frustrated with this situation, the British sent Lord George Macartney to Ch'ien Lung's court in 1793 to request more equitable trading policies. Arriving on Ch'ien Lung's eightieth birthday, Macartney brought British manufactured goods carefully selected to impress the Chinese with the latest in Western technology. The emperor responded in a famously short-sighted letter to Britain's King George III, writing, "We have never valued ingenious articles, nor do we have the slightest need of your country's manufactures."

In 1780, Ch'ien Lung fell under the sway of Heshen, a young Manchu guard whose corruption epitomized the empire's growing problems. Heshen became the aging emperor's most trusted adviser. Heshen used his powerful position to enrich himself on an imperial scale, amassing a fortune estimated at 800 million pieces of silver.

To show respect for his grandfather Kangxi's long reign by not surpassing it, Ch'ien Lung officially abdicated in 1796 after nearly sixty-one years on the throne. However, he continued to hold power until his death in 1799, when his fifth son, Jiaqing (r. 1796–1820), took full control of the throne. The new emperor forced Heshen to commit suicide and confiscated his massive fortune.

See also: KANG XI; MING DYNASTY.

FURTHER READING

Fairbank, John King. *China, A New History.* Cambridge, MA: Harvard University Press, 1992.

Paludan, Ann. *Chronicle of the Chinese Emperors.* New York: Thames and Hudson, 1998.

Spence, Jonathan D. *The Search for Modern China.* 2nd ed. New York: W.W. Norton, 1999.

CHILDERIC I. *See* CLOVIS I

CHIMÚ EMPIRE (900–1460 C.E.)

Pre-Columbian state that developed on the northern coast of Peru and grew into a powerful military society with a complex, well-organized social system. Originating in the Moche Valley, the Chimú state expanded south to Huarmey and north to Lambayeque. Chan Chan, its capital city, covered an area of about 2.3 square miles and reached a population of between 25,000 and 69,000 inhabitants.

AUTONOMOUS RULERS

According to oral accounts recorded by Spanish conquerors and officers during the sixteenth and seventeenth centuries, the founder of the Chimú dynasty was Taycanamu. According to traditional accounts, Taycanamu arrived at Moche by sea in the early tenth century, claiming he had been sent by a great lord of afar to govern the territory, and he was accepted as ruler by the natives. After establishing the first settlement, Taycanamu was succeeded by his son Guacricaur, who completed the conquest of the Moche Valley. Guacricaur was in turn succeeded by Ñançenpinco who, around 1350, conquered a number of neighboring valleys, including Saña, Pacasmayo, Chicama, Virú, Chao, and Santa.

CONQUEST BY THE INCAS

After a series of unnamed rulers, a seventh or eighth ruler named Minchançaman came to power. Around 1450, Minchançaman expanded the Chimú Empire to its greatest territorial extent, conquering as far as to the Tumbes Valley in the north and to Chillón in the south.

Around 1460, the Incas began the conquest of Chimú. After fierce and prolonged fighting, invading forces led by the Inca lord Topa Yupanqui (who later ruled the Inca Empire as Topa Inca, r. 1471–1493) conquered the city of Chan Chan around 1470 and subdued the Chimú Empire.

Following customary strategy, the Inca took Minchançaman to Cuzco, their capital city, as a royal hostage. Although the Inca nominally respected the integrity of the Chimú Empire, they gradually reduced the authority of the native dynasty to the Moche Valley.

From approximately 1470 to 1532, the series of Chimú rulers under Inca dominion included Chumuncaur, Guamanchumo, and Ancocuyuch. By the time of the Spanish conquest of Peru in 1532, the Chimú ruler was Cajaçimçim, who became Christian and took the name of Don Martín.

ECONOMIC AND SOCIAL ORGANIZATION

The primary economic activity in the Chimú Empire was agriculture, and the Chimú built a large network of irrigation canals to raise crops in the valleys of their empire. This irrigation system required an extensive bureaucracy as well as several administrative centers, led by the capital city of Chan Chan.

Founded between 850 and 900, Chan Chan was constructed of adobe bricks. Each of the Chimú rulers had his own palace in the city, and when the king died, his residence became a mortuary monument. Chimú society was divided in a rigid hierarchy of classes led by a hereditary nobility. The nobles demanded labor from their subjects and employed them in construction projects, the manufacturing of goods, and as artisans and technical specialists.

See also: INCA EMPIRE; MOCHE KINGDOM.

CH'IN (QIN) DYNASTY

(221–207 B.C.E.)

First national Chinese imperial dynasty, for which China is named, that was established after the period of the Warring States (403–221 B.C.E.). Recruiting talented advisers from other areas to give them an advantage over their rivals, the Ch'in also applied their advanced military techniques to conquer the various other states in China.

Around 361 B.C.E., a leader named Shang Yang from the kingdom of Wei was put in control of the reform program of the Ch'in (Qin) state. A staunch proponent of legalism, in which the absolute power of the ruling class was ensured by harsh punishments, he believed that the interests of the state came first.

Shang Yang removed power from the hereditary landowners in Ch'in by replacing the feudal system with counties, each of which was administered by an appointed magistrate. He instituted a code of laws that meted out harsh punishment for infractions and divided the population into groups, making each group responsible for any wrongdoing by one of its members. In this way, he encouraged the groups to inform on each other and reinforced obedience to the Ch'in state. Shang Yang's legislative reforms in-

Ch'in Dynasty	
SHIH HUANG TI	221–210 B.C.E.
ERH SHIH HUANG TI	210–207 B.C.E.
CH'IN WANG	207 B.C.E.

creased agricultural productivity and tax revenues, which, in turn, supported the Ch'in army.

Despite Shang Yang's achievements, he fell from grace and was executed in 338 B.C.E. Yet, his policies had greatly strengthened the Ch'in state, and by 221 B.C.E. it had gained dominance over the other Chinese feudal states. The Ch'in ruler, King Zheng, who had led successful military campaigns against rival states, established a new Ch'in dynasty and declared himself Shih Huang Ti (Shihuangdi), or "First August Emperor," of a united Chinese empire.

Shih Huang Ti (r. 221–210 B.C.E.) and his chief minister Li Ssu (Li Si) applied the legalist practices established by Shang Yang to the governing of the new empire. The territory was divided into thirty-six regional districts, each of which was ruled by a civil governor and a military commander. Imperial inspectors oversaw the actions of those two leaders and reported back to the emperor to ensure that the balance of power was maintained. Aristocratic families from former feudal states were relocated to the Ch'in capital of Xianjang so that their activities could be monitored more easily. They also were forced to relinquish their weapons, which were melted down to form statues.

Once a centralized government was in place, Shih Huang Ti implemented other unifying reforms. He had his government standardize weights, measures, and currency, as well as the system of writing. Laborers, often conscripted into service, built over four thousand miles of roads and cut waterways and canals that extended water transport for twelve hundred miles between the Yangzi and Guangzhou rivers. Even the axles of carts had to be a certain width so that ruts in the road would be uniform. Shih Huang Ti also began the construction of the Great Wall to serve as fortification against northern invaders.

Suppression of dissent and harsh laws enforced the cohesiveness of the Ch'in Empire. According to historians, hundreds of books were burned during Ch'in rule. One ancient historical account accuses Shi Huang Ti of burying over four hundred scholars alive as a warning to others not to defy his will.

ROYAL PLACES

The Tomb of Shih Huang Ti

Located near the ancient imperial city of Xi'an in north-central China, the tomb of Shih Huang Ti is a remarkable testament to the organizational ability and ambition of China's first emperor. Long before he became emperor, Shih Huang Ti, King Zheng of the Ch'in state, began construction of his tomb. Sima Qian, a later court historian, described it as a microcosm of the heavens and earth. Within the main tomb, pearls set in a copper-domed ceiling represented stars and planets, while mercury ran in miniature rivers and oceans created on the floor of the tombs. The entrance to Shih Huang Ti's tomb has not yet been discovered, but in March 1974, farmers digging a well near Xi'an uncovered a piece of a warrior figure made of terra cotta, or earthen pottery. Subsequent archaeological excavation revealed an army of over 7,000 terra cotta foot soldiers—an army perhaps created to accompany Emperor Shih Huang Ti in the afterlife.

The emperor's army lay in three large pits. The first pit excavated held over 6,000 infantry, with some chariots and horses; the second pit had 1,400 soldiers and cavalry, as well as chariots; the third pit was the army headquarters, with sixty-eight officers. Although all the figures were broken, over one thousand have been restored to reveal the remarkable craftsmanship of the Ch'in period. The various parts of the soldiers were made from a mold, but then several layers of fresh clay were applied to the figures and finished by hand so that each is unique.

In preparation for his death, Shih Huang Ti, founder of the Ch'in dynasty, had a vast tomb complex built near the capital of Xianyang in the third century B.C.E. An army of life-sized terra cotta warriors, each with unique facial and other features, were erected to accompany him to the afterlife. More than seven thousand soldiers, horses, and chariots were discovered by archaeologists in 1974.

Above and beyond these factors, it was the force of Shih Huang Ti's character and his active leadership that held the empire together. After Shi Huang Ti's death in 210 B.C.E., his son, Hu Hai, or Erh Shih (Er Shi) ("Second Emperor") (r. 210–207 B.C.E.), tried to follow in his father's footsteps. The dynasty quickly declined, however. Peasants, tired of heavy taxes and harsh repressive laws, revolted in various parts of the kingdom. In 207 B.C.E., the Second Emperor's unscrupulous adviser, Chao Kao (Zhao Gao), occupied the imperial palace with his own loyal troops and forced the emperor to commit suicide.

The third Ch'in ruler, Erh Shi's nephew Prince Ch'in Wang (r. 207 B.C.E.), dispatched Chao Kao but could not defend his throne against Liu Pang (Liu Bang), a rebel leader and future founder of the Western Han dynasty (206 B.C.E.–8 C.E.). Ch'in Wang surrendered the throne to Liu Bang less than two months after becoming emperor, bringing the Ch'in dynasty to an end.

See also: HAN DYNASTY; LIU BANG (GAODI); WEI DYNASTIES.

FURTHER READING

Qian, Sima. *Records of the Grand Historian.* Trans. Burton Watson. New York: Columbia University Press, 1995.

CH'ING (QING) DYNASTY
(1644–1912 C.E.)

Chinese dynasty founded by the Manchus which marked the end of imperial rule in China. The Ch'ing came from southeast Manchuria, a region on China's northern frontier.

In the late sixteenth century, the tribal Manchu chieftain Nurhaci consolidated the disparate tribes of southeastern Manchuria into an effective "banner"

THE CH'ING (QING) DYNASTY, ca. 1800

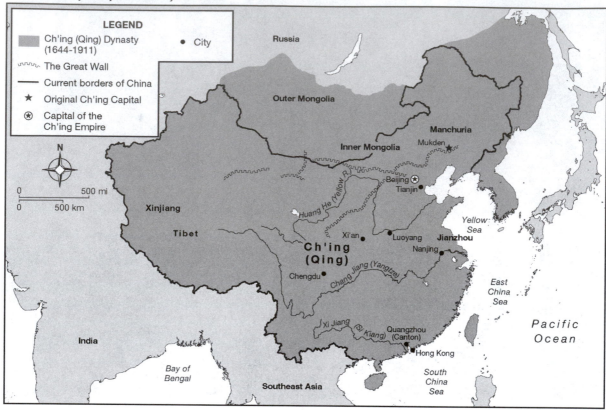

system, in which all tribesmen were assigned to a banner or flag of a particular color. From their capital at Mukden in north China, the Manchus proclaimed the Ch'ing ("pure") dynasty. Capitalizing on the turmoil of the late Ming dynasty, they seized Beijing in 1644 and proclaimed Shun Chih (Shunzhi) (r. 1638–1661), Nurhaci's six-year-old grandson, the first emperor of the Ch'ing dynawsty.

ESTABLISHING AUTHORITY

China's new Ch'ing rulers required that all male Chinese prove their loyalty to the dynasty by adopting the traditional Manchu hairstyle of a shaved forehead and a queue, or long braid, worn at the back of the head. To establish themselves as China's legitimate rulers, the Ch'ing adopted traditional Confucian rituals and morality. They maintained many Chinese institutions, including the examination system that selected the brightest scholars to serve in the government. The Ch'ing leaders balanced this adherence to Chinese traditions with maintenance of their Manchu ancestors' vigorous way of life, celebrating their martial traditions on

regular hunting trips to Inner Mongolia. This balance between Manchu and Chinese extended to the government, where one Chinese and one Manchu were assigned to jointly administer important agencies.

A CENTURY OF STABILITY

For more than one hundred years, the Ch'ing dynasty enjoyed stability and prosperity under three strong, conscientious rulers. During his sixty-one-year reign, K'ang Hsi (Kangxi) (r. 1661–1722) secured Ch'ing power by quashing the Three Feudatories revolt in southern China. To keep informed about the true state of affairs in his empire, he set up a system of direct communication in which provincial officials sent messages that were read only by the emperor. His grandson, Ch'ien Lung (Qianlong) (r. 1735–1796), expanded the Chinese Empire to its greatest extent. By the end of Ch'ien Lung's long reign, the Ch'ing controlled Taiwan and parts of Central Asia, including Mongolia and Tibet.

The Ch'ing court welcomed Jesuit scholars from

Ch'ing Dynasty

SHUN CHIH	1644–1661
K'ANG HSI	1661–1722
YUNG CHENG	1722–1735
CH'IEN LUNG* (QIANLONG)	1735–1796
CHIA CH'ING	1796–1820
TAO KUANG	1820–1850
HSIEN FENG	1850–1861
T'UNG CHIH	1861–1875
KUANG HSÜ* (GUANG XU)	1875–1908
PU YI*	1908–1912

*Indicates a separate alphabetical entry.

Europe because of their knowledge of Western advances in science. Chinese trade and manufacturing expanded, as European demand increased for Chinese silk, porcelain, and especially tea. By the time of Ch'ien Lung's reign, the growing British appetite for Chinese tea had created a trade imbalance that brought large quantities of silver into China. At the same time, technological improvements in agriculture combined with new crops introduced from the New World to produce a population explosion in China.

REBELLION AND INVASION

The Ch'ing's glory days came to an end in the nineteenth century. Weak rulers and a corrupt bureaucracy could not respond effectively to a century of internal rebellion and foreign invasion. Overpopulation contributed to poverty and land shortages, providing rebel leaders with willing followers among the desperate peasantry. More than 20 million Chinese died in the Taiping Rebellion (1851–1864), which was a revolt against the Ch'ing by the supporters of a would-be dynasty called the Taiping.

Like the Ming before them, the Ch'ing were uninterested in relations with foreign nations. Trade was severely restricted, and all foreign envoys were expected to *kowtow* (touch their foreheads to the floor) before the emperor, thereby showing their acknowledgment of Chinese superiority. In 1793, the British sent a mission led by Lord George Macartney to request more favorable trade conditions between Britain and China. Macartney, hoping to impress Emperor Ch'ien Lung with gifts representing the latest in European technology, instead found himself summarily rebuffed. In a letter to Britain's King George III (r. 1760–1820), Ch'ien Lung explained that the Chinese had no need for Western goods.

The Europeans soon found that by exchanging opium for tea and other Chinese goods they were able to reverse the flow of silver into China. Opium addiction spread rapidly throughout the Ch'ing Empire. When the Chinese tried to stop the opium trade, the British attacked and easily defeated China in the Opium War (1840–1842). The resulting Treaty of Nanjing, which gave the British control of Hong Kong, was only one of many such treaties that took land from the Chinese and forced foreign will on the weakened empire.

In 1898, antiforeign sentiment in China culminated in the Boxer movement, which called on the Chinese people to attack foreigners in the country. In 1900, the Boxers laid siege to foreign legations in Beijing until Western forces entered the city to dispel them.

The last fifty years of Ch'ing rule were dominated by the empress dowager Tz'u Hsi (Cixi). Recognizing China's need to reform, Emperor Kuang Hsü (Guang Xu) challenged Tz'u Hsi's power in 1898 and joined with reformers to call for sweeping changes to modernize the country. However, the conservative Tz'u Hsi suppressed the reformers and had Kuang Hsü imprisoned. Tz'u Hsi eventually agreed to reforms, promising a constitutional government, but it was too late. In 1911–1912, the revolutionary leader Sun Yat-sen led a successful rebellion against the Ch'ing, ending the short reign of Pu Yi, China's last emperor, and instituting a republic.

See also: CH'IEN LUNG (QIANLONG); KANG XI; KUANG HSU (GUANG XU); MING DYNASTY; PU YI; TZ'U HSI (CIXI).

CHOLA DYNASTY. *See* MYSORE KINGDOM

CHOLA KINGDOM. *See* COLA

KINGDOM

CHORASMIAN KINGDOM. *See*

CENTRAL ASIAN DYNASTIES

CHOSON KINGDOM (1392–1910 C.E.)

Name given to Korea by the Yi dynasty during its reign from 1392 to 1910.

The Choson kingdom was created in 1392 when General Yi Songgye overthrew the Koryo monarch Kong-yang (r. 1389–1392), founded the Yi dynasty, and changed the country's name to Choson. Yi selected the name to honor a kingdom that had existed on the Korean Peninsula in the fourth through first centuries B.C.E. For Yi, the name had a deeply symbolic meaning. The original Choson was the earliest recorded civilization in Korean history. By naming his kingdom Choson, Yi implied that a new, but traditional, civilization was emerging.

For centuries, an insurmountable social stratification had characterized the Koryo kingdom and its predecessors. To facilitate the new Choson civilization, Yi and his successors attempted to overturn this stratification. In Koryo, wealthy families, called the *yangban*, had occupied the highest social level and controlled much of the farmland, thereby retaining the profits generated in Koryo's agricultural economy. To reduce this financial power, Yi confiscated all these vast estates and gave ownership to the state. Although their wealth was greatly diminished, the *yangban* still held a prominent position in the new Choson society because they were better educated than other citizens. The local peasantry also viewed each *yangban* family with a patriarchal reverence.

Another important class, the literati, had originated during Koryo's existence. The literati were an educated class primarily responsible for running the government. To install these officials, the Yi monarchs devised two civil service examinations. When individuals passed both exams, they could attain a government position. To prevent these positions from being filled solely by the *yangban*, the monarchy opened the exams to all Choson citizens and created public schools to educate them. However, the *yangban* still received the best education, and many of the literati continued to come from the *yangban* class.

Commoners, or peasants, and slaves occupied two lower positions in Choson society. The Yi monarchs also strove to reform these two classes. During the seventeenth century, the monarchy instituted a new taxation system that determined taxes by the amount of land each individual owned. This new system greatly alleviated the tax burden on small landowners. Concurrent improvements in farming methods created new affluence among the peasant class. The government also reduced restrictions that the Koryo rulers had placed upon merchants in the peasant class. Consequently, merchants began to expand their businesses and import new products from other Asian countries. By 1801, the government had even freed all remaining slaves.

Eventually, these reforms created a deep rift in Choson society. During the nineteenth century, countries such as China, Japan, and Russia, each looking to control the Korean Peninsula, were pressuring Choson to modernize its government and economy. The *yangban* and literati feared that such modernization would undermine their social positions and give greater power to merchants and farmers. The merchants and farmers shared this belief; they had already profited from modern agricultural and economic practices, and they hoped to further advance their social position.

The conflict between the social classes soon became violent. In 1884, a group of peasants named the Enlightenment Party attempted to overthrow the monarchy and institute reforms similar to those of the Meiji in Japan. Although the insurrection failed, the movement encouraged both China and Japan to participate more heavily in Choson affairs. After Japan defeated China in the Sino-Japanese War of 1895, the Japanese government compelled Choson to adopt the Kabo Reforms, which opened the government to all classes and specified huge expenditures on public projects such as schools. Alarmed by these events, a group of literati called the Independence Club sought to expel all foreigners from Choson and preserve the kingdom's autonomy. However, under pressure from Japan, the Choson monarch forced the group to disband.

Kyongbok Palace in Seoul, Korea, was built as the residence of the rulers of the Choson Kingdom in the late fourteenth century. The staggering cost of its construction was a factor in the decline and eventual downfall of the kingdom. Destroyed by Japanese invaders in 1592, the palace was reconstructed in 1867. It originally contained some 350 buildings, including Hyangwon Pavilion, shown here.

The hostility between organizations such as the Enlightenment Party and the Independence Club severely weakened Choson society. In 1905, Japan designated Choson as an official protectorate. Five years later, the Japanese removed the Yi monarch and declared Choson to be a colony. The Yi dynasty's reforms had brought a new prosperity to Choson for several centuries. But the class struggles that had plagued the preceding Silla and Koryo kingdoms also eventually doomed Choson.

See also: KORYO KINGDOM; YI DYNASTY; YI SONGGYE.

FURTHER READING
Eckert, Carter J., et al. *Korea Old and New.* Cambridge, MA: Harvard University Press, 1990.

CHOU (ZHOU) DYNASTY
(ca. 1045–221 B.C.E.)

Early Chinese dynasty that produced a golden age in philosophy. Following the Hsia and the Shang dynasties, the Chou was the last of China's three ancient dynasties. The longest dynasty in Chinese history, the Chou lasted nearly one thousand years. Although the Chou period was an era of constant political turmoil, it also produced some of China's most influential thinkers.

EARLIER OR WESTERN CHOU

The Chou dynasty was founded by two brothers, the sons of King Wen, ruler of the Chou, a state on the western frontier of the Shang dynasty. After defeating the Shang armies in 1050 B.C.E., one of the brothers, Wu Wang, became the first Chou ruler. On Wu's death, his brother, Chou Gong, served as regent for Wu's young son. Chou Gong expanded Chou territory, conquering the Yellow River plain. With its capital near the modern-day city of Xi'an,

this period, known as the Earlier or Western Chou, endured for more than four hundred years.

Chou kings ruled indirectly during the Western Chou period, establishing vassal states that sent tribute to the Chou king and provided him with soldiers. The Chou exerted limited central control through an imperial army and the beginnings of a bureaucracy. In 771 B.C.E., the Chou capital was sacked by the armies of tribal rivals and vassal states. The Chou reestablished their capital to the east at the city of Luoyi, the site of modern-day Luoyang, marking the beginning of the Later or Eastern Chou period.

LATER OR EASTERN CHOU

Twenty-two kings ruled the Eastern Chou for more than five hundred years, but Chou kings held little

Western Chou		**Hsi Wang**	681–676
Wu Wang	1045–1043 B.C.E.	Hui Wang	676–651
Ch'eng Wang	1043–1006	Hsiang Wang	651–618
K'ang Wang	1006–978	Ch'ing Wang	618–612
Chao Wang	978–957	K'uang Wang	612–606
Mu Wang	957–918	Ting Wang	606–585
Kung Wang	918–900	Chien Wang	585–571
I Wang	900–873	Ling Wang	571–544
Hsiao Wang	873–866	Ching Wang	544–519
Yi Wang	866–858	Ching Wang	519–475
Li Wang	858–841	Yuan Wang	475–468
Regency	841–827	Chen Ting Wang	468–440
Huan Wang	827–781	K'ao Wang	440–425
Yu Wang	781–771	Wei Lieh Wang	425–401
		An Wang	401–375
		Lieh Wang	375–368
Eastern Chou		Hsien Wang	368–320
P'ing Wang	770–719	Shen Ching Wang	320–314
Huan Wang	719–696	Nan Wang	314–256
Chuang Wang	696–681	Tung Chou Chun	255–249

power over the states in their realm. Rival states within the Chou territory engaged in near-constant warfare. The Eastern Chou is generally divided into two periods, the Spring and Autumn period (722–481 B.C.E.), which is known for the chivalry of its nobles, and the Warring States period (ca. 403–221 B.C.E.), when several powerful states vied for supremacy.

A hierarchy of aristocrats emerged during the Later Chou period, with nobles ruling their individual states from palaces surrounded by walled cities. In the latter years of the era, several states gained power and dominated the others. One of these was the state of Ch'in in the northwest, whose leader deposed the last Chou king in 256 B.C.E. In a series of long campaigns, the Ch'in conquered the fragmented Chou territory, defeating the last of its rivals in 221 B.C.E. and founding the Ch'in (Qin) dynasty.

LIFE UNDER THE CHOU

Chou society was highly stratified, with the king at the pinnacle of a social hierarchy that included the nobility, a small class of artisans, and an emerging merchant class. At the bottom were the peasants, who comprised the majority of the population and were bound to the land in serf-like conditions. Agriculture was the basis for the Chou economy, but trade also flourished. In 500 B.C.E., metal coins were first introduced to China under the Chou, replacing silk as the primary form of currency.

From their Shang predecessors, the Chou inherited divination, ancestor worship, and the custom of ritual sacrifices in honor of a pantheon of gods. The Chou introduced the idea that the emperor was the link between heaven and earth and that he ruled according to the will of heaven. If heaven disapproved of the actions of the king, or "Son of Heaven," natural disasters and other omens would occur, signaling the end of a king's mandate to rule. Succeeding dynasties adopted this concept throughout China's history.

Constant warfare between rival states contributed to technological advances in the Chou period. Among these advances were the adoption of the crossbow in the fourth century B.C.E. and the introduction of cavalry during the Eastern Chou period. Horseback riding, borrowed from Central Asia, became common in China for the first time with the development of the saddle in the 800s B.C.E. Around 500 B.C.E., China entered the Iron Age, with iron replacing bronze in the making of tools and weapons.

A GOLDEN AGE OF PHILOSOPHY

During the Later Chou period, nobles, seeking the knowledge to help them defeat rival states, recruited scholars to their courts. These numerous centers of learning allowed a variety of schools of philosophy to flourish, and the period became known for its "One Hundred Schools of Thought."

Two of China's most important philosophies, Confucianism and Taoism (Daoism), emerged in this period. The philosopher Confucius (551–479 B.C.E.) argued that rulers should set a moral example through ethical conduct and the performance of rituals. Confucianism sought to maintain the existing social hierarchy, advocating the performance of traditional roles and obedience to authority. The *Five Classics* emerged from the Chou period. These Confucian texts served as the basis for China's philosophical, political, and ethical systems until the twentieth century C.E. Taoism, founded by the philosopher Lao Tzu (Laozi), advocated the merging of the individual with the *Dao*, or Way.

See also: CH'IN (QIN) DYNASTY; HSIA DYNASTY; SHANG (YIN) DYNASTY.

CHRISTIANITY AND KINGSHIP

Christianity was the primary force shaping the ideas and practices of kingship in the European world from the Middle Ages to early modern times. The Christian idea of kingship grew out of the Bible and earlier forms of kingship in the Roman Empire and among Germanic tribes in Europe.

CHRISTIAN IDEAS OF KINGSHIP

The first influence on Christian ideas of kingship were the New Testament writings about Jesus, who described himself as a king, though his kingdom was "not of this world" (John 18:36). In other New Testament writings, Jesus is described as a high priest. Above all, he was called the Messiah, the "Anointed One," a sacred king expected by the Jews.

The Christian concept of kingship in the Middle Ages was also influenced by ideas about the relationship between church and state that developed during the later Roman Empire. Roman emperors had acted as the *Pontifex Maximus*, or chief priest, of the state religion. Constantine (r. 307–337), the first Christian emperor, believed that he too should be a religious leader;

ROYAL RELATIVES

CLOTILDA, QUEEN OF THE FRANKS (ca. 470–544 C.E.)

Clotilda, wife of Clovis, the pagan king of the Franks, became responsible for making much of Europe Christian when she converted her husband and the people of his kingdom to Christianity.

Clotilda was the daughter of King Chilperic of Burgundy and a Gallo-Roman mother. Clovis, the king of the Salian Franks, heard of her beauty and asked for her hand in marriage. At first Clotilda refused him because he was a pagan, but when Clovis threatened war against her uncle and guardian, she agreed to the marriage. Clovis and Clotilda were married in 493.

Clotilda often tried to convert her husband to Christianity but without success. She nevertheless insisted on having their children baptized as Christian. Clovis was devastated when their first child died after the baptism, believing that he had died because he had not been dedicated to the pagan gods. But when Clovis went to war against the Alemanni and the Suevi in 496, and saw that he was about to be overcome, he prayed to his wife's God, and the battle turned in his favor. That same year, he received baptism from Saint Remigius, the bishop of Reims, and became the first Christian king of France

After Clovis died in 511, Clotilda turned to religious life, founding the religious communities of St. Peter in Lyon and Les Andelys and St. Ouen in Rouen. Female monasticism soon flourished in Merovingian Gaul, and monasteries became havens for the poor and persecuted.

Clotilda's conversion of Clovis and his people cemented an alliance between the Frankish rulers and Catholic Christianity, centered in the papacy, that lasted throughout the Middle Ages.

he convened the First Council of Nicaea in 325 to solve a religious dispute. The idea that a secular ruler could decide religious questions frequently led to conflict between kings and popes during the Middle Ages.

Another influence on Christian ideas of kingship was the idea of kingship held by the ancient, pre-Christian Germanic tribes in Europe. The early Germanic tribes had two kinds of kings: the *reik* or warrior king, and the *thiudan* or priest-king. The early Christian writer Ulfilas, who translated the Bible for the Goths, used the word *thiudan* for Jesus's kingship. But both forms of kingship influenced the Christian ideal of a king.

In the Middle Ages, some considered the anointing of kings a sacrament. In early medieval France, for example, the oil used to anoint kings was thought to be the same oil brought from heaven for the coronation of Clovis (r. 481–511), the first Christian king

of the Franks. Because the Frankish king was regarded as the anointed (*Christus*) of the Lord, he was often considered another Christ, and, like Christ, both a priest and a king.

The *Via Regia* (Royal Way), written by the medieval hagiographer (writer of lives of the saints) Smaragdus of St. Mihiel (d. ca. 843), shows how kingship was perceived during the Carolingian period. Smaragdus stressed that the king acquires a holy character through sacred anointing and that he must display all the Christian virtues: justice, mercy, compassion, and courage. According to Smargdus, a king should recall that seeking the kingdom of God is more important than earthly government. The king's life, nevertheless, is different from that of an ascetic monk because the king is more deeply involved in the world. These instructions given to kings were the basis of lay spirituality in the later Middle Ages.

tude deso̅n puep̅le par la main · mess̅ire sai̅nt Remi archeuesque de Rains ·

Ce sire saint remi fut tout maintenant les

In the early Middle Ages, kingship and Christianity were inextricably linked, and the anointing of kings was considered a holy sacrament. This fourteenth-century illustration shows Clovis I, the first Christian king of the Franks, being baptized and anointed by St. Remigius, bishop of Rheims.

Most Christian monarchs did not live up to these responsibilities; nevertheless, a number of them were actually canonized as saints, including Edward the Confessor of England (r. 1042–1066), Louis IX of France (r. 1226–1270), and the Holy Roman emperor Henry II (r. 1002–1024) and his wife Cunegunde. From the eleventh century onward, people believed that French and English kings, like the earlier Germanic kings, could cure scrofula by touching the sufferer.

It was from anointing by the bishop that the king received his sacred character, and the Church and bishops had primary authority during the earlier Middle Ages and sought to control kings. In the eleventh century, a strengthened and reformed papacy under Pope Gregory VII sought to rein in the emperor's claims to control the selection of bishops and their power to rule, a dispute called the Investiture Controversy. The imperial side often took the position that kings and popes were equal and that the king was God's vicar in secular matters.

Toward the end of the Middle Ages, jurists developed the idea that the king had two "bodies." One was his natural body, which was subject to sin, imperfection, and corruption; the other was his "body politic," which was incorruptible and passed on from king to king so that rule was preserved. Beginning with the funeral of Charles VIII of France (r. 1483–1498) in 1498, the king's natural body, which had formerly been buried with all his regalia, was now clothed only in a white sheet. The regalia adorned his funeral effigy, symbol of the "body politic," on top of the monarch's coffin.

BYZANTINE KINGSHIP

The rulers of the Byzantine Empire (330–1453) shared not only the despotic tradition of eastern kingships, but the exalted conception of the ruler of the late Roman Empire. In Byzantium, the emperor's sacred character was highly developed under the influence of an ascetic approach to Christianity. Relations between the papacy and the Byzantine emperors were distant, especially after the schism that divided the Eastern from the Western Church in 1054. As a result, the Byzantine emperor had a good deal of control over his clergy. The sacred character of society was centered in the emperor, who was considered the living law. His seat was physically located under an icon of Christ, which showed his identification with the kingship of Christ.

RENAISSANCE AND POST-REFORMATION KINGSHIP

The Protestant Reformation, which began in the sixteenth century, changed the concept of Christian kingship in Protestant countries. After breaking with the pope, Henry VIII of England (r. 1509–1547) declared himself head of the Church in England. Henry was now the vicar of God for his kingdom, without priestly competition. The king was now seen as ruling by "divine right" in both temporal and secular matters and thus answerable to no one but God.

The sacramental system of the Catholic Church, with its symbolism and use of religious images, was suppressed during the Reformation. As a result, the cult of the ruler replaced the real presence in the Eucharist (holy communion) as a subject of view and worship in Protestant countries. Royal rituals were secularized, becoming grandiose civic pageantry rather than sacramental rites. At the coronation of Elizabeth I of England (r. 1558–1603) in 1558, more attention was given to the queen's procession than to the scaled-down coronation mass.

There was a change in Catholic countries as well, due to the secular ideas of the Renaissance. Supporters of absolutism in France used the pagan mythological figure of Apollo, the sun-god, to symbolize the divinity of the monarch. This idea reached its height under Louis XIV (r. 1643–1715), who was known as the Sun-King.

In the seventeenth and eighteenth centuries, the idea of the "body politic" came to be centered not in the king's body, but in the more impersonal state. Divine conceptions of the monarch largely ended with the almost total secularization of society during the French Revolution.

See also: ACCESSION AND CROWNING OF KINGS; BODIES, POLITIC AND NATURAL; DIVINE RIGHT; DIVINITY OF KINGS; ENTHRONEMENT, RITES OF; HEALING POWERS OF KINGS; HEAVENS AND KINGSHIP; SACRAL BIRTH AND DEATH; SACRED KINGSHIPS; SACRED TEXTS.

CHRISTINA (1626–1689 C.E.)

Queen of Sweden (r. 1632–1654) who, for religious reasons, abdicated her throne at age twenty-eight. Queen Christina is especially remembered for her wit and charm and her lavish patronage of the arts.

The fortunes of monarchs often change radically during their lifetimes. The destiny of Christina of Sweden was unique in European history, both in its originality and in the degree to which it was self-directed.

Christina was the daughter of King Gustavus II Adolphus of Sweden (r. 1611–1632) and Maria Eleanora of Brandenburg. When Maria presented her warrior husband with a daughter rather than a son, that valiant defender of Protestants accepted this reversal of plans with brave equanimity. Christina, in turn, grew up as boyishly as was possible given her social position. Her father put her under the care of the intelligent and loyal Count Axel Oxenstierna and, when Gustavus II was killed in 1632, Christina became queen at the age of six.

Oxenstierna educated the eager young girl so well that when she reached maturity, Christina immediately and successfully opposed him regarding the Thirty Years' War (1618–1648) and became one of the prime movers of the difficult Peace of West-

phalia (1648), which began the modern European state system.

Under Christina, Sweden became a cultural haven; men of letters and the arts from all over the Western world were lured by her open-handed patronage. The queen built hospitals, colleges, and universities; she supported public education; and she adjudicated and quelled feuds both within her own realm and internationally.

Christina's courtiers did not universally applaud her patronage of the arts and humanities. Courtly relations were strained further by the queen's pacifism, her wilting wit, and her reluctance to wed any of the royal suitors who came constantly to her court.

Christina noticed this discontent, but she thought such problems superficial; she was dedicated to the life of the mind and to the cold comforts of philosophy. In her boldest adventure in self-education, Christina sent an admiral and ship to collect René Descartes—the greatest philosopher of his time—so that he might personally instruct her in his new system of thought. The great philosopher came to Stockholm, but succumbed to the harshness of Sweden's weather and the schedule kept by the queen, who insisted on beginning her lessons at 5 A.M. Descartes died of pneumonia not long after his arrival.

Christina continued her spiritual quest and was led, ironically, to Catholicism. Sweden was not only Lutheran; it was profoundly anti-Catholic. Attracted to Catholicism, and weary of her royal duties, Christina made a decision that shocked not only her subjects, but all of Europe; she abdicated the throne in favor of her cousin, Charles X Gustav (r. 1654–1660) in 1654 and left her homeland. Curiously, Christina's importance to European history had hardly reached its zenith at this point.

After brief stays in the Netherlands and Paris, Christina found a spiritual home at Rome. For another thirty-five years she played on the European political stage. In 1657, Christina participated in an abortive French plot to give her the Crown of Naples. Several years later, at the urging of Pope Clement IX and under his sanction, she traveled to Poland in an attempt to assume the throne of that kingdom. In 1660, Christina returned to Sweden upon the death of Charles X Gustavus in hopes of regaining the throne. She failed, however. Refused entrance to the capital of Stockholm because of her Catholic faith, she was forced to return to Italy.

During her exile from Sweden, Christina also volunteered her personal fortune to help continue the crusade against the Turks, the only military action she ever sanctioned. No matter where her travels took her, Christina always returned to Rome and to her magnificent Palazzo Riario and to the Accademia dell'Arcadia, which she founded and which became the gathering place for the greatest philosophers, musicians, and artists of her day. Thus, the patronage that Christina had begun in the frozen North blossomed in the Italian sun. Christina was the discoverer or primary patron of the musicians Alessandro Scarlatti and Arcangelo Corelli, and the sculptor Giovanni Bernini, Her library was considered the best in Rome and is now part of the Vatican Library. She also built Rome's first public opera house. Christina died in her adopted home of Rome in 1689 and is entombed at St. Peter's Basilica.

See also: GUSTAVUS II (ADOLPHUS); QUEENS AND QUEEN MOTHERS; SWEDISH MONARCHY.

FURTHER READING

Buckley, Veronica. *Christina, Queen of Sweden: The Restless Life of a European Eccentric.* New York: Fourth Estate, 2004.

CHULALONGKORN (1853–1910 C.E.)

Fifth king (r. 1868–1910) of the Chakkri dynasty of Thailand, who is remembered as a great modernizer.

Chulalongkorn (also known as Rama V) was born in the royal palace in Bangkok, Thailand (then called Siam), on September 20, 1853. He was the eldest son of King Mongkut (r. 1851–1868), who is immortalized in the novel *Anna and the King of Siam* and the popular musical play and film, *The King and I*, which were based upon the actual memoirs of a British tutor who served in the Siamese court in the mid-1800s. From birth, Chulalongkorn was destined to succeed his father to the throne.

Although King Mongkut traveled throughout his realm, the Thai royal family rarely ventured beyond the palace walls. Chulalongkorn and his many siblings (they numbered in the hundreds, for Mongkut kept a very large harem) received their education from private tutors. Chulalongkorn's father, determined that his children would understand the Western powers that were colonizing many parts of Southeast Asia, supplemented their traditional course of study with tutelage in English, for which he hired an English widow, Anna Leonowens. From her, Chulalongkorn gained fluency in the English language as well as a solid grounding in European academic subjects.

At age nine, Chulalongkorn's education was expanded to include studies in the martial arts and horsemanship, and four years later he underwent a ritual haircutting that marked his entry into young manhood. Soon after he began studying for the Buddhist priesthood. In 1868 King Mongkut died and Chulalongkorn was made king, but he was still too young to rule in his own right. Instead, a regency of court ministers handled the operation of the government, and these regents were highly resistant to any policies that threatened the established order.

During the regency period, Chulalongkorn traveled outside of Thailand, becoming the first Thai king to do so. During his travels he came to believe that Thailand needed to make significant changes if it ever hoped to retain its independence from the European powers that were colonizing the region. On November 16, 1873, Chulalongkorn was finally old enough to rid himself of the regents who stifled his attempts at change. He at once embarked upon a program of modernization, while attempting to maintain those elements of Thai culture that gave his people a unique identity.

Chulalongkorn's mission to maintain Thai independence suffered some setbacks during the latter decades of the 1800s, when he lost territory to the French (in present-day Laos and Cambodia). Still, he managed the considerable feat of retaining his nation's sovereignty. This can be attributed to former king Mongkut's foresight in providing Chulalongkorn with a solid understanding of the West and its aims.

Chulalongkorn's efforts at modernization and development won him the admiration of his subjects but the enmity of his ministers, who saw their traditional power being undermined. Chief among Chulalongkorn's early reforms was his promotion of education and literacy, which culminated in the creation of Chulalongkorn University in Bangkok in 1902. Equally important was his abolition of slavery, a change that the noble families of Thailand fought bitterly, but that was finally signed into law in 1905. By that time the king was seriously ill, having battled a variety of physical ailments since childhood and now suffering from chronic kidney disease. On October 23, 1910, he finally died, at the age of fifty-seven. He was succeeded by his son, Vajiravudh (r. 1910–1925).

See also: CHAKRI DYNASTY; MONGKUT (RAMA IV); SIAM, KINGDOMS OF.

CIXI. *See* Tz'u Hsi

CLASS SYSTEMS AND ROYALTY

Factors related to a hierarchical system of social groupings and its relationship to monarchial forms of government. Throughout history, one of the primary motivators of social change has been the relationship between various economic classes. The history of monarchy is by no means exempt from this social change. In fact, the growth of a large and powerful middle class in the sixteenth through nineteenth centuries was a fundamental factor in the gradual movement away from monarchy and toward democratic forms of government. Monarchs throughout history sought to appease tensions between the classes while still maintaining royal power.

ORIGINS AND BACKGROUND

The history of class development is difficult to trace since socioeconomic classes did not emerge until near the end of the Middle Ages. Whereas today most people consider social classes and economic classes to be one and the same thing, a clear or direct overlap did not exist in the ancient world. It was by no means uncommon for a person in the ancient world to be of a different social class than someone who was of roughly the same economic level. Into the modern era, India has witnessed the perpetuation of a caste system, wherein rigid social distinctions are only partly based on economic factors. The one constant characteristic in the evolution of the relationship between monarchs and class systems is that monarchs, with a few notable exceptions such as Chinese emperor Hung Wu (Hongwu) (r. 1368–1398), almost always originated from the upper classes.

ANCIENT EGYPT AS A MODEL

The ancient Egyptian kingdoms were among the first to grow and prosper, as well as among the first to decline. This decline was largely the result of the effect that growth and prosperity had on the relationship between the monarchs (pharaohs) and the upper classes. Originally, the pharaohs ruled with the support of a powerful priestly class.

As Egypt grew into an important commercial empire in the Mediterranean, however, many individuals grew wealthy and consequently challenged the authority of the pharaohs, demanding more local power. The diffusion of wealth around the country made it extremely difficult for the pharaohs to maintain central control.

The collapse of the Egyptian kingdoms was to a great extent brought about by this phenomenon, which would become the dominant pattern for monarchical development throughout the world. This pattern involved a consolidation of royal power with the acquiescence of the wealthy in society, followed by economic growth and the assertion of power by increasingly wealthy individuals and groups, concluded by internal collapse.

THE ROMAN EMPIRE AND THE FEUDAL STATE

The Roman Empire followed the example of the ancient Greeks in its experimentation with democratic governments. This fostered an eventual collapse of class distinctions in early Rome, but they returned in the middle and later periods as Rome moved from a republic to an empire. The rise of powerful emperors such as Augustus (r. 27 B.C.E.–14 C.E.) was facilitated by the upper classes, but these same elite members of society rebelled against later emperors, and the empire rapidly decentralized, crumbling throughout the third and fourth centuries.

The collapse of the central authority of the Roman Empire set Europe on the road to an economic and political system known as feudalism. Under feudalism, the monarch was ostensibly in charge of all lands under his or her domain, but the wealthy nobles who administered small areas of lands held much of the real political power. Thus, the monarchy was, to some extent, subject to the will of the upper classes. The poor, who constituted by far the largest class in feudal societies, were a matter of little concern to either monarchs or wealthy nobles. By the time feudalism began in Europe in the ninth century, it was already widely practiced throughout Asia, albeit in slightly altered forms. Feudalism was significant to monarchical development because it perpetuated the influence of local, upper-class authorities.

THE RISE OF THE MIDDLE CLASS

As technological advances in Europe in the fourteenth and fifteenth centuries integrated local economies in new ways, the feudal system began to be challenged by a new class of people who were not as wealthy as the nobles but who had many more peers: the middle class. Feudal towns grew and prospered, and merchants and artisans sprang up to fill the needs of larger populations, thus constituting the foundations of the middle class. Though no one person of the middle class could compete with a feudal lord, the middle class as a whole quickly outnumbered the feudal lords and thus put pressure on the lords for more political control.

Simultaneously, monarchs throughout Europe, realizing their own weakness, began to consolidate their power, citing royal prerogatives in order to dispense with feudal lords. As tension between the feudal lords and the monarchy mounted, the middle class sided with the monarchy, believing that they could ultimately get more local authority under a strong central monarch than under a strong local noble. The sixteenth and seventeenth centuries saw many feudal societies crumble and monarchs reach new heights of power with the support of the middle class.

THE COLLAPSE OF MONARCHY

The trouble for European monarchies, however, was that the middle class kept growing and by the eighteenth century was agitating for more power in government. In Britain, the monarchy relented and turned significant power over to Parliament. Elsewhere, however, most monarchs resisted the demands for more diffuse power, until the French middle and lower classes rose up against King Louis XVI (r. 1774–1792) in the French Revolution. Although monarchies continued to be moderately important throughout the nineteenth century, the French Revolution is generally taken to mark the end of widespread monarchical authority, as the ideals of the Revolution quickly spread throughout Europe.

In the late-nineteenth and early twentieth centuries, Japan and China also witnessed this phenomenon. In 1889, the Japanese Meiji emperor, Mutsuhito (r. 1867–1912), was forced to grant a liberalized constitution in Japan, and China's Ch'ing (Qing) dynasty (1644–1911) was overthrown in a class revolt in 1911.

Most monarchs gave in to the demands of the middle class in their societies rather than face violent uprisings. As a result, the nineteenth and twentieth centuries were characterized by the growth of democratic governments around the world, most of which were—and still are—dominated by the will of the middle class.

See also: CASTE SYSTEMS; COMMERCE AND KINGSHIP; FEUDALISM AND KINGSHIP; POWER, FORMS OF ROYAL; RIGHTS, CIVIL.

CLAUDIAN DYNASTY. *See* JULIO-CLAUDIANS

CLAUDIUS (10 B.C.E.–54 C.E.)

Emperor of Rome (r. 41–54) whose moderate rule contrasted markedly with the cruelty of Caligula (r. 37–41), who preceded him, and Nero (r. 54–68), who followed him.

Claudius was born Tiberius Claudius Drusus Nero Germanicus in the Roman province of Gaul, near modern-day Lyons, France. His father, Drusus, had won honor and acclaim for military service; his mother, Antonia, was the daughter of the great military officer Marcus Antonius (Mark Antony). Claudius's step-grandfather and great uncle was the Roman emperor Augustus (r. 27 B.C.E.–14), and his uncle, Tiberius (14–37) also held the throne.

Claudius suffered from physical frailties from childhood and throughout his life and so was never expected to rule. He was born with a deformed leg, his speech was impaired, and he had tremors in his limbs. Because of these physical defects, his family considered him to be mentally impaired as well, but Claudius ultimately proved himself to be an intelligent, able ruler.

Because no one ever expected Claudius to achieve a prominent position in government, he was given none of the early responsibilities in Roman society or the military that would normally fall to a member of an imperial family. This proved to be a blessing in later life, for Claudius never had the opportunity to participate in the intrigues that were rife in Roman politics of the time.

Instead, Claudius became something of an historian, chronicling the reign of his grand uncle, Augus-

The fourth emperor of Rome, Claudius never expected to take the throne. He was spared assassination by his predecessor and nephew, Caligula, only because he did not appear to pose a threat. Despite his impaired speech and other physical disabilities, Claudius, portrayed here in an agate cameo, was a competent ruler.

tus, and writing histories of the Etruscan region of Italy and of the great North African city of Carthage. It was expected that Claudius would live out his life in scholarly obscurity, and he would have done so were it not for the self-destructiveness of Emperor Caligula.

When Claudius was forty-seven years old, Caligula became the fourth emperor of the Roman Empire. For nineteen years, this mentally unstable man ruled with increasing brutality, until even his Praetorian Guard (a special military unit charged with protecting the emperor) could no longer tolerate his cruel and violent behavior.

A member of the Praetorian Guard assassinated Caligula in 41. Prior to his death, Caligula, in paranoid fear of conspiracy by rivals, had managed to kill off most of the adult males of the imperial line; only

Claudius remained alive, largely because Caligula did not consider him a threat. The assassination of Caligula plunged Rome into political disarray, and the Roman Senate began debating the possibility of eliminating imperial rule and returning to a republic. The Praetorian Guard, however, forestalled this decision by proclaiming Claudius the new emperor.

After the violence of Caligula, the Emperor Claudius proved to be a welcome change. He instituted a domestic program of public works, improved harbors and farmlands, and attempted to inspire the Senate to a greater sense of public duty. Militarily, he reformed the pay scales and living conditions of the army, and even accompanied his troops during the invasion and conquest of Britain in 43.

During his lifetime, Claudius took four wives. The last of these was his niece Agrippina, whom he married in 49. Agrippina was thirty-four years old at the time and came to the imperial marriage with a son, Nero, who had been born of an earlier marriage. Hoping to increase her son's prospects for power, Agrippina participated in palace intrigues, and she succeeded in convincing Claudius to legally adopt her son. Because Claudius was by this time growing more sickly, Agrippina seized the opportunity to acquire increasing control over the administration of the empire.

Claudius died in 54 after eating a poisonous mushroom. At the time, many believed that Agrippina had provided the fatal morsel to ensure that her son would inherit the throne. Although never proven, this belief was perpetuated by early Roman historians. Whether or not Claudius's death was the result of accident or foul play, Nero (r. 54–68) did ascend the imperial throne and swiftly brought to an end the relatively peaceful prosperity that characterized Claudius's rule.

See also: AUGUSTUS; CALIGULA; NERO; ROMAN EMPIRE; TIBERIUS.

CLEOPATRA VII (69–30 B.C.E.)

Queen of Egypt (r. 51–30 B.C.E.), a member of the Ptolemaic dynasty, and one of history's great romantic heroines.

Born in 69 B.C.E. in the Egyptian capital of Alexandria, Cleopatra was the third daughter of King Ptolemy XII (r. 80–51 B.C.E.). Her family was descended from Ptolemy I (r. 323–282 B.C.E.), the founder of the Ptolemaic dynasty, who served as a general in the army of Alexander the Great (r. 336–323 B.C.E.). Cleopatra received an extensive education. The future Egyptian ruler is said to have been fluent in nine languages and to have been a gifted mathematician. She was also trained in the arts and in statecraft.

When Cleopatra was eleven years old, the Egyptians revolted against her father, forcing him to flee to Rome. The rebels then chose Cleopatra's elder sister Berenice to serve as ruler in her father's stead. In exile, Ptolemy turned to Roman General Gnaeus Pompeius Magnus (Pompey) for support. He raised an army and returned to Egypt to reclaim his throne in 55 B.C.E., whereupon he had Berenice beheaded for her treachery in supporting the rebellion against him. During Berenice's rule, the next oldest child in

Cleopatra VII of Egypt is perhaps best known for her relationship with the Roman ruler Julius Caesar, with whom she had a son named Caesarion, also known as Ptolemy XVI. She is depicted here with Caesarion at the Temple of Hathor on the bank of the Nile in southern Egypt.

the family, Cleopatra VI, had died of illness, leaving Cleopatra VII as the heir apparent.

Ptolemy XII died within three years of returning to Egypt and Cleopatra, who was now about eighteen years old, inherited the throne. Egyptian royal custom decreed that only a child of two equally royal (and thus divine) parents could inherit the throne. Cleopatra, therefore, was obliged to take as consort and co-regent a blood relative, primarily to ensure the birth of a successor. She wed the elder of her two young brothers, twelve-year-old Ptolemy XIII (r. 51–47 B.C.E.), who became co-ruler. Cleopatra, however, ruled with great independence, angering the regents who looked after Ptolemy XIII's interests. One of these regents, Pothinus, led a conspiracy that forced Cleopatra into exile in Syria.

Like her father before her, Cleopatra did not accept exile. She recruited an army and marched back to Egypt, waiting for the proper time to attack. Meanwhile, in the Roman Empire, two great generals, Pompey and Julius Caesar, vied for imperial control. Pompey sought the support of Ptolemy XIII just as, years previously, Ptolemy's father had sought Pompey's assistance. Ptolemy, however, supported Caesar and ordered Pompey to be assassinated upon his entrance to Alexandria. When Caesar arrived outside the city, Ptolemy sent emissaries to the general with a gift: Pompey's head.

This ploy to curry favor with Caesar backfired. Although the two Roman generals had been rivals, they had also once been friends. Offended by Ptolemy's brutality, Caesar ordered his troops to storm Alexandria and seize the palace. Aware of the rivalry between Ptolemy and Cleopatra, Caesar called them both before him, intending to choose one to govern the Roman province of Egypt. Cleopatra, fearing that her brother's supporters would kill her when she entered the city, had herself wrapped in a rug and smuggled into the palace to avoid detection.

Writers of the period have said that Cleopatra was extraordinarily charismatic. She certainly made a powerful impression on Caesar, and soon after this first meeting, the two became lovers. Caesar named Cleopatra his new governor of Egypt, which outraged Ptolemy. In protest, Ptolemy called up an army of followers and attempted to regain the palace in Alexandria. The attempt failed, and Ptolemy was drowned while trying to flee across the Nile River. Cleopatra promptly replaced him as consort by marrying her youngest brother, eleven-year-old Ptolemy XIV (r. 47–44 B.C.E.).

Cleopatra and Caesar now embarked upon a long journey up the Nile, during which Cleopatra became pregnant with a son, Caesarion ("little Caesar"). Caesar then returned to Rome, but in 46 B.C.E. he summoned Cleopatra, along with her husband, son, and retainers to stay in his villa outside Rome. Cleopatra remained in Italy for two years, and Caesar lavished her with gifts, honors, and titles. Their affair became the subject of scandalized gossip (Caesar already had a wife), and was one of many factors that led to Caesar's assassination in 44 B.C.E. With her protector dead, Cleopatra fled home to Alexandria. At about this time, her young husband died in suspicious circumstances (it was rumored that Cleopatra had him poisoned). Cleopatra now named her four-year-old son Caesarion as co-regent, giving him the royal name of Ptolemy XV (r. 36–30 B.C.E.).

Egypt truly needed Cleopatra's attention at this time, for it was suffering from prolonged drought. The annual flooding of the Nile had been inadequate for several years in a row, resulting in poor harvests and famine. Cleopatra ordered repairs to the levees and canals that regulated the Nile's waters, but she also kept an eye on Rome, which was in the throes of a power struggle. When the time came for Egypt to choose sides, Cleopatra chose Marcus Antonius (Mark Antony) and set out to seduce him as she had Julius Caesar. Once again, Cleopatra's charm and charisma served her well, and Antony followed her to Alexandria.

In the spring of 42 B.C.E., Cleopatra gave birth to twins: Cleopatra Selene and Alexander Helios. Antony, though married to a Roman woman named Fulvia, was believed to be their father. In 46 B.C.E. Fulvia died, raising speculation that Antony would marry Cleopatra. Instead, he found it politically expedient to marry Octavia, the sister of one of his rivals (Octavian, later called Augustus). He continued to see Cleopatra, however, using war with the Parthians as a pretext for their meetings. Cleopatra provided an Egyptian fleet and other support for Antony's armies. In return, Antony acknowledged paternity of her twins, granting them title to the lands of Cyprus, Phoenicia, Judaea, Arabia, and part of Syria. Even with Cleopatra's support, however, Antony failed in his military campaign. He withdrew to Syria in 36 B.C.E. and then traveled to Egypt to join Cleopatra. The Roman Senate was outraged by

Antony's behavior; angriest of all was his brother-in-law, Octavian.

In 34 B.C.E. Antony decided to conquer Armenia and once again turned to Cleopatra for support. Victorious, he returned to Alexandria rather than to Rome, sparking further outrage in the Senate. In 37 B.C.E. Antony divorced Octavia, intending to marry Cleopatra. Octavian responded to this insult by declaring war on Egypt. After a series of battles, Octavian's forces captured the city of Alexandria in 30 B.C.E. Antony committed suicide rather than face capture, and Cleopatra was taken prisoner.

Unlike Antonius and Caesar, Octavian was impervious to Cleopatra's charm. He offered her only one fate: to be kept captive and to be carried from city to city throughout her former realm, set on display for all to revile. The humiliation was more than the proud queen could accept, and she committed suicide. Upon her death, her son Caesarion inherited the title of king, but Octavian had the boy strangled. Cleopatra's other children were taken away to be raised by Octavia. With this action, the Ptolemaic dynasty came to an end.

See also: EGYPTIAN DYNASTIES, PERSIAN, HELLENISTIC, AND ROMAN; PTOLEMAIC DYNASTY; PTOLEMY I.

FURTHER READING

Boardman, John, Jasper Griffin, and Oswyn Murray. *The Oxford History of the Classical World.* New York: Oxford University Press, 1986.

Starr, Chester. *A History of the Ancient World.* New York: Oxford University Press, 1991.

Weigall, Arthur. *The Life and Times of Cleopatra, Queen of Egypt.* New York: G.P. Putnam's Sons, 1974.

CLOVIS I (ca. 466–511 C.E.)

Merovingian king of the Franks (r. 481–511), who is credited with establishing the Franks as an important power and laying the earliest foundations for the monarchy and nation of France. Clovis also established Paris as the capital of the Franks and championed the spread of Roman Christianity in his realm. His laws, codified in the *Lex Salica* (Salian Law), became the basis for the laws of the Mergovingian and Carolingian dynasties, as well as for the Holy Roman Empire.

Clovis was the son of Childeric I (r. 460–482), king of the northern (Salian) Franks, one of several Germanic tribes in northwestern Europe. Although little is known of Childeric, he seems to have been a natural leader who allied himself with both the Romans and the Christian Church in Gaul (the Roman name for the area that is present-day France).

When Clovis inherited his father's kingdom in Gaul around 481, it was only one of many Frankish kingdoms. In order to consolidate power and expand his own kingdom, Clovis first conquered, bargained with, or assassinated other Frankish kings. He also set out to claim territory from other Germanic groups, including the Thuringians and the Alamanni, whom he defeated in 491 and 506, respectively.

One of Clovis's most significant military victories came in 486 with his defeat of Syagrius, the last Roman general of Gaul. As a result of this victory, Clovis claimed all of northern France for the Franks. After attacking the rival Burgundians in 500, he persuaded them to join with him in an attack on the Visigoths in the region of Aquitaine in southwestern France. This campaign, in 507, resulted in another important military victory for Clovis.

Around 493, Clovis married the Christian princess Clotilda, the daughter of the Burgundian king Chilperic. A few years after their marriage, around 496, Clovis converted to Christianity and was baptized at Reims by Bishop Remigius. Clovis's adoption of Christianity helped establish and strengthen his rule by making allies of both the Gallo-Romans and the Church. Recognized as the legitimate ruler of Gaul in 507, Clovis received the honorary titles of consul and Augustus from the Holy Roman emperor.

Clovis died in Paris in 511. According to old Germanic custom, his kingdom was divided equally among his four sons: Theodoric I (r. 511–533), whose kingdom was centered at Reims; Clodimir (r. 511–524), whose capital was at Orleans; Childebert I (r. 511–558), with his capital at Paris; and Clotaire I (r. 511–561), who ruled from Soissons and became sole king of the Franks in 558 at the death of his last surviving brother.

See also: BURGUNDY KINGDOM; FRANKISH KINGDOM; MEROVINGIAN DYNASTY; MEROVINGIAN-FRANKISH KINGDOM; VISIGOTH KINGDOM.

CONGO KINGDOM. *See* KONGO KINGDOM

CNUT I (ca. 994–1035 C.E.)

Ruler of England (r. 1016–1035), Denmark (1019–1035), and Norway (1028–1035); also known as Canute or Knud, who united these kingdoms under his rule and forged friendly relations with the Holy Roman Empire.

The son of Sweyn or Sven "Forkbeard" of Denmark (r. 1013–1014), Cnut was one of the four Danish kings of England at the beginning of the eleventh century. Cnut was the only one of these rulers, however, who was able to consolidate power in both England and Scandinavia for a sustained period of time. After his death in 1035, Cnut's Scandinavian domains in Denmark and Norway began warring among themselves.

CONQUEST OF ENGLAND

In 1013, Cnut accompanied his father Sweyn on an expedition to England, during which Sweyn forced the Anglo-Saxon ruler, Aethelred II (r. 978–1016) of Wessex, into exile in Normandy. Sweyn assumed rulership of England, and upon his death in 1014, the Danes in England swore their allegiance to Cnut. That same year, however, Aethelred returned to England at the request of Anglo-Saxon nobles and forced Cnut back to Denmark. where he later took the throne after the death of his brother, King Harald II (r. 1014–1019).

After regrouping and strengthening his forces, Cnut re-invaded England in 1015. King Aethelred died during the military campaigns against the Danes, and his son and successor, Edmund II Ironside (r. 1016), took the throne of Wessex. Edmund died soon after, however, and Cnut, who conquered most of Wessex and Northumbria, became sole ruler of England.

RULE IN SCANDINAVIA

While Cnut ruled in England, there was considerable unrest and dynastic infighting in his native Scandinavia. When Cnut's older brother, King Harald II (r. 1014–1019) of Denmark, died in 1019, English forces supported Cnut's campaign to enforce his claim to the throne, and Cnut became king. He later turned over rule of Denmark to his son, Harthacnut (r. 1028–1042), so that he could concentrate on ruling England. While Cnut ruled Denmark, he maintained strong support for Christianity, even sending English missionaries to the kingdom to counter the growing power of German archbishops. He also introduced a system of coinage copied from that used in England.

In Norway, Cnut exploited struggles between Norwegian landowners and King Olaf II (r. 1016–1028). Cnut drove Olaf from the throne in 1028 and wielded Danish power through a native chieftain, Haakon. When Haakon died in 1030, Cnut sent his illegitimate son Sweyn and Sweyn's mother, Aelfigifu, to rule Norway. Sweyn and his mother ruled the kingdom for several years. But in 1035, Olaf II's son, Magnus I (r. 1035–1046), rallied the Norwegians against the unpopular foreigners and took back the throne.

ACHIEVEMENTS AS KING

During his reign, Cnut generously supported the Christian Church in England as well as in Denmark. Although he maneuvered successfully on the European political stage, and negotiated the marriage of his daughter to the son of Emperor Conrad II (r. 1027–1039) of the Holy Roman Empire, his political control of his own kingdoms was never very secure.

As ruler of England, Cnut is best known for his lawful, peaceful, and prosperous reign. He protected Baltic trade routes in the north and promulgated ecclesiastical and secular laws based on the English tradition (especially "Edgar's law" from the reign of that Saxon ruler). Cnut also protected England against external dangers, including the threat of fresh Viking attacks. In 1018, for example, he retained a fleet of forty ships that forced back a Viking assault.

Cnut also showed considerable political acumen in choosing a wife. Before being acknowledged king of England in 1016, Cnut had fathered two illegitimate sons, Harald "Harefoot" and Sweyn, with Aelfigifu of Northumbria, the daughter of a Saxon ealdorman. Then, in 1017, he married Emma of Normandy, the widow of King Aethelred II, and established that only their joint children should be able to succeed to the English kingship after his death. Cnut and Emma had a son, Harthacnut.

When Cnut died in 1035, the English nobles did not attempt to restore the Anglo-Saxon line of kings, and Cnut was succeeded by his sons, Harald I Harefoot (r. 1037–1040) and Harthacnut (r. 1040–1042). However, both of Cnut's sons failed to secure deep-seated English support, and they waged a continuous struggle against each other. Both were widely unpopular during their short reigns. Har-

thacnut was succeeded by his half-brother, Edward the Confessor (r. 1042–1066), who, as the son of Aethelred II, restored the Anglo-Saxon line to the English throne.

See also: ANGLO-SAXON RULERS; DANISH KINGDOM; EDWARD THE CONFESSOR; ENGLISH MONARCHIES.

FURTHER READING

Haywood, John. *The Penguin Historical Atlas of the Vikings.* New York: Penguin, 1995.

Jones, Gwyn. *A History of the Vikings.* 2nd ed. New York: Oxford University Press, 2001.

Sawyer, Peter. *Kings and Vikings.* New York: Methuen, 1982.

———. *The Oxford Illustrated History of the Vikings.* New York: Oxford University Press, 1997.

Stenton, Sir Frank M. *Anglo-Saxon England.* 3rd ed. New York: Oxford University Press, 2001.

COINAGE, ROYAL

Means of exchange used by monarchs from the sixth century B.C.E. until the present day to facilitate trade for their nations and to promote their names or faces nationally and internationally.

ORIGINS OF COINAGE

The earliest known coins in the Western world were minted in the kingdom of Lydia in Anatolia (present-day Turkey) in the sixth century B.C.E. Electrum, a natural alloy of gold and silver, was found in the riverbeds of Lydia during the reign of King Croesus (r. ca. 560–547 B.C.E.). Croesus had coins minted using this metal and then, later in his reign, had pure silver and pure gold coins minted as well. The impact of this innovation on the king's fortunes is commemorated in the phrase, "rich as Croesus."

In ancient China, small clay token tablets and cowrie shells had been used as a medium of exchange since approximately 1100 B.C.E., during the Shang dynasty. The use of these objects as a means of exchange continued through the Chou dynasty (ca. eighth century B.C.E). The succeeding Ch'un Chiu dynasty, however, issued knife money (in the form and shape of knives), spade money (in the shape of small shovels), and devil-faced money; all of these forms of tokens were cast in copper.

The numismatic breakthrough in Asia came when the Ch'in emperor, Shih Huang Ti (r. 221–210 B.C.E.), completed the conquest of his neighbors and effectively united China. Shih Huang Ti outlawed all previous forms of currency and issued the new Pan-liang coin (around 200 B.C.E.), now familiar as the round Chinese copper with a square hole in the center.

COINAGE IN EUROPE

In Europe, Philip II of Macedon (r. 359–336 B.C.E.) popularized the use of gold coins during his reign. His illustrious son, Alexander the Great (r. 336–323 B.C.E.), was the first Western monarch to use coinage to spread his own name and image throughout the world. Prior to Alexander, coins had borne the images of animals, plants, heroes, or gods. Alexander minted silver and gold coins with the image of a seated Zeus on one side and his own image (thinly disguised as a god) on the other. Many of these "Alexanders" are still extant and may be found in numerous museums and private collections today.

After Alexander's death, rulers in Greece and Rome continued using the image of the divine Alexander on their coins. Ptolemy I of Egypt (r. 323–282 B.C.E.) was the first of Alexander's successors to put his own image on his coins (around 306 B.C.E.). He was soon followed by Seleucis I (r. 312–281 B.C.E.) of the Seleucid kingdom in Syria. Both kings pictured themselves on their coins as gods. This practice died out within a few decades but was revived when Julius Caesar placed his own bust on the Roman gold aureus in 46 B.C.E.

THE MIDDLE AGES

Proper design, smelting, and minting is a complex process requiring the cooperation of numerous industries, trades, and artisans. After the fall of Rome in the fifth century C.E., barter again became the more frequent and trusted means of exchange.

There were notable exceptions, however. For example, as the Merovingian Franks consolidated their power in ancient France, Clovis I (r. 481–511) struck great quantities of gold coins with his own image. His immediate descendants followed his lead.

With limited supplies of gold in northern Gaul, the Carolingian ruler, Pepin III, the Short (r. 751–768), substituted silver for gold in his imperial coinage. The result was a coin called the *denier*, which would be the basis of the treasury of his famous son, Charlemagne (r. 768–814), as well as the basis for most European coinage throughout the Middle Ages.

TOWARD THE MODERN ERA

Throughout antiquity and the Middle Ages, the practices of coin cutters, or "shorters," posed a great nuisance and threat to economies that increasingly relied on coinage. Consequently, prior to the ninth century, the value of coinage was directly related to the material of which it was made.

In the modern era, the Industrial Revolution improved coining techniques, greatly discouraging the practices of coin "clippers" who had hitherto easily removed portions of any coin they wished to alter. By this time, most Asian economies and monarchs had established a standardized system of silver coinage, and European nations had established a gold standard. Today the use of royal images on coins, first begun more than two thousand years ago, remains a common practice, even in countries that no longer have recognized monarchs.

See also: ALEXANDER III, THE GREAT; COMMERCE AND KINGSHIP; CROESUS; PHILIP II OF MACEDON; TAXATION; TRIBUTE.

COLA KINGDOM (ca. 850–1279 C.E.)

Kingdom in southern India (also spelled Chola), dating from the middle of the eighth century, which became one of the leading and most powerful states in the southern part of the Indian subcontinent.

Historical records note the existence of the Cola people as early as the third century B.C.E. However, little is known about events between that time and the ascendancy of the first Cola monarch, Vijayalaya (r. ca. 846–871), around 846. Vijayalaya conquered the region of Thanjavur around 850 and ruled over it until 870.

The Cola kingdom survived at this time despite being surrounded by more powerful neighbors, such as the Pandya and Pallava kingdoms. There is evidence that, during Vijayalaya's reign, the Cola kingdom expanded north into the Tondaimandalam region. But the conquest of Tondaimandalam was not completed until the early years of the reign of Aditya I (r. ca. 871–907), Vijayalaya's son and successor.

FURTHER EXPANSION

Aditya continued the policy of expansion begun by his father. In addition to conquering Tondaimanadalam, he also targeted the Kongumandalam, a territory on the western border of his kingdom and Tondaimandalam. In 880, Aditya began wars of conquest against his southern neighbors, the Pandyas. Archaeological evidence suggests that Aditya died around 898. His death seems to have sparked instability in the Cola court, since there is no record of another king until Parantaka I (r. ca. 907–947), Aditya's son.

The reign of Parantaka I was a crucial period for the future development of the Cola kingdom. Although Cola lost Tondaimandalam during the interregnum, the period between the reign of Aditya and Parantaka, Parantaka managed to recapture it. He then proceeded to conquer the Banu region north of Tondaimandalam. Like his father, Parantaka pursued the conquest of his southerly neighbor, the Pandya kingdom.

After conquering Pandya, Parantaka subdued the kings from Ceylon (Sri Lanka) who were allies of the Pandya king, Rajasimha II (r. ca. 902–920). This success extended the boundaries of the Cola kingdom to the most southern tip of the Indian subcontinent. By the end of Parantaka's reign, the Cola kingdom had more than tripled in size, and it had increased its security by reducing the number of neighbors with which it shared borders.

MAINTAINING POWER

The expansion of the Cola kingdom allowed the next ruler, Gandaraditya (r. 955–957), to pursue other means of developing the kingdom beyond geographic and political conquest. This does not mean that the conquered territories were entirely secure. In fact, it required a great deal of work by Gandaraditya's successors to maintain Cola sovereignty over Tondaimandalam.

The Pandya territory was not fully secured until the tenth century, during the reign of Rajaraja I, the Great (r. 985–1016). In addition to securing the frontiers of the empire, Rajaraja I was notable for the extent to which he regularized the structure and organization of the kingdom.

Rajaraja's successors made additional claims to territory, such as the addition of southern Ceylon to the kingdom. As the eleventh century began, the Cola kingdom also took measures to ensure that its lucrative maritime trade suffered as little disruption as possible, even if doing so required aggressive campaigns against rivals.

FALL OF THE COLAS

Ultimately, Cola control of its domains did not last. Early in the twelfth century, Cola lost territory to both the Vengi dynasty of the Mysore region and the Hoysala kingdom of the eastern Deccan region. Despite reconquering some of the lost territory, the Colas were unable to withstand the expansionary conquests of Hoysala.

During the twelfth century, as the Cola kingdom weakened under later monarchs, including Rajendra III (r. 1070–1122) and Rajaraja III (r. 1150–1173), Pandya declared its independence. By 1279, the Hoysala kingdom and the Kakatiya dynasty of the Warangal kingdom annexed the remainder of the Cola kingdom and so the Cola kingdom ceased to exist.

See also: INDIAN KINGDOMS; MYSORE KINGDOM; PANDYA DYNASTY; SOUTH ASIAN KINGDOMS.

COLONIALISM AND KINGSHIP

Relationship between colonialism and kingship, and the impact that colonial rule has had on the various kingdoms and monarchies throughout the world. The European encounter with, and conquest of, the non-European world between the fifteenth and twentieth centuries produced an ongoing dialogue between the interests of the colonial powers and the systems of monarchy and kingship in place within the various empires.

Despite the popular image, European colonialism in many cases avoided outright annexation of kingdoms in favor of working through local rulers or collaborating elites, often of a monarchical type. This system of "indirect rule" served to further the political and economic requirements of imperialism, as well as to buttress or undermine existing monarchies, depending upon their ability to adapt to the new leadership.

In the Americas, Asia, Africa, and the islands of the Pacific Ocean, colonialism had a diverse and complex effect on the structures of kingship present in the existing states of those regions. (For the purposes of this entry, colonialism is understood to

EUROPEAN COLONIAL EMPIRES, 1914

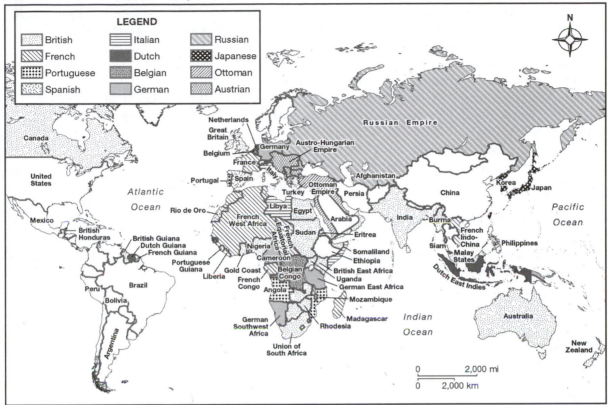

mean the "Western" experience in the centuries defined above.)

EARLY COLONIAL EMPIRES IN THE NEW WORLD

The first colonial empires to be established by Europeans—those of Spain and Portugal in the late fifteenth and early sixteenth centuries—experienced dramatically different encounters with kingdoms on several continents. In Central and South America, the overwhelming biological and social impact of the Old World confronting an isolated New World served rapidly to overwhelm existing political structures, most famously the Aztec Empire in Mexico and the Inca Empire in Peru. In the latter case, the Spanish tolerated a king for a few years after the conquest of the Inca Empire in 1532, but both the Aztecs and Incas rapidly disintegrated under the combined impact of superior European military technology and communicable diseases.

With few exceptions, the Spanish Empire in the New World was centralized under governors who had minimal respect for existing Native American political structures, most of which were badly un-

dermined in any case. A similar pattern can be discerned in Portuguese Brazil during the sixteenth and seventeenth centuries. With the exception of more remote political units—which were often first contacted by Jesuits and other religious orders—the larger empires and monarchies in what would become Latin America vanished within a generation.

PORTUGUESE AND SPANISH COLONIALISM IN AFRICA AND ASIA

In Africa and Asia, circumstances forced the Portuguese to work through the existing political structures because they did not have the advantage of numbers, technology, or new communicable diseases, and they encountered sophisticated kingly states. In West Africa, Portuguese contact with coastal kingdoms in the sixteenth century gave rise to the slave trade to offshore islands and then to the Americas.

In the Indian Ocean, the Portuguese established trade relations and made war on Islamic city-states in East Africa, the Persian Gulf, and the East Indies. They also established relations with the Mogul Empire in Delhi as well as princely rulers in Goa and other coastal cities of India. In 1513, the Portuguese also attempted to establish relations with the Ming dynasty of China, and later in the century with the Yi dynasty in Korea and the last rulers of the Ashikaga shogunate in Japan. None of these dynasties ever submitted to a colonial relationship with Europeans, however. Meanwhile, in the Philippines, the Spanish encountered small island states that were quickly brought under Spanish authority. As in Latin America, it was often the Catholic religious orders that provided the point of contact with local chiefs or headmen.

OTHER EUROPEAN POWERS

The other European empires of the early modern era, those of England, France, and the Netherlands, followed a broadly similar pattern in Africa and Asia. The Europeans made agreements with African coastal kingdoms to facilitate the slave trade, which, as it grew, enriched coastal African kingdoms like Benin and Dahomey at the expense of their defeated rivals in the interior. Many of the slaves shipped to the Americas were prisoners taken in the wars between African kingdoms.

As with the Portuguese, the later European colonial powers found it necessary to work through existing princely states in parts of East Africa, the Persian Gulf, India, and the East Indies. Until at least the eighteenth century, many of these Islamic and Hindu kingdoms operated on a basis of rough equality with their European trading partners. Only in India in the early nineteenth century did the British East India Company begin to have a significant political impact as the Mogul Empire declined and the numerous princely rulers formed alliances with various European and/or Indian power blocs. In most

For over a century, India was a colony of Great Britain, and the English monarch was considered its emperor. King George V and Queen Mary traveled to India for enthronement ceremonies in December 1911, becoming the first English rulers ever to visit the colony.

cases, the trade-oriented nature of the mercantile empires of the day made working through existing structures the most stable and cost-effective method.

COLONIALISM IN NORTH AMERICA

In North America, the French and English respected the independence and dignity of Native American rulers and chiefs to a much greater degree than was the case with the Spanish and Portuguese in Latin America. In the seventeenth and early eighteenth centuries, the English and Dutch formed trade and political relationships with the Iroquois Confederacy, among others, and the French established close relations with the Huron and Algonquin peoples.

Unlike the Asian monarchies, which often had a clear hierarchy and power structure that was recognizably similar to European monarchies, the native states of the Americas and Africa varied enormously in the type of political structure that existed. Usually, the Islamic states of Asia had a clear kingly ruler, but other societies operated through councils or other nonhereditary structures. The term *monarchies* in such cases is necessarily elastic.

A number of Native American nations, however, maintained their integrity well into the nineteenth century, only gradually succumbing to the combined assaults of European settlement, disease, and warfare. Even today, the recognition of "chiefs" by certain Native American nations reflects the last remnant of indigenous North American kingship.

EFFECT OF INDIRECT RULE

The dramatic growth of the European empires in the nineteenth and early twentieth centuries, and their transformation from primarily economic to primarily political units, brought about the age of "High" Imperialism and the more direct need to define the relationship between European and local interests. The system of "indirect rule" evolved largely out of the necessity to preserve social order and minimize the administrative cost to the colonial power.

British India perhaps provides the best example of this evolution. In 1858, rule by the East India Company gave way to formal British sovereignty, yet British India contained within its borders not only British territory (in which the British monarch was sovereign) but an array of more than five hundred princely states of great variety. Each was under British "protection" but enjoyed varying degrees of

local autonomy. Some were tiny, while others, such as Hyderabad and Kashmir, were significant kingdoms in their own right. The last remnant of the Mughal Empire, the kingdom of Delhi, was abolished by the British in 1858. This vast series of Indian kingdoms came to an end with the independence of India and Pakistan in 1947.

As the British Empire expanded in the late nineteenth century, a similar pattern of indirect rule was applied in parts of Africa, particularly Nigeria, the Gold Coast, and Uganda; the Persian Gulf emirates, such as Bahrain and Oman; and the Pacific, where kingdoms such as Tonga and Fiji were placed under British protection. In the Middle East, the British elevated the Khedive of Egypt to full kingship in 1922, and they established two Hashemite princes as kings of Iraq and Transjordan. The homeland of these princes, the kingdom of the Hejaz around Mecca, disappeared into Saudi Arabia in the 1920s.

Although the British were perhaps the best known exemplars of the application of indirect rule, similar patterns could be found in most of the other European empires in Africa and Asia. To some degree, the survival of precolonial kings depended on the level of political centralization employed by each empire; for example, the French tended to reduce kingly power to a minimal level in Africa and French Indochina (as in Morocco, Tunisia, Cambodia, and Laos), preferring to work through colonial administrators. The Dutch practiced indirect rule in the Dutch East Indies (modern Indonesia) among various Muslim and Hindu princes. At the local level, village chiefs or headmen in the various empires often provided the connecting link to the colonial authorities. The later African empires—such as those of Germany, Italy, and Belgium—generally employed some form of indirect rule for a time, but all three European powers moved toward centralization and the abolition of local institutions in response to resistance to colonial rule.

THE IMPERIAL EXPERIENCE

Imperial experience in the twentieth century ensured that few precolonial kingdoms survived to the present day. Some were subsumed into larger states that were granted independence but retained some local authority, such as the Asante kings in Ghana and the kings of Buganda and Bunyoro peoples in Uganda. Others were toppled by coups or revolutions that often were unleashed by the responses to colonialism—nationalism and radicalism. Examples of the latter include French Indochina, where indigenous monarchies disappeared in communist revolutions (although Cambodia's monarchy has been restored).

In Africa, only Morocco, Lesotho, and Swaziland retain their precolonial monarchies as independent states. Indeed, revolutions of various kinds have proven far more damaging to the survival of monarchies than the initial colonialism. Monarchies in Iraq, Iran, Egypt, Tunisia, Burundi, and Ethiopia all were overthrown by internal revolutions between the 1950s and 1970s.

Western colonialism did not only include the European powers. Japan and the United States also constructed colonial empires that necessitated dealing with kingly rulers. Japan displaced the indigenous monarchies in Okinawa (1873) and Korea (1910) through colonial annexation, and they established a puppet monarchy in Manchuria (renamed Manchukuo) under the last emperor of the Ch'ing (Qing) dynasty, Pu Yi, between 1932 and 1945. The United States terminated the Hawaiian monarchy through its annexation of that territory in 1898.

In sum, Western colonialism served to enhance the power of some monarchies, but more often than not it forced them to conform to new models of government and sovereignty. Survival usually depended on cooperation with colonial powers. Those monarchies that eventually did emerge from colonialism then had to confront the forces of nationalist state-building or revolutions opposed to traditional elite rule. Few monarchies thus survive outside of Europe and the Middle East in the twenty-first century.

See also: BODIES, POLITIC AND NATURAL; CONQUEST AND KINGSHIPS; EMPIRE; IMPERIAL RULE; NATIONAL IDENTITY; NATIONALISM; POSTCOLONIAL STATES.

FURTHER READING

Ansprenger, Franz. *The Dissolution of the Colonial Empires.* New York: Routledge, 1989.

Darwin, John. *Britain and Decolonization.* New York: Macmillan, 1988.

Fieldhouse, D.K. *The Colonial Empires from the Eighteenth Century.* New York: Dell, 1965.

COMMERCE AND KINGSHIP

Economic activities that include interchange of goods and services, large-scale trade, and buying and selling between political units such as cities, nations, and kingdoms.

Commerce has often been an activity of rulers and their advisers. These individuals have provided the chief market for goods and have been the principal benefactors of the economic transactions that take place. Strong commerce with other kingdoms ensured economic stability for the nation. In addition, rulers encouraged and financed trading expeditions in search of needed resources as well as luxuries and exotic goods for their courts.

EARLY COMMERCE AND TRADE

The ancient empires of Egypt and Babylon, which produced enough grain to export, conducted a lively trade with other kingdoms. Among the most sought after trade items were fabrics, rare woods, jewelry, pottery, tapestries, and unusual animals. There was also a significant slave trade among these empires.

The Phoenician city of Carthage, a maritime center located on the coast of North Africa, engaged in extensive trade throughout the Mediterranean region, along the coast of Europe, and in Africa. In fact, it may have been the necessity of keeping records of complex trade accounts that prompted the Phoenicians to develop the alphabet, which became the basis of the Latin alphabet and, through that, of our own Western alphabet today.

When the ancient Greeks colonized and mapped the Mediterranean and Black Sea regions in the late centuries B.C.E., commerce grew. Excellent Greek harbors and ports facilitated the exchange of goods from inland, and Greek cities such as Corinth and Hellas became great economic centers. In the 330s and 320s B.C.E., Alexander the Great (r. 336–323 B.C.E.) launched trade between the Mediterranean world and Central Asia as far as India, and the city of Alexandria in Egypt became the most important commercial hub of the Western world.

MEANS OF EXCHANGE

The earliest traders bartered goods, with livestock serving as an important means of exchange. As travel among kingdoms increased, however, commodities were purchased with easier to transport items, such as precious and semiprecious metal ingots. King Croesus of Lydia (r. ca. 560–547 B.C.E.), whose name is synonymous with wealth, is said to have minted the first gold coins as a means of exchange.

Once coins were in common use, banking began

to develop in large commercial centers, adding to the financial power of the countries in which they were located. By about 600 B.C.E., private banking existed among many Mediterranean societies, and it was developed considerably by the Greeks, Romans, and Byzantines. Commercial banking first became established in Italy during the Renaissance. Since monarchs retained control of the minting of coins, which often bore the likeness of the rulers, they had great influence on commerce.

COMMERCIAL REVOLUTION

Beginning in the eleventh century, the changes in economic structure resulting from increased world commerce led to the so-called Commercial Revolution. The economies of many kingdoms became increasingly tied to trade, more people lived in towns and cities and received wages, and business transactions were carried out with money.

Prince Henry the Navigator, the son of King John I (r. 1385–1433) of Portugal, was largely responsible for Portugal's rise as a maritime power in the 1400s. Henry brought together cartographers, shipbuilders, instrument makers, and sailors trained in navigation techniques to prepare for discovering a route to the East following the coast of Africa. After many expeditions, Henry's ships succeeded, and Portugal soon established a preeminent position in commerce.

Hoping to open new westward trade routes to India and increase their treasuries, the Spanish rulers Ferdinand of Aragon (r. 1479–1516) and Isabella of Castile (r. 1474–1504) financed the journeys of Christopher Columbus. When Columbus returned from his initial voyage to the Americas with gold, "Indians," and other valuable commodities, he was soon dispatched a second time, with more ships, men, and trade items and the imperative to claim the new lands for the Spanish Crown.

Along with the Spanish, the Dutch and Italians became significant commercial powers in the 1500s and 1600s. In an effort to strengthen its own economic interests, England passed, in 1651, the Navigation Acts, which required all goods exported or imported by English colonies to be carried on English ships. This legislation vastly increased the amount of trade for England and ensured its dominance in world commerce.

Trade routes opened earlier to China and the Far East had created markets in Europe for spices, silks, tea, dyes, and porcelain, and sustained commerce between the East and West. The East India Company, which received its original royal charter in 1600 from Queen Elizabeth I (r. 1558–1603) to conduct sea trade with the Americas, later became the major force behind English imperialism in Asia.

Ironically, the expansion of commerce, so strongly supported by sovereign rulers as a means of strengthening their wealth, created a merchant class powerful enough to challenge the absolute authority of monarchs and wealthy enough to emulate the lifestyle of aristocrats.

See also: COINAGE, ROYAL; CROESUS.

COMNENIAN DYNASTY

(1081–1185 C.E.)

Dynasty that ruled the Byzantine Empire in the eleventh and twelfth centuries.

The Comnenian dynasty came to power in 1081, when Alexius I Comnenus (r. 1081–1118), a popular military leader, became ruler of the Byzantine Empire. Several years earlier, in 1073, Alexius had become well known in military circles after he led several successful military campaigns, in alliance with Venetian forces, against the Normans in France.

Alexius used his political influence among Byzantine society—elite military leaders and wealthy relatives—to create a new aristocracy and eventually a dynasty. He had the support of many influential people because he provided them with power and status. They, in turn, shielded him against dissension and supported his rise to power.

Alexius's rule began at the end of a long period of turmoil following successful expansion under Basil II (r. 976–1025) of the Macedonian dynasty. Basil had extended the empire to encompass the Balkan region north to the Danube River, a large section of southern Italy, as well as control of Anatolia (present-day Turkey) and the Black Sea. His successors, however, had been unable to balance the divergent cultures within the Byzantine Empire, and a series of military failures, financial losses, and rebellions characterized much of Byzantine history in the eleventh century.

When Alexius I gained control in 1081, the empire was threatened on every side. His primary threat was from the Turks to the east and south and from the Normans, who were in southern Italy and prepared to invade Albania. Alexius continued his campaign against the Normans first, relying on the fact that the Normans were operating with the full support of the Roman Catholic Church. The Byzantine people had a long history of animosity toward the Roman Catholic Church and were willing to support a long military campaign that they saw as a bulwark against it.

After losing several battles, Alexius began using ambush techniques that he had learned from Turkish military strategists. The Byzantines thus began to win decisive military victories throughout the late 1080s. Ultimately, outside distractions on other fronts, including several civil wars in Norman territories, gave Alexius time to concentrate and consolidate power throughout his territories in the Balkans.

Alexius had many dissenters in his territories arrested, then imprisoned or executed. He also confiscated their property and scattered their families throughout the empire. Balkan rulers attempted to fight back, but Alexius repeatedly reclaimed lost territory. His control over the Balkans, however, was never stable, but rather a series of gradual and unsteady military occupations.

Alexius's reign was not entirely focused on the acquisition of land. The Comnenian dynasty also spent much effort casting out heretics and reforming the clergy. Included in such reforms was an attempt to resolve the differences between the eastern and western Christian churches. Alexius was unsuccessful in uniting the churches, however, and this failure alienated the Comnenian dynasty from the social change brought on by the Crusades.

In 1095, Alexius asked Pope Urban II to help him recover Anatolia from the Seljuk Turks, which helped to initiate the First Crusade. He forced people who joined his crusade to take an oath of allegiance to his leadership when they arrived in Constantinople a year later. The crusaders helped Alexius regain control of western Anatolia. However, he failed to prevent them from establishing independent states in Syria and Palestine, and the successful alliances he had made across Christian cultures during the Crusades began to break apart.

In 1098, Alexius failed to rescue a group of crusaders from a Turkish invasion because they had refused to take an oath of loyalty. As a result, many crusaders began to doubt Alexius's trustworthiness and refused to join in military and economic al-liances with the Byzantines, which had been one of the great sources of Alexius's success and power.

Over the next sixty-seven years, Alexius's four successors—John II (r. 1118–1143), Manuel I (r. 1143–1180), Alexius II (r. 1180–1183), and Andronicus (r. 1183–1185)—continued to gain and lose territories. This continued until 1185, when successful military raids on Byzantium by an alliance formed, in part, from the Norman nobility Alexius I had made his mark defeating, were able to topple much of the Byzantine Empire. The riots that ensued in the city of Constantinople after these raids ended the Comnenian dynasty and ushered in a new era of leadership for the humbled Byzantine Empire under the Angelus dynasty

See also: BYZANTINE EMPIRE; CRUSADER KINGDOMS; NORMAN KINGDOMS.

FURTHER READING
Angold, Michael. *The Byzantine Empire 1025–1204.* New York: Longman Group, 1984.

COMPETITION, FRATERNAL

Competition between brothers for kingship or political power. Fraternal competition has varied between different types of monarchies or royal families. The custom of primogeniture (inheritance by the oldest son), followed by most medieval and modern European monarchies, has limited the power of fraternal competition by establishing the oldest brother as the unquestioned successor.

Even so, a number of European royal brothers have engaged in political intrigue or even military action against each other. In the late 1100s and early 1200s, for example, John of England (r. 1199–1216) fought his elder brother Richard I (r. 1189–1199) before acceding to the throne on Richard's death. Situations in which two brothers claimed the throne, however, have been rare.

The very sharp distinction in European monarchies between "legitimate" children born to wives and "illegitimate" children born to mistresses, also limited fraternal competition by rendering it impossible for illegitimate sons ever to be accepted as monarchs. Fraternal competition could also be limited, though not suppressed, by monarchs who divided their empires among their sons, as did Charlemagne (r. 768–814) and Genghis Khan (r. 1206–1227). The division of the empire led to conflict between the sons of these rulers, but the conflict did not extend to fratricide or dethronement.

Monarchies that have lacked an impersonal mechanism to designate the successor but relied on a royal father to designate one of his sons (rarely daughters) as sole heir to an undivided realm have fostered intense competitiveness among brothers, sometimes extending to outright killing. Polygamous systems, in which all of the children of a monarch and his many wives or concubines are equally legitimate, also encourage fratricidal conflict.

Royal fraternal competition was perhaps greatest in the Muslim world, and particularly the early Ottoman Empire, which combined a stable imperial house, a tradition of imperial unity, a harem of concubines whose children were of equal legitimacy, and an open succession to the throne. The practice of fratricide in the Ottoman Empire was introduced by Sultan Bayezid I (r. 1389–1402), who on his accession in 1389 had his brother Yakub executed.

The early Ottoman sultans established their numerous sons as army leaders or provincial governors, and the death of a sultan was sometimes followed by civil wars in which the defeated brothers either fled the empire or were killed by their siblings. The *ulema*, or body of scholars of Islamic law, grudgingly accepted fratricide as superior to unending civil war or the fragmentation of the empire. The practice of fratricide also had the advantage of usually providing competent sultans. Ottoman fratricide reached its peak with Sultan Mehmed III (r. 1595–1603), who on his accession in 1595 had nineteen of his brothers strangled.

Beginning in the late 1500s, the Ottomans switched from fratricide to a system in which royal sons were kept in a special section of the palace known as the "cage" until they died or were raised to the throne. This practice of isolating potential heirs often produced inexperienced, and sometimes insane, sultans. Another great Muslim dynasty known for its fratricidal succession conflicts was the Mughal dynasty of India.

See also: INHERITANCE, ROYAL; ISLAM AND KINGSHIP; LEGITIMACY; OTTOMAN EMPIRE; PRIMOGENITURE; ROYAL FAMILIES; SIBLINGS, ROYAL; SUCCESSION, ROYAL.

CONCUBINES, ROYAL

Women who cohabit with monarchs without being married to them. The distinction between a concubine and a secondary wife in a polygamous system is not always clear, but generally, concubines are distinguished from wives by enjoying few legal protections and by the fact that their children are not recognized as heirs. A concubine is usually selected for her beauty or charm rather than for wealth or family connections, and her position depends on her hold over the monarch's affections or lust.

CONCUBINE OR MISTRESS?

Another word used for a man's sexual partner outside of marriage is "mistress"—a word that suggests a woman who is sought after, wooed, and loved, and may have a husband and social position independent of her relationship with the monarch. The word "concubine" most often implies a woman who is of low social status and who serves her master's purpose, not her own. But the line between these concepts is not always clear either. In Western societies, royal mistresses have often been referred to as concubines by people who dislike them and wish to underplay their importance. This happened with Jane Shore, the beautiful and high-spirited lover of England's King Edward IV (r. 1461–1470), and to Anne Boleyn, the second wife of King Henry VIII (r. 1509–1547), who gained the title of queen only to be executed for alleged sexual misconduct.

YANG GUIFEI

Through the ages, concubines have sometimes transcended their essentially lowly status to achieve distinction, at least in literature or in folk memory, and sometimes to reach real material power. Yang Guifei was the low-born favorite concubine of the T'ang emperor of China, Hsuan Tsung (Xuanzong) (r. 712–756).

It was said that Hsuan Tsung's passion for Yang Guifei was so great that he failed to tend to the business of his empire. A terrifying rebellion, which forced the court to flee the capital for a time, was blamed by the palace guards on Yang Guifei and her brother. The guards insisted that the emperor order that both be executed. The emperor complied but, heartsick at his loss, he abdicated soon after.

Yang Guifei became known as one of the Four Beauties of ancient China, and her tragic story is the subject of a renowned poem, "Song of Everlasting Sorrow," by Bai Juyi.

LADY NIJO

Another famous concubine was Nakanoin Masatada no Musume, also known as Lady Nijo. Born around 1257 to an aristocratic Japanese family, she grew up in the imperial palace, where her father held important positions. Emperor Go-Fukakusa (r. 1246–1260), fifteen years older than Lady Nijo, took her as a concubine when she was fourteen years old.

Nijo's father, who might have been able to exert some influence to secure a position for her as a secondary wife to the emperor, died only two years later, leaving Nijo dependent on the emperor. It does not seem to have bothered Go-Fukakusa that she had at least two other lovers, but when the empress, who had always resented Nijo's presence, circulated a rumor that Nijo had begun an affair with the emperor's brother and political rival, Go-Fukakusa banished her from the court.

Nijo lived in seclusion for several years and then began to travel around Japan as a Buddhist nun. After Go-Fukakusa's death in 1260, she wrote her story, which has been published in English as *The Confessions of Lady Nijo*. It is an intimate confession, full of intense feeling not just about Nijo's own plight but about the lives of the ordinary people she met during her travels.

MADAME DE POMPADOUR

One of the most famous royal concubines in France was Madame de Pompadour, born Jeanne-Antoinette Poisson to a middle-class Paris family in 1725. When Jeanne was nine years old, a gypsy fortuneteller predicted that she would become mistress to the king. Her family made a joke of it, calling her Reinette (little queen). But she seems to have taken the prophecy seriously and to have set about acquiring the accomplishments—writing in a beautiful script, playing the harpsichord, painting, and making witty and intelligent conversation—that would make her fit to be mistress to a king.

As a young woman, Jeanne-Antoinette made a wealthy marriage and soon became known for her exquisite style of dress and the dinner parties to which she invited the most intelligent people in France. In 1745, she managed to meet King Louis XV (r. 1715–1774) at a masked ball; her beauty and charm captivated him, and before long she had left her husband and was installed in an apartment at the royal palace of Versailles.

The king showered Jeanne with honors. She became the Marquise de Pompadour, a center of social life at court, an important patroness of the arts, and the focus of much hatred throughout the land. Her physical relationship with the king ran its course, however, and he had many other extramarital affairs, but the deep friendship between Louis and Madame Pompadour ensured that she maintained her position until her early death at age forty.

See also: CONSORTS, ROYAL; HENRY VIII; LOUIS XV; MARRIAGE OF KINGS; POLYGAMY, ROYAL.

CONNAUGHT KINGDOM

(358–1585 C.E.)

The smallest of the five kingdoms of early Ireland. The Gaelic name for the kingdom of Connaught is said to derive from Connmac, one of the sons of the legendary goddess Maeve, whose legendary residence was located in the kingdom.

EARLY RULERS

According to ancient Irish legends, Connaught was the home of the Fir Bolg, a pre-Gaelic people who invaded Ireland around 1972 B.C.E. After the Fir Bolg were conquered by the Dé Dannnan people, Sreng, one of the defeated warriors, was given Connaught as a peace settlement. The early capital of Gaelic Connaught was located at Cruachain. Most of the genealogical sources for the Connaught kings start with Beochaich Moydedon (r. 358–366), who was also the high king of Tara.

The dominant dynasty in Connaught from the late fifth to mid-eighth century was the Ui Fiachrach. They were supplanted by the Uí Bríuin. Both traced their descent from Eochu Mugmedón, a fourth-century high king of Ireland. The Ui Fiachrach were the descendants of Eochu's, son Fiachra Foltsnaithech. The Uí Bríuin traced their descent from Bríon, Fiachra's brother, who was also a brother of Niall, the founder of the Uí Neill dynasty, who were later kings of Ulster. The Uí Bríuin later took the name Conchohbair (O'Connor), from Conchobar, a king who died in 973.

THE O'CONNORS

Until the eleventh century, Connaught played little part in the affairs of Ireland. It was Turloch O'Connor (r. 1106–1156), who unexpectedly made his dynasty a great power in Ireland. A warrior and statesman, he also was a kingmaker, forcing the O'Brien high king to accept the treaty of Glonmire in 1118, which partitioned Munster into northern and southern kingdoms. In 1121, on the death of the Uí Neill king, Domnall Ua Lochlainn (r. 1119–1121), Turloch seized the high kingship of Tara by force, though he continued to face opposition from the kingdoms of Desmond, Thomond, and Leinster, as well as the Uí Neill kings.

In 1150, Miurchertach Ua Lochlainn (r. 1156–1166) established himself as a rival to Turloch for the high kingship. Turloch won a famous battle at Moin-mor in Tipperary in 1151, where he defeated the forces of Turloch O'Brien, the king of Thomond. Turloch O'Connor was a centralizing monarch; he developed and improved the area's roads and bridges and established a strong naval force at the mouth of the Shannon River.

Upon Turloch's death in 1156, his son, Ruaidri (Rory) O'Connor (r. 1156–1186), gained the kingship of Connaught by blinding his eldest brother, who was thought most qualified to be king. When Ruaidri tried to gain the high kingship, however, he was defeated by Miurchertach Ua Lochlainn. In 1166, after Muiurchetach killed some princely hostages and was driven from the kingship, Rory O'Connor joined forces with Tigernan Ua Ruairc of Breifne (r. 1124–1172) and Diarmait Ua Máel Sechnaill of Meath (r. 1160–1169), and won a series of victories that made him high king of Ireland.

STRUGGLE WITH ENGLAND

Rory O'Connor's reign started well, but in 1169 he had to fight the Norman knights and later the troops of Henry II (r. 1154–1189) who had invaded Ireland. In 1175, he signed the Treaty of Windsor, acknowledging the English king as his overlord. He continued to reign as a vassal king, as did his successors after he abdicated in 1186.

In 1235, an English army laid waste to the kingdom of Connaught, and the Normans seized land to make estates for themselves. The O'Connors were almost exterminated at the battle of Athenry, fought against the English in 1316.

At the end of the fourteenth century, the kingdom was divided between two branches of the dynasty, called the O'Connor Roe (red) and the O'Connor Don (fair-haired). In 1543, the O'Connors relinquished their titles and agreed to obey the English Crown, while still intending to fight for their hereditary lands.

Beginning in 1571, Diarmuid mac Eogan Chaoic (r. 1550–1585) of the O'Connor Don, and the head of the O'Connor Roe, Tadhg Óg O'Connor (r. ?–1585), waged war against the English overseers of Connaught but were defeated. In 1585, Tadhg Óg O'Connor agreed to the Composition of Connaught, which abolished all Gaelic titles in the kingdom. Diarmuid died that same year, ending the line of Irish kings in Connaught.

See also: IRISH KINGS; LEINSTER KINGDOM; MEATH KINGDOM; ULSTER KINGDOM.

FURTHER READING

Byrne, Francis John. *Irish Kings and High-Kings.* 2nd ed. Portland, OR: Four Courts Press, 2001.

Ellis, Peter Beresford. *Erin's Blood Royal: The Gaelic Nobel Dynasties of Ireland.* New York: Palgrave Macmillan, 2002.

O Corrain, Donnchadh. *Ireland Before the Normans.* Portland, OR: Four Courts Press, 2004.

CONQUEST AND KINGSHIPS

A method of acquiring territory by force used by rulers and kings throughout much of early history. Conquest often had lasting and profound political, administrative, and social effects on the defeated state or people. Conquest was considered a legally valid means of acquiring territory until the twentieth century, when nations and statesmen began to challenge this idea. Following World War I, the acquisition of territory through force, especially by waging war, was considered a violation of international law.

HISTORICAL NOTION OF CONQUEST

Historically, sovereign states were said to have a legal right to conquest, and other states recognized territory gained through conquest as legally valid. The right to conquest is closely associated with the concept of state sovereignty, or the ability of a state to possess primary power over its own borders without accountability to any other state. It was a generally

ROYAL RITUALS

DIVINE RIGHT AND CONQUEST

In early history, people believed that kings were entitled to conquest by the same rules that governed their accession to the throne—divine right. In 1399 C.E., the English Parliament recognized Henry Bolingbroke as King Henry IV (r. 1399–1413) by agreeing that he had gained the throne through conquest, which was a right God had given him. People also thought that kingship was above the law and that kings retained their sovereignty through the will of God. Regardless of how a king gained the throne—through descent, election, or conquest—the kingship was thought to be the will of God, and kings were, therefore, infallible.

accepted notion that a sovereign state had the right to wage war for whatever reason it saw fit, including the desire to acquire territory.

The expansion of many of the great empires throughout history was achieved through conquest. Conquest was one of the primary means by which various cultural, political, and social ideas spread from one part of the world to another.

Conquests of Alexander the Great

Alexander III, the Great, of Macedon (r. 336–323 B.C.E.) launched the greatest series of conquests the world has ever seen, and his short reign marked a significant moment in the history of Europe and Asia. At the height of Alexander's rule, his vast empire stretched from the Ionian Sea near Greece to the northern part of India.

The Roman Empire, the spread of Christianity, and the Byzantine Empire were all, to some degree, the results of Alexander's conquests, which included Greece, virtually all of Asia Minor (present-day Turkey), and the empires of Persia, Babylon, Phoenicia, Palestine, and Egypt. Alexander's victories created a single cultural and economic world, known as the Hellenistic, that allowed for the social and economic exchange of various ideas and goods.

Norman Conquest

The Norman Conquest was the military conquest of England by Duke William of Normandy in 1066 C.E.. The culmination of the conquest came at the battle of Hastings on October 14, 1066. After a full day of

fighting, with the battle's outcome in doubt, the English line eventually collapsed and the Normans crushed the enemy with vigor. With this victory, the Norman Conquest was completed, ending Anglo-Saxon rule of England. Duke William became King William I (r. 1066–1087)

Following the Norman Conquest, England was changed to suit its conquerors. The majority of the Saxon aristocracy, along with the upper levels of clergy, were killed or replaced by the Normans. The invaders also imposed a system of military feudalism on the Saxon populace. In addition to drastically altering the social and political structure of England, the Norman Conquest also had a great impact on the English language. English dialect was completely replaced by Latin, and then Norman French, as the language for laws and literature. This impact can still be seen today, with a large portion of English vocabulary based on either Latin or French.

Mongol Conquests

Genghis Khan (r. 1206–1227), known as one of the world's fiercest conquerors, was able to unite the nomadic tribes of Mongolia into a disciplined military state for the first time. His grandson, Kublai Khan (r. 1260–1294), cemented Mongol conquests in Asia by conquering China and moving the Mongol capital to Beijing in 1271.

The Mongol Empire was the only foreign dynasty ever to rule all of China. At its greatest extent, the empire stretched from Korea to Hungary and as far as Vietnam in the south, an area that comprised one of the largest empires in history. The Mongols were noted for improving the Chinese road systems running into Russia and for promoting trade throughout the empire and with Europe. They are also remembered for their most notable trait—a ferocious military force.

MODERN NOTION OF CONQUEST

At the beginning of the twentieth century, the idea that a state had a legal right to forcibly acquire territory from another state was challenged by various nations, statesmen, and scholars. One of the primary underpinnings of this new view was the principle of self-determination, which was adopted by the international community after World War I. Self-determination—the ability of a group with a national identity to form its own state and determine its own government—was accepted as one of the key factors behind the peace settlement that ended the war.

The League of Nations, which was created at the end of the war as an organization for international cooperation, held that war for the purpose of territorial acquisition was unjust. The United Nations, which grew out of the League of Nations, now considers conquest a violation of international law.

See also: BYZANTINE EMPIRE; MONGOL EMPIRE; PERSIAN EMPIRE; ROMAN EMPIRE.

FURTHER READING

Korman, Sharon. *The Right of Conquest: The Acquisition of Territory by Force in International Law and Practice.* New York: Clarendon Press, 1996.

CONRAD II (ca. 990–1039 C.E.)

German king (r. 1024–1039) and Holy Roman emperor (r. 1027–1039), who was first emperor of the Salian dynasty. A champion of the minor nobles and the common person, Conrad established the German monarchy as an independent power.

Conrad II was a Franconian noble and descendant of Holy Roman Emperor Otto I (r. 962–973). (The duchy of Franconia was a region of Germany that occupied the northern part of the present-day state of Bavaria.) In 1024, the German ruler, Henry II (r. 1014–1024), the last of the Saxon dynasty, died without an heir. German princes elected Conrad—

the matrilineal heir of Otto I—as Henry's successor, but Conrad's stepson, Ernest of Swabia, contested the accession along with the Italian nobility and the Lotharingians, whose land roughly comprised the present-day Netherlands, Belgium, Luxembourg, Alsace, and northwest Germany.

After putting down uprisings led by Ernest and the Lotharingians, Conrad marched toward Milan and was crowned king by the archbishop of Milan in 1026. Conrad brought the other city-states of northern Italy into submission and was crowned Holy Roman emperor at Rome in 1027. Conrad suppressed two more revolts by Ernest in 1027 and 1030, and he won the region of Lusatia from Poland in 1031. In 1034, he annexed Burgundy under the terms of an earlier treaty between his predecessor, Henry II, and Rudolf III (r. 993–1032) of Arles, whose realm included Burgundy.

Conrad then returned to northern Italy, where the greater nobility, with support of the archbishop of Milan, were fighting against the lesser nobility. Conrad, who was powerful enough not to need the support of either the nobility or the church, sided with the lesser nobility and the common man. He deposed the archbishop of Milan and his allies in 1036, and made the title to the lands under the control of the lesser nobles hereditary. Conrad then established the ministeriales, a new hereditary bureaucracy manned by the common people, who replaced the clergy in the civil service. Upon Conrad's death in 1039, he was succeeded on the throne of both Germany and the Holy Roman Empire by his son, Henry III (r. 1039–1056).

See also: FRANCONIAN DYNASTY; HOLY ROMAN EMPIRE; LOTHAIR I; OTTO I, THE GREAT; SALIAN DYNASTY.

CONRAD III (1093–1152 C.E.)

First member of the Hohenstaufen dynasty to rule as German king (r. 1138–1152) and contender for Holy Roman emperor, though he was never confirmed or crowned emperor by the pope.

Conrad was the son of Frederick, duke of Swabia, and Agnes, the daughter of Holy Roman emperor Henry IV (r. 1084–1105) of the Salian dynasty. In 1125, Conrad's brother, Frederick, lost the imperial election for Holy Roman emperor to Lothair of Saxony, who became Emperor Lothair II (r. 1125–1137). In the aftermath of this electoral defeat, the two brothers rebelled against Lothair and set up Conrad as a rival king. Conrad went to Milan to seek recognition and was crowned king there in 1128. However, when he failed to gain power at Lothair's expense, Conrad finally submitted to the emperor in 1135.

When Lothair died in 1137, the German imperial electors feared increasing the power of Lothair's son-in-law, Henry the Proud of Bavaria, by electing him as successor. As a result, they elected Conrad III king of the Romans (emperor). Conrad annexed the duchies of Saxony and Bavaria from Henry, which led to civil war.

The war between Conrad and the supporters of Henry continued even after Henry's death in 1139, as Henry's brother Guelph and the Saxons supported the claims to the throne of Henry's son, Henry the Lion. Two opposing political groups—the Guelphs and Ghibellines—emerged from this conflict. A short-lived truce was made between the opposing forces in 1142, but the Guelph-Ghibelline conflict reemerged periodically for many years afterward.

In 1146, Conrad met the Crusader, Saint Bernard of Clairvaux, and was persuaded to take part in the unsuccessful siege of Damascus, from which Conrad returned to Europe in 1149. Because the pope never crowned Conrad, he was never officially confirmed as Holy Roman emperor. However, upon his death in 1152, he was succeeded as German king by his nephew, Emperor Frederick I Barbarossa (r. 1152–1190).

See also: FREDERICK I, BARBAROSSA; HENRY IV; HOHENSTAUFEN DYNASTY; HOLY ROMAN EMPIRE; LOTHAIR I; SALIAN DYNASTY.

CONSORTS, ROYAL

Individuals whose royal status is dependent on marriage to a royal person. Consorts are not sovereigns, and not all royal spouses fall into this category.

Some European monarchies offered the possibility of marriage to a king without acquiring the position of queen consort through the institution of morganatic marriage. This is a form of marriage in which a wife of lower status does not acquire the status of her husband. The most famous royal morganatic marriage was that of Louis XIV of France (r. 1638–1715) to Madame de Maintenon.

Another form of royal marriage is co-rulership, in which both partners are sovereign. Famous examples of co-rulership in European monarchies are Ferdinand II of Aragón (r. 1479–1516) and Isabella I of Castile (r. 1474–1504) who, though they ruled Spain jointly, actually ruled their kingdoms of Aragón and Castile separately. Another example of co-rulers are William III (r. 1689–1702) and Mary II (r. 1689–1694) of England, whose co-rulership was a compromise after William refused the status of consort to Mary, who had the legitimate claim to the English Crown.

In Europe, royal or noble status is usually a prerequisite for a queen to be considered a full consort. Royal consortship is not a status held for life, however. Upon the death of a king, his queen consort becomes queen mother or queen dowager rather than remain queen consort.

Female monarchs have faced particularly difficult challenges in finding a role for their partners. In patriarchal societies, the difficulty of a reigning queen maintaining her independence if married was one factor that led some queens, notably Elizabeth I of England (r. 1558–1603) or Christina of Sweden (r. 1632–1654), to remain unmarried despite the problems caused by the lack of a direct heir. Male royal consorts are usually referred to as prince consorts because it has been difficult to separate the title of "king" from actual power.

Although consorts usually lack institutionalized political power, they can exert influence in many ways. It is rare but not unheard of for a consort to become a ruler in her own right. This possibility is most likely in kingdoms that lack a clear law of succession. The best-known example is Catherine II of Russia (r. 1762–1796), originally a German princess from a minor house who married into the Romanov dynasty.

Consorts can act as regents for their spouses, as Catherine of Aragón did for her husband, Henry VIII of England (r. 1509–1547), while he was on campaign in France. Consorts can also exercise influence behind the scenes, depending on the personalities of the ruler and consort. A well-known example is Prince Albert, consort to Queen Victoria of Great Britain (r. 1837–1901), whose influence over her was so powerful that he was allowed to play a leading role in English life.

See also: CONCUBINES, ROYAL; DUAL MONARCHIES; KINGS AND QUEENS; MARRIAGE OF KINGS;

POLYGAMY, ROYAL; QUEENS AND QUEEN MOTHERS; SUCCESSION, ROYAL.

FURTHER READING

Cook, Petronelle. *Queen Consorts of England: The Power behind the Throne*. New York: Facts on File, 1993.

CONSTANTINE I, THE GREAT

(274–337 C.E.)

Roman emperor (r. 306–337) and the first Roman ruler to be converted to Christianity. He founded Constantinople (now Istanbul), which remained the capital of the Byzantine Empire, or the Eastern Roman Empire, until the empire's fall in 1453. Constantine is best known for unifying an empire on the verge of collapse, reorganizing the Roman state, and setting the stage for the victory of Christianity at the end of the fourth century.

RISE TO POWER

The son of Constantius I, a Roman military commander, Constantine was born Flavius Valerius Constantinus in Nis, in what is present-day Serbia. While his father was away fighting, the young Constantine stayed at the court of the Emperor Diocletian (r. 284–305). When Diocletian resigned from the emperorship in 305, Galerius (r. 305–311), who was co-emperor of Rome with Constantius I (r. 305–306), sent Constantine to join his father in Britain.

While in Britain, Constantine became very popular with the Roman soldiers, who proclaimed him emperor after the death of Emperor Constantius in 306. Galerius still held the co-emperorship, however, and there were other claimants to the throne. Through much political maneuvering, Constantine managed to hold on to his rule, but for the next twenty years, he continually had to fight to maintain his control of the throne, which was often challenged.

The Arch of Constantine in Rome was built in 315 C.E. This triumphal arch was erected in honor of the Emperor Constantine I after his victory over Maxentius, a rival for the imperial crown, at the battle of the Milvian Bridge in 312 C.E.

CONVERSION TO CHRISTIANITY

For much of his early life, Constantine relied on his faith in the Roman sun-god, Sol. However, by 312, he had converted to Christianity. At first, Constantine associated Christ with the sun-god, but he ultimately abandoned all his previously held pagan beliefs and converted fully to Christianity. Even so, he still tolerated paganism among his subjects.

Constantine was converted to Christianity following a vision in which he believed a higher power indicated an upcoming victory. Soon after, he defeated his imperial rival, Maxentius (r. 307–312), at the battle of the Milvian Bridge in 312, a victory that earned Constantine the reputation as savior of the Roman people. Viewing the Christian God as responsible for his victory, Constantine called for an end to the persecution of Christians with the Edict of Milan in 313. Soon after, Constantine began to challenge his co-emperor, Licinius (r. 308–324), for power, emerging as sole ruler of the Roman Empire in 324.

REFORMS AND POLICIES

After becoming sole ruler, Constantine began to implement many reforms of the empire. He reorganized the Roman army and separated civil and military powers. He returned a great deal of authority to the Roman Senate, which had lost much of its power in the third century. Constantine also issued new gold coins called *solidi*, which remained the currency until the end of the Byzantine Empire.

Constantine began building the city of Constantinople in 326. Built on the site of the ancient Greek city Byzantium, Constantinople was completed in 330, although it was later expanded. The new capital city was given the best of Roman institutions, while being graced with the beauty of ancient Greek works of art. The emperor also began building churches in the Holy Land, where his mother claimed to have found the cross on which Jesus was crucified. As the first Christian emperor, Constantine played an instrumental role in expanding Christianity in the Roman Empire. He received his own baptism on his deathbed in 337.

Constantine had done much to reunify the Roman Empire. But upon his death, the empire was divided again, as his three sons, Constantine II (r. 337–340), Constans (r. 337–350), and Constantius II (r. 337–361) vied for power.

See also: BYZANTINE EMPIRE; CHRISTIANITY AND KINGSHIP; DIOCLETIAN; ROMAN EMPIRE.

FURTHER READING

Grant, Michael. *Constantine the Great: The Man and His Times.* New York: Scribner's, 1994.

————. *The Emperor Constantine.* London: Weidenfeld & Nicolson, 1993.

Pohlsander, Hans A. *The Emperor Constantine.* New York: Routledge, 1996.

COOKS, ROYAL

People who prepare food for royalty. Food in the royal courts was hardly an ordinary affair; elaborate presentations and amazing quantities of exotic foods unknown to the common man were all but the norm for monarchs. Marriages between kings and queens of various countries did much to help introduce and popularize previously unknown foods into a new region. The marriage of Henry VII of England to Catherine of Aragón of Spain, for example, introduced the king to the artichoke and fueled a passion for fruit resulting in the planting of a royal cherry orchard at Kent in 1533. Monarchs treasured new food experiences. After becoming empress of India in 1876, England's Queen Victoria (r. 1819–1901), fascinated with the subcontinent she had not traveled to, employed a young Indian man, Abdul Karim, who became her confidant. She then hired two Indian chefs to cook curry lunches for her in the event she had an Indian visitor.

Monarchs honed their appreciation for great food by employing some of the most talented chefs in the world to serve and delight their courts. Food played an integral role in the coronation celebration of England's James II in 1685. The feast consisted of 145 dishes served in the first course and 30 in the second; over his lifetime, the king's master chef Peter Lamb prepared over 1,400 dishes.

GREAT ROYAL CHEFS

Marie-Antoine Careme (1784–1833) was the founder of French haute cuisine and by the age of twenty-one served as chef de cuisine to the popular French politician and diplomat Charles Maurice de Talleyrand-Perigord (1754–1838). He served in the royal courts of George IV of England (r. 1820–1830) and Emperor Alexander I of Russia (r. 1801–1825). Marie-Antoine penned several books on cookery and the history of French cooking; each volume comprised hundreds of recipes and menus. He died at forty-eight and is remembered as the "chef of kings and the king of chefs."

Georges August Escoffier (1846–1935) began cooking at the age of thirteen, when he went to work in his uncle's kitchen in Nice. Escoffier modernized the cooking systems founded by Careme and was widely considered to be the chef of emperors. He was held in high esteem by Kaiser Wilhelm II of Germany (r. 1888–1918).

CÓRDOBA, CALIPHATE OF

(756–1031 C.E.)

An independent Muslim emirate, centered at the city of Córdoba, that unified Moorish Spain in the eighth century and brought a flowering of commerce and culture. In 756, Abd al-Rahman, a prince of the Umayyad dynasty of Damascus in Syria, defeated the governor of al-Andalus—the parts of Spain under Moorish control—and founded the politically independent emirate of Córdoba, thus unifying all of Moorish Spain.

Abd al-Rahman II, who ruled from 912 to 961, proclaimed Córdoba a caliphate in 929 and named himself caliph. (A caliph is an Islamic leader who is thought to be related to the prophet Mohammad, and a caliphate is the geographical area over which he rules.) Until this time, al-Andalus had been under the jurisdiction of the caliphate of Baghdad, so Abd al-Rahman's action was especially significant. For the first time, the rulers of al-Andalus were independent both religiously and politically. Abd al-Rahman developed a strictly controlled and well-organized administration that included a treasury and centralized accounting.

Because Córdoba's economy was based on the use of currency, as opposed to an economy based on barter, it became an important economic center of medieval Europe. At the height of its power, the city of Córdoba had more than one hundred thousand residents, making it Europe's largest city. Moreover, after Caliph al-Hakam II (r. 961–976) came to power, Córdoba became an extremely important cultural center. Al-Hakam founded a library that

eventually housed hundreds of thousands of books. Because of a policy of religious tolerance, Muslim, Jewish, and Christian scholars were able to teach students from all over Europe who came to Córdoba to study and learn. Muslim thinkers were particularly adept in medicine, mathematics, and astronomy, and, in general, Muslim culture in Spain was very much more advanced than any culture in Europe at the time, not only in education and religious tolerance but also in the quality of life. At its height, Córdoba had 700 mosques, 300 public baths, paved streets, and streetlights. Wealthy residents even had heat ducts running under the mosaic floors of their homes.

When al-Hakam died in 976, his son and heir Hisham II (r. 976–1009) was only twelve years old. A *hajib*, or court chamberlain, named al-Mansur took over the government and, in 981, forced Hisham to grant him complete authority over Córdoba. Al-Mansur became a powerful dictator, who was seen as a defender of orthodox Islamic faith, partially because of his *jihad*, or holy war, against the Christian kingdoms to the north of al-Andalus. Al-Mansur died in 1002 and was succeeded by his son, Abdul-Malik, who died only six years later, probably murdered by an assassin.

Because the Umayyad dynasty had been usurped for twenty-two years of dictatorship, the people in the caliphate came to question the dynasty's legitimacy. Hisham was deposed in 1009, restored, and then killed in 1013. In the same year, the city of Córdoba was sacked by a group of Muslim dissidents. For the next twenty-three years, rival claimants to the throne further weakened central authority in the caliphate until 1031, when it collapsed. After the collapse of the caliphate of Córdoba, Moorish Spain fractured into about thirty *taifas*, or smaller kingdoms, each ruled by local leaders. Some of these *taifas*, such as Granada, Seville, and Toledo, eventually grew into strong Moorish principalities.

See also: ABD AL-RAHMAN; GRANADA, KINGDOM OF; UMAYYAD DYNASTY.

FURTHER READING

Collins, Roger. *Early Medieval Spain: Unity in Diversity, 400–1000.* 2nd ed. New York: St. Martin's Press, 1995.

Fletcher, Richard. *Moorish Spain.* Berkeley: University of California Press, 1993.

Councils and Counselors, Royal

Various bodies and individuals who function as assistants to the royal personage.

Very few monarchs throughout history have ruled completely without counselors, and, in some cases, the men and women who have helped monarchs in decision-making processes have grown to be more powerful than the monarchs they were ostensibly serving. The increasing power of royal councils and counselors ultimately contributed to the decline of monarchies and the rise of more democratic forms of government.

EARLY ROYAL COUNCILS

Royal councils and counselors served a crucial function for monarchs, for ruling even a small kingdom is a difficult and complex task. Similar to modern governments, which generally have different branches and offices serving a variety of diverse public needs, most monarchs throughout history depended on counselors or ministers to aid them in performing the assorted duties of governance.

In ancient Egypt, for example, priests assisted the pharaohs in administrative duties, as well as serving as royal scribes. Egyptian nobles also were known to be important royal counselors, as the influence of Horemheb on the Pharaoh Tutankhamun (r. 1334–1325 B.C.E.) attests. Eventually, the broad powers granted to royal counselors, especially priests, usurped the power of the pharaohs themselves. Later Egyptian dynasties are characterized by an increase in political power among the priestly class and the consequential weakness of the pharaohs.

The fifth through first centuries B.C.E. saw several developments issue from royal councils that greatly modernized political organization. The Greek city-states of the fifth and fourth centuries B.C.E. were the first democracies and had their political roots in aristocratic councils that had overtaken the monarchy in political importance.

The Roman Empire that followed the Greeks was notable for its Senate, an anomalous political organization that fell somewhere between a noble council and a representative democracy. The Roman Senate lost much of its political power during the time of Julius Caesar and the Emperor Augustus (r. 29 B.C.E.–14 C.E.).

In China, the third century B.C.E. saw the emergence of the Ch'in dynasty and the rise of Li Ssu, counselor to Shih Huang-ti (r. 221–209 B.C.E.), the first emperor of the Ch'in. Li Ssu is often credited with unifying China, as he standardized the legal code and alphabet, allowing greater communication among the people of China's far-flung regions.

THE *WITENAGEMOT* AND EMERGENCE OF DEMOCRACY

One of the most notable royal councils in history was the *witenagemot*, which was composed of various organizations of Anglo-Saxon nobility that served as advisors and even electors for monarchs in England in the years following the collapse of the Roman Empire. Although the Anglo-Saxon monarchy was ostensibly in control of the *witenagemot*, the latter was generally invested with rudimentary legislative power. Only rarely would early Anglo-Saxon monarchs act without the approval of the *witenagemot*, which would have provided a stiff challenge in a civil war because of its broad local powers.

The Norman conquest of England in 1066 drew the era of the *witenagemot* to a close, but a body known as the *Curia Regis* quickly sprang up in its place. The differences between the two are not drastic, but the *Curia Regis* did serve more as a royal court, with less real power than the *witenagemot*. The *Curia Regis* is generally regarded as an early model for the eventual formation of the English Parliament.

The collapse of feudal societies in the late Middle Ages was followed by a brief period during which several monarchs, most notably France's Louis XIV (r. 1643–1715), attempted to rule absolutely and had little use for royal counselors. Louis's power, however, was established by one of the most famous royal counselors in history, Cardinal Richelieu, who served under Louis XIII (r. 1610–1643) and who effectively ran France from behind the throne for nearly twenty years.

REVOLUTION AND DECLINE

The seventeenth and eighteenth centuries were marked by the stirrings of democratic movements that challenged monarchical supremacy, and many of these movements began with or were supported by groups that traced their origins back to royal councils. The British Parliament, for instance, finally achieved power over the monarchy with the Glorious Revolution of 1688, in which William III (r.

1689–1702) took the throne under an agreement granting Parliament nearly full sovereignty. The 1789 French Revolution, which ignited numerous democratic movements throughout the world, was begun by a revolt in the Estates-General, a national council that ostensibly advised the monarchy and served as a check on royal power.

The decline of monarchical forms of government in Europe in the years following the French Revolution also signaled a decline in the importance of royal counselors. Several well-known and powerful figures served, at least superficially, as royal counselors during this period—perhaps most notably Otto von Bismarck of Germany, who served under Kaiser Wilhelm I (r. 1861–1888). But these officials acted more as modern prime ministers than as actual royal counselors, frequently circumventing the monarchy in order to promote their own political agendas.

The most significant royal counselor of the twentieth century was Koichi Kido, adviser to Japanese emperor Hirohito (r. 1926–1989). Kido mediated between the Japanese military and Hirohito during the closing days of World War II, and he was almost singlehandedly responsible for convincing the emperor to surrender to the Allied forces at the end of the war.

See also: ANGLO-SAXON RULERS; BUREAUCRACY, ROYAL; COURTS AND COURT OFFICIALS, ROYAL; EUNUCHS, ROYAL; FEUDALISM AND KINGSHIP; POWER, FORMS OF ROYAL; PRIESTS, ROYAL; PROPHETS, ROYAL; REGENCIES; SERVANTS AND AIDES, ROYAL.

COURTS AND COURT OFFICIALS, ROYAL

The people who live in the official home of a queen or king and who work for or advise them.

A monarch's court might encompass a moderate number of individuals, including the members of the ruler's immediate family and the most prominent members of government. In many monarchies, however, the court might be immense, with nobles, high officials, petty officers, and even commoners included. The monarch had the sole authority to determine members of his or her court. In fact, in royal courts, it was difficult to differentiate between the official and personal, between favored friend and civil servant.

COURT HIERARCHY

Members of a royal court were not all equal. There was a highly developed hierarchy in most courts, and one's duties and social position were often very specific. These distinctions often led to elaborate court protocol concerning who should bow to or salute whom and which terms of address were appropriate. Since court positions were given and taken at the monarch's whim, few could feel secure in the offices they obtained. Corruption was a way of life among many royal courts, with bribery and flattery more likely to lead to advancement than true service to the country.

In ancient Egypt, it was usually nobles and priests who were appointed to court positions. The pharaoh's chief administrator was the vizier, who had the important duty of collecting taxes. Under the vizier were a number of scribes who maintained the government records; some of these scribes rose from the lower classes.

The royal court system was highly developed in ancient India as well. Along with political administrators, Brahmin priests, artists, and musicians were among members of the court. *The Arthashastra*, a guidebook for political and social life written in the fourth century B.C.E., gives details of the behavior expected of nobles, aides, and servants at Indian royal courts. When they met together, courtiers were arranged in specific positions following a strict formal hierarchy. Prostration before the sultan, or even before the empty throne, was also often required.

Although a few court positions were hereditary, crowned heads in the East and West held the power to grant offices and titles and to award pensions. Once one received a court position, that individual also could wield great influence. Often this influence was for sale to the highest bidder, the one most willing to pay the courtier for an audience with the king or for a friendly word in the queen's ear. The administrators in the court of the notoriously parsimonious Queen Elizabeth I of England (r. 1558–1603) learned to take advantage of opportunities to sell their access to the queen.

THE ZENITH OF COURT LIFE

Some historians ascribe the advent of the royal court as an adjunct to the seat of English power to Elizabeth's grandfather Henry VII (r. 1485–1509) and to her father Henry VIII (r. 1509–1547). These Tudor rulers sought to diminish the power of the local lords

In 1713, King Louis XIV of France was attended by a court of hundreds in the gardens at the palace of Versailles.

throughout the country and to consolidate government in the hands of the monarch. Yet, royal courts had been seats of influence long before the Tudors. In fact, Elizabeth's court had much in common with the court of an earlier English queen, Eleanor of Aquitaine, the wife of Henry II (r. 1154–1189), including many young men who used the techniques of courtly love to flatter and woo the queen.

The epitome of medieval court life was Eleanor of Aquitaine's court at Poitiers in southwestern France. Eleanor, who was married first to Louis VII of France (r. 1137–1180) and then to Henry II of England, left England during a period of estrangement from Henry and established a court in her native land, the duchy of Aquitaine. Life at Poitiers, the capital of the duchy, attracted knights, ladies, artists, musicians, and visiting royalty from throughout Europe. Eleanor's daughter, Marie de Champagne, undertook the task of tutoring young squires and maidens in court manners. She engaged the writer Andreas Capelanus (Andre le Chapelain) to write a handbook of proper court behavior. The resulting

Book of the Art of Loving Nobly and the Reprobation of Dishonorable Love, though probably not a factual representation of court life, greatly influenced the image of chivalry during that period, which has been passed down through literature.

The royal court of the French Sun-King, Louis XIV (r. 1643–1715), at Versailles is often seen as the archetype of later European court life. The most sought-after court offices at Louis's court were those with minimal duties, large pensions, and substantial influence. Even the most ordinary events in the king's life—going to bed, saying his prayers, getting dressed—were carried out with great ceremony and with the assistance of members of his court. Within Louis's court there were as many as thirty individuals whose sole duty was to serve the king his dinner. Regulations for court dress permitted only certain fabrics and colors.

When not absorbed with duties to King Louis XIV, members of the court spent their days in pleasurable pursuits and luxury, but life there was not without hazards. When financial adviser Nicholas Fouquet began to irritate Louis by displaying his wealth, the king had him imprisoned for life. Maintaining his royal court allowed Louis to keep French lords under his control and to display his power to other nations. But the extravagance of Versailles cost the country dearly; upon his death, Louis XIV left his nation nearly bankrupt.

In spite of the cost of maintaining lavish courts, other monarchs such as Peter the Great (r. 1682–1725) tried to construct their own households in similar fashion. England also fell under the influence of the French court. After the execution of England's King Charles I (r. 1625–1649), his son Charles II (r. 1660–1685), sometimes known as the Merry Monarch, spent years in exile in the court of Louis XIV. When Charles II was restored to the throne in 1660, he brought many of the excesses of the French court with him.

Women in the royal court might include the queen herself, princesses, other noble relatives, ladies in waiting, servants, and mistresses of the king. King Mongkut of Siam (r. 1851–1868), best known as the king in *Anna and the King of Siam*, had eighty-two children with his thirty-nine wives, all members of the royal court. It was said that an additional 9,000 women lived in his harem. Biblical kings such as David (r. 1010–970 B.C.E.) and Solomon (r. 970–931 B.C.E.) included their many concubines in their royal courts.

Among the effects of the historic system of royal courts was the development of craftsmanship and artistry. Monarchs who wished their courts to be places of beauty, opulence, and advancement frequently became patrons of the arts and sciences. Many of the world's greatest works of art, architecture, music, literature, and science were created for rulers and their royal courts.

See also: ART OF KINGS; BEHAVIOR, CONVENTIONS OF ROYAL; CLASS SYSTEMS AND ROYALTY; COUNCILS AND COUNSELORS, ROYAL; ELEANOR OF AQUITAINE; GROOMS OF THE STOOL; HAREMS; LITERATURE AND KINGSHIP; MUSIC AND SONG; PALACES; PARKS, ROYAL; RITUAL, ROYAL.

CROATIAN KINGDOM (960–1918 C.E.)

Kingdom in the Balkan region that was historically controlled or affiliated with the Austrian Habsburg dynasty and the Ottoman Turks.

Originally part of the ancient Roman province of Pannonia, Croatia was settled in the seventh century by a people known as the Croats, who, in the ninth century, accepted Christianity as their state religion. Croatia became a kingdom in the tenth century. Its rulers conquered surrounding regions, including Dalmatia, leading to much disagreement with the Republic of Venice over control of that territory. Ultimately, the kingdom of Croatia claimed Dalmatia.

The Croatian kingdom reached the height of its power in the eleventh century. However, internal struggles soon weakened the kingdom, allowing it to be conquered by Hungary between 1097 and 1102. In 1102, Croatia and Hungary officially united under a single monarch. Although the two kingdoms remained joined for the next 800 years, Croatia often chose its own rulers independently of the Hungarian Crown.

In 1526, most of Croatia came under Turkish rule after a series of successful invasions by the Ottoman Empire. The next year, in 1527, Croatian feudal lords agreed to accept the Habsburg rulers of Austria as their kings. In return, the Habsburg dynasty provided a defense of Croatia against the Turks, while the Croatian lords retained their power and privileges. However, under Habsburg rule, the independent kingdom of Croatia ceased to exist.

For a period of about a century, Croatia served as a buffer, helping defend the Austrian Empire of the Habsburgs against the Turkish onslaught. However, the centralizing and Germanizing tendencies of the Habsburgs began to weaken the Croatian nobility by gradually reducing their influence and power, causing dissension among the Croats. This threat to their autonomy awakened in the Croats a strong sense of nationalism. Joseph Jellachich, a Croatian lord, gathered forces to march against the Habsburgs in 1848–1849.

In 1867, when the dual Austro-Hungarian monarchy was established, Croatia was included in the kingdom of Hungary. One year later, in 1868, Croatia united with Slavonia and became an autonomous Hungarian crownland. During this period, Croatian and South Slavic cultural and political organizations began to come into existence, most notably the Croatian Peasant Party, founded in the early twentieth century.

The collapse of the Austro-Hungarian Empire at the end of World War I saw the unification of the Balkan kingdoms into the kingdom of Serbs, Croats, and Slovenes. The formation of this unified new state, which later became known as Yugoslavia, marked the end, once again, of the Croatian kingdom.

See also: AUSTRO-HUNGARIAN EMPIRE; OTTOMAN EMPIRE; SERBIAN KINGDOM.

FURTHER READING

Guldescu, Stanko. *The Croatian-Slavonian Kingdom, 1526–1792.* The Hague: Mouton, 1970.

Mazower, Mark. *The Balkans: A Short History.* New York: Modern Library, 2000.

CROESUS (ca. 596–547 B.C.E.)

Last ruler (r. ca. 560–547 B.C.E.) of Lydia, an ancient kingdom located in western Asia Minor in what is now part of Turkey, who was known primarily for his great wealth.

There is no reliable information concerning the early years of Croesus's life. It is known that he was born to the royal family in or near the city of Sardis in Asia Minor, that his father was named Alyattes, and that he attained the throne after defeating the rival claim of a half brother.

Croesus is best remembered for his wealth: the phrase "as rich as Croesus" is commonly used to describe a person who controls fabulous riches. There are many reasons for this reputation, not least of which is the fact that Lydia held great deposits of gold and silver, and mining these precious metals was an important industry during the time that Croesus ruled. However, other factors also contributed to the idea that Croesus was extraordinarily wealthy. For instance, the first known action of Croesus's reign was the conquest of several Greek cities along the western (Mediterranean) coast of Asia Minor. Among the most important of these was Ephesus, a key trading center, which fell to Croesus in approximately 550 B.C.E. Whoever controlled Ephesus also controlled an east-west trade network that linked the Mediterranean world to places as far away as China.

Although Croesus coveted the wealth of the Greeks, he was a political realist who recognized the need to maintain cordial relations with the powerful independent Greek city states that were his neighbors. After taking Ephesus, he thus set out to repair the political damage his action might have caused. He welcomed Greek visitors to Lydia and offered generous donations to the most important of Greece's temples and oracles. This policy of hospitality and generosity only increased Croesus's reputation for fabulous wealth.

There are various versions of the story of how Croesus fell from power. The most credible holds that Croesus became embroiled in a war with the powerful Persian Empire. To improve his chances in the war, he attempted to negotiate a military alliance with Babylon, Egypt, and Sparta, but Persia struck the Lydian capital of Sardis in 547 B.C.E., before the alliance was fully established. The Persians captured the city, and the kingdom of Lydia became a possession of the Persian Empire.

The details of Croesus's final years are also uncertain. Some sources claim that he was sentenced to death by the Persian ruler, Cyrus the Great (r. 559–530 B.C.E.), but that Cyrus relented and appointed Croesus governor of a Persian province. Popular legend claims that Croesus was sentenced to death by fire, but the god Apollo sent a rainstorm to douse the flames and spare his life. The ancient Greek historian Herodotus records that Croesus cast himself upon a funeral pyre after his defeat by Cyrus the Great.

See also: CYRUS THE GREAT; LYDIA, KINGDOM OF; PERSIAN EMPIRE.

CRUSADER KINGDOMS

(1098–1561 C.E.)

A loose collection of states, principalities, and kingdoms established by groups originating from the Crusades. Among the crusader states were the kingdom of Jerusalem (1099–1291) and its associated states; the Principality of Antioch (1098–1268); the counties of Edessa (1098–1144) and Tripoli (1109–1289); and the island states of Rhodes (1309–1523) and Malta (1530–1798).

OUTREMER

When the Frankish and Norman armies of the First Crusade landed in *Outremer* (literally, "across the sea") in 1097, an integral part of their plan was to appropriate the territory from the Muslims. Jerusalem was the primary goal because of its religious significance.

Many of the crusader knights were younger sons of European noble families that rigorously practiced primogeniture, the right of the first-born son to inherit everything from his father. The Crusades thus offered younger sons an opportunity to stake claim on "fresh" land and establish their own domain, for the Roman Catholic Church had sanctioned the Crusades and had assured participants that the heathen Saracens (Arab Muslims) did not have genuine rights to these Christian lands.

The first area to fall to the crusaders was Antioch, long the most important city in the northwest corner of *Outremer*, which was conquered by Bohemond in 1098. Bohemond was a noble of Norman origin, from the recently formed duchies of southern Italy and Sicily. The principality of Antioch remained primarily in Norman hands until it was captured and razed by the Mamluks in 1289.

In 1098, the coastal county of Edessa was taken by crusaders led by Baldwin of Boulogne, who ruled as King Baldwin I of Edessa (r. 1098–1100) until he turned it over to a cousin two years later. The fall of Edessa to the Muslims in 1144 precipitated the Second Crusade.

Jerusalem was successfully stormed in 1099 by the crusader army of Godfrey of Bouillon, and its Muslim inhabitants were massacred. Once in possession of the holy site, Godfrey stated that only Jesus Christ could be the true king of Jerusalem; Godfrey thus took the title of Defender of the Holy Sepulcher. However his brother, Baldwin, the king of Edessa, disagreed with this view and was crowned as the first king of Jerusalem upon Godfrey's death in 1100.

The fourth crusader state established around the time of the First Crusade was the county of Tripoli, centered along the north coast of Palestine below the Principality of Antioch. French noble Raymond of Toulouse began a siege there in 1102 but died before the city was taken in 1109. His relatives remained in power in Tripoli until 1187, when Raymond III (r. 1152–1187) died from wounds received at the disastrous battle of Hattin. Control of Tripoli then passed to Bohemond III (r. 1163–1201, the prince of Antioch.

On his way to the Third Crusade, to recover Jerusalem from the Muslim leader Saladin, Richard Lionheart of England stopped on the Christian island of Cyprus in 1192 and took control of it from the Byzantine Empire. Richard gave the island to Guy of Lusignan, the king of Jerusalem (r. 1186–1192), who had recently participated in the great defeat of the Europeans at the battle of Hattin.

Jerusalem was not restored to the Europeans in the Third Crusade (1189–1192), but they continued to name kings of the holy city. In 1224, the Egyptian sultan, al-Kamil Muhammad II (r. 1218–1238), gave Jerusalem back to the Christians as part of a treaty he signed with Holy Roman Emperor Frederick II (r. 1212–1250). (Frederick crowned himself the new king of Jerusalem and then summarily left the city.) Jerusalem fell twenty years later to the Islamic Ayyubid dynasty, and it was never regained by Europeans.

ELSEWHERE IN THE MEDITERRANEAN

After the city of Acre in Palestine fell to the Muslims in 1291, *Outremer* was lost to the Europeans for good. However, a religious-military order, the Hospitalers (the Sovereign Order of the Knights of the Hospital of St. John of Jerusalem, of Rhodes, and of Malta) laid siege to the island of Rhodes in 1307 and, in 1309, took control of it from the Roman adventurer who had held it previously. The Hospitalers built a thriving mercantile empire on Rhodes that lasted over two hundred years, until 1523, when the young Ottoman ruler, Suleyman the Magnificent (r. 1520–1566), ousted them from the island.

The Hospitalers languished for seven years until the Holy Roman emperor Charles V (r. 1519–1558) offered them a new home on the rocky island of Malta. The Hospitalers ruled Malta until they were ousted by the Egypt-bound Napoleon Bonaparte in 1798.

See also: BALDWIN I; CHRISTIANITY AND KINGSHIP; CONQUEST AND KINGSHIPS; FRANKISH KINGDOM; LUSIGNAN DYNASTY; MAMLUK DYNASTY; NORMAN KINGDOMS; RICHARD I, LIONHEART; SALADIN; SULEYMAN I, THE MAGNIFICENT.

FURTHER READING

Hillenbrand, Carole. *The Crusades: Islamic Perspectives.* New York: Routledge, 2000.

CURSES, ROYAL

Condemnations or words meant to call down some type of evil or injury upon an individual or group or a calamity upon a state or a society.

The practice of issuing curses or condemnations has a history that reaches as far back as the ancient Mediterranean cultures of the Egyptians, Assyrians, and Israelites. Curses have been used by peoples all over the world and in many periods for personal gain, to frighten others into submission, to dissuade enemies from taking action, and to protect sacred places.

Ancient curses commissioned by royalty have been found inscribed on tablets throughout the Mediterranean world. These curses were used primarily to deter the people in the society from disobeying royal authority or to dissuade potential enemies from contesting royal power. Other royal curses were issued to protect certain religious and burial sites from desecration and destruction.

Early scholars believed that curses were inscribed on the entrances to royal tombs in Egypt to prevent the desecration of these burial sites. Recent studies, however, have concluded that most royal tombs did not contain curses, although a large number of tombs for nonroyalty did have curses attached. Such curses appeared most frequently in tombs from the Middle Kingdom period of Egypt, and a number of these tombs belonged to administrators of the Egyptian pharaohs. One such tomb is that of Amenhotep, an administrator for Pharaoh Amenhotep III (r. ca.1386–1349 B.C.E.), which contains a lengthy description of curses against potential desecrators of his tomb.

A number of royal tombs from ancient Assyria contain a standard curse used to deter potential enemies from defacing and destroying the rulers' inscribed names. This curse, standard throughout Assyria, is found on the tombs and temples of Assyrian kings of the tenth century B.C.E., including those of Ashur-dan II (r. 934–911 B.C.E.) and Tiglath-pileser II (r. 966–935 B.C.E.). The standard curse began as follows, with a threat of possible death or injury added afterward:

He who erases my inscribed name and writes his (own) name or discards my steles, hands them over for destruction, consigns them to oblivion, covers them with dirt, burns them with fire, throws them into the water, puts them into a Taboo house where there is no visibility, or because of these curses, he incites a stranger, a foreigner, a malignant enemy, a man who speaks another language or anyone else to do any of these things, or conceives of and does anything injurious.

May the god Ashur, the exalted god, dweller of Ehursagkurkurra, the gods An, Enlil, Ea and Ninmah, the great gods, the Igigu of heaven, the Anunnaku of the underworld.

In addition to the Assyrians and Egyptians, the practice of formalized cursing was well established in ancient Israel, where curses appeared in a number of biblical prophecies, often directed against the enemies of Israel.

Cursing in the ancient Mediterranean world, especially royal curses, was conducted in the context of highly developed legal and religious ceremonies. It appeared to serve almost the same function as the common law—acting as a restraint, a corrective, and a stimulant to better the behavior of those in society. It was probably the increasing appropriation of curses for private uses that led to official disapproval of the practice during the Roman period. By the eighth century C.E., the practice of cursing had almost disappeared throughout the Mediterranean world.

Curses also feature prominently in Indian literature, namely, in the *Mahabharata* epic, composed between 200 B.C.E. and 200 C.E. The royal background of the Pandavas and Kauravas, the main characters of the epic poem, justified use of the curse motif as an example of royal curses. There are nearly eighty-four references to curses in the whole of the epic excluding the *Harivamsa*, a text that served as an appendix to the larger work. The most pervasive curse in the *Mahabharata* concerns disrespect and insult targeted at a great spiritual teacher, and this curse was meant to cause the perpetrator to suffer great pain and possibly death.

In ancient Cambodia in the seventh century, inscriptions placed in the vicinity of religious foundations (*sthapana*) gave the donor the right to share his merits (*punya*) with whomever he chose. These accounts and commemorations often were preceded by a vow directed at future visitors, written in the form of a blessing (*vara*) on the benevolent and a curse (*sapa*) on all others. The composite term used to describe this vow—*varasapa*—represents these two antithetical aspects of the vow.

Other instances of the use of royal curses on stone inscriptions can be found in Sumatra. An inscription on the island of Bangka contains a lengthy warning directed against potential rebels and traitors. Another at Palembang, called the Telaga Batu, contains a more elaborate version of the same warning, framed with carved *naga* (serpent) heads.

According to ancient Chinese sources, the vassals and officials of a king had to perform a ritual in which water was poured over a stone. This water was then collected from the spout at the bottom and drunk. If a vassal or official broke his oath of loyalty to the king, he would be poisoned by the water of the curse and die.

See also: DIVINATION AND DIVINERS, ROYAL; HEALING POWERS OF KINGS; OATHS AND OATH-TAKING; RELIGIOUS DUTIES AND POWER; SACRED TEXTS.

FURTHER READING

Gager, John, ed. *Curse Tablets and Binding Spells from the Ancient World.* New York: Oxford University Press, 1992.

Jenner, Philip. *Dated Inscriptions from the Seventh and Eighth Centuries (AD 611–781).* Honolulu: Southeast Asian Studies, Asian Studies Program, University of Hawaii, 1980.

Jessup, H.I., and T. Zephir, eds. *Sculpture of Angkor and Ancient Cambodia: Millennium of Glory.* Washington, DC: National Gallery of Art, 1997.

Miksic, John, ed. *Indonesian Heritage: Ancient History.* Vol. 1. Singapore: Archipelago Press, 1995.

Ramankutty, P.V. *Curse as a Motif in the Mahabharata.* Delhi: Nag Publishers, 1999.

CYAXARES (645–585 B.C.E.)

King of Media (r. ca. 625–585 B.C.E.), an ancient kingdom in northwestern Iran, who played an important role in the final overthrow of the Assyrian Empire. Also known as Huvakhshtra (the Iranian form of the Greek name Cyaxares), he raised the kingdom of the Medes to a major power in the ancient Near East.

Soon after taking the throne around 625 B.C.E., Cyaxares conquered the Scythians, who had ruled Media for twenty-eight years, and he greatly expanded the Median realm. According to the ancient Greek historian Herodotus, Cyaxares was the first ruler to reorganize his army by dividing it into groups of soldiers using the same weapons—such as archers, lance carriers, and cavalry. This reorganization of the army greatly strengthened the Median kingdom.

Cyaxares went to battle again a decade later, this time against the Assyrians, with whom the Medes had fought on and off for years. In 614 B.C.E. he conquered Assur, the ancient religious center of Assyria. Two years later, in 612 B.C.E, Cyaxares formed an alliance with Nabopolassar of Babylon (the Assyrian governor of Chaldea) and with his former enemies, the Scythians, and overthrew the Assyrians and took control of their great capital of Nineveh. Fighting against the Assyrians continued until their final defeat in 609 B.C.E.

Around the same time, the Medes under Cyaxares apparently defeated the kingdom of Mannai (in present-day northwestern Iran). In 609 B.C.E., they conquered Urartu (Armenia) and invaded eastern Anatolia, starting a war with the Anatolian kingdom of Lydia that ended in 585 B.C.E. when an eclipse of the sun was interpreted as an omen that the battle should stop. Media and Lydia both accepted the Halys River (now the Kizil Irmak River in north-central Turkey) as the boundary between the two countries. Cyaxares died soon after and was succeeded on the throne by his son, Astyages (r. 584–ca. 550 B.C.E.).

See also: ASSYRIAN EMPIRE; MEDES KINGDOM; NABOPOLASSAR; SCYTHIAN EMPIRE.

CYRUS THE GREAT (ca. 580–530 B.C.E)

Founder (r. 559–530 B.C.E.) of the Achaemenid dynasty of the Persian Empire, who was known for his military successes and innovative administration.

The Persians, originally a nomadic or semi-nomadic people of Central Asia, began moving south and west as early as the 1500s B.C.E. Led by a series of strong chieftains, they conquered neighboring peoples as they went along, gaining in wealth and power. They ultimately arrived in the region now known as Iran, whereupon they decided that this land would become their permanent home. Unfortunately, a people called the Medes had already settled here and had established a thriving empire that included the region known as Assyria.

For a time, the Persians existed as a vassal state under the Medes, but this situation eventually changed. According to legend, the Median king, Astyages (r. ca. 584–550 B.C.E.), received a prophecy that his daughter would bear a son who would one day overthrow his rule. To forestall fate, Astyages married off his daughter to Cambyses, a loyal soldier from among the Persians. When the couple bore him a grandchild around 580 B.C.E., Astyages decided to have the boy killed and sent a trusted soldier to do the deed. The soldier balked at his orders, however, and instead gave the infant to a peasant couple to raise. The boy, named Cyrus (also spelled Kurash or Kourosh), was said to be extraordinarily beautiful, and eventually he came to the attention of Astyages.

Astyages is said to have repented of his earlier orders, but he punished the disobedient soldier by having that man's own son killed. Nursing resentment, the soldier is said to have urged Cyrus to overthrow the old Median king, and to have expedited the revolt by convincing his fellow soldiers to support Cyrus in this undertaking. Whatever truth may reside in this legend, Cyrus did indeed overthrow the Median king in 550 B.C.E., and he went on to unite the Medes and Persians into a single empire that became the most formidable military power in the region.

The rise of Persia did not go unnoticed by the other powerful kingdoms of the day. In the kingdom of Lydia in Anatolia (present-day Turkey), King Croesus (r. ca. 560–547 B.C.E.), worried that his newly powerful neighbor would attack, called upon Egypt, Babylon, and the Greek city-state of Sparta to form an alliance to combat the Persian threat. This alliance did not move quickly enough, however, and Cyrus struck Lydia in 548 B.C.E., well before its allies could organize a defense. By 546 B.C.E. Cyrus had taken the Lydian capital of Sardis. Babylon fell next, surrendering without a fight in 539 B.C.E.

Having gained control of the whole of Asia Minor, Cyrus pushed eastward and eventually extended the Persian Empire well into Central Asia and southeast-ward to the border of India. Each success further strengthened Cyrus's military, for he required every conquered kingdom to send a quota of men to serve in the Persian army. In this way, Cyrus had enough military manpower not only to maintain order within his empire, but also to fill the ranks of his armies of conquest.

Domestically, Cyrus created a new system of government, realizing that the traditional loose affiliation of independent settlements would be inadequate to maintain the security of his expanding territory. He invented a system of *satrapies*, or provinces, the satraps, or governors, of which were appointed by and answerable to the king. Cyrus also built a great roadway that stretched 1,700 miles from the city of Sardis in Asia Minor to the Persian capital of Susa in southwestern Iran. The roadway enabled him to establish what was probably the world's first postal system, which facilitated communication throughout the vast and far-flung Persian Empire.

For all his administrative innovations, Cyrus was not content to remain in his capital while his armies went to war. His insistence on accompanying his troops, however, led to his fall. In 530 B.C.E., while campaigning in the East, he was killed in battle. His son, Cambyses (r. 529–522 B.C.E.), assumed the throne, but not without a power struggle in which he killed his brother, Smerdis, who also sought to take the Achaemenid throne. Cambyses continued his father's expansionist policies and ultimately succeeded in adding Egypt to the imperial holdings of the Persian Empire.

Cyrus the Great's success in war earned him renown throughout the ancient Near East, but he was also famous for his treatment of the peoples he brought into his empire. He forbade his soldiers to loot or pillage the towns and cities they conquered, and he incorporated local rulers into his imperial government, establishing them as governors to whom he offered a great degree of autonomy. He is also famous for freeing slaves. For example, Babylon had a large population of Jews who were kept there as an enslaved class. When Cyrus conquered Babylon, he issued a decree allowing the Jewish population to return to Palestine.

See also: ACHAEMENID DYNASTY; CROESUS; PERSIAN EMPIRE.

DACIA KINGDOM (60 B.C.E.–106 C.E.)

Ancient kingdom, located in what is now present-day Romania, that predated the Roman occupation of the region south of the Danube River. Under the emperor Trajan (r. 98–117 C.E.), the Dacia kingdom was incorporated into the Roman Empire as a province.

Historical references to Dacia date back to at least around 450 B.C.E. In some early sources, including works by the Greek historian Herodotus and the Roman poet Horace, the Dacians were referred to as the Getae, or Geto-Dacians.

The early history of Dacia is filled with conquests, both attempted and successful, by foreign armies. These include losses to the Persian rulers, Darius I the Great (r. 521–486 B.C.E.) and Xerxes (r. 485–465 B.C.E.) in the fifth century B.C.E. In the third century C.E., the Dacians managed to fend off an invasion by the Celts.

EARLY KINGS

Between 450 and 60 B.C.E., Dacia experienced a succession of kings that predate the establishment of a stable monarchy. These kings include Dromikhaites (early 200s B.C.E.) in the third century B.C.E., and Oroles (r. early 100s B.C.E.) and Ruboostes (r. mid-100s) in the second century B.C.E.

Dacia developed into a stable monarchy only with the accession of Burebista (r. ca. 60–45 B.C.E.) to the throne in 60 B.C.E. His accession was made possible by the expulsion of the Celts and his ability to win the support of the religious establishment in Dacia. The support of religious leaders, however, brought with it a move toward a stricter moral code in the kingdom.

During his fifteen-year reign, Burebista expanded the Dacia kingdom into Bohemia, western Austria, the northern areas of Carpathia, areas around the Black and Adriatic seas, and the Balkans. Burebista was eventually killed during a civil uprising in 45. After his death, control of the Dacia kingdom passed to the religious elite, who ruled Dacia for another fifteen years. During the time that Dacia was a theocracy, the kingdom shrank and was splintered ethnically into five tribal kingships.

STRUGGLE WITH ROME

Dacia's most sustained conflict was its enduring struggle with the Romans, which began with the campaigns of the Roman general Licinius Lucullus early in the first century B.C.E. Dacia at that time, under the leadership of Burebista, was highly respected militarily. This respect created a sense of fear in their Roman neighbors.

After Burebista's death, however, the tribal kings of Dacia assisted various factions within Rome's own internal power struggles. One example of such assistance was the association of Cotison, a Dacian tribal king, with the assassination of Julius Caesar. The period of ethnic fragmentation that ensued after the death of Burebista forced Dacia into a defensive mode to keep the Romans out of Dacian territories. This defensiveness lasted until the late first century B.C.E.

By the first century C.E., the power of the Dacians was at its height. The Dacian kings Duras (r. 68–87) and his successor Decebalus (r. 87–106), led the Dacian resurgence. Both of these kings were able to make Rome pay tribute to Dacia. This change in status tarnished Rome's prestigious image.

The Romans soon recognized the potential threat that their declining image would have on their ability to force others to pay tribute to the Roman Empire. As a result, the Roman emperor Trajan began taking steps to conquer Dacia at the start of the second century. By 106, the military conquest of Dacia by the Romans was complete, and Dacia ceased to exist as an independent kingdom.

The military conquest of Dacia was made even more final by a subsequent cultural conquest, which resulted in the linguistic and cultural Romanization of the former kingdom. This cultural conquest became the seed that would form present-day Romania.

See also: ROMAN EMPIRE; TRAJAN.

DAGOMBA KINGDOM

(1300s C.E.–Present)

One of several small kingdoms of northern Ghana and Burkina Faso that existed from the fourteenth century to the present. The Dagomba kingdom of today maintains its royal capital at Yendi, in the northern region of Ghana. Tradition holds that the kingdom was founded sometime in the 1300s by one of two brothers, the second of whom simultaneously founded the Mamprusi kingdom of western Africa.

The region occupied by the Dagomba kingdom was fortuitously located on the southern reaches of the great Trans-Saharan trade route. Trade in the area was monopolized by a group of Mande trading specialists known as Dyula. From about the 1300s onward, these traders arrived in Dagomba in ever-increasing numbers, drawn by the opportunity for trade. For a time, traditional rulers retained control of the kingdom, but by the end of the sixteenth century C.E., power and control of the Dagomba kingship passed to the Mande, who retained control until the start of the eighteenth century.

The Dagomba people of today are divided into three groups. The first comprises the royal families, who claim descent from the early invaders who entered the region from the northeast and established rule over the indigenous peoples. The second are Muslims—descendants of the Mande Dyula traders who came to the region from the Sahel, as well as local peoples who converted to Islam. The final group are descendants of the farmers, fishermen, and hunters who originally inhabited the region. Membership in one or another of these groups is largely fixed by birth, with the exception of the merchant class, to which a commoner may aspire upon conversion to Islam.

Today, Dagomba land is controlled by the ruling class, which shares stewardship with ritual specialists called earth priests. Subordinate to the king, but still classified as royals, are local chiefs. Only members of the royal class can succeed to Dagomba leadership, and only royals may employ symbols of their class—the horse and animal skins upon which they seat themselves.

See also: AFRICAN KINGDOMS; MAMPRUSI KINGDOM.

DAHOMEY KINGDOM. *See* FON

KINGDOM

DAI VIET, KINGDOM OF. *See*

VIETNAMESE KINGDOMS

DANISH KINGDOM

(900s C.E.–Present)

Scandinavian kingdom founded in the Middle Ages, which exists today as a constitutional monarchy. The kingdom of Denmark has its roots in several small kingdoms of the Viking era (ca. 790–1000) and earlier centuries. What little history is known of these pre-Christian kingdoms comes from legendary accounts. One of the earliest historical records is the *Gesta Danorum*, a work written in Latin by medieval Danish chronicler Saxo Grammaticus, which deals with early Danish history in a colorful but not necessarily reliable manner.

Danish history becomes more definite with the reign of Gorm the Old (died ca. 940), the first king of all Denmark. Gorm's son, Harald Bluetooth (r. ca. 940–986), was the first Christian king of Denmark. The monarchy was an elective one at this time, with kings chosen from within the royal family.

From the eighth to the eleventh centuries, Danish Vikings raided and settled in England and Ireland, and in the tenth century they founded the duchy of Normandy in northern France. In 1013 the Danes under King Svend Forkbeard (r. 986–1014) conquered England. Svend's son Knud (Cnut the Great, r. 1016–1035) ruled England, Denmark, and Norway. Danish rule of England ended in 1042 with the death of Knud's son Hardeknud (r. 1040–1042), at which point Denmark was briefly ruled by Magnus the Good of Norway (r. 1035–1047).

Knud's nephew, King Svend Estridsen (r. 1047–1074), left the Danish kingdom to his five sons. The death of the last of these sons, Niels (r. 1104–1134), led in 1134 to a period of civil war that ended in 1157 when Svend Estridsen's great-grandson Waldemar I, the Great (r. 1157–1182), became king. Under Waldemar and his son, Waldemar II (r. 1202–1241), Denmark became a great power in the Baltic region, although its territorial gains were short-lived. Much newly conquered territory was lost when Waldemar II was imprisoned for two years by Count Henry of Schwerin in a dispute over a fief. While Waldemar was imprisoned, Denmark fell into chaos, and even after the king's release it never regained its former conquests.

For a brief period, Scandinavia was united under a Danish ruler, Margrethe I (r. 1387–1412). Margrethe was the daughter of Waldemar IV of Denmark (r. 1340–1375), wife of King Haakon VI of Norway (r. 1355–1380) and mother of Olaf II of Denmark (r. 1376–1387), who also ruled Norway as Olaf V. Olaf was elected king of Denmark at age five, with his mother as regent. Margrethe also became regent of Norway when her husband, King Haakon VI, died in 1380. In addition, The Swedish nobility, at odds with their king, Albert of Mecklenburg (r. 1364–1389), invited her to become ruler of Sweden, which she did after a victory over Albert at the battle of Falköping in 1389. By then, her son Olaf was dead, but she persuaded all three kingdoms to acknowledge her great-nephew Eric as heir. Effected in 1397, this joining of three Crowns was known as the Kalmar Union.

The Kalmar Union was dissolved in wars between Denmark and Sweden, which began in 1451 and continued for many years. However, the Crowns of Denmark and Norway were united by the Treaty of Bergen in 1450. This dual monarchy remained in existence until 1814, when Norway was joined to Sweden.

In 1448, the House of Oldenburg came to the throne of Denmark with the election of Christian I (r. 1448–1481). Elective monarchy within the royal family remained the official means of succession until Frederick III (r. 1648–1670) instituted hereditary succession in 1661. In 1665, the "king's law" gave the king absolute power. This law remained in effect until 1849, when Frederick VII (r. 1848–1863) conceded to demands for reform and approved a constitution. Despite the change to a constitutional monarchy, the king continued to hold a great deal of power over government.

The accession of Christian IX (r. 1863–1906) to the Danish throne marked the end of the Oldenburg dynasty and the beginning of the Glucksburg dynasty. In 1915, a new constitution greatly limited the powers of the monarchy, with legislative powers vested in the monarch and the elected parliament. The 1953 Act of Succession allowed the eldest daughter to succeed to the throne if there were no sons, whereas previously women were barred from the succession. Denmark's first female ruler under this law, Margrethe II (r. 1972–present) was crowned queen on January 14, 1972.

See also: CNUT I; JUTLAND KINGDOM; KALMAR UNION; MARGARET OF DENMARK; NORWEGIAN MONARCHY; OLDENBURG DYNASTY; SWEDISH MONARCHY; WALDEMAR I, THE GREAT.

FURTHER READING

Butler, Ewan. *The Horizon Concise History of Scandinavia.* New York: American Heritage, 1973.

Kirby, David. *Northern Europe in the Early Modern Period: The Baltic World 1492–1772.* New York: Longman, 1990.

Nordstrom, Byron J. *Scandinavia Since 1500.* Minneapolis: University of Minnesota, 2000.

Toyne, S.M. *The Scandinavians in History.* 1948. Reprint, New York: Barnes and Noble, 1996.

DAR FUR SULTANATE. *See* FUR

KINGDOM

DARIUS I, THE GREAT

(r. 522–486 B.C.E.)

One of the greatest of the Achaemenid monarchs of ancient Persia, who created the political and administrative structures that kept the Persian Empire together for nearly two hundred years.

A member of a side-branch of the Achaemenid dynasty, Darius came to power in 522 B.C.E. through a violent coup, which he later described in a monumental inscription on a cliff wall at Behistun in southern Anatolia (present-day Turkey). The inscription claimed that a man posing as Bardiya, the brother of the just-deceased Persian king Cambyses II (r. 530–522 B.C.E.), had usurped power in the interests of the Magi, the hereditary priests of the Persian state religion. Darius led a group of seven nobles to dethrone and execute this impostor.

Whether or not this is true, in the six years following his coronation Darius had to fight off eleven uprisings across the realm and in border areas from India to Thrace. In the process, he extended the Persian Empire at both its eastern and western margins. To ward off future rebellions, Darius followed up his victories by dividing the vast Persian Empire, with its 50 million people, into twenty provinces, appointing a Persian noble to govern each one. Other officials,

A member of the Achaemenid Dynasty, Darius I was one of the greatest rulers of the Persian Empire. Among his achievements was the construction of the imperial capital at Persepolis, where his likeness was carved in bas relief on the walls of several palaces. He is shown here accepting homage from a Median officer.

including military governors and royal inspectors, were put into place to assist and watch over the satraps, as the governors were called. These officials were also of Persian or other Iranian extraction. They all worked with local officials to collect and store the immense tax revenues that now poured into the royal treasury. Darius also reorganized the Persian army around the core guard of "Ten Thousand Immortals," all of whom were ethnic Persians.

STRUGGLES IN THE WEST

Early in his reign, in 513 B.C.E., Darius led a major expedition into the region of Scythia north of the Black Sea. To bring his massive forces into place, he had a pontoon bridge built across the Bosporus strait and had another bridge extended across the Danube River. Although Darius made no lasting gains in Scythia, he pacified Thrace and Macedon along the way and made the region a Persian satrapy. This invasion of European lands by an Asian power made the world seem smaller to people on both sides of the divide, thus setting the psychological preconditions for the conquest of Asia by Alexander III, the Great (r. 336–323 B.C.E.) of Macedon two centuries later.

Like his predecessors, Darius employed many Greek advisers and mercenaries, but relations between Persia and the Greek city-states began to deteriorate during his reign. In 499 B.C.E., several of the Ionian Greek cities on the eastern shore of the Aegean Sea revolted against Persian rule. After suppressing the rebellion, Darius decided to invade Greece itself to punish the city-state of Athens for supporting the rebels. The invasion force he landed was wiped out by the Greeks at the battle of Marathon in 490 B.C.E., which became a key event in the national consciousness of the ancient Greeks.

STRENGTHENING THE EMPIRE

Darius took an active role in developing a new written code of laws for the Persian Empire. In the provinces, he streamlined preexisting local laws and set up permanent courts to enforce them. His government introduced standard weights and measures, and imposed Aramaic as the exclusive language for all legal documents. A Semitic language, Aramaic was already widely spoken in Mesopotamia and Syria.

The king instituted a massive program of road repair and construction, including a 1,300-mile Royal Road from Susa in Persia to Sardis in Anatolia near the Aegean Sea. The roads, guarded and provided with waystations at periodic intervals, facilitated rapid delivery of the Royal Mail and stimulated commerce. Darius also completed another old project, construction of a Nile-to-Red-Sea canal. He minted gold and silver coins, the first outside Asia Minor and Greece to have a standard content and weight.

Darius reasserted Persian religious and linguistic traditions. He is said to have helped devise a hieroglyphic system for the Old Persian language, which until then had remained unwritten, in order to record his exploits in stone. He assembled materials and craftsmen from throughout the empire to build palaces and other public buildings across the ancestral Persian homeland, especially at Persepolis.

At the start of his reign, Darius had married the two surviving daughters of Cyrus the Great (r. 559–530 B.C.E.) in an attempt to reinforce his legitimacy. Atossa, the elder daughter, served as an important imperial adviser. In that capacity, she succeeded in advancing the royal prospects of her son Xerxes I (r. 485–465 B.C.E.), whom Darius designated as his successor a year before his own death in 486 B.C.E.

See also: ACHAEMENID DYNASTY; CAMBYSES II; EGYPTIAN DYNASTIES, PERSIAN, HELLENISTIC, AND ROMAN; PERSIAN EMPIRE.

DARIUS II (OCHUS) (d. 404 B.C.E.)

King of Persia (r. 423–405 B.C.E.) whose unpopular and unsuccessful rule caused a period of decline for the Persian Empire.

One of the illegitimate sons of Artaxerxes I (r. 464–424 B.C.E.), Darius was originally named Ochus, but he took the name Darius when he wrested the throne from his half-brother, Sogdianus (Secydianus) (r. 424 B.C.E.). At first, he promised to let his brother rule half the kingdom, but Darius later ordered him executed. As the son of a concubine, Darius was sometimes known as Darius Nothus (bastard).

The royal court of Darius II was a dangerous place, rife with plots and intrigue. Before taking the throne, he married his half-sister, Parysatis, a vicious political schemer who helped him in the suppression of Sogdianus and another brother, Arsites. Together, Darius and Parysatis presided over increasingly corrupt courtiers.

In military matters, Darius was plagued by uprisings in Syria, Lydia, and Media—all of which he halted promptly and harshly. Then, hoping to recover the coastal cities of Asia Minor (present-day Turkey) from Athens, he forged an alliance with the Greek city-state of Sparta in 407 B.C.E. With the help of Sparta, Darius recovered the coastal cities, finally defeating Athens in a naval battle at Aegospotami in 405 B.C.E. The next year, however, Darius succumbed to an illness and was succeeded by his son, Artaxerxes II (r. 404–359 B.C.E.).

Parysatis plotted with her favorite son, Cyrus the Younger, to take the throne from Artaxerxes. But the rebellion Cyrus led against his brother crumbled, and he was killed at the battle of Cunaxa in 401 B.C.E. The cunning Parysatis dominated Artaxerxes II throughout his reign and proved to be the real power behind the throne.

See also: ARTAXERXES I; ARTAXERXES II; PERSIAN EMPIRE.

DARIUS III (CODOMMANUS)

(d. 330 B.C.E.)

Ruler of Persia (r. 335–330 B.C.E.), last of the Achaemenid dynasty, whose defeat at the hands of Alexander III the Great of Macedon (r. 336–323 B.C.E.) marked the end of the Persian Empire and the beginning of the Hellenistic period in the eastern Mediterranean.

A cousin of Artaxerxes III (r. 358–338 B.C.E.), Darius was selected for the kingship by Bagoas, a palace eunuch, who had poisoned the two previous kings, Artaxerxes III and his son Arses (r. 337–336 B.C.E.). Bagoas, finding Darius less pliable than he had hoped, attempted to poison Darius as well but was caught in the attempt and forced by the king to drain the cup of poison himself.

Darius may have been involved in the assassination of King Philip II of Macedon (r. 359–336 B.C.E.) in 336 B.C.E. Philip had gathered troops to recover the Greek cities of Asia Minor that were under Persian rule. Following in his father's footsteps, Alexander the Great proceeded with Philip's plan with such success that by 333 B.C.E., with the battle of Issus, he had recovered the Greek cities. Darius fled the Persian capital, leaving behind his mother, wife, and children, who were subsequently taken into custody by Alexander.

In an attempt to recover his family, Darius offered Alexander his daughter in marriage and a large ransom. Instead, Alexander crossed the Tigris and Euphrates rivers and engaged in a final contest with Darius at the battle of Gaugamela in 331 B.C.E. Fleeing once more, this time leaving his subordinates to fight, Darius escaped to the region of Bactria, where the satrap (governor) Bessus had him killed. As Bessus was unable to resist Alexander's forces, the Persian Empire came to a close.

See also: ACHAEMENID DYNASTY; ALEXANDER III, THE GREAT; ARTAXERXES III; DARIUS II (OCHUS); PERSIAN EMPIRE; PHILIP II OF MACEDON.

DAVARAVATI KINGDOM. *See* SIAM, KINGDOMS OF

DAVID (r. 1010–970 B.C.E.)

King of ancient Judah and Israel (r. 1010–970 B.C.E.), who unified the twelve Israelite tribes into a powerful regional state and is revered by Jews, Christians, and Muslims.

The second king of ancient Israel, David is celebrated in the Bible for his martial feats, charismatic personality, piety, and skills as a poet and musician. In later Jewish and Christian political thought, he was regarded as the model monarch. Millions of Jews and Christians have believed that the messiah, or savior, will be a descendant of David, while the Koran regards David as a great prophet.

Most of what is known about King David comes from the accounts of his life in the Bible. Unlike many of the later Hebrew kings, David's name does not appear clearly in the surviving chronicles of Egypt or Mesopotamia. Only three stone inscriptions from that era have been found which seem to refer to a king named David or to the "House of David."

Described in scripture as a wise and powerful monarch, King David ruled during a golden age in Israel's ancient history. In this section of the Landauer Altarpiece, completed in 1511, the Renaissance artist Albrecht Dürer portrayed King David with his signature harp beside Moses and the Ten Commandments.

According to biblical accounts, David was born in Bethlehem, the youngest son of Jesse, who was a grandson of Ruth, whose story in the Bible reflects the idea of redemption. David served for several years in the court of King Saul (r. 1020–1010 B.C.E.), the first king of the twelve tribes of Israel. There he befriended Jonathan, the king's son, and married Michal, one of Saul's daughters.

While still young, David was credited with several impressive victories against the Philistines, who lived along the Mediterranean coast and had been a constant danger to the Israelites. In particular, he used a slingshot to kill the great Philistine hero Goliath. Jealous of his popularity, Saul tried to have David killed, but David escaped and survived with the help of his friend Jonathan and the Philistines. Living with a band of outcasts, David continued to garner popular support through his raids against the Amalekites and other traditional enemy tribes.

Saul and Jonathan were killed in a battle against the Philistines sometime around 1010 B.C.E. Their deaths inspired a poetic lament by David, the first of his works to be recorded. Jewish tradition also credits David with writing the Book of Psalms.

After Saul's death, the men of Judah (the region to the south of Jerusalem) anointed David king in the city of Hebron. At first, the tribes in Israel (the region to the north) recognized Saul's son Ishbosheth as king, but the latter was eventually assassinated by his courtiers, and all the tribes came to accept David as their ruler.

Seven years after his anointment in Hebron, David captured Jerusalem, which was then controlled by the Jebusites, a Canaanite tribe. This conquest linked together the two halves of David's kingdom, and he made the city its capital. David endowed Jerusalem, and the monarchy itself, with religious sanctity when he brought the previously itinerant Holy Ark containing the Law of Moses to the fortified city. Although David came to be seen as a symbol of God's relationship with Israel, he did not build a temple to house the Ark because, as the prophet Nathan told him, God had disqualified him for his sins.

David's reign was marked by a long series of successful military encounters. He subdued the Philistines and attached their lands to his realm. Other petty kingdoms, including Moab, Edom, and Ammon, became tributaries. David ensured national unity through his policies of conciliation and his marriages to wives from several of the Israelite tribes.

Toward the end of David's realm, a rebellion led by Absalom, his son and heir, forced the king to flee across the river Jordan. David soon rallied his forces, and Absalom was captured and killed. The king then promised the succession to Solomon, his son with his favorite wife, Bathsheba. The choice received the support of the prophet Nathan, even though David's relationship with Bathsheba was initially adulterous, and the king had had her husband killed.

Nathan told David that kingship would always remain with his descendants. With this promise, the principle of hereditary succession was enshrined in Jewish thought. Any subsequent pretender to a Jewish throne, in ancient or even medieval times, had to demonstrate descent from the House of David. Eventually, Judaism developed the concept of an anointed savior, who was to be an "offshoot of Jesse,"

David's father. Early Christians believed that Jesus was such a person, and thus the Christian gospels stressed his birth in Bethlehem, which was David's birthplace as well.

David died peacefully around 970 B.C.E., leaving a strong united kingdom to his son Solomon (r. 970–931 B.C.E.)

See also: HEBREW KINGS; ISRAEL, KINGDOMS OF; JUDAH, KINGDOM OF; JUDAISM AND KINGSHIP; SOLOMON.

DAVID I (1084–1153 C.E.)

King of Scotland (r. 1124–1153) who expanded Scotland's southern territory and became involved in English succession battles.

The youngest son of King Malcolm Canmore (r. 1058–1093) and Queen Margaret, David spent much of his adolescence at the English court as a sign of goodwill between the two countries. During the reign of his older brother Alexander I (r. 1107–1124), David ruled as earl of Cumbria, and upon marrying Matilda, the heiress of the earl of Northumbria, he acquired the English title of earl of Huntingdon.

David I inherited the Scottish throne after the death of Alexander in 1124. He went on to rule Scotland successfully and peacefully. He encouraged commerce and foreign trade, introduced silver coinage, promoted education, and gave generously to religious orders, helping to establish a number of important abbeys in southern Scotland. David also granted land to many prominent Anglo-Norman families, laying the foundation for the development of the Scottish feudal aristocracy.

David shrewdly took advantage of a succession crisis in England to pursue territorial gains. During the long struggle between his niece, Queen Matilda, and King Stephen for the throne of England, he sided with Matilda. However, after Stephen's triumph at the Battle of the Standard in 1138, David made peace with him in order to pursue his claim to Northumbrian territory through his wife's inheritance. David's claim was successful and Stephen granted him the earldom. By the time of David's death in 1153, when he was succeeded by his grandson Malcolm IV (r. 1153–1165), the Scottish border extended further south than ever before.

See also: SCOTTISH KINGDOMS; STEPHEN.

DAVID II (1324–1371 C.E.)

King of Scotland who inherited the throne in 1329 at the age of five upon the death of his father, Robert the Bruce. When David was four, a marriage had been arranged for him to Joan, sister of Edward III of England. Through this marriage, Edward sought to regain influence over Scotland, which had been lost during the previous reign. England's constant wars against Scotland forced the young Scottish King David to flee to France for safety, where King Philip VI gave him safe asylum.

In 1341 David returned to Scotland. In gratitude to the French, in 1346, David assisted them in an invasion of England. The English captured him at Neville's Cross, imprisoned him, and from 1346 to 1357 he lived as a pampered captive of England.

The Scottish aristocracy promised to pay a ransom to England to restore their king. After signing the Treaty of Berwick, with harsh terms for Scotland, David returned to his country to rule ably until his death in 1371. Despite a second marriage, this time a love match to Margaret Logie in 1364, he died childless, ending the male line of the Bruce dynasty.

See also: ROBERT I (ROBERT THE BRUCE); SCOTTISH KINGDOMS; STEWART DYNASTY.

DEACCESSION

The loss of a throne by a living monarch. While most hereditary rulers reign for life, it is not uncommon for a monarch to leave a throne while still living.

INSTITUTIONALIZED RETIREMENT
Monarchs rarely have had fixed terms, as do most elected offices in republics. One attempt to institutionalize fixed-term monarchy occurred in the late Roman Empire with the institution of the Tetrarchy, so called because it divided power among four rulers. The Emperor Diocletian (r. 284–305 C.E.), the inventor of the system, planned that the two senior emperors of the East and West would each retire after twenty years and be replaced by their junior emperors.

Diocletian himself faithfully carried out this mandate, but the system quickly collapsed because of the emperors' unwillingness to actually give up power.

Limited-term monarchy has worked better in postcolonial Malaysia, where monarchs are largely figureheads. There, the nine regional sultans rotate in five-year terms as monarch of the whole country. Although it did not use fixed terms, Japan in the premodern period also accepted retirement as a normal phase of a ruler's career. Released from ceremonial duties, retired Japanese emperors and shoguns often wielded more power than reigning ones.

VOLUNTARY RETIREMENT
In most monarchical systems, voluntarily resigning the throne is definitely the exception rather than the rule. One motivation for giving up a throne is the monarch's concern over the state of his or her soul.

Some of history's most powerful monarchs have renounced their thrones in old age to concentrate on their spiritual salvation. According to legend, Chandragupta Maurya (r. ca. 322–297 B.C.E.), the founder of the Maurya dynasty of India, eventually became a Jain monk and even starved himself to death as was the practice of the Jain sect. Charles V, Holy Roman emperor (r. 1519–1558) and king of Spain (r. 1516–1558), resigned all his titles to spend the last few years of his life near a Spanish monastery, even rehearsing his own funeral.

Abdicating the throne in this manner has the advantage of putting the ex-monarch in a structured environment removed from political power, enabling his successor to rule independently. The most famous abdication of modern times, that of King Edward VIII (r. 1936) of England, was prompted not by religious fervor but by romantic love and the unwillingness of the English people and political elite to accept his marriage to American divorcee, Wallis Warfield Simpson. Edward's difficulties in finding a role after his abdication (he was granted the title duke of Windsor) shows how awkward it can be for an ex-monarch in a system like the British, which lacks a formal position for such persons.

INVOLUNTARY LOSS OF RULERSHIP
More common than voluntary retirement or abdication is involuntary loss of a throne—dethronement—which is usually the consequence of political or military defeat by domestic or foreign foes. Involuntary dethronement can take various forms. In the most radical, the monarchy itself is simply eliminated, as occurred in France during the French Revolution with the proclamation of a Republic. King

Louis XVI (r. 1774–1792) was executed not as king of France but as Citizen Louis Capet.

More common is forcible ejection from a throne by a rival claimant. James II (r. 1685–1688) of England was declared to have abdicated following his defeat by William of Orange in the so-called Glorious Revolution of 1688. James fled the country but never accepted his abdication and continued to claim the throne until his death. Generally, those who have overthrown monarchs have found it safer either to kill them or to keep them on as puppets rather than forcing their resignation.

See also: ABDICATION, ROYAL; DETHRONEMENT; REGICIDE.

DEHEUBARTH KINGDOM

(900s–1200s C.E.)

Medieval kingdom in southwestern Wales that was eventually conquered by England along with the rest of Wales. In the early centuries of post-Roman Britain, the term *Deheubarth* was used to indicate the general region of southern Wales.

Hywel Dda (r. 942–950) is credited with founding the kingdom of Deheubarth by joining his small territory of Seisyllwg with the kingdom of Dyfed, which he claimed through his wife. Hywel also ruled Gwynedd and Powys, which, along with Deheubarth and Powys, became separate kingdoms again after Hywel's death in 950.

In the eleventh century, Deheubarth was located between the kingdoms of Dyfed in the west and Brycheiniog on the English border, and it contained territory that was formerly part of these other kingdoms. Its boundaries continued to change, for throughout the eleventh and twelfth centuries Deheubarth lost territory as a result of attacks and settlement by the Normans.

In 1039, Gruffydd ap Llywelyn (r. 1039–1063) of the kingdoms of Powys and Gwynedd drove out Hywel ab Edwin, prince of Deheubarth, as part of an attempt to make himself ruler of all southern Wales. Deheubarth was not fully conquered, however, because Hywel continued to resist. Following Hywel's death in 1044 another prince, Gruffydd ap Rhydderch (r. 1044–1055), took control of Deheubarth and held it against Gruffydd ap Llywelyn until the former's death in 1055. During Gruffydd ap Rhyd-

derch's rule, he led raids into England and forced the English to adopt more vigorous defensive measures against the Welsh.

Gruffydd ap Llywelyn continued to rule in southern Wales after the death of Gruffydd ap Rhydderch. An ally of the earls of Mercia in England, he fought in various English disputes. Eventually forced into central Wales by Harold Godwinson, earl of Wessex, Gruffydd was killed by his own men in 1063. Following his death, southern Wales broke up into its former kingdoms, which were ruled by men who were essentially client-kings of the English monarchs and who often styled themselves as "prince" rather than "king." Deheubarth was first ruled by Maredudd ab Owain ab Edwin (r. 1063), a nephew of Hywel ab Edwin. Other princes of this period included Rhys ab Owain (r. 1072), Rhys ap Tewdwr (r. 1078–1093), and Gruffydd ap Rhys (r. 1135).

In 1137, four brothers inherited the rule of Deheubarth from their father, Gruffydd ap Rhys. They shared power peacefully while making war on their neighbors and increasing Deheubarth's territory. The expansion of the kingdom brought the last surviving brother, Rhys ap Gruffydd (r. 1153–1197), into conflict with Henry II of England (r. 1154–1189). Rhys submitted to Henry but rebelled several times in the 1160s. Then, in 1172, Henry appointed Rhys as his representative in Wales; thereafter, Rhys acted for the king and helped him put down a Welsh rebellion in 1173–1174.

In the thirteenth century, Deheubarth suffered from various disputes within its ruling family and was never again a power in Wales. Deheubarth finally came under direct English rule, along with the rest of Wales, following the conquest of the region by Edward I of England (r. 1272–1307) in 1283.

See also: ANGLO-SAXON RULERS; EDWARD I; ENGLISH MONARCHIES; HAROLD II GODWINSON; HENRY II; WELSH KINGDOMS.

DELHI KINGDOM (1206–1526 C.E.)

Muslim kingdom in north-central India, sometimes referred to as the Delhi sultanate, which ruled a large portion of India from the early thirteenth century to the early sixteenth century.

The Muslim state known as the Delhi kingdom or Delhi sultanate originated with the invasions of Delhi by the Ghurids of Afghanistan, which began in 1194. The kingdom officially came into existence in 1206, when Qutb-ud-din Aibak (r. 1206–1210) took to the throne as the first sultan of Delhi. At this time, the sultanate included not only Delhi but also the Punjab region and much of Bengal. Already, it rivaled the earlier Gupta Empire.

THE SLAVE DYNASTY

Qutb-ud-din Aibak, who at one time was a slave, was succeeded by other former slaves, creating what came to be known as the Mu'izzi dynasty, or "Slave dynasty." This dynasty included the next two sultans, Aram Shah (r. 1210–1211) and Iltutmish (r. 1211–1236). During the succession process, the Delhi kingdom lost some of its territory. But by the end of Iltutmish's reign, all of the territory that Delhi had lost had been regained, and new territory was added, including the important region of Sind.

Iltutmish was followed, after a succession struggle between his children, by his daughter Radiyya (r. 1236–1240). She, in turn, was succeeded by various brothers, as struggles between opposing military factions arose once again to complicate the succession process. Finally, the throne came to rest with Nasir-ud-din Mahmud Shah (r. 1246–1266), also known as Mahmud Shah I, who reigned for a relatively long period and was followed by his father-in-law, Ghiyath-ud-din Balban (r. 1266–1287).

The reigns of both Nasir and Balban saw the beginning of significant invasion threats from the Mongols, Turks, and Hindus. Despite these invasions and uprisings within the kingdom, Balban's rule was one of stability and order unlike any that the kingdom would see again. Within four years of Balban's death in 1286, the Slave dynasty had come to an end owing to a lack of suitable successors.

THE KHALJI DYNASTY

The seeds of the Delhi sultanate's decline were sown during the early years of the Khalji dynasty, the successor to the Slave dynasty, when an invading army of Mongols was permitted to leave India without hindrance.

The first Khalji sultan, Jalal-ud-din Firuz Shah II (r. 1290–1296), who was a Turk, lost his throne to his nephew, Ala-ud-din Muhammad I (1296–1316), who usurped power in 1296 after deposing Firuz Shah's son, Ibrahim I (r. 1296). During his reign, Muhammad I conquered much of the Deccan region. Inse-

cure about his hold on the throne, Muhammad I was known to forcefully remove any potential threat to his power. In addition to his Deccan conquest, Muhammad I also conquered the Gujurat region of India in 1297. After this success, he increased his attacks on the Deccan throughout the early fourteenth century.

The Delhi sultans held on to their conquered lands by executing threats, such as introducing Muslim Mongol settlers to the largely Hindu populations near Delhi, and administrative measures. These measures included attempts to discourage black markets, price fixing, and other provisions that increased the sultan's ability to raise the funds needed to finance an army to hold off the potential Mongol invaders. Muhammad I's forceful hold on power was not as tyrannical as that of his son, Qutb-ud-din Mubarak (r. 1316–1320), who took the throne upon his father's death in 1316. Mubarak's barbaric reign spawned a reaction by those around him that ended the dynasty in 1320.

THE TUGHLUQ DYNASTY

The overthrow of Mubarak in 1320 created a sense of disorder in the Delhi kingdom. This disorder forced the nobility of the sultanate to approve a central figure on the throne to make their control of annexed territories easier. The individual was Ghiyath-ud-din Tughluq I, the founder and first ruler of the Tughluq dynasty.

Nevertheless, political infighting continued and resulted in the rise of Muhammad Shah I (r. 1325–1351), who murdered his father, Tughluq I, and took the throne in 1325. Within three years of taking power, Muhammad Shah I put down two separate rebellions in the kingdom. During his reign the capital was moved from Delhi to Daulatabad.

Muhammad Shah I faced increasing threats from the Mongols. Between 1328 and 1329, the Mongols invaded repeatedly and advanced as far as Delhi with relative ease. This threat, combined with abortive and unsuccessful ventures by Muhammad into northern territories and the fact that the kingdom had reached its geographic limits, led the Delhi sultanate into a slow process of decline.

In 1338, the kingdom faced a serious revolt by Bengal, followed by several years of famine and the rise of two new kingdoms within India, Vijayanagar and Bahmani. These events, all occurring within ten years of each other, conspired to hasten the kingdom's decline.

THE SULTANATE'S DECLINE

By the late 1300s, the Delhi kingdom faced one of its direst threats, the great Mongol conqueror, Tamerlane. Tamerlane invaded the sultanate in search of India's reputed wealth and to take advantage of a power vacuum that developed during the later years of the Tughluq dynasty.

In 1398, Tamerlane invaded and occupied Delhi and was briefly named its king. When he left the following year, Delhi slipped further into anarchy and chaos. A second power vacuum lasted until 1414, when the Sayyid dynasty rose to power and took control of Delhi after the last Tughluq ruler, Dawlat Khan Lodi (r. 1413–1414), was deposed.

The Sayyids ruled Delhi until 1451, when their dynasty was overthrown by an Afghan ruler, Bahlul Khan Lodi (r. 1451–1489), who established the Lodi dynasty. During his reign, Bahlul Khan attempted to regain control of territories formerly under the administration of the Delhi kings.

The Lodi dynasty maintained Delhi as an independent sultanate until its last sultan, Ibrahim II (r. 1517–1526), was defeated by the Mughals led by Babur (r. 1526–1530). From this point until the nineteenth century, Delhi was part of the Mughal Empire.

See also: GUPTA EMPIRE; INDIAN KINGDOMS; MUGHAL EMPIRE; MU'IZZI (SLAVE) DYNASTY; TUGHLUQ DYNASTY.

DELHI SULTANATE. *See* DELHI

KINGDOM

DESCENT, ROYAL

Membership in a royal dynasty or family line, which may or may not provide eligibility for kingship.

Many people in history have claimed royal descent, but this claim often has little meaning. With the passage of time, royalty has uncounted millions of descendants in the world today, and tracing "royal descent" is something of a cottage industry for genealogists. As subsequent generations of descendants moved further and further away from the monarch,

ROYAL RITUALS

MASS AT THE COURT OF LOUIS XIV

The closeness in familial relationship to the monarch determined rank between royal descendants, as can be seen from this description of a Catholic mass during the reign of Louis XIV of France. The writer of the following passage, the German princess Liselotte von der Pfalz, was married to Louis's brother, Philippe d'Orleans. As Philippe was the son of Louis XIII, the couple ranked as "children of France," taking precedence over the princes and princesses of the blood, whose connection with the royal family was more distant. In 1710, she wrote to her aunt Sophie, Duchess of Hanover:

You must remember that here distinctions of rank are observed in the mass. For example, only granddaughters of France are allowed to have a chaplain give the responses during mass and hold a candle from the *Sanctus* of the *Preface* to the *Domine non sum dignus*. Princesses of the blood are not allowed a candle or chaplain of their own, and their pages must give the responses. At the end of the mass the priest brings the *corporal* [the cloth under the bread and wine as they are consecrated] to be kissed: this goes only so far as the children of France. As for the chalice in which wine and water are served, only we are entitled to drink from it, and it is not passed to the princes of the blood. Here, as you see, there is ceremony in everything, even religion.

they usually fell into the general population. At what point a person stopped being royal was sometimes strictly defined. The French monarchical system, for example, contained a separate category, the "Princes of the Blood," for legitimate descendants of monarchs in the male line past the third generation. In addition to having a claim on the throne in the event the main line failed, the princes had certain honorary privileges that put them above other members of the French nobility.

Royal descent is sometimes a liability. In some cases dissolution of a dynasty has been followed by the new regime's extermination of anyone having a claim on the throne through the old dynasty. For example, when the Abbasids took over the Islamic caliphate from the Ummayads in 750 C.E., the new regime killed all the ruling Ummayad family except Abd-ar Rahman who fled to Spain and founded an independent emirate.

LEGITIMATE AND ILLEGITIMATE DESCENT

European monarchy, as it developed in the Middle Ages, differed from other monarchical systems in drawing a sharp distinction between the king's legitimate children born in marriage and illegitimate children born to mistresses. (European marriage law lacked the intermediate category of "concubine.") In theory, only legitimate children and their legitimate descendants could have a claim on the throne. Illegitimate children, if recognized, could receive high honors, titles of nobility, aristocratic spouses, and even political responsibilities, but they could not inherit the throne. Louis XIV of France (r. 1643–1715) fought a long battle to have his illegitmate sons accepted in the line of succession to the throne after all the legitimate claimants. His eventual victory alienated a good portion of the French high aristocracy.

GENDER AND ROYAL DESCENT

Another factor creating differences between different lines of royal descent is gender. European countries following the Salic Law (first announced in fourteenth-century France) barred even legitimate royal daughters and their descendants from any claim to the throne, restricting possible claims to the purely male line.

The spread of European models of monarchy has led other kingdoms to adopt European ideas of patrilineal descent. For example, the gradual replacement of a chiefly society with a monarchy loosely modeled after that of Britain in nineteenth-century Tonga, in the South Pacific, was accompanied by a greater emphasis on the power of royal descent, although not the Salic Law (which never applied in Britain itself). King George Tupou II (r. 1893–1918) of Tonga married a woman from a lower social class, violating the Tongan practice whereby a person's social status descended from the mother. His daughter, Salote Tupou III (r. 1918–1965), succeeded to the throne as the heir of her father.

See also: BLOOD, ROYAL; CONCUBINES, ROYAL; DYNASTY; GENDER AND KINGSHIP; INHERITANCE, ROYAL; LEGITIMACY; POLYGAMY, ROYAL; PRIMOGENITURE; ROYAL FAMILIES; ROYAL LINE; SIBLINGS, ROYAL; SUCCESSION, ROYAL.

DESSALINES, JEAN-JACQUES

(1758–1806 C.E.)

Emperor of Haiti (r. 1804–1806), who declared that country's independence in 1804.

Born a slave in Grande-Riviere-du-Nord, in the French colony of Saint-Dominque (present-day Haiti), Jean-Jacques Dessalines toiled in slavery until 1791, when he joined a slave uprising that erupted in the colony. Dessalines became a fearless chief lieutenant of the black leader Toussaint L'Ouverture who, after battling the French, became governor-general of Saint-Dominque with nominal loyalty to Revolutionary France.

In 1802, however, Napoleon Bonaparte of France betrayed a promise of amnesty, arresting Toussaint-L'Ouverture and sending a French expedition to reconquer the colony. Realizing that Napoleon intended to reinstitute slavery (which the French had abolished in 1794), Dessalines and other black and mulatto leaders revolted. A number of fierce battles ensued, and gradually the rebel army, led mainly by Dessalines, gained ground and triumphed against the French forces. On January 1, 1804, Dessalines proclaimed the colony's independence under its West Indian name, Haiti. He was immediately designated governor-general for life by the leaders of the rebellion, and eight months later he was crowned emperor of Haiti under the name Jacques I.

In spite of his power, Dessalines did not succeed in restoring stability or wealth to Haiti. Instead, he initiated cruel and despotic acts, such as forced labor on plantations, in order to avoid returning to a mere subsistence economy. Dessalines was also much harder on whites than on blacks in Haiti. He took away land belonging to whites and made it impossible for them to legally own any land. Possibly fearful that the whites would turn against him if there were another French attack, he had thousands of them killed.

Dessalines undertook these harsh measures to ensure that white dominance over blacks, who accounted for more than 80 percent of Haiti's population, would not recur. He also treated the mulattoes of Haiti, many of whom were wealthier and more successful than blacks, unfairly. In 1806, Dessalines was ambushed and murdered by the mulatto leader Alexandre Sabès Pétion. After that, Haiti was divided between Pétion and the black leader Henry Christophe.

DETHRONEMENT

The process of removing a monarch from power, usually by force or the threat of force. Unlike abdication, in which a monarch willingly relinquishes the Crown, dethronement implies some sort of struggle or resistance on the part of the ruler, though monarchs often have abdicated rather than risk being dethroned.

Although forced dethronement was decidedly more common in earlier periods, it has occurred throughout history and into the modern era, where it has often been seen as an instrument to bring about modern democratic forms of government. The list of dethroned monarchs includes kings and queens from every period of history and nearly every nation on the globe.

RIGHTS OF DETHRONEMENT

Because early forms of monarchy were usually based on military power, royal houses generally were overthrown and their kings and queens dethroned when rivals or opponents defeated royal armies. In fact, the early Greek kingdoms coined a name—tyrant—for any ruler who came to power by overthrowing a preceding monarch. Though today we associate tyranny with malicious and despotic rule, the early Greeks simply considered tyranny as one form of government among many.

The Greek tyrants generally were able to dethrone their predecessors by focusing on one issue or set of grievances that had broad popular appeal, and then mounting a strong enough opposition to force the reigning monarch from the throne. In many cases, the monarchies established by tyrants ultimately were superseded by rudimentary forms of democracy.

As in many other nations, China saw its ruling house change hands numerous times during its history, almost always because of royal dethronement led by internal forces. The Shang, Chou (Zhou), Ch'in (Qin), and Ming dynasties all began as a result of a violent overthrow of preceding rulers. Forced dethronement continued in China until the overthrow of its last emperor, Pu Yi (r. 1908–1912), by pro-democracy forces in 1912.

Many dethronements throughout history occurred not because of some internal disagreement or strife but because of international conflict. When one monarchical nation invaded and conquered another, the losing monarch would almost always be dethroned or even killed and an emissary government set up in place of the former royal house. It was in this way that Alexander the Great (r. 336–323 B.C.E.) overthrew Darius III (r. 336–330 B.C.E.) of the Persian Empire in the third century B.C.E. This kind of dethronement was generally thought to be a necessary condition of conquest; if the ruling house of a defeated nation was left with any power, it might well attempt to mount an uprising and regain the kingdom and the throne.

Conquest dethronements continued to be common throughout the history of monarchy, but the feudal and postfeudal eras in Europe saw dethronements that were led not by conquering nations or internal opposition but by the Roman Catholic Church. Papal power in Europe reached its height during the Middle Ages and early modern era; many popes were able to command foreign military forces to political ends, which frequently involved the ouster of unsympathetic ruling houses. This occasionally led to major shifts of political power. French control of Italy, for example, collapsed when Charles of Durazzo (r. 1381–1386), acting on the orders of Pope Urban VI (r. 1378–1389), overthrew Joanna of Naples (r. 1343–1381) in 1381.

DETHRONEMENT OF MONARCHY ITSELF

In the seventeenth and eighteenth centuries C.E., three dethronements occurred that served as crucial defeats for monarchical forms of government and pointed to the rise of democracies. The first was the dethronement of King Charles I (r. 1625–1649) of England in 1649. Charles's attempt to crush the power of Parliament and rule autocratically led England into a civil war between the Royalists and the Parliamentarians. When the Parliamentarians proved victorious, they executed Charles in 1649, thereby leaving the institution of Parliament in a powerful position.

The power of Parliament proved critical during England's second great dethronement, the nonviolent Glorious Revolution of 1688. In this instance, James II (r. 1685–1688) was dethroned as a result of the invasion of England by William of Orange (King William III, r. 1689–1702), a Dutch prince who was acting with the support of Parliament. By guaranteeing the throne to William—whose wife Mary was the daughter of the deposed James II—Parliament was able to secure sovereignty for itself, thereby taking a major step toward democratic government.

In eighteenth-century France, dethronement would not prove as peaceful as in England's Glorious Revolution. During the French Revolution, antimonarchists overthrew King Louis XVI (r. 1774–1792) and his wife, Marie Antoinette, and executed them both in 1793. Although the Revolutionaries did not meet many of their original goals, the French Revolution incited a wave of popular democratic movements throughout the world over the next two centuries. Numerous monarchs were dethroned, forced to abdicate, or compelled to give major concessions to pro-democratic forces in order to avoid the same fate as Louis XVI and Marie Antoinette.

See also: ABDICATION, ROYAL; CONQUEST AND KINGSHIPS; TYRANNY, ROYAL.

DEWAS KINGDOMS (1728–1948 C.E.)

Kingdoms in central India, now a part of the state of Madhya Pradesh, that were agricultural trading centers and major junctions for overland transportation.

In the early 1700s, two brothers, Tukoji and Jivaji Puar (Parmar), played an important role as generals in the conquest of central India by the Maratha Confederacy. In 1728, the peshwa, or chief minister, of the Satara region of the Maratha Confederacy

granted the brothers the area of Dewas on the Malwa plateau. Tukoji and Jivaji divided the kingdom in two, with Tukoji in control of the Dewas Senior Branch and Jivaji ruling the Dewas Junior Branch (J.B.). The two states were totally separated, each having its own administration and infrastructure. Yet, both kingdoms also became deeply entwined.

The Paur brothers claimed descent from the ancient Parmar dynasty, which had ruled central and northwestern India in the first century B.C.E. Tukoji (r. 1728–1753) was succeeded as ruler of Dewas Senior by his adopted son, Krishnaji Rao (r. 1753–1789), who fought the disastrous battle of Panipat in 1761, during which the Afghan prince, Ahmad Shah (r. 1747–1773), overcame the Marathas. Krishnaji was followed on the throne by his adopted son, Tukoji Rao II (r. 1789–1827). When Jivaji (r. 1732–1755) died in 1755, he was succeeded on the throne of Dewas Junior by Sadashiv Raj (r. 1755–1803), Rukmangad Rao (r. 1803–1817), and Anand Rao (r. 1817–1840.)

In 1818, the British entered into a treaty of friendship and alliance with Tukoji Rao II of the Senior Branch and Anand Rao of the Junior Branch. Two decades later, in 1841, both Dewas kingdoms came under the control of the British Central India Agency.

Krishnaji Rao II (r. 1860–1899), the successor of Yakmangad Rao (r. 1827–1860), was a poor administrator and plunged Dewas Senior deeply into debt. He was succeeded by Tukoji Rao III (r. 1899–1937), an adopted son from another branch of the family. In Dewas Junior, Anand Rao was succeeded by Hebant Rao (r. 1840–1864), Narayan Rao (r. 1864–1892), Malhar Rao (r. 1892–1934), and Sadashiv Rao (r. 1934–1943).

Dewas Senior and Dewas Junior both acceded to the Dominion of India in 1947 and joined the state of Madhya Bharat in 1948, with Dewas Senior under the leadership of Vikram Singh Rao (r. 1937–1947) and Krishna Ji Rao (r. 1947–1956) and Dewas Junior under Yashwant Rao (r. 1943–1956). Both states merged with the state of Madhya Pradesh in 1956.

See also: INDIAN KINGDOMS; MARATHA CONFEDERACY; SOUTH ASIAN KINGDOMS.

DIDO. *See* CARTHAGE, KINGDOM OF

DINGISWAYO (ca. 1770s–1816 C.E.)

Last paramount chief (r. ?–1816) of the Nguni confederation before the rise of Shaka Zulu (r. 1816–1828) and the formation of the Zulu kingdom.

Born in the 1770s, Dingiswayo was the son of Jobe, a chief of the Mtetwa people, one of many groups that made up the peoples called the Nguni. Dingiswayo was not first in line to inherit his father's rule, which initially passed to one of his brothers. But Dingiswayo disputed the legitimacy of his brother's succession and proclaimed himself the rightful ruler of the Nguni. To make good this claim, he set out to create a powerful military force. Among the youths recruited into Dingiswayo's rapidly growing army was a young man named Shaka, whose military prowess greatly impressed Dingiswayo. He made Shaka his general and with his help claimed the throne upon the death of his father.

Having secured his position as ruler of the Nguni, Dingiswayo set out to unify neighboring chiefdoms into a single entity, with the goal of militaristic expansion throughout the region. To further this goal, he created a new political organization composed of subchiefs selected by and answerable only to him. These officials were charged with maintaining order among the citizenry and creating a powerful military. In the course of consolidating and expanding his rule, however, he created many rivals for himself. Among them was Zidwe, whose followers from the Ndwandwe clan succeeded in killing Dingiswayo in ambush in 1816. Upon the death of Dingiswayo, his chief general Shaka, assumed leadership, giving rise to the Zulu kingdom.

See also: MZILIKAZI; SHAKA ZULU; ZULU KINGDOM.

DIOCLETIAN (ca. 240–311 C.E.)

Capable ruler (r. 284–305) of the late Roman Empire, who made many important reforms of imperial governance but is remembered also for his persecution of Christians.

Born Diocles in 240, Diocletian was the son of peasants who lived in the Roman province of Dalmatia (present-day Croatia). As a young man, Diocletian distinguished himself by his loyalty and military skills. He rose quickly through the ranks of the Roman army, and by 270 he had been made commander of imperial troops in Moesia, a province bordering the Black Sea at the outer reaches of the empire. In 283 or 284, Diocletian became commander of the Imperial Guard of Emperor Numerian (r. 283–284).

GAINING THE THRONE

Numerian was assassinated in 284, and Diocletian swore to avenge his death. When an officer was accused of the crime, Diocletian personally carried out the execution. There were several claimants to the throne, including Numerian's brother Carinus (r. 283–285), who already ruled. However, the Imperial Guard was greatly impressed by Diocletian's act to avenge the emperor's death, considering it a powerful demonstration of his loyalty to the empire. The guard thus acclaimed Diocletian the new ruler.

Diocletian's rise to power was challenged by others, on the grounds that the manner of his ascent to the throne violated tradition. It took two years to settle the issue. With the backing of the powerful Imperial Guard, Diocletian ultimately defeated all rivals and, in 286 he adopted the imperial name Gaius Aurelius Valerius Diocletianus.

The Roman Empire at the time extended north into Europe and the British Isles, south and west into North Africa, and east into Asia Minor. Control over this vast territory had already begun to break down, particularly on the frontier, where the army was stretched too thin to defend effectively against attacks from neighboring peoples.

The empire also had internal problems: inflation was rampant, and the political system was in disarray as competing factions within the Senate indulged in petty squabbles that sometimes erupted into violence. Worse still, this continual infighting had led to a century of political instability, as one emperor after another was toppled from the throne.

POLITICAL AND ECONOMIC REFORM

To create greater stability, Diocletian introduced several reforms. First, he undertook a fundamental restructuring of power, dividing the empire into two separate political units, each to be governed by an emperor called an *Augustus*, who was to be assisted by a subordinate called a *Caesar*. The *Augustus* would serve a ten-year term, after which he would leave office and his *Caesar* would become *Augustus* and appoint a new *Caesar*. By means of this new administrative structure, called a tetrarchy or "rule of four," Diocletian hoped to ensure an orderly transition of power, ending the contentiousness that had become an unavoidable element of imperial politics over the past hundred years.

Diocletian entrusted the western half of the empire—which included Italy, Gaul (now France and part of Germany), the British Isles, and Spain—to Maximian, a friend and fellow soldier. Diocletian took the wealthier eastern half of the empire, which included Greece, Asia Minor, Syria, and Egypt. In addition, Diocletian retained imperial authority over both the eastern and western political units.

Diocletian's reorganized administrative structure was very effective. With less overall territory to oversee, the *Augusti* could maintain better internal control over their subjects. In addition, Diocletian greatly increased the size of the Roman armies, so that the defense of the border regions was more effective.

Diocletian's reforms extended beyond the administrative and defensive. He sought to improve the imperial economy by setting price controls, which brought inflation to an end. He also established a uniform tax code. In the provinces, he established smaller, more efficient administrative units and appointed local governors to oversee them. The result was greater stability throughout the empire.

LAST YEARS

Toward the end of his reign, Diocletian inaugurated a policy of persecution against Christians. Christianity was still a relatively new religion, but it was spreading rapidly throughout the Roman Empire.

Diocletian was incited to take action against the Christians by his *Caesar,* Galerius Valerius Maximianus, who sought to restore the religion of Mithraism to the preeminence it had enjoyed for the previous 300 years. In 303, at Galerius's urging, Diocletian ordered that places of Christian worship throughout the empire be destroyed and that the right of Roman citizenship be taken away from all those who refused to reject Christianity.

In his zeal to overcome the threat of Christianity to his authority, Diocletian soon allowed extreme brutality in the campaign against the new religion. His campaign of persecution continued until 305, when he retired from office and returned to Salonae, the town of his birth. Diocletian convinced his fellow *Augustus,* Maximian, to retire at the same time, and

the two men who had served as *Caesari* were duly promoted to *Augusti.* This was to be the first test of Diocletian's plan for orderly succession, and it failed utterly. Both of the newly annointed *Augusti* had grown sons, and these sons were ambitious.

Constantius I (r. 305–306), who replaced Maximian as *Augustus,* lived only a year before he died in Eboracum, a Roman town (now York) in the British Isles. His son, Constantine, was at his side when he died and was acclaimed the new *Augustus* by the troops there.

Meanwhile, Maximian's son, Maxentius (r. 307–312), enlisted the support of the Praetorian Guard and advanced his own claim to the title of *Augustus.* After a bloody civil war, Constantine's faction carried the day. He took the imperial name of Constantine I (r. 307–337), eliminated the office of *Caesar,* and became sole ruler of the western half of the empire. In 324, Constantine I defeated Licinius (r. 308–324) and then *Augustus* of the eastern half of the empire, bringing an end to Diocletian's tetrarchy.

See also: CONSTANTINE I, THE GREAT; ROMAN EMPIRE.

FURTHER READING
Grant, Michael. *The Roman Emperors.* New York: Charles Scribner's Sons, 1985.

Nardo, Don. *The Roman Empire.* San Diego: Lucent Books, 1994.

Starr, Chester. *A History of the Ancient World.* 4th ed. New York: Oxford University Press, 1991.

DIPLOMACY, ROYAL

Official communication and negotiation between rulers and kingdoms. Monarchs have varied greatly in the skill and interest with which they have conducted diplomacy. Control over foreign policy is often the last area of effective power that monarchs have relinquished. When the individual states of the Holy Roman Empire won the right to conduct their own foreign policies at the Treaty of Westphalia in 1648, it marked the end of the Holy Roman emperor's central power. Monarchs have often avoided the day-to-day work of diplomacy, however, leaving it to ministers and ambassadors. Although less physically taxing and dangerous than military leadership, diplomacy also offers fewer chances for glory.

MONARCHS AND DIPLOMATIC PROTOCOL

In monarchical societies, monarchs receive ambassadors, even if it is their ministers who negotiate with them. Many societies have developed elaborate protocols for impressing foreign envoys with their wealth and power, as embodied in the splendor of their monarchs.

The Book of Rituals, adopted by Byzantine emperor Constantine VII Porphyrogenitos (r. 913–959), is one of the earliest books on diplomatic procedure. It contains detailed recommendations for the reception of ambassadors in Byzantine territory, ranging from how ambassadors should be housed while journeying to the empire's capital at Constantinople to the culminating exchange of gifts with the emperor.

Issues of protocol, or proper diplomatic behavior, can be thorny and complex, particularly in royal courts accustomed to seeing themselves as exercising universal primacy. In 1792, for example, British diplomats' hopes of establishing permanent representation in Beijing, China, were frustrated, in part, by their refusal to perform the ritual "kowtow" before the emperor, which required them to lie face downward on the floor in front of the emperor.

On occasion, monarchs have bypassed ambassadors in order to meet directly with other sovereigns. Many attempts at head-to-head royal diplomacy have proven fraught with difficulty, however. The avoidance of the suggestion that one ruler is inferior to the other makes protocol difficult, and it is hard to resolve personality conflicts when neither partner to a negotiation answers to any higher authority. The Field of the Cloth of Gold, the famous meeting of Henry VIII (r. 1509–1547) of England and Francis I (r. 1515–1547) of France in 1520, was marked principally by lavish competitive displays of wealth and splendor (hence the name), but did not have any important diplomatic results. The 1807 meeting at Tilsit between Emperor Napoleon I (r. 1804–1815) and Tsar Alexander I (r. 1801–1825) of Russia did produce a treaty of alliance, but despite the mutual admiration of the two sovereigns, their countries were at war a few years later.

PERSONAL AND "NATIONAL" MONARCHICAL DIPLOMACY

One handicap monarchical diplomacy has had to confront since the development of nationalism has been the difference between the national and the dynastic or personal interests of a monarch. Given the importance to the state of such familial matters as the marriage of a monarch or a monarch's children, it is often impossible to fully disentangle the two. Monarchs have frequently been accused (in some cases justly) of putting the interests of their dynasties or families ahead of national interests. This is a particularly difficult problem when monarchs rule multiple realms.

The Hanoverian kings of Great Britain in the eighteenth century—George I (r. 1715–1727), George II (r. 1727–1760), and, to a lesser degree, George III (r. 1760–1820)—were frequently accused of putting the interests of their continental electorate of Hanover ahead of those of their island realm of England. Their contemporary Louis XV of France (r. 1715–1774) ran a whole clandestine foreign policy parallel to that of his official ministers—the "King's Secret." It was not very successful.

The monarchs' loss of actual political power in the twentieth century has actually increased their usefulness in public diplomacy. The visit of King Edward VII of Great Britain (r. 1901–1910) to Paris in 1903, for example, is often credited with smoothing the way for the alliance known as the Entente Cordiale between France and Britain, which was concluded the following year. Edward's affability and genuine affinity for France helped dissolve some of the French hostility to Britain engendered by the history of conflicts between the two states and by ongoing colonial rivalries. By contrast, the impulsive and arrogant behavior of Edward's nephew, Kaiser Wilhelm II of Germany (r. 1888–1918), posed perpetual diplomatic headaches for his government. Modern monarchs also play the traditional diplomatic role of heads of state in receiving the credentials of newly appointed foreign ambassadors.

See also: AMBASSADORS; POWER, FORMS OF ROYAL.

DISEASE AND ROYALTY

The relationship and effects of disease on royalty.

The unique position monarchs held in society as hereditary rulers led to unique ideas about the nature of royal bodies and royal illness. The idea that kings and queens were divinely appointed influenced notions not only about royal health, but also about the relationship between the monarch and the health of his or her subjects.

Although monarchs were traditionally responsible for the welfare of their subjects in a broad sense, many ruling dynasties in Europe claimed that God had given them the ability to heal their subjects of illness. Beginning in the twelfth century in France, rulers began "touching" sufferers of disease in the manner of many Christian saints. The practice of royal healing gained popularity both in the popular mind and in medical literature because illness was thought to be caused in part by the sick person's sins.

As the Middle Ages wore on, the healing claims of various dynasties became more sophisticated. A kind of specialization developed when certain dynasties began to touch the sufferers of specific diseases. The most popular and prolific practice was in France and England, where monarchs touched to cure the "king's evil"—the disease scrofula (*Tuberculous lymphadenitis*), a glandular form of tuberculosis. Other dynasties touched for a variety of different diseases. The kings of Hungary, for example, claimed the ability to cure jaundice. English kings also distributed "cramp rings" that were intended to cure all manner of muscle cramps and epilepsy.

The practice of touching gained popularity in the sixteenth century with the Protestant Reformation and the Catholic Counter-Reformation, and with the rise of the absolutist theory of monarchy. It also first appeared in medical literature of that time, although it does appear that university-educated physicians considered this a treatment of last resort after conventional medical treatments had failed. Touching also stemmed from the practice of royal charity and mirrored developments in the field of educated medicine. Ultimately, royal touching died out after the seventeenth century, although the Bourbon restoration monarchy of nineteenth-century France revived it briefly.

Although members of royal families were believed to have healing powers, they were victims of the same diseases as their subjects. Several members of royal houses died in the periodic bouts of plague that swept through Europe, and royal women were susceptible to the dangers of childbirth and infection. However, royalty occupied a unique and often physically separate place in society that shielded them from the dangers faced by most people. Monarchs generally lived some distance from the polluted and disease-infested neighborhoods of their capitals. Royal families also enjoyed rich and varied diets and did not usually suffer from the diseases brought on by the malnutrition that often afflicted their subjects.

Royalty and nobility were more prone to certain types of diseases, usually stemming from their lifestyle. Medical practitioners and commentators in the early modern era believed that royalty was more likely to contract diseases like dropsy and gout stemming from overeating, inactivity, or even too frequent sexual intercourse. Indeed, Henry VIII of England (r. 1509–1547) was legendary for his excess in food, wives, and illness. The dynastic practices of some royal families may also have increased the presence of hereditary disease in some ruling houses. Traditionally, historians have blamed the practice of intermarriage between royal houses as the cause of genetic illnesses like hemophilia and insanity. In ancient Egyptian dynasties, marriage between royal siblings was common and has been linked to bone deformities. However, it is uncertain that genetic illness was really more common among royalty, and some monarchs, like those in Asia, did marry non-royals. When illness did occur, however, it could have dramatic dynastic and political consequences. Hemophilia in the Tsarevich Alexis, the heir of Tsar Nicholas II of Russia (r. 1894–1917), contributed to the success of the Bolshevik Revolution led by Vladimir Ilyich Lenin.

Disease in a monarch presented a crisis for the government. Because monarchs governed through appointment by God, an incompetent monarch could not easily be removed. Sick rulers often were replaced by relatives or ministers, who ruled either "behind the throne" or as regents. When George III of England (r. 1760–1820) became mentally ill with what was probably an inflammatory disease of the brain, the English government tried to establish a regency to rule for him (1788–1789). Other rulers were compelled to abdicate. Emperor Thanh Thai of Annam (Vietnam) (r. 1889–1907) was forcibly deposed in 1907 after he became ill, setting a dangerous precedent for later rulers of that country. When it came to disease, the sacral character of monarchy was a mixed blessing, bringing the ability to cure disease in others, but also making royalty more prone to an unhealthy lifestyle and to certain hereditary illnesses.

See also: ABDICATION, ROYAL; HEALING POWERS OF KINGS; REGENCIES; SUCCESSION, ROYAL.

FURTHER READING

Bloch, Marc. *The Royal Touch, Sacred Monarchy and Scrofula in England and France.* Trans. J.E. Anderson. New York: Dorset Press, 1990.

Kagan, Donald, et al. *The Western Heritage.* Upper Saddle River, NJ: Prentice Hall, 2002.

Lindemann, Mary. *Medicine and Society in Early Modern Europe.* New York: Cambridge University Press, 1999.

DIVINATION AND DIVINERS, ROYAL

The act of trying to foretell the future or explore the unknown, and the individuals who perform this service for kings and other rulers.

Monarchs in almost all societies and periods of history have both been divined about and employed diviners. The earliest collections of omens, dating from the civilizations of the ancient Near East, include many relating to the fate of kings.

EXAMPLES OF DIVINATION

One well-known early example of divination related to monarchs is that of King Saul (r. ca. 1020–1010 B.C.E.) of ancient Israel, whom the Bible describes as consulting a woman at Endor who was said to contact spirits. Many Israelites condemned Saul for his action, which violated the precepts of their god.

Another example of the royal use of divination was told by the ancient Greek historian Herodotus about King Croesus of Lydia (r. 560–547 B.C.E.) Croesus consulted the oracle of the god Apollo at Delphi to learn if he should meet the Persian army of Cyrus the Great (r. 559–530 B.C.E.) in battle. The oracle replied that should he do so, Croesus would destroy a mighty empire. Thinking that this meant Persia, Croesus attacked. Only after he was defeated and his kingdom annexed to Persia did Croesus realize that the mighty empire the oracle referred to was his own. This is one of many legends detailing how foreknowledge of the future fails to prevent disaster, or may even bring it on.

Despite the disasters that befell both Saul and Croesus, divination was commonly practiced for western monarchs and courtiers through ancient and medieval times. In the twelfth century C.E., the English philosopher, John of Salisbury, wrote a treatise denouncing different forms of divination as practiced at the royal court of England.

ASTROLOGY

Astrology was a particularly popular form of divination in late medieval Europe. Several rulers, including Charles V of France (r. 1364–1380) and the Holy Roman emperor, Frederick II (r. 1212–1250), were notorious for their reliance on astrologers. Charles V founded an astrological college, and Frederick II's court astrologer, Michael Scot, was one of the most famous magicians of the Middle Ages.

Another popular divination technique was geomancy, which involved divining by studying the patterns formed by thrown earth. Wenceslas II of Bohemia (r. 1278–1305), Richard II of England (r. 1377–1399), and Charles V of France all owned finely made manuscripts of geomancy.

ATTITUDES TOWARD DIVINATION

Christian societies have always condemned recourse to magical divination. In other cultural traditions, divination has been practiced more openly, and its association with rulers has been more explicit. In Far Eastern cultures, for example, divination has been much more accepted over the ages.

Divination in China goes as far back as the Shang dynasty (ca. 1750–1040 B.C.E.), when court officials divined by heating bones and tortoise shells and reading the cracks that the heat produced. Along with dream interpretation, divining was presented as a way in which the Shang rulers communicated with the gods.

Under China's Chou (Zhou) dynasty (ca. 1046–221 B.C.E.), divination began to spread more widely in society. Chinese imperial divination broadened over the dynasties to take in other techniques, such as astrology. Determining auspicious days for the monarch to perform certain tasks or undertake certain activities was one responsibility of the imperial astrologers.

DIVINATION IN AN AFRICAN SOCIETY

Divination was central to the power of the kings of the Azande, a central African people. Azande men divined by a technique known as the "poison oracle." A specially prepared poison was fed to fowls, and their reactions revealed hidden truths. Azande kings employed special oracle interpreters, who were required to be men of good character and observe certain taboos. Questions of criminal guilt, judgments, household affairs, and other matters were submitted to the oracle, although the king retained freedom of action. Poor answers could be blamed on the incompetence or malice of the interpreter and thus were disregarded. The king was also believed to have the best poison, and others sought to employ the king's oracle, enhancing his importance to Azande life.

PENALTIES AGAINST DIVINATION

Divination about monarchs, when practiced outside the monarch's authority, has been viewed with great suspicion in most societies. In the Roman Empire, for example, even casting the emperor's horoscope carried a penalty of death. It was feared that if a magician claimed that the emperor was soon to die, this would encourage rebellion. The T'ang dynasty (618–907 C.E.) in China attempted to restrict divination as practiced outside the court for similar reasons, though ineffectively.

Eleanor Cobham, an aunt of King Henry VI of England (r. 1422–1471) by marriage, was condemned as a witch in 1441. She was condemned partly because she had asked an astronomer named Roger Bolingbroke to divine her future, the implication being that she wanted to know if the king would die and if her husband, Duke Humphrey of Gloucester, would then become king.

See also: CURSES, ROYAL; PRIESTS, ROYAL; PROPHETS, ROYAL; WITCHCRAFT AND SORCERY.

FURTHER READING

Carey, Hilary M. *Courting Disaster: Astrology at the English Court and University in the Later Middle Ages.* New York: St. Martin's Press, 1992.

Evans-Pritchard, E.E. *Witchcraft, Oracles and Magic among the Azande.* Oxford: Clarendon Press, 1937.

Smith, Richard J. *Fortune-Tellers and Philosophers: Divination in Traditional Chinese Society.* Boulder, CO: Westview Press, 1991.

DIVINE RIGHT

The notion that monarchs hold their authority by decree of God and that this authority may be passed down to royal offspring.

The principle of divine right is as old as monarchy itself. It has been used throughout history to justify the reign of particular monarchs, to quell political discussion unfavorable to the ruling party, and to ensure that powers of governance stay within the same family. The rise of proto-democratic movements in Europe in the seventeenth and eighteenth centuries, particularly in England and France, did much to dispel the notion of the divine right of kings. Nevertheless, variants of this ideology could be seen in Asia until the twentieth century.

ORIGINS OF THE IDEA

The earliest known versions of the theory of the divine right of kings occurred in ancient Egypt, where ruling pharaohs, especially in the early dynasties, frequently invoked the god Horus as a symbol of their divinity. Represented by a crowned falcon, Horus was thought to be the last in a line of gods that ruled over the earth, and the human kings who followed in his path were considered material representations of him. In fact, early Egyptian hieroglyphics frequently represent an image of Horus preceding the name of all royal personages. Later Egyptian pharaohs, mostly from the Fourth dynasty onward, invoked the sungod Re as a representation of themselves, and they also used his name and symbol as a prefix to royal names.

A similar development occurred in China under the Chou (Zhou) dynasty, in which a theory of the divine right of kings known as *t'ien ming* was developed. *T'ien ming*, which roughly translates as "mandate from heaven," held that whatever changes in power occurred did so because of the will of a divine spirit. Thus, the victory of the Chou over their predecessors, the Shang (Yin) dynasty, in 1045 B.C.E. was a sign from heaven that the Chou were better fit to rule than the Shang. This can be distinguished from European notions of divine right, because *t'ien ming* suggests that rulers who failed to fulfill their obligations to their subjects would be removed from power, whereas European kingly divinity suggested that monarchs were essentially infallible.

The theory of divine right was given new form by the early Church father, Saint Augustine of Hippo, in his classic work, *City of God*, written in the early 400s C.E. during the waning years of the Roman Empire. Saint Augustine presented a version of history characterized by human progress out of paganism and toward Christianity. Although Augustine did not propose a political theory of monarchy in the way later thinkers would, he did suggest that rulers were granted certain privileges—and consequently took on certain obligations—by virtue of divine will. Versions of Augustine's ideas about the relationship between monarchs and divinity came to characterize European monarchies for the next thousand years.

AGES OF DECLINE

The divine right of kings went more or less unchallenged in Europe throughout the medieval period, even as monarchies across the continent changed hands continually. The emergence of early democratic movements during the Renaissance began to put pressure on the notion of monarchical divinity, and this tension finally spilled over into a major conflict in seventeenth-century England.

James I (r. 1603–1625), the first English monarch of the Stuart dynasty, believed strongly in the divine right of kings and consequently gave Parliament little say in the governance of Britain. James also courted controversy by issuing a series of religious mandates aimed at stifling Puritanism and Roman Catholicism; James believed that his authority for issuing these doctrines was granted to him by God. James dissolved Parliament in 1611, and when he died in 1625, his son Charles I (r. 1625–1649) inherited a deeply troubled nation.

Charles I was equally convinced of the divine right of kings, but his struggle with Parliament took a much more violent turn than his father's. Charles's frustrations with the demands of Parliament arose immediately. He dismissed Parliament in 1629 and ruled alone for eleven years, during which time he drove England further and further toward bankruptcy. When Parliament reconvened in 1640, it refused to grant Charles total authority, a move that led to civil war. The Parliamentarians ultimately defeated and executed Charles. This victory of Parliament over the king effectively ended the idea of divine right in England.

Meanwhile, in France, the long reign of Louis XIV (r. 1643–1715) in the seventeenth and early eighteenth centuries was characterized by Louis's firm belief in his kingly divinity. This led to a consolidation of power around the throne that bordered on absolute monarchy. Although Louis's reign went relatively unchallenged, the wasteful financial consequences of his absolutism led to the gradual weakening of the monarchy, which finally collapsed with the antiroyalist French Revolution of 1789 and the beheading of Louis XVI (r. 1774–1792) in 1793.

See also: CHRISTIANITY AND KINGSHIP; DIVINITY OF KINGS; HEAVENS AND KINGSHIP; POWER, FORMS OF ROYAL; RELIGIOUS DUTIES AND POWER; SACRED KINGSHIPS.

DIVINITY OF KINGS

Belief that kings are incarnations or direct descendants of a deity. The idea that kings are greater than ordinary men by virtue of their divine nature has flourished in many cultures and ages. Divine kingship is often associated with Christianity, which provides a model for the concept in the person of Christ. Yet the story of a god who sends a son (or daughter) to earth to establish civilization is not restricted to the New Testament. Monarchs throughout the world have based the legitimacy of their rule on precisely these grounds.

DIVINE ANCESTORS

In ancient Peru, among a people known as the Tihuanaco, the story was told of a creator god named Viricocha, whose own son, Inti, also came to be revered as a god. Inti decided to gather all the true people of the earth together so that they could learn to live in a civilized fashion. He ordered his own son and daughter, Manco Capac and Mama Ocllo, to wed and go to earth to bring the people together. They found the Tihuanaco people by the waters of Lake Titicaca and carried out the task ordained by their father. From these two, all rulers of the Tihuanaco, and later of the Incan Empire, traced their descent.

Stories such as this are found in the oral histories of all the great civilizations of Latin America. They are found, too, in the traditions of the great Egyptian pharaohs, in the monarchical culture of pre-World War II Japan, and among many of the peoples of Africa. In every case, they provide the legitimacy for a dynasty's right to rule and a rationale for maintaining the status quo in terms of practice and ritual. This idea, that a people and their civilization are the direct products of the labors of a founding ancestor born of the gods, is perhaps the most commonly encountered variation on the theme of divine kingship.

This variation is not the only one, however. In pre-Enlightenment Christian Europe, the case was

ROYAL RELATIVES

THE DIVINE KINGS OF SCANDINAVIA

The Skioldung dynasty, from which the modern royal families of Sweden and Denmark are descended, is one of the most ancient in Europe. Royal genealogies trace the lines of descent from King Ragner Lodbrok of Denmark (r. 750–794) with a high degree of reliability. Records before 750 are less dependable but tell of much more ancient connections going back to Skiold, a son of the chief Norse god, Odin, and a mortal wife. Skiold married the minor goddess Gefjon, and they founded the city of Lethra, which became a center of worship.

made somewhat differently. Christ was not himself invoked as the founder of the ruling dynasties of France or England, for example. Rather, he served as a model for the rule of the king, whose divinity was derived from the simple expediency of God's order. In this instance, the king was seen not as a direct descendant of God, but rather as a man who, upon assuming the throne, attained his divinity through the agency of his office and therefore transcended his humanity. Nonetheless, belief in the divinity of the king, and in the sacredness of his person in office, was fundamental to the legitimacy of the throne.

FUNDAMENTALS OF DIVINE KINGSHIPS

The nature of the ruler's relationship to the divine may take a number of forms. It may be a direct, one-to-one correspondence, as when a monarch is held to be the incarnation or manifestation of a god, or it may be a less direct relation between the two, as when the monarch is understood to be the divinity's representative or agent. In other words, a divine king may be viewed as a god in and of himself, or he may be understood as the god's high-priest and spokesperson. In either case, a number of things must be true before one can consider a monarch to be divine. These include:

1. The belief that the monarch is the receptacle of divine power, bearing within his or her living form the essence of godhood.

2. The belief that the king is responsible for the prosperity and fertility of his people. Literally, it is the king, through his divine nature, who forestalls disasters, guarantees the harvest, and ensures the coming of future generations.

3. The belief that the monarch stands apart from the normal run of humanity, with a direct connection with god through which he achieves his inspiration and his strength.

These elements of belief find expression in a variety of ways. Because of his divinity, the king must be addressed in ways that mark him as different from his subjects. This may mean that he lives in deep seclusion, never directly approachable by mere mortals. This was true of the Japanese emperors, who were rarely seen outside their residences except for religious celebrations. Alternatively, the king may be expected to travel frequently among his people. This was true in Peru, where the stately passage of the Great Inca throughout his domain was an important part of his responsibilities, a ritual passage that served to remind the populace to whom they owed allegiance.

Tracing the king's genealogy to the founding divine ancestor was essential in maintaining his claims to the throne. Some of the earliest recorded history consists of lists of kings such as those of Egypt and Sumer. Within kingdoms asserting divine descent of their ruler, demonstrating the purity of the descent was paramount. The goal of ensuring a divine heir explains why, for example, the Egyptian pharaoh might have been encouraged to marry a woman of his own family, including his sister or half-sister. It is said that the wives of Ramses II (r. 1279–1213 B.C.E.) included one of his sisters and three of his daughters. The offspring of such unions were considered true inheritors to the throne, for they shared in the pure blood of the god.

Although kings were often considered divine, they were not immortal. In order to preserve the appearance of divinity, ritualized transference of divine rule developed. The need for preserving divinity was met through ceremonies of divestiture and investiture, marking the reversion of the ailing king to mortal status and the elevation of his successor. Many cultures tied these ceremonies to their religion, giving the priest the sacred duty of carrying out the rituals and reinforcing the link between king and god. Charlemagne (r. 800–814) began the practice of having the pope crown the Holy Roman emperor; this practice would last for centuries.

DIVINITY MANIPULATED

In *The Golden Bough* (1940), Sir James Frazer attempted to explain the rationale underlying the belief in divine kingship. He argued that the belief was a logical outgrowth of a belief system based on ancestral worship, one of the earlier forms of religious belief. Frazer also presupposed that the office of king arose from an earlier political structure in which priests held the ultimate office.

For anthropologist E.E. Evans-Pritchard, who did fieldwork in the eastern Sudanic kingdom of the Shilluk, experience did not bear out Frazer's long-accepted assumptions. For instance, Frazer maintained that the king was held sacred in the very specific sense that he was descended from, and thus part of, the creative center of the universe. Evans-Pritchard's observations told a different story, suggesting that the Shilluk were fully aware of the man beneath the royal regalia but saw their monarch's sacredness as springing from his role as symbol of their larger society. In such a case, attributions of divine descent become capable of being manipulated to suit the needs of society or the ambitions of an individual.

That the divinity of a king could be subject to manipulation has many historical examples. Great Inca Huayna Capac (d. 1525) attempted to do just that when he elevated his son, Atahuallpa, to king of half of the Incan Empire, even though this son was not born of the true, that is, "divine" marriage. By doing so, he caused internal conflict in the empire that ultimately led to its destruction. Similarly, the emperor of Japan, Hirohito, was by tradition divinely entitled to rule. Yet throughout his life there was evidence that Hirohito knew this idea to be a fiction, regardless of its usefulness in inspiring the unswerving devotion of his people—particularly his military—during World War II. Therefore, when Japan fell to the Allies at the end of the war, it was no great problem for him to formally renounce his divinity and revert to the status of mortal man.

The history of monarchies throughout the world is filled with tales of the miraculous return of lost or hitherto unknown heirs to divine leadership. That these claims to power might have been made with calculation seems beyond dispute. The tradition of the Aztec divine kings, for example, seems to have been lifted directly from the Toltecs, whose own empire had existed centuries earlier, but whose memory was still strong in the Valley of Mexico among Toltec descendants whom the Aztecs intended to conquer. What better way to legitimize a new ruler than to lay claim to the religiopolitical beliefs of the locals?

Other rulers sought to formalize their right to rule in similar ways. In the thirteenth century, the Amhara conquerors of Ethiopia asserted their right to rule by claiming their descent from the first king of Ethiopia, the son of Solomon and the queen of Sheba. Ancient Irish kings declared they were descendants of Milesius, a Spanish king who conquered Ireland and was himself a direct descendant of Adam.

A LASTING CONCEPT

The idea of having a divinely ordained ruler is still present in some cultures. Within Japanese society, a movement is in process to restore the (divine) Chrysanthemum Throne, the ancient traditional throne of Japan. Some independent states of Africa find the remnants of once powerful kingdoms invoking their traditions, including their divinely royal lineages, in a desire to return to their former glory. King Mswati III (r. 1986–   ) of Swaziland, Africa's last absolute monarch, insists upon his divine rights, even that of capturing girls to add to his harem.

In the Middle East, the drive toward establishing Islamic theocracies reflects a desire to establish a divine king or at least to install a semidivine ruler. The idea of a divinely inspired ruler underlies the philosophy of the Shi'ite Muslims, who installed the Ayatollah Khomeini (1979–1989) as the head of the Iranian state. Khomeini was acclaimed not as a direct descendant of Allah, but as one of Muhammad's holiest followers, the so-called Hidden Imam who disappeared from public view in 939 C.E. and waited through the centuries until he might be called to rule by Allah.

Even societies that have established more democratic forms of government sometimes cling to vestiges of traditions of divine rule. The ceremonies and regalia associated with the British royalty, for example, can be understood as survivals of such a time, and although they no longer carry the meaning they once possessed, their symbolic power remains strong.

See also: AZTEC EMPIRE; DIVINE RIGHT; GENEALOGY, ROYAL; HIROHITO; INCA EMPIRE.

FURTHER READING

Engnell, Ivan. *Studies in Divine Kingship in the Ancient Near East.* Oxford: Basil Blackwell, 1967.

Evans-Pritchard, E. E. *Divine Kingship of the Shilluk of the Nilotic Sudan.* Cambridge: Cambridge University Press, 1948.

Frazer, James, Sir. *The Golden Bough.* London: Macmillan, 1922.

Piggott, Joan R. *The Emergence of Japanese Kingship.* Stanford, CA: Stanford University Press, 1997.

Seligman, C. G. *Egypt and Negro Africa: A Study in Divine Kingship.* New York: AMS Press, 1987.

DJOSER (ca. 2737–2717 B.C.E.)

Variously credited as either the first or second king of Egypt's Third dynasty (d. ca. 2649 B.C.E.) and the first to be entombed within a stone pyramid upon his death.

The actual dates of Djoser's birth and death (and the years of his rule) are still in dispute. Nonetheless, he is one of the best known of the Egyptian kings who made their capital in the ancient city of Memphis, situated at the apex of the Nile Delta. Djoser (also called Netjerikhet) was born sometime after 2700 B.C.E. His father was probably Khasekhemwi, who was the last king of Egypt's Second dynasty, If this is so, his mother was Nimaathapu, whose name in inscriptions is often followed by the epithet "Mother of the King." The dates attributed to Djoser's life and reign are only estimates, based on scholarly attempts to interpret the king lists left behind by the pharaohs of ancient Egypt. These are

not straightforward documents, however, and several lists exist that contradict one another.

Details of Djoser's early life, his age at marriage and the name of his wife, and the names of his children (if he had any) are all unknown. He is thought to have ruled for about nineteen years, but some sources claim that he ruled for as many as thirty-seven. He is believed to have extended the territory of Egypt down to the First Cataract of the Nile, but this, too, is subject to debate. In fact, Djoser is remembered so well today primarily because of his innovation in creating his own tomb. Prior to Djoser's rule, Egypt's pharaohs were entombed after death, but their burial sites were mounds of earth and rock, topped with a low, oblong tomb covering made of mud bricks. Djoser, however, commissioned his grand vizier, Imhotep, to design a much more elaborate mortuary complex, one that would exalt the rule of the pharaoh and stand for all time.

Imhotep's response to Djoser's command was to design a unique, monumental stone structure. Pyramidal in shape and flattened at the top, its four sides consisted of ascending steps leading to a surface that could be used for ritual purposes. Inside were burial chambers destined to hold the body of the pharaoh, the corpses of his retainers, and the possessions that were deemed necessary to guarantee a life of ease in the next world. The pyramid remains standing today, at its original site near the city of Saqqara on the west bank of the Nile River.

See also: EGYPTIAN DYNASTIES, ANCIENT (BEFORE EIGHTEENTH DYNASTY).

DMITRI, GRAND PRINCE (1350–1389 C.E.)

Russian ruler (r. 1359–1389), often known by the sobriquet Dmitri Donskoi ("of the Don"), who briefly freed Muscovy from control by the Tatars, who dominated parts of Russia after the Mongol invasions of the 1200s.

Dmitri Ivanovich was the son of Grand Prince Ivan II (r. 1353–1359) and Aleksandra. When Ivan II died in 1359, he divided Muscovy among his three sons, Dmitri and two younger brothers. Both Dmitri's young age and the devastating prevalence of the plague throughout Muscovy initially limited Dmitri's power. Furthermore, since 1236, the Mongol Tatars had controlled Muscovy as a feudatory state. Although the grand prince oversaw local affairs, he paid an enormous tribute to the Tatars and ultimately answered to the Tatar khan.

In 1362, Dmitri and his brothers gained control of the influential Grand Princedom of Vladimir. a principality that bordered Novgorod, Muscovy's most serious rival in the region. Rather than attacking Novgorod, Dmitri married Evdokia Dmitrievna, a royal princess from the rival state. Their marriage created an alliance between Muscovy and Novgorod. The death of Dmitri's brother, Ivan, further solidified his control of Muscovy.

After unifying Vladimir and Novgorod with Muscovy, Dmitri sought to eliminate Tatar control. In 1380, he engaged the Tatar Golden Horde at the battle of Kulikovo. The battle was extremely bloody with heavy casualties, but the Russian forces emerged victorious. The triumph was Dmitri's foremost act, and he augmented his victory by assuming control of the Riazan territory, which had aided the Tatars, and by appointing his own representative to lead the Orthodox Church in Moscow.

Dmitri's victory, however, was temporary. Enraged by Dmitri's actions, the new Tatar khan, Tokhtamysh (r. 1376–1390), reassembled the Tatar army. His forces captured Russian ships on the Volga River, occupied Bolgar, Riazan, and Novgorod, and slaughtered over twenty-four thousand citizens when they raided Moscow.

Although Tokhtamysh's presence ensured that Muscovy would not attain total freedom, Dmitri had significantly expanded Muscovy's political and military influence. During his reign, the economy expanded because Dmitri instituted a monetary system and allowed new settlers to farm much of the land he had conquered. He also acquired the Principality of Vladimir as a permanent part of Muscovy. Most importantly, Dmitri's victory over the Tatars, though not permanent, presaged the eventual elimination of Tatar control in Russia.

The cause of Dmitri's death in 1389 is not certain, although the suspicious deaths of several of his key supporters suggest that he may have been assassinated. His son, Vasilii I (r. 1389–1425), inherited a united Muscovy–Vladimir princedom that his father had significantly strengthened.

See also: GOLDEN HORDE KHANATE; RUS PRINCEDOMS.

DUAL MONARCHIES

A form of political organization in which one monarch has sovereignty over two kingdoms. The best example of this formation is the Austro-Hungarian Empire of the nineteenth and twentieth centuries C.E., although dual monarchies have existed at least since biblical times. Although there are certainly some advantages to organizing two states as a dual monarchy, historically it has led to internal fractures that make it difficult for the monarchy to maintain power.

DUAL MONARCHY IN BIBLICAL TIMES

The best known early example of a dual monarchy is that of the biblical kingdoms of Israel and Judah. According to the Second Book of Samuel in the Old Testament, David, the successor of King Saul (ca. 1020–1010 B.C.E.), was made king of Judah, in southern Palestine, sometime around 1010 B.C.E. At the same time, Saul's son, Ishbosheth, was crowned king of the northern kingdom of Israel. War soon broke out between the two kingdoms. As Israel's forces were being badly beaten, two of Ishbosheth's officers entered his home and killed him, intending to make peace and curry favor with David. The leaders of the northern kingdom then came to David and anointed him head of the united kingdoms of Judah and Israel (r. ca. 1010–970 B.C.E.). The dual monarchy was short-lived, however, as David's grandson Rehoboam (r. 930–914 B.C.E.), the son of King Solomon (r. ca. 970–931 B.C.E.), was unable to hold the kingdoms together, losing Israel to Jeroboam I (r. 931–910 B.C.E.). The Bible has little to say about the nature of this dual monarchy, however, and physical evidence for a combined kingdom has not been found.

DUAL MONARCHY IN MEDIEVAL AND RENAISSANCE EUROPE

The major postbiblical examples of international unions include the tempestuous and never-complete union of France and England under the Angevin, Plantagenet, and Lancaster dynasties; the Kalmar Union of Denmark, Norway, and Sweden under Queen Margaret (r. 1387–1396 C.E.); and the Danish-Norwegian union under the Oldenburg dynasty. Only the last named endured, and it is historically significant largely for the ease with which the two kingdoms came and stayed together. As Norway had no internal administration under the Oldenburgs, the union of that country and Denmark was a dual monarchy in name only.

Occasionally, the term *dual monarchy* is applied to the English rule of William and Mary (r. 1689–1702; 1689–1694). This is not technically accurate, however, since William and Mary reigned over only one kingdom. The fact that both rulers were equal inheritors to the throne has led to this description, though their reign is most commonly known as a joint monarchy.

DUAL MONARCHY IN THE MODERN ERA

The only successful and lasting example of dual monarchy in the modern era is that of Austria-Hungary. Hungary, under control of the Austrian Habsburg dynasty since the 1600s, began to agitate for self-rule during the revolutionary years of the 1840s and continued to do so for the next several years. Weakened by its defeat in the Austro-Prussian War of 1866, Austria granted domestic autonomy to the Hungarians, provided that Emperor Franz Josef (r. 1848–1916) maintained his title of sovereign, as well as control of Hungarian foreign policy. The Hungarians agreed, and, in 1867, Franz Joseph was crowned king of Hungary and emperor of Austria.

The Austro-Hungarian Empire was a powerful economic and political force, but from its inception it was fraught with internal tension. Nationalist movements quickly sprang up among the marginalized ethnic groups within the empire, most notably the Slavs. Calls for independence came from many groups under the aegis of the empire. The Hungarians, meanwhile, came to resent Austria for not granting them complete autonomy, and the economic exploitation of the working classes in Hungary only exacerbated the situation. All of these problems continued to worsen until 1914, when Francis Ferdinand, heir to the Austro-Hungarian throne, was assassinated by a Slavic nationalist, thereby igniting World War I.

As the defeat of Austria-Hungary grew increasingly apparent near the end of the war, pro-independence movements within the empire found new energy, and 1918 saw numerous groups, including Hungary, declare their independence from

Austria, thus bringing the dual monarchy to an end.

See also: Austro-Hungarian Empire; Habsburg Dynasty; Israel, Kingdoms of; Judah, Kingdom of; Kalmar Union; Nationalism; Oldenburg Dynasty.

DUTCH KINGDOMS. *See* Netherlands Kingdom

DYFED KINGDOM (ca. 400s–1000s C.E.)

One of the four major kingdoms of medieval Wales, located in the extreme southwestern part of the region.

The kingdom of Dyfed was established by Irish migrants to Wales in the fifth century. As with most of the small Welsh kingdoms of the early medieval period, however, few facts are known about the kingdom until the eighth or ninth century.

Geographically, Dyfed was the Welsh kingdom most remote from England, but its location in the far west did not protect it from Anglo-Saxon incursion during the early Middle Ages. The kingdom was accessible from the sea, and the terrain was not as mountainous as that of the interior of Wales.

King Offa of Mercia (r. 757–796) (who had Offa's Dyke built to mark the border between Wales and England) attacked Dyfed in 778, and in 818 another Mercian king, Cenwulf (r. 796–821), raided the kingdom as well. In 878, a ruler of Dyfed named Hyfaidd ap Bleddri was among five Welsh princes who turned to King Alfred the Great of Wessex (r. 871–899) for protection, allying themselves with him to increase their own power and authority. Alfred's son and successor, Edward the Elder (r. 899–924), was acknowledged as overlord of the western part of Wales, including Dyfed. The rulers of some of the Welsh kingdoms paid tribute to Edward's successor Athelstan (r. 924–939) and acknowledged him as their overlord, attending his court and witnessing charters. Dyfed's alliance with Wessex continued into the 940s, when forces from Dyfed played a role in an English invasion of the kingdom of Strathclyde (now Cumbria in northern England).

Hywel Dda (the Good) was one of the Welsh kings who attended Athelstan's court. Hywel became king of Dyfed in 904. He ruled the territories of Ceredigion and Ystrad Tywi along with his brother, and he acquired the kingdom of Gwynedd in 942, thus uniting the western coast of Wales under one ruler for the first time. He is celebrated as the codifier of Welsh law.

Following Hywel's death in 950, the Welsh kingdoms separated once more and Dyfed never again achieved any importance in relation to the other kingdoms of Wales. In 1073, the Normans invaded Dyfed, establishing Pembroke Castle as a base. King William I of England (r. 1066–1087) named the Norman lord Arnulf as earl of Pembroke, with the task of governing western Dyfed. The eastern half of Dyfed had also come under Norman rule by the early twelfth century, finally ending its existence as an independent kingdom.

See also: ALFRED THE GREAT; ANGLO-SAXON RULERS; GLYWYSING KINGDOM; GWENT KINGDOM; GWYNEDD KINGDOM; NORMAN KINGDOMS; POWYS KINGDOM; WELSH KINGDOMS.

DYNASTY

A ruling family that holds a throne for a period of time, generally several generations.

In most countries, the right to the throne is hereditary and is passed on from one generation to the next. It is usually passed on to the eldest son, although in some cases, as with the Picts of England, the right of succession was passed from the father through the daughter to her husband. In either case, the same family keeps the throne for several generations, thus creating a dynasty.

In many cases, dynasties provide stability to the countries that they rule. However, a series of weak and inept monarchs, or the lack of a direct heir, can result in civil war or instability, as various members of the ruling class contend for the right to rule. For example, in the fifteenth century, the kingdom of Castile on the Iberian Peninula was ruled successively by John II (r. 1406–1454) and Henry IV, the Impotent (r. 1454–1474). Both monarchs were unable to handle the political and military problems that Castile faced at the time. Henry IV, in particular, bankrupted the treasury of

the kingdom by showering money and gifts on his favorites. The paternity of his daughter, Juana la Beltraneja, was also in question, leaving the succession unclear. Consequently, for more than fifty years, Castile lacked political guidance and suffered continual warfare and corruption while the nobility fought among themselves or rebelled against the Crown.

Similarly, in fifteenth-century England, the roots of the Wars of the Roses (1455–1485) go back, in part, to the incompetence of Richard II (r. 1377–1399). Henry IV (r. 1399–1413) of the house of Lancaster deposed Richard and seized the Crown. Henry and his son, Henry V (r. 1413–1422), ruled efficiently, but Henry VI (r. 1422–1471) inherited the throne at the age of nine months. As an adult, Henry VI was inept; he favored his supporters and appointed his family to positions of honor, thus creating factions. In 1471, he was deposed by Edward, duke of York, who became Edward IV (r. 1461–1470) of the house of York. England then descended into civil war as the Yorkists and Lancastrians warred among themselves for the throne. The conflict was finally ended by Henry Tudor (of the house of Lancaster), whose marriage to Elizabeth of York, the daughter of Edward IV, united the two houses and began the Tudor dynasty. He ruled as King Henry VII (r. 1485–1509).

Dynasties can also create instability when, through marriage or otherwise, they acquire a claim to the throne of a particular country. In 1700, for example, Philip V (r. 1700–1724) became the first member of the Bourbon dynasty to inherit the Spanish throne. Philip was descended from Louis XIV (r. 1643–1715) of France and Philip IV (r. 1621–1665) of Spain; hence, many in Spain saw his accession as a great moment for unity between France and Spain, who had long been rivals. Some, however, opposed such an alliance. Moreover, many countries opposed Philip's claim, fearing that a union between France and Spain would upset the balance of power in Europe. In 1701, England, Austria, and Holland formed an alliance, and the War of the Spanish Succession (1701–1714) began. Although Philip ultimately was recognized as king of Spain, the country lost much of its empire, with France replacing Spain as the most powerful nation in Europe.

See also: RICHARD II; SUCCESSION, ROYAL.

EARTH AND SKY, SEPARATION OF

A concept that arose in ancient myths as an explanation of cosmic order and that, in many cultures, helped establish the divinity of kingship on earth. In the creation myths of many lands, the separation of earth and sky not only established order in the universe, but also forced a separation between humans and gods. Both gods and humans continually engaged in a battle against chaos; the gods fought against chaotic forces in the sky, while kings and emperors fought against chaotic forces on earth. The separation of earth and sky therefore led to a separation of powers, and that led, in turn, to the concept of kings and emperors as divine rulers.

The notion that kingship arose from the need for world order permeated early myths, quite noticeably the myths of ancient Mesopotamia and Egypt. Early people recognized order in the heavens when they watched the celestial bodies move in regular patterns, so they considered the gods who ruled the sky to be the ultimate defenders of the cosmos. But the sky gods could not maintain order on earth once they separated from earth and rose above it. And so, it was said, they endowed kings and emperors with powers that enabled them to assume this function, and divine rulers thus took power in many lands.

In many myths, earthly rulers emerged as actual manifestations of the sky gods, often the god of the sun. Ancient peoples recognized the supremacy of the sun because they watched it rise and set, turn the seasons, and renew the world; they understood that the movement of the sun guaranteed life. The Egyptians worshiped their pharaohs as direct descendants of the sun-god, as the Inca and Japanese did their emperors and as people of many other lands did the rulers they considered divine. People who believed their kings got power from the sun worshiped these kings as solar deities, or sun-gods. This guaranteed the rulers' supremacy and affirmed their ability to keep the earth in tune with the heavens.

Believing that earthly rulers had divine origin established the notion of power on earth, and as long as people yielded to the power of their kings, they could recognize godly power in the earthly realm. Creation myths tell how the gods ordered the cosmos, but many of them also show a progression from the creation of the universe to the founding of kingship. In Egyptian myth, for instance, the creator god Atum emerged from chaos, separated from the earth and retreated to the sky, and then put his power to work in the world by giving the earthly rulers a divine right to fight the forces of chaos.

The noted religious scholar Mircea Eliade asserts that the separation of earth and sky established a relationship between gods and humans, and that this necessitated the need for an intermediary. When the creator god ascended to the sky, he needed an earthly power in which to manifest his own power and essence. So he manifested himself as king, pharaoh, or emperor, a ruler who often held the position of priest and who bridged the gap between earth and sky.

See also: DIVINE RIGHT; DIVINITY OF KINGS; ENTHRONEMENT, RITES OF; FUNERALS AND MORTUARY RITUALS; HEAVENS AND KINGSHIP; KINGLY BODY; MONARCHY FORMATION, MYTHS OF; MYTH AND FOLKLORE; SACRAL BIRTH AND DEATH; SACRED KINGSHIPS.

FURTHER READING

Andrews, Tamra. *Legends of the Earth, Sea, and Sky: An Encyclopedia of Nature Myths.* Santa Barbara: ABC-CLIO, 1998.

Eliade, Mircea. *Patterns of Comparative Religion,* New York: Sheed and Ward, 1958.

Leeming, David Adams. *Encyclopedia of Creation Myths.* Santa Barbara: ABC-CLIO, 1994.

EAST ASIAN DYNASTIES

The kingdoms and dynasties of China, Japan, and Korea, which have historically been cohesive despite their very pronounced national differences. The three countries share centuries-old ties based on either shared ethnic origins or shared values adopted from Chinese culture and religion, or both.

The East Asian kingdoms ruled over an amalgam of peoples shaped by ancient migrations and centuries of conquest. Not all these disparate peoples were Chinese, but their common history was so old that their common references created an identifiable grouping. Within that grouping, each country—China, Japan, Korea—evolved into a unique nation displaying deep national pride.

Geographically, East Asia encompasses the regions of northeastern and eastern China, the Korean Peninsula, and Japan. This area is in the nontropical monsoon belt above the more tropical regions of Southeast Asia. The region includes many relatively low mountain ranges separated by small, irregular plains and alluvial lowlands.

The monsoon climate and many mountainous areas of East Asia are factors of historical importance to regional travel, agricultural advances, military campaigns, and fortress building, among other East Asian endeavors.

EAST ASIAN CONFLICTS

Historically, the national consciousness of the three East Asian countries was forged by the ability of each society within the region to resist invasion by its neighbors, either alone or in shifting alliances with each other or against each other.

For example, in the early fourth century, the Koguryo and Paekche kingdoms of Korea initially expelled the Chinese from the Korean Peninsula. Then they and the Silla kingdom (the third of Korea's "Three Kingdoms") waged war among themselves until the Silla kingdom won out in 668, with the support of the T'ang Dynasty of China.

Yet it was the earlier victories of the Koguyro kingdom over invading Chinese armies that had preserved Korea's autonomy for the future. In 612, the Koguyro rulers had successfully repulsed a massive invasion of over a million Chinese soldiers led by the Sui emperor of China. Again in 642, the Koguyro forces triumphed over the invading armies of the T'ang emperor, Tai Tsung (r. 626–649).

In the mid-fourth century, the Japanese raided Korea and established a foothold colony on the tip of the Korean Peninsula, which encouraged Korean migration to Japan for more than two centuries. The Korean "continentals" brought with them to Japan the silkworm and metal working, and they con-

The social organization of the kingdoms of East Asia owed much to the ideals of Confucianism, the philosophy established by the Chinese scholar Confucius in the sixth and fifth centuries B.C.E. This Korean painting, dating from the seventeenth century C.E., depicts a Confucian classroom.

tributed greatly to raising the level of education of the early Japanese aristocracy.

In the late sixteenth century, Japan's abortive efforts to conquer China via Korea earned Japan centuries of enmity from the Koreans. Organized by the Japanese samurai warlord, Toyotomi Hideyoshi (r. 1536–1598), the invasions in 1592 and 1597 by an army of over 200,000 Japanese nobles and retainers left Korea devastated and dependent upon assistance from the ruling emperor of the Chinese Ming dynasty.

Native Chinese and Korean rulers were overrun in the thirteenth and fourteenth centuries by the Yuan dynasty established by the Mongol leader Kublai Khan (r. 1260–1294), the grandson of the great Genghis Khan (r. 1206–1227). Korea remained a vassal state to China from 1231 to 1336.

Japan, on the other hand, resisted the Mongol invasions. Two massive invasions by Kublai Khan's forces in 1274 and 1281 were repulsed by spirited Japanese

CHINESE DYNASTIES (1766 B.C.E.–1912 C.E.)

SHANG (YIN) DYNASTY*	1766–1045 B.C.E.
WESTERN CHOU DYNASTY*	1045–771 B.C.E.
EASTERN CHOU DYNASTY*	770–249 B.C.E.
CH'IN DYNASTY*	221–207 B.C.E.
WESTERN HAN DYNASTY*	207 B.C.E.–9 C.E.
HSIN DYNASTY	9–24
EASTERN HAN DYNASTY*	25–220

Three Kingdoms Period

WEI DYNASTY	220–266
MINOR HAN DYNASTY	221–263
WU DYNASTY	222–280
WESTERN CHIN DYNASTY	266–316

Southern Dynasties

EASTERN CHIN DYNASTY	317–420
LIU SUNG DYNASTY	420–479
SOUTHERN CH'I DYNASTY	479–502
LIANG DYNASTY*	502–557
CH'EN DYNASTY	557–589

Northern Dynasties

NORTHERN WEI DYNASTY*	386–534
EASTERN WEI DYNASTY	534–550
NORTHERN CH'I DYNASTY	550–557
WESTERN WEI DYNASTY	535–557
NORTHERN CHOU DYNASTY	557–581

SUI DYNASTY*	581–618
T'ANG DYNASTY*	618–907

Five Dynasties Period

LATER LIANG DYNASTY	907–37
LATER T'ANG DYNASTY	923–937
LATER CHIN DYNASTY	937–947
LATER HAN DYNASTY	947–951
LATER CHOU DYNASTY	951–960
NORTHERN SUNG DYNASTY*	960–1127
SOUTHERN SUNG DYNASTY*	1127–1279
YUAN (MONGOL) DYNASTY*	1206–1368
MING DYNASTY*	1368–1644
CH'ING (MANCHU) DYNASTY*	1644–1912

KOREAN KINGDOMS AND DYNASTIES (37 B.C.E.–1910 C.E.)

KOGURYO KINGDOM*	37 B.C.E–668 C.E.
PAEKCHE KINGDOM*	18 B.C.E.–661 C.E.
SILLA KINGDOM*	57 B.C.E.–935 C.E.
KORYO KINGDOM*	918 C.E.–1392 C.E. (Wang Dynasty)
CHOSON KINGDOM (YI DYNASTY)*	1392–1910

JAPANESE IMPERIAL COURTS AND SHOGUNATES (ca. 40 B.C.E.–Present)

Imperial Courts

YAMATO DYNASTY*	CA. 40 B.C.E–707 C.E.
NARA EMPERORS*	707–781

Japanese Imperial Courts *(continued)*		MODERN EMPERORS	1867—PRESENT
HEIAN EMPERORS*	781–1185		
KAMAKURA EMPERORS	1183–1318	**Shogunates**	
DUAL DYNASTIES		KAMAKURA SHOGUNATE*	1192–1333
SOUTHERN COURT	1318–1392	ASHIKAGA SHOGUNATE*	1338–1573
NORTHERN COURT	1331–1382	TOKUGAWA SHOGUNATE*	1603–1868
MUROMACHI EMPERORS	1382–1586		
TOKUGAWA EMPERORS	1586–1867	*Indicates a separate alphabetical entry.	

resistance, aided by two enormous storms that engulfed the Mongol fleets. The typhoons were called *kamikaze* (divine winds), and their appearance to foil the Mongol fleets reinforced the enduring Japanese belief that the gods were protecting their land.

POST-FIFTEENTH CENTURY

From the sixteenth to the nineteenth century, most East Asian rulers imposed upon their realms strict isolation from the Western world as well as from each other. During this period, the countries of the region enjoyed relative peace under formal, strict, hierarchical regimes and increasingly self-centered, if not corrupt, leaders.

While Western missionaries, traders, and U.S. gunboat diplomacy successfully forced China and Japan to reopen the gates of East Asia in the last half of the nineteenth century, Korea resisted Western demands. However, by 1874, Japan was strong enough to force Korea to grant extra favorable trading terms and privileges; similar Korean treaties followed with the Europeans and Americans.

By the end of the nineteenth century, Meiji Japan had once again demonstrated the nation's ability to study, learn, absorb, and internalize foreign ideas and influences, this time from the West. Well on the way to becoming a major industrial and military power of the twentieth century, Japan was victorious in the armed clash with China over Korea during the Sino-Japanese War (1894–1895) and again in the Russo-Japanese War (1904–1905) fought over Korea and Manchuria. Korea became a colony of Japan in 1910, ending more than five hundred years of independent rule. It would remain a colony until the end of World War II.

SHARED CULTURAL VALUES

Across the ages, East Asian culture has been marked by Korea and Japan's willingness to borrow from China. Korean and Japanese leaders, together with their societies, regularly incorporated Chinese ideas, institutions, religion, art, and other cultural influences without sacrificing their own distinctive national cultures.

Both Korea and Japan adopted the Chinese characters for their written script, even though their languages were structurally different from Chinese. It is generally acknowledged that the Koreans passed the Chinese character script to the Japanese sometime around the early to mid-fifth century, even though it was likely not unknown in Japan as early as the first century.

The influence of Chinese literature and culture in the East Asian kingdoms reached a high point during the T'ang dynasty (618–907). During the Nara Period in Japan (710–794), the Japanese elite looked to China for cultural and political inspiration, and the Japanese imperial court maintained extensive contact with China via embassies of several hundred men.

Having subjugated both the Paekche and Koguryo kingdoms in Korea, the ruler of Silla then forced out the Chinese in 676 and created the Unified Silla kingdom on the Korean Peninsula, which lasted until 935. The military success of the Silla against the Chinese provided the frame for a unique, local culture with historical writings, elegant pottery, and a distinct architectural style.

At the end of the eighth century, both the new Japanese capital at Heian-kyo (modern Kyoto) and the new Korean capital of Kyongju were laid out to mirror the grid of the T'ang capital city of Chang-an.

Nonetheless, to the Japanese and Korean aristocracies, China was at times an inspiration and at other times simply a bother. By the late ninth century, for example, the leading Japanese scholar of Chinese literature, Sugawara Michizane, refused an ambassadorship to China because he claimed that China had nothing more to teach Japan.

Social Organization

The social organization of the East Asian nations at key historical moments owed much to the classical Chinese Confucian model and was deeply influenced across the centuries by both Confucian and Buddhist tenets of law, ethics, and class organization.

Both Japan and Korea incorporated Chinese Confucian concepts of centralized administration and the appointment of "qualified" government officials. Korea closely modeled its official examination system upon the Chinese Confucian model but went even further by requiring not one but two examinations.

The centralized governmental institutions set up in Japan during the Taika Reforms of 645, which rapidly evolved into a highly centralized system of administration, were copied from the Chinese Confucian model with significant Japanese modifications. But the rule of merit in Japan more often than not lost out to powerful traditions of clan loyalty and privilege.

Land and Taxes

Historically, the East Asian societies were land-based economies that relied on hierarchical bureaucratic institutions to collect local taxes and maintain order at the local levels. Sometimes, the central government would claim all land, which it would then allocate for production; sometimes local aristocracy or local administrators controlled or owned the land, and collections proceeded "up the ladder."

Generally, direct or indirect taxes on rice and agricultural production subsidized the central authorities and the military in East Asia and weighed heavily on the peasants and rural villages. The tension and competition between ruling houses and clans and the outlying aristocracy, administrators, and/or tax-exempt landowners is a recurring theme in the history of the East Asian kingdoms.

CONFUCIANISM

The all-encompassing Chinese humanistic philosophy of Confucianism is a way of life rather than an organized religion. Classical Confucianism never prevented its East Asian followers from also being Buddhists, Christians, Shintoists, Taoists, or adherents of any other religious tradition. Along with Buddhism, Confucian teaching permeates the culture and institutions of East Asian kingdoms. It is based upon the ideas and writings of Chinese scholar/philosopher Confucius, which date from the sixth and fifth centuries B.C.E.

Confucianism and Neo-Confucianism have been continually studied and reinterpreted over the centuries in East Asia. It is extremely difficult to summarize outside a given historical context the precise relationship between Confucian moral idealism and the concrete social and political realities of any given era in any given East Asian society.

Confucian philosophy focuses on ideas of harmony as related to law, economics, and politics, and constantly redefines the proper relationships between ruler and ruled, between justice and obligation. Confucianism usually implies a strong central government, a ruler of virtue, a viable court system, and an educated bureaucracy of responsible administrators. The classical Chinese model prescribed rigid qualifying examinations for civil servants.

After periods of social and political unrest, East Asian rulers frequently invoked Confucianism to reestablish order and the authority of the central government. For example, the founder of the Ming dynasty in China immediately reinstituted the rituals of Confucianism, which had been neglected or corrupted by the preceding Yuan dynasty, which was of "foreign" Mongolian origin.

Intent upon centralizing control over the aristocracy, the first ruler in the Yi dynasty of Korea, T'ae-jo (r. 1392–1398), officially adopted Confucian ethics in place of Buddhism. He also set up Confucian learning centers and adopted the Chinese system of civil examinations.

The social organization of the Tokugawa shogunate in Japan (1603–1868) was a reaction against the nearly three centuries of ceaseless civil conflict that preceded it. The Japanese warlord, Tokugawa Ieyasu (r. 1603–1605), instituted a new, rigid hierarchy of four social classes, each with its own subclasses and its designated role in society—warrior, peasant, artisan, and merchant. The peasants represented the bulk of the Japanese population, produced the rice, and in the neo-Confucian philosophy were more important than artisans or merchants because they were the essential "producers." The Meiji restoration in Japan after 1868 banned Buddhist practices from imperial ceremonies, in favor of Confucian and Shinto rites that institutionalized the role of the divine emperor.

Confucianism probably reached maximum influence in China under the Ch'ing dynasty (1644–1912).

Ch'ing rulers based their highly centralized political system of control on Confucian ideals.

BUDDHISM

Buddhism is the other major ideology that permeates East Asian thinking and history. The religion originated in India, and it first took hold in China during the second century alongside Taoism and Confucianism. Buddhist ideas became influential in fourth-century China, although Buddhism suffered a setback in China during a period of persecution in 845 under the T'ang revival of Confucianism.

The Korean kingdom of Koguryo adopted Buddhism as the state religion in 372 and set up the National Confucian Academy. About the same time, the ruler of the Paekche kingdom supported the introduction of Buddhism. The state religion of the Silla kingdom was Buddhism, and some of the finest Buddhist monuments were built in southeastern Korea during this period.

Although Korean refugees introduced Buddhism to Japan as early as the fourth century, the Paekche ruler of Korea officially introduced it to the Japanese imperial court in the mid-sixth century with a gift of sacred writings and a grand Buddhist image. Japanese prince Shotoku (r. 574–622) converted and championed the introduction of things both Chinese and Buddhist to Japan.

The Japanese emperor Shomu (r. 724–749) was a devout Buddhist who blamed the suffering of the people on his own inadequacies. He commissioned Buddhist temples for each province of Japan as well as the imperial capital at Nara. The Buddhist centers were meant to be the physical instruments that unified the spiritual and political realms.

The cultural legacy of the Japanese warrior society from the Ashikaga shogunate through the Tokugawa shogunate reflected the Zen Buddhist ideals of simplicity, restraint, discipline, and meditation—in contrast to almost constant outside disorder.

Buddhist monasteries in East Asia were often wealthy, powerful institutions that controlled their own land and sometimes their own military forces. Historically, there was a recurring tension in East Asia between the Buddhist strongholds and the political rulers, leading from time to time to repression or destruction of the monasteries.

In 1392, for example, the founder of the Yi (Choson) dynasty of Korea confiscated Buddhist temple lands and set up strict controls over Buddhist monks.

The Japanese samurai warlord Oda Nobunaga burned out the Mount Hiei Buddhist monastery in 1571, slaughtering about three thousand individuals, and in 1574, he burned the Buddhist complex at Nagashima, home of the fanatical Ikko sect of Buddhists, massacring an estimated twenty thousand men, women, and children.

See also: BUDDHISM AND KINGSHIP; KOGURYO KINGDOM; PAEKCHE KINGDOM; SILLA KINGDOM.

EDO KINGDOM. *See* BENIN KINGDOM

EDUCATION OF KINGS

The schooling required to prepare the prince (and sometimes the princess) to rule the kingdom.

The education of kings has two goals: to prepare the heir apparent to be an effective ruler; and to embed into the consciousness of the heir apparent a profound and enlightened understanding of what is expected of the next monarch. The first goal encompasses the skills needed to be an effective administrator, legislator, judge, and/or mediator; the second, the development of personal qualities of leadership and honor. Historically, the two goals of princely education are neither synonymous nor even necessarily complementary.

The content of the curriculum for a king-to-be is determined by the political and religious philosophies of the society into which the prince is born, by the beliefs of those closest to the throne, and by the economic trends and realities of the day. How much history or fine arts, how many and which languages, how much music or dancing, how much poetry or literature, how much science or religious philosophy, how much geography or commerce, how much math and engineering, how much economics and politics, how much horseback riding and shooting—are all weighted by time and place in the royal curriculum, even when the student shows distinct personal interests and aptitudes.

SOCIAL CONTRACT

The obligations of a ruler to his people form the basis of the social contract. High on the list of subjects that should be studied are the arts of war and diplomacy necessary to a nation's survival. Equally important in learning the fine art of governing is an awareness of the popular expectation, or tenuous hope, that rulers will be wise in the choice of advisers, fair in rendering justice, and firm in maintaining order.

Kings must learn when and how to observe popular cultural taboos and to respect the proprieties of court life down to the finest detail: Do they eat alone or at the head of the table? How must they dress in public and at court? How are their subjects allowed to approach them? How many temples must they build to atone for national misfortunes? What sports please the populace? What earns the loyalty of the nobles? What sacrifices do they owe the populace?

APPOINTED TUTORS

Historically, it was unusual for a crown prince to be enrolled in a formal school or university; instead, learning took place at a royal palace or in special classrooms. In addition, it was unusual for the ruling king or queen to personally oversee the day-to-day training of the royal heir, no matter how involved the current ruler may be in shaping the curriculum.

Whether for a child king awaiting coronation at maturity or a grown prince assuming the throne at the death of the former ruler, the education of a designated heir has been generally placed in the hands of nurses, tutors, doctors, regents, queen mothers, councilors, wealthy courtiers, powerful politicians, and/or religious leaders and sages. Such arrangements foster intrigue and plotting at court among the prince's entourage and the ruler's councilors and are the informal base of the heir's political education.

Both the two leading European Renaissance treatises on the education of kings—*The Prince* (1513) by Niccolò Machiavelli, and *Education of a Christian Prince* (1516) by Desiderius Erasmus—stress the necessity of giving the heir apparent the ability to recognize and resist sycophants and flatterers.

Neither Henry VIII of England (r. 1509–1547) nor Peter the Great of Russia (r. 1682–1725) was educated as an heir apparent but rather with other royal children, and both took the thrones only after their older brothers' untimely deaths. Their biographers often cite this fact when describing their inquisitive intellects, their personal confidence, and their athletic prowess, implying that both were extremely lucky to have escaped the stultifying atmosphere in which their brothers were trained to be kings.

The court of child-king Louis XIV (r. 1643–1715) in France was turbulent during the regency of the queen mother, Anne of Austria, and her adviser, Cardinal Mazarin, and the politics of the time provided the Sun-King with an entirely different set of lessons from his formal schooling.

The court of Henry II of England (r. 1154–1189) and his wife Eleanor of Aquitaine held literature, learning, and music in very high esteem, which may have inspired the restless adventures of their children, Richard I the Lionheart (r. 1189–1199) and his younger brother, John (r. 1199–1216).

DIVINE DESCENT

Under a "sacred kingship," kingship may be divinely bestowed upon the descendants of the gods or divinely blessed by the sanction of religion, or the ruler may be considered the personification of a divine being.

When the king is considered a divine being, the religious leaders control the king's schooling, and usually a mystical or cult relationship exists between the ruler and the priests, as with, for example, the Incan and Aztec rulers and the Egyptian pharoahs. Tribal myths and rituals play a key role in this case, and the heir is anointed via ritual initiations and mystical ceremonies. Even in modern monarchies, vestiges of religious ritual permeate coronation oaths and prayers.

On the other hand, divine rulers, such as the puppet emperors of Japan during the period of the shogunates, were sometimes more important as an icon of legitimacy than as a sacred ruling force. For centuries up to the Meiji restoration in 1868, Japanese emperors were educated to their ceremonial roles, being highly trained in refined cultural arts like the tea ceremony or haiku poetry, but lacking training in the political or military arts.

CHRISTIAN KINGS

In Christian kingdoms, the Church sanctioned the divine rights of kings and laid out the monarch's obligation to defend the faith, maintain order, protect the poor, render justice, and protect the realm from its enemies. In addition to the religious responsibili-

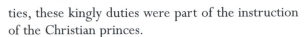

ties, these kingly duties were part of the instruction of the Christian princes.

During the medieval period in Europe (ca. late 400s–early 1500s), the lessons of chivalric duty between lords and vassals were crucial parts of a royal education. The king was a lord among lords fighting for his realms, and his military might depended as much upon maintaining the support of the noble knights as upon his own skill on horseback with a lance and sword.

By the seventeenth century, the curriculum of kings, like that of the European universities and upper classes, embraced the concepts of rationalism enunciated by French philosopher René Descartes: learning was based on reason as the source of all knowledge. Over the eighteenth century, secularism grew, and the curriculum expanded to include the sciences and courses taught in the popular languages instead of Latin or Greek. Pedagogy became an intellectual discipline on its own.

HEREDITY OR ELECTION

Elected rulers must be educated in politics and diplomacy as well as administrative and military competence. There are fewer elected rulers in history than those born to the throne. Such rulers tend to be found in societies that are not overly hierarchical and that have multiple seats of power. In Europe, for example, elected rulers were mostly the earlier kings who rose to power after the decline of the Roman Empire, including the Holy Roman emperor.

Hereditary kings, on the other hand, are of necessity well schooled in the dynasties and families of other royal and aristocratic houses. They are also schooled in the art of procreation, for the royal marriage has two explicit goals: to acquire lands by marriage; and to produce an heir to hold the realm together. The rules of marriage and inheritance are fundamental to the culture of each monarchy and contribute greatly to treacheries such as coups, assassination, abductions, and palace conspiracies.

See also: ACCESSION AND CROWNING OF KINGS; CONSORTS, ROYAL; ENTHRONEMENT, RITES OF; INHERITANCE, ROYAL; LEGITIMACY.

FURTHER READING

Erasmus, Desiderius. *Education of a Christian Prince.* Trans. Neil M. Cheshire and Michael J. Heath. New York: Cambridge University Press, 1997.

Marvick, Elizabeth Wirth. *Louis XIII: The Making of a King.* New Haven, CT: Yale University Press, 1986.

Painter, Sidney. *French Chivalry: Chivalric Ideas and Practices in Mediaeval France.* Ithaca, NY: Cornell University Press, 1969.

EDWARD I (1239–1307 C.E.)

King of England (r. 1272–1307), known also as Edward Longshanks, who embodied most of the kingly attributes admired by the people of the time. Edward I joined a Crusade to the Holy Land, administered justice and laws fairly to his people, and ruthlessly campaigned to expand and protect what he saw as his birthright. The futures of Wales and Scotland were particularly affected by his actions.

Born in 1239 to King Henry III (r. 1216–1272) of the Angevin dynasty and to Eleanor of Provence, Edward was raised in a disciplined and highly cultured environment. At age fifteen, he traveled to Spain to meet and marry the nine-year-old Eleanor of Castile. When he returned, his father bequeathed him the royal holdings in Ireland, Wales, the Channel Islands, and Gascony (in France) to support him and his household. This gift presaged Edward's future preoccupations with the borders of the English realm.

Henry III was not a well-loved monarch, and Edward was embroiled in complex court intrigues at an early age. Henry's brother-in-law, Simon de Montfort, was the most powerful of the king's opponents, and for a brief time Edward allied with Montfort against his father. However, during the Baron's War (1263–1267), Edward switched his allegiance back to his father and was captured by Montfort in 1265. Edward cleverly escaped and shortly thereafter defeated Montfort at the battle of Eavesham, ending Montfort's threat and his life.

In 1270, Edward I pledged to travel to the Holy Land to join Louis IX (r. 1226–1270) in a Crusade. When he reached Palestine, Edward learned that Louis had died shortly earlier in Tunis, and the remaining Crusaders were quarrelsome and in complete disarray. Undaunted, Edward pledged to raise the siege at Acre (which he did) and to prosecute the holy war against the Muslims completely on his own, if necessary.

Edward was partially successful in rallying the

King Edward I of England left a legacy of accomplishment in civic administration, law, justice, and conquest. Portrayed here in a nineteenth-century engraving, Edward was said to embody the best and noblest attributes of a medieval monarch.

Christians—enough so that the Egyptian sultan Baibars hired a member of the Hashashin (a secret Islamic sect) to assassinate this troublesome newcomer. Edward foiled the assassin's attack but was poisoned grabbing a poison-covered blade during the struggle. Miraculously, he survived but decided to return to England. When he reached Sicily, he learned that his father was dead. Edward hastened back to England and was crowned king at Westminster in 1272.

During his reign, Edward determined to enforce the English Crown's claims to all of the British Isles. He began with a successful war in Wales (1277–1282) against Llewelyn ap Gruffyd (r. 1246–1282), prince of Gwynedd, who had insulted him by refusing to come to his coronation. Edward raised a large sum to build a ring of defensive castles along the northern Welsh coast and defeated the prince at every encounter. Llewellyn's death in battle in 1282 marked the end of Welsh autonomy.

Edward's other passion, and his most lasting con-

tribution, was his skill and devotion to administration and parliamentary procedure. He summoned Parliament twice a year until 1286. Then, in 1295, he summoned the so-called Model Parliament, which was the first ever to have representatives not just from the barons, the knights, and the Church, but from every borough and town in England.

Although his primary purpose in summoning these Parliaments was to raise funds for his treasury, Edward was assiduous as a lawmaker as well. His legacies include the regulating of wool; levying just and reasonable taxes and licenses; curbing corruption by local magistrates and officials; codifying and regularizing local laws that defined royal rights, privileges, and abuses; limiting feudal rights and entailments (thus restricting the power of the barons); and establishing equal rights for all.

When the Scottish king, Alexander III (r. 1249–1286), died in 1286 and his heir Margaret, the Maid of Norway, died four years later, the Scottish nobles asked Edward to decide the Scottish succession. Edward's beloved Eleanor died the same year, and with her passed one of his two best advisers. Edward claimed sovereign lordship of Scotland and decided in favor of the claimant John Balliol.

In 1294, Edward's longtime chancellor, Robert Burnell, died; his death removed the last check on Edward's strong will. Shortly thereafter, Edward summoned Balliol to Westminster on a pretense. Offended, the Scottish nobles approached King Philip IV of France and signed an alliance against England and Edward. Edward retaliated in 1296 by sacking Berwick-upon-Tweed, an important Scottish gateway to the Lowlands and the North Sea coast. He then took Edinburgh and stole the Stone of Scone, a relic that was required for Scottish coronations. Faced with this humiliating loss, John Balliol surrendered Scotland to Edward and retired to exile in France.

Returning victorious from Scotland, Edward faced huge debts, rebellious nobles, and a recalcitrant clergy. He gladly signed a treaty with Philip IV of France in 1303 in which the English claim to Gascony in southwestern France was affirmed. However, Edward's policies in Scotland continued to haunt him. He narrowly defeated the popular rebel leader, William Wallace, at Falkirk in 1298. But one of his hand-picked Scots, Robert the Bruce (r. 1306–1329), rebelled and was crowned king of Scotland in 1306.

On his way to another campaign in Scotland in 1307, Edward died at age sixty-eight. He was succeeded by his son, Edward II (r. 1307–1327). For the next two hundred years, Edward's black marble tomb in Westminster held burning candles commemorating this remarkable king's achievements.

See also: ANGEVIN DYNASTIES; EDWARD II; ENGLISH MONARCHIES; LLYWELYN AP GRUFFYDD; PHILIP IV, THE FAIR; PLANTAGENET DYNASTY; ROBERT I (ROBERT THE BRUCE); SCOTTISH KINGDOMS; WELSH KINGDOMS.

FURTHER READING

Durant, Will. *The Age of Faith.* New York: Simon and Schuster, 1950.

Prestwich, Michael. *Three Edwards: War and State in England, 1272–1377.* London: Routledge, 1980.

EDWARD II (1284–1327 C.E.)

King of England (r. 1307–1327) whose policies and favoritism toward certain retainers led to rebellion and his eventual abdication from the throne.

Edward was the son of King Edward I (r. 1272–1307) and Eleanor of Castile. Born in Wales, he became the first English heir to the throne to receive the title prince of Wales, which he received in 1301. As heir to the throne, and later as ruler of England, Edward II received little respect from his contemporaries. His father, Edward I Longshanks, possessed all the medieval kingly requisites: physical size and prowess, keen intellect, enormous appetites, and a ferocious temper. Edward, on the other hand, was a beautiful, meek, and sensitive individual who preferred bricklaying to swordplay and conversation to coercion. Longshanks' bitter disappointment in his son is recorded in a number of chronicles from the period.

Edward I not only dominated his son in terms of character, but he even chose his son's wife, Isabella of France. Isabella was the daughter of the notoriously cunning King Philip IV of France (r. 1285–1314). Her abilities and temperament proved equal to her father's and, eventually, too much for her hapless husband. Caught between the powerful characters of his father and his wife, Edward II was often considered a weak ruler; his own weaknesses and failings did little to contradict that view.

Edward's first great failing was the trust he put in Piers Gaveston, an intimate friend and adviser whom Edward raised to the earldom of Cornwall. Edward seems to have been the only person who saw great things in the new earl. Gaveston was intensely disliked and resisted by the other English aristocracy, partly because of Edward's favoritism toward him. Despite Edward's continued but ineffectual attempts to protect his friend, Gaveston was murdered by the earl of Warwick in 1312. Edward mourned Gaveston, whom tradition has labeled as Edward's lover, but Edward did not punish Warwick for the deed.

In 1314, Edward decided to continue his father's war on Scotland. He raised a great army and marched on Stirling Castle, but was beaten by the forces of Robert the Bruce in the vale of Bannockburn on June 24, 1314. It was the worst defeat of English forces on their own island since the defeat of King Harold II Godwinson (r. 1066) by the forces of William the Conqueror at the battle of Hastings in 1066.

This catastrophe in Scotland did not enhance Edward's reputation, and he had increasing difficulty finding any English barons who would support him or his policies. Two who did—Hugh Le Despenser, the earl of Winchester, and his son, also named Hugh—became Edward's new court favorites. The Despensers gained increasing power, making them as unpopular as the ill-fated Piers Gaveston and leading in 1321 to a revolt against them led by Edward's cousin, the earl of Lancaster. However, the revolt failed to remove the Despensers, who continued to dominate Edward.

Meanwhile, Queen Isabella, alienated by Edward's neglect toward her, was living with her brother in France. While there, she became the lover of Roger Mortimer, an English baron who had participated in the revolt against Despensers and afterward escaped to France. Isabella and Mortimer gathered forces and invaded England in 1326. They trapped and assassinated the Despensers and captured Edward, forcing him to abdicate the throne. Imprisoned, Edward was murdered in 1327, no doubt at the orders of Isabella and Mortimer. Isabella proclaimed her son, the fifteen-year-old Edward III (r. 1327–1377), the new king and assumed the role of regent until 1330.

See also: DETHRONEMENT; EDWARD I; EDWARD III; HOMOSEXUALITY AND KINGSHIP; PLANTAGENET,

House of; Regicide; Robert I (Robert the Bruce).

EDWARD III (1312–1377 C.E.)

King of England (r. 1327–1377) of the House of Plantagenet, who is often cited as the model for medieval chivalry and kingship. Although considered a role model, Edward began and presided over the early stages of the ruinous Hundred Years' War with France (1337–1453). Ultimately, the damages caused by that war, as well as the ravages caused by the first incursions of the Black Death into England, marked Edward's reign more indelibly than his chivalrous demeanor.

EARLY LIFE AND RULE

Edward III was born in 1312 to King Edward II of England (r. 1307–1327) and to Isabella, the daughter of King Philip IV of France (r. 1285–1314) and sister of King Louis X of France (r. 1314–1316). In 1325, Edward was taken to France by his mother, who had become alienated from her husband because of his neglect. Edward became king of England two years later, at age fifteen, when his mother and her supporters overthrew his father, forced Edward II to abdicate, and later killed the king. Isabella and her lover, Roger Mortimer, ruled England as regents for three years. When Edward turned eighteen, however, he rebelled against the regents, executed Roger, and sequestered away his mother.

As Isabella's son, Edward III had a claim on the throne of France as well. He first claimed the French crown in 1328 upon the death of Charles IV (r. 1322–1328). He renewed his claim again in 1337, during the reign of Philip VI (r. 1328–1350). He launched two unsuccessful invasions of France in 1339 and in 1340, and, undeterred, named himself king of France in 1340, despite the fact that Philip VI still reigned. Edward's actions mark the beginning of the Hundred Years' War, which eventually would decimate the populations of both England and France and which would not be resolved until well into the fifteenth century.

WAR, PLAGUE, AND PARLIAMENT

Edward III was himself a strong and successful warrior, but he relied primarily on the abilities of his son and heir, Edward (called the Black Prince), for the promotion of his war in France. Edward III's most famous battle against the French was the victory at Crècy in 1346, where a larger force of French troops armed with crossbows was overwhelmed by the English and their longbows.

A catastrophe even more costly in human lives than the Hundred Years' War began during the reign of Edward III: the coming of the Black Death, the term used at the time for the bubonic plague. The first outbreak of the plague in England occurred in 1348, and it returned with devastating effect in 1361 and again in 1369.

The Black Death killed millions of people; the population losses it incurred had dramatic cultural and economic effects throughout Europe. In England, the depredations suffered by the populace as a result of both the war and plague were so great that Edward enacted the Statute of Labourers in 1351 in a futile attempt to freeze wages and prices. The population and, therefore, the labor pool had shrunk so considerably that serfs and laborers were able to begin "asking a price" for their work because of the shortage of workers. The increased power of feudal serfs and laborers was ultimately to prove a mortal blow to the feudal system.

Edward's military campaigns resulted in an important new development in the English Parliament. During Edward's reign, the House of Commons gained increasing power in Parliament. The king's need for revenue to pay for his wars enabled the Commons to assert their right to have a say in matters of taxation, and Edward was forced to grant them concessions in order to secure support.

FINAL YEARS

Edward's wife, Philippa of Hainault, died in 1369, leaving the king without one of his trusted advisers. Meanwhile, his son, the Black Prince, was occupied in the wars in France. As a result, during his later years, Edward was guided by two advisers. The first was his son John of Gaunt (father of the future King Henry IV), who led his aging, more pliable father in matters of statecraft and the disposition of laws and privileges. The second was Edward's mistress, Alice Perrers, who, to the dismay of the court, directed the king's attentions in all personal matters.

When Edward died in 1377, he had been on the throne for fifty years. He had established the Order of the Garter in 1342 to promote chivalry, had had his own Round Table built, conducted innumerable tournaments and pageants, and had refused an offer to become the Holy Roman emperor in 1348. In short, he had been a model of late medieval kingship. On the other hand, he had begun a ruinous, unwinnable war against France, had the bad luck to be king during the worst outbreak of plague that England had yet known, and had generally lost the confidence of his people. Edward's oldest son and heir, Edward, the Black Prince, predeceased his father by one year. The king was thus succeeded by his grandson, the ten-year-old Richard II (r. 1377–1399), who was the son of the Black Prince.

See also: DISEASE AND ROYALTY; EDWARD I; EDWARD II; ENGLISH MONARCHIES; HENRY IV (ENGLAND); LITERATURE AND KINGSHIP; MILITARY ROLES, ROYAL; PHILIP IV, THE FAIR; PLANTAGENET, HOUSE OF; RICHARD II.

FURTHER READING

Ormrod, W.M. *The Reign of Edward III.* New Haven: Yale University Press, 1990.

EDWARD THE CONFESSOR

(ca. 1003–1066 C.E.)

King of Wessex and England (r. 1042–1066), who was known more for his piety than his effectiveness in ruling. Edward was canonized a saint in 1161; it was because of his piety that he is known as "the Confessor." His lack of an heir led to the Norman Conquest in 1066.

Edward was the son of Ethelred II the Unready (r. 978–1016) and Emma of Normandy. After the death of Ethelred in 1016, Edward's mother married Cnut the Great (r. 1016–1035) of Denmark, and Edward was sent to be raised at the home of his uncle in Normandy. After the death of Cnut in 1035, Edward unsuccessfully challenged Cnut's sons to claim the English throne; the title eventually was won by Edward's half brother, King Harthacnut (r. 1040–1042). When Harthacnut died without an heir in 1042, Edward, a descendant of Alfred the Great (r. 871–899), was the chosen heir to the English throne. He was crowned at Canterbury in 1042.

Edward's life in Normandy prior to becoming king had a significant influence on him, and he bestowed favors on Normans at the expense of the Anglo-Saxon nobles in England. Disputes over this and other issues led to the exile in 1051 of the powerful Anglo-Saxon earl, Godwin of Wessex. Godwin raised an army and forced Edward to yield him his former political power and to exile some of the Norman nobles.

After Godwin died in 1053, his son, Harold Godwinson, became the most powerful man in England. Overshadowed by Harold in political matters, Edward the Confessor withdrew to a life of religious devotion and focused his energy on supervising the rebuilding of Westminster Abbey in London.

Edward married Edith, the daughter of Godwin of Wessex, in 1045 when he was forty-two years old and she was at most twenty-five. The couple had no children, and there were rumors that the marriage had never been consummated. As a result, Edward had no direct heir to the throne. When he died on January 5, 1066, a rivalry between Harold II Godwinson and Duke William of Normandy (William the Conqueror) to succeed him led to the battle of Hastings and the Norman conquest of England.

See also: ALFRED THE GREAT; ENGLISH MONARCHIES; NORMAN KINGDOMS; WESSEX, KINGDOM OF; WILLIAM I, THE CONQUEROR.

EDWARD VI (1537–1553 C.E.)

King of England (r. 1547–1553), a member of the Tudor dynasty, whose brief and youthful reign is noted primarily for advancing Protestantism in England.

Edward was the only son of King Henry VIII (r. 1509–1547) and the king's third wife, Jane Seymour. When Henry VIII died in 1547, Edward succeeded him as Edward VI. Edward was only nine years old at the time. As a result of Edward's youth, his ministers governed more than he did, although his involvement did increase as he matured. For the first few years of his reign, Edward's uncle, Edward Seymour, the duke of Somerset, ruled as regent. After Somerset's fall from power, he was replaced by John Dudley, the duke of Northumberland.

Edward VI has a reputation for being deeply Protestant, but because of his youth, it is difficult to determine whether decisions regarding religion, as well as other matters, were his own or those of his ministers. Very early in his reign, in 1549, Somerset organized Protestant worship with the Act of Uniformity, which required use of the Book of Common Prayer. Reaction to this religious change led to civil unrest between Protestants and Catholics in southwest England that same year. The rebellion was suppressed by military force. Unrest also arose in Norfolk in 1549; the issue was not religion, however, but the action of local landlords in setting high rents and enclosing public lands. Blamed for the civil unrest, the duke of Somerset lost power in 1549 and was executed in 1552.

In 1550, John Dudley, the earl of Warwick and a former member of Henry VIII's government, became lord president of the Royal Council. In 1551, he was named duke of Northumberland, and he became Edward's regent the following year. Under Dudley, the Church of England issued a Second Prayer Book in 1552. It eliminated all Catholic dogma and practices from the Protestant service. Dudley also ordered the destruction of many objects used in the mass, as well as religious artwork with Catholic themes.

Northumberland's power depended on Edward's kingship, and when Edward became sick in February 1553, Dudley's position was in jeopardy. A combination of Protestant loyalty and Northumberland's influence led Edward to declare that the succession would skip his half-sisters Mary and Elizabeth. Instead, the Crown would pass to Lady Jane Grey, a great-granddaughter of Henry VII (r. 1485–1509) and, conveniently, the daughter-in-law of the duke of Northumberland.

Edward died in 1553 after a few months of illness, most likely a pulmonary infection. He was only fifteen years old. Lady Jane Grey was declared queen upon Edward's death, but this was successfully challenged a short time later by Edward's half-sister, Mary I (r. 1553–1558).

See also: ELIZABETH I; ENGLISH MONARCHIES; HENRY VIII; MARY I, TUDOR; TUDOR, HOUSE OF.

EGYPTIAN DYNASTIES, ANCIENT (BEFORE EIGHTEENTH DYNASTY) (ca. 3100–1570 B.C.E.)

The first dynasties of ancient Egypt, important for establishing the country and bringing it to levels of great power and influence in the ancient Near East.

The 3,000-year history of ancient Egypt's dynas-ties is one of endurance, vitality, and high culture. The kings of ancient Egypt, called pharaohs, were seen not as mere mortals but rather as god-kings whose power and authority within the kingdom were absolute and divinely given.

EARLY DYNASTIC PERIOD

Scholars have arranged the early Egyptian dynasties into periods, the first of which is called the Early Dynastic Period (ca. 3100–2755 B.C.E.) This period marks the unification of Upper Egypt and Lower Egypt and thus the beginning of a more centralized Egyptian kingdom.

According to Egyptian tradition, Menes (r. ca. 3100–3066 B.C.E.) was responsible for bringing the two lands together around 3100 B.C.E. and is considered the first pharaoh of Egypt. Historians disagree, however, over whether Menes was an actual pharaoh, whether this was another name for the early pharaoh also known as Narmer, or whether the story of Menes was merely legend.

Whatever the truth, Menes and the First dynasty (ca. 3100–2905 B.C.E.) is credited with building the first capital of Egypt at Memphis, near where Lower and Upper Egypt meet, and with successfully molding the variety of separate cultures along the Nile River into one cohesive country. Menes was believed to be descended from the Egyptian sun-god, Horus, who was usually represented as a falcon or a man with a falcon head. This First dynasty developed a calendar and encouraged the use of hieroglyphic writing.

During the Third dynasty (ca. 2755–2680 B.C.E.), Pharaoh Djoser (r. ca. 2737–2717 B.C.E.) had his final resting place built at Sakkarah in the form of a step pyramid. This pyramid was the first large-scale structure built out of stone and is a testament to the mastery and technical skill of the architects and builders of the time. It also attests to the pharaoh's place in society as a supreme ruler of enormous significance.

OLD KINGDOM

The period known as the Old Kingdom (ca. 2680–2255 B.C.E.) started with the Fourth dynasty (ca. 2680–2544 B.C.E.). This was a time of great wealth, stability, and cultural advances in architecture and sculpture for Egypt. By this time, the pharaohs had garnered the respect not only of their own people, but also of those in the rest of the ancient Near East as well.

Construction of the pyramids at Giza was perhaps the greatest engineering feat of the ancient world. Built by the pharaohs of the Fourth dynasty between about 2589 and 2530 B.C.E., these colossal tombs were named by Greek and Roman authors as one of the Seven Wonders of the World.

The Great Pyramids

The Fourth dynasty is probably best known for the pyramids that were built during this time. Snefru (r. 2680–2585 B.C.E.), the first pharaoh of this dynasty, built a pyramid at Dahshur, and his son and successor, Khufu (r. 2585–2560 B.C.E.), built the Great Pyramid at Giza. It and the three other pyramids built in the same vicinity became known as marvels of the ancient world.

During the Old Kingdom period, pharaohs were beginning to claim to be descended from the sun-god, Re. It is thought that the pyramid design may have been inspired by this attention to the sun, perhaps with the top of the pyramid pointing upward to guide the pharaoh to his afterlife in the heavens.

Nomes and Nomarchs

During the Old Kingdom period, Egypt was divided into districts called *nomes* that were ruled by *nomarchs*. Although the pharaohs initially appointed the nomarchs, they eventually came to see their power as

their own and passed it along to family members. Great economic stress was prevalent at this time, caused by the huge expense of building pyramids. It is also believed that the climate began to change; a sustained period of drought along the Nile caused hardship and famine.

All of these problems came to a head during the Sixth dynasty (ca. 2407–2255 B.C.E.), particularly during the long reign of the last important pharaoh of that dynasty, Pepy II (r. 2288–2194 B.C.E.). After Pepy's death, there was little central power to hold the country together. The nomarchs took control, and Egypt was maintained as a separate feudal state in which land was held by vassals in return for political and military service to the pharaoh. The country now entered a weakened period known as the First Intermediate Period (ca. 2255–2035 B.C.E.).

FIRST INTERMEDIATE PERIOD

During this period, Egypt was divided in two. Nomarchs of the Ninth and Tenth dynasties (ca. 2235–2035 B.C.E.) ruled from Herakleopolis in Lower Egypt. Somewhat simultaneously in Upper Egypt, monarchs of the Eleventh dynasty (ca. 2134–1991 B.C.E.) ruled from Thebes. The Upper and Lower Egyptian regimes warred with each other until the reign of Mentuhotep (r. ca. 2134–2118 B.C.E.) of the Theban Eleventh dynasty. Mentuhotep was able to conquer Herakleopolis with the help of the Nubians and to reunite the country.

MIDDLE KINGDOM

The reunification of Upper and Lower Egypt under Mentuhotep marks the beginning of the so-called Middle Kingdom (ca. 2134–1786 B.C.E.) and a period of strength and growth for a united Egypt. The first pharaoh of the Twelfth dynasty (ca. 1991–1786 B.C.E.), Amenemhet I (r. ca.1991–1962 B.C.E.), founded a city near Memphis called Itjtawy, which he made his capital. He and his successors were responsible for conquering Nubia as far as the second cataract, and then they moved north into Palestine where trade was increased. The Twelfth dynasty was also a period of renewed creativity in the arts, and literature flourished as did sculpture and painting. Egypt was restored to greatness.

SECOND INTERMEDIATE PERIOD

The Thirteenth dynasty (ca. 1786–1668 B.C.E.) and Fourteenth dynasty (ca. 1720–1665 B.C.E.), however, saw a weakening of royal power, and Egypt was invaded by a group of foreigners called the Hyksos—nomads who came from the northeast and settled near Egypt's eastern border in the city of Avaris. The Hyksos established what is called the Fifteenth dynasty (ca. 1668–1560 B.C.E.), which was the Third dynasty of the Second Intermediate Period (ca. 1680–1539 B.C.E.).

The Sixteenth dynasty (ca. 1665–1565 B.C.E.) and Seventeenth dynasty (ca. 1668–1570 B.C.E.) occurred nearly simultaneously with the Fifteenth dynasty of the Hyksos. While the Hyksos maintained control of the middle and northern parts of Egypt, the smaller and less influential Sixteenth dynasty had some control over parts of the delta and middle Egypt and the Seventeenth controlled the south from a base in Thebes.

See also: DJOSER; EGYPTIAN DYNASTIES, ANCIENT (EIGHTEENTH TO TWENTY-SIXTH); HYKSOS DYNASTY; KHUFU; MENES; NUBIAN KINGDOMS; THEBES KINGDOM.

FURTHER READING

Baines, John, and Jaromir Málek. *Atlas of Ancient Egypt.* New York: Facts on File, 1996.

Casson, Lionel. *Ancient Egypt.* Alexandria, VA: Time-Life Books, 1978.

Metz, Helen Chapin, ed. *Egypt: A Country Study.* 5th ed. Washington, DC: Federal Research Division, Library of Congress, 1991.

Silverman, David P., ed. *Ancient Egypt.* New York: Oxford University Press, 2003.

EGYPTIAN DYNASTIES, ANCIENT (EIGHTEENTH TO TWENTY-SIXTH) (ca. 1570–525 B.C.E.)

Series of dynasties that included some of the most famous and important pharaohs of ancient Egypt.

When the Eighteenth dynasty came to power in Egypt around 1570 B.C.E., the written record of Egyptian history was already some fifteen hundred years old, as many years as separate our own contemporary era from the fall of Rome. Egypt, from the Mediterranean Sea to Nubia at the cataracts of the Upper Nile River, was a single political, cultural, linguistic, and economic unit that had maintained its integrity even under the foreign rule of the Hyksos dynasty.

Nine hundred years later, by the end of the Twenty-fifth, or Kushite, dynasty, Egypt was still recognizably Egypt, but dramatic changes had occurred within the country and abroad. Egyptian independence, whether political or cultural, was no longer a given; in fact, it was not to last much beyond this era.

THE NEW KINGDOM AND THE EMPIRE

Ahmose I (r. 1570–1546 B.C.E.) is considered the first pharaoh of the Eighteenth dynasty. His reign also inaugurated what historians call the New Kingdom. After throwing off the "Asiatic" Hyksos overlords of the Sixteenth dynasty, Egypt's rulers made the fateful decision to build their own foreign empire, on the far side of the Sinai Desert.

Ahmose ascended the throne as a child, while the Hyksos still ruled from their capital at Avaris in the Nile Delta. His mother, Ahhotep I, ruled as regent, following the tradition of effective, powerful women set by Tetisheri, grandmother of Ahmose. Ahmose's wife Nefertari performed the same function during the childhood years of her son Amenophis I. All three women were revered after their deaths.

As soon as Ahmose reached his maturity, he turned north and waged a determined five-year campaign against the Hyksos, gradually retaking the old northern capital of Memphis, the entire Nile Delta, and then the last remaining Hyksos strongholds in southern Palestine. Sailing south down the Nile, he restored Egyptian control over Nubia as well, and then he set about restoring the administration of government. Training of civil bureaucrats became more institutionalized. Many officeholders in the New Kingdom were appointees from the ranks of the military, as fewer offices were passed along within bureaucratic families.

Ahmose probably extended Egyptian influence into the Ancient Near East. Cities in Syria are known to have paid tribute to his son, Amenhotep I (r. 1551–1524 B.C.E.). In any case, regular trade with the Near East resumed; prosperity and raw material imports led to an upsurge of artistic production.

The New Kingdom monarchs were intensely devoted to the Theban god Amon-Re, whose priests apparently supported the new imperial policies. The spoils of war were transferred to the temple cults;

This colossal statue shows the Egyptian pharaoh Akhenaten, also known as Amenhotep IV. A member of the Eighteenth Dynasty, he briefly revolutionized his people's religion by focusing devotion on only one god. After his death, however, the Egyptians abandoned the new religion and returned to their old gods.

these funds financed a long succession of major temple and tomb construction projects. The New Kingdom avoided above-ground funeral monuments; nearly all its pharaohs were buried in concealed graves in the Valley of the Kings near Thebes.

The next three pharaohs, Thutmose I (r. 1524–1518 B.C.E.), Thutmose II (r. 1518–1504 B.C.E.), and Thutmose III (r. 1504–1450 B.C.E.) expanded and consolidated Egyptian power in Asia. Naval power played a role in these campaigns, as Egyptian ships ferried troops to Phoenician ports for deployment inland. Egypt's influence was at its peak, as tribute poured in from Babylon, Assyria, and the Hittite Empire, but the dominant Mitanni kingdom was never actually defeated.

Egyptian conquests in Syria and Palestine were not directly integrated into the Egyptian state. Garrisons were left to ensure loyalty and collect tribute, but local government remained in place. The sons of local royal families were often educated at the Egyptian court before assuming local power as vassals of the empire. On the other hand, Nubia seems to have been fully incorporated at this time, its estates handed over to Egyptian temples, and its indigenous culture suppressed.

A powerful woman played a role in this period as well. Hatshepsut (r. 1503–1483 B.C.E.), a daughter of Thutmose I, ruled as regent, and for a while as king, during the childhood of her stepson Thutmose III. She ruled for some twenty years, supervising vast construction programs at Thebes. Hatshepsut was usually shown as a man in statues and documents.

The next several pharaohs seemed to shift the emphasis in Asia from conquest to diplomacy, with the first of a series of royal marriages with women from the Mitanni kingdom, located in Syria. Egypt seemed to be opening up to foreign influence as never before in the historic record. Imported or tribute goods from Syria, Phoenicia, Crete, and the Aegean Islands appear on Egyptian sculptural bas reliefs. Raw materials (especially silver) and finished art works found their way to Egypt, and foreign styles were often copied by Egyptian artisans.

Temples and inscriptions to Near Eastern gods like Reshef and Astarte also appeared in Egypt during this era. They were imported by some of the many immigrants who settled in Egypt and even rose to important positions in the administration. These gods were usually worshiped in Egyptian style and were eventually associated with native Egyptian deities.

These eclectic artistic influences competed with archaic tendencies, as pharaohs exploited the prestige of their ancient predecessors by imitating the style of their reliefs and inscriptions. It was Amenhotep III (r. 1386–1349 B.C.E.), in particular, who revived religious-political rituals of the past; ironically, his own son, Amenhotep IV (r. 1350–1334 B.C.E.), also known as Akhenaten, tried to make a clean break not only with the distant past, but with contemporary religious, political, artistic, and literary traditions.

THE AMARNA REVOLUTION

In the fourth year of Amenhotep IV's reign, the monarch changed his name to Akhenaten, to honor the Aten, or sun-disk. Egyptian religion had come to focus more and more on the sun-god, usually called Amun-Re, whose temples controlled much of the

New Kingdom	1570–1070 B.C.E.

Eighteenth Dynasty (at Thebes) — 1570–1293 B.C.E.

AHMOSE I*	1570–1546 B.C.E.
AMENHOTEP I	1551–1524 B.C.E.
THUTMOSE I	1524–1518 B.C.E.
THUTMOSE II	1518–1504 B.C.E.
QUEEN HATSHEPSUT*	1498–1483 B.C.E.
THUTMOSE III*	1504–1450 B.C.E.
AMENHOTEP II	1453–1419 B.C.E.
THUTMOSE IV	1419–1386 B.C.E.
AMENHOTEP III	1386–1349 B.C.E.
AKHENATEN* (AMENHOTEP IV)	1350–1334 B.C.E.
SMENKHKARE (CO-REGENT)	1336–1334 B.C.E.
TUTANKHAMEN*	1334–1325 B.C.E.
AY ITNEJER	1325–1321 B.C.E.
HOREMHEB	1321–1293 B.C.E.

Nineteenth Dynasty (at Thebes) — 1293–1185 B.C.E.

RAMSES I	1293–1291 B.C.E.
SETI I*	1291–1278 B.C.E.
RAMSES II*	1279–1212 B.C.E.
MERNEPTAH	1212–1202 B.C.E.
AMENMESES	1202–1199 B.C.E.
SETI II	1199–1193 B.C.E.
SIPTAH	1193–1187 B.C.E.
QUEEN TWORE	1187–1185 B.C.E.

Twentieth Dynasty (at Thebes) — 1185–1070 B.C.E.

SETNAKHT	1185–1182 B.C.E.
RAMSES III	1182–1151 B.C.E.
RAMSES IV	1151–1145 B.C.E.
RAMSES V	1145–1141 B.C.E.
RAMSES VI	1141–1133 B.C.E.
RAMSES VII	1133–1127 B.C.E.
RAMSES VIII	1127–1126 B.C.E.
RAMSES IX	1126–1108 B.C.E.
RAMSES X	1108–1098 B.C.E.
RAMSES XI	1098–1070 B.C.E.

Third Intermediate Period — 1069–525 B.C.E.

HIGH PRIESTS (AT THEBES)	1080–945 B.C.E.
HERIHOR	1080–1074 B.C.E.
PIANKH	1074–1070 B.C.E.
PINEDJEM	1070–1032 B.C.E.
MASAHERTA	1054–1046 B.C.E.
MENKHEPERRA	1045–992 B.C.E.
SMENDES II	992–990 B.C.E.
PINEDJEM II	990–969 B.C.E.
PSUSENNES III	969–945 B.C.E.

Twenty-first Dynasty (at Tanis) — 1069–945 B.C.E.

SMENDES I	1069–1043 B.C.E.
AMENEMNISU	1043–1039 B.C.E.

Twenty-first Dynasty (continued)

PSUSENNES I	1039–991 B.C.E.
AMENOPHTHIS	993–984 B.C.E.
OSORKON	984–978 B.C.E.
SIAMUNY	978–959 B.C.E.
PSUSENNES II	959–945 B.C.E.

Twenty-second Dynasty (at Tanis)   945–860 B.C.E.

SHESHONQ I	945–924 B.C.E.
OSORKON I	924–889 B.C.E.
SHESHONQ II	890 B.C.E.
TAKELOT I	889–874 B.C.E.
OSORKON II	874–850 B.C.E.
HARSIESE (AT THEBES)	870–860 B.C.E.
TAKELOT II	850–825 B.C.E.
SHESHONQ III	825–773 B.C.E.
PIMAY	773–767 B.C.E.
SHESHONQ V	767–730 B.C.E.
OSORKON IV	730–715 B.C.E.

Twenty-third Dynasty (at Leontopolis) 818–715 B.C.E.

PEDIBASTET	818–793 B.C.E.
SHESHONQ IV	793–787 B.C.E.
OSORKON III	787–759 B.C.E.

TAKELOT III	764–757 B.C.E.
RUDAMON	757–754 B.C.E.
IUPUT	754–715 B.C.E.

Twenty-fourth Dynasty (at Sais)   727–715 B.C.E.

TEFNAKHT	727–720 B.C.E.
BAKENRANEF	720–715 B.C.E.

Twenty-fifth Dynasty (Kushite)   747–656 B.C.E.

PIANKHY	747–716 B.C.E.
SHABAKA	716–702 B.C.E.
SHEBITKU	702–690 B.C.E.
TAHARQA	690–664 B.C.E.
TANTANAMI	664–656 B.C.E.

Twenty-sixth Dynasty (at Sais)   664–525 B.C.E.

PSAMMETICHUS I	664–610 B.C.E.
NECHO	610–595 B.C.E.
PSAMMETICHUS II	595–589 B.C.E.
APRIES	589–570 B.C.E.
AMASIS	570–526 B.C.E.
PSAMMETICHUS III	526–525 B.C.E.

*Indicates a separate alphabetical entry.

Egyptian economy. Akhenaten narrowed the focus by, on the one hand, stressing the god's non-manlike manifestation as the sun disk, source of warmth and life, and on the other emphasizing his own personal relationship with the god.

After devoting the first few years of his reign building massive temples to Aten at Thebes, including an open air temple that contrasted with the dark recesses of the temple of Amun at Karnak, Akhenaten decided to build a new capital city. He chose an unoccupied site along the Middle Nile, isolated on three sides by cliffs. He named the city Akhetaten (the horizon of the aten, or sun), but the later name for its ruins, Tel el-Amarna, has lent its name to the entire period. Temples, palaces, and residential quarters were built, and broad boulevards were laid out for the king's daily processions in imitation of the sun's movements across the sky.

From a modern perspective, the Amarna cult seems rather monotheistic and spiritual. But in practical terms the new cult revolved around the pharaoh himself to a degree that was unprecedented even in Egypt. Akhenaten was considered to be the son of Aten and his co-ruler. Only the king could have knowledge of Aten, and only he could mediate the benefits that Aten bestowed.

The pharaoh's queen, Nefertiti, seems to have played a major role in these rituals. The pair, together with their six daughters, were commemorated endlessly in public and private reliefs all over Amarna, usually in naturalistic poses and settings quite out of keeping with Egypt's stylized traditions. Both in literature and the arts, Amarna tried to break with past conventions. All official texts, even religious hymns, were written in a new official language that was close to vernacular-spoken Egyptian. These new modes survived into the subsequent era, even though Amarna was abandoned and the new cult suppressed shortly after Akhenaten died.

As the years went by, the royal couple became more and more intolerant of other cults. The temples of Amun were shut down, and references to that god were erased from inscriptions all over the country. But few individuals outside the court actually adopted the new faith; even at Amarna the ruins of workers' housing have turned up numerous relics of non-Aten practices.

Court officials were appointed from the humble classes, especially from the army, whose support was indispensable for a king who had to fight the dispossessed elite classes while suppressing a popular religion.

Akhenaten's son, Tutankhamen (r. 1334–1325 B.C.E.), ascended the throne at the age of nine. Three years later, he moved from Amarna to Memphis and abandoned his father's religion. In a reversal of his father's action, the young king signaled his new religious allegiance by changing the "aten" in his name to "amun." It was as Tutankhamen that the young pharaoh earned worldwide fame, after his tomb and its treasures were discovered by archeologists in 1922.

THE LATER NEW KINGDOM

Although the pharaohs who came after the Amarna period tried to blot out its very name, some of its innovations may have had a lasting effect. A variety of separate deities were gradually consolidated into three, who were themselves occasionally considered as different manifestations of each other. Tomb paintings of nobles and officials, which previously showed scenes from their public lives, were now increasingly devoted to religious and mythological themes. In general, there seems to have been a greater degree of piety and consciousness of the presence of the gods in daily life, judging from surviving writings.

The Nineteenth dynasty saw a stabilization of economic and political life in Egypt, and a reassertion of the Egyptian presence in Asia, which may have slackened during the Amarna era. The founder of the dynasty, Ramses I (r. 1293–1291 B.C.E.), was a military officer from a non-noble military family in the Nile Delta, which now assumed a greater role in the governance of Egypt. His son, Seti I (r. 1291–1279 B.C.E.), established the dynasty on a firm domestic footing and fought off enemies in Libya and Syria. He thus passed along a secure throne to his son, Ramses II, the Great (r. 1279–1212 B.C.E.).

Ramses II, possibly the pharaoh of the biblical story of Exodus, had one of the longest reigns in the history of any monarchy. He spent most of that time constructing colossal monuments to himself all over the country; as a result, he became a symbol of ancient Egyptian civilization for latter-day Greek historians, who added "the Great" to his name. Although his huge statues and elaborate reliefs celebrate his reign as a time of great victory, his years were relatively peaceful.

Ramses II built a new capital city in his native Nile Delta region, calling it Pi-Ramesse and adorning it with gardens, orchards, and canals. The city's name and location have led some scholars to identify it with Ramses, the "store city" built by the Children of Israel, according to the Book of Exodus in the Hebrew Bible. In fact, Egyptian records show that the "Apiru" (usually identified with the Hebrews) were among Ramses II's brick makers and stone quarriers. Ramses II also suffered the premature death of his heirs, which also conforms to the Exodus account in the Bible.

There is no Egyptian record of a slave revolt at this time, or of an exodus of Near Eastern immigrants or captives. The first mention of Israel in Egyptian inscription occurs in a victory poem of Ramses II's son and heir, Merneptah (r. 1212–1202 B.C.E.), which states that "Israel is desolate and has no seed."

Most of the remaining New Kingdom pharaohs of the Nineteenth and Twentieth dynasties could boast little in the way of solid accomplishment. An exception was Ramses III (r. 1182–1151 B.C.E.), who defeated major military threats from Libyans and from "Sea Peoples," including the Philistines. By keeping out foreign soldiers, he may have inadvertently delayed the introduction of Iron Age technology into Egypt, with dangerous consequences for the country's future.

Both the economy and administrative efficiency seem to have deteriorated toward the end of the Nineteenth dynasty. Literary output did not suffer, however. A large number of manuscripts have survived, including vigorous tales reflecting folk mythology.

THE THIRD INTERMEDIATE PERIOD

As Egypt's foreign empire dissipated, central control decreased, and imperial revenues declined, the Theban high priests seem to have accumulated more and more power, which was often passed along in hereditary fashion. During the so-called Third Intermediate period, their powers often equaled those of the kings. Eventually, a new dynasty, the Twenty-first (ca. 1070–946 B.C.E.), arose in the Nile Delta, with its capital at Tanis, while the Theban priests ruled the rest of the country. This era of weakness and contraction provided an opportunity for the kingdom of Israel to arise under King David (r. 1010–970 B.C.E.). David's son and successor, King Solomon (r. 970–931 B.C.E.), even married a daughter of Pharaoh Siamun (r. 979–960 B.C.E.); Egypt had ac-

cepted brides from Asia but had never before offered one of its sacred daughters on the altar of diplomacy.

It was now left to minority ethnic or regional groups to try to reinvigorate Egypt. The kings of the Twenty-second and Twenty-third dynasties were of Libyan ancestry and mostly had military names, though they were thoroughly acculturated. Deriving from military backgrounds, their rule was enforced by local garrisons under officers who eventually acted as feudal lords. Urbanization advanced, especially in the Delta region.

THE LATE PERIOD

Perhaps the last major effort to arrest the decline of the old Egyptian society was made by the Twenty-fifth dynasty, also known as the Kushite dynasty. The kings of this dynasty hailed from the independent kingdom of Kush on the Upper Nile, an area that had been controlled by Egypt in its heyday. It is not known whether the dynasty descended from Egyptian colonists or from Egyptianized Kushites, but the explicit policy of the Kushite rulers was to purge new-fangled practices and piously restore the old ways.

The pharaohs Piankhy (r. 747–716 B.C.E.) and Shabaka (r. 716–702 B.C.E.) brought the entire country under one rule for the first time in generations. But the arrangement lasted only a bit upwards of a century. By 664 B.C.E., an Assyrian army under Ashurbanipal II (r. 668–627 B.C.E.) defeated the last Kushite king, Tantanami (r. 664–656 B.C.E.). They sacked Thebes, burnt its temples, and carried off the sacred treasures of Amun; this was a staggering propaganda loss for Egyptian religion. Tantanami fled back to Napata, the Kushite capital; his kingdom survived another thousand years, maintaining the Egyptian language, religion, and civilization long after they disappeared in their homeland.

The Twenty-sixth dynasty arose from Sais, one of the petty principalities that had sprung up in the Nile Delta. By judiciously allying himself with Assyria, Psammetichus I (r. 664–610 B.C.E.) was able to reunite Egypt under his rule. He waged a punitive campaign against the Libyans, and he garrisoned the countries' borders, largely with foreign troops such as Libyans, Nubians, Greeks, Carians, Phoenicians, Syrians, and Jews, many of whom had been displaced by Assyrian conquests in Asia.

Foreign merchants and even Greek intellectual tourists streamed into the country in this era, but

Psammetichus fought to maintain artistic and religious purity, even suppressing foreign worship. He moved administrative departments to Memphis, the original capital of united Egypt two thousand years before, and he deliberately imitated cultivated traditional language in government documents.

The last kings of the Twenty-sixth dynasty presided over political and artistic resurgence, benefiting from the rapid collapse of Assyrian power. The population is said to have reached more than seven million, a number it would not exceed for more than two millennia. But the armies became too reliant on foreign mercenaries and allies, who were not to stand fast in the face of the triumphant ranks of Persia. In 525, Psammetichus III (r. 526–525 B.C.E.), who had assumed the throne just the previous year, was defeated and captured by king Cambyses II (r. 529–522 B.C.E.) of Persia. Venerable Egypt now became just one province in the vast, well-run empire of the Persians and Medes.

See also: AKHENATEN; HATSHEPSUT; HYKSOS DYNASTY; KUSH, KINGDOM OF; NEFERTITI; RAMSES II, THE GREAT; SETI I; TUTANKHAMEN.

EGYPTIAN DYNASTIES, PERSIAN, HELLENISTIC, AND ROMAN (ca. 525 B.C.E.–330 C.E.)

An extended period during which Egypt was under the rule of three successive foreign powers, following thousands of years of Egyptian power and cultural superiority in the ancient Near East.

PERSIAN RULE

In 525 B.C.E., the Persian king, Cambyses II (r. 529–522 B.C.E.) successfully invaded the country, ending the Twenty-sixth dynasty of Egypt. For the first time, Egypt became a province of a foreign empire—Persia. This period, usually called the Twenty-seventh dynasty (525–404 B.C.E.), was one in which the Egyptians chafed under harsh Persian rule. Although Cambyses attempted to align himself with the Egyptian gods, his rule was often oppressive.

Cambyses was succeeded on the Persian throne by Darius I, the Great (r. 521–486 B.C.E.) who was a more benevolent leader. Darius built temples in Egypt and also had a canal dug between the Nile River and the Red Sea, which allowed for easy trade between Persia and Egypt, bringing greater prosperity to the Egyptians.

Egyptians, particularly in northwestern Egypt, never accepted Persian rule and so launched a number of rebellions with help from the Greeks, with whom they traded food for military aid. In 404 B.C.E, a leader named Amyrtaios from Sais in Egypt's delta managed to sustain a revolt and brought Egyptian rule back to Egypt, though only briefly, with three dynasties—Twenty-eighth (404–399 B.C.E.), Twenty-ninth (399–380 B.C.E.), and Thirtieth (380–343 B.C.E.).

For this sixty-year period, Egypt was able to regain some of its former pride in self-government, and it managed to hold off a Persian attack in 385 B.C.E. The Thirtieth dynasty was the last dynasty with native rulers to rule Egypt, however. In 343 B.C.E., the Persian king, Artaxerxes III (r. 343–338 B.C.E.), succeeded in reconquering Egypt, and once again the country was reduced to provincial status.

This second period of Persian rule is known as the Thirty-first dynasty (343–332 B.C.E.). Because the Persians had had to fight so hard to regain the territory, their rule was harsher this time. Thus, when Alexander the Great of Macedonia (r. 336–323 B.C.E.) defeated the Persians in 332 B.C.E. and conquered Egypt, the Egyptians eagerly accepted him as their new king.

HELLENISTIC PERIOD

The next 300 years of Egyptian history are known as the Hellenistic period, a time during which Greek culture and learning were at the forefront of cultural activities. Alexander the Great founded a city, Alexandria, at the mouth of the Nile River on the Mediterranean coast to serve as his capital. Alexandria became a great cultural and intellectual center, with a library, museum, and university.

Alexander's life was cut short about a decade after he conquered Egypt. One of his faithful military commanders, Ptolemy I Soter (r. 306–282 B.C.E.), was left in charge of Egypt as governor, but he eventually declared himself king. The Ptolemaic dynasty (306–30 B.C.E.) ruled Egypt for more than two hundred and fifty years.

Under the Ptolemaic dynasty, Egypt was ruled as a separate entity under its own monarch, although, at times, two monarchs ruled together. During this Hellenistic period, Egyptian culture was gradually

Twenty-seventh Dynasty

CAMBYSES II*	530–522 B.C.E.
DARIUS I*	521–486 B.C.E.
XERXES I*	485–465 B.C.E.
ARTAXERXES I*	464–424 B.C.E.
DARIUS II*	423–405 B.C.E.

Twenty-eighth Dynasty

AMYRTAIOS	404–399 B.C.E.

Twenty-ninth Dynasty

NEPHERITES I	399–393 B.C.E.
PSAMMUTHIS	393 B.C.E.
HAKORIS	393–380 B.C.E.
NEPHERITES II	380 B.C.E.

Thirtieth Dynasty

NECTANEBO I	380–362 B.C.E.
TEOS	365–361 B.C.E.
NECTANEBO II	361–343 B.C.E.

Thirty-first Dynasty

ARTAXERXES III*	343–338 B.C.E.
ARSES	333–336 B.C.E.
DARIUS III	335–332 B.C.E.

Macedonian Kings

ALEXANDER III THE GREAT*	332–323 B.C.E.
PHILIP ARRHIDAEUS	323–317 B.C.E.
ALEXANDER IV	317–304 B.C.E.

Ptolemaic Dynasty

PTOLEMY I*	306–282 B.C.E.
PTOLEMY II	282–246 B.C.E.
PTOLEMY III	246–222 B.C.E.
PTOLEMY IV	222–205 B.C.E.
PTOLEMY V	205–180 B.C.E.
PTOLEMY VI	180–145 B.C.E.
PTOLEMY VII	145 B.C.E.
PTOLEMY VIII	170–163 AND 145–116 B.C.E.
CLEOPATRA III AND PTOLEMY IX	116–107 AND 88–80 B.C.E.
AND PTOLEMY X	107–88 B.C.E.
CLEOPATRA BERENIKE	81–80 B.C.E.)
PTOLEMY XI	80 B.C.E.
PTOLEMY XII	80–58 AND 55–51 B.C.E.
BERENIKE IV	58–55 B.C.E.
CLEOPATRA VII* AND PTOLEMY XIII	51–47 B.C.E.
AND PTOLEMY XIV	47–44 B.C.E.
AND PTOLEMY XV	44–30 B.C.E.

*Indicates a separate alphabetical entry.

Hellenized, or made more Greek: Greek became the language of the government, Egyptians adopted Greek dress, and Greek styles were incorporated into Egyptian art and architecture.

Although the Hellenistic period was mostly a peaceful time, native Egyptians were considered to be of a lower social class than the immigrant Greeks. This social superiority, together with the continued draining of Egyptian resources by the Greeks, created Egyptian resentment that erupted in periodic revolts.

By the first century B.C.E., however, the real prob-

ROYAL RITUALS

RULERS AS GODS

It was around the time of the Fifth dynasty that Egyptian kings claimed to be directly descended from the sun-god, Ra, and were thus part-god, part-human. Reliefs were carved on temple walls in a special motif known as a cartouche, an oval with the hieroglyphs of the ruler's name, to represent the king's divine birth and his function as a representative of the gods. Though not native-born, the foreigners who ruled Egypt during the Hellenistic and the Roman periods had the conventional divine attributes assigned to them, and, to protect the ancient religion, they accepted this divine role. Thus, Alexander and his successors were depicted on the walls of existing temples and also in some cases had new temples built with their names carved as Egyptian god-kings.

lem facing the Greeks was the growing power of the Roman Empire, which began interfering in Egyptian affairs. After the death of Roman dictator Julius Caesar (r. 49–44 B.C.E.) in 44 B.C.E., Cleopatra VII of Egypt (r. 51–30 B.C.E.), a mistress of Caesar, mistakenly aligned herself with Mark Antony in the ensuing power struggle with Octavian over control of the Roman Empire. When Octavian—the future emperor Augustus (r. 27 B.C.E.–14 C.E.)—won this power struggle, Cleopatra committed suicide rather than surrender. After her death in 30 B.C.E., Egypt became a province of Rome, and it remained under Roman control for nearly seven hundred years.

ROMAN RULE

Emperor Augustus later declared himself king of Egypt and accepted the god-king status that had been the tradition of the Egyptian pharaohs. Roman Egypt was governed by a prefect, who reported directly to the emperor and who was commander of the army and official judge. Over time, Latin replaced Greek as the language of government. Greek nobles were still considered to be of a higher class than native Egyptians.

Egypt became a very important province of the Roman Empire, and it was tightly controlled administratively from Rome. The Egyptian grain harvest, its manufactured goods, and its taxes were vital to the Roman economy. As a center of trade between India, Arabia, and other Mediterranean countries,

the Egyptian city of Alexandria was one of the great cities of the Roman Empire. Although Rome governed Egypt, the cultural institutions founded by Alexander the Great continued to thrive.

Egypt was relatively peaceful under the Romans. In 211 C.E., Emperor Caracalla (r. 211–217) officially made the Egyptians citizens of the Roman Empire. When Emperor Constantine I (r. 307–337), the first Christian emperor of Rome, established a new capital at Byzantium (which he renamed Constantinople) around 330, Egypt became part of the Eastern Roman Empire, also called the Byzantine Empire. Egypt remained under Byzantine control until the Muslim Arab conquest of it in the mid-seventh century.

See also: ALEXANDER III, THE GREAT; AUGUSTUS; BYZANTINE EMPIRE; CLEOPATRA VII; CONSTANTINE I, THE GREAT; EGYPTIAN DYNASTIES, ANCIENT (BEFORE EIGHTEENTH DYNASTY); EGYPTIAN DYNASTIES, ANCIENT (EIGHTEENTH TO TWENTY-SIXTH); MACEDONIAN EMPIRE; PERSIAN EMPIRE; PTOLEMAIC DYNASTY; PTOLEMY I; ROMAN EMPIRE.

FURTHER READING

Baines, John, and Jaromir Málek. *Atlas of Ancient Egypt.* New York: Facts on File, 1996.

Casson, Lionel. *Ancient Egypt.* Alexandria, VA: Time-Life Books, 1978.

Metz, Helen Chapin, ed. *Egypt: A Country Study.* 5th

ed. Washington, DC: Federal Research Division, Library of Congress, 1991.

Silverman, David P., ed. *Ancient Egypt*. New York: Oxford University Press, 2003.

EGYPTIAN KINGDOM, MODERN

(1805–1952 C.E.)

Final period of monarchy in Egypt, from the waning of Ottoman rule to the emergence of a new republic in 1952 under Gamal Abdel Nasser.

Although nominally under the Ottoman Empire from 1802, Egypt was ruled quite independently by military officials called pashas headquartered in Cairo. The first pasha was Muhammad (Mehmet) Ali (r. 1805–1848), whose rule marked the beginning of the state system and modernization in Egypt. After completing a successful military campaign of Albanians and Turks against the French, Mehmet Ali, who commanded the Albanian forces, was named governor (viceroy) of Egypt in 1805. He remained in that post until 1848, founding a dynasty that lasted until 1952.

After strengthening his command at the beginning of his rule, Mehmet Ali focused on military and economic expansion. He advanced Egypt's manufacturing and trade, especially of textiles, and constructed the first dam across the Nile River to improve irrigation. He thought highly of European civilization and had European educators teach Egyptian students both at home and abroad. Ali also was well-regarded for his administrative skills and is credited with creating Egypt's new constitution, army and navy, tax system, import and export system, health laws, schools, colleges, and publishing enterprises. Through his new administrative and military institutions, the world became accustomed to viewing Egypt as an independent state with capable government and military leaders who sought Western reforms and Egyptian autonomy.

The next Egyptian pasha was Abbas I (r. 1848–1854), who inherited rule from his grandfather Mehmet. More of a traditionalist than Mehmet Ali, Abbas was less interested in the westernization of Egypt. He was murdered mysteriously in 1854 and succeeded by his uncle, the more effective Said Pasha (Mohammed), who governed from 1854 to 1863. A successful military leader, Said resumed national civil and social projects begun by his father, Mehmet Ali.

Said was succeeded by his nephew, Ismail Pasha (r. 1863–1879). Ismail obtained credit for extravagant schemes from Egypt's very valuable Egyptian cotton crop, and as a result of his actions the country went into serious debt. In 1875, he was forced to sell his stockholdings in the Suez Canal to Great Britain, and the following year he had to put Egypt's finances in the hands of a debt commission representing French and British bondholders. When Ismail tried to get rid of foreign control in 1879, the Ottoman sultan unseated him and replaced him with Ismail's son, Tewfik Pasha (r. 1879–1892).

Tewfik Pasha ruled as khedive, a title that differentiated Egypt's viceroy from other Ottoman governors. In 1880, he agreed to let the French and British have joint control over the country's finances, a decision that led to conflicts and ended with Great Britain's having sole control of Egyptian finances. Tewfik usually took a Western point of view and was quite committed to improvements in Egypt's educational and legal systems.

The next, and last, khedive of Egypt was Tewfik's son, Abbas II (Abbas Hilmi), who ruled from 1892 to 1914. Though still nominally under the Ottoman Empire, Egypt was really controlled by the British. Abbas II tried unsuccessfully to resist British rule; but during World War I, Egypt became a British protectorate (1914) and Abbas II was deposed.

Egypt became nominally independent in 1922, when Britain set up a constitutional monarchy headed by King Fuad I (r. 1922–1936). Fuad was especially interested in military and cultural progress for his country, and he established the University of Cairo in 1906. However, he had problems dealing with external pressure from the British and internal pressure from the Wafd nationalist political party in Egypt. Upon Fuad's death in 1936, his son Farouk succeeded him as constitutional monarch.

King Farouk (r. 1936–1952) also had internal and external political problems. Because of his pro-German and Italian leanings during World War II, the British forced him to accept a pro-British premier in 1942. In 1948, Farouk's forces were defeated in the Arab-Israeli War. Four years later, in 1952, he was overthrown by a group of army officers that included Colonel Gamal Abdel Nasser, who became the first president of the new republic of Egypt.

See also: FAROUK; FUAD; MUHAMMAD ALI.

ELEANOR OF AQUITAINE

(ca. 1122–1204 C.E.)

Queen consort of France from 1137 to 1152 while married to Louis VII (r. 1137–1180), and of England from 1154 to 1204 while married to Henry II (r. 1154–1189); mother of Henry, Geoffrey, Richard I, Lionheart (r. 1189–1199), and John (r. 1199–1216). Eleanor wielded considerable influence and power, taking an active part in administering and advising her husbands and sons. One of the most influential women of medieval times, she also was an important patron of the arts, especially the poetry of courtly love.

Eleanor was the daughter and heiress of William X, the wealthy and powerful duke of Aquitaine and count of Poitou. When William died in 1137, Eleanor became a ward of King Louis VI of France. In July 1137, at age fifteen, she married the heir to the French throne, who later that year became King Louis VII.

Eleanor played a very active role in Louis's government, and even accompanied him on the Second Crusade from 1147 to 1149. Her independent spirit, however, resulted in her arrest because of disobedience to her husband the king. She was returned to France, and, despite the fact that they had two daughters, Louis annulled their marriage in 1152.

Later the same year, Eleanor married Henry Plantagenet, the duke of Normandy and count of Anjou. Henry also was heir to the English throne and became Henry II in 1154. Between her inheritance of Aquitaine and her marriage to Henry, she became very powerful as queen consort of England, Normandy, and a large part of France.

Henry's adultery eventually resulted in their separation, and in 1171 Eleanor returned to her home in Poitiers and established her own court there. When her son Richard and others revolted against Henry in 1173, she was accused of aiding them. Henry imprisoned Eleanor in 1174, and she was not released until he died and her son Richard became king in 1189.

While her son Richard was on the Third Crusade from 1189 to 1192, Eleanor administered his government. She was instrumental in raising the ransom to buy Richard's freedom after he was taken captive in Austria.

Richard died without an heir in 1199, and Eleanor used her considerable political power and influence to ensure that her son John became the next king. Of her eight children, her son Henry ruled as co-regent (r. 1170–1183), two sons were crowned king of England (Richard I and John), and two daughters married kings. Her daughter Eleanor married Alfonso VIII (r. 1158–1214), king of Castile, and her daughter Joan married William II (1166–1189), king of Sicily and then Raymond VI (r. 1194–1222), count of Toulouse. Although two sons died young, the fifth son, Geoffrey, was duke of Brittany. Eleanor's third daughter, Matilda, married Henry the Lion, duke of Saxony and Bavaria.

See also: AQUITAINE DUCHY; BRETAGNE DUCHY; FRANKISH KINGDOM; HENRY II; JOHN I; LOUIS VII; RICHARD I, LIONHEART; SICILIAN, KINGDOM OF.

ELECTION, ROYAL

The selection of a monarch by election rather than by inheritance alone.

Although modern monarchies are generally hereditary, this was not always the case. In the past, many monarchies have been elective. Most authorities agree that the prehistoric Germanic and Scandinavian tribes of Northern Europe had an elective monarchy whereby a king was chosen from among members of the royal family, often as a leader in time of war. Kings among these tribes could also sometimes serve as sacrificial victims. The most likely means of electing these tribal kings was by acclamation among an assembly of the free men of the tribe.

ANGLO-SAXON AND EARLY ENGLAND

In the post-Roman period, forms of elective kingship continued among these same peoples. In the early Anglo-Saxon kingdoms in England, the succession could pass to a brother or other near relative of the deceased king rather than to his son, particularly if that son was a minor. As in the English kingdom of Kent—where Hlothere (r. 673–685) succeeded his brother Egbert (r. 664–673) as king and was later overthrown by Egbert's son Eadric (r. 685–686)—this often resulted in civil strife between rival claimants.

There was no formal electoral procedure in the early Anglo-Saxon kingdoms. Often a king would designate his successor during his lifetime, and that successor would then be acknowledged or formally acclaimed king by the leading men of the kingdom. Primogeniture, in which the succession descends to the eldest (usually the eldest male) child, quickly became the normal pattern of succession, but as late as the eleventh century a king could be chosen by the combination of designation as successor and acclamation by the nobles. Harold II Godwinson (r. 1066) claimed his legitimacy as English monarch on these grounds.

THE HOLY ROMAN EMPIRE

Elective kingship persisted in the Holy Roman Empire, which by the twelfth century consisted of a number of principalities. The Holy Roman emperor was chosen by the princes of these states, and by the mid-twelfth century, the title "elector" (for example, the elector of Hanover) began to be used for those princes who had the right to take part in choosing the emperor. Six, and later eight, princely electors made up the electoral college. Three were archbishops of Mainz, Treves, and Cologne; the others were rulers of the Rhine Palatinate, Saxony, Bohemia, Brandenburg, and Hanover. Eventually there were thirteen electors. Heredity played a role in imperial elections as well, since only royal candidates were considered.

The election of the emperor was often a source of conflict in the Holy Roman Empire. At times, the papacy, which claimed the right to appoint or approve the emperor, and the electors would designate rival claimants. Sometimes two elections would be held, with different factions among the electors supporting different emperors. In 1198, for example, Otto IV (r. 1198–1218) of the Welf dynasty was chosen as a rival to Philip of Swabia (r. 1198–1208), a Hohenstaufen, resulting in civil war.

OTHER ELECTIVE MONARCHIES

Poland also had an elective monarchy from the sixteenth century until 1796, when that kingdom ceased to exist. After the separation of Norway and Sweden in 1905, a Norwegian monarchy was reestablished through the election of a king. The new Norwegian government invited a Danish prince to become king; Haakon VII (r. 1905–1957) accepted this invitation only after a referendum of the Norwegian people approved his election, although his successors inherit by right of primogeniture. The official acclamation of the British monarch at his or her coronation is a symbolic remnant of Anglo-Saxon elective monarchy and the right of the people to approve their new ruler.

At least one elective monarchy still exists today. In Malaysia, which has a constitutional elective monarchy, a group of nine hereditary state rulers elect a leader, the *yang dipertuan agong*, from among their number every five years. Like the current constitutional monarchs of Europe, the *yang dipertuan agong* acts as symbolic head of state but has little real power.

See also: ACCESSION AND CROWNING OF KINGS; ANGLO-SAXON RULERS; FRANKISH KINGDOM; HOLY ROMAN EMPIRE; PRIMOGENITURE; SUCCESSION, ROYAL.

FURTHER READING

Blair, Peter Hunter. *An Introduction to Anglo—Saxon England.* 2nd ed. New York: Cambridge University Press, 1977.

Haverkamp, Alfred. *Medieval Germany: 1056–1273.* 2nd ed. Trans. Helga Braun and Richard Mortimer. New York: Oxford University Press, 1992.

Kern, Fritz. *Kingship and Law in the Middle Ages.* Trans. S.B. Chrimes. Westport, CT: Greenwood Press, 1985.

Nicolson, Harold. *Kings, Courts, and Monarchy.* New York: Simon and Schuster, 1962.

Spellman, W.M. *Monarchies, 1000–2000.* London: Reaktion Books, 2001.

Todd, Malcolm. *The Early Germans.* Oxford: Basil Blackwell, 1992.

ELIZABETH I (1533–1603 C.E.)

Queen of England (r. 1558–1603), whose reign marked the high point of the English Renaissance. Elizabeth was the daughter of King Henry VIII (r. 1509–1547) and his second wife, Anne Boleyn. Henry established the Church of England, which launched the Protestant Reformation in England, in order to divorce his first wife and marry Anne. As a result, Elizabeth was raised as a Protestant.

LIFE AND REIGN

Elizabeth was born at Greenwich Palace and brought up in a household at Hatfield apart from her parents. Her father had her mother executed on charges of adultery when Elizabeth was just a child.

Despite this traumatic event, Elizabeth was treated well as a child and received an excellent education in the classics, history, and philosophy. When her half-sister Mary became Queen Mary I (r. 1553–1558) in 1553 and reestablished Catholicism in England, Elizabeth saved her own life by going along with Mary's changes. Secretly, however, she resolved to restore the Church of England.

When Mary died in 1558, Elizabeth succeeded to the throne. She was instantly popular with the English people, not least because of her religious preferences. Elizabeth rid her body of advisers, the Privy Council, of Catholics and reopened the Protestant churches. She also selected a new group of political advisers that included many influential Protestant noblemen.

One of the key concerns that many people in England had about Elizabeth was the fact that she was a woman. Women, even queens, were considered naturally inferior to men. Although Elizabeth had an education superior to that of most Englishmen of the time and an indomitable will, she had to prove herself superior in order to relieve the doubts of her subjects. One way in which she established her power was by never marrying. As "the Virgin Queen" Elizabeth never had to subject herself to a husband, who most likely would have tried to assume much of her power. Elizabeth also created a quasireligious aura around herself, which she encouraged through court ritual and costume.

Her Protestant subjects, in particular, wanted Elizabeth to marry and produce an heir because the next individual in line for the throne was Mary, Queen of Scots, a staunch Catholic. Elizabeth avoided the problem of Mary succeeding to the throne not by marrying and producing an heir but by taking advantage of Mary's weakness. When Mary was forced to abdicate the Scottish throne after suspicions that she had murdered her husband, Elizabeth offered her sanctuary in England in the hopes of neutralizing her as a threat to Elizabeth's Protestant succession. The sanctuary turned into a long imprisonment in England, and Mary was eventually executed in 1587 on grounds of plotting in a scheme to murder Elizabeth.

Throughout her reign, Elizabeth faced a number of other threats to Protestant stability. These included a conspiracy to take her life, the Ridolfi Plot in 1571; a rebellion in the north of England in 1569; and papal excommunication in 1570. Perhaps her

Queen Elizabeth I of England, shown here in a sixteenth-century portrait, was one of the great monarchs of European history. A member of the Tudor Dynasty, she maintained political stability and presided over a period of flourishing culture that became known as the Elizabethan Age.

greatest challenge came in the 1580s, when England became involved in a war with Spain. Phillip II (r. 1556–1598), the Catholic king of Spain, attempted to conquer England with his famed Armada. In 1588, the English fleet defeated the Spanish Armada, saving England from an imagined Catholic takeover.

As Elizabeth approached old age, many wondered about her choice of successor to the throne. She had no heirs, no living siblings, and no nieces or nephews. In fact, the closest heirs to the throne were fairly distant relatives, any one of a number of whom had equally valid claims. Elizabeth kept people guessing until almost the end of her life. Eventually, she announced that she had selected as her heir James VI of Scotland (r. 1567–1625), the son of the murdered Mary, Queen of Scots, and a descendant of Margaret Tudor, the sister of Elizabeth's father, Henry VIII. Elizabeth's death in 1603 brought an end to England's Tudor dynasty, while the accession of James as King James I (r. 1603–1625) ushered in the Stuart dynasty.

THE ELIZABETHAN AGE

The period of Elizabeth's rule, known as the Elizabethan Age, is considered a golden age of English history. During this period, England briefly resolved its violent internal religious and dynastic conflicts to become a major world power. The Elizabethan Age was also a time of financial prosperity, brought about in large part by the exploration of the New World. Among the most notable explorers of Elizabeth's reign was Sir Francis Drake.

The Elizabethan period was also an age of distinguished and accomplished courtiers—"Renaissance men" such as Sir Walter Raleigh; Robert Devereux, the earl of Essex; and Robert Dudley, the earl of Leicester. These three courtiers, among others, became royal favorites of Elizabeth: she lavished honors and estates on them, and gossip would regularly circulate that she was about to marry each of them.

The Elizabethan period is perhaps most distinguished, however, for its astounding burst of literary achievement. The many works of literature produced in this period include *The Faerie Queene* of Edmund Spenser, which was dedicated to the queen; the poetry of Sir Philip Sidney; the dramas of Christopher Marlowe; and, most notably, the sonnets and early plays of William Shakespeare.

See also: HENRY VIII; JAMES I OF ENGLAND (JAMES VI OF SCOTLAND); MARY, QUEEN OF SCOTS; MARY I, TUDOR; QUEENS AND QUEEN MOTHERS; STUART DYNASTY; THEATER, ROYAL; TUDOR, HOUSE OF.

FURTHER READING

Jenkins, Elizabeth. *Elizabeth the Great.* New York: Berkley, 1972.

Johnson, Paul. *Elizabeth I: A Study in Power and Intellect.* London: Weidenfeld and Nicolson, 1988.

Regan, Geoffrey. *Elizabeth I.* New York: Cambridge University Press, 1988.

Smith, Lacey Baldwin. *Elizabeth Tudor: Portrait of a Queen.* Boston: Little, Brown, 1975.

Williams, Neville. *The Life and Times of Elizabeth I.* Garden City, NY: Doubleday, 1972.

ELIZABETH II (1926 C.E.–)

Queen of Great Britain and Northern Ireland (r. 1952–present), who rules as a constitutional monarch and serves as head of state, head of the Church of England, and head of the British Commonwealth. As is true of other modern British monarchs, her duties are primarily ceremonial and a symbol of nationhood. In 2002, she celebrated her Golden Jubilee, marking fifty years as reigning monarch. Only three English monarchs have reigned longer. Five archbishops of Canterbury and ten prime ministers have served during her reign.

Born on April 21, 1926, Elizabeth is the daughter of George VI (r. 1936–1952), and the granddaughter of King George V (r. 1910–1936) and Queen Mary. Although not in direct line of succession to the throne at the time of her birth, she became heir apparent at the age of ten, when her father unexpectedly became King George VI. As next in line of succession to his brother Edward VIII (r. 1936), George became king following a scandal in which Edward abdicated in order to marry Mrs. Wallis Simpson, an American divorcee, after Edward could not gain approval from government ministers to wed.

In 1947, Elizabeth married Philip, duke of Edin-

In 2002, on the fiftieth anniversary of her succession to the throne, Queen Elizabeth II became one of the five longest-reigning monarchs in English history. Her ancestors, Queen Victoria and King George III, ruled for 64 and 60 years, respectively. Henry III ruled for 56 years, Edward III for 50 years.

burgh, earl of Merioneth, and baron of Greenwich; they have four children (Charles, Anne, Andrew, and Edward) and six grandchildren. The heir apparent is their eldest son Charles, prince of Wales.

Although Elizabeth has no control over government or military policy, she has played a significant role in strengthening English morale and unifying her subjects, especially during times of crisis. She began this role in 1940 during World War II, when, at the age of fourteen and long before she was queen, she broadcast a message of support to the children of Britain. She has continued to be an emblem of British nationalism during subsequent military engagements, such as the Suez crisis (1956), the Falklands War (1982), the first Gulf War (1991), the war in Iraq (2003), and the ongoing unrest and violence that has been recurring in Northern Ireland since 1968.

During her reign, Elizabeth has seen the continued devolution of the former British Empire: at least forty former territories have gained independence since she took the throne in 1952. There has also been a move to decentralize domestic power in the United Kingdom. The National Assemblies for Wales in Cardiff and the Scottish Parliament in Edinburgh were founded in 1999 as part of these move toward devolution. At the same time, ties with Europe have become stronger during her reign; Britain joined the European Economic Community in 1973 and is one of its strongest members.

Elizabeth's reign has also witnessed personal changes to the British monarchy, both real and symbolic. In 1993, after much public pressure and controversy, Elizabeth voluntarily agreed to begin paying income and capital gains taxes, from which she had previously been exempt. At about the same time, in the early 1990s, the marital difficulties and divorces of her children became a cause of public embarrassment. Despite widespread public disapproval of her children's behavior, Elizabeth herself has remained a popular monarch.

See also: WINDSOR, HOUSE OF.

EMISSARY LETTERS

Official messages carried by a representative of one government or monarch to another.

Until the transportation advancements of the twentieth century, travel and communication between distant governments was slow. Only under special circumstances, such as war or religious pilgrimages, did rulers leave their own lands and journey to another. Yet, monarchs still were able to exercise complete authority over such matters as war and peace. Emissaries to foreign nations carried out much necessary political and trade negotiation through diplomatic letters expressing the sovereign's wishes. The letters were often elaborately concealed and bore seals and other marks of authenticity.

Among the oldest existing letters carried by emissaries are a series of about 400 clay tablets, dating from the fourteenth century B.C.E., from the ancient city of Amarna in Egypt. These ancient clay documents, written in a cuneiform script, were sent by the Pharaoh Amenhotep III (r. ca. 1386–1349 B.C.E.), and his son, Akhenaten (r. ca. 1350–1334 B.C.E.), to surrounding realms and cities under their control. The Amarna letters concerned various matters of state, such as taxes, the provision of soldiers, and the diplomatic exchanges of gifts.

Individuals from various professions, including clergymen, served their monarchs as emissaries. The Franciscan friar John of Pian de Carpine was one of four monks dispatched by Pope Innocent IV to the Far East. Friar John traveled to Mongolia around 1245 C.E. to deliver papal letters to the Great Khan, Kuyuk Khan (r. 1241–1248), urging him to stop killing Christians and to embrace the Christian faith. When Friar John returned to Italy, he brought letters to Pope Innocent from the khan; not only had the friar not converted him, but the khan said he would continue efforts to conquer more territory and told the pope to surrender to his power.

The mistrust between Christian and Mongol nations continued, and other Western diplomatic missions to the East met with varying degrees of success. In 1289, for example, the king of France, Philip IV (r. 1285–1314), negotiated with Arghun Khan (r. 1284–1291), promising to support the khan's invasion of Egypt. In return, the khan promised France control of the city of Jerusalem.

Historically, much diplomacy has been carried out secretly, with only monarchs, a few trusted advisers, and emissaries fully aware of treaties or clauses in treaties. In the thirteenth century, two envoys posing as Franciscan monks carried out clandestine negotiations among Peter III of Aragon (r. 1276–1285), the pope, and Emperor Michael VIII of Byzantium (r. 1261–1282). These negotiations resulted in an uprising in Sicily, known as the Sicilian Vespers, against Duke Charles I of Anjou (r. 1246–1285).

Throughout the Renaissance, world exploration led to interest in other cultures and to efforts to establish diplomatic relationships. Elizabeth I of England (r. 1558–1603) dispatched emissaries to India to the court of Akbar the Great (r. 1556–1605). Elizabeth also sent the mathematician and astronomer John Dee on a secret diplomatic mission to the court of Holy Roman Emperor Rudolf II (r. 1576–1612) in Prague. The mission served Elizabeth's Protestant interests in having an eye and ear in the Holy Roman Emperor's capital city.

Diplomatic initiatives also were carried out by other European nations. By 1596, for example, the Spanish had established themselves in the Philippines. When the king of Angkor in Cambodia needed soldiers for protection against attack, he sent a request to the Spanish governor of Manila, who came to his aid. This appeal is the first known exchange between the West and Cambodia.

Other governments have used emissary letters to ask for aid from allies. In the eighteenth century, the kingdom of Georgia in the Caucasus region found itself threatened by the expanding Ottoman and Persian empires. Through an envoy, King Vakhtang VI of Georgia (r. 1703–1724) sent a petition for help to King Louis XIV of France (r. 1643–1715). Fearing that France's interests would be harmed, Louis ignored the plea. In 1723, the Ottoman Turks were able to occupy eastern Georgia.

Emissary letters have been sent for a variety of purposes. For example, Guru Gobind Singh (r. 1675–1708), the Muslim leader of the Sikhs of India, sent two emissaries with his well-known Epistle of Victory (or Zafarnamah) to Mughal emperor Aurangzeb (1658–1707), criticizing the emperor's conduct in war and advocating the application of strict morality in all human activities. It seems that Aurangzeb was so impressed with the letter that he requested Gobind Singh to meet with him to establish a peace. Unfortunately, Aurangzeb died before the Guru could reach the palace, but the Sikhs still venerate the letter as a treatise on moral conduct.

See also: AMBASSADORS; DIPLOMACY, ROYAL.

EMPERORS AND EMPRESSES

Monarchs who reign over an extended area, usually one that includes several subject nations.

The term *emperor* has its origin in ancient Rome. In 31 B.C.E. Octavian, the nephew of Julius Caesar (r. 49–44 B.C.E.), emerged as sole victor in the civil wars that followed Caesar's assassination in 44 B.C.E. Octavian, who became the Emperor Augustus (r. 27 B.C.E.–14 C.E.). In 29 B.C.E., the Roman Senate bestowed a number of titles on Augustus, one of which was *imperator*. The term meant *power, command,* and *dominion,* and was usually used in a military sense.

The title *imperator* (or emperor) was retained by all of Augustus's successors, even after the Roman Empire split into two parts in 395 C.E. For centuries after the final fall of Rome, the rulers of the Eastern Roman Empire continued to see themselves as the heirs of Rome. Because the center of the Eastern Empire was Byzantium, it became known as the Byzantine Empire; its rulers continued to use the title emperor until the collapse of the empire in 1453 at the hands of the Ottoman Turks.

The Western half of the Roman Empire collapsed in 476, following the Germanic conquests, and its territory was broken up into various kingdoms. In 800, Pope Leo III bestowed the title of emperor on the Frankish king Charlemagne (r. 768–814) following his conquest of most of Western Europe. Although his son Louis (r. 814–840) inherited the title, the Frankish Empire did not survive long.

By the tenth century, the dukes of Saxony, who had come to the German throne beginning with Henry I (r. 919–936), ruled much of Central Europe. Henry's son, Otto I (r. 936–973), conquered Italy and was crowned emperor of the Romans by the pope in 962. As such, Otto is generally regarded as the founder of the Holy Roman Empire and the first Holy Roman emperor. Throughout Europe at the time, the title "emperor" remained associated with Rome and with the German Crown.

By the sixteenth century, however, the term *emperor* ceased to be tied to Germany or to ancient Rome, and other kings began to use the title. By 1610, it was used to designate the Ottoman sultan, as well as to refer to the heads of earlier ancient empires such as Babylonia and Assyria. By the early seventeenth century, Russia saw itself as the heir to

Byzantium and, hence, as the third Roman Empire. Consequently, Russian ruler Peter the Great (r. 1682–1725) used the title *imperator*, and Catherine the Great (r. 1762–1796) was styled "Empress of all the Russias."

Although the term *emperor* was originally understood to mean a ruler who had control over several kingdoms, by the beginning of the nineteenth century, the title came to be much overused. Napoleon (r. 1799–1815), who became dictator for life, was granted imperial status by the French Senate and was crowned emperor by the pope in December 1804. This led to a number of European rulers proclaiming themselves emperors, including even the Habsburg ruler of Germany, who was a vassal of the Holy Roman emperor.

The Westernized term *emperor* has also been applied to the rulers of non-Western empires. In both China and Japan, for example, the individuals who ruled over the centuries are now termed emperors, and Japan still has an emperor. Other countries in other periods, including Ethiopia, Mexico, Brazil, and India, have also been ruled at one time or another by rulers now termed *emperors*.

See also: DYNASTY; EMPIRE; IMPERIAL RULE; KINGDOMS AND EMPIRES; REALMS, TYPES OF.

EMPIRE

A large extended area, usually including several subject nations, which is ruled by the same monarch. The ruler of an empire may be called by various titles, including caesar, emperor or empress, tsar or tsarina, kaiser, khan, or even king or queen.

When an empire develops and expands, its ruler sometimes leaves the monarchs of conquered states to serve as puppet rulers or administrators; in other cases, an emperor may choose to appoint his own administrators. Historically, as empires age, they often grow corrupt and overextended, leaving them weakened and unable to defend themselves militarily.

Many times in history, a weakened empire has been conquered by another state. In some cases, the conquering state was one that was expanding and building its own empire. In other cases, it might have been an imperial territory or subject state whose ruler or people revolted against imperial power because of harsh rule, resentment over paying tribute,

dealing with the whims of corrupt rulers, or unpopular imperial policies.

A number of times throughout history, empires have become too powerful, threatening the balance of power. Such was the case, for example, with Spain in the early 1600s. When Charles II of Spain (r. 1665–1700) died childless in 1700, ending the powerful Habsburg line on the Spanish throne, the successor was Philip V (r. 1700–1724) of the French House of Bourbon. The Wars of the Spanish Succession (1701–1714) followed; ultimately, Spain lost many of its territories and its power and became, instead, a puppet state of France.

An empire often provides military protection to subject nations and, in return, expects some form of tribute from its vassals. In addition, empires frequently expect, and take steps to develop, some type of cultural, economic, and political conformity. As with the Roman or British empires, for example, the state encourages the development of a common language, a common monetary unit, and a common set of ideals throughout the empire. This helps to create a common bond, and the use of a common language—whether Latin, Spanish, or English—makes communication between different peoples easier and helps to consolidate imperial power. For these reasons, empires frequently see themselves as a civilizing influence, although vassal nations will usually regard the imperial power with resentment.

Empires can be acquired through marriage as well as through battle and conquest. Should a king marry the daughter of another monarch, their child will then be in line to inherit both thrones. Such was the case in fifteenth-century Spain, when the marriage Ferdinand of Aragón (r. 1479–1516) and Isabella of Castile (r. 1474–1504) united the two most important kingdoms of Iberia. In the generation following Ferdinand and Isabella, marriages among their children forged alliances with Austria and the powerful Habsburg dynasty, ultimately giving Spain an extended empire.

In recent years, since the decline of the British Empire in the first half of the twentieth century, the word "empire" has taken on increasingly negative connotations, as peoples around the world reject the notion of imperial rule and claim the idea of self-rule as the basic foundation of government.

See also: DYNASTY; EMPERORS AND EMPRESSES; IMPERIAL RULE; KINGS AND QUEENS; KINGDOMS AND

EMPIRES; REALMS, TYPES OF; ROYAL FAMILIES; SUCCESSION, ROYAL; TRIBUTE.

FURTHER READING

Miller, Townsend. *The Castles and the Crown. Spain: 1451–1555.* New York: Coward-McCann, 1963.

ENGLISH MONARCHIES

(400s C.E.–Present)

One of the world's oldest surviving monarchies, which has experienced a succession of rulers and dynasties from the early Middle Ages to the present. Over the past sixteen centuries, the English monarchy has survived in an almost continuous line of succession. One reason the English monarchy has endured is its ability to adjust to changing historical circumstances. England's kings and queens have ruled over territories of different sizes, have wielded greater and lesser degrees of power, and had widely varying responsibilities.

HISTORY

The history of the English monarchy begins in the so-called Dark Ages. England itself takes its name from fifth century invaders—the Germanic tribes known as the Angles, Saxons, and Jutes. Prior to this time, the Celtic people of Britain, the Britons, were under the dominion of the Roman Empire. The same northern Germanic warlords who destroyed Rome eventually made their way to Britain and established small kingdoms beginning in Kent in the southeast and spreading to the north and west.

Eventually, the Anglo-Saxons established seven small separate kingdoms in England that battled each other for control of their small territories almost constantly for nearly four centuries. These small, weak kingdoms of the Saxon heptarchy (seven kingdoms) were first united at the beginning of the ninth century under Egbert (r. 802–839), the first king of a unified England whose borders roughly correspond to those of today.

During the ninth and tenth centuries, the Anglo-Saxon monarchs were fairly successful in fending off threats from Viking invaders. But they were unable to repel the Norman invasion of 1066, when they were forced to cede control of England to William of Normandy (the Conqueror), who established a new,

French-speaking royal dynasty and ruled England as William I (r. 1066–1087).

During the Middle Ages, the Norman kings made significant increases in the size of the territory controlled by the English Crown, gaining tenuous holds on Wales, Ireland, and Scotland. The dominion of the English kings over their Celtic neighbors reached its height in this period under Edward I (r. 899–924), while England briefly gained power over France under Henry V (r. 1413–1422). Scotland presented perhaps the biggest obstacle to the Normans; the two nations engaged in bloody skirmishes along the England–Scotland borders for most of the medieval period.

Skirmishes between England and Scotland came to an end in 1603 when James VI of Scotland (r. 1567–1625) succeeded to the throne of England as James I (r. 1603–1625) after the death of his distant relation, Elizabeth I (r. 1558–1603). James's Union of the Crowns united the former rival nations under one monarch, a union that was cemented with the Act of Union of 1707, which united the parliaments of England and Scotland. In 1800, Ireland became part of the United Kingdom, losing its separate parliament. But most of Ireland, except Northern Ireland, regained its independence in the twentieth century.

Beginning in the sixteenth century, England began a course of New World exploration, establishing colonies for trade throughout the world. In the centuries that followed, English monarchs ruled over American colonies, Canada, Australia, India, South Africa, and other parts of the world. While America gained its independence from England in the eighteenth century, many of England's other colonial ventures did not become independent until well into the twentieth century.

POWER

Just as the English monarchs ruled over vastly different-sized territories, they also possessed radically different degrees of power throughout history. Many other Western European nations eventually abandoned the monarchical form of government. France, for example, first abolished its monarchy in the French Revolution of 1789, and it has not had a monarch, even a symbolic one, since the nineteenth century.

England, however, has been through revolution, yet the monarchy remains. England's revolution took

Kings and Queens of England

House of Wessex

Egbert	802–839
Ethelwulf	839–858
Ethelbald	858–860
Ethelbert	860–866
Ethelred I	866–871
Alfred the Great*	871–899
Edward I*	899–924
Ethelstan	924–939
Edmund I	939–946
Edred	946–955
Edwig	955–959
Edgar I	959–975
Edward II*	975–978
Ethelred II	978–1016
Edmund II	1016
Edward III [The Confessor]*	1042–1066
Harold	1066

House of Normandy

William I [The Conqueror]*	1066–1087
William II [Rufus]*	1087–1100
Henry I*	1100–1135

House of Blois

Stephen*	1135–1154

House of Plantagenet

Henry II*	1154–1189
Richard I*	1189–1199
John*	1199–1216
Henry III	1216–1272
Edward I*	1272–1307
Edward II*	1307–1327
Edward III*	1327–1377
Richard II*	1377–1399

House of Lancaster

Henry IV*	1399–1413
Henry V	1413–1422
Henry VI	1422–1461

House of York

Edward IV	1461–1483
Edward V	1483
Richard III*	1483–1485

House of Tudor

Henry VII	1485–1509
Henry VIII*	1509–1547
Edward VI*	1547–1553
Mary I*	1553–1558
Elizabeth I*	1558–1603

House of Stuart

James I*	1603–1625
Charles I*	1625–1649

House of Stuart *(continued)*			George III*	1760–1820
Charles II*	1660–1685		George IV	1820–1830
James II*	1685–1688		William IV	1830–1837
			Victoria*	1837–1901

House of Orange

William III*	1689–1702
and Mary II*	1689–1695

House of Stuart

Anne*	1702–1714

House of Hanover

George I*	1714–1727
George II*	1727–1760

House of Saxe-Coburg-Gotha (House of Windsor since 1917)

Edward VII	1901–1910
George V	1910–1936
Edward VIII	1936
George VI	1936–1952
Elizabeth II*	1952–

*Indicates a separate alphabetical entry.

place a century before that of France, and its subsequent restoration of the king was more successful. Nevertheless, the powers of the monarchy in England have been significantly reduced since that time.

The current ruler of England, Queen Elizabeth II (r. 1952–), is mainly a figurehead, with little political influence or military power. However, she retains an important role as a national symbol, an object of English pride, and a living representative of centuries of English history.

Although English monarchs today possess little actual power, the height of the monarchical power in England was reached during the Renaissance under the Tudor and Stuart dynasties. Notable Tudor rulers include Henry VIII (r. 1509–1547), who broke with the Catholic Church in order to end his marriage to Catherine of Aragon. In the process, Henry destroyed Catholic monasteries, seized the wealth of the English churches for himself, and ordered the murder of Thomas More, chancellor of England, who refused to acknowledge Henry's authority over the Church. Another notable Tudor monarch was Henry's daughter Elizabeth I (r. 1558–1603), who also executed political enemies, such as Mary, Queen of Scots.

Although the Tudors increased the power of the throne through violence, their successors, the Stuarts, brought the English monarchy to the verge of despotism. To the Stuarts, kingliness was next to godliness. The first Stuart king of England, James I (r. 1603–1625), believed passionately in the divine right of kings—the belief that the king was God's representative or steward on earth, divinely selected and infallible. The Stuart kings were also proponents of the "royal touch," the belief that the touch of a divinely appointed monarch could heal certain ailments, such as scrofula ("the king's evil").

The despotism of the Stuarts, combined with a growing religious conflict between Catholics and Puritans, led to the English Civil War in 1642. The reigning monarch at the time, Charles I (r. 1625–1649), and the royalist nobles who remained loyal to him, defended themselves against the supporters of Puritanism and the Parliament. Charles was eventually executed in 1649, and in his place, the parliamentary general Oliver Cromwell became the Lord Protector of England.

After Cromwell's death and the brief rule of his son Richard, the English people invited the exiled Stuarts to resume the throne in 1660. But the En-

Originally built in the seventeenth century, Buckingham Palace was remodeled under the direction of architect John Nash in 1828. Beginning with Queen Victoria in 1837, the palace has served as the official London residence of British sovereigns.

glish Civil War had changed the country. When James II (r. 1685–1688) angered a large portion of the English people by promoting religious tolerance, particularly toward Catholics, he was forced from the throne in the Glorious Revolution of 1688, so-called because no blood was shed.

James's successors, William (r. 1689–1702) and Mary (r. 1689–1695), relinquished a large portion of the monarch's power to Parliament and the Privy Council, the advisers to the Crown. This compromise, in which power was shared by Parliament and the throne, returned England to a state closer to the Anglo-Saxon kingdoms, in which monarchy was semi-elective and the *witenagemot*, the Saxon equivalent of a parliament, possessed some power.

RESPONSIBILITIES

Over time, the responsibilities of English monarchs have fluctuated along with their power. First and foremost, the monarchs controlled political and military aspects of the kingdom. This involved every-

thing from policymaking to leading the country to war. In the medieval period, English kings actually led armies in battle. Henry V (r. 1413–1422), for example, led the English army to a great victory over the French at the battle of Agincourt (1415), while Richard III (r. 1483–1485) died on the battlefield in a civil conflict that ended the Wars of the Roses (1455–1485). Since Henry VIII, the kings and queens of England have also been their country's spiritual leader as head of the Church of England.

Certain English monarchs have had immense influence in the cultural realm. In the world of letters, the patronage of a king or queen could lead to the success or failure of a particular writer. English authors who made their fortune in part through royal patronage include Geoffrey Chaucer, William Shakespeare, Ben Jonson, and Sir Walter Scott. A few English monarchs were even authors themselves. James I wrote treatises not just on kingship but on witchcraft and tobacco, while Elizabeth I wrote poetry. In the nineteenth century, Queen Victoria (r. 1837–1901) set trends in all fields of culture. In stark contrast to the decadence of the earlier nineteenth century, the Victorian era ushered in a stricter sense of morality, a new emphasis on domestic values and family life, and a more conservative style of dress.

The power of the English monarchy has weakened significantly since the days of Saxon warlords and medieval kings who were thought to be able to heal illness with a touch of the hand. Even so, royalty still has the ability to capture the imaginations of the world; witness the remarkable influence that Princess Diana, the wife of Prince Charles, current heir to the throne, had during her lifetime.

See also: ENTRIES ON INDIVIDUAL ENGLISH MONARCHS; ANGLO-SAXON RULERS; COLONIALISM AND KINGSHIP; DIVINE RIGHT; HEALING POWERS OF KINGS; LANCASTER, HOUSE OF; NATIONAL IDENTITY; PLANTAGENET, HOUSE OF; STUART DYNASTY; WINDSOR, HOUSE OF; YORK, HOUSE OF.

FURTHER READING

Ashe, Geoffrey. *Kings and Queens of Early Britain.* Chicago: Academy Chicago, 1998.

Brendon, Piers, and Phillip Whitehead. *The Windsors: A Dynasty Revealed, 1917–2000.* London: Pimlico, 2000.

Longford, Elizabeth, ed. *The Oxford Book of Royal Anecdotes.* New York: Oxford University Press, 1989.

ENTHRONEMENT, RITES OF

Ceremonies in which a king or queen is seated on a chair or throne, often the last stage in the coronation or inauguration, indicating that the ruler has now reached the fullness of royal power. The throne is the place from which the sovereign dispenses justice and law. When enthroned, the ruler is also traditionally manifested symbolically to the people as a semidivine being.

SYMBOLISM OF THRONES

Throughout history, rulers in both ancient and modern societies have used the throne as a symbol of their royal status. Thrones are frequently associated with divinity, as a link to the gods who sit on thrones in the heavens. Jupiter's throne was strewn with stars, and the God of the Old Testament is supposed to have said to the ancient Hebrews, "Heaven is my throne and the earth is my footstool."

For earthly kings and rulers, thrones symbolize their role as intermediaries between heaven and earth. According to tradition, the sacred Chrysanthemum Throne of Japan was established at the time the heavens and the earth were separated. The emperor of Japan himself is thought to descend from heaven. The Dragon Throne of China was said to unite heaven and earth, and when the emperor was seated on it, he radiated his presence through the entire world.

Ancient Sumerian mythology describes the royal throne as being carved from a cosmic tree, the tree that in many cultures connects the various realms of the world: the home of the gods, the earth, and the underworld. A Sumerian myth describes how the huluppu tree grew beside the Euphrates River and was found by the goddess Innana. Out of it, the hero Gilgamesh carved a throne and regalia for her. It is from Inanna and her throne (which she wore on her head) that the Sumerian kings received their power. In the medieval period, the imperial throne of the Byzantine emperor was under a starred canopy and was made like a chariot to symbolize cosmic movement.

ENTHRONEMENT RITES

Enthronement rites in many societies are designed as a rite of passage, symbolizing a death to the monarch's previous ordinary life and a rebirth as ruler. Often, the throne represents the body of the Great Mother or earth goddess; the king sits in it as though sitting on her lap and is reborn. Christian terminology employs the same theme. At the council of Ephesus in 431 C.E., the Virgin Mary was declared to be "The Mother of God, the Throne of God." In fact, Mary is often shown in the same way as older mother goddesses, with the divine king Jesus seated on her lap.

French historian Jacques Le Goff described a French coronation ritual from the thirteenth century as a rite of passage in which the king goes from the ordinary world to the sacred one. The rite begins with the king's ceremonial rising from bed, and it continues with his procession to the cathedral in Reims, where his transformation into a king takes place. In the final part of the rite, the king mounts the throne, the place of new life and new power.

In Japan, the emperor and empress have been traditionally regarded as descendants of the goddess Amaterasu. Before they could rule, they underwent a Great Enthronement ceremony during which Amaterasu was said to enter their bodies. The Japanese imperial candidate entered a special enthronement palace in front of the imperial palace alone in the middle of the night and passed first into one sacred hall, then another. In each hall, there was a *kami* (divine) couch. The nature of the rite was kept secret, but it involved being symbolically united to the goddess.

In the Akuapem kingdom in Ghana, the king is installed on a special throne called a Black Stool, on which human blood, usually from his lineage, has been poured. The blood is considered the source of the stool's power. When the king is installed on the Black Stool, it unites him to the spirit of his ancestors and gives him power to rule.

A ruler on a throne is a symbol of power, but at times, the throne itself is such a symbol. For example, in the eighteenth century in China, on the imperial feast day, the emperor himself would remain hidden behind a screen, and the people would prostrate themselves before the empty throne, which is where his power lay.

Thrones remain an important part of royal ritual throughout the world's surviving monarchies. They still give a sense of exaltation and power, even when the original sacred origins of the rites have long been forgotten.

See also: ACCESSION AND CROWNING OF KINGS; DIVINITY OF KINGS; EARTH AND SKY, SEPARATION OF.

FURTHER READING

Bertelli, Sergio. *The King's Body: Sacred Rituals of Power in Medieval and Early Modern Europe.* Trans. R. Burr Litchfield. University Park: Pennsylvania State University Press, 2001.

Cannadine, David, and Simon Price, eds. *Rituals of Royalty: Power and Ceremonial in Traditional Societies.* New York: Cambridge University Press, 1992.

ESARHADDON (r. 680–669 B.C.E.)

Assyrian king who consolidated his power, enlarged his kingdom, and rebuilt the city of Babylon. Esarhaddon was the youngest son of King Sennacherib of Assyria (r. 705–681 B.C.E.) and Queen Naqija.

In 689 B.C.E., Sennacherib sacked Babylon and appointed Esarhaddon governor of Babylonia. When the king was murdered by his older sons in 681 B.C.E., Esarhaddon moved quickly to face his brothers' rebel forces, massed in western Assyria. Most of these forces promptly deserted to Esarhaddon, and his brothers were forced to flee. Esarhaddon returned to Nineveh, the Assyrian capital, where an Assyrian council appointed him king. This appointment was probably a controversial one because Esarhaddon, unlike his father and most powerful Assyrian politicians of the time, was a supporter of the Babylonians. Many scholars speculate that his mother, Queen Naqija, assisted Esarhaddon in his successful bid for power.

Esarhaddon had a number of superstitious practices that affected his reign. Perhaps the most striking of these was a strong fear of eclipses of the moon, three of which occurred while he held the throne. Each time, Esarhaddon decided to remove the risk of ill luck by not remaining as the head of state. Instead, he had a replacement king take the throne, while he masqueraded as a peasant. After a brief sojourn on the throne (and the return of the moon), the temporary kings were killed, and Esarhaddon resumed the throne.

Soon after becoming king of Assyria, Esarhaddon ordered the reconstruction of Babylon, warning the Babylonians that their city had been destroyed by his father as punishment by the god Marduk. Esarhaddon gained Babylonian support by referring to himself as governor of Babylonia rather than as king of Assyria.

A short time into his reign, Esarhaddon signed a peace treaty with the Elamites, who occupied an independent kingdom southeast of Assyria. This allowed him to turn his attention away from traditional disputes over the border between Elam and Assyria and to focus instead on Egypt, Assyria's greatest rival. When Egypt, under the leadership of the Pharoah Taharqa (r. 690–664 B.C.E.), began to foment revolt in Assyrian-controlled Phoenicia, Esarhaddon established a garrison of Assyrian troops on the Egyptian border and quelled the rebellion. He then marched on Egypt, taking the Egyptian capital of Memphis in 671 B.C.E., and making Egypt a vassal state of Assyria.

Esarhaddon's older son, Shamash-shum-ukin, was unpopular, so the king named his younger son, Ashurbanipal, as his successor in 672 B.C.E., leaving

Shamash-shum-ukin as Crown Prince of Babylon. Three years later, in 669 B.C.E., Esarhaddon died while trying to put down a rebellion in Egypt led by Taharqa, who Esarhaddon had overthrown in his conquest of Egypt several years earlier. Ashurbanipal succeeded his father on the throne, ruling Assyria from 668 to 627 B.C.E.

See also: ASHURBANIPAL; ASSYRIAN EMPIRE; EGYPTIAN DYNASTIES, ANCIENT (EIGHTEENTH TO TWENTY-SIXTH); SENNACHERIB.

ETHELRED II, THE UNREADY.

See ANGLO-SAXON RULERS; EDWARD THE CONFESSOR

ETIQUETTE, ROYAL

The ceremonies and forms of acceptable behavior expected of royalty. Kings and queens were governed by the etiquette that they or their royal predecessors constructed. Etiquette for royals often differed greatly from the rules of comportment that governed their subjects and thus became a reflection of the title and status awarded the person, whether king, queen, princess, or prince. The etiquette in place in royal courts governed the sovereigns, often equating them with godlike figures while thoroughly discouraging any attempt at social climbing by courtiers and subjects. Ritualized interaction between a monarch and subjects was important because it reinforced continuity and displayed power.

SHAPERS OF ETIQUETTE

France's most powerful king, Louis XIV (1638–1715), did much to shape the way royal etiquette was interpreted. Louis ascended the throne in 1642, though his reign really began after the death of Cardinal Mazarin in 1661. After being victorious in two wars in 1682 and determined to rule directly unlike previous kings who ruled through their ministers, Louis did so in the grandest style possible from the palace of Versailles. The palace was home to 5,000 nobles and roughly that same number in the surrounding neighborhoods. Versailles became the center of power, both socially and politically; for a noble not to be active at Versailles was tantamount to invisibility.

By using etiquette and ceremony as tools of power, Louis XIV was able to influence the behavior of the courtiers since they were falling over themselves to please him and secure their place at Versailles. The courtiers would interpret Louis's smallest gesture of displeasure or happiness as a sign of a shift in power—and indeed these gestures often were signs, resulting sometimes in unusual behavior on the part of the king.

QUEEN VICTORIA

The reign of Queen Victoria of England (1819–1901) was punctuated by a complex set of mores and etiquette that governed good society. During Victoria's reign, England was immensely wealthy, and wars were largely confined to the colonies. Queen Victoria withdrew from society after the death of her husband, her German cousin, Prince Albert. The etiquette of the era governed nearly every aspect of upper-class society, from dancing and the need for a modest demeanor in women, to the conduct of business and appropriate behavior during visits to private homes.

In Tudor England (the fifteenth and sixteenth centuries), royal etiquette dictated that where one's marriage took place hinged on one's noble rank. For example, a knight's wedding could take place inside the chapel door, while an earl's could take place inside the church. Those of a lesser rank could not be married physically inside the church.

CONSUMPTION

Alcohol consumption in ancient Egypt was widespread, even among women and royals. Unlike their counterparts in Europe, Egyptians imbibed and indulged openly and often to excess. A woman depicted in a tomb illustration is shown vomiting, presumably after overindulgence, while a king-like figure is shown in a limestone drawing looking rather haggard and dissipated. Forensic scientists have found traces of cocaine and nicotine in twenty-one dynasty mummies; it is unclear, however, whether these traces are the result of drug use or contamination or ingestion of similar plants.

See also: BEHAVIOR, CONVENTIONS OF ROYAL.

FURTHER READING
Cressy, David. *Birth, Marriage and Death: Ritual, Religion and the Life Cycle in Tudor and Stuart England.* New York: Oxford University Press, 1994.

ETRUSCAN KINGDOMS

(flourished 700s–300s B.C.E.)

First great urban civilization of ancient Italy, whose culture strongly influenced the development of Rome and the Roman Republic. Etruscan civilization was centered in the Italian region of Etruria (which comprises present-day Tuscany and parts of Umbria), although at their height, the Etruscans ruled most of Italy. The Etruscans were well known in the ancient Mediterranean world for the freedom they allowed women, the relatively comfortable status of their slaves, and their elaborate divination rituals.

ORIGIN OF THE ETRUSCANS

Debated since ancient times, the origin of the Etruscans is still a mystery. Three contradictory theories have emerged: the Etruscans came from Lydia in Asia Minor (present-day Turkey); they were an indigenous people of Italy; or they migrated to Italy from somewhere to the north. None of these theories has been proven conclusively, although modern scholars have largely discredited the third—that the Etruscans came from the north.

Scholars have used two kinds of evidence in their efforts to solve the mystery of the Etruscans' origins: archaeological and linguistic. Some archaeological evidence has led archaeologists to claim that the "civilized" Etruscans arrived in a region inhabited by the more "primitive" Villanovans, who flourished from the tenth to eighth centuries B.C.E. Other modern archaeologists suggest that the source of the cultural shift that took place in Etruria after 700 B.C.E. resulted from the growing influence of Greece rather than from a foreign migration.

Linguistic analyses have been limited by a poor understanding of the Etruscan language. Some scanty evidence suggests that a dialect related to Etruscan was spoken on the Aegean island of Lemnos, in the direction of Lydia. Inscriptions found in the Alps suggest the Etruscan presence there as well. Until the obscure language of the Etruscans is fully translated, the origin of the Etruscans will probably remain a mystery. In the meantime, scholars are relying on archaeology to learn about Etruscan life.

ETRUSCAN CIVILIZATION

Whatever its origins, Etruscan civilization developed rapidly in Etruria during the seventh century B.C.E. By the sixth century B.C.E., Etruscan power and wealth reached its peak, and Etruscan influence extended throughout much of the Italian Peninsula. The Etruscan civilization was relatively short-lived, however, especially compared to their successors, the Romans. By the fifth century B.C.E., it had begun to decline, and around 500 B.C.E. the Romans overthrew the Etruscans and established a new civilization in Italy.

Language and Writing

The Etruscan language remains largely unintelligible to modern scholars. Their writing system, however, was adapted from that of the Phoenicians, and their alphabet is reasonably well understood. Indeed, it was from the Etruscans that the Romans received the alphabet which they adapted to Latin and which is the basis of the alphabet used in English and other Western languages today.

Unfortunately, no Etruscan literature has survived from ancient times. The Roman emperor Claudius (r. 41–54 C.E.) wrote a history of the Etruscans based on sources that existed in the first century C.E., but all copies of this history have also been lost. Although more than 13,000 known inscriptions in Etruscan exist, most are very short and consist of no more than the name of a person or object.

Religion

Divination was a very important aspect of Etruscan religion, particularly as derived from examining weather and the livers of animals. Etruscan diviners were responsible for determining the orientation of cities, and Etruscan cities were among the first planned cities in the ancient world. Etruscan priests, augurs, and diviners were employed in Rome for centuries after the Etruscan kingdom had lost its independence to the Romans.

Early Etruscan religious objects show little evidence of a belief in humanlike gods. But later contact with the Greeks and Romans had a great influence, and Etruscan deities became increasingly identified with the pantheons of Greek and Roman gods and goddesses. Earlier Etruscan art suggests a conception of a happy afterlife, but funerary art after the fourth century B.C.E. shows a much darker vision of life after death—perhaps also a result of the influence of Greek and Roman traditions.

Government and Social Structure

The Etruscan government was never centralized; rather, it comprised a number of autonomous city-

The ancient Etruscans developed the first urban culture in Italy from the eighth to the first century B.C.E. Much of what is known about this enigmatic civilization comes from tombs in sprawling necropolises, or cemeteries, like this one in Cerveteri, Tuscany.

states connected by common cultural ties. In early Etruscan history, these city-states were ruled by kings, probably drawn from the wealthy aristocracy. Every year, a council of leaders from twelve cities, called the League of the Twelve Peoples, met at a shrine to the Etrurian god Voltumna, although the purpose of this meeting seems to have been as much religious as it was political. By the end of the fifth century B.C.E., however, it appears that most Etruscan governments had shifted to oligarchies, which included elected assemblies and magistrates.

By the sixth century B.C.E., a growing middle class had begun to emerge in Etruscan society. Although the Etruscans depended upon slaves for labor, it is clear that the position of slaves at that time was far better than that of slaves in the rest of the ancient world. Indeed, Greek and Roman authors repeatedly

remarked on the comfortable position of slaves in Etruscan society. Etruscan slaves could own their own homes, and they were freed with relative ease into a society that allowed ex-slaves to rise easily in status.

Women in Etruscan society enjoyed civil liberties that scandalized their Greek and Roman counterparts. According to Roman stories, Etruscan women could take an active part in public life, including involving themselves in political affairs, acting as highly educated augurs, and dining freely with their husbands and friends.

Leisure
Etruria was a wealthy region, and the upper classes of Etruscan society enjoyed a significant amount of leisure. Etruscan frescoes and painted pottery are renowned for the skill and liveliness of their depic-

tion of Etruscan life. Many decorative scenes show elaborate dinners, attended by men and women, with entertainment provided by musicians and dancers. Others show that the Etruscans adopted a number of sports from the Greeks, and that hunting and fishing may have been popular forms of recreation. The Etruscans also played board games and used devices of chance, such as knucklebones and dice, although these may have played a role in divination as well as in recreation.

War and Trade

The Etruscans were a significant military power on both land and sea. According to the Roman orator Cato the Elder, almost all of Italy was once under Etruscan control. Rome itself was an Etruscan colony during the early years of its history.

Although the Etruscans had to compete with the Greeks for maritime supremacy, they managed to establish an extensive trade network. Etruscan goods were exported throughout the Mediterranean world, including the Iberian Peninsula, France, the Balkan region, Greece, Anatolia (present-day Turkey), and North Africa.

DECLINE OF THE ETRUSCANS

Until the Etruscan dynasty of the Tarquins assumed control of it, Rome was a rural backwater, hardly more than a collection of agricultural huts built in a swamp. Under the Etruscan kings of Rome—Lucius Tarquinius Priscus (r. ca. 616–579 B.C.E.), Servius Tullius (r. ca. 578–535 B.C.E.), and Lucius Tarquinius Superbus (r. ca. 524–510 B.C.E.), Rome was transformed into the city that would one day rule the world. The Etruscan rulers of Rome built the Cloaca Maxima, a sewer that helped to drain the marshy soil around the Tiber River. They constructed the walls of the Capitoline hill, replaced huts with brick houses, paved roads, and built the city's first temples.

Nevertheless, by 510 B.C.E., the Romans had become dissatisfied with the rule of the Etruscan kings and had expelled the Tarquins from the city. The Romans then established a republic, just as its Etruscan counterparts were doing in the rest of Italy. The overthrow of Etruscan rule in Rome, however, marked the beginning of the decline of Etruscan power in southern Italy.

Beginning of the End

When the Etruscans lost control of Rome, they lost their land route to the cities of the fertile region of Campania in southern Italy. This loss was tolerable as long as the Etruscans maintained their naval routes. But when the Etruscan navy was destroyed by Hieron I (r. 478–466 B.C.E.) of Syracuse in 474 B.C.E., contact with Campania was completely cut off and the region soon fell to restive Umbro-Sabellian tribes.

In 395 B.C.E., the Etruscan city-state of Veii, one of the twelve cities of the confederation, fell to the Romans. At the same time, Celtic peoples from the north invaded as far as the heartland of Etruria, and the Gallic Senones people took possession of Picenum on the east coast of Italy. The invaders threatened the entire Etruscan civilization, and in the mid-fourth century B.C.E., the Etruscans barely escaped total destruction.

Roman Rule

The Etruscan city-states, threatened on all sides by hostile groups and weakened by internal class struggles, fell to Rome one by one over the next century. By the mid-third century B.C.E., all of Etruria was under Roman control, although most of the Etruscan states preserved at least a pretense of political autonomy. In 90 B.C.E., Rome granted citizenship rights to its Italian vassal states, and the Etruscan states were incorporated into the growing power of the Roman state.

During the Roman civil wars (80–79 B.C.E.), many of the Etruscan cities chose the wrong side, and the victor, the Roman general Lucius Cornelius Sulla, exacted brutal retribution. Sulla established his soldiers in several Etruscan districts, granting them Etruscan land in return for their past services. This led to a vicious cycle of Etruscan revolt and Roman reprisal, until the reign of the emperor Augustus (r. 27 B.C.E.–14 C.E.) finally brought peace to the land. By this point, Rome had either incorporated or discarded much of Etruscan culture.

See also: DIVINATION AND DIVINERS, ROYAL; RIGHTS, CIVIL; ROMAN EMPIRE; TARQUIN DYNASTY; TARQUIN THE PROUD.

FURTHER READING

Brendel, Otto, and Francesca R. Serra Ridgeway. *Etruscan Art.* New Haven, CT: Yale University Press, 1995.

Haynes, Sybille. *Etruscan Civilization: A Cultural History.* Los Angeles: Paul Getty Museum Publications, 2000.

Macnamara, Ellen. *The Etruscans*. Cambridge, MA: Harvard University Press, 1991.

EUNUCHS, ROYAL

Castrated men who served as advisers and top officials for monarchs in many countries and periods.

The cruel practice of castrating men in order to provide pliable slaves or loyal servants for royal masters occurred in many civilizations. Many died during the painful and unsanitary removal of the testicles (and sometimes the penis as well), and most of the rest lived miserable lives. But oddly, small numbers of royal eunuchs were able to use their peculiar status to amass and wield great power, even controlling the destiny of empires.

ROLES OF THE EUNUCH

The Greek word *eunouchus*, from which the English "eunuch" derives, meant "keeper of the bedchamber." That was perhaps the most well-known task that eunuchs performed—protecting the ruler's sexual monopoly over his wives and concubines.

In many empires and kingdoms, the monarch had hundreds or even thousands of female consorts, and any one of their many sons might aspire to the throne. To prevent the legal and religious catastrophe of an illegitimate king, eunuchs would guard the royal harem to keep out any man but the monarch.

Eunuchs, however, also filled many other functions that required trust and loyalty to the monarch. Universal taboos prevented them from ever becoming rulers themselves. Perhaps more important, these childless men could not build rival dynasties and did not have families requiring support or an inheritance. They were expected to devote all their energies to their jobs and their monarchs.

Monarchies as varied as ancient Egypt, Babylon, Persia, and Rome, the Byzantine and early Arab empires, the Muslim courts of Turkey, Persia, and India, and probably all the dynasties of China, used eunuchs. They all developed systems of recruiting or purchasing boys, slave or free, and castrating them to produce eunuchs for palace and government work.

When political and religious custom kept monarchs isolated in palace complexes, eunuchs were the only men with regular access to the ruler, and they became his advisers, ministers, and generals. Wives, concubines, and queen mothers would often ally themselves with prominent eunuchs to gain a measure of power and promote the interests of their own children.

THE SYSTEM IN CHINA

The eunuch system was most deeply entrenched in China, where it is first mentioned in records from the eighth century B.C.E., though it probably long predated that era. By the end of the Ming dynasty (1368–1644 C.E.), more than seventy thousand eunuchs served in the imperial court. The subsequent Manchu dynasty (1644–1912) drastically reduced these numbers, in an attempt to lessen eunuch intrigues. Nevertheless, as late as 1887 a British scholar reported that there were two thousand eunuchs in the Forbidden City in Beijing, while outside the palace, dozens of imperial relatives were also allowed to employ fixed numbers of eunuchs, as a privilege of rank.

Classic Chinese historians repeatedly accused eunuchs of corruption and treachery, and blamed them for imperial inaction or misdeeds. These historians may have been biased, as they all came from the highly educated and generally aristocratic Mandarin class, while their eunuch competitors were of lower class origin and had not spent long years studying the Confucian classics.

Chinese imperial armies, especially the palace armies of the T'ang dynasty (618–907), were often led by eunuchs. Under the later Mings, one celebrated eunuch was Admiral Zheng He (1371–1435), whose fleets of more than three hundred ships explored and traded all across the Indian Ocean.

Whatever the exalted status of some individuals, however, most Chinese held eunuchs in contempt and excluded them from many religious rites. They saw eunuchs as deformed and pitied them for not having children to revere them after their deaths, a key concept in Chinese religion.

SLAVE EUNUCHS IN TURKEY

In China, most eunuchs were sold as boys by poor parents. In some cases, young men with no resources had themselves castrated in the hope of getting palace jobs. In contrast, the eunuchs of the Ottoman Empire were generally of slave origin; by the sixteenth century, most Ottoman eunuchs were black Africans. Neither their race nor their legal status prevented some of these eunuchs from rising to positions of great power. The Chief Black Eunuch was often one of the most powerful officials at the Ottoman court. In fact, the only blacks ever to rise in the Ottoman imperial service were eunuchs.

In the early nineteenth century, European observers reported on castration "factories" in southern Egypt, where several hundred young black boys were prepared each year for sale as eunuchs. When castration was banned in Egypt around 1860, the operation moved south to the Sudan. According to informants, a large majority of the boys (from 97 to 99 percent) survived, about the same success rate claimed in nineteenth-century China.

Only four hundred seventy eunuchs still lived in the Forbidden City in Beijing in 1911 when the Chinese Revolution overthrew the Manchu dynasty. In 1924, the new Nationalist republic formally abolished the eunuch system. At the other end of Asia, in Ottoman Turkey, the revolution of 1908 ultimately led to the same result. When the reformist republican government in 1924 disbanded the seraglio (harem) in Istanbul, the last stronghold of the royal eunuch, respected and deplored for millennia, had finally disappeared.

See also: MING DYNASTY; OTTOMAN EMPIRE; T'ANG DYNASTY.

EUROPEAN KINGSHIPS

The dominant style of European political rule from the fall of the Roman Empire to the era of democratic revolution (ca. 500–1800). The oldest European kingdoms came into existence during the early Middle Ages. Over the next millennium, powerful kingdoms arose in England and France, Germany flirted with centralized monarchy in the Holy Roman Empire, and kingdoms took shape in Spain, Sweden, Russia, and other places. After 1500, all these kingdoms faced serious challenges from the rise of democracy. The role of monarchs after 1800 changed dramatically for those who survived the democratic revolutions. Kingdoms became republics and constitutional monarchies and gave their once powerful rulers only limited or symbolic roles to play.

MEDIEVAL ORIGINS
After the fall of the Roman Empire in the fifth century, Europe split into a series of kingdoms roughly corresponding to the locations of the various Germanic peoples who had migrated there. These Germanic kingdoms rarely lasted more than a few generations. Meanwhile, the armies of the Islamic caliphate conquered Visigothic Spain in 711, and Merovingian France divided and united repeatedly as a result of battles between competing heirs. The true ancestors of European kingdoms came into being in the tenth century.

THE RISE OF THE CENTRALIZED STATE
In the early Middle Ages, kings exercised power through personal ties with lesser nobles known as vassals. In return for protection from the king and the right to adjudicate their lands as they wished, vassals provided the monarch money and service. Authority such as exercising justice was privately owned. This system of governance, known as feudalism, began breaking down because it lacked a single powerful central authority. Beginning in England and France, kings began to erode feudal rights and centralize their authority through war, legal means, and wealth.

In England, this process began under Norman rule following the invasion and conquest by William the Conqueror in 1066. As King William I (r. 1066–1087), he erased the existing Anglo-Saxon aristocracy of England and replaced it with Norman lords. As a result, William was able to establish unchallenged rule. His government was efficient and hierarchical, overcoming the weaknesses of a feudal system. By the thirteenth century, English monarchical government was well established despite periods of royal uncertainty. One such period occurred during the reign of King John (r. 1199–1216) when France seized English continental territories. In order to raise an army to fight the French, John raised taxes. When the war went badly for John, the English barons revolted and forced John to accept limitations on his power by signing the Magna Carta (1215). The English king was now subject to law and bound to his nobles.

In France, beginning in the tenth century, the Capetian dynasty gradually centralized power by fighting against entrenched feudal lords and consolidating their own rule. The first Capetian monarch, Hugh Capet (r. 987–996), was elected by an aristocratic assembly and owed his authority to them. As a result, the French monarchy took much longer to centralize authority than their English counterparts.

ROYAL RITUALS

THE ROYAL TOUCH

Monarchs throughout Europe were often assigned supernatural as well as political powers because of their special position in European society. One such example was the legend that the kings could cure illness, especially epilepsy and a painful skin disease known as scrofula. French kings from the Middle Ages onward met their public on ceremonial occasions to touch the ill and infirm. The ritual was practiced much more often during the Middle Ages than later. Nonetheless, Louis XIV, who detested commoners, touched over 1,000 persons on numerous occasions, and in 1774 Louis XVI made a point of performing the ritual upon his coronation.

English kings also practiced the ritual of the royal touch. All the kings from Henry VIII through the Stuarts met their people as healers. Henry reportedly believed thoroughly in his powers, while Elizabeth I was a skeptic. The Stuart king Charles II touched over 100,000 persons in the ritual act over the course of his reign.

By the twelfth century, however, Capetian kings had begun to extend royal power beyond central France. Louis the Fat (r. 1108–1137) and his trusted adviser Suger, the abbot of St. Denis, defended royal authority and, through careful propaganda, built an image of the French king as both saint and hero. Several generations later, Philip Augustus (r. 1180–1223) consolidated French power through a series of conquests and managed to incorporate much of Normandy and northern France into his domain. These kings laid the groundwork for a strong French monarchy.

THE EARLY MODERN PERIOD
(ca. 1500–1800)

Most European kingdoms followed a centralizing course from the sixteenth to the nineteenth centuries. During this time, however, they took several different paths and faced very different futures.

England and Constitutionalism

In 1603, Elizabeth I of England (r. 1558–1603) died without an heir. The closest male relative was James Stuart, who had been raised in France and influenced by the French court's style and politics. When James I (r. 1603–1625) took the throne, he attempted to install a French-style absolutist monarchy in which the king had unchallenged power. Since the Magna Carta, however, English kings had shared power with an assembly of notables, and this arrangement had been institutionalized as Parliament over the previous several centuries. James's political and religious views thus angered and worried many Englishmen.

When James's son Charles I (r. 1625–1649) took the throne, he went even further than his father in his attempts to establish absolute power. Parliament resisted his initiatives, and Charles retaliated by sending soldiers into the House of Commons. Open civil war followed. In the end, Charles I was executed in 1649 and replaced not by a king, but by Oliver Cromwell, who ruled as Lord Protector of a Puritan Protectorate. Cromwell's republic proved unpopular, however. After his death, the new Parliament of 1660 invited Charles II (r. 1660–1685), the son of the executed king, to return as monarch.

The Stuarts still had not learned their lesson, however, and both Charles II and his brother James II (r. 1685–1688) pursued absolutist and Catholic initiatives. When James produced a male Catholic heir, Parliament appealed to William of Orange (r. 1689–1702), the husband of James's Protestant daughter Mary (r. 1689–1695), to displace James and take the English throne. James fled to France, and William and Mary took the throne as co-monarchs. England returned to a stable monarchy, but the political direction of the country was decidedly constitutional. The monarch's power was limited by law and precedent, and the power of Parliament was clearly on the rise.

France and Absolutism

By 1600, France faced a set of problems similar to those in England. The monarchy was well established, but it was dependent upon a powerful and entrenched nobility. To rid itself of this challenge, the French monarchy, beginning with Louis XIII (r. 1610–1643), adopted a political philosophy known as absolutism. This philosophy asserted that the king was the sole authority in the kingdom and subject to challenge by no other power. Some individuals, such as the philosopher Jean-Bénigne Bossuet, went so far as to claim that the French king's authority was second only to God's. Bossuet called this concept the "divine right of kings."

Louis XIV (r. 1643–1715) carried the philosophy of absolutism and divine right to its extremes. As a child, he had witnessed a civil war, the Fronde (1648–1653), during which aristocrats, judges, and commoners had all challenged monarchical power. In response, Louis sought to tame the forces that challenged his rule. He established his court outside Paris at the luxurious palace of Versailles, and he avoided commoners (except his officials) at all cost, never returning to Paris as an adult. Louis is said to have declared, "L'état, c'est moi" ("I am the state"). To insure that he remained a monarch with no united challengers, he created a body of bureaucrats and aristocrats who owed their careers and livelihoods to the king alone. His power was unmatched and unquestioned.

Other Monarchies

Other European nations possessed powerful and well-established monarchies as well. In Russia, for example, princes and then tsars had ruled from Moscow with an iron fist since around 910. The Spanish monarchy emerged with the unification of Aragón and Castile under Ferdinand II (r. 1479–1516) and Isabella (r. 1474–1504). Germany began its long road to unification under the military rulers of Prussia, beginning with Frederick I (r. 1701–1713). The Holy Roman Empire and the Austrian Empire influenced European history under Habsburg rule from the late fifteenth century. Other monarchies saw more limited periods of glory, Sweden and Poland-Lithuania being just two examples.

DEMOCRACY AND MODERN MONARCHY

In the late eighteenth century, a distinct change in the political values of the Western world resulted in a series of democratic revolutions. Beginning with the American Revolution (1776–1783) and the French Revolution (1789–1799), Americans and many Europeans rejected arbitrary government and authoritative monarchy once and for all. The United States rejected monarchy entirely, forming the first large and stable republic in the modern era. France also rejected monarchy, executing Louis XVI (r. 1774–1792) in 1793. Other monarchies, such as the English, survived, but were no longer active political institutions. Instead their roles became more and more symbolic and cultural. European monarchs such as Denmark's Queen Margrethe II (r. 1972–Present) and Belgium's King Albert II (r. 1993–Present) still exist today, but none has any real power.

See also: BOURBON DYNASTY; CAPETIAN DYNASTY; DIVINE RIGHT; ENGLISH MONARCHIES; FRENCH MONARCHIES; HABSBURG DYNASTY; HOLY ROMAN EMPIRE; IBERIAN KINGDOMS; RUSSIAN DYNASTIES; SPANISH MONARCHIES; SWEDISH MONARCHY; TUDOR, HOUSE OF; VALOIS DYNASTY.

FURTHER READING

Collins, James. *The State in Early Modern France.* New York: Cambridge University Press, 1999.

Fraser, Antonia, ed. *Lives of the Kings and Queens of England.* Berkeley: University of California Press, 2000.

Venturi, Franco. *The End of the Old Regime in Europe, 1768–1776: The First Crisis.* Trans. R. Burr Litchfield. Princeton, NJ: Princeton University Press, 1989.

EWYAS, KINGDOM OF. *See* GWENT KINGDOM

EXCHANGE, MEANS OF. *See* COINAGE, ROYAL

EXECUTIONS, ROYAL

Sanctioned executions of monarchs, often carried out for political purposes, particularly during disputes over the Crown. Royals were often executed by members of their own government under the pretext of treason. Sometimes, however, this charge was simply a way of justifying the execution of a monarch in order to serve other political motivations.

In general, a king was executed only in extreme circumstances. For example, in 1782, King Taksin of Cambodia (r. 1768–1782) was executed by his ministers after he had removed himself to a monastery, thereby allowing rebellion and the breakdown of his government.

The execution of King Charles I of England (r. 1625–1649) in 1649 was an exceptional event, even in an age when public execution was common. Charles I claimed to rule with divine right, or with the will and authority of God. The idea of executing the divine head of state aroused great passion among the populace because it was considered a direct challenge to God's authority. When Charles's son, Charles II (r. 1660–1685) was restored to the throne of England eleven years later, the men who signed his father's death warrant were tried and executed. Only the executioner, who had worn a mask concealing his identity, was spared retribution.

The execution of King Louis XVI of France in 1792 (r. 1774–1792) was an important historic event in that it signified the end of the French monarchy following the French Revolution. The fate of the former king had been the first great political issue confronting the National Convention, which had ruled France since September 1792. When it was decided to try the former king for crimes against the nation, the deputies spent days agonizing over whether they had the authority to kill him and whether they should use that authority. Ultimately, they decided to execute the former king, and Louis XVI was guillotined in the Place de la Révolution in Paris on January 21, 1793. The French also used the guillotine for the executions of the former king's Austrian queen, Marie-Antoinette. Many of the French aristocracy also met their fate at the guillotine during the revolutionary period.

Throughout much of history, the execution of a king has marked a radical shift in a country's form of government. The execution of Charles I of England, for example, signified the change in government from the monarchy to the Commonwealth (1649–1653) with the Parliamentary leader Oliver Cromwell as head of state. The execution of French king Louis XVI also marked the end of the French monarchy and the beginning of the First Republic. (The monarchy was restored in 1804, but lasted only until 1870.)

Modes of executing royalty have varied over the ages. In the sixteenth and seventeenth centuries, Germany and England used the Headman's Axe to execute both royal and nonroyal individuals. In England, the Tower of London was the site of many notable beheadings and was used for only the aristocracy. Tower Green, an area outside the Tower, was reserved for royal executions, and the public did not attend. The Tower Green saw the beheadings of two of the wives of Henry VIII (r. 1509–1547)—Anne Boleyn and Katherine Howard—as well as Lady Jane Grey, who took the throne of England briefly after the death of Henry's son and successor, Edward VI (r. 1547–1553).

See also: DEACCESSION; DETHRONEMENT; DIVINE RIGHT; REGICIDE; TREASON, ROYAL.

FAISAL I (1885–1933 C.E.)

Hashemite ruler (r. 1921–1933) who rebelled against Ottoman rule and became the first king of a sovereign Iraq. Faisal was a member of the Hashemite dynasty, an old Arabian noble family that had been influential in the city of Mecca since pre-Islamic times. In the twentieth century, the Hashemites briefly dominated the areas that are now Saudi Arabia, Jordan, Syria, and Iraq.

Faisal's father, Al-Hussein bin Ali, was the *sherif* of Mecca, a local ruler subordinate to the powerful Ottoman Empire that ruled over most of the Middle East. Faisal spent several years of his youth in Constantinople, the Ottoman capital, but in 1908 he returned to Mecca with his father to help govern the Hejaz region of Arabia. In 1916, Hussein and his sons led the Arab Revolt, a British-backed uprising against Ottoman rule.

During the Arab Revolt, Faisal established himself as a competent leader, fighting alongside British adventurer T.E. Lawrence in the deserts of Jordan. In 1918, Faisal conquered the Syrian city of Damascus and set up a government there, and in 1920 he declared himself king of "Greater Syria." However, the French government drove him out and established a semicolonial mandate government in Lebanon and Syria.

Faisal lived in exile in Britain until the British government offered him the throne of Iraq in exchange for temporary British mandate authority over the new state. Faisal agreed and became king of Iraq in 1921 after winning 96 percent of the vote in a plebiscite. He ruled Iraq as a constitutional monarch during the mandate period and after the country gained its independence.

Faisal governed capably, managing to moderate between the diverse ethnic and religious power blocs within Iraq. Under his leadership, Iraq became a fully independent nation and a sovereign member of the League of Nations in 1932. Just under a year later, Faisal I died of heart problems at a clinic in Switzerland, leaving his hard-won throne to his son Ghazi (r. 1933–1939).

See also: HASHEMITE DYNASTY.

FAN SHIH-MAN (d. 225 C.E.)

Considered the greatest ruler (r. ca. 205–225) of the ancient Funan kingdom, which covered the area that is present-day Myanmar (Burma), Thailand, Cambodia, and southern Vietnam.

The details of Fan Shih-Man's reign are poorly documented, and nothing is known of his early life before taking the throne. According to ancient Chinese historical records, Fan Shih-Man ruled at the height of the Funan kingdom and was known for his attacks and conquests of neighboring kingdoms, both by land and sea. According to some sources, he extended the size of his kingdom by as much as 1,500 miles, as far as the lower Mekong River. Fan Shih-Man recognized conquered states as his vassals.

So successful was Fan Shih-Man in his endeavors that he proclaimed himself Great King. Historical documents indicate that Fan Shih-Man died while exploring Chin-lin, a state believed to have been located in lower Burma or the Malay Peninsula. After his death in 225, his nephew, Fan Chan, killed Fan Shih-Man's son, the rightful heir to the throne, and declared himself king.

See also: CAMBODIAN KINGDOMS; FUNAN KINGDOM; VIETNAMESE KINGDOMS.

FANTE KINGDOM. *See* AKAN KINGDOMS

FAROUK (1920–1965 C.E)

Last reigning king of Egypt (r. 1936–1952), whose allegedly corrupt governance and unpopularity with the military led to the collapse of the Egyptian monarchy and the establishment of a republic in 1952.

Farouk succeeded to the throne of Egypt in 1936, upon the death of his father, the unpopular King Fouad (r. 1917–1936). The first of the Mohammed Ali Pasha dynasty to speak fluent Arabic and a proponent of nationalism, Farouk seemed to be a king destined for popularity. But the young king, still a minor, entered the political stage at a turbulent time. Royal power in Egypt was waning and giving way to growing compromise between the imperial interests of Great Britain on the one hand and the nationalist demands of the popular Wafd Party on the other. Farouk's diplomatic skills were not great enough to transcend his circumstances.

For the first year of his reign, Farouk could do little but watch as the Wafd prime minister, An-Nahh-as—who became a recurring antagonistic figure during Farouk's reign—renegotiated Egypt's treaties with Britain. However, when Farouk reached the age of majority in July 1937, he immediately went about securing his control of all the powers accorded to him as a king of Egypt. By December of that same year, An-Nah-h-as had been dismissed.

Great Britain, concerned primarily with preserving control of the Suez Canal, maintained a strong military and cultural presence in Egypt, and in 1939, the British insisted that Farouk reinstate An-Nah-h-as as prime minister. Farouk refused but was forced to comply when the British and the Wafd Party joined forces in 1942.

When the prime minister negotiated the groundwork for the foundation of the Arab League in 1944, Farouk took advantage of An-Nah-h-as's loss of Britain's favor and dismissed him once more, planning to name himself head of the League. The Arab cause in Palestine was popular in Egypt, and despite allegations of corruption, political instability did not threaten Farouk's hold on power until the unexpected crushing defeat of the Egyptians in the first engagement of the Arab-Israeli War (1948–1949). Many of Egypt's military officers blamed Farouk personally for Egypt's defeat, citing his incompetence in ridding Egypt of British military occupation as a symptom of his political ineffectiveness.

In July 1952, a group calling itself the Free Officers, led by Colonel Gamal Abdel Nasser, staged a political coup in Egypt, forcing Farouk to abdicate the throne. Farouk's son, Fouad (Fu'ad) II (r. 1952–1953), was named king, but in less than twelve months, Nasser had transformed the country into a republic, leaving Farouk to live out the remainder of his life abroad. Fouad II was also exiled to France.

See also: ABDICATION, ROYAL; DETHRONEMENT.

FATIMID DYNASTY (909–1171 C.E.)

Islamic Shi'ite dynasty that ruled North Africa, especially Syria and Egypt, and often contended with the Abbasid dynasty for the title of caliph. The name of the dynasty is derived from Fatima, the daughter of the Prophet Muhammad and wife of Ali, from whom the dynasty claimed descent.

ORIGINS

The Fatimid dynasty first emerged in North Africa from relative obscurity in 909, when a Shi'ite leader named Ubaydullah arrived in Tunisia, claiming to be caliph by right of his descent from the Prophet's family. Ubaydullah backed his claim with adequate military force to take North Africa from the Aghlabid dynasty.

The Fatimids strengthened these claims in the next half-century, finally taking Egypt from the Ikshidid dynasty in 969. In Egypt, the Fatimids built their new capital, al-Qahirah, which we call Cairo. Ruling from the new capital, the Fatimids expanded the empire into Syria and Palestine. While concentrating their rule and focus in Egypt, however, the Fatimids subsequently lost Tunisia.

The Fatimid rulers took the titles of caliph and imam, reflecting their dual roles in temporal and spiritual leadership. As imams, they claimed religious dominion over all Islam, and Egypt became the center from which Shi'ite Muslims proselytized in Syria, Iran, and Yemen. Yet the Fatimids made no real efforts to convert the Egyptians, who were primarily Sunni Muslims, and they dealt with Christian and Jewish inhabitants with peaceful tolerance.

PERIOD OF TYRANNY

One notable exception to the open-minded religious policy of the Fatimids was the caliph al-Hakim (r. 996–1021), whose madness prompted him to execute or assassinate almost anyone unfortunate enough to trigger his wrath, including several of his viziers (ministers of state).

Al-Hakim persecuted Christians and Jews, destroying synagogues and churches. His destruction of the Church of the Holy Sepulcher in Jerusalem provided one of the rallying points for Christians in the Crusades.

Not satisfied with these religious pogroms, al-Hakim declared himself a god and sent missionaries to carry word of his divinity throughout the Muslim world. Oddly, when some of these missionaries were killed, he restored Christians and Jews to favor and rebuilt many of their holy places. These religious activities were cut short when al-Hakim died abruptly under mysterious circumstances in 1021.

FATIMID RULE

As caliphs, the Fatimids ruled a wealthy empire. Centered in the extremely fertile Nile Valley, the empire generated considerable agricultural wealth, augmented by extensive and profitable trade along the Mediterranean basin and the Red Sea. The Fatimid caliphs underlined their power by judicious display of their wealth, riding on horseback in elaborate processions through the streets of Cairo, attended by soldiers and holders of civil office.

Fatimid administration was similar to that practiced by the Abbasid caliphs in Baghdad. However, under the Fatimids, civil office became a meritocracy in which advancement was based on merit. Here again, the religious tolerance of the Fatimids was evident, as Sunnis were as likely as Shi'ites to hold public office. In general, even Christians and Jews were eligible to serve in government and were promoted based on their skill.

Egypt generally prospered under the Fatimids, who by and large promoted architecture, the arts, and scholarship. The culture of the Fatimids reached its apex during the caliphate of al-Mustansir (r. 1036–1094), but it began to decline toward the end of his reign as well.

END OF THE DYNASTY

Like many other eastern rulers, the Fatimids chose their soldiers from outside the populations they ruled, choosing to fill their military ranks with mercenary Berbers, Sudanese, and Turks. In 1076, Turkish mercenaries rebelled against Mustansir, running roughshod through the palace and carrying away a fortune in jewels and art treasures. They were also said to have loaded twenty camels with priceless manuscripts, many of which were used later to light fires.

When Mustansir died in 1094, the Fatimid army broke into factions among the Berbers, Sudanese, and Turks. The country followed suit, with Morocco, Palestine, and Syria falling away from central Fatimid control. In 1171, the Ayyubid leader Al-Nasir Yusuf removed the last Fatamid caliph, al-Adid (r. 1160–1171), from power, bringing the Fatimid dynasty to an end. Yusuf, better known as Saladin, soon became sultan of Egypt (r. 1175–1193), bringing the Ayyubid dynasty to power.

See also: ABBASID DYNASTY; AYYUBID DYNASTY; CALIPHATES; IKHSHIDID DYNASTY; SALADIN.

FURTHER READING

Armstrong, Karen. *Islam: A Short History.* New York: Random House, 2002.

FERDINAND I (1751–1825 C.E.)

Despotic monarch of the short-lived kingdom of the Two Sicilies, who ruled Sicily from 1816 to 1825). Both Ferdinand I and his grandson, Ferdinand II (r. 1830–1859), left behind a legacy of violence toward their people and obstinacy toward democracy.

Ferdinand I was born in 1751 to Charles, ruler of the independent kingdoms of Naples and Sicily (r. 1735–1759). After his father became King Charles III

of Spain (r. 1759–1788) in 1759, Ferdinand reigned as King Ferdinand IV of Naples and Ferdinand III of Sicily. Ferdinand's father Charles, an enlightened despot, instituted many progressive policies that continued after Ferdinand took the throne under the regency of Bernardo Tanucci. However, Ferdinand's 1768 marriage to Marie Caroline of Austria, sister of the future queen of France, Marie Antoinette, marked the beginning of more authoritarian policies.

After the Napoleonic Wars threw all of Europe into upheaval, Ferdinand abused his powerful position to eliminate the Sicilian constitution and then, in 1816, declared himself Ferdinand I of the new kingdom of the Two Sicilies. Though Ferdinand signed a new, Spanish-style constitution in 1820, his severe persecution of his political opponents never ceased. He died peacefully in 1825, and the Crown passed to his son Francis I (r. 1825–1830), who continued the ruthless and reactionary policies of his father.

See also: CHARLES III; MARIE ANTOINETTE; NAPLES, KINGDOM OF; POWER, FORMS OF ROYAL; SICILY, KINGDOM OF.

FERDINAND II (1810–1859 C.E.)

Ruler of the kingdom of the Two Sicilies (r. 1830–1859), whose harsh and despotic policies in reaction to the liberalizing trends of the time hastened the downfall of the kingdom.

The son of Francis I (r. 1825–1830) and grandson of Ferdinand I (r. 1816–1825), Ferdinand II continued the ruthless administration that had been established by his grandfather and continued by his father. Gaining the throne in 1830 upon the death of Francis I, Ferdinand II began his rule with promises of reform. These promises were quickly broken or forgotten, however, and he became an absolute despot who used repression to further his goals. Furthermore, Ferdinand continued the policy of taking political prisoners that had characterized the reigns of his predecessors.

After a few unsuccessful insurrections in the 1830s, the people of the Two Sicilies finally forced Ferdinand II to sign a new constitution in 1848, which granted liberal reforms and limited royal power. A string of violent demonstrations in Naples, however, led Ferdinand II to dissolve the constitution in 1849, and he began attacking his own people with bombs and artillery. These actions caused international and domestic outcry against Ferdinand and earned him the epithet "King Bomba."

Upon Ferdinand's death in 1859, the devastated kingdom passed to his son, Francis II (r. 1859–1860), a weak ruler who let his ministers continue the reactionary policies of his father. The movement for Italian unification, led by the future king of Italy, Victor Emmanuel II (1861–1878), forced Francis II to surrender in 1861, thus dissolving the kingdom of the Two Sicilies.

See also: NAPLES, KINGDOM OF; NATIONALISM; SICILY, KINGDOM OF; VICTOR EMMANUEL II.

FERDINAND II AND ISABELLA I

(1452–1516 C.E.; 1451–1504 C.E.)

Fifteenth-century Spanish monarchs of the Trastarmara dynasty, also known as the Catholic Monarchs, whose marriage united the two most important kingdoms of Iberia and set the foundation for making Spain the most powerful nation in Europe.

ISABELLA OF CASTILE

Isabella of Castile (r. 1474–1504) was born in the town of Avila on April 22, 1451. Her half-brother, Henry IV of Castile (r. 1454–1474), was a corrupt ruler against whom the Castilian nobles openly rebelled. In July 1468, the nobles offered the crown to Isabella, who demanded, instead, that the rebels acknowledge Henry IV as monarch. The rebellious nobles did so, but they required Henry to acknowledge Isabella as his lawful heir.

Henry IV tried to arrange a marriage for Isabella with several undesirable choices. The worst of these, Pedro Giron, was a debauched middle-aged man who asked for Isabella's hand in exchange for deserting the nobles in their revolt against Henry. Isabella, however, had her own plans and corresponded secretly with Ferdinand of Aragón, the son of King John II of Navarre (r. 1425–1479) and Aragón (r. 1458–1479). Ferdinand and Isabella were married in October 1469, without Henry's consent.

FERDINAND OF ARAGÓN

Born on March 10, 1452, Ferdinand was given rule of Sicily in 1468 by his father, King John II. The next year he married Isabella. Upon the death of his father in 1479. Ferdinand became king of Aragón, but the Crown of Navarre passed through marriage to the French House of Foix instead. After Henry IV of Castile died on December 13, 1474, Isabella accepted the Crown of that kingdom.

Through their marriage, Ferdinand and Isabella united Aragón and Castile, two of the most powerful kingdoms in Iberia. Although they ruled the kingdoms jointly, the union of Crowns was a personal one and not an official unification. Nevertheless, their joint reign marked the beginnings of a united Spain.

REFORMS AND CONQUESTS

The Catholic Monarchs faced abundant obstacles upon coming to the throne. They inherited a bankrupt treasury, a corrupt court, a rebellious nobility, and a clergy badly in need of reform. Among the monarchs' first tasks was to take control of the country and administer justice against those who had committed crimes. Ferdinand and Isabella curbed the power of the *cortes,* or legislature, and they confiscated the lands of many nobles to weaken their power. They also took over the administration of many of the rich holdings of the various religious and military orders in Spain, both reducing the powers of those orders and increasing their own.

Military Conquests

Immediately after Isabella's coronation, Alfonso V of Portugal (r. 1438–1481), who was betrothed to Henry IV's daughter, Juana, invaded and captured the Spanish city of Toro. Ferdinand and Isabella gathered an army and besieged the city, but they quickly ran out of supplies and retreated in disarray. Learning from their mistakes, Ferdinand and Isabella raised another army and returned, better supplied. In 1476, they won a decisive battle over the Portuguese, who did not attempt another invasion.

In 1476, Muley Hacen, the emir of Granada, in southern Iberia, broke a truce with Castile and captured the city of Zahara. The attack allowed the Christian Monarchs to renew the reconquista, or war against the Moors, making it a religious crusade to regain all of Iberia from the Muslims who had conquered much of the peninsula in the 700s.

Granada was well fortified, however. Only gradually did the war take on a new character as the Span-

Ferdinand II of Aragón and Isabella I of Castile laid the foundation for a unified Spanish kingdom. Known as the Catholic Monarchs, they also helped launch the Age of Discovery by funding the expeditions of Christopher Columbus, portrayed here in an audience before the king and queen.

ish army learned new tactics and underwent reform. Eventually, the Spanish acquired a reputation as one of the ablest military forces in Europe. Ferdinand and Isabella encamped with their army, sharing the hardships of the common soldiers and keeping their respect. This final war against the Moors lasted ten years.

Granada finally surrendered to the Christian Spanish forces in 1492. The Spanish, however, did not keep the promises of toleration that they had given years before. In 1502, Ferdinand and Isabella issued an edict that ordered all unconverted adult Moors to leave Spain or face the Inquisition.

Religious Reform and Exploration

In 1495, Isabella appointed the Franciscan prelate, Ximénez of Cisneros, as archbishop of Toledo. Cisneros reduced the grandeur of the episcopal palace in Toledo and set about reforming the clergy. However, he met stiff resistance to reform in both Spain and Rome. Isabella sent emissaries to Rome, arguing persuasively for her cause. In the end, Pope Alexander VI (r. 1492–1503) issued a papal bull, or edict, supporting Isabella.

One of Cisneros's acts was to enforce the power of the Spanish Inquisition. He was supported in this action by Isabella, who favored purging Spain of all its non-Christians. In 1492, the Inquisition had decreed that all Jews convert or be expelled from Spain within three months. Most chose exile; an estimated 200,000 Jews emigrated. Of those who converted to Christianity, some became convinced Catholics, but many risked the Inquisition to practice Judaism secretly.

In 1492, Isabella financed Christopher Columbus,

a Genoan navigator who sought to discover a trade route to the East by sailing west across the unknown reaches of the Atlantic Ocean. Provided with three ships, Columbus sailed from Spain in August. On October 10, 1492, he landed on the island of San Salvador in the present-day Bahamas. This discovery marks the beginning of Spain's empire in the Western Hemisphere.

LAST YEARS

When Isabella died in 1504, her daughter, Juana, should have become heir to the kingdom of Castile. However, Juana was emotionally unstable, and her husband, Philip of Habsburg, duke of Burgundy, was pro-French, which did not endear him to the Castilian nobility. With the approval of the *cortes*, Ferdinand ruled Castile as regent.

In 1504, Ferdinand remarried, taking as his second wife Germaine de Foix, the niece of King Louis XII (r. 1498–1515) of France. Isabella's will had contained provisions for the Castilian succession should Ferdinand have children by a second marriage, but this marriage remained childless.

In the early 1500s, Ferdinand became involved in wars with France over control of Italy. In 1508, he launched a campaign against Venice, and in 1511 he joined the Holy League against France. In 1512, he annexed much of the kingdom of Navarre, basing his claim on his marriage to Germaine. With this annexation, he regained much of the patrimony that had belonged to his father.

For the remainder of his life, Ferdinand ruled Aragón as king and Castile as regent, first for his daughter Juana and then for his grandson Charles, who later became King Charles I of Spain (r. 1516–1556) and Emperor Charles V (r. 1519–1558) of the Holy Roman Empire. Ferdinand died in 1516, leaving Charles a united Spain, as well as the kingdoms of Naples, Sicily, Sardinia, and an overseas empire.

Isabella and Ferdinand were long considered Spain's greatest monarchs. Together they centralized Spain's government, overcame its rebellious nobility, and established the beginnings of a vast overseas empire. Today, however, historians are more critical of the Catholic Monarchs, especially condemning the intolerant policies they adopted toward the Jewish and Muslim populations of Spain.

See also: Aragón, Kingdom of; Castile, Kingdom of; Charles V; Christianity and Kingship; Granada, Kingdom of; Navarre, Kingdom of; Spanish Monarchies.

FEUDALISM AND KINGSHIP

Political structures that frequently struggle for control of a state or nation. This struggle is between the monarch and the most powerful class of the nation, who are generally members of a landed aristocracy.

FEUDALISM DEFINED

Feudalism may be defined as a social, political, and economic system in which the power of one class becomes dominant over the majority of the population in society. Most often, but not always, the difference in power between the classes is based on military strength or economic access to military power.

The societies founded in medieval Europe between about 1100 and 1500 C.E. furnish many excellent and well-documented examples of feudalism. Some scholars actually define feudalism as precisely that: the economic and social system of medieval Europe. Within this context, medieval feudalism was based on a simple trade: the economic and physical resources of an individual or family were pledged to a lord in return for the use of land and the lord's physical protection of that land. The grantee, or vassal, was under obligation to provide arms, goods, or services to the grantor, or lord, upon request. Usually penalties—either implicit or explicit—were imposed when a vassal failed to fulfill his agreement under the terms of the feudal arrangement. Each vassal had the option to oppose his lord militarily and attempt to become a lord himself, or to move elsewhere and become vassal to another lord.

Some recent scholars have suggested that medieval Europe did not necessarily operate under this so-called feudal system. As evidence, they often point to the postmedieval invention of the term *feudalism* (which came from late-sixteenth-century Italian legal documents). Although they are not able to supply an alternative sociopolitical system that describes Europe as thoroughly as the commonly accepted definition of feudalism, their theories and facts are under close inspection by modern historians.

Study of the inherent conflict between feudalism and kingship has it roots primarily in the philosophy

During the feudal period in the Middle Ages, peasants were bound to the land by political, economic, and social obligations to the upper classes. This scene of feudal life is from the famous *Tres Riches Heures,* an illustrated manuscript created by the Limbourg Brothers of Flanders for Duke Jean de Berry, one of the highest ranking nobles in fifteenth-century France.

of the nineteenth century. German philosopher George Frederich Hegel saw history as a dynamic tension created by the struggle between the opposing forces of the desire for freedom and the will to power, and political systems as the social expressions of this struggle. In the case of monarchy, the will to power of an individual overcomes the desire for freedom of all others in the society. In feudalism, it is the will to power of a chosen class that supersedes both the will to power of any single ruler and the desire for freedom of the common people. Conversely, in democracy, the will to power and desire for freedom among the common people triumphs over both individual and aristocratic aspirations for power.

Mirroring their sociopolitical contrasts, the administrative structures of feudalism and monarchy differ in significant ways as well. Feudalism is, by its very nature, decentralized, while a successful monarchy requires a strong central government. The dynamic tension between central and local governments is echoed in the political platforms of modern states. Based on the lack of historical evidence to the contrary, such conflict seems inevitable whenever the body politic becomes large enough to require more than local controls.

The resulting ebb and flow of political control has followed similar patterns for the last four millennia. The ancient Egyptian pharaohs, for example, ruling the longest-running successful monarchy in human history, maintained tight control over their aristocracy. Ancient Egypt had a thriving middle class for centuries but very few noble families other than immediate relatives of the ruling royal clan. The pharaohs safeguarded this system by jealously guarding all their rights and privileges and, to a lesser degree, their sources of wealth.

THE ARISTOCRACY AND FEUDALISM

Aristocracy arose in the West because most of Europe in the eleventh through fourteenth centuries was governed by chieftains or warlords, each defending a small area. Most of these petty lords owed fealty, or allegiance, to another lord, who perhaps had slightly more land. That greater lord, in turn, often answered to yet another chieftain or perhaps to a king. As a result of these complex and tenuous hierarchies of fiefdoms, most medieval monarchs exerted only minimal coordination and control.

The history of the relationship between the English monarchy and aristocracy illustrates the complicated power shifts seen throughout Europe during the Middle Ages. William I, the Conquerer (r. 1066–1087), is a perfect example of a controlling, consolidating monarch. After his conquest of England in 1066, William destroyed the Anglo-Saxon aristocracy, took a thorough census of his new subjects and holdings, and claimed essentially all temporal power for the kingship.

William's descendants and successors in the house of Plantagenet followed his lead in retaining as much power for the Crown as possible given the large, complicated nation they had to rule, perhaps culminating in the absolute despotism of kings Henry I (r. 1100–1135) and Henry II (r. 1154–1189). However, William's unfortunate descendant, King John (r.

1199–1216), was forced to succumb to the strength of his vassals and give over to his barons many rights that had hitherto been reserved to the Crown when he signed the Magna Carta in 1215. The pendulum of power had now swung heavily in the direction of feudalism over kingship.

John's successors, particularly the powerful King Edward I (r. 1262–1307), regained much of the ground lost by the English monarchy and played well the game of royal demagogue, in which the king made himself the best hope of the downtrodden classes, their champion against the cupidity of the aristocrats.

The Tudor monarchs, Henry VIII (r. 1509–1547) and Elizabeth I (r. 1558–1603), were the last English rulers to enjoy both despotic control and the full favor of the common folk of England. However, despite their popularity and successes, the power and influence of the aristocracy had been weakened a century earlier in the long internecine struggles over succession to the throne during the Wars of the Roses (1455–1485). The parallel religious struggles between Catholics and Protestants, which eventually caused a general loss of faith in the English Crown, were cleverly, though temporarily, derailed by Henry VIII's audacious creation of the Church of England in 1534.

By the time the autocratic powers of the English monarchy expired with the execution of King Charles I (r. 1625–1649) by the headsman's axe, feudalism had long been dead in England. However, the power of kingship had also been dramatically reduced as well.

See also: CLASS SYSTEMS AND ROYALTY; DIVINE RIGHT; JOHN I; LABOR, FORMS OF; NORMAN KINGDOMS; RIGHTS, LAND; WILLIAM I, THE CONQUEROR.

FURTHER READING
Bloch, Marc. *Feudal Society.* New York: Routledge, 1989.

FIVE DYNASTIES AND TEN KINGDOMS (907–959 C.E.)

Series of northern dynasties and southern kingdoms that struggled to control China after the collapse of the Tang dynasty in 907.

By the end of the ninth century, repeated peasant rebellions had irreparably weakened China's T'ang dynasty (618–907). In 875, Huang Chao, a minor bureaucrat, launched the most serious of these rebellions. Chao's general, Chu Wen, betrayed Chao and allied himself with the T'ang, receiving a provincial governship as a reward. However, Chu recognized that the T'ang dynasty was failing. In 907, he organized the northern *fubing*, or militia, and seized the T'ang capital of Changan. After assassinating the last T'ang monarch, Zhaoxuang, Chu founded the Liang dynasty.

Chu despised both the bureaucracy and the aristocracy. To ensure his power, he executed the highest government officials and members of the nobility. Those who survived fled China. Chu replaced them with military commanders and officials from his own provincial government. He also broadened the political power of the rapidly expanding merchant class. Chu's actions overturned T'ang society. As his officials seized the aristocracy's vacant land, they formed a new gentry class that attained a permanent prominence in Chinese affairs.

Chu was unable to control his family, however. In 912, his son Modi murdered him, and for ten years, Chu's sons battled one another for control of the dynasty. Their internecine struggle ruined any chances of the Liang dynasty's survival or imminent Chinese reunification. Consequently, the Liang dynasty easily fell when Zhuangzong, a Shato Turk who had protected the T'ang's western borders, led an attack against the Liang capital at Luoyang. In 923, he founded the Later T'ang dynasty.

Zhuangzong (r. 923–926) was a T'ang loyalist who wished to restore the T'ang social order. He began with the conquest of Shu, the richest of the Ten Kingdoms. But when Zhuangzong was assassinated in 926, his successor, Minzong (r. 926–933), retained the Liang political structure. Minzong was a weak ruler who failed to capitalize on Zhuangzong's actions.

Not surprisingly, therefore, the Later T'ang dynasty was shortly dispatched. In 937, Shi Jingtang, who came from the same region as Zhuangzong, defeated the final Later T'ang ruler and established the Later Jin dynasty. Shi Jingtang achieved power by forming an alliance with the Khitan, Mongol tribes who repeatedly raided China's northern provinces. In return for sixteen prefectures located south of the Great Wall, the Khitan military helped Jingtang assume control. But the Khitan presence would disrupt Chinese affairs for over a century.

In fact, the alliance soon crumbled because the Khitan immediately threatened to occupy more territory. Shi Jingtang realized that the Khitan must be expelled to maintain China's existence, but he died shortly after assuming the throne. His successor organized an army to attack the Khitan. In 946, the two armies met, and the Khitan massacred the Jin forces. The Khitan may have overrun China, but their emperor died in 947 and an internal struggle erupted in the Khitan court.

Because the Khitan were disorganized, the Jin forces were able to rally and push the Khitan back to the northern prefectures. The most prominent Jin general, Liu Zhiyuan, then deposed the Jin emperor and founded the Later Han dynasty. The Later Han controlled the northern areas of China and also gained control of Shanxi, one of the key Ten Kingdoms. But despite its efforts, the Later Han dynasty failed to further expand its power.

In 951, a Jin general, Guo Wei, staged yet another military coup and deposed Liu Zhiyuan. The Jin monarchy fled to Shanxi, where it maintained limited control for twenty years. Guo initiated the Later Zhou dynasty, the last of the Five Dynasties. When Ghou seized control, the Chinese society was in shambles. War with the Khitan had significantly weakened the military, the government was highly corrupt, and the economy was severely depressed. Wei's successor, Chai Rong, took strong steps to correct these ailments. First, he completely reorganized the military. Second, he seized Nan Tang, the most agriculturally rich kingdom in the south. This acquisition revitalized the dynasty's economy.

Chai Rong died during combat in 959. His oldest children had been slaughtered in an earlier coup, and only a six-year-old survived. Predictably, the child was soon deposed. General Zhao Kuangyin seized control in 960 and founded the Song dynasty, which lasted for over 300 years. The Five Dynasties period was over, but during the period, a new gentry class had replaced the old, entrenched aristocracy. As F. W. Mote notes in *Imperial China* (1999), "this profound social change established the conditions under which a new, more egalitarian elite based on merit was able to emerge under the Song."

See also: LIANG DYNASTIES; T'ANG DYNASTY.

FURTHER READING

Mote, F. W. *Imperial China.* Cambridge, MA: Harvard University Press, 1999.

FLANDERS, COUNTY OF

(864–1576 C.E.)

State in northwestern Europe, roughly encompassing modern-day Belgium, which was ruled by a series of counts from the ninth through sixteenth centuries.

Celtic Gauls originally inhabited the region of Flanders, but the Germanic Franks moved into the area between 300 and 600, creating a regional split between Latin-speaking Gallo-Romans and German-speaking Franks. This division is still evident today in the Belgian linguistic division between French and Dutch.

At the beginning of the Frankish period, Flanders was the center of the Frankish kingdom. However, as the Frankish kings pushed their landholdings south and moved their capital to Paris, Flanders became a peripheral county in a growing empire. Flanders officially became a county in 864, when the Frankish emperor Charles I (r. 840–877) of the Carolingian dynasty made his son-in-law Baldwin I, Iron Arm (r. 864–879), its ruler. From this date, Flanders became a fief of the French Crown, although, as a frontier region, it remained largely autonomous.

During the tenth and eleventh centuries, the counts of Flanders extended their territory eastward. These territories, though within the county of Flanders, were enfiefed to the Holy Roman emperor, not the French king. This confusing array of medieval political connections cost Flanders its French territories in the twelfth century, as the kingdom of France extended its direct sovereignty northward into the county.

By the twelfth century, many Flemish cities had gained the rights of privileges of a commune from the French Crown. A commune was a city that had united as a single association and earned the right to self-governance from monarchs in return for promises of taxes or other services. Flemish cities such as Ghent, Bruges, and Ypres benefited from this arrangement and became commercial centers of a growing textile industry. By the thirteenth century, the Flemish cloth trade was the most prosperous and respected in Europe.

With prosperity came conflict. Within Flemish cities, guild workers and town elites clashed over rights, money, and politics. Workers tended to support an independent Flanders, while town elites favored the French Crown. Although the roots of this division were social rather than political, the departure of the count of Flanders, Baldwin IX (r. 1195–1205), on the Fourth Crusade in 1204 touched off an international conflict over the wealthy region. While Baldwin led the Crusaders against Constantinople, Philip II of France (r. 1180–1223) moved into Flanders.

The next hundred years were marked by almost continual warfare between France and Flemish, English, and German armies. In 1322, the pro-French noble Louis I of Nevers (r. 1322–1346) became count of Flanders, sparking a civil war. Although initially successful, Louis faced a growing economic crisis in the county. Edward III of England (r. 1327–1377) banned all wool exports to Flanders as a prelude to the Hundred Years' War (1337–1453).

For a brief period beginning in 1337, a number of Flemish cities, led by Ghent, broke away from Flanders and allied themselves with England. This independence proved short-lived, as the pro-French Count Louis I put down the rebellion after the death of its leader, Jacob van Artevelde, in 1345. However, Ghent remained a site of rebellion against French sovereignty in Flanders for the next half-century.

In 1384, Count Louis II de Male of Flanders (1346–1384) died without a direct heir. The duke of Burgundy, Philip the Bold (r. 1363–1404), assumed the title of count and brought Flanders under the control of the Habsburg dynasty. At first, under Philip and his heir Mary of Burgundy, Flemish commerce and art flourished in Flanders. But the Habsburgs saw the county as little more than a rich source of tax revenue and ignored the political rights and privileges of its cities.

In 1506, Flanders passed to the Spanish Habsburg line, which exploited Flemish commerce even more than their predecessors. Less than a century later, in 1576, Flanders County joined with the rest of the Netherlands in revolt against King Philip II of Spain (r. 1556–1598). The Dutch eventually succeeded in driving out the Spanish, but the Flemish did not succeed. Most of the county passed back to Austrian Habsburg control in 1714, although the French annexed parts of it in the seventeenth century. The region of Flanders was alternately controlled by the French and the Dutch until Belgian independence in 1830.

See also: BURGUNDY KINGDOM; CAROLINGIAN DYNASTY; EDWARD I; HABSBURG DYNASTY; PHILIP II.

FURTHER READING
Cantor, Norman F. *The Civilization of the Middle Ages.* New York: HarperCollins, 1993.

FOLKLORE AND MYTHS. *See* MYTH AND FOLKLORE

FOLKUNG DYNASTY (1250–1387 C.E.)

Medieval dynasty that ruled Sweden (1250–1364), Norway (1319–1387), and Denmark (1375–1387), which expanded Sweden's territory and effected the union of Norway and Denmark.

The Folkung dynasty first rose to power in Sweden in 1250 with the election of Waldemar I (r. 1250–1275) as king. During Waldemar's rule, the monarchy centralized its power and passed laws giving more protection to the rights of women, the church, and the courts. Sweden's wealth grew significantly as a result of territorial expansion to the east and increased trade. In 1275, Waldemar's brother, Magnus I (r. 1275–1290), overthrew Waldemar with Danish aid and was elected king. During his reign, the Folkung monarchy grew stronger through improved taxation in the kingdom.

Magnus was followed on the throne by his son Birger (r. 1290–1318), who ended a decade-long revolt against the monarchy led by his brothers Erik and Waldemar. Birgir invited them to a feast in 1317, imprisoning them, and allegedly starving them to death. However, their followers rose against Birger and forced him to flee the country; he died in exile in Denmark.

Erik's son Magnus, already ruler of Norway (through his mother) as Magnus VII (r. 1319–1355), was elected King Magnus III of Sweden (r. 1319–1364) by the nobles in 1319. His reign saw the establishment, in 1350, of a single law code for Sweden. He named his son Erik as co-regent of Sweden in 1344 in an attempt to ensure the succession. Erik wanted more power, however. With the aid of the nobles, he forced his father to share the throne from 1356 until Erik's death in 1359.

In 1344, Magnus agreed to abdicate the throne of Norway in favor of his son, Haakon VI (r. 1355–1380), and he did so in 1355. Haakon married Margaret, the daughter of Waldemar IV of Denmark (r.

1340–1375), which led to the union of the Crowns of Denmark and Norway under their son, Olaf, who ruled as Olaf IV of Norway (r. 1380–1387) and Olaf II of Denmark (r. 1376–1387). Magnus and Haakon lost most of Sweden in 1363 to an invasion by Magnus's nephew Albrecht (r. 1364–1389), but Folkung rule continued in Norway and Denmark until the death of Olaf in 1387.

The legacy of the Swedish Folkung dynasty was, ironically, the union of Sweden with Denmark and Norway. The ambition of the Folkung monarchs for greater territory, which they fulfilled largely through strategic marriages, culminated in 1397 with the Kalmar Union. This merger of the three Scandinavian kingdoms was accomplished through the ambition and political skills of Queen Margaret, the mother of Olaf.

See also: DANISH KINGDOM; HAAKON VI; KALMAR UNION; MARGARET OF DENMARK; NORWEGIAN MONARCHY; SWEDISH MONARCHY.

FURTHER READING

Anderson, Ingvar. *A History of Sweden.* Trans. Carolyn Hannay. London: Weidenfeld and Nicolson, 1956.

Butler, Ewan. *The Horizon Concise History of Scandinavia.* New York: American Heritage, 1973.

Larsen, Karen. *A History of Norway.* Princeton, NJ: Princeton University Press for the American-Scandinavian Foundation, 1948.

Toyne, S.M. *The Scandinavians in History.* 1948. Reprint, New York: Barnes and Noble, 1996.

FON KINGDOM (1600s–1894 C.E.)

Also called Dahomey, a kingdom that arose in the early 1600s in the area known today as the Republic of Benin; the name Fon refers to the indigenous people of the region, who also comprised the majority of the kingdom's subjects.

The Fon kingdom was founded in the early 1600s by a group of immigrants who came into the region from the neighboring land of Allada and were of Aja ethnicity. These newcomers, who had experience with centralized government, were more accomplished in the exercise of authority than the indigenous Fon, who until this time had lived in small, scattered, and independent villages.

By 1650 the Aja immigrants had welded the Fon villages into a single political entity and had established a capital at Agbome, installing a leader named Wegbaja (r. 1645–1685), as king. Wegbaja declared all land in the kingdom to be the property of the king, and he charged his subjects a tax for the right to farm it. Wegbaja undermined local authority by limiting kingly succession to the eldest son of a reigning king, thus restricting rulership to descendants of the Aja, and excluding all Fon from the throne.

Wegbaja further strengthened his hold on power by introducing new rituals centered upon sacrificial offerings to the king, or, more precisely, to the kingly lineage. Sacrificial subjects were usually war captives, thus providing incentive for the people to support Wegbaja's military campaigns against neighboring peoples.

Wegbaja and his successors were well acquainted with the Atlantic slave trade. In Allada, slave raiding was common and may even have been the impetus behind their migration to Fon territory. The Fon kingdom, too, participated in the trade, with hopes of becoming the preeminent supplier of slaves to the European traders. This meant embarking upon a vigorous campaign of raiding and conquest throughout Fon territory. Exchanging slaves for European goods brought a steady supply of European firearms into the king's armory, further enhancing the military power of the Fon kingdom and its supremacy over most of its neighbors. By the 1720s, the present ruler, Agaja (r. 1716–1740) had succeeded in eclipsing and, finally, occupying his coastal rivals in the trade.

In the first half of the eighteenth century, only the kingdoms of Fon and Oyo were left as true powers on the Atlantic coast, and they struggled for dominance. The Oyo finally gained the upper hand militarily, and they forced King Agaja to pay tribute to the Oyo rulers in order to retain his throne. As a client state to Oyo, the Fon kingdom remained prosperous through the eighteenth century. With the collapse of the Atlantic slave trade, however, both kingdoms suffered drastic losses in revenues. The Fon kingdom was conquered by the French in 1892–1894.

See also: AFRICAN KINGDOMS.

FURTHER READING

Ajayi, J.F.A., and Michael Crowder, eds. *History of West Africa.* 2nd ed. New York: Columbia University Press, 1976.

GENERAL INDEX

BIOGRAPHICAL INDEX

Photo Credits Volume One

WORLD MONARCHIES, PRESENT DAY

LEGEND
- Non-Monarchies
- Monarchies